Germanic Language Histories 'from Below'
(1700 – 2000)

W
DE
G

Studia Linguistica Germanica

Herausgegeben

von

Christa Dürscheid
Andreas Gardt
Oskar Reichmann
Stefan Sonderegger

86

Walter de Gruyter · Berlin · New York

Germanic Language Histories 'from Below' (1700–2000)

Edited by
Stephan Elspaß
Nils Langer
Joachim Scharloth
Wim Vandenbussche

Walter de Gruyter · Berlin · New York

♾ Printed on acid-free paper which falls within the guidelines of the ANSI
to ensure permanence and durability.

Library of Congress Cataloging-in-Publication Data

Germanic language histories 'from below' (1700–2000) / edited by
Stephan Elspass ... [et al.].
  p. cm. – (Studia linguistica germanica ; 86)
  Includes bibliographical references and index.
  ISBN 978-3-11-019335-0 (alk. paper)
  1. Germanic languages – History.   2. Germanic languages – Variation.   3. Germanic languages – Standardization – History.   4. Germanic languages – Standardization – Political aspects.   I. Elspass,
Stephan.
  PD75.G45   2007
  430.9 – dc22

                                                         2007012654

Bibliographic information published by the Deutsche Nationalbibliothek

The Deutsche Nationalbibliothek lists this publication in the Deutsche Nationalbibliografie;
detailed bibliographic data are available in the Internet at http://dnb.d-nb.de.

ISBN 978-3-11-019335-0
ISSN 1861-5651

Printed in Germany.

Disk conversion: OLD-Satz digital, Neckarsteinach
Cover design: Christopher Schneider, Berlin

ACKNOWLEDGEMENTS

In April 2005 we were able to organise a conference on "Language History from Below. Linguistic Variation in the Germanic Languages from 1700 to 2000" with the support of the *Institute for Advanced Study at the University of Bristol*, the *University of Bristol Institute for Research in the Arts and Humanities*, the *Linguistics Association of Great Britain*, the *British Academy*, and the *Vrije Universiteit Brussel* in Clifton Hill House at the University of Bristol. This volume presents a selection of 30 contributions to this conference and continues the tradition of alternative approaches to the history of the Germanic languages initiated by "Standardization. Studies from the Germanic languages" (ed. by Andrew Linn and Nicola McLelland, Benjamins 2002) and "Linguistic Purism in the Germanic Languages" (ed. by Nils Langer and Winifred Davies's, de Gruyter 2005). We are grateful to the editors of the *Studia Linguistica Germanica* for accepting the book in this series and to Angelika Hermann and Heiko Hartmann from de Gruyter publishers for their assistance with its publication. We would like to thank the student helpers in Bristol for looking after the conference delegates (Louise Hughes, Sarah Spencer Bernard, Helen Pope, Hannah Evans, Aled Seys-Llewellyn); thanks are also due to the Augsburg team (Michaela Negele, Stefan Dettl, Raphael Doderer) for their assistance during the editing process of this book, especially to Alex Mangold (Aberystwyth).

Stephan Elspaß (Augsburg)
Nils Langer (Bristol)
Joachim Scharloth (Zürich)
Wim Vandenbussche (Brussel)

CONTENTS

Introduction

IV. Language choice and language planning

X

V. Reflections on alternative language histories

Introduction

Stephan Elspass (Augsburg)

A twofold view 'from below': New perspectives on language histories and language historiographies

Up until the late 20th century, language historians were primarily concerned with unification and standardization processes and fostered what could be called a 'language history from (and of) above'. This approach was deeply entrenched in 19th and early 20th century political ideologies: in Germany, for instance, which like so many European countries in the 19th century was still en route to a nation state, philologists collaborated with politicians, historians and writers in constructing a picture of a unified nation with autonomous cultural traditions. Language and literature played a central role in the idea of nationhood; literary and linguistic traditions were projected back to the Middle Ages and beyond (cf. Durrell 2000, Reichmann 2001, etc.). Generations of scholars and teachers have viewed language history as the inexorable march towards a uniform standard and, by narrowing their view on standard varieties, presented a "tunnel vision version" of language history (Trudgill and Watts 2002: 1). Language change appeared to be of interest only when it contributed to the linguistic architecture of a modern standard language. Up to the late 20th century, textbooks were clearly dominated by this teleological view, portraying 'the best' authors – like classical Schiller and Goethe in Germany (or rather the 19th-century editions of their works) – as role models of language norms and style, and therefore 'true' representatives of the national language as such. Analyses of literary texts (representing a 'high' variety that was only practiced by a tiny minority of the population), were used to support the orthodox belief that the German language had been standardized by the time of the 'classics', that is by the turn of the 18th/19th century. That this was not an isolated phenomenon particular to German can be seen, for example, in the research by James Milroy (1999, 2005) who identified similar standard language ideologies in the historiography of English.

In this 'language history from above' approach, the histories of non-standardized languages and language varieties were widely ignored. The whole range of texts and varieties that oscillate between formal written and informal spoken language are the other side of the coin, which has only just begun to be looked at more closely.[1] Variation and other linguistic 'digressions' from a pre-supposed 'standard' have often been shrugged off as 'bad' language (cf. Davies and Langer 2006) and disqualified as invalid or simply 'wrong' data for linguistic research. 'Non-standard' variation other than traditional dialect was regarded as corrupt and vulgar, so that in an act of "sanitary purism", non-standard forms were often cleansed out from textbooks (Milroy 2005: 324). The result of this selection – or rather manipulation of linguistic data – is that modern standard languages sometimes seem not to have changed at all for 200 years.

The inevitably consequence of these practices for language historiography are incomplete language histories full of 'blank areas' ("witte vlekken", as Marijke van der Wal 2006 puts it) that need not be there, as this insufficiency is not necessarily due to a lack of data. In recent decades, this has become particularly obvious for a number of national language histories of the last three or four centuries. Hand-written, rather than printed texts have always been available, but philologists took hardly any notice of them (unless they were composed by writers, artists, politicians, aristocrats or other members of the elites). The neglect of texts 'below' the surface of printed language, which was mostly homogenized by professional proof-readers, has led to a language historiography in which a major part of both the language community (i.e. those writers with no access to printing) and their written language production is simply not represented. It is therefore essential to look at text sources that represent informal and 'everyday' language in the past and to think about diverse or even new methodologies to reconstruct the full picture of our languages in the past. We are convinced that this full picture may contribute to a better understanding of both past *and* present-day linguistic changes.[2]

This rough outline and critique of the traditional 'language histories from above' may give an idea of what inspired the editors of this volume to strongly plead for an alternative and long overdue 'language history *from below*' approach (cf. Elspaß 2005a). As in the concept of 'history from below', it implies a radical change of perspective from a 'bird's eyes' to a 'worm's eyes' view. This entails basically two aspects:

Firstly, a 'language history from below' focuses on the oral as well as written language use of larger sections of the population, particularly the lower and lower middle classes. In traditional language historiography, these are the people who – if at all – mainly appear as speakers of rural dialects, but hardly

---

[1] Traditional dialects always formed an exception, but they were mostly considered suitable for diachronic analysis only in their oldest and purest form, which was supposedly represented by the stereotypical 'nonmobile older rural males' (NORMs).

[2] Cf. Elspaß (2005b: 27ff.) for an illustration with some examples from German grammar.

ever as people whose *texts* contributed to the history of our modern languages. From early modern times, however, reading and writing was no longer a privilege of the upper and upper middle classes, who never constituted more than 5% of the population anywhere in Western and Central Europe. Large parts of the 'ordinary' population (like farmers, artisans, soldiers, housemaids etc.), and not only members of the social elite, were able to put pen (or pencil) to paper, particularly as a result of massive literacy drives in the 18th and 19th century. Although they had rarely reason or opportunity to do so, the sheer mass of people produced a wealth of private letters, diaries, inventories, cooking books, petition letters, lay theatre plays, and so on.

'Language history from below', however, is not only a plea for a long overdue emancipation of more than 95% of the population in language historiography. Secondly and more importantly, the concept of 'from below' pleads for a different starting point of the description and explanation of language history. In linguistics, the shift of perspectives involves an acknow-ledgment of language registers which are basic to human interaction and which are prototypically represented by speech in face-to-face-interaction. I refer to Peter Koch's and Wulf Oesterreicher's (1985) well-known concept of 'lan-guage of proximity' or 'conceptual orality' (as opposed to 'language of dis-tance' or 'conceptual written language'). A 'language history from below' would thus set off with the analysis of "material as close to actual speech as possible, only in written form" (Sević 1999: 340; cf. also Schneider 2002). Such material is maybe best represented in ego-documents, be they written by paupers (cf. Tony Fairman in this volume) or by members of the nobility (cf. Steffen Arzberger in this volume). Thus, a historical grammar of the (early) modern period 'from below', i.e. from the beginning of standardisation efforts, would not start from the language of literature, but from texts representing everyday language (cf. Ágel and Hennig 2006).

In his paper on 'lower order' letters in this volume, Tony Fairman rightly cautions that a view from below may be as one-sided as a view from above and he proposes "a panorama of all forces, formal and informal". In general, language historiography should certainly aim at getting the full picture, including as many text genres and as many linguistic and metalinguistic data – on indigenous and contact languages – as possible. However, as textbooks on language history have mainly presented formal (or fictitious informal) language and concentrated on writer elites in the past, it appears to be justified to focus on a view from below for some time – at least until it can be assured that a significantly high number of formerly unknown or forgotten data 'from below' will a) be made available and b) actually be considered in language historiography.

Whether it may be disputed that a 'language history from below' is feasible for each individual language and language period, the contributors to this book may all agree that it is necessary to work on a change of perspective and some sort of 'alternative histories' of our languages (Watts and Trudgill 2002). The volume contains 30 papers on histories from ten 'big' as well as 'small' Germanic languages and varieties in the last 300 years.[3] Nearly all papers are deeply rooted within the concepts of Historical Sociolinguistics[4] and Historical Pragmatics.[5] The topics covered in this book accordingly include language variation and change and the politics of language contact and choice, seen against the background of standardization processes, of written and oral text genres and from the viewpoint of larger sections of the population. Methodologically, the contributions range from grapheme analysis (Anja Voeste) to discourse analysis (Nicola McLelland) and the reconstruction of communicative genres (Angelika Linke).

The five chapters of this volume outline major topics and research fields of an alternative 'language history from below'.

An alternative approach requires new sets of data, i.e. primary data, not textbook data, representing so-called 'non-standard' varieties as the starting point of linguistic analyses – or rather: varieties and variants other than what is traditionally considered as 'standard'. A lot of hand-written data which could be relevant in this field, have not even been unearthed from the archives yet, let alone been transcribed and digitalised. The five papers in the first section concentrate on the analysis of language variation in 18th and 19th texts written by members of the lower and lower middle classes, mainly consisting of private correspondence, but also of lay theatre plays (Reershemius). Contributions to some of the following chapters use spoken data of recent non-standard varieties of Germanic standard languages.

Likewise, it is justified to move away from formal written registers and text types, which represent the most 'static' part of modern language histories, and focus on orality and informal everyday language instead: everyday language comes more 'natural' to the speaker and to the writer. It represents the unmarked end of the varieties scale, while formal registers such as written standard varieties clearly stand for markedness in sociolinguistic terms. Unmarked communication, as represented in informal everyday language in recent history, is at the core of *change* from below. Most of the papers in

---

[3]   The volume contains two papers which, strictly speaking, study language variation and change before 1700, i.e. Anja Voeste's investigation of spelling in Early New High German and Richard Dury's paper on the address system in Early Modern English.

[4]   Cf. Willemyns and Vandenbussche (2006) for a critical overview of current developments in Historical Sociolinguistics; cf. also the European Historical Sociolinguistics Network (HiSoN; http://www.philhist.uni-augsburg.de/ hison/) which was established at the Bristol conference.

[5]   For a state-of-the-art overview on Historical Pragmatics cf. Taavitsainen and Fitzmaurice (2007).

section II explicitly refer to William Labov's concept of 'language change from below'. Labov characterized this as "systematic changes that appear first in the vernacular and represent the operation of internal, linguistic factors"; in Labov's terms, they refer primarily to changes "below the level of social awareness", and he stresses that they "may be introduced by any social class, although no cases have been recorded in which the highest-status social group acts as the innovating group" (Labov 1994: 78). Here again, it becomes apparent that much of language variation and changes past and present will go unnoticed if one does not acknowledge language material that is close to 'vernacular' language.

The emphasis on contact between different varieties and registers, also between different language communities, makes clear – and this is essential for a sociolinguistic approach – that 'external' factors in language variation and change play a central role in an alternative language historiography. Following Labov's axiom that 'there are no single style speakers' it may be safely assumed that none of the speakers of the Germanic language varieties between 1700 and 2000 had a competence that was limited to one variety only. In this respect, not only the use and choice of more prestigious ('high') and less prestigious ('low') varieties and variants according to situation and interaction partners must be addressed, but also the more fundamental question in how far the cultural history of a society is reflected in its language history: how come that a specific variant or variety has gained prestige? Prestige in what context? Where do language norms come from? Where did prescriptive norms come from? How did or do they get into people's heads? And why do people still make 'mistakes'? What effect does professionalism and routine in writing have? Such issues on language norms in view of standardization processes are addressed in section III of this volume.

The papers in section IV focus on questions of language choice and language planning. In the tradition of 19th century language historiography, particularly as part of the "Neogrammarian legacy", as Ernst Håkon Jahr (1999: 119) put it, scholars have followed a monocentric, single-language path in the account of language histories. An alternative language history 'from below' is more interested in the linguistic interaction of individuals or groups of speakers/writers from different varieties or languages. This may not only reveal cross-linguistic similarities in communicative patterns of discourse or even similarities in 'internal' language change, but also language change which is induced by language contact. A further aspect of the co-existence of different languages in multilingual societies is the language choice of individuals or distinct populations and the language policy in these societies, which could even lead to language conflict.

The two final papers of this book by Angelika Linke and Richard Watts reflect on the wider issue as to how traditional 'language history from above' and an alternative 'language history from below' may be integrated in a more general concept of a cultural history of language and discourse (section V).

Finally, two other issues of an alternative language historiography, which are not confined to special sections of this volume, deserve special attention. Firstly, it is both desirable and necessary not only to tell the histories of the 'big' languages, like traditional historical linguistics tends to, but also of smaller languages and language varieties, e.g. Yiddish, Luxembourgish, or Creoles (cf. Reershemius, Horner and de Kleine in this volume). Secondly, traditional language history has mostly told the history of male language. Women have been greatly underrepresented in accounts of language history, often (but not solely) due to a lack of original sources. It may not be possible to correct the gender disparity in language historiography, but it is feasible and also high time to study whether and how men and women in the past differed in their discursive use of language (cf. Nevalainen 2002, and Nicola McLelland in this volume).

For practical reasons, the present volume remains confined to the histories of Germanic language varieties. However, the topics raised here are not purely 'Germanic' problems and can most certainly be matched with the methodological defeats and challenges of scholars of other language histories. Therefore it is hoped that this book will give a new impetus for a true social and pragmatic history of all European languages, across national and linguistic borders.

References

Ágel, Vilmos and Mathilde Hennig (eds.). 2006. *Grammatik aus Nähe und Distanz. Theorie und Praxis am Beispiel von Nähetexten 1650–2000.* Tübingen: Niemeyer.

Davies, Winifred V. and Nils Langer (eds.) 2006. *The Making of Bad Language. Lay Linguistic Stigmatisations in German: Past and Present.* Frankfurt am Main: Lang.

Durrell, Martin. 2000. Standard Language and the Creation of National Myths in Nineteenth-Century Germany. In Jürgen Barkhoff, Gilbert Carr and Roger Paulin (eds.), *Das schwierige neunzehnte Jahrhundert. Germanistische Tagung zum 65. Geburtstag von Eda Sagarra im August 1998. Mit einem Vorwort von Wolfgang Frühwald.* Tübingen: Niemeyer, 15–26.

Elspaß, Stephan. 2005a. *Sprachgeschichte von unten. Untersuchungen zum geschriebenen Alltagsdeutsch im 19. Jahrhundert.* Tübingen: Niemeyer.

Elspaß, Stephan. 2005b. Language norm and language reality. Effectiveness and limits of prescriptivism in New High German. In: Nils Langer and

Winifred V. Davies (eds.), *Linguistic Purism in the Germanic Languages.* Berlin, New York: de Gruyter, 20–45.

Jahr, Ernst Håkon. 1999. *Language change: Advances in Historical Sociolinguistics.* Berlin, New York: Mouton de Gruyter.

Koch, Peter and Wulf Oesterreicher. 1985. Sprache der Nähe – Sprache der Distanz. Mündlichkeit und Schriftlichkeit im Spannungsfeld von Sprachtheorie und Sprachgeschichte. *Romanistisches Jahrbuch* 36: 15–43.

Labov, William. 1994. *Principles of linguistic change. Part 1: Internal factors.* Oxford, UK and Cambridge, USA: Blackwell.

Milroy, James. 1999. The consequences of standardisation in descriptive linguistics. In Tony Bex and Richard J. Watts (eds.), *Standard English. The widening debate.* London, New York: Routledge, 16–39.

Milroy, James. 2005. Some effects of purist ideologies on historical descriptions of English. In: Nils Langer and Winifred V. Davies (eds.), *Linguistic Purism in the Germanic Languages.* Berlin, New York: de Gruyter, 324–342.

Nevalainen, Terttu. 2002. Women's writings as evidence for linguistic continuity and change in Early Modern English. In Richard Watts and Peter Trudgill (eds.), *Alternative histories of English.* London: Routledge, 191–209.

Reichmann, Oskar (2001): Nationale und europäische Sprachgeschichtsschreibung. *Mitteilungen des Deutschen Germanistenverbandes* 48: 530–537.

Schneider, Edgar W. 2002. Investigating Variation and Change in Written Documents. In J. K. Chambers, Peter Trudgill and Natalie Schilling-Estes (eds.), *The Handbook of Language Variation and Change.* Malden, MA & Oxford: Blackwell, 67–96.

Sević, Radmila B. 1999. Early Collections of Private Documents: The Missing Link in the Diachronic Corpora. In Christopher Beedham (ed.), *Langue and Parole in Synchronic and Diachronic Perspective. Selected Proceedings of the XXXIst Annual Meeting of the Societas Linguistica Europaea, St Andrews 1998.* Amsterdam u. a.: Pergamon, 337–347.

Taavitsainen, Irma and Susan Fitzmaurice. 2007. Historical pragmatics: What it is and how to do it. In Susan M. Fitzmaurice and Irma Taavitsainen (eds.). *Methods in Historical Pragmatics.* Berlin, New York: Mouton de Gruyter, 11–36.

Trudgill, Peter and Richard Watts. 2002. Introduction. In the year 2525. In Richard Watts and Peter Trudgill (eds.), *Alternative Histories of English.* London and New York: Routledge. 1–3.

Wal, Marijke van der. 2006. *Onvoltooid verleden tijd. Witte vlekken in de taalgeschiedenis.* Amsterdam: Koninklijke Nederlandse Akademie van Wetenschappen.

Willemyns, Roland and Wim Vandenbussche. 2006. Historical Sociolinguistics: Coming of Age? *Sociolinguistica* 20: 146–165.

I. Language variation in letters, diaries
and other text sources from below

MARINA DOSSENA (BERGAMO)

"As this leaves me at present" –
Formulaic usage, politeness, and social proximity
in nineteenth-century Scottish emigrants' letters

1. Introduction

This paper discusses linguistic usage as recorded in unpublished letters written by encoders of Scottish origin who migrated to America and Australia in the nineteenth century. Its aim is to identify the extent to which specific usage (whether diatopically or diastratically marked) is maintained in individual texts and the ways in which this contributes to the reinforcement of social bonds between participants, despite their geographical distance and the considerable time span which might elapse between one letter and the other. The letters examined derive from a collection of complete texts which are currently being transcribed from original manuscript or typescript sources for inclusion in the Corpus of Nineteenth-Century Scottish Correspondence (19CSC: Dossena 2004). The corpus will include both private and non-private letters, written by men and women of varying ages at a crucial time in the history of Scots and in the development of Scottish English. Following the eighteenth century, i.e. the grand age of prescriptivism, but also of the inception of the 'vernacular revival' in literature, the aim to 'improve' language by bringing it closer to southern models of usage was still forcefully pursued by Scottish speakers and writers in the nineteenth century. Although some commentators expressed concern at the loss of vernacular elements (for instance, see Cockburn 1856), many grammars were still published practically reporting lists of proscribed Scotticisms that had already appeared in the previous century (Dossena 2005). In this context, it may thus prove especially interesting to investigate such an important genre as letters. First of all, private correspondence may be discussed in terms of its speech-relatedness (see Biber 1995: 283–300), thus shedding light on possible uses in spoken language. Indeed, Görlach (1999: 149–150) stresses that letters "reflect the social and functional relations between sender and addressee to a very high degree – only spoken texts can equal this range." In this respect, then, the possibility of identifying patterns in which Scots types of usage actually diverged from southern ones proves very appealing and may clearly concern syntax, morphology, lexis and, in particular, spelling. This in turn may be quite fruitful for the reconstruction of phonological realizations and their geographical and social distribution.

The corpus is expected to include a proportional quantity of both private and business letters, so that usage may be compared in formal and informal registers alike. The aim is to have a total of at least 500,000 words; all the letters are to be transcribed integrally, recording writers' self-corrections, amendments, and details relating to paratextual features such as the recipient's title(s) and address. Original (non-) capitalization is maintained throughout and original word and line division is signalled (see Dury 2006).[1] As regards the selection of texts, the samples discussed in this study have been selected from those available in the National Archives of Scotland or in the National Library of Scotland; at a later stage the inclusion of privately-held documents is also envisaged.[2] Letters by literary figures that had previously been edited elsewhere were deliberately excluded.[3] At the moment, 19CSC comprises 355 letters (for a total of ca. 89,000 words); 229 letters (ca. 42,000 words) concern business, while 126 letters (ca. 47,000 words) are of private origin; of these, 42 letters (ca. 27,000 words) were written by emigrants and constitute the subcorpus which will be analyzed in this study. In general, the time span of the letters investigated here ranges from 1815 to 1892, though most letters pertain to the second half of the century.[4]

As for informants in the subcorpus of emigrants' letters, we have 2 women and 13 men: 8 letters were written between 1859 and 1867 by a Fife woman who emigrated to Argentina with her brothers. To these, another letter may be added that was sent by a woman, though it is somewhat different in that it is a formal note of thanks to the Duke of Sutherland for a donation of £ 7, which enabled the encoder to emigrate and join her husband:

---

[1]   In the examples provided in this paper, however, line division is only indicated when it is deemed to be significant for the presentation of overall textual mapping.

[2]   Individual letters for inclusion in the corpus have been chosen both randomly and on the basis of their being the response or follow-up to a previous text (whether a letter or a brief note). In the future a similar policy will be followed, though a constant attempt at creating a balanced set of samples of both male and female writers will be made.

[3]   In fact, linguistic issues in some of these have been studied elsewhere – see, for instance, Dossena (1997 and 2002).

[4]   As a matter of fact, emigration rates increased with the first Highland Clearances: according to Whatley (2000: 242), in the Highlands "most landowners (in the north and west) were steadfastly opposed to emigration until the 1820s".

> My Lord Duke, # I had the honor of receiving the sum of 7 £ sterling through the generosity of your grace, for which I beg to offer my most sincere thanks, and heart-felt gratitude, as by that reason myself and family can now be enabled to join my husband without any delay. # I have the honor to be # Your Grace's most Ob^t and H. S^t

The text was probably written by somebody familiar with the conventions of formal letter-writing, and it might actually be more appropriate to classify this as a business letter; our decision to place it here, however, derives from its relation to the kind of formal register recorded at the other end of the cline, from the unschooled register usually found in familiar letters.

As a matter of fact, 8 out of 13 male informants encode letters that seem to convey full-schooling (albeit with idiolectal traits), 1 appears to be minimally schooled, while the other 4 are partially schooled;[5] 6 encoders address relatives in Sutherland, St Andrews and Dunbar; in 7 cases it has not been possible to trace the origin of the encoder, and as the envelope is missing and there is no address on the letter itself, further archival investigations will be required. Suffice it to say that, for the moment, on the basis of internal evidence, such encoders are clearly of Lowland origin, as no interference from Gaelic has been observed. Indeed, even the letters addressed to Sutherland are encoded in English; the only reference to Gaelic is in the following paragraph, in which two Scotticisms occur: the use of the article before the names of languages ("the Gaelic", "the English") and the Scots adjective *bonnie*:

> there is quite a few Scotch Canadians here who can speak the Gaelic better than the English so we have a good time of it here once in a while when Ihere the Gaelic songs. it reminds me of the good old times when Iused to here the Gaelic song in the Bonnie Highlands

Such distinctive uses will be discussed at greater length in the second part of this paper.

---

[5] These terms referring to the encoder's level of schooling are adopted from Fairman's studies (2000 and 2003).

1.1 Register and dialect in personal letters

As we mentioned above, "[p]rivate letters can contain valuable evidence on informal usage" (Görlach 1999: 150). The same author, however, denies that they may have any significant value from the dialectologist's point of view, as "[t]hey rarely include dialect [...]. Writing is so much connected with the school and standard language that composing a letter in dialect is a breach of sociolinguistic convention", and therefore "[m]ost letters written in dialect are literary fabrications". At the same time, "[m]any non-standard features are found in letters by emigrants, who were forced to communicate in written form although not fully qualified for this". This is indeed a crucial issue, pointing to an area of study worth investigating. As a matter of fact, the point is discussed only briefly in Görlach (2004: 211f.), where it is stressed that "sociolinguistic conventions did not permit the use of Scots in [private letters]. [...] If you wrote anything, including private letters, you would do so in *English* (though possibly not *Standard* English), Scots being reserved to oral communication." (original emphasis).

This reference to a standard form, however, begs the question of what Standard English was actually like in nineteenth-century Scotland, especially among partially schooled writers – an issue discussed by Elspaß (2002) in relation to German. As we shall see, in the letters encoded by partially schooled writers the density of Scots elements is quite high, thus pointing to the early existence of the cline still identified by present-day scholars (e.g. McClure 1994). At the one end we have Scots, while at the other end we have Scottish Standard English: in between, Scots lexis, syntax, and morphology may be employed more or less self-consciously and more or less frequently. Even fully-schooled encoders did occasionally choose to use Scots lexis and phrases as markers of solidarity and involvement, while partially-schooled encoders employed Scots lexis and syntax unselfconsciously, providing us with examples of authentic usage beyond the dicta of anglicizing schoolbooks, of which encoders may nonetheless have been aware;[6] indeed, as Fairman (2000, 2003) points out, attempts to follow models associated with full-schooling could often result in varying lexical usage and discourse structure.[7]

Concerning partially-schooled encoders, relatively little (if anything) may be known in relation to the social networks to which writers and recipients

---

[6] For instance, on the influence of Standard English on Northern varieties see Petyt (1992); the complex relationship between Scots and English is discussed by Dossena (2003 and 2005).

[7] In addition, such attempts may be seen as instances of the encoder's social aspirations (Elspaß 1998), of his attempts to 'improve' himself (McColl Millar 2003).

belonged,[8] especially when comparing the situation of gentry and businessmen, where fairly detailed information may be gathered as to what connections existed both in terms of genealogy and of social proximity (see Fitzmaurice 2002; Tieken-Boon van Ostade 1999, 2002 and 2003). On the other hand, emigrants' letters were almost exclusively written to family and neighbours, thus pertaining to a fairly close-knit social group. We may therefore expect instances of informal usage to occur, although geographical distance and the (often stressful) circumstances in which the letters were written may have dictated more formal uses. This is observed most clearly when encoders adopt a more solemn tone on the occasion of someone's death; in which case references to the obedience owed to the Lord's decrees is expressed in terms that echo religious discourse.[9] The following quotation is an example:

> My Dear parents the death of my Husband is a warning to us and showes us how unsertan our times in this world that we know not the day nor the hour that is to call us to account may the Lord look down upon us and enable us to say: Lord thy will be done.

In the next section we shall discuss the linguistic strategies that encode politeness and involvement, whether through formulas or more 'spontaneous' choices.

---

[8]   None of the informants included in this study, for instance, is mentioned among the 130 biographies presented by Bryan (1997). However, it would be incorrect to assume that it was only the most destitute who emigrated – in fact, in the 1830s "emigration [...] was an option only for the better-off" (Whatley 2000: 254). For instance, an indication of the costs a prospective emigrant might incur, apart from transport, is given in a letter from 1818, which recommends: "Be sure to Bring your self shoes enogh to last you 3 or 4 years [...] I want you to lay it out in the following articols as farder as they will go you may lay out 20 pounds sterling in shoemakers threed this article will dubel its valey Easey but it must be of the best kind fetch one pice of the best kind of blue cloth [...] I want you to bring 5 of the best kind of watches [...] Be sure to fetch the fowling articols which you will find greatly to your advantage that is 4 packs of the best kinds pototies 2 pecks of the best wheat 2 Do of oats 2 of teans e of Reygras seed all of them articols you will find a profiet in more then you are aware of Each you will do well to bring one of the best kind of single Bareld shot guns with you as Geam is hear verey plenty Try to bring 3 of the Best kind of pear trees 3 Do of Appels 3 of plumbs + 3 of gusbereys + 10 gallon cas of the best kind of West Cuntry Herrings fetch them things if you find it convenant likewis 10 or 12 Botels of the best Scotch Whisky 2 pecks of Barly [...] NB Bring 2 of the best kind of 10 gallon Bras Bottels".

[9]   This is discussed more extensively by Dossena (forthcoming).

2. Formulaic usage and involvement strategies

First of all, we are going to investigate the connection between formulaic usage and politeness on the one hand and the encoding of social proximity by means of dialectal features on the other. The occurrence of geographically and socially marked syntax and morphology, in addition to phonetic spellings, will be discussed as instances of in-group language in partially-schooled texts.

2.1 Opening and closing formulas

If we exclude the letter addressed to the Duke of Sutherland and concentrate on the remaining 41 letters addressed to family members, we can see that the recipient is typically addressed with *Dear* followed by a term of kinship: "Dear Brother," / "Dear Father and Mother". The possessive *my* is only added when

a. the letter expresses strong emotion, as on the occasion of someone's death:

> My Dear Mother Brothers + Sisters # It is with sorrow that I pen you these few lines in our sad bereavement, I got a letter from Danie last night intimating Dear Fathers unexpected death,

b. the encoder is a woman[10] – this is, for instance, the case in Jane Campbell's letters, where we find "My dear parents" or "My dear Father and Mother";

c. the recipient is a woman or a child; in these cases the first name is also added: "My dear Bella," / "My dear Johnnie".

As can be seen, male encoders generally prefer less involved forms of address, unless a change is dictated by the subject matter or the type of addressee (of a different sex and/or of younger age).

Similarly, closing greetings may also vary and be more or less emphatic, depending on the degree of social or psychological proximity the encoders wish to signal. In formal letters (both private and business) the signature is preceded by phrases like "Yours Most Sincerely" or "I am # Gentlemen # Your very Obedt Servt". Closeness and familiarity, instead, are signalled by formulas like "believe me ever & ever Your Most Affectionate" or "I remain your most sincere Friend". Indeed, the type of relationship existing between encoder and recipient in these cases is made explicit, as in "Your ever faithful

---

[10]   On gender-specific usage see also McLelland (this volume).

& affectionate Husband" or "your Affectionate Nephew". Even in these instances, in which we occasionally find the repetition of the vocative, signatures usually include both name and surname, thus showing that, as late as in the nineteenth century, intimacy was seldom conveyed by the use of first names only.[11]

- I am Dear Brother your affectnet brother and welwisher # Thomas Wilson
- I remain your Affectionate Nephew Malcolm Beaton
- beleve me to be ever your affectionate sister # Jane Campbell

Deeper involvement was therefore encoded by means of other linguistic strategies – for instance, through evaluative lexis expressing appreciation for letters, newspapers, or other items received:

- I am happy to be able to enform you that your Parcel has arreived at last we were very glad to see it and to see it came all right
- I received your letter this morning and the Box of Cloth Which I was Glade to see them all right and safe ,, which I will Recompence you for it if even I live and God spairs me,,
- I am just after receiving and reading your Note, and I have to say that I am really proud of it.

The very first paragraph of the letter, however, is often similar in different texts. In fact, some encoders show very little variation in the way they start their letters and generally follow the models dictated by letter-writing manuals – a few examples are given below:

- Your most welcome letter I duly received the other day and was most glad to learn from it that you were all enjoying good health as this leaves me at present and sincerely hoping it may find you all in the same manner.
- I write you these few lines in the expectation that they will find you all enjoying good health, as this leaves me at present.
- It is with much pleasure that I write you […] to let you know that

The paragraph that announces that the letter is about to conclude, a kind of 'envoy', is also conventional in many cases; either another letter is promised, not necessarily by the same encoder, or apologies are offered for the brevity, haste, poor hand-writing, or other forms of supposed inadequacy of the current

---

[11] On eighteenth-century usage see Tieken Boon-van Ostade (2003), Austin (2000 and 2004) and Bijkerk (2004).

letter. The latter is clearly a positive politeness strategy, based on the maxim of modesty (Leech 1983)[12] – the encoder wishes to avoid that the recipient should equate inaccuracies with neglect and lack of consideration for themselves: a possibility which letter-writing manuals were careful to stress (see Dierks 2000 and Schultz 2000). The following quotations include a few examples:

- as George is writting I will come to a close
- I will not extend this letter further but will write when I get back to Iowa.
- you must excuse me at present for my short letter I will write you soon again

Lack of time and, indeed, lack of paper is often invoked as the reason for closing the letter:

- But I have not time to say more so good bye for the present
- I am sorry my paper is done I would have given you the detail

Very often someone else's greetings are added, or the encoder asks to be remembered to another 'virtual' recipient:

- I must close at present Danie joins with me in sending his best regards to you all.
- I have nomor to say at present but my love to My uncle + Aunts not forgetting yourself and wife and familie
- Remember me kindly to all old friends,

Of course, the parting lines are always the ones where the encoder finds it most difficult to tear oneself away from the virtual contact with the recipient – for this reason, this is where we find expressions of hope concerning the current and future welfare of the recipients:[13]

- hoping you are all enjoying good health hoping all freinds in the like manner

An interesting twist in time reference can also be found where encoders sign off with such a specific greeting as "good night" – clearly, it is very likely that the reader will see it at a different time, but the participants choose to ignore this possibility and implicitly agree on a fictitious time coincidence, so that psychological proximity may be established:

---

[12] In such cases the letter may even be called 'a scrawl'.
[13] In such expressions the deontic value of the phrase encompasses both present and future time reference.

- I am looking for a litter every packet as yet none has come yet but I hope to get one soon Good night and joy be with you

So reluctant are encoders to sign off that very often the conclusion can only be dictated by deontic necessity:

- I must bid you goodbye
- I must conclude with our best compliments to you

In fact, this is also the part of the letter in which spoken interaction is imitated more closely – this is shown, for instance, by the frequent occurrence of *well* as a discourse marker indicating a change of subject and the approaching conclusion, as in "Weel I have no news of any importance to let you know".

2.2 Involvement strategies within the body of the letter

In the cases above we have observed involvement strategies in which the connection between participants is mainly dependent on the conventions of formulaic usage. Within the body of the letter, however, we see that encoders express their psychological proximity to their recipients by means of other linguistic devices.[14] It is not uncommon for the writer to describe the place where (s)he is, perhaps with minute details (especially concerning the weather) that may help the reader visualize the context:

> Weather cold frosty +a little snow when the sun has not melted it today looks very bad +like a big snow storm.

In later letters 'visualization' is made explicit when encoders refer to 'likenesses' being taken, sent, or expected: in these cases the virtual presence of the participants is surrogated by their photos or, occasionally, other realia such as 'Baby's hair'.

On a different level, epistemic modality is frequently employed to predict the recipient's reactions or the encoder's suppositions about what is going on at home – again, distance is shortened through virtual participation in each other's lives:

---

[14] As a matter of fact, Austin (2000: 52ff.) has identified instances in which the formulas dictated in model letters were both adopted and jocularly adapted by the encoders, and indeed the same encoders seem to have been deeply aware of the gap existing between what was conventionally expected to appear in a letter and its actual body.

- You will smile, I daresay, at the idea of my finding any difficulty in managing so small a number,
- I suppose you will be having long ceilidhs in the old familiar way.

The most involving topics in these cases concern village life (births, deaths, marriages and even gossip on unexpected pregnancies, also local politics), wages overseas and at home, and other emigrants from the neighbourhood, with whom a local connection might be established:

- You have no idea what part of America John Murray came too. what girl did he leave in the family way. I understand that his brother James Murray came to America last year I would like to know what part of America they are in.
- I suppose you will be talking Election in the Highlands now as the time is fast approaching when the people loyality will be put to the test and I sincerely hope that they will come forward for men and show that they have no more use for landlords or their oppressive tyrants
- wedges hear for a common mason is about 2 dollars + ¼ or half a gunie for boy

On a metalinguistic level, involvement is also signalled where dialect is employed humorously in letters by fully-schooled encoders – participants deliberately choose an idiom reflecting a *we*-code, which stresses their common cultural background (see Dossena 2002). The function of such 'overt Scotticisms' (Aitken 1979) is therefore to establish common ground through the evocation of shared (past) (linguistic) experience:

- Tom used to be a funny laddie in the days of auld lang syne
- I hope by this time you have recovered your former health and that Margaret is aye the auld saxpence yet and be sure when ye write to gi us a guid lang letter about Dalry an the folk int.

In particular, we may observe that this typically happens with quotations (from Burns, in the case of "auld lang syne") and idioms ("aye the auld sixpence"). In both cases the phrase is somehow 'framed' in the sentence and either follows or introduces another dialectal element ("laddie" in one case, "a guid lang letter" in the other).

At the same time, it would be incorrect to argue that dialect is otherwise entirely missing. In fact, users often employ geographically and socially marked syntax and vocabulary unselfconsciously – that is as 'covert Scotticisms' (Aitken 1979) – and this makes it all the more interesting to analyze their letters, as they may allow us to witness authentic usage beyond the so-called 'observer's paradox'. These traits will be the object of the next section.

3. Grammar and syntax in partially-schooled texts

3.1 The verb phrase

As regards verbs, it is interesting to observe that it is not just 'irregular' forms that occur, but actual variation in tense and aspect construction; for instance, we have instances of *wrot* as participial form:

- I have wrot to John Admson 3 tims since I landed hear
- My Dear parents I should have wrot you long before this but

In the formation of past conditionals we see that, in addition to *ben* as another 'irregular' participial form, in two cases we also record the omission of *have* – a construction that was certainly not uncommon in Older Scots:[15]

- I would ben better pleased without that help but since it is the ceas I may as well have it
- I had had no one to work with me this season although I could now had work for 5 or 6

Other 'non-standard' features are observed in the expression of duration. Indeed, in such cases the perfect tense may be replaced by a simple tense in phrases in which the time adverb is introduced with *since*:

- I see that you have stormy weather since a while at home
- she said that her mother was not keeping very well since some time ago,
- he says he wrote you two or three letters since he went to Kansas City

The perfect aspect may also be expressed by means of an adverbial phrase introduced by *after*, as in "I am just after receiving and reading your Note".[16]

Finally, we observe numerous instances of the so-called 'Northern Subject Rule', according to which a plural subject is followed by a verb with 3rd-

---

[15]   See DOST: "The same North Berwick Law This carling *wald* away <u>carreit</u>"; Gyre-carling 31. (b); "The bischops *wold* gladlie <u>passed</u> by the said petitions"; Rothes Affairs Kirk 7. (2). Grant / Dixon (1921: 120) also illustrate this omission of *have* after *should* and *would*, especially in negative clauses, with a quotation from Burns: "'Have' (*hae, 'a*) is constantly dropped after the auxiliaries 'would', 'should', etc. especially when followed by *-na* [...] "O, Tibbie, I hae seen the day Ye wad na been sae shy." Burns (Song).

[16]   Here the influence of Gaelic may be traced (see Hickey 2004).

person singular ending (if it is a noun or if it is a pronoun plus a noun –
generally, the rule does not apply if the subject is exclusively a pronoun):

- the dresses is to be made short sleaved and low low in the body for eveing
  partes
- he and Dr Willison has known Angus for upwards of 20 years

3.2 Conjunctions and prepositions

Scots forms occur in distinctive uses of conjunctions and prepositions. We
have *for* introducing concessive clauses, as, for instance, in the famous line "A
man's a man for all that":

- my famly all sem to grow uncomenley fast for I do not think that you would
  know them alredy for the short time they have ben out of your sight

We then find a subordinating use of *and*, a case still occurring in present-day
Scottish Standard English:

- i have quiet made up my mind to take a home of my own and to serve my
  brothers no longer first serving one and then the other and getting nothing *and*
  me at the age that I am if there is a easy life alloted for me i think it is quiet time
  iI had it
- Dear Fathers unexpected death, and I can not tell you who how I received such a
  heavy stroke it is hard on me *and* me so far away from you all, but it is the will
  of Almighty God

Scots forms are also found in the use of *nor* instead of 'than' in comparative
clauses:

- there is great opertuinety of well douing here if popel be carful and if they be
  not carful they will not do good hear mor *nor* at hom onley money is easer
  earned hear *nor* what it is at home

3.3 Articles

Typically Scots uses of the deictic *the* occur in time phrases like "the day"
(= 'today') or "the year" (= 'this year') and in the expression "in the fishing",
indicating the activity in which the encoder or the recipient are employed:

- we are to go on board the steamer by twelve o clock the day
- what do they pay in the fishing the year.
- I suppose you will be hard at the potato lifting by this time

In addition, like we saw above, the definite article may occur with the names of languages ("the Gaelic").

4. Lexis and orthography in partially-schooled texts

Phonetic spellings are very frequent in emigrants' letters. Indeed, such spellings typically co-occur with such Scots uses as in the case of *mind* meaning 'remember':

> I mind when I was at denner time after I had supped sume cale and whean a pease of pork I youst to slink about the house untill My Mother gott the swins pitcher to geather up the taty pleallings and sume left Cale into the pitcher away she *gou* to feed the swine with the pitcher in wone hand and the other hand under her apron

When we find instances of self-corrections, it is typical to insert a grapheme that had been omitted, misplaced, or confused

- Johnny hes runing about always in ~~mischefeth~~ mistchef
- we have lost a good many lambs on a count of the ~~Shp~~ Sheep not having milk

or to correct slips of the pen due to an almost automatic inception of a formulaic phrase not corresponding to the actual meaning that was intended:

- I am sory to ~~inform~~ hear by your letter that
- if she comes ~~send me~~ let me know of it
- a Dr William Willson who is a Airshire man has also been kind and ~~attive~~ *atintive* to me at the time Angus died

4.1 Punctuation

As observed by Fairman (2000: 71), partially- or minimally-schooled encoders use punctuation and capitalization quite differently from what can be found in documents by fully-schooled encoders. Indeed, in some cases punctuation is not employed at all:

> when I do remove I will writ you but I am sorow that you have so much posteg to pay for I se that you have to pay $2/6^{1/2}$ but I hop that you will not grudge it I have wrot to John Admson 3 tims since I landed hear but I have not heard from them yet

> but I am going writ this weak to him with a man that is going to the place wheir he is but thair is a grait distence betwen him and me nearley 1[torn] miles but it is not hard to travel to that place onley thair is about 900 miles of sea along the Coast of america will Coast about 3£ for Each person and from that we can have a passage in waggens almost for nothing as they com down that way with the produice of ther land and goes hom empty and had it not ben to wait on Andrew I would have gon of in the cours of 2 monts to wher John Admson is but I will wait now for Andrew or an answer from him

In other cases, punctuation is restricted to the full stop or a dash. In addition, several encoders show a tendency to make their writing faster and more fluent through the use of abbreviations (+ for 'and') and linking words – typically, the first person singular subject and the ensuing verb, or the verb and its infinitive marker:

> As you remark it will be very jolly when I return home with a hatful of money +Iintend this year tostick in + make a nest egg to send home tho' as to farming there on a small scale Ihave my doubts of.

As regards paragraph division, it is not unusual to see that the vocative is repeated whenever the encoder intends to signal a change of subject:

> Dear uncle I have to inform you that John is better at the present time but he will soon be ill again
> Dear uncle I have to relate to you that any of us was never a day ill since we came to Australia […]
> Dear uncle I have to acknowledge that any of us never heard a serimon since we left home we are 50 miles from any Minister and if it was only that against the bush it was Enoug Dear Uncle as soon as I will get an answer from you I intend to go to Melbourne for there is good wages there Dear Uncle I wish you would be so good is to send Mary Walker out here

5. Concluding remarks

As our investigation shows, partially- and minimally-schooled encoders employed a broad range of linguistic strategies aimed at encoding politeness, psychological proximity, and solidarity with their addressees. In addition to the typical formulas adopted from letter-writing manuals, the choice of pragmatic strategies like the 'visualization' of the context or a fictitious bridge across the time-space gap existing between the act of writing and the act of reading could convey messages aimed at maximizing modesty, generosity, tact, and approbation. As regards microlinguistic variation, we see that conscious choices of Scots lexis and idioms only occur in the texts encoded by fully-schooled writers. This is consistent with the nineteenth-century perception of dialect as being inappropriate for written communication outside humorous or jocular contexts. On the other hand, in the texts of partially- and minimally-schooled encoders, geographically marked grammar and syntax are employed unselfconsciously and give us a better picture of authentic usage than any prescriptive or literary text might provide, thanks to the spontaneity that had been recommended by Hugh Blair and had also been appreciated by the nineteenth-century manuals (see Schultz 2000: 118). In the case of our encoders, this spontaneity is indeed so unaffected that the freshness of their messages still has an appeal that cannot but supplement and enrich their (already great) linguistic value.

References

Aitken, Adam Jack. 1979. Scottish Speech: a Historical View with Special Reference to the Standard English of Scotland. In Adam Jack Aitken and T. McArthur (eds.), *Languages of Scotland*. Edinburgh: Chambers, 85–118.

Austin, Frances. 2000. Letter Writing in a Cornish Community in the 1790s. In David Barton and Nigel Hall (eds.), *Letter Writing as a Social Practice*. Amsterdam: Benjamins, 43–61.

Austin, Frances. 2004. "Heaving this importunity": The Survival of Opening Formulas in Letters in the Eighteenth and Nineteenth Centuries. *Historical Sociolinguistics and Sociohistorical Linguistics* 4: online at <www.let. leidenuniv.nl/hsl_shl/> (accessed 14.03.2007).

Barton, David and Nigel Hall (eds.). 2000. *Letter Writing as a Social Practice*. Amsterdam: Benjamins.

Biber, Douglas. 1995. *Dimensions of Register Variation: A Cross-linguistic Comparison*. Cambridge: Cambridge University Press.

Bijkerk, Annemieke. 2004. *Yours sincerely* and *Yours affectionately*. On the Origin and Development of two Positive Politeness Markers. *Journal of Historical Pragmatics* 5: 297–311.

Bryan, Tom. 1997. *Rich Man, Beggar Man, Indian Chief. Fascinating Scots in Canada and America*. Insch/Scotland: Thistle Press.

Cockburn, Henry. 1856/1971. *Memorials of His Time*. Edinburgh: Adam and Charles Black / James Thin.

Dierks, Konstantin. 2000. The Familiar Letter and Social Refinement in America, 1750–1800. In David Barton and Nigel Hall (eds), *Letter Writing as a Social Practice*. Amsterdam: Benjamins, 31–41.

Dossena, Marina. 1997. Attitudes to Scots in Burns's Correspondence. *Linguistica e Filologia* 4: 91–103.

Dossena, Marina. 2002. 'A Scots accent of the mind': The Pragmatic Value of Code-switching between English and Scots in Private Correspondence. A Historical Overview. *Linguistica e Filologia* 14: 103–127.

Dossena, Marina. 2003. Scots. In Ana Deumert and Wim Vandenbussche (eds.), *Germanic Standardizations – Past to Present*. Amsterdam: Benjamins, 383–404.

Dossena, Marina. 2004. Towards a Corpus of Nineteenth-century Scottish Correspondence. *Linguistica e Filologia* 18: 195–214.

Dossena, Marina. 2005. *Scotticisms in Grammar and Vocabulary*. Edinburgh: John Donald.

Dossena, Marina. Forthcoming. "Thank God for his great blessing": Faith and Formulas in Nineteenth-century Scottish Correspondence. In M. Luisa Maggioni (ed.), *The Language(s) of Religion: a Diachronic Approach*.

Dossena, Marina and Charles Jones (eds.). 2003. *Insights into Late Modern English*. Bern: Lang.

Dury, Richard. 2006. A Corpus of Nineteenth-Century Business Correspondence: Methodology of Transcription. In Marina Dossena and Susan M. Fitzmaurice (eds.), *Business and Official Correspondence: Historical Investigations*. Bern: Lang, 193–205.

Elspaß, Stephan. 1998. 'Bridging the Gap: Fixed Expressions in Nineteenth-Century Letters of German Immigrants'. In *Defining Tensions: A Fresh Look at Germans in Wisconsin*. Online at <csumc.wisc.edu/mki/Resources/ Online_Papers/proceedings/elspa.html> (accessed 14.03.2007).

Elspaß, Stephan. 2002. Standard German in the Nineteenth Century? (Counter-) Evidence from the Private Correspondence of 'Ordinary People'. In Andrew R. Linn and Nicola McLelland (eds.), *Standardization – Studies from the Germanic Languages*. Amsterdam: Benjamins, 43–65.

Elspaß, Stephan. 2005. *Sprachgeschichte von unten. Untersuchungen zum geschriebenen Alltagsdeutsch im 19. Jahrhundert*. Tübingen: Niemeyer.

Fairman, Tony. 2000. English Pauper Letters 1800–34 and the English Language. In David Barton and Nigel Hall (eds.), *Letter Writing as a Social Practice*. Amsterdam: Benjamins, 63–82.

Fairman, Tony. 2003. Letters of the English Labouring Classes 1800–34 and the English Language. In Marina Dossena and Charles Jones (eds.), *Insights into Late Modern English*. Bern: Lang, 265–282.

Fitzmaurice, Susan M. 2002. *The Familiar Letter in Early Modern English: A Pragmatic Approach*. Amsterdam: Benjamins.

Görlach, Manfred. 1999. *English in Nineteenth-century England – An Introduction*. Cambridge: Cambridge University Press.

Görlach, Manfred. 2004. *Text Types and the History of English*. Berlin: Mouton.

Grant, William and James Main Dixon. 1921. *A Manual of Modern Scots*. Cambridge: Cambridge University Press.

Hickey, Raymond. 2004. Standard Wisdoms and Historical Dialectology: The Discrete Use of Historical Regional Corpora. In Marina Dossena and Roger

Lass (eds.), *Methods and Data in English Historical Dialectology*. Bern: Lang, 199–216.

Leech, Geoffrey. 1983. *Principles of Pragmatics*. London: Longman.

McClure, J. Derrick. 1994. English in Scotland. In Robert Burchfield (ed.), *The Cambridge History of the English Language*, vol. 5. Cambridge: Cambridge University Press, 23–93.

McColl Millar, Robert. 2003. 'Blind attachment to inveterate custom'. Language Use, Language Attitude and the Rhetoric of Improvement in the First Statistical Account of Scotland. In Marina Dossena and Charles Jones (eds.), *Insights into Late Modern English*. Bern: Lang, 311–330.

Petyt, K.M. 1992. The Influence of the Standard Variety on Northern Forms of British English. In Jan A. van Leuvensteijn and Johannes B. Berns (eds.), *Dialect and Standard Language in the English, Dutch, German and Norwegian Language Areas*. Amsterdam: The Netherlands Academy of Arts and Sciences, 106–118.

Schultz, Lucille M. 2000. Letter-Writing Instruction in Nineteenth Century Schools in the United States. In David Barton and Nigel Hall (eds.), *Letter Writing as a Social Practice*. Amsterdam: Benjamins, 109–130.

Tieken-Boon van Ostade, Ingrid. 1999. Of formulas and friends: Expressions of Politeness in John Gay's Letters. In Guy Tops, Betty Devriendt and Steven Geukens (eds.), *Thinking English Grammar*. Leuven/Paris: Peeters, 99–112.

Tieken-Boon van Ostade, Ingrid. 2002. Robert Lowth and the Corpus of Early English Correspondence. In Helena Raumolin-Brunberg et al. (eds.), *Variation Past and Present. VARIENG Studies on English for Terttu Nevalainen*. Helsinki: Société Néophilologique, 161–172.

Tieken-Boon van Ostade, Ingrid. 2003. Lowth's Language. In Marina Dossena and Charles Jones (eds.), *Insights into Late Modern English*. Bern: Lang, 241–264.

Whatley, Christopher A. 2000. *Scottish Society 1707-1830. Beyond Jacobitism, Towards Industrialization*. Manchester: Manchester University Press.

TONY FAIRMAN (INDEPENDENT RESEARCHER)

'Lower-order' letters, schooling and the English language, 1795 to 1834

1. Introduction

Between 1795 and 1834, English Poor Laws permitted people living in distress outside their parish to apply for relief to their home parish in person or writing. Although a few wrote for relief before 1795, distressed people didn't apply in large numbers till after 1800. The over 10,000 applications I have seen are usually filed as 'correspondence' in the parish overseers' records in County or Metropolitan Record Offices (also called Archives).[1]

Overseers' records contain letters on the many branches of parish business for which the overseers were responsible. Some are drafts of the overseers' own letters, but most, and linguistically perhaps the most interesting, are the applications, written by or for the applicant. A few are from informants about someone who, the writer alleges (sometimes wrongly), is cheating the parish. Most are addressed to parish officials, but a few are addressed to friends and relatives and have ended up in the overseers' records because they include requests for assistance.

I have a corpus of over 1500 letters, comprising about 230,000 'orthographic units' – that is, groups of graphs which the writers separated from other groups by spaces before and after. Most units coincide with dictionary words. The language of the letters ranges from un- and partly-schooled on all linguistic levels (handwriting, orthography, lexis, grammar, discourse and punctuation) to (for about fifty) fully schooled[2] for the early

---

[1] There are other letters in partly-schooled English in other files, but the overseers' files contain the largest collections. I haven't visited Welsh or Scottish Record Offices.

[2] 'Unschooled, schooled, schooling' refer to a, perhaps *the* primary agent through which recognised, or self-appointed authorities on language, supported by textbooks and pedagogues of all types, try to control language. 'Schooled language' is achronic. 'Standard' refers to the accumulation of features in the mid to late 1900s, when authorities made great efforts to get the whole English-using community to write and speak alike. In the early 1800s, the authorities' main aim seems to have been to 'refine' English, not to make everyone use it alike.

1800s. The aim of this paper is to try to construct an overall view of these different letteracies.[3]

2. Three scripts

The first script[4] was written in December 1821 by John Ansell near Hull in north-east England to his parish New Romney, some two hundred miles (320 km) south.[5] The letter includes mistakes and alterations because he probably had no money for paper for a rough copy and may not have thought of making one.[6]

Establishing who wrote such letters is often impossible, because we cannot prove that the person whose name appears at the end did the writing. This letter, however, reads as if the writer wrote it himself. But in 1821 there were three John Ansells in New Romney. Two were 18-year-old youths. One of them was the son of a 62-year-old man, the other was illegitimate, and was probably the writer – his mother could sign her name and may have taught him.

Plate 1. John Ansell's letter

Transliteration		Comments
from John Ansell North Cave Yorkshea$_r$		
frends this coms from me with a		
gret deel of un eas for to think how	*dll*	*h* written above.
werry i am ~~of~~ bad of and i should		
5 be glad if you yould send me acup	orig?: *glas--*	
ple of pounds for i am yerry		
bad of and if you yount i suld	orig?: *basi* *i* inserted later.	
fall seek on this parrish and	*pa* or *po*	
thay well breng me home	orig: *brend.* *h* started before *me.*	
10 Sick send it sune to for		
i am bad of i wish that i was	*i an.*	*i* doubtful mark before *wish.*
back agane at my home a		
gane for hear is bread as		
black as my at and i have	*blas.*	*i ha* rising loop started.

---

[3]   In the early 1800s, people who could read counted as literate. But, since it is difficult to discover the reading ability of lower-class writers, I discuss only writing. 'Letteracy' means 'writing' and the ability to produce it.

[4]   'Script' means handwritten discourse. 'Text' is printed discourse. Scripts may contain their own history and provide information about writers which texts don't.

[5]   Centre for Kentish Studies, Maidstone (CKS(M)): New Romney, P309/18/17.

[6]   Unlike now, paper did not lie in the streets in those days. William Hone's biographer says Hone (1780–1842, father a copy-clerk) "plundered rubbish bins [for reading matter] with the desperation of a drug addict" (Wilson 2005: 26).

15 mot ad no work sence   orig: *h* and another letter. orig. *at.*
    harvest   *n har.*
    [ON REVERSE SIDE]
    pleas Mr Glover Show this to the   *M* looks like *W. Sha.*
    gentlemem and if you gentle   *genthe-*: final *m* is doubtful. *if* over *y.*
    nen ob beay i shall yarrer   *of.* First *r* of *yarrer* as in *harvest.*
20 sune send an ser back agane   *an ser* written separately, then joined.
    and dereck it at Robbard ~~Hew~~   orig: *and l.*
    Hewson North Cave Yourkshea_r
       Weten Weten

Answd by [writing to the [War Office [9th Dec [TW^7

Handwriting

Ansell was an inexperienced pointillist writer; that is, he didn't write his words but drew them graph by graph, as pointillist painters build an image dab by dab. In fact, he was a minimal pointillist because he drew some graphs with more than one stroke of the pen, as calligraphers do – lower case <m>, for example. Other graphs he didn't produce in schooled shape – his lower case <y> looks slightly upper case. As learner writers still do, he confused <b, d, g, p> (l. 9). One might guess from his many false starts that forming graphs took up so much of his attention that he lost track of his message (l. 4). This guess is supported by comparing the names *John Ansell, Robberd Hewson* and the two instances of *North Cave* with the rest of his writing. His pen formed the names with long, smooth strokes and good calligraphic swells on the down strokes. As a learner he must have practised his own names many times. The other names were strange to him. Someone, therefore, may have written them for him, with the unschooled spelling, which isn't unique. When copying these names, therefore, he concentrated entirely on producing 'a fair hand'.

Lexis

1) His vocabulary and phrasing are almost entirely Anglo-Saxon. His Latinate words had been in the English language so long that they looked Anglo-Saxon. For example, partly-schooled writers throughout England used the lexeme [UN]EASE (l. 3);
2) *fall seek on* (l. 8) and *bad of* (ll. 4, 7, 11): language authorities tried to refine such metaphorical and phrasal usages out of English.
3) *for* (l. 6): writers like Ansell rarely wrote 'because'.

---

7   The bracket [in running script = line break.

Orthography

There is much to say about this level, but I point out two features: 1) *werry, yerry, yarrer* (ll. 4, 6, 19): this is a rare example of dialect influence. Kentish speakers in those days pronounced /w/ for the schooled initial /v/ and spelt accordingly.[8] 2) *you yould, you yount, thay well* (ll. 5, 7, 9): Ansell must have learnt not to write his spoken abbreviations, but, like other partly-schooled writers,[9] he was unsure how to unpack them into schooled spellings. As with other partly-schooled writers, uncertainty about forming <v, w> and <y> may have increased his uncertainty about unpacking.

Grammar

My corpus has examples of *for to* (+INFIN) (l. 3) and double negation (l. 15) throughout England.

Discourse

1) Ansell didn't know the schooled openings and endings of a letter.
2) Like other writers who had learnt no more than to form graphs and to copy, Ansell seems to have thought in formulas, which sometimes led him to repeat words and phrases too often for the requirements of schooled styles. For example, *I am bad of,* and *back agane* and *home agane* (ll. 12–13).[10]

The annotation at the end shows that lack of schooling didn't deter TW (Thomas Woollett, the New Romney overseer) from relieving applicants. It didn't deter other overseers either. Partly-schooled letteracy was effective and those who wrote it felt no need for a schooled script.

The second script was sent to another overseer of New Romney by Stephen Wiles, three days before his nineteenth birthday.[11] Wiles was apprenticed to a watch and clockmaker in Rye, Sussex (south east), a few miles from New

---

[8]   For example, *gorge plum*mer. No date, 1806? it [is not in my powr to come to [the westrey. CKS(M): Farningham, P145/18/1.

[9]   For example, Catarine Pea*ce. Febry 17 1834. you promised you [Ould a foard me some assstens* Somerset R.O (south west), Curry Rivell, D/P/cur.r/13/10/3.

[10] German scholars speak of "Stilzusammenbruch" ('stylistic collapse'. See Vandenbussche 1999: 53, quoting from Mattheier. All translations from German to English are my own.), which views discourse from above. But the concept of formulaicity views discourse panoramically (see Wray 2000). Partly-schooled writers in England weren't concerned to follow schooled stylistic requirements.

[11] CKS(M): New Romney, P309/18/15.

Romney. Thomas Woollett had taught Wiles to read and 'write'. Many of Woollett's letters survive, showing that he wrote good schooled English of his time. But, like other teachers, he didn't think it was his task to teach Wiles (then aged 10 to 15 years) to compose in schooled English.

Plate 2. Stephen Wiles's letter

Rye May 8th 1821
Mr Cohen , — — —
Sir I have taken the liberty
of writing a few lines wich I should be
5   very much a bleidge to you if you will
have the Goodness to Git my trowers
Donn by Satuarday if you please — —
Sir/ this Wheskett peace i add Given me
if you will have the Goodness to make me
10   a Wheskett i Should be very much a bleidge
to you Sir/ I am very much a bleidge
to you for the things that you
Sent me a Satuarday
from yours Respectfully
Stephen Wiles —

Wiles's handwriting is pointillist in places, but his script is more schooled than Ansell's. Perhaps its most striking feature, which isn't unique in my corpus, is the vocative punctuation, *Sir/*, which Wiles used before (not after) each proposition. Other writers punctuated verbally before they changed the subject, instead of starting a new paragraph. Few partly-schooled writers used punctuation, perhaps because most spelling-books introduced it at the end of the book, as an aid to reading aloud.[12] For example, Joseph Guy in *A New British Spelling Book* (1810), which Woollett used when teaching Wiles, wrote

> A *comma* is a pause, or resting in speech, while you may count *one* [...] A *semicolon* is a pause while you may count *two* [...] A *colon* is a pause while you may count *three* [...] A *period*, or full stop, denotes the longest pause, or while you may count *four*. (Guy 1810: 149)

The left dislocation, *this wheskett peace i add given me* (l. 8), wasn't a schooled structure, and still isn't – 'a feature of colloquial style [...] very loose and informal spoken English' says the Quirk team (1985: 1416). But it isn't ungrammatical and is easy to understand. There seems no reason why it should

---

[12]   Several teachers demonstrated the efficacy of their teaching by staging annual Public Recitations. See Canterbury Cathedral Archives: Dover St Mary's, U3/P30/25/10, from 1871 to 1901, and Caffyn (1998) for Sussex in the 1700s.

be unschooled, except perhaps that it wasn't used in Latin – then still the
model for schooled English.

I include the third script for contrast with the other two. It was written by
Philip Papillon from his boarding school in what is now a north London suburb
to his parents in Canterbury.[13]

Plate 3. Philip Papillon's letter

April 26nd, 1834

My dear Mama
    I hope Lawrence is better give
my love to Papa & Sisters give my love to
M[rs] scrain. I likeed been at school very
much I took such a long walk the first day
& I walked with Johny & fredy we had our
diner at the inn I drank tea with M[r] Burron
the first night I make a very nice breakfast
of the cocoa I am able to pa^ly at all the
games that the boys play at tell Papa that
[NEXT PAGE]
I have not began to learn my gramar
so good bye my dear mama your dutiful son
P O Papillon

Papillon was a gentleman's son and had probably been privately tutored at
home before he went to school. He must also have benefited from his literate
and well-schooled home environment. His handwriting (calligraphic and
minimal pointillist) and content are childlike (he was seven years, eight
months old), but all his graphs are well formed and, because he wrote between
double lines, regular. Like Ansell and Wiles, Papillon didn't punctuate. But,
young as he was, he had the concept of sentence.

If we count unschooled spellings in the first 82 units in the bodies of the
letters as a letteracy marker, the figures for Wiles's first and his last surviving
letter one year and five months later are 13/82 (for Ansell 23/82) and 8/82, and
he still punctuated vocatively. During that time he was learning to repair and
make watches and clocks. Papillon's figures are 6/82 and 2/82, including
words like *Colossians, filberts* and *because*. During that time Papillon took
notes of Sunday sermons, stopped pointillism, and began to use punctuation
and learn Latin – *we now have two Latin lessons every day*.[14]

---

[13] CKS(M): Osborne, U1015/C122/1.
[14] CKS(M): Osborne, U1015/C122/4. Papillon's letters seem 'uncorrected'.

Stem cell script and causation

These three scripts were probably the writers' first compositional writing. In the New Romney records, for example, the first letter about Wiles's need for new shoes and clothing is from Mary Wiles, his sister or sister-in-law, and is dated more than two years before desperation drove Stephen himself to write.

Like Stephan Elspaß, discussing similar German letters (2002: 49), I am not inclined to take a one-sided view from above and 'shrug off' the language of these letters simply because it isn't schooled.

Such first scripts, or, since it's impossible to be sure they really were first scripts, such near-first scripts are of interest to teachers and linguists, because they are the sites at which the language user changes from being only a speaker to being a speaker and a writer. Such scripts I call 'stem cell scripts'. The National Institutes of Health website says a stem cell has:

> the potential to develop into many different cell types. When a stem cell divides, each new cell has the potential to either remain a stem cell or become another type of cell with a more specialized function.

Two questions arise concerning stem cell scripts: 1) What happened before them? 2) What, if anything, did the writer produce afterwards? To answer the first question I propose four factors:

1) *age*: What effect does age have on a writer's first composition? A young child's linguistic ability isn't fully developed. But in the early 1800s, unlike nowadays, adults also wrote stem cell scripts. I shall not discuss this factor;

2) *speech and writing*: Modern researchers take their data from the speech and writing of people who are (or were) fully-schooled writers and focus on similarities of features in speech and writing (Biber 1988; Street 1995). But I focus on a more basic level, on the point at which speakers became writers too, before they had learnt much about schooled writing.

3) *social background*: The linguistic environment within which the learner writer lives;

4) *schooling*: How is writing taught?

Speech and writing

Researchers classify writing as either Standard or non-standard, which they subdivide into dialect and failed Standard. My letters have few dialect features, few, at least, according to standard reference books. But since the letters contain words and meanings which the books don't record, there may be more regional features than we know of. Furthermore, written dialect is a special category, invented in the early 1800s by writers who either had never spoken it, or had done so, but, after learning schooled English, had invented printed dialects when there was a market for them after about 1850. Printed dialects differ from partly-schooled writing.

As for failed standard (the ultimate shrug-off category), we must not assume stem cell scripts are interlanguages on the way to full Standard (Richards 1974). In theory, they could change in any direction, or not at all. Certainly, we *can* take a view from above and sort the letters into a continuum according to their approximation to full schooledness. It is also certain that some initially partly-schooled writers became fully-schooled, for there are single letters, written in practised hands, which the writers might have written after just such a change. But I have seen no sequence in which the letteracy developed from partly- to fully-schooled. So far I have seen only two series where the writer changed the letteracy in an unschooled direction: 1) Rachel Clark's three increasingly 'impudent' letters in 1826; 2) the vocabulary of William King, shoemaker, gradually became more religious in fourteen applications for relief which he wrote from London to his home parish in Essex between 1828 and 1834.[15] Most series of partly-schooled letters I have seen remain unchanged over many years.[16] Their writers were not on a continuum to anywhere. If they altered anything, they usually altered only to make better sense.

Wim Vandenbussche (1999), writing of Belgian scripts, says many, perhaps most writers seem to have regarded letteracy as 'a onefold' task. They aimed to express themselves clearly, and not also in schooled language. But, in fact, as I discussed above, some writers did have two tasks: making sense, and what Vandenbussche and I, who both produce fully-schooled scripts with comparative ease, don't see as a task at all – the purely mechanical task of forming graphs.

These letters and other types of writing, such as bills, form a body of language, which doesn't fit into the categories which linguists have developed for classifying schooled or dialect writing.

Despite Street's arguments (1995: passim), I maintain that scripts are sites both of the socially defined requirements for letteracy and of what he calls 'autonomy'. For example, even the least-schooled language users didn't write, like, fillers and phatic communication, which they probably said, know what I mean. The scripts of writers with little or no training in composition, or who

---

[15] 1) Essex (East Anglia) R.O. (Colchester): St. Botolph's, Colchester, D/P 203/18/1; 2) Essex R.O. (Chelmsford): Braintree, D/P 264/18/24. See also Sokoll (2001).

[16] James and Frances Soundy, for example, Berkshire (just west of London) R.O.: Pangbourne, DP/91/18/4–11 (1818–1829).

perhaps had been exposed to discourses (Biblical, for example) which were unlike what they wanted to put down on a blank sheet of paper – the scripts of these writers are sites where we might be able to detect both what writers do which speakers don't and informal forces of language conventionalisation.

One rarely mentioned factor in successful communication is the reader's input. Kate Parry (1988), discussing English as a second language, quotes Frank Smith that for writing to have meaning 'readers have to draw all the time on "the theory of the world in the brain".' A reader who knows nothing of cigarettes, for example, cannot understand what 'NO SMOKING' is intended to mean. Parry discusses a good example of reader's input – a moving letter she once received from a Nigerian student. Readers without African experience find this letter a puzzle, if not incompetent. If, therefore, readers of English partly-schooled letters find them incomprehensible, they should not blame only the writer, but should consider what types of reading skills they do and don't bring to the script.

Social background

Ansell and Wiles lived in largely orate environments; Papillon in a literate [sic] one. Another difference is that educationists, family members and others expected Papillon, as a gentleman's child, to write what they might find worth reading. But from Ansell and Wiles, as members of the lower orders, they expected little more than bills for services rendered.

Patrick Colquhoun, lawyer and social activist (1745–1820), calculated the population of England and Wales in 1803 by status and occupation (1806: 23). The less than well-schooled letters in my corpus were written by members (and their spouses) of occupational classes such as shopkeepers, lesser landholders, master craftsmen, artisans, soldiers, clerks and other business assistants, labourers, servants, pedlars, publicans and paupers, totalling 83.7% of Colquhoun's population of 9,343,561. This occupational range is too wide to be a useful determiner of letteracy.

Furthermore, the overseers' records contain letters in well-schooled English by other members of these classes. We must, therefore, beware of the concept of *eine Arbeiterschriftsprache* ('a workers' letteracy'), which German scholars (Mattheier 1990, Klenk 1998) have tried to identify in similar German letters in the same period. It might be true that a certain letteracy is predominantly workers' letteracy, but it isn't true that workers had no other letteracy.

Secondly, from the Industrial Revolution in the mid 1700s onwards more and more people became socially mobile. William Cobbett, for example, started his working life as a copy-clerk and ended it as a landowner and member of parliament, and the author Charles Dickens also came from a working-class family.

Thirdly, in the 1970s in Africa many students' parents were agricultural labourers very like those in Europe in the early 1800s. I find no trace of anything I want to call an Africanised labourers' letteracy. Street discusses something similar on Pacific Ocean islands (1995: 77ff.).

Finally, researchers often cannot relate letteracy to class because we don't know who wrote the letters, and if we do, we often know little about the writers beyond the date of their baptism and, after 1812 when such details were first required to be recorded at baptisms, their father's occupation.

The schooling of letteracy

No one just picks up writing. We must be schooled. By this I don't mean only attendance at school. Many children – of rich and poor parents alike – were schooled at home.

There are two difficulties to accounting for letteracy by schooling. First, whereas we can often link an upper-class child with schooling because records have survived, we cannot link a lower-class child with schooling because usually none have survived. For example, Stephen Wiles is the only writer out of hundreds in my corpus whose schooling I know something about. Secondly, home schooling is almost unrecoverable.

Nevertheless, if poor people went to school, most attended one type – a free, or charity school. I have written elsewhere (Fairman 2005) about such schooling. So, here I mention only two key features. First, teachers were untrained and their methods must have differed syn- and diachronically. This resulted in different letteracies and probably literacies too. Secondly, until after 1870 teachers taught letteracy in two distinct stages. All learners started the first stage, which we might call 'the mechanical part of the instruction'.[17] This method had hardly changed since Quintilian in the first century AD: pupils learnt to form and join graphs regularly, moving from left to right in straight lines, from top to bottom of the page (Kress 2000). They would then practise 'WRITING in all its useful Hands'[18] by copying religious or moralising texts into their copy (not exercise) books. Lower-order children could spend three years doing this.

---

[17]   Cheshire (north Midlands) R. O.: Regulations, 1814, Warrington Female School of Industry, P316/5448/195.

[18]   An advert for a boys' school in Mayfield, Sussex, 1771 (Caffyn 1998: 201). Schooling the poor for 'usefulness' was often stressed.

Only children whose parents could afford the fees started the second stage of letteracy, 'liberal education', though others taught themselves later. Stage-two letteracy was narrower than modern letteracy. The National Curriculum for England (1999), for example, expects an eleven-year-old child to write 'narratives, poems, playscripts, reports, explanations, opinions, instructions, reviews, commentaries'.

This two-stage instruction in letteracy had three consequences. First, Elspaß's question 'To what extent, and for how long, did regional influences prevail in [the teachers'] actual written language production and their teaching' (2002: 45) arises only partly for those English writers who weren't taught to compose and who copied from books, not from their teachers. They may have learnt from each other *after* their basic instruction. Such informal traditions are as much forces for language conventionalisation as schooled formal instruction with all its supporting means is.

Secondly, there was "keine für Volksschulen geeignete Grammatik" ('no grammar suitable for elementary schools', Klenk 1998: 326). The children of the poor learnt no grammar, neither in the modern nor in the old sense, which included all levels of language. Robert Lowth, the first modern English grammarian, defined grammar as "the Art of rightly expressing our thoughts by Words" (1762: 1), which suggests a reason why the lower-orders were thought to need no grammar: they were "so trained up, as to make them [...] not only fit, but willing to be employed [as copy-clerks] either in trade, service, husbandry, or any other business".[19] They were expected to copy others' words,[20] not write their own.

Thirdly, if they did write for themselves, their letteracy was more open to unschooled influences than that of fee-paying scholars. Finally, since their partly-schooled applications for relief were granted, they didn't need to write schooled scripts.

Partly-schooled writers wrote according to conventions which extended informally throughout England. For example, 1) some began letters to social superiors with 'Frends' and ended 'so nomore from [NAME]'; 2) they used words like *dark* (blind), *shift* (make a living), *nourish(ment)* (tonic), *tramp* (look for work), which the *OED* doesn't mention, or defines as obsolete, or dialect; 3) for 'precision' schooling authorities demanded different words for different meanings, but partly-schooled writers combined the same words (*be,*

---

19 Charity school regulations, 1824. Berkshire R.O., Binfield: D/P18/25/7.

20 But they did need grammar. Cobbett, copy-clerk, says: 'I could not read the pot-hooks and hangers of Mr. Holland [...] I was of but little use to him; for [...] my want of knowledge in orthography, gave him infinite trouble' (*Life and Adventures of Peter Porcupine*. William Cobbett. Port Washington, London: Kennikat Press. 1970: 29).

come, go, make, take, etc.) with different particles to convey different meanings by phrases.

In this volume we are invited to view the history of language from below. But a view from below is as one-sided as a view from above. I try to adopt a position from where we can have a panorama of all forces, formal and informal, which conventionalise letteracies. The term 'convention' includes those forces which insist on a single way to write (or speak) and those which result merely in ways in which writing is done.

References

Biber, Douglas. 1988. *Variation across Speech and Writing*. Cambridge: Cambridge University Press.

Caffyn, John. 1998. *Sussex Schools in the 18th Century*. Lewes: Sussex Record Society.

Colquhoun, Patrick. 1806. *A Treatise on Indigence*. London: Hatchard.

Elspaß, Stephan. 2002. Standard German in the 19th Century? (Counter-) evidence from the private correspondence of 'ordinary people'. In Nicola McLelland and Andrew Linn (eds.), *Standardization Studies from the Germanic Languages*. Amsterdam and Philadelphia: Benjamins, 43–66.

Fairman, Tony. 2005. Schooling the Poor in Horsmonden, 1797–1816. *The Local Historian* 37.2: 120–131.

Klenk, Marion. 1998. Briefe preußischer Bergarbeiter von 1816 bis 1918. Eine soziologische Studie zur Arbeiterschriftsprache im 19. Jahrhundert. In Dieter Cherubim, Siegfried Grosse and Klaus J. Mattheier (eds.), *Sprache und bürgerliche Nation: Beiträge zur deutschen und europäischen Sprachgeschichte des 19. Jahrhunderts*. Berlin and New York: de Gruyter, 317–340.

Kress, Gunther. 2000. *Early Spelling: Between convention and creativity*. London: Routledge.

Lowth, Robert. 1762. *A Short Introduction to English Grammar*. London: Routledge/Thoemmes Press.

Mattheier, Klaus J. 1990. Formale und funktionale Aspekte der Syntax von Arbeiterschriftsprache im 19. Jahrhundert. In Anne Betten (ed.), *Neuere Forschungen zur historischen Syntax des Deutschen. Referate der internationalen Fachkonferenz Eichstätt 1989*. Tübingen: Niemeyer, 286–295.

National Curriculum for England: English. 1999. London: The Stationery Office.

Parry, Kate. 1988. Letter from Mohammed. *Geolinguistics* 14: 16–27.

Quirk, Raymond, Sidney Greenbaum, Geoffrey Leech and Jan Svartvik. 1985. *A Comprehensive Grammar of the English Language*. London and New York: Longman.

Richards, Jack C. (ed.). 1974. *Error Analysis: Perspectives on Second Language Acquisition*. London: Longman.

Sokoll, Thomas (ed.). 2001. *Essex Pauper Letters, 1731–1837*. Oxford: Oxford University Press.

Street, Brian. 1995. *Social Literacies: Critical Approaches to Literacy in Development, Ethnography and Education*. Harlow: Pearson.

Vandenbussche, Wim. 1999. 'Arbeitersprache' in Bruges during the 19th century. In Helga Bister-Broosen (ed.), *Beiträge zur historischen Stadtsprachenforschung*. Wien: Edition Praesens.

Wilson, Ben. 2005. *The Triumph of Laughter: William Hone and the Fight for the Free Press*. London: Faber & Faber.

Wray, Alison. 2000. The functions of formulaic language: an integrated model. *Language and Communication* 20: 1–28.

NICOLA MCLELLAND (NOTTINGHAM)

"Doch mein Mann möchte doch mal wissen ..." A discourse analysis of 19th-century emigrant men and women's private correspondence[1]

1. Introduction: Gender and discourse

Since the 1970s at least, it has been suggested that men and women differ in their discursive use of language (Lakoff 1973, 1975). The last twenty years or so have seen much work that explores this contention (e.g. Bergvall et al. 1996, Cameron 1996, Cheshire and Trudgill 1998, Holmes 1995, Kotthoff and Wodak 1997, Talbot 1998, Tannen 1995, Wodak 1997) and tests it against German data (e.g. Günthner and Kotthoff 1992, Linke 2002, Schoenthal 1998) in addition to the larger body of work available for English. It has been suggested that in conversation women are more prone than men to use epistemic modality forms – those forms used to indicate the speaker or writer's confidence, or lack of it, in the truth of what they are saying (*perhaps, I think, probably*, modal verbs, etc.) (Holmes 1995), as well as hedging phrases such as *sort of, really*; and tag questions like *doesn't it, won't they? nicht wahr?*, which invite the participation of others and which have been interpreted as evidence for a greater co-operativeness in the structuring of women's discourse, as opposed to a more competitive discourse style, which is more often adopted by men (also Coates 1989 [1998], Erickson et al. 1978, Thimm 1998). It has further been suggested that, when issuing instructions, women are more likely to use less direct means than men, minimizing the difference in power or status between themselves and their interlocutor (Kuhn 1981/82, Kuhn 1992a, Kuhn 1992b). However, apparent gender differences of this sort in discourse remain difficult to pin down and interpret. For instance, Thimm (1998) found that (as we might have hypothesized) the women in her

---

[1] Thanks are due to Dr Tom Reader for assistance with the statistical analysis and for helpful comments on an earlier draft of this paper. Any remaining shortcomings are of course my own. Thanks also to Stephan Elspaß, who made available the corpus of letters used in the second study reported on below.

boss/secretary role-play study used more questions than the men, who used more commands, and that the women used more metacommunicative formulations such as *da hätte ich noch eine Bitte* .... – but she found that the men in her study used more softeners such as particles, diminutives, and subjunctive forms.

Part of the lack of clarity in research into gender and discourse patterns is the result of the fact that discourse analysis tends to be qualitative rather than quantitative. Problems arise when data that are essentially anecdotal in nature are treated as if indicative of general trends without appropriate statistical analysis. An influential but not isolated example – included both in a standard sociolinguistics reader (Cheshire and Trudgill 1998) and, translated, in a German collection of studies of gender in institutional settings (Günthner and Kotthoff 1992) – is West (1990). In a detailed qualitative analysis, West demonstrates how in her data male and female doctors use differing strategies to issue instructions to their patients. West then suggests that there is also a *quantitative* difference between genders in the frequency with which the strategies adopted meet with patient compliance. Unfortunately, this suggestion is not supported by appropriate statistical analysis, and a closer examination reveals that the apparent trend could easily have appeared by chance. The success rates of strategies used by men and women did not differ significantly when analysed statistically. (Chi-squared tests on the raw data as presented by West herself: for women, $\chi^2_{(df)} = 5.53_{(3)}$, $p = 0.137$; for men, $\chi^2_{(df)} = 7.94_{(6)}$, $p = 0.242$. That is: there was a >13% chance (for women) and a >24% chance (for men) of patterns at least as extreme as those observed in the data occurring if the null hypothesis, that there was no difference in compliance regardless of strategy used, was correct.) Thimm's (1998) study referred to above, with its 109 participants, is a serious attempt to identify trends in the general population, but again my own analysis shows that none of the raw data presented (Thimm 1998: 336) are indicative of statistically significant effects of gender.[2]

The present paper aims to look at gender and discourse features from a historical sociolinguistic perspective, but also – in the light of the methodological problems with discourse analysis noted above, and with the advantage of a relatively large, easily searchable corpus – to produce quantitative results that are robust and generalizable.

---

[2]   In all cases, $\chi^2_{(df)} < 4.67_2$, $p > 0.097$. On the other hand, Thimm tells us that her results for syntactical complexity *are* significant, though she does not present the raw data.

2. Language and gender
in 19th-century German emigrant letters

Elspaß' studies of linguistic variation in letters written by German 19th-century emigrants to the USA (Elspaß 2002a, Elspaß 2005) have drawn attention to a rich resource[3] that allows us to study the written production of ordinary people writing for private consumption. Elspaß has investigated these letters from a number of different perspectives, including considering possible differences attributable to gender (Elspaß 2002b). He found that there was no difference between genders in the use of non-standard grammatical features, nor in syntactic complexity, and that gender only seemed to play a role where it interacted with the social aspirations of the writers. For example, he noted the fondness of some young female working class writers for expressions such as *sich amüsieren* which had connotations of a bourgeois lifestyle.

While Elspaß found no real difference in men and women's basic written *competence*, the present study considers features of *discourse* that research has suggested can vary between men and women in 20th-century linguistic practice. Not only are we dealing with linguistic data from a century or so earlier than that considered by the research I have referred to above, we are also looking at the specific, *written* text-type of the letter. Looking at these rather different data should add a dimension to our understanding of possible interactions between gender and discourse strategies, so far largely based on latter 20th-century discourse.

The study was conducted in two phases. A small corpus of letters was first investigated manually. In the second phase a larger corpus was investigated using a concordancing programme. All results were tested for statistical significance using appropriate statistical analysis.

3. The first study

3.1 Methods

The corpus for the first study consisted of 22 letters by women and 23 by men, totalling approximately 30,000 words, covering the period 1850–1900, and representing seven female and eight male writers. The features investigated have all been identified by previous work as possibly differing according to gender in late 20th-century German spoken discourse:

---

[3] See www.auswandererbriefe.de.

(1)   particles (softening / hedging / emphatic)
(2)   formulations such as *ich denke* preceding a proposition
(3)   tag questions, specifically *nicht wahr*
(4)   intensifying adverbs such as *sehr, ziemlich, so*
(5)   superlatives
(6)   metacommunicative formulations (*ich möchte Dich bitten; nun will ich Euch auch schreiben, daß ...*).
(7)   imperatives

It was hypothesized that letters written by women would show a higher frequency of items 1–3, and that men's letters would have a higher instance of imperatives (item 7). Work on features 4, 5, and 6 in 20th-century discourse has usually suggested that these would be used more frequently by women than by men, though Burgoon et al. (1991) suggested that men do also use features of verbal intensity effectively, in some contexts at least.

In addition, the following features specific to the discourse type of letter were investigated:

(8)   language used in expressing the desire for a reply.

Since this is a common speech act in the corpus, it can provide roughly comparable data giving an indication of how directly or otherwise requests/ instructions are formulated.

(9)   the use of the opening and closing formulae *die Feder ergreifen* and *ich will schließen* (and their variants).

Here it was hypothesized – in the light of research suggesting that women attempt to adhere to standard language forms more so than men – that women might tend to conform more to the 'rules' of letter-writing, and hence to use such formulae more frequently.

(10)   apostrophising the recipient(s) (addressing the recipient by name / title in the letter after the initial salutation).

This is a strategy to involve the recipient and to overcome the essential monologic constraint of a letter. In this sense, it is comparable in function with tag questions in conversation, and so it was hypothesized that like tag questions, it would be used more frequently by women than by men.

Frequency was measured per line. Where more than one letter was written by one writer, a single average frequency for all letters by that writer was fed into the analysis, so that writers of multiple letters were not over-represented in the data. In all cases, orthographic variants (such as *nuhr*, *mahl*, etc.) were also considered.

3.2 Results

(1) The use of particles

The frequency of the following particles was measured: *doch, (ein)mal, schon, nun, wohl, ja, eben, halt, immer [noch], sogar, nur, gerade, eigentlich, überhaupt, nämlich, erst, durchaus, also*. Only their use in the function of particles was counted. (Thus *wenn ich nur Zeit hätte* would count as an instance of the particle *nur*; *Es waren nur sechs Leute da* would not count.) Because it was often difficult to determine whether tokens of *auch* were used as particles or in the full semantic sense of 'in addition', it was discounted from the analysis.

	Men		Women	
	Total	Per line	Total	Per line
Particles	138	0.154	207	0.124
Total lines sampled	892		1662	

Table 1: Frequency of particles by gender in Corpus 1

Overall, as hypothesized, the frequency of particles was higher for women than for men (one-tailed *t*-test adjusted for unequal variance, $t=1.989$, $df=9.3$, $p=0.039$) (Figure 1), though with considerable variation between authors within each gender (Figure 2).

Nicola McLelland

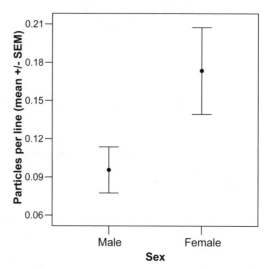

Figure 1: Male and female use of particles in Corpus 1

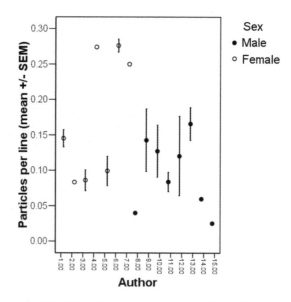

Figure 2: Male and female use of particles in Corpus 1
(individual authors; no error bar indicates that the author only contributed one letter to the corpus)

It turns out that *doch* alone drives the significant result: the difference in frequency of *doch* is significant (adjusted *t*-test: $t = 3.11$, $df = 6.6$, $p = 0.010$) (see Figure 3), while the difference in frequency for the remaining particles is not (*t*-test: $t = 1.13$, $df = 14$, $p = 0.134$). Furthermore, the usage patterns of individual authors (Figure 4) reveal two female 'outliers' with particularly high frequences of *doch*. This is not enough alone to drive the significant result, but certainly contributes to its strength; with the small corpus size, then, the finding needs to be treated cautiously.

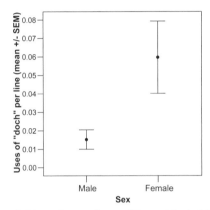

Figure 3: Men and women's use of the particle *doch* in Corpus 1

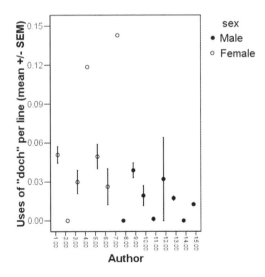

Figure 4: Men and women's use of *doch* (individual authors) in Corpus 1

Given our finding for *doch*, further analysis of the data was undertaken to see if the difference in frequency could be explained by differences between males and females in *how* they use *doch*. All instances of the particle were categorized according to function: contrastive (*aber doch ein Armer*), with a command (*denk' doch nicht*), explanatory (not found in the data), expecting agreement (*Hoffentlich habt Ihr sie seitdem doch jede Woche erhalten*), stating something assumed to be known (*Es ist doch Winter*), expressing a wish (*wenn er doch hier währ*), and emphatic (*doch gar viele*). The results of the categorization are given in Table 2 below:

Function of *doch*	Males	Females
contrastive	8	10
with a command	7	8
explanatory	0	0
expecting agreement	0	2
stating something assumed to be known	6	7
expressing a wish	1	9
emphatic	2	11

Table 2: Functions of *doch* in letters by male and female writers (raw figures) in Corpus 1

Given that the corpus of female letters is smaller than that of the males, the raw data in the first five categories already reflect a higher frequency per line in the female data. However, it is the final two categories – expressing a wish and emphatic usage – that account for most of the 'extra' *doch* occurrences in the letters written by women. The differences between genders are not significant ($\chi^2_{(df)} < 8.43_{(5)}, p = 0.134$), though the trends here do accord with established findings that women are more likely to use emphatic language such as *so, very*, etc. The occurrences in clauses expressing a wish may simply reflect an overall higher frequency of wishes in the female data, in line with work on late 20th-century data suggesting that women are more likely to express emotions linguistically than are men.

(2) *Ich denke, ich sage immer* etc. preceding a proposition

As Figure 5 shows, the women writers use significantly more such introductory clauses, which soften the definiteness of the following statement (Mann Whitney U test: $U = 9.5, n = 15, p = 0.028$).

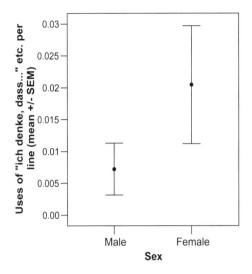

Figure 5: Men and women's use of *ich denke, ich sage immer*, etc.
preceding a proposition in Corpus 1

(3)–(7) Tag questions, intensifying adverbs such as *ziemlich, sehr* and *so*,
superlatives, metacommunicative formulations, and imperatives

Only one occurrence of the tag *nicht wahr* was found in the data (produced by
a woman). There were no significant differences between the sexes in their use
of intensifying adverbs (*t*-test: $t = 0.941$, $df = 13$, $p = 0.364$ for all intensifiers;
for individual intensifiers, in all cases $t < 1.290$, $df = 13$, $p > 0.220$), nor in
their use of superlatives (*t*-test: $t = 1.223$, $df = 13$, $p = 0.243$) – in the case of
the superlatives, there were only 7 occurrences each in the male and female
letters.

	Women		Men	
	Total no. of tokens	Per line	Total no. of tokens	Per line
Intensifying adverbs	96	0.107	120	0.072
Superlatives	7	0.007	7	0.004
Total no. of lines sampled	892		1662	

Table 3: Men and women's use of intensifying adverbs and superlatives in Corpus 1

There were also no significant differences for metacommunicative formulations such as *ich möchte dich bitten* (adjusted *t*-test: $t = 1.615$, $df = 6.453$, $p = 0.154$),[4] nor in the frequency of imperatives between the genders (*t*-test: $t = 0.184$, $df = 12$, $p = 0.857$).

(8) Language used to request a reply

Since imperatives were counted without regard to their function, including instances such as *Grüße meine Tante!* or *Lebet wohl!*, a finer analysis of expressions used to request a reply might have revealed differences in directness missed in a simple count of imperatives. It is clear from reading the letters that the writers yearn for a reply – indeed the absence of a hoped-for reply and possible reasons or excuses are frequent topics in the letters. Both genders use the set phrase *in der Hoffnung auf / hoffe auf (eine) baldige Antwort* (four each for both groups). The scanty data (presented in Table 4 below) show considerable overlap in male and female practice, but suggest women soften the imperative *schreib* with *bitte* or *und viel*; men leave *gleich* or *sobald ....* unsoftened, and strengthen the effect of *bald* with *recht bald*. However, caution is called for here. Elspaß' study (2002: 92) gives in passing an instance from a female writer which is more in line with the male practice found here: *schreib doch auch recht bald wie es Dir geht* (Wilhelmine Wiebusch, letter from 1884, in Elspaß 2002: 92).

Men	Women
ich bitte dich ...	*seie so gut und ...*
mal, doch mal	*mal* x2, *man*
doch gleich	*doch kleicht*
gleich x 2	*bald*
sobald [...] x 2	*bitte ... bald* x 2
recht bald	*bald und viel*
nur recht bald	

Table 4: Phrases accompanying the imperative *schreib(e)(t)!* in Corpus 1

---

[4] Thimm's (1998) finding that women used more metacommunicative formulations was in the context of issuing an instruction to a secretary, and it appears that in that context they served as a means of embedding and thus softening the command. However, some instances found in the present data have more in common with the use of verbs of claiming and asserting that Thimm called features of verbal intensity, and which she found to be more frequently used by males. Consider Ludwig Weber, a farm-hand, afraid that his sister may sell his father's tools in his absence: *Und dier sach ichs noch einmal bewahre alles guth bies ich dier wieder schreibe* (June 1881). *Ich sach es dier noch einmahl verwahr alles gut* (August 1881).

(9) Opening and closing formulae

The nature of an opening formula means that it can only occur once at most in each letter. On inspection, just four of the 22 female letters (three different writers) use the phrase *die Feder ergreifen* (or a variant), and only one of the 23 male letters, so that the data are too sparse to be interpretable. Just over 70% of the letters use a closing formula *nun will ich schließen* (and variants), distributed very evenly between the genders. The hypothesis that women might rely more on formulaic phrasing was therefore not supported here.

(10) Apostrophising the recipient(s)

Six female and six male writers use apostrophising addresses such as *lieber Heinrich, liebe Tante* in the course of their letters. There is no significant difference in the occurrence or in the relative frequency per line of appeals to the recipients ($t = 0.136$, $df = 13$, $p = 0.894$), and the initial hypothesis that women would make greater use of this strategy to involve their recipients is not supported.

3.3 Preliminary discussion

In this small corpus many of the features investigated showed no differences between the genders. However, female writers in this corpus use the particle *doch* more frequently and use phrases such as *ich denke* to soften assertions more often than men. Furthermore, finer analyses of the data suggest tentatively that women may soften imperatives, express more wishes, and are more emphatic in their formulations than are men.

4. The second study

4.1 Methods

In the second phase, a larger corpus (henceforth Corpus 2) of 182 letters from the same collection of emigrant letters (totalling just over 84,000 words, compared to 30,000 for Corpus 1) was investigated, 91 each by men and women, from 38 different writers in each case. With a handful of exceptions, male and female members of the same families contribute equal numbers of letters to the male and female sub-corpora, and – as far as the entire collection of available letters permitted – the two sub-corpora cover a similar spread of dates from 1843–1909. None of the letter writers has any higher education. The average letter length is 618 words, and any letters over 1500 words in length were excluded. No single writer contributed more than eight letters and/or more than 3000 words to Corpus 2. Though this is still not ideal, a trade-off was necessary, in order to keep the corpus as large as possible whilst still matching numbers of male and female letter writers. Since Corpus 2 is in electronic form, it was possible to perform word counts, and so the frequency data for this second study are expressed in the more usual form of a frequency per 10,000 words, rather than per line as for Corpus 1. Again, orthographic variants such as *nuhr*, *mahl*, etc., were included, though – since the searches were performed automatically – it is possible that very idiosyncratic spellings may have been overlooked.

On the other hand, the size of Corpus 2 meant that it was not feasible to examine the practice of individual writers. Results for men and women are therefore presented as averages over all the letters, rather than as averages over all letter-*writers*, as in the first study (and are therefore analysed using Chi-squared tests rather than *t*-tests). Because of these differences in analysis, the data for the two sub-corpora are not directly comparable, but the overall findings of significant patterns can nevertheless be validly compared.

The same features were investigated for Corpus 2 as in the first study, with the exception of a count of all imperatives, which was not feasible with this larger (untagged) corpus. Two further features were investigated that may be taken as indicators of a writer's emotional involvement in their writing: 11. Exclamatory *ach* / *o*, and 12. Use of *ich* / *mich* / *mir*. Data were collected using the shareware concordancing programme ConCapp by Chris Greaves.[5]

4.2 Results

(1) Use of particles

In contrast to the finding in the first study, there were no significant differences in the overall frequency of particle use ($\chi^2_{(df)} < 0.003_1$, $p = 0.955$, nor for any individual particles (in all cases, $\chi^2_{(df)} < 1.52_1$, $p = 0.05$) .

---

[5]   See http://www.edict.com.hk/PUB/concapp.

	Women	Men	Women per 10,000 words	Men per 10,000 words
all particles	407	484	107.1	104.8

Table 5: Overall frequency of all particles in Corpus 2

Looking at the top nine particles, which account for over 90% of all particles in the data, it is interesting to note that, as in Corpus 1, *doch* is again by far the most frequent (with *schon, mal/einmal, nun, wohl* and *ja* again occupying 5 of the next 6 places – *nur* is more frequent here than in the first study, however). Yet the frequency of *doch* here is remarkably consistent between the genders at 22.1 and 22.6 per 10,000 words – a marked contrast to the finding in the first study.

	Women	Men	Women per 10,000 words	Men per 10,000 words
doch	86	102	22.6	22.1
nun	59	71	15.5	15.4
schon	52	65	13.7	14.1
mal/ einmal [6]	45	36	11.8	7.8
wohl	40	47	10.5	10.2
nur	39	33	10.3	7.1
ja	31	28	8.2	6.1
gar	21	33	5.5	7.1
eben	4	14	1.1	3.0
Total	377	429	99.2	92.9

Table 6: Frequency of top 9 particles in Corpus 2

Again, further analysis was undertaken of the different functions of *doch* (table 7), and again it appears women's use of *doch* is higher in the expression of wishes and in emphatic use, but also in commands as a softening strategy, while men's use is higher in the functions that express an assumed view about a fact (explanatory, expecting agreement, assumed knowledge), but lower in those with an affective function (contrastive, command, wish, emphatic). However, this apparent difference is not significant ($\chi^2_{(df)} = 1.69_6, p = 0.194$).

---

[6]   Incl. 1 x *man*.

Finally, the *doch* data from Corpus 2 were re-analysed by individual author, so that on this one measure the results could be *directly* compared with those from Corpus 1. This simply confirmed what the initial analysis had shown: that the greater use of *doch* by women in Corpus 1 is *not* replicated in Corpus 2 ($t = 0.698$, $df = 37$, $p = 0.487$).

	Women	Men	Women per 10,000 words	Men per 10,000 words
contrastive	21	18	5.5	3.9
in command	25	23	6.6	5.0
explanatory	5	13	1.3	2.8
expecting agreement	5	9	1.3	1.9
stating something assumed to be known	5	11	1.3	2.4
expressing a wish	6	4	1.6	0.9
emphatic	19	13	5.0	2.8
Total	86	91	22.6	19.7

Table 7: Frequency of *doch* by function

An analysis of the functions in which the particle *nur* was used by males and females was also undertaken, since casual inspection had suggested a relatively high frequency of *nur* in the male corpus in commands, where it arguably reinforces the strength of the admonition. The data do indeed suggest such a tendency (see Table 8 below), but, again, the difference was not found to be statistically significant ($\chi^2_{(df)} = 1.749_3$, $p = 0.186$).

	Women	Men	Women per 10,000 words	Men per 10,000 words
as admonishment etc. in (indirect) command (*wen du fort gehst, so nehme nur alles Werkzeug mit*)	7	14	1.8	3.0
surprise (reproach/ admiration)	9	5	2.4	1.1
urging hearer to give info.	1	1	0.3	0.2
wishes / unreal	22	13	5.8	2.8
Total	39	33	10.3	7.1

Table 8: Frequency of *nur* by function in Corpus 2

(2) ich denke, ich glaube, ich sage (immer) preceding a proposition

As a group, these introductory clauses do not differ between the genders ($\chi^2_{(df)}$ = 2.365_1, p = 0.124), but women do use the most common, *ich denke*, significantly more ($\chi^2_{(df)}$ = 6.17_1, p = 0.012). The cases of *ich glaube, ich sage* were not significant ($\chi^2_{(df)} < 0.378_1$, $p > 0.539$).

	Women	Men	Women per 10,000 words	Men per 10,000 words
ich denke	22	11	5.8	2.4
ich glaube	8	11	2.1	2.4
ich sage	2	3	0.5	0.6
Total	32	25	8.4	5.4

Table 9: *Ich denke / glaube / sage* + a proposition in Corpus 2

(3) Tag questions

Not surprisingly, given the text-type, the data here are once again too scanty to be interpretable. There is just one occurrence of *nicht wahr* (in the male corpus).

(4) Intensifying adverbs such as *sehr, ziemlich, so*

In the first study no significant differences were found in the two genders' use of intensifying adverbs. In this corpus, however, there is a significant overall difference ($\chi^2_{(df)}$ = 7.76_1, p = 0.016), driven by highly significant differences for *so* ($\chi^2_{(df)}$ = 17.96_1), *ziemlich* (χ^2 = 7.72) and *recht* ($\chi^2_{(df)}$ = 8.54_1) ($p < 0.005$ in all three cases).

	Women	Men	Women per 10,000 words	Men per 10,000 words
immer + comparative (*immer kleiner/mehr* etc.)	8	16	2.1	3.5
sehr	104	123	27.4	26.6
so	109	70	28.7	15.2
ziemlich	10	32	2.6	6.9
recht	85	64	22.4	13.9
ganz as intensif. adverb	31	47	8.2	10.2
Total	347	352	91.3	76.2

Table 10: Use of intensifying adverbs in Corpus 2

(5) Superlatives

The total number of 192 tokens of superlatives found include many in addresses to the recipient (*theuerste Eltern*, etc.), which are counted in the analysis, since, after all, the superlative is a stylistic choice in such cases. At face value, the difference in total frequency of superlatives seems to tend to support the hypothesis that women use superlatives more frequently than do men (the difference is just outside the significant range, at $p = 0.053$; $\chi^2_{(df)} = 3.740_1$). However, many of the tokens refer to an oldest / youngest sibling or child, and in such cases the superlative is not hyperbolic, but simply the only way of making an unambiguous reference – and it turns out that it is precisely this usage that produces the significant difference between men and women's usage. This in itself begs an explanation – one might hypothesize that women write about family members more, in line with a tendency found in some research for women to discuss topics more in terms of people, while men discuss the same topics in more abstract terms (Hultmann and Westmann 1977, Johansson 1995). Without further investigation, however, this remains pure speculation here. At any rate, once such superlatives are factored out, the significant result is lost.

	Women	Men	Women per 10,000 words	Men per 10,000 words
Total superlatives	100	92	26.3	19.9
superlatives referring to oldest / youngest sibling etc.	16	8	4.2	1.7
remaining superlatives (esp. frequent are *liebst-*, *theuerst-*, *best-*, *herzlichst-*, *innigst-*)	84	86	22.1	18.6

Table 11: Superlatives in Corpus 2

(6) Metacommunicative formulations
(*ich möchte Dich bitten, nun will ich Euch schreiben, daß ...*)

The gender difference here overall is not significant, though it is in the direction hypothesized, with women using more of such formulations, perhaps as a softening strategy ($\chi^2_{(df)} = 3.168_1$, $p = 0.075$). Compared to men, women also use the less direct *ich möchte* more frequently than *ich will*, but far from significantly so ($\chi^2_{(df)} = 0.209_1$, $p = 0.648$).

meta-com-municative formulations with the phrase ...	Women	Women %	Men	Men %	Women per 10,000 words	Men per 10,000 words
... *ich möchte bitten / Euch wissen lassen* etc.	8	21.05	5	16.67	2.1	1.1
... *ich will* ...	30	78.95	25	83.33	7.9	5.4
Total	38	100.00	30	100.00	10.0	6.5

Table 12: Metacommunicative formulations in Corpus 2

(7)–(8) Imperative forms and asking for a reply: *schreib(e)(t)!*

As noted earlier, it was not feasible to count all imperative forms in Corpus 2, but, as with Corpus 1, the modifiers accompanying all imperatives requesting the recipient(s) to write back were noted. Analysis again showed no clear difference in the frequency with which men and women use an imperative of *schreiben*, soften an imperative (with *mal*, an introductory phrase such as *ich bitte Dich*, or *liebe(r)* + name), or use an intensifying *doch* (Table 13). There is again an apparent tendency for men to use intensifiers such as *recht (bald)* more frequently (Table 14), but with so few tokens, the trend is not significant ($\chi^2_{(df)} = 1.717_1, p = 0.190$).

	Women	Women %	Men	Men %	Women per 10,000 words	Men per 10,000 words
no softener	5	23.81%	5	21.74%		
1 softener (*mal, lieber X, ich bitte dich*)	7	33.33%	5	21.74%		
2 softeners	0	0.00%	2	8.70%		
Total no. of tokens with softeners	7	33.33%	7	30.43%		
Total no. of tokens of the imperative of *schreiben*	21		23		5.53	4.98

Table 13: Qualitative analysis of imperative *schreib(e)(t)*

	Women	Men
Total no. of intensifiers, incl. *bald, recht (bald), geschwind* etc.	6	11
doch as strengthener of imperative	4	4

Table 14: Frequency of *doch* or other intensifying adverb with *schreib(e)(t)*

The higher frequency of either *bitte(n) / Bitte* or *sei(d) so gut* in the women's letters is likewise significant overall ($\chi^2_{(df)}$ = 5.025$_1$, p = 0.025), driven by women's significantly greater use of *bitte(n)/ Bitte* ($\chi^2_{(df)}$ = 9.56$_1$, p = 0.002). (*Sei(d) so gut* shows no significant difference ($\chi^2_{(df)}$ = 1.553$_1$, p = 0.213). (See Table 15).

	Women	Men	Women per 10,000 words	Men per 10,000 words
bitte / Bitte / bitten where the writer's wish is being expressed	39	21	10.26	4.55
sei(e)(d) so gut	4	10	1.05	2.17
Total	43	31	11.31	6.71

Table 15: *Bitte / Sei so gut* to make a request

(9) The use of opening and closing formulae *die Feder ergreifen, nun muss ich schließen* and their variants

Table 16 shows the use of opening and closing formulae in Corpus 2. Recall that, since such a formula normally occurs only once per letter, and the male and female corpora both consist of 91 letters, the raw figures are directly comparable here. As can be seen, the women's letters do contain more formulae, as hypothesized, but the difference is not significant ($\chi^2_{(df)}$ = 0.881$_1$, p = 0.348).

	Women	Men
die Feder ergreifen, etc.	6	9
schließen (*ich will jetzt mein Schreiben schließen,* etc.)	28	19
Total	34	28

Table 16: the use of opening and closing formulae in Corpus 2

(10) Apostrophising the recipient(s)
(within the letter itself, not as part of initial salutation)

As hypothesized, women address the recipients of their letters significantly more frequently than do men ($\chi^2_{(df)} = 11.415_1$, $p < 0.001$).

	Women	Men	Women per 10,000 words	Men per 10,000 words
apostrophising *lieb-* + name / title, not at start of letter	157	124	41.3	26.9
apostrophising *t(h)euer-* + name / title, not at start of letter	0	4	0.0	0.9
Total	157	128	41.3	27.7

Table 17: Apostrophising letter recipient(s) in Corpus 2

In the light of the above finding, two other phenomena were investigated for Corpus 2, for which higher use might indicate greater expression of emotional involvement. Firstly, it was found that women refer to themselves with the pronoun forms *ich, mich, mir* significantly more frequently than do men ($\chi^2_{(df)} = 20.675_1$, $p < 0.001$).

	Women	Men	Women per 10,000 words	Men per 10,000 words
ich	893	953	235.0	206.4
mich	122	108	32.1	23.4
mi(e/h)r	234	209	61.6	45.3
Total	1249	1270	328.7	275.0

Table 18: Frequency of the 1st person pronoun singular in Corpus 2

Secondly, women use significantly more exclamations, as measured here by the frequency of *o* and *ach* (where the figures below exclude a few tokens that occur as part of quotations from hymns or when quoting another speaker) ($\chi^2_{(df)} = 7.688_1$, $p < 0.01$).

	Women	Men	Women per 10,000 words	Men per 10,000 words
o	8	4	2.1	0.9
ach	9	2	2.4	0.4
Total *o* and *ach*	17	6	4.5	1.3

Table 19: Frequency of exclamatory *o* and *ach* in Corpus 2

5. Discussion and conclusions

Our most puzzling result is the contrast between the strong finding that women use *doch* more than men in Corpus 1, and the equally clear finding that there is no difference in Corpus 2. Given that in the larger Corpus 2 male and female letters are matched (approximately) both for date and for social background (by using males and females from the same families), and given that in both corpora the use of all other particles seems to be evenly distributed between genders, it seems most likely that the *doch* finding for Corpus 1 is an artefact of using such a small number of letter-writers. Amongst the women of Corpus 1, one writer out of the seven contributes over one-third of all occurrences of *doch* (16 of 46), and her language also shows many features suggestive of less education (including non-standard spellings such as *mier* for *mir* and de-rounding of vowels, highly paratactic style), as in the following sample:

> *ihr habt doch wohl die Kide* [= Güte] *und Siet doch mal wie es Meine Geschwister ihn Offenbach Geht* (Margarethe Wetz, servant-girl in Germany, farmer's wife in America, ca.1852).

It is worth noting, though, that this writer's letter is the earliest (1852) in the female part of Corpus 1, and so her less standardized style, more reminiscent of speech, may be less a marker of her low level of education compared to the other writers than a reflection of the relatively early date of her letter. For a significant negative correlation was indeed found between date of letter and frequency of *doch* in Corpus 1 (Pearson's correlation: $r = -0.525$, $n = 15$, $p = 0.044$): it occurs more frequently in the earlier letters than in later ones. (Unfortunately the same analysis could not be readily repeated for Corpus 2.) If frequent use of *doch* can be interpreted as an indication of colloquial, speech-like behaviour, this correlation might reflect a development towards greater adherence to *Schriftsprache* norms during the course of the second half of the 19th century. In sum, though, the data on particles here yield no firm conclusion. At most, we can say that, on the whole, there is no difference between the genders in their use of particles, with the possible exception of *doch*.

Several of our other hypotheses about possible differences between male and female linguistic practice in the letters also received little or no support. Formulae, superlatives, and metacommunicative formulations had all been identified as features that women might use more frequently than men, but analysis revealed no clear differences between the genders for these features in either corpus. Nor are there any significant differences either in the frequency of imperatives (investigated for Corpus 1 only), or in the ways in which the imperative *schreib(e)(t)* is modified (in both corpora) – whether intensified or softened with additional adverbs. In short, there is no evidence of differences in those areas of language connected with directness and politeness (imperatives, metacommunicative formulations, particles), nor with a potential orientation to standard discourse models (letter-writing formulae). The only hedging strategy for which a clear significant result was found is women's tendency to use an introductory *ich denke* or similar more often to soften the force of statements. This is significant in Corpus 1; likewise, their more frequent use of *ich denke* (but only of *ich denke*) is significant in Corpus 2.

There *is* a strong finding in Corpus 2 that women are more likely to make a request using *bitte(n) / Bitte* (or, to a lesser extent, with *sei(d) so gut*). While this might indicate a greater use of politeness strategies on the part of women, it may equally simply reflect a greater tendency to make requests *at all* (unfortunately it was not feasible to make a count of all requesting speech acts in the data). The latter explanation would accord with the anecdotal observation in our analysis of *doch* and *nur* that women use them more for expressing their wishes than do men, and, taken together, one might be tempted to use these findings to suggest that 19th-century women writers are more ready to express wishes and desires than are men. However, this is a very tentative claim at best and arguably does no more than pander to the stereotype of the more emotional woman.

And yet – the most significant group of results are those that can indeed be understood as reflecting emotional involvement. Firstly, women use more intensifying adverbs – specifically *ziemlich, recht*, and *so* – in Corpus 2, with a similar, though not significant tendency in the smaller Corpus 1. Secondly, women are far more likely in Corpus 2 to address the recipient in the body of the letter, something which can be interpreted as an involvement strategy that attempts to overcome the monologic nature of the text-type. Thirdly, women make more exclamations beginning *o* or *ach*. Finally, women refer to themselves using some form of the 1st person singular pronoun more often than men – the frequency remains higher than for men even if only those tokens involving a subject *ich* are counted. I am inclined to count this too as a mark of personal involvement in what is related.[7] Perhaps women's greater use of *ich denke* can also be seen as part of this same tendency to display greater personal involvement.

In this study, I have considered a moderately large body of naturalistic data by discourse analysis standards – though still tiny by corpus linguistics standards – to yield more robust quantitative findings about gender and

---

[7] It is interesting, however, to note the contrast here with Thelander (1986), who, according to Linke (2002), found that in a very different text-type – political discourse – Swedish men used *jag* ('I') most frequently of all pronouns, while it did not even rate amongst the top five pronouns used by women.

discourse in 19th-century correspondence than at least some of those for the present day noted at the start of this paper. The matter of interpreting the results is no easier, however. Taken together, the findings suggest that 19th-century emigrant women are more likely to use discourse strategies that express personal involvement in their letters than are men – but that in their use of other discourse features the genders do not differ. What are we to make of this? The data here are both earlier than, and in a different medium to, those from the 20th-century discourse analysis studies on the basis of which our initial hypotheses were generated. Does the different medium – and the specific text-type of the letter, often copied out 'neat' by unpractised writers after a rough draft – mean that there is no need for many of the strategies that are variously adopted by the genders to manage spontaneous face-to-face interaction?[8] Or is the earlier date the deciding factor? Could it be that apparent gender differences in directness and politeness strategies correlate with particular roles adopted by the genders in post-industrial western society, and that that is why we find so little evidence of them in our corpora from the 19th century? This in turn brings us to more fundamental questions: the extent to which the gender differences found here and in other studies are the result of socially constructed roles or of universal, biologically determined propensities, as well as how gender interacts with other social factors (see for discussion of such questions Bing and Bergvall 1996, Cameron 1996). Of course, as long as so much of our data on gender and discourse today remain essentially anecdotal, these questions are all the harder to answer.[9] Any answers will at any rate need to take into account the fact that only *some* of the differences found in 20th-century women's discourse are likewise present in 19th-century German women's written discourse too: those features expressing emotional involvement.

---

[8] Here it would also be interesting to know whether, for instance, particle frequency in the letters correlates with the gender of the *recipient*, in line with a body of research showing that in oral interactions the gender of the addressee affects particle frequency (Holmes 1995: 108f.)

[9] This is not to deny the value of fine-grained qualitative research – but we must be cautions about making any generalizations from such research not also supported by robust qualitative data.

References

Bergvall, Victoria L., Janet M. Bing and Alice F. Freed (eds.). 1996. *Rethinking language and gender research*. London: Longman.

Bing, Janet M., and Victoria L. Bergvall. 1996. The question of questions: beyond binary thinking. In Victoria L. Bergvall, Janet M. Bing and Alice F. Freed (eds.), *Rethinking language and gender research*. London: Longman, 1–30.

Burgoon, Michael, T. Birk and J. Hall. 1991. Compliance gaining and satisfaction with physician-patient communication: an expectancy theory interpretation of gender difference. *Human Communication Research* 18: 177–208.

Cameron, Deborah. 1996. The language-gender interface: challenging co-optation. In Victoria L. Bergvall, Janet M. Bing and Alice F. Freed (eds.), *Rethinking language and gender research*. London: Longman, 31–54.

Cheshire, Jenny, and Peter Trudgill (eds.). 1998. *The Sociolinguistics Reader. Vol. 2. Gender and discourse*. London: Arnold.

Coates, Jennifer. 1989. Gossip revisited: language in all-female groups. In Jenny Cheshire and Peter Trudgill (eds.), *The Sociolinguistics Reader. Vol. 2. Gender and discourse*. London: Arnold, 127–152.

Elspaß, Stephan. 2002a. Standard German in the 19th-century? (Counter-) Evidence from the private correspondence of 'ordinary people'. In Andrew Robert Linn and Nicola McLelland (eds.), *Standardization. Studies from the Germanic Languages*. Amsterdam: Benjamins, 43–65.

Elspaß, Stephan. 2002b. Sprache und Geschlecht in Privatbriefen „einfacher Leute" des 19. Jahrhunderts. In Gisela Brandt (ed.), *Bausteine zu einer Geschichte des weiblichen Sprachgebrauchs V: Vertextungsstrategien und Sprachmittelwahl in Texten von Frauen. Internationale Fachtagung Dresden 10. –12.09.2001*. Stuttgart: Heinz, 89–108.

Elspaß, Stephan. 2005. *Sprachgeschichte von unten. Untersuchungen zum geschriebenen Alltagsdeutsch im 19. Jahrhundert*. Tübingen: Niemeyer.

Erickson, B., A. E. Lind and W. M. O'Barr Johnson. 1978. Speech styles and impression formation in a court room setting: the effects of "powerful" and "powerless" speech. *Journal of Experimental Psychology* 14: 266–279.

Günthner, Susanne, and Helga Kotthoff. 1992. *Die Geschlechter im Gespräch: Kommunikation in Institutionen*. Stuttgart: Metzler.

Holmes, Janet. 1995. *Women, men and politeness*. London: Longman.

Hultmann, Tor G., and Margaretha Westmann. 1977. *Gymnastistssvenska*. Lund: Liber Läromedel.

Johansson, Catrin. 1995. *Skrivande och kön i utbildingsdebatten. En undersökning av journaliststudentersdebattartiklar i könperspektiv.* Uppsala: Uppsala Universitet.

Kotthoff, Helga, and Ruth Wodak (eds.). 1997. *Communicating gender in context.* Amsterdam: Benjamins.

Kuhn, Elisabeth. 1981/82. *Geschlechterspezifische Unterschiede in der Sprachverwendung.* Linguistic Agency University Duisburg.

Kuhn, Elisabeth. 1992a. *Gender and Authority: Classroom diplomacy in German and American universities.* Tübingen. Narr.

Kuhn, Elisabeth. 1992b. Geschlecht und Autorität. Wie Lehrende ihre Studenten/innen zur Mitarbeit bewegen. In Susanne Günthner and Helga Kotthoff (eds.), *Die Geschlechter im Gespräch: Kommunikation in Institutionen.* Stuttgart: Metzler, 55–72.

Lakoff, Robin. 1973. The logic of politeness. In *Papers from the Ninth Regional Meeting of the Chicago Linguistics Society,* 292–305.

Lakoff, Robin. 1975. *Language and Women's Place.* New York: Harper & Row.

Linke, Angelika. 2002. Das Wort in der feministischen Sprachreflexion. Eine Übersicht. In D. Alan Cruse, Franz Hundsnurscher, Michael Job and Peter Rolf Luzteier (eds.), *Lexikologie. Ein internationales Handbuch zur Natur und Struktur von Wörtern und Wortschätzen.* Berlin: de Gruyter, 121–129.

Schoenthal, Gisela (ed.). 1998. *Feministische Linguistik – Linguistische Geschlechterforschung. Ergebnisse, Konsequenzen, Perspektiven.* Hildesheim: Olms.

Talbot, Mary. 1998. *Language and gender. An introduction.* Oxford: Blackwell.

Tannen, Deborah. 1995. *Gender and discourse.* Oxford: OUP.

Thelander, Kerstin. 1986. *Politikerspråk i könsperspektiv.* Malmö: Liber Förlag.

Thimm, Caja. 1998. Frauen, Sprache, Beruf: Sprachliches Handeln am Arbeitsplatz. In Gisela Schoenthal (ed.), *Feministische Linguistik – Linguistische Geschlechterforschung. Ergebnisse, Konsequenzen, Perspektiven.* Hildesheim: Olms, 325–343.

West, Candace. 1990. Not just 'doctors' orders': directive-response sequences in patients' visits to women and men physicians. *Discourse and society* 1: 85–113.

Wodak, Ruth (ed.). 1997. *Gender and discourse.* London: Sage Publications.

GERTRUD REERSHEMIUS (ASTON, BIRMINGHAM)

Remnants of Western Yiddish in East Frisia

1. Traces of a language believed dead since the 19th century

1.1 Introduction

Whereas Eastern Yiddish was a thriving language used by millions of speakers until the Second World War and the Holocaust, Western Yiddish, the language of Ashkenazic Jewry spoken in Western Europe, had been proclaimed extinct a comparatively short time after the Enlightenment, due to the Jewish minority's shift from the traditional Hebrew-Yiddish diglossic set-up to German during the 19th century (see e.g. Gerzon 1902, Mieses 1924). From the 1950s on, however, it became apparent through field-work by Florence Guggenheim-Grünberg that Western Yiddish varieties had remained a current medium of discourse well into the 20th century in remote provinces of Switzerland, Alsace, and the Southwest of Germany. Furthermore, field workers for the 'Language and Culture Atlas of Ashkenazic Jewry' (LCAAJ) realized that the extent of linguistic assimilation to Standard German or German dialects had been overestimated. In 1969 Steven Lowenstein pointed out that many facts about Jewish speech could still be collected in the 1950s and 1960s to such an extent that regional patterns could be distinguished (Lowenstein 1969). Beem (1954, 1967, 1970) showed that in the North, in Dutch-speaking areas, traces of a Jewish vernacular could also be found. It appears that rural Jewish communities in some remoter provinces of the German and Dutch language area seem to have preserved an in-group vernacular which was based on Western Yiddish varieties well into the 20th century. A gradual process of linguistic assimilation and language change makes it impossible to call most of these vernaculars 'Western Yiddish', although they clearly originate from it. A number of scholars use the term 'Judeo-German' for the younger variants based on Western Yiddish (Weinberg 1981, Matras 1991). Jacobs (1996) suggests 'post-Yiddish Ashkenazic speech' for varieties based on language shift from Yiddish in general. Western Yiddish used to be the Jewish variety spoken in the Dutch, German, and Low German linguistic areas of Europe, the western part of the countries Jews referred to as 'Ashkenaz', using the Biblical name of a people and a country bordering on Armenia and the Euphrates (cf. Genesis 10,3 and Chronicles 1,6).

The Yiddish language originates from medieval times and developed through language contact. Jewish speakers of Old High German and later Middle High German varieties enriched these vernaculars with a component, mainly in the lexicon, from Hebrew and Aramaic. These languages of the scriptures and religious practice served as written and high varieties in a situation of di- or triglossia. The language was written mainly for informal purposes, such as private letters, memoirs, notes, and entertaining or devotional literature, addressed to those who were unable to read and write in Hebrew, such as women. We do not know whether in early stages the vernacular was identical with the varieties spoken by non-Jews; a majority of scholars in the field of historical Yiddish linguistics assume that Yiddish developed on the substrate of an older spoken Jewish language, either Aramaic or a Romance-based Jewish variety (Jacobs 2005, 9–56).[1] In their view, the language spoken by Jews has always been distinct from the varieties used around it, and it clearly is the case that the Germanic component in Yiddish developed a form distinct from German varieties (Timm 2005). Another hotly discussed topic in Yiddish linguistics is the question whether Yiddish originates from the Upper Rhine valley (Weinreich 1980) or from an area between Regensburg and Prague (Katz 1991, Eggers 1998). We have written sources of the Jewish language from the late 13th century on. These sources are easily recognizable as Jewish, since they are written in Hebrew letters. From the beginning of the 16th century on, they prove Yiddish to be clearly distinct from German varieties in both lexicon and phonology (Timm 1987).

Whereas Yiddish in the West (Western Yiddish) remained in contact with spoken German varieties and the slowly evolving German standard language, the migration of Jews to Slavic-speaking areas in Eastern Europe, due to oppression and persecution in the West ever since the First Crusade, gave Eastern Yiddish its final and well-known form. Language contact led to a Slavic component, especially in the lexicon. Slavic impact on morphology and syntax remained comparatively weak, while it did play a considerable role in phonology and word formation (Weinreich 1958). Whereas Eastern Yiddish thrived from the 18th century on and became a full-fledged language able to cover all oral and written linguistic domains of modern life and to contribute to world-class literature, Western Yiddish was given up by its speakers after the Enlightenment and died out in the course of the 19th century.

---

[1]   Paul Wexler's (1991) hypothesis that Yiddish is a relexified variant of Sorbic has been rejected by most scholars in the field, see e.g. Eggers (1998).

1.2 Rural Jewish communities

Or did it? The immense Jewish contribution to German culture and society tends to be perceived as one of an urban minority, and this certainly does apply to the century before the Holocaust as well as to medieval times until approximately 1400 to 1450. Those medieval Jews who had survived the Plague and the pogroms and did not migrate to Eastern Europe were subject to drastic restrictions and taxation in larger towns and cities of the German speaking countries. From around 1600 many settled in small rural towns or villages as a result and adapted to a completely new way of life. During the 17th and 18th century, 90% of Jews in the German-speaking countries lived in the countryside, and the figure was still 80% at the beginning of the 19th century. It is only fairly recently that historians have started to focus on rural Jewish life (see e.g. Richarz and Rürup 1997), and slowly a picture is emerging which shows a German-Jewish culture remarkably different from urban German-Jewish life. Economically these rural communities depended on small trade, especially cattle- or horse-trading, and butchery. The latter originates in the fact that Jews were obliged to observe the halachic rules of daily life, even when they lived in some isolation in the countryside, away from the ritual services a larger community would be able to provide. This meant, among other things, that they had to prepare meat in a specific ritual way. Since Jews were not supposed to eat the whole animal, parts of it could be sold usually cheaply. Butchery led to trading, and what started as the means to fulfil certain religious obligations became the economic basis for life in rural Jewish communities. Spiritual life changed too: whereas in the old centres of Ashkenaz the learned study of the scriptures, mainly the Talmud, had been the centre around which Jewish life had circulated, in rural communities a Jewish folklore emerged which put much emphasis on certain traditions and customs and could not keep up with learned studies of the scriptures. According to most accounts of life in Jewish rural communities, the celebration of the Sabbath and annual festivals became the focal point of spiritual life.[2]

Knowledge of Hebrew went into decline along with the study of the scriptures and the importance of Western Yiddish grew. Between the 16th and the 18th century, more books covering a wider range of topics were published in Western Yiddish and were read by a wider audience. During the 19th century, however, printing in Western Yiddish went into decline (see e.g. Römer 1995).

---

[2]   See e.g. Breuer (1997) or Cahnman (1979).

1.3 Jewish communities in Low-German speaking East Frisia

East Frisia, a peninsula in the most northwesterly part of Germany bordering on the Netherlands, belongs to the Low German language area. After a turbulent history of language contact and linguistic change from Frisian to Low German with Dutch and later Standard German as written varieties, a situation of stable diglossia established itself which lasted well into the second half of the 20th century: Low German served as the spoken variety, Standard German as written and institutional language (Reershemius 2004). At the beginning of the 20th century, twelve small towns and villages in East Frisia had significant Jewish communities. Sources of Jewish life in the region describing the period before the Holocaust make the point that East Frisian Jews were linguistically integrated into the general diglossic set-up of the region,[3] which means that they spoke Low German and learned Standard German only when they started school.

Recently I discovered sources for a Jewish vernacular which used to be spoken in the town of Aurich in East Frisia. At the beginning of the 20th century, approximately 400 Jews lived in Aurich, counting for 7% of the town's population and depending economically on cattle trading, butchery, and small trade. Previously nothing was known about a Jewish variety spoken in the region. The sources date from 1902 to 1985 and consist of two amateur theatre plays, an unpublished memoir, word lists, and an extended correspondence between survivors of the Aurich Jewish community and a retired teacher. The sources cover two periods: the older and much longer of the two amateur plays refers to the Jewish vernacular spoken in the second half of the 19th century. All the other sources concern the linguistic situation in the 1920s.

Sources for spoken Western Yiddish are rare and difficult to find for a number of reasons. Firstly, most speakers or persons with some recollection of the Jewish vernaculars were forced to emigrate or killed during the Holocaust. Those very few who are still alive today are very old. Secondly, Western Yiddish books, which were distributed and read throughout Ashkenazic Jewry between the 16th and the 18th century, were published in a supra-regional, highly stylized language, which does not allow insights into regional variation. This makes most printed Western Yiddish sources practically useless for the reconstruction of spoken language. Katz (1983) pointed out that the main sources for spoken Western Yiddish are dictionaries in Latin transcription, satirical plays written during the Enlightenment period, and the few remaining individuals who have some recollection of the spoken vernaculars. Taking this

---

[3]   WS, private archive JD.

into account, the sources discovered can be seen as an opportunity to shed light on a regional linguistic set-up previously very little explored.[4]

Within the limits of this article, it will not be possible to analyze in detail the oldest source, a longer amateur play written in 1902, which is by far the most complex of the texts discovered. Instead, a preliminary overview of first results will be given to present the linguistic background of the Aurich Jewish community. The play shows phonological, morphological, and syntactic features of the Jewish vernacular in context, not merely isolated lexical items and expressions. Furthermore, it does not focus exclusively on the Hebrew component words, but it stresses the differences between Low German and the High German based Jewish vernacular, as well as it shows traces of borrowing from Low German. The play was written by a moderately well known author of children's books called Isaac Herzberg, who grew up in Aurich and contributed the play to the 100th anniversary of the local Jewish Women's Organization. He claims to have written it in the Jewish vernacular he had spoken in his youth, in the 1860s.

It becomes evident that, during the second half of the 19th century, Jews in Aurich and, presumably, in the whole region used a Western Yiddish based variety for in-group communication and Low German as the spoken language with non-Jews. Thus, a complex linguistic set-up emerges: in addition to their in-group vernacular, East Frisian Jews spoke Low German. Both Dutch and Standard German served as written languages for communicating with the non-Jewish world, while Hebrew and Aramaic were the languages of the Jewish scriptures. In addition to this, a special parlance of cattle-traders and butchers was used which was not identical with the Jewish vernacular but made extensive use of its Hebrew component in order to serve as a secret language (Guggenheim-Grünberg 1954).[5] The knowledge of Hebrew, however, seems to have been limited in Jewish rural communities and was usually restricted to a few men educated in the Jewish traditions.

The later sources furthermore indicate that Low German became the dominant variety for in-group use during the first half of the 20th century. 20th century references to the Jewish variety underline the fact that it was mostly older people who were familiar with the language. In the 1902 audience of the above-mentioned amateur theatre play, however, a majority must have been able at least to understand the language in order to enjoy the play.[6]

---

[4]   Three informants for the LCAAJ came from East Frisia, see Baviskar et al (1992).

[5]   The sources discovered indicate that such a special parlance of cattle-traders had been in use in Aurich too.

[6]   All sources mentioned will be published and analyzed in a planned monograph on the Jewish variety in East Frisia.

1.4 Remnants of the Jewish vernacular in the 1920s

The later sources convey a picture of the linguistic situation in the Aurich Jewish community during the 1920s. They indicate that the language did not disappear in the 20th century, but amalgamated into the spoken vernaculars, both Low German and Standard German based. The later sources consist of a rhymed dialogue by an anonymous writer, called *Zwiegespräch in Auricher Judendeutsch* 'dialogue', which was performed in 1929,[7] and two extended word lists – containing 294 and 222 words – compiled by two speakers in 1980 and 1990 respectively. Both speakers were born in 1911 and emigrated to Israel and the United States respectively. By means of these word lists, they recollect elements of the language as it was still in use in the community when they were children, although spoken mainly by older people, as they both state.[8] One of them has also written an unpublished memoir, which gives insights into the function and significance of the Jewish vernacular for daily communication in the Jewish community of Aurich in the 1920s.[9]

The second part of this paper will be devoted to the analysis of the *Zwiegespräch*, which is presented below with translations of the Hebrew-component words or of words which are not common in German or Low German.

---

[7] A copy of the *Zwiegespräch* was given to the then headmaster of the local school who had been trying to get in contact with survivors of the Aurich Jewish community ever since the 1960s. He passed it, together with other related documents, to the *Niedersächsisches Staatsarchiv* in Aurich (StAA, Dep. 66, 4). The donor, who was born in Aurich in 1914 and who emigrated to the United States during the early 1930s, had been one of the performers of the *Zwiegespräch*. She claimed that it had been written and performed on the occasion of the 125th anniversary of the Jewish Women's Organization in Aurich in 1929. The local newspaper *Ostfriesische Nachrichten*, however, featured an article about this event in its issue of 31 January 1928 (StAA, Dep. 66, 5). Since the 100th anniversary of this organization had been celebrated in 1902, it seems that the donator must have mixed up the years: it is almost certain that the event in question took place in late 1927.

[8] The word lists, compiled such a long time after the variety had been used by the speakers, focus mainly on Hebrew-component words. This applies to most research done into remnants of Western Yiddish and gives a somewhat distorted picture, since the Hebrew-component words were only one of the features which distinguished Western Yiddish from regional varieties of German or Standard German.

[9] Both speakers died some years ago.

2. *Zwiegespräch in Auricher Judendeutsch*
('Dialogue in the Aurich Jewish Variety')

2.1 Text

Male, a Jewish housewife who lives in Aurich, is busy preparing the Sabbath meal. She expects her husband Itzig, a cattle-trader, to return from a business trip.

Male:	Was hot man am Fratig zu rennen, zu laufen,	
	Challes zu backen, *Krain* zu reiben,	חלה 'white bread'; 'horseradish'
	Fisch zu sieden, Kind zu hüten,	
	de Müh ist *osser* nicht zu beschreiben,	אסור 'surely not'[10]
	Händ hot man nur zwa,	
	alles liegt uf de Fra.	
	G'tt, was bleibt heut mein Itzig so lang,	
	es wird doch *osser* im Leben	
	kein *Schlemassel* mehr geben,	'mess'
	der Schuster war heit al poormal do,	
	wollt's Geld für die Schuh,	
	hot's aber nicht bekumen,	
	hot er's mich gleich arg übbel genommen.	
	So, nun geih ich hen, hol ihm sein *Schabbos*hemd,	שבת 'Sabbath'
	sein Halstuch mit de große Blumen,	
	unterdes' werd er kummen.	
	Wer kummt denn dor zur Tür herein?	
	Am Schritt nach kunnt's mein Itzig sein.	
	Itzig, bist do?	
Itzig:	Jo!	
Male:	Host de *Beheimes* verkofft?	בהמה 'cow'
Itzig:	Jo!	
Male:	Wie *jauker* host se denn verkofft?	יקר 'expensive'
Itzig:	Das kann dich *koscher* sein, ich hob's verkofft.	כשר 'kosher'
Male:	Itzig lieb, wie kommst du mich denn vor,	
	bist mich *osser* nicht recht klor!	
	Host de Hunger, willst de Sup,	
	bist daheim in deiner Stub,	

---

[10] See Stern (2000), 155.

brauchst dich *osser* nicht zu genieren,
kumm her, tu's probieren,
ich schneid a kla *Challe* an.

Itzig: Na!

Male: Itzig lieb, was ist dich denn passiert?
Wie mich der Mann pressiert!

Itzig: Ich hob mich de Daume verstacht!

Male: G'tt, wie ist das ne Mann!
Wie kann man de Daume verstachen!
No, kumm her, ich will dich *brochen*!   verb derived from ברכה 'blessing'
"Der Herr der Ratten und der Mause,
der Flöhe, Wanzen und der Lause,
hör auf die Bitten deiner Male,
und tu deinm Itzig de Daume hale.
R'fuoh Schlelemo   רפואה שלמ ה 'get well soon'
hal doch geschwind!"
Du bist auch so kritik wie a Kind,
wie kann man so'n *mies Ponim* machen   מיאוס 'ugly', פנים 'face'
um so ne geringe Sach!
Ich bin erschrocken bei mein Leben,
kann kein Tropfen Blut mehr geben,
wie mich all die Oder schlogen,
alles Umglück muß ich trogen,
nichts als Ärger, nichts als Schand,
hob kein Ruh,
mein größtes Joch bist du!

Itzig: Male, nun mucht ich erzählen dir jetzt,
was unterwegs gesogt worden ist.
Es soll hier sein a kleine Feier.
Der Eintritt ist der Zeit entsprechend nicht teier.
No, s' Essen kost ja auch nicht viel,
de ganze Wuch gibt's *milchding Achiel*.   'dairy dish'
Ich hoff, daß du heit obend gebacken host,
gebroten a gut Stück Pökelbrust!
Dann bin ich de ganze Wuch auch satt,
und du hast mit mich kein *Sho* mehr Last.   שעה 'hour'
Doch a de tust de *Schabbos*kerz anzünden,
laß uns noch a Stückche singen!

Beide singen nach einer Melodie aus „Zar und Zimmermann":

Einst reist ich mit *S'raure* und Tücher durchs Land,   סחורה 'goods'
verkaufte den Leuten viel Ware und Band.
Lieb Male, meine Gattin, du brachtest mir viel Glück,
froh kehrt ich in's *Bajis* des Gatten zurück.   בית 'house'
Ach, wie wird's ei'm allweil vor sein *Chajis* so mies,   חיות 'life'

wenn man sieht, wie die Welt heut so neimodisch ist.
De jungen Leit essen *treife*   טרפה 'not kosher'
und *charpen* sich nicht,   based on חרפה 'shame',
                                                            'to be ashamed of'

am *Schabbos* zu rauchen! – Ist das noch a Jid?
Wir leben ganz *bejiddischlich*, ganz wehr ohne Fehl,   'according to the
                                                             Jewish way of life'

essen alle *Schabbos* a *Kuggel*,   'traditional Sabbath dish'
aus ran *Matzemehl*   'flour from matzo'
machen Kiddusch, machen *Broche* über'n Becher voll Wein.
Nur fröhlich, ihr Lieben, a Jid muß man sein!

2.2 Analysis

Needless to say, the *Zwiegespräch* does not portray the Jewish vernacular as spoken by the Aurich community in the late 1920s, but rather recollects certain elements of the language.

The *Zwiegespräch* is a rather crudely rhymed text. Its main function seems to be to provide an opportunity to use as many well-known elements of the Jewish vernacular as possible. Its content is simple: a Jewish housewife complains about her hard life, then her husband returns from a business trip and has hurt his thumb, she speaks a blessing, and finally they both sing a song which nostalgically invokes the good old days of traditional Jewish life. The song, however, can be seen as the key to the text: whereas young people smoke on the Sabbath and do not follow the Jewish dietary laws, the two singers claim to lead a life according to the traditional rules. Language complements the content: the Jewish vernacular is the language of the old days, when people did not try to be modern and were happy with the ways of traditional Jewish life. In this respect, the *Zwiegespräch* works as a means to idealize the past in a folkloristic and entertaining way.[11]

When analyzing the language of the *Zwiegespräch*, we cannot take it as a transcription of the Jewish vernacular – if only due to the fact that it is in rhymed form. The writer, whoever he or she was, involuntarily alternated Yiddish and German forms, e.g. the definite article is sometimes noted as *de*, sometimes it follows the German *der*, *die*, *das* paradigm. The text contains a number of Hebrew-component words which seem to have been among the most frequently used in the vernacular, since they are all mentioned in all the

---

[11] In Jewish dramatic plays, especially comedies, the use of Western Yiddish in order to characterize more traditional Jews has been an established feature ever since the end of the 18th century (see Lowenstein 1979: 184). Currently the same pattern applies to Low German in the region (see Reershemius 2004).

sources discovered in Aurich. Some of them, e.g. *koscher, Schlamassel*, were established borrowings even in the non-Jewish Low German spoken in the region. Also interesting is the recollection of certain phrases like *mies ponim, R'fuoh Schlelemo, milchding Achiel, Itzig lieb* or the interjection *no* as pragmatic markers of the Jewish vernacular.[12] There is clear indication that even as late as the 1920s, speakers or semi-speakers of the vernacular were aware of its distinct phonology, which contrasted with spoken Low German, since it was High German based. Later sources, such as the two word lists compiled in 1980 by two speakers in their seventies, focus on the more exotic Hebrew-component words.

The writer of the *Zwiegespräch* indicates the following distinct phonological features, such as

- *Fratig* 'Friday'; *zwa* 'two': Middle High German (MHG) /eɪ/, Aurich Western Yiddish (AWY) /a:/, Standard German (SG) /aɪ/
- *Fra* 'woman': MHG /ou/, AWY /a:/, SG /au/
- *erschrucken* 'frightened'; *kumm* 'come!': MHG /u/, AWY /u/, SG /o/
- *host* 'have'; *gesogt* 'said': MHG /a:/, AWY /o/, SG /a/
- *teier* 'expensive'; *Leit* 'people'; *neimodisch* 'modern': MHG /y:/, AWY /aɪ/,[13] SG /ɔɪ/

In the older source Western Yiddish phonological features were used more frequently throughout the text than in the *Zwiegespräch* but the fact that they are still known as late as 1928 underline the continuity between the older and the younger sources of the Aurich vernacular.

As regards morpho-syntax, the general impression is that the writer of the *Zwiegespräch* consciously uses features of the Aurich Jewish variety but forgets to apply them throughout the text: most phenomena listed below have exceptions in the text. This may be due either to the dominance of Standard German as a written language in the 1920s and the fact that the *Zwiegespräch* is, after all, a written text, or to a shift of the Western Jewish based variety to German. The phenomena observed are as follows: Towards the end the writer uses the subordinate conjunction *a(z)* 'while'. A number of Western Yiddish morphological features are applied which happen to be Low German as well: a) The definite article *de* is used without indication of case; b) No distinction is made between accusative and dative for personal pronouns in the 1. and 2. sg;

---

[12] It is an indicator of language shift in progress when speakers or semi-speakers of a language refer to certain set phrases frequently as a token of the variety about to be given up (see Reershemius 2004 for Low German in East Frisia).

[13] In a recording from 11.11.1988 one of the speakers who compiled the word lists reads the *Zwiegespräch* aloud. He pronounces *ei* in *teier* as /ai/ (WST, private archive JD).

c) The 2. sg. pronoun tends to be dropped in the nominative; d) Apocope of *-e*, especially with the 1. Sg. of verbs; e) the diminutive form is *-che* as in Low German and f) the Zwiegespräch shows three examples of marking the predicate with the verb *tun* 'to do' as an auxiliary. These phenomena underline that features which distinguish the Jewish vernacular from Standard German seem to be remembered best when they coincide with Low German. In addition the adverbs *al*, *hen* and *dor* are borrowed from Low German.

Florence Guggenheim-Grünberg categorizes the results of her fieldwork in Switzerland, Alsace and Southwest Germany into three stages: 1) the Western Yiddish vernacular ("jiddische Vollmundart"), 2) mixed Western Yiddish vernacular ("jiddische Mischmundart") and 3) remnants of Yiddish ("Reste des Jiddischen") (Guggenheim-Grünberg 1964). It appears that the amateur play from 1902 features 1) and 2), and the later sources, among them the *Zwiegespräch* 3), remnants of Western Yiddish. Thus the sources of the Aurich Jewish vernacular bridge a period of linguistic change and transition.

A survivor of the Aurich community, born in 1911, recalls his uncle's linguistic preferences, which he refers to as "mauscheln" in his unpublished memoirs:

> Gern mauschelte er, zum Leidwesen meiner Tante. Juden unter sich gebrauchten diesen dem Jiddischen ähnlichen Dialekt, viele konnten kein richtiges Hochdeutsch sprechen, eher noch Plattdeutsch.[14]

> 'He liked to 'mauschel', very much to the dislike of my aunt. Jews among themselves used this vernacular which was similar to Yiddish; most could not speak proper Standard German, they rather spoke Low German'.

This recollection further underlines the fact that the vernacular was still well known and used in the 1920s but spoken only by a minority of the Aurich community. The predominant spoken language mentioned here as in many other sources is Low German. In a letter another survivor of the Aurich community, also born in 1911, writes:

> Die Sprache wurde nicht mehr in unserem Hause gebraucht aber die ältere Generation machte Gebrauch davon. Die Sprache ist nicht jiddisch sondern ein Jargon, der nur in Aurich gesprochen wurde.[15]

---

[14] WS, private archive JD. For the term *Mauschelsprache* see Althaus (2002): Its etymological origin is not clear, but the term has pejorative, sometimes anti-semitic connotations. Surprisingly, Aurich Jews used *mauscheln* or *Mauschelsprache* as positive words describing the Jewish vernacular and its use (WST, private archive JD).

[15] BW 31.03.1986 (StAA, Dep.66, 4)

'The language was not spoken in our house any more but the older generation used it. The language is not Yiddish but a jargon which was only spoken in Aurich.'

Both statements indicate that the vernacular was still known in the 1920s although used mainly by the older generation and, as the *Zwiegespräch* indicates, by a growing number of semi-speakers. The simple fact that the *Zwiegespräch* was performed in 1927 proves that a majority in the audience must have had some idea of the vernacular, otherwise it would have been pointless to use it as a form of entertainment. The writer of the memoir furthermore recalls that children were severely punished when they called non-Jewish children *kloben* ('dogs'): "Als ein Kind den hässlichen Ausdruck Kloben (eigentlich Hunde) für nichtjüdische Kinder gebrauchte, setzte es eine grosse Tracht Prügel." (WS, private archive JD) Thus, the sources indicate that elements of the Jewish variety could be used as a secret parlance.

Abbreviations

AWY: Aurich Western Yiddish
BW: Letters of a survivor of the Aurich Jewish community
JD: Johannes Diekhoff, Aurich
LCAAJ: Language and Culture Atlas of Ashkenazic Jewry
MHG: Middle High German
SG: Standard German
StAA: Staatsarchiv Aurich
WS: Unpublished memoir of a survivor of the Aurich Jewish community
WST: Recording of a reading by a survivor of the Aurich Jewish community

References

Althaus, Hans Peter. 2002. *Mauscheln. Ein Wort als Waffe*. Berlin and New York: de Gruyter.

Baviskar, Vera et al. (eds.). 1992. *The Language and Culture Atlas of Ashkenazic Jewry*. Vol. 1: *Historical and Theoretical Foundations*. Tübingen: Niemeyer.

Beem, Hartog. 1954. Yiddish in Holland: Linguistic and Sociolinguistic Notes. In Uriel Weinreich (ed.), *The Field of Yiddish. Studies in Yiddish Language, Folklore, and Literature*. New York: Linguistic Circle, 122–133.

Beem, Hartog. 1967. *Resten van een taal. Woordenboekje van het Nederlandse Jiddisch*. Assen: Van Gorcum.

Beem, Hartog. 1970. *Jiddische spreekwoorden en zegswijzen uit het Nederlandse Taalgebied*. Assen: Van Gorcum.

Breuer, Mordechai. 1997. Jüdische Religion und Kultur in den ländlichen Gemeinden 1600–1800. In Monika Richarz and Reinhard Rürup (eds.), *Jüdisches Leben auf dem Lande. Studien zur deutsch-jüdischen Geschichte.* Tübingen: Moor, 69–78.

Cahnman, Werner J. 1979. Village and Small-Town Jews in Germany. A Typological Study. *Leo Baeck Institute Year Book (LBI)* 19: 107–130.

Eggers, Eckhard. 1998. *Sprachwandel und Sprachmischung im Jiddischen.* Frankfurt/Main: Lang.

Gerzon, Jacob. 1902. *Die jüdisch-deutsche Sprache. Eine grammatisch-lexikalische Untersuchung ihres deutschen Grundbestandes.* Köln: Salm.

Guggenheim-Grünberg, Florence. 1950. *Die Sprache der Schweizer Juden von Endingen und Lengnau.* Zürich: Verlag Jüdische Buch-Gemeinde.

Guggenheim-Grünberg, Florence. 1954. The Horse-Dealers' Language of the Swiss Jews in Endingen and Lengnau. In Uriel Weinreich (ed.), *The Field of Yiddish: Studies in Language, Folklore and Literature.* New York: The Linguistic Circle, 48–62.

Guggenheim-Grünberg, Florence. 1958. Zur Phonologie des Surbtaler Jiddischen. *Phonetica* 2: 86–108.

Guggenheim-Grünberg, Florence. 1961. *Gailinger Jiddisch.* Göttingen: Vandenhoeck.

Guggenheim-Grünberg, Florence. 1964. Überreste westjiddischer Dialekte in der Schweiz, im Elsass und in Südwestdeutschland. In Lucy Dawidovicz et al. (eds.), *For Max Weinreich on his Seventieth Birthday. Studies in Jewish Languages, Literature and Society.* The Hague: Mouton, 72–81.

Guggenheim-Grünberg. 1966. *Surbtaler Jiddisch.* Frauenfeld: Huber.

Guggenheim-Grünberg, Florence. 1973. *Jiddisch auf alemannischem Sprachgebiet.* Zürich: Juris.

Herzog, Marvin et al. (eds.). 2000. *The Language and Culture Atlas of Aschkenazic Jewry.* Vol. 3: *The Eastern Yiddish – Western Yiddish Continuum.* Tübingen: Niemeyer.

Jacobs, Neil G. 1996. On the investigation of 1920s Vienna Jewish Speech: Ideology and Linguistics. *American Journal of Germanic Linguistics & Literatures* 8.2: 177–217.

Jacobs, Neil G. 2005. *Yiddish. A Linguistic Introduction.* Cambridge: CUP.

Katz, Dovid. 1983. Zur Dialektologie des Jiddischen. In Werner Besch, Ulrich Knoop, Wolfgang Putschke and Herbert Ernst Wiegand (eds.), *Dialektologie. Ein Handbuch zur deutschen und allgemeinen Dialektforschung.* Berlin and New York: de Gruyter, 1018–1041.

Katz, Dovid. 1991. The children of Heth and the ego of linguistics. A story of seven Yiddish mergers. *Transactions of the Philological Society* 89.1: 95–121.

Lowenstein, Steven. 1969. Results of Atlas Investigations among Jews in Germany. In Marvin I. Herzog, Wita Ravid and Uriel Weinreich (eds.), *The*

Field of Yiddish. Studies in Language, Folklore and Literature. 3rd ed. The Hague: Mouton, 16–35.

Lowenstein, Steven. 1979. The Yiddish Written Word in Nineteenth-Century Germany. *LBI Yearbook* 24: 179–192.

Matras, Yaron. 1991. Zur Rekonstruktion des jüdischdeutschen Wortschatzes in den Mundarten ehemaliger „Judendörfer" in Südwestdeutschland. *Zeitschrift für Dialektologie und Linguistik* 63/3: 267–293.

Matras, Yaron. 1996. Sondersprachliche Hebraismen: Zum semantischen Wandel in der hebräischen Komponente der südwestdeutschen Viehhändlersprache. In Klaus Siewert (ed.), *Rotwelsch-Dialekte.* Wiesbaden: Harrassowitz, 43–58.

Mieses, Matthias. 1924. *Die jiddische Sprache.* Berlin and Wien: Harz.

Reershemius, Gertrud. 2004. *Niederdeutsch in Ostfriesland. Zwischen Sprachkontakt, Sprachveränderung und Sprachwechsel.* Stuttgart: Steiner.

Richarz, Monika and Reinhard Rürup (eds.). 1997. *Jüdisches Leben auf dem Lande. Studien zur deutsch-jüdischen Geschichte.* Tübingen: Moor.

Römer, Nils. 1995. *Tradition und Akkulturation. Zum Sprachwandel der Juden in Deutschland zur Zeit der Haskalah.* Münster: Waxmann.

Simon, Bettina. 1991. Zur Situation des Judendeutschen im 19. Jahrhundert. In Rainer Wimmer (ed.), *Das 19. Jahrhundert. Sprachgeschichtliche Wurzeln des heutigen Deutsch.* Berlin and New York: de Gruyter, 178–184.

Stern, Heidi. 2000. *Wörterbuch zum jiddischen Lehnwortschatz in den deutschen Dialekten.* Tübingen: Niemeyer.

Timm, Erika. 1987. *Graphische und phonische Struktur des Westjiddischen unter besonderer Berücksichtigung der Zeit um 1600.* Tübingen: Niemeyer.

Timm, Erika. 2005. *Historische jiddische Semantik.* Tübingen: Niemeyer.

Toch, Michael. 1997a. The Formation of a Diaspora: The Settlement of Jews in the Medieval German Reich. *Aschkenaz* 7: 55–78.

Toch, Michael. 1997b. Die ländliche Wirtschaftstätigkeit der Juden im frühmodernen Deutschland. In Monika Richarz and Reinhard Rürup (eds.), *Jüdisches Leben auf dem Lande. Studien zur deutsch-jüdischen Geschichte.* Tübingen: Moor, 59–67.

Weinberg, Werner. 1981. Die Bezeichnung Jüdischdeutsch. Eine Neubewertung. *Zeitschrift für deutsche Philologie* 100 [Sonderheft]: 253–290.

Weinreich, Max. 1980. *History of the Yiddish Language.* London and Chicago: University of Chicago Press.

Weinreich, Uriel. 1958. Yiddish and colonial German in Eastern Europe: The differential impact of Slavic. In *American contributions to the fourth International Congress of Slavicists, Moscow.* The Hague: Mouton, 369–421.

Wexler, Paul. 1991. Yiddish – The Fifteenth Slavic Language. A Study of Partial Language Shift from Judeo-Sorbian to German. *International Journal of the Sociology of Language* 91: 9–150.

Marijke van der Wal (Leiden)

Eighteenth-century linguistic variation from the perspective of a Dutch diary and a collection of private letters[*]

1. Introduction

For decades, research of the Dutch standardization process has focused mainly on the first stage of codification and selection during the sixteenth and seventeenth centuries. Less attention was paid to the subsequent eighteenth century, which has been considered a less remarkable period of linguistic consolidation. In this still widespread view of the eighteenth century, a more or less uniform written language is assumed to have developed as a result of successful micro-selection. In the following article, I will demonstrate that this view relies only on eighteenth-century printed sources. When 'ego documents' such as diaries and private letters are taken into account, a more complex linguistic reality of variation arises.

In sections 2 and 3, I will briefly discuss selection at the macro and micro levels in the Low Countries, questioning the accepted view on the eighteenth-century linguistic situation. After an introduction to the chosen sources (a diary and private letters) in sections 4 and 5, three morphological phenomena will be examined: diminutives (section 6), personal pronoun variation *mij/mijn* (section 7), and verbal variation (section 8). In section 9 evidence from the diary and the collection of private letters will be evaluated and some conclusions will be drawn.

[*] My research was carried out within LUCL (Leiden University Centre for Linguistics). I thank Nicola McLelland (Nottingham) for her useful comments on an earlier draft of this article.

2. The standardization process:
macro selection in the Low Countries

In the sixteenth and seventeenth centuries, the Low Countries encompassed an area with various dialects. Leaving aside the French speaking provinces and Frisian speaking Friesland, the main Dutch speaking areas were Flanders, Brabant, Holland, and the eastern part of the Low Countries. The division into the southern dialects (both Flemish and Brabantian), the Hollandish dialect, and the eastern dialects is shown on map 1.

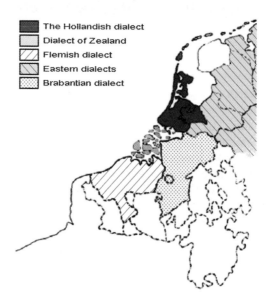

Map 1: Dialects in the Low Countries

Initially, in the second half of the sixteenth century, standardization took place in the South of the Low Countries as well as in the North. This is evident from early codification activities such as the *Nederlandsche Spellinghe* 'Dutch orthography' (1550), written and published by the printer Joos Lambrecht in the town of Ghent, in the South, and the first printed Dutch grammar, the *Twe-spraack vande Nederduitsche letterkunst* 'Dialogue of Dutch grammar' (1584), written by the Amsterdam Chamber of Rhetoric *In Liefd Bloeyende* and published in the town of Leiden, in the North. This joint standardization 'enterprise', however, was brought to an end by major political and economic developments. The wealthy South gradually lost its prosperity after the fall of Antwerp in 1585, when this main trade centre of the South finally succumbed to Spanish government. Holland, on the other hand, flourished and became powerful and wealthy during the second half of the sixteenth century. Due to these well-known historical factors, the Dutch standard language developed in the northern part of the Low Countries, in Holland in particular. The eastern dialects barely contributed to the standard language, for, at the beginning of the seventeenth century, they had little or no prestige. For the southern dialects, this was different. The standard language comprised southern (Brabantian and Flemish) elements thanks to the influential written and printed language, which had exhibited southern characteristics for centuries. Another factor that may have strengthened the position of southern linguistic elements was the influence of a considerable number of immigrants who fled to the North after the fall of Antwerp. In the Northern towns, they were a prestigious group of merchants, scholars, printers, schoolmasters, etc.[1]

This brief sketch of selection at macro level and of the external factors involved raises the question of the actual selection of competing variants, the so-called selection at micro level for the developing Dutch standard language.

3. Selection at micro level
and eighteenth-century linguistic variation

Selection of variants takes place through the language usage of speakers and writers who avoid particular variants. As Stein (1994: 1) put it: "sorting out the variants"; a sorting out into "goodies" and "baddies", leading to a difference in prestige between standard and dialectal forms. This selection at micro-level becomes apparent in the Low Countries during the seventeenth century. By the eighteenth century, the Dutch standardization process had made considerable progress, and the written language shows the results of selection at micro level. Particular variants, still present in seventeenth-century texts, are not found in most eighteenth-century printed publications.

For many decades this view on the progress of standardization has led to a lack of interest in the eighteenth century, which was seen as a less remarkable period of both linguistic consolidation and elaborate prescriptivism. Yet this view needs to be questioned in various respects. Did the previous linguistic variation largely vanish from usage? Did literate people in everyday life write according to the norms of the preferred variants? These variants were mainly those from the province of Holland, in particular the variants of 'the well-

---

[1] Cf. Van der Wal (1995: 30–36). Doubt has been cast on both the influence of these southern immigrants and the southern influence in written language by Boyce and Howell (1996) and Van der Sijs (2004). Instead of southern influence, Van der Sijs assumes influence from German and the eastern dialects, a view that has been an issue of debate recently (cf. Van der Wal 2005).

educated in the towns and cities', whose language usage is repeatedly
mentioned by contemporaries as exemplary for 'good Dutch'.[2] Did the usage
of writers from various backgrounds show these preferred variants, or did large
groups of native speakers still prefer other dialectal and sociolectal variants?
Answers to these questions may be found in a particular kind of text material
that may reveal an as yet under-researched area of the eighteenth-century
linguistic usage. This study investigates both a diary and a recently published
collection of private letters to present us with a more differentiated picture of
eighteenth-century Dutch.

4. Sources for this study:
a collection of private letters and a diary

In 2003 the historian Perry Moree published a collection of private letters that
he had discovered in the Public Record Office London. This private
correspondence is a collection of twenty letters addressed to Hermanus Kikkert
(1749–1806), a sailor employed by the VOC (Verenigde Oost-Indische
Compagnie 'East Indian Company'). The letters were written by his wife,
Aagje Luijtsen (1756–1797), who stayed behind on the island of Texel, the
most northern part of the province of Holland. Hermanus and Aagje, both born
and bred in Den Burg, the largest village on the island of Texel, were members
of much respected, protestant families, and both were educated at the local
primary school. Furthermore, Hermanus is believed to have received his
nautical training in the town of Den Helder, leading to a successful career with
the VOC fleet. A few months after his marriage to Aagje on June 2 1776,
Hermanus sailed out as a navigating officer on a VOC ship heading for the
East (Moree 2003:14ff.).

For the newly-weds, writing letters was the only way to keep in contact.
That is what they did, and, fortunately, twenty of Aagje's letters, sent to her
husband during his two voyages in the years 1776–1780, miraculously
survived the turmoil of life at sea.[3] These letters are little jewels not only for
historians who appreciate first-hand information about daily life, but for

---

[2]   Cf. the Dutch author and playwright Joost van den Vondel (1587–1679), who in 1650
      explicitly mentions the spoken language of the well-educated in the towns of The Hague, the
      centre of government, and of Amsterdam, the centre of trade (Van der Wal 2004: 220). The
      Dutch linguist Lambert ten Kate (1674–1731) also points at the highest social groups ("de
      Deftigsten") for the best pronunciation (Ten Kate 1723, I: 146f.).

[3]   The letters received by Hermanus Kikkert were confiscated in an attack by English war ships
      at The Cape of Good Hope in 1781. They are kept in the High Court of Admiralty-Archive
      No-30 of The National Archives (TWA) in Kew (UK).

linguists as well. They are far from being brief notes full of standard formulae, clumsily written by a barely literate woman. On the contrary, Aagje, native speaker of the (Hollandish) dialect of the island of Texel, was a skilled writer who was able to express herself well in an informal style of writing. Her elaborate, intimate letters contain no more than a few standard formulae, in particular opening and closing phrases.

In addition to these interesting letters from the last quarter of the eighteenth century, I examined yet another source which might show linguistic variation. This second source was a diary written forty years earlier, in 1736, by two sisters from Zealand who made a journey to Batavia in the company of their brother, an employee of the VOC. The two sisters, Maria (1709–1738) and Johanna (1713–1737) Lammens, were from a well-to-do protestant family of burgomasters in the province of Zealand.[4] The diary kept by the sisters during their voyage to Batavia is a lively report of daily life aboard. Apart from some recurrent participle constructions, the style of the diary can be characterized as informal.[5]

The Lammens sisters were familiar with the dialect of Zealand, which shares quite a few characteristics with the southern dialects. It is important to note that the sisters did not write in their local dialect, but intended to write well, i.e. to write according to the developing standard variety.[6] They seriously aimed at achieving that goal and doubt whether they had succeeded, when, at the end of the diary, they apologize for their style and orthography.

Although members of respected families, as females both Aagje Luytsen and the Lammens sisters must have received less education than did their male well-educated counterparts. Therefore, both by their education and by their local origin, they were quite different from the exemplary and well-educated inhabitants of the Hollandish towns and cities, and their writings constitute the kind of text material that could reveal evidence of non-standard linguistic variation not found in contemporary printed publications.[7]

---

[4]   The Lammens family moved from the village of Axel in the eastern part of Zealand-Flanders to the town of Vlissingen where the sisters remained until the time of their departure to Batavia (Barend-Van Haeften 1996: 22–24).

[5]   The sisters' diary was preserved in a copy made by their brother Pieter (Barend-Van Haeften 1996: 27).

[6]   Cf. also Elspaß (2002: 47) and Vandenbussche (2002: 34f.), who have made this observation for nineteenth-century private letters. The 'intended standard language' was meant by the writers to function as standard language, but does not meet various standard language characteristics such as consistent spelling and grammatical correctness.

[7]   I am most grateful to both Marijke Barend-van Haaften and Perry Moree (and publisher Theo Timmer) for providing me with their electronic texts of the diary and the letters respectively.

5. Examples of linguistic variation

In order to assess whether the linguistic usage in the diary and the letters differs from that in printed publications, a sample of printed sources needs to be examined as well. As representatives of eighteenth-century printed sources, a description of a journey to an imaginary country and a selection of issues from a Dutch *Spectator* magazine were chosen. The *Beschryvinge van het magtig Koninkryk Krinke Kesmes* ('Description of the mighty kingdom of Krinke Kesmes'; 1708) was published by H. Smeeks (?–1721), a surgeon in the town of Zwolle. Justus van Effen (1684–1735), a journalist born in the town of Utrecht, was the editor and author of *De Hollandsche Spectator* (1731–1735), the successful Dutch imitation of Steele and Addison's *Spectator*.[8]

Although linguistic variation can be examined at the various levels of orthography, morphology, syntax and the lexicon, within the limits of this article I will focus chiefly on illustrative examples at the morphological level: diminutives (section 6), personal pronoun variation (section 7), and verbal variation (section 8). After having drawn conclusions at the morphological level, I will briefly touch upon variation at other levels in section 9.

6. The diminutives

In seventeenth-century texts, we find diminutive variation of the suffixes *-ken* and *-jen*. In his grammar of 1625, the Dutch grammarian Christiaen Van Heule even explicitly mentions this suffix variation as a dialect-bound phenomenon, and he himself shows preference for *-ken:*

Holland	*het mannetje, het wijfje, het diertje* 'little man, woman, animal'
Flanders	*het mannekjen, het wijfkjen, het dierkjen*
Brabant	*het manneken, het wijfken, het dierken*

Almost thirty years later, the grammarian Petrus Leupenius had to admit that *-jen* was far more usual than *-ken* (Van der Wal 1992: 123). The use of Brabantian *-ken* had decreased; *-ken* had given way to Hollandish *-jen*. Ultimately, for the standard language the diminutive *-je*, i.e. *-jen* with loss of final *n* was

---

8   Both publications are to be found in an on-line collection of Dutch texts, the DBNL (www.dbnl.org). I examined the whole of Smeeks (1708) (150 pages) and the following selection from the *Hollandsche Spectator*: the issues from May 26 till July 7, 1732 (pages 43–122), those from September 11 till October 5, 1733 (pages 45–106) and those from January 1 till February 12, 1734 (pages 287–374).

selected, and *-ken* was only maintained in archaic usage such as in the States Bible, the Dutch Authorized Version of the Bible, published in 1637. Apart from the diminutive variants mentioned by the grammarians Van Heule and Leupenius, yet another variant, the suffix *-ie*, occurred in the seventeenth century, a variant which had developed from the Hollandish diminutive *-jen* (*boekjen-* > *boekjie-* > *boekie* 'little book'; Van Loey 1964: 230). The *-ie*-diminutive was not accepted into the standard language; it was considered a colloquial, low variant alongside the current *-jen* and the high, archaic variant *-ken*.

Against the background of these seventeenth-century data, I examined, first of all, the two eighteenth-century printed texts. These appeared to reveal a remarkable uniformity: apart from one single instance of *-ken*, only the diminutive *-je(n)* is found, mostly with loss of final *n,* and neither text shows any sign of *-ie*.[9]

In 1736, i.e. about the same time as Van Effen's texts were published, the sisters Lammens do not use any *-ke(n)*-diminutive. In their diary we mainly find the *je*-suffix and its variants *-tje/-etje* in examples such as the following: [10]

> *copje* 'little cup', *schuijtje* 'little boat', *koekjes* 'cookies'; *uurtje* 'little hour', *koeltje* 'gentle breeze', *maantje* 'little moon', *schoteltjes* 'little saucers', *voogeltjes* 'little birds'; *spulletjes* 'little things'.

The data look rather straightforward, but on closer examination they include a few remarkable instances:

> *coptje* (4) versus regular *copje* (5) 'little cup'
> *gebacktjes* (1) versus regular *gebakjes* (1) 'little pastries'
> *steektje* (1) versus regular *steekje* (0) 'little stitch'
> *stucktje* (1) versus regular *stuckje* (1) 'little piece'

The occurrence of the incorrect diminutives *coptje, gebacktjes, steektje, stucktje* (versus the correct diminutives *copje, gebackjes, steekje, stuckje*; cf.

---

[9]   Smeeks' only *-ken* instance is *steedeken* 'little town'. In Van Effen's texts *-ken* derivations do not occur apart from a lexicalized adverb *allengskens* 'gradually'. The original *-jen* occurs in a few of Smeeks' examples.

[10] Note that the occurrence of the variants *-tje* and *-etje* depends on the phonetic context: *-tje* in the case of nasals and liquids preceded by a long vowel and in the case of a preceding unstressed syllable with a sjwa; *-etje* in the case of nasals and liquids preceded by a short vowel. Assimilation of *-tje* into *-je* is shown in four cases: *beesjes* (twice), *resje, nagje*.

footnote 10) demands explanation.[11] To explain these particular data, attention must be paid to another small set of data in the diary:

ansjovisie (1) 'little anchovy'
buurpratie (1) 'little chat, gossip'
mutsie (1) 'little cap'
ontbijtie (2) 'little breakfast'
plaetsie (1) 'little place'

These six instances can be seen as slips of the pen against the 130 instances of diminutive *-je* and its variants, but they undoubtedly show that the Lammens sisters were familiar with the *-ie* diminutive.[12] Returning to the earlier problem of the incorrect *-tje* diminutives, we may doubt whether the sisters mainly wrote what they actually spoke. I would assume that *coppie, stuckie* etc. was what they said in daily conversation but did not write down in their diary, knowing that the *-ie* variant was not acceptable. They wrote what they were taught to write and, apart from a few slips of the pen, applied the suffix *-tje*, in a few cases even hypercorrectly or incorrectly.

Aagje's letters offer a different picture. Apart from the suffix *-ke* in *Lamke*, the name for little Lammert, her son, we predominantly find diminutives spelled as *-ije*, e.g. the following nouns: *hartije* 'little heart', *livertije* 'darling', *lief schatije* 'darling', *kindertijes* 'little children', *pottije* 'little pot', *traantije* 'little tear', *winkeltije* 'little shop', *zieltije* 'little soul', and proper names such as *Aagije, Antije, Kikkertije, Naantije*.[13] These diminutives sometimes alternate with *-je* (*hartje* 'little heart', *schatje* 'darling', *Aagje*) or with *-ie* (*Aagie*); the latter also occurs in *versie* 'little song', *huysie* 'little house', *Avie, Leysie*. An analysis of Aagje's orthography leads to the conclusion that the highly frequent spelling *-ije* is a variant of the spelling *-ie*.[14] Therefore, the stigmatized diminutive *-ie* is found to be Aagje's usual suffix, and, in this respect, her usage differs considerably from both the diary and the printed sources.

---

[11] The diminutive s*tormtje*, which occurs twice in the diary and differs from the modern Dutch *stormpje*, is assumed to be a regular form in the Zealand dialect of the eighteenth century (Magda Devos (Ghent): personal communication). The variation *speenvarkje* (1) versus *varktje* (1) is also found in the diary.

[12] In two cases the *-ie* diminutives alternate with the *-je* diminutives in the diary: *visjes* (2) 'little fishes' and *(buur)praetje* (2).

[13] The proper name *Lamke* occurs seven times against a single occurrence of *Lammertije*.

[14] The *ij*-token likewise represents an *i*-spelling in words such as *huijs*, etc. Aagje's letters offer a wealth of diminutives: apart from the proper names, 180 instances of the *ije*-diminutives occur (against only 19 *-je*-diminutives).

For the diminutives we may conclude that both the Lammens sisters from Zealand and Aagje from Texel are familiar with the Hollandish diminutive *-ie*, a diminutive that does not occur in the printed publications examined. The Lammens sisters may have been well aware of the low status of the *ie*-variant in the written standard language: they mainly write *je/(t)je*, even hyper-correctly. Aagje, on the other hand, does not hesitate at all to write *ije/ie*: it is her most frequently used diminutive.

7. *mij/mijn* variation

The second case to be discussed is variation *mij* versus *mijn*. In northern Dutch of the seventeenth century, the first person pronoun *ik* (subject) occurs in the object forms *mij* and *mijn*. The form *mijn,* which is still preserved in some Dutch dialects, belongs to the dialect of the province of Holland. Ultimately, *mijn* was not accepted into the standard language and the form has disappeared from the educated written language. Seventeenth-century grammarians do not comment on this variation, but the translators of the States Bible do. In order to decide which variant among the competing forms should be used for the Bible translation, they discussed various questions of language and made a note on *mijn.* This variant was rejected as being low or too colloquial: "nunquam *myn*, ut vulgus hic loquitur" ('never use *mijn* as the lower class people do') was their opinion (Van der Wal 1992: 124).

The stigmatized object form *mijn,* which also occurred in prepositional phrases, is clearly present in Aagje's letters, which show about 55% *mijn* versus 45% *mij*. Even quoting from the Bible, Aagje writes *mijn*: "ik zal *mijn* buijgen na het paleis Uwer heijligheijd" ('I will bow [myself] towards the palace of your holiness', Ps. 5:8; emphasis added). In the diary of the Lammens sisters, however, we find no examples of *mijn*, nor does Smeeks' book offer any *mijn*-instances.[15] The only two examples to be found in Van Effen's *Spectator* are, on closer examination, remarkable ones:

(1) de oudst […] ruim twintig jaar *met myn* en men Vrouw verscheelt
     'the oldest differs from me and my wife more than twenty years in age'
     (emphasis added)
(2) […] afgronten die *myn* zyn aangedaan
     'offences done to me' (emphasis added).

---

[15] The only example of *mijn* in Smeeks' book (page 80 *dat* [...] *hy mijn altijd Gods-kind noemde* 'that he always called me a child of God') may be safely discounted. Inspection of the copy of the original (UBL 1496G21: 1) has shown that this line does not preserve its original type-setting.

The first instance occurs in a quotation from an elderly man's conversation and the second one in an imaginary letter to the editor, texts which both show various characteristics of spoken language.

The evidence from Smeeks' book and Van Effen's texts reveals not only the absence of *mijn* from eighteenth-century printed and standard written language, but also its survival in spoken language. From that perspective, the absence of *mijn* in the diary raises a few questions. Did the Lammens sisters avoid the *mijn*-variant, knowing that it was considered too colloquial? Or were they not familiar with the *mijn*-variant in their Zealand dialect? The latter appears not to be the case: the *mijn* personal pronoun occurred in the Zealand dialect as well as in the Hollandish dialect.[16] The Lammens sisters must therefore have deliberately avoided *mijn* and chosen the acceptable *mij* variant. For Aagje Luijtsen, however, *mijn* is not an improper variant to be discarded in written language, but a variant on a par with *mij*.

8. Verbal variation

Apart from the nominal and pronominal variation discussed above, verbal morphological variation occurs both in the letters and in the diary. Aagje's letters show, for instance, verbal variants such as *ic/hij gong* 'went' (versus regular *ging*), *stong, sting* 'stood' (versus regular *stond*), *ic gaen, doen, sien* 'I go, do, see' (versus regular *ga, doe, sie*). In the diary both *gong* and *vong* 'caught' (versus regular *ving*) are found, variants that occur in the printed sources as well, cf. Table 1.

The numbers in the table should be interpreted against the frequency of the other, 'regular' alternatives. Against Smeeks' single instance of *gong* and Van Effen's two instances, 88 and 22 instances of *ging* respectively occur.[17] The verb *vangen* itself is less frequently used: Smeeks' two instances of *vongen* occur versus six of *vingen;* Van Effen only shows two instances of *ving*. The variations *moet/mot, moeten/motten, moest(en)/most(en),* still present in seventeenth-century texts, do not occur in Van Effen's publications. In Smeeks' book, six instances are found, all of them *most (ik/ men most)*, versus 163 instances of *moest*. It is striking that the *most* variant is a frequent phenomenon in Aagje's letters too (28 instances versus 2 instances of *moest*), whereas her present tense and infinitive forms show no variation at all (151

---

[16] Cor van Bree (Leiden): personal communication.

[17] Interference between the verbs *gaan, staan, vaan/vangen* led to the variants *sting* (cf. regular *ging, ving*), *vong* and *gong* (cf. *stong/ stond*) (cf. Van Loey 1964: 178). Both Smeeks and Van Effen even each show a single instance of *hong* 'hang'.

instances of *moet(en)* versus not a single instance of *mot(ten))*. In the diary only the 'regular' variants *moet(en), moest(en)* occur.

Verbal variants	printed text Smeeks	printed text Van Effen	private text Lammens	private text Aagje Luijtsen
gong	1	2	5	1
stong, sting	-	-	-	2
vong	2	-	3	-
ic gaen[18]	-	-	-	3
ic doen	-	-	-	5
ic sien[19]	-	-	-	2
mot, motten	-	-	-	-
most/mosten	6	-	-	28

Table 1: Verbal variants

We conclude that in all four sources the verbal variants discussed are marginal phenomena, with the one exception of *most(en)*. There is a striking difference between the present and infinitive on the one hand and the preterite on the other. The preterite *most,* which still occurs in Smeeks' book, is even the most frequent variant in Aagje's letters.

9. Reflection and conclusions

From the cases discussed, we can see that variants such as the diminutive suffix *-ie* and the personal pronoun *mijn* had disappeared from printed sources by the eighteenth century but occurred frequently in Aagje's letters. The diary has a position somewhere in between: from the data in the diary, we get the impression that the Lammens sisters aimed at avoiding these colloquial variants, but without succeeding in all respects. The verbal variation is more complex. *Mot, motten* appears to be absent in all four sources, whereas the preterite *most/mosten* still occurs in Smeeks' book and even appears to be Aagje's usual variant. The Lammens sisters, however, stick to the *moeten/ moesten* variants.

The results of our examination at the morphological level clearly illustrate that both Aagje's private letters and the diary of the Lammens sisters show a linguistic reality richer and more complex than the picture based on printed

---

[18] Apart from these forms the imperative *gaan* and the first person plural present *wij gaanen* also occur. Similar instances of the verb *staan* (*ic staen*) are not found in any of the four sources.

[19] Apart from this form the infinitive *sienen* occurs as well.

sources. These findings, which I could have extended to the phonological, syntactical, and lexical level as well, once more prove the value of ego documents for linguistic research. Having said this, a caveat should be made as well. We have to realize that not all diaries or private correspondences are equal, and the value of their data should be determined in each case. This means establishing in what respects these ego documents represent the actual spoken language. In Aagje's letters we indeed find the reflex of the contemporary spoken language. For instance, particular spellings such as *begreijpe* 'to understand' indicate that the final *n* of infinitives was not pronounced. Her spelling also suggests that many French loans were adopted by conversation and not by reading. Compare the following quotations from Aagje's letters:[20]

    (3)   Mar ik zijn met Leijs en Aavei heele *vammeljare* vrindinne
            'but I am very familar friends with Leijs and Aavei'
            (*vammeljare = familiare* 'familiar')
    (4)   Sijmon Kikkert is bij *sikkertaares* vandaan
            'Sijmon Kikkert went away from the secretary'
            (*sikkertaares = secretaris* 'secretary')
    (5)   ik *vielesteere..*/ ik *fielsseteer*/ *feleseteer* u
            'I congratulate you'
            (*vielesteere/ fielsseteer/ feleseteer = feliciteer* 'congratulate')

Particular syntactic patterns of the letters also reflect the spoken language, such as the repetition of the subject *Heijn van der Markt* by the demonstrative *die* in (6) and the *noun + possessive pronoun + noun* pattern to express the possessive in (7):[21]

    (6)   Heijn van der Markt *die* wagt der na
            'Heijn van der Markt (he) waits for it'
    (7)   ik heb een brief van *de captijn zijn vrouw* gehad
            'I got a letter from the captain his wife/ the captain's wife'

These orthographical and syntactical examples, however, should not obscure the fact that ego documents may not only reflect the spoken language, but also the language taught. In order to understand the earlier morphological results, in particular those of the diary, we have to bear in mind that the writers of diaries and letters were taught to write a developing standard language and, therefore,

---

[20]   To these examples I could easily add many from the diary of the Lammens sisters, who used much more French vocabulary than Aagje did, and who likewise show a deviant orthography. Cf. also Stroop (1997: 194ff.).

[21]   For similar syntactic patterns in German letters written by 'ordinary people' cf. Elspaß (2005).

to avoid dialectal or sociolectal unacceptable variants. It is not only highly probable that people were instructed, during their primary or secondary school education, to avoid unacceptable linguistic variants. Convincing evidence of this can be found in a little eighteenth-century dictionary, written about 1730 by an anonymous schoolmaster from The Hague and published in 1780 (Van der Wal 1994; Kloeke 1938). Aiming at correcting so-called street language, the author of the dictionary lists all kinds of stigmatized pronunciations, among which we find the verbal forms *most, mot, motten* (preferred variants: *moest, moet, moeten*) and nouns such as *sikkertaris* (preferred variants: *geheimschryver, secretaris*). This particular publication is convincing proof of an undoubtedly more widespread practice in the Netherlands.

Private letters and diaries reflect actual usage on the one hand and the taught written language on the other, and a thorough analysis is therefore needed to disentangle both elements. It is the rewarding analysis of private documents such as these that reveals a more diverse picture of the eighteenth-century linguistic situation than we had to date. Such a diverse picture must underpin a history of the Dutch language that describes the complex standardization process and pays attention to language change from above as well as from below.[22]

References

Barend-Van Haeften, M.L. (ed.). 1996. *Op reis met de VOC. De openhartige dagboeken van de zusters Lammens en Swellengrebel.* Zutphen: Walburg Pers.

Boyce, Jennifer and Robert Howell. 1996. Rewriting the History of Dutch: On the Use of Social History to Explain Linguistic Change. In William Z. Shetter and Inge Van der Cruysse (eds.), *Contemporary Explorations in the Culture of the Low Countries.* Lanham: Univ. Press of America, 25–38.

Effen, Justus van. 1731–1735. *De Hollandsche Spectator.* www.dbnl.org

Elspaß, Stephan. 2002. Standard German in the 19th Century? (Counter) Evidence from the private correspondence of 'ordinary people'. In Andrew R. Linn and Nicola McLelland (eds.), *Standardization. Studies from the Germanic Languages.* Amsterdam and Philadelphia: Benjamins, 43–65.

Elspaß, Stephan. 2005. *Sprachgeschichte von unten. Untersuchungen zum geschriebenen Alltagsdeutsch im 19. Jahrhundert.* Tübingen: Niemeyer.

---

[22] When describing language history, we must be aware of the ambiguity of the notions *change from above* and *change from below*, as David Denison rightly points out in this volume. The ambiguity between a change driven by systematic factors below or above the level of conscious awareness and a change initiated by those lower down or higher up the social scale needs to be taken into account.

Kate, Lambert Hermansz ten. 1723. *Aenleiding tot de kennisse van het verhevene deel der Nederduitsche sprake*. Amsterdam: Wetstein. [Repr. Jan Noorde-graaf and Marijke van der Wal (eds.), 2 vols. Alphen a/d Rijn: Canaletto 2001].

Kloeke, Gesinus G. 1938. Haagse volkstaal uit de achttiende eeuw. *Tijdschrift voor Nederlandse Taal- en Letterkunde* 57: 15–56.

Loey, Adolphe van. 1964. *Schönfelds historische grammatica van het Neder-lands*, 7th ed. Zutphen: Thieme.

Moree, Perry et al. (eds.). 2003. *Kikkertje Lief. Brieven van Aagje Luijtsen, geschreven tussen 1776 en 1780 aan Harmanus Kikkert, stuurman in dienst van de VOC*. Den Burg Texel: Het Open Boek.

Smeeks, Hendrik. 1708. *Beschryvinge van het magtig Koninkryk Krinke Kesmes*. www.dbnl.org.

Stein, Dieter. 1994. Sorting out the variants: Standardization and social factors in the English language 1600–1800. In Dieter Stein and Ingrid Tieken-Boon van Ostade (eds.), *Towards a Standard English 1600–1800*. Berlin: Mouton de Gruyter, 1–17.

Stroop, Jan. 1997. Over het 'journaal' van de gezusters Lammens (1736). In Ariane van Santen and Marijke van der Wal (eds.), *Taal in tijd en ruimte*. Leiden: SNL, 193–199.

Sijs, Nicoline van der. 2004. *Taal als mensenwerk: het ontstaan van het ABN*. Den Haag: SDU.

Vandenbussche, Wim. 2002. The standardization of Dutch orthography in lower, middle and upper class documents in 19th century Flanders. In Andrew R. Linn and Nicola McLelland (eds.), *Standardization. Studies from the Germanic Languages*. Amsterdam, Philadelphia: Benjamins, 27–42.

Wal, Marijke J. van der. 1992. Dialect and Standard Language in the Past: the Rise of the Dutch Standard Language in the sixteenth and seventeenth Centuries. In Jan A. van Leuvensteijn and Johannes B. Berns (eds.), *Dialect and Standard Language*. Amsterdam et al.: North Holland, 119–129.

Wal, Marijke J. van der. 1994. Straattaal en slechte woorden: sociolinguïsti-sche onderscheidingen in observaties en taalbeschouwing vóór 1800. In Philippus H. Breuker, Hendrik Derk Meijering and J. Noordegraaf (eds.), *Wat oars as mei in echte taal, Fryske Stúdzjes ta gelegenheid fan it ôfskie fan prof. dr. A. Feitsma as heechlearaar Fryske Taal en Letterkunde*. Leeuwarden/Ljouwert: Fryske Akademy, 231–244.

Wal, Marijke J. van der. 1995. *De moedertaal centraal. Standaardisatie-aspecten in de Nederlanden omstreeks 1650, reeks Nederlandse cultuur in Europese context*. Den Haag: SDU.

Wal, Marijke van der (in cooperation with Cor van Bree). 2004. *Geschiedenis van het Nederlands*, 4th ed. Utrecht: Spectrum.

Wal, Marijke J. van der. 2005. Review of Nicoline van der Sijs, Taal als mensen-werk: het ontstaan van het ABN. *Nederlandse Taalkunde* 10: 353–359.

II. From past to present:
Change from above – change from below

JOAN C. BEAL (SHEFFIELD) AND KAREN P. CORRIGAN
(NEWCASTLE)

'Time and Tyne': a corpus-based study of variation and change in relativization strategies in Tyneside English

The Newcastle Electronic Corpus of Tyneside English (NECTE) incorporates data from two periods within the 20th century. It amalgamates two separate corpora of recorded speech, one collected in the late 1960s as part of the Tyneside Linguistic Survey (TLS) (Strang 1968), and the other in 1994 for the Phonological Variation and Change in Contemporary Spoken British English (PVC) project (Milroy et al. 1997). This database is an ideal source for the type of statistical comparison which has become the bedrock of current variationist investigations into dialect levelling and the causes and mechanisms of linguistic change. Furthermore, research into the efficacy of the 'apparent-time' method which predominates in this framework is also possible since the corpora in question are both intra-generational and longitudinal in nature and the fieldwork techniques that were employed in their collection are essentially commensurate.

In a previous paper (Beal and Corrigan 2000), we examined speech samples from three generations of working-class and middle-class informants drawn from each corpus with a view to determining the social trajectories of non-standard relativization and subject-verb concord strategies. The tentative conclusions drawn from this small-scale study indicated that, with regard to changes in relativization, both 'real'- and 'apparent'-time analyses pointed to an increase in the use of *wh*-relatives in Tyneside English taking place in the course of the 20th century. In this paper, we both extend the analysis to a larger subsample of the NECTE corpus, and, as in Beal and Corrigan (2005), break down the analysis according to clause (restrictive vs. non-restrictive) and antecedent type.

1. Introduction: the NECTE corpus

The *Newcastle Electronic Corpus of Tyneside English* (NECTE) has brought together recordings of Tyneside speakers made at two different periods in the 20th century and 'future-proofed' them. The two data sets which make up NECTE are (i) the surviving materials, including 89 recordings of loosely-structured, one-on-one interviews from the *Tyneside Linguistic Survey* (TLS) project, collected in Gateshead c. 1969 and (ii) recordings of all 18 dyadic conversations from the *Phonological Variation and Change in Contemporary Spoken British English* (PVC) project, collected in Newcastle upon Tyne in 1994. Gateshead and Newcastle are respectively on the south and north banks of the river Tyne, in the far north-east of England. Although they are administered by separate authorities, Newcastle and Gateshead both form part of the Tyneside conurbation, and there is an increasing tendency for organisations involved in tourism and cultural activities to represent them as a single entity with the name Newcastle-Gateshead. In terms of the traditional dialect areas used by the *Survey of English Dialects* (SED), Gateshead was located in County Durham and Newcastle in Northumberland, but the urban dialect on both sides of the Tyne is relatively homogenous, and popularly referred to as 'Geordie'. The TLS informants, when asked whether it might be possible to distinguish between a Newcastle and a Gateshead accent, all reply in the negative. An example of such an interchange is:

[TLS/G01] Do you ever think that people specifically from Gateshead are more recognisable to Gateshead you-know? Does anybody ever guess that you come from Gateshead specifically rather than Newcastle?

[TLS/G29] – I've never had that happen. They've always just said, "Oh er you come from Geordie-land" or "Tyneside".

The NECTE corpus thus provides an ideal data-set for studies of variation and change in the dialect of Tyneside, since both the TLS and the PVC collected data from male and female informants whose ages ranged from 16 to over 60, and who could be categorised as working-class or middle-class. Further details of the NECTE corpus, and of the aims and methodologies of the TLS and PVC projects, can be found on the NECTE website (www.ncl.ac.uk/necte).

2. Real and apparent time

Traditional histories of English (e.g. Baugh and Cable 1978, Freeborn 1992), infer changes in the language from comparisons of texts produced in successive periods of time, identifying distinct stages such as 'Old English', 'Middle English' and 'Modern English'. Where differences are observed between texts from one century and comparable texts from a later century, a change is assumed to have occurred. Over the last forty years, studies of language variation and change have tended to use the 'apparent-time' methodology pioneered by Labov (1963). Setting out to challenge the view put forward by Bloomfield (1933), that the process of linguistic change could never be directly observed, Labov formulated the hypothesis that, when other extra-linguistic factors such as gender, social class, education, etc. are kept constant, patterns of variation in the language of different age groups reflect change in progress, since the oldest speakers tend to be the most conservative, and the youngest the most innovative. The assumption behind the apparent-time hypothesis is that an individual speaker's usage reflects the stage of his or her language's development when he or she reached adolescence, generally viewed to be the age at which the vernacular stabilises. Thus, a sixty-year-old recorded in 1969 would reflect usage typical of the 1920's, but a sixteen-year-old recorded in the same year would represent that of the 1960's, and any consistent differences between the language of these two age cohorts would be deemed to provide evidence of change in the language or dialect concerned. Since Labov's groundbreaking study, the use of apparent-time methodology has become the norm in investigations of language variation and change (see, for instance, the studies in Foulkes and Docherty 1999). However, Bailey warns us that "apparent time data are only a *surrogate* for real-time evidence, and apparent-time data cannot uncritically be assumed to represent diachronic linguistic developments" (2002: 314). He points out that the phenomenon of 'age-grading', whereby linguistic behaviour is associated with a particular stage of life rather than a point in time, and doubts concerning the stability of adult vernaculars raised by, e.g. Cukor-Avila (2000), signal a need for caution. He concludes that "in the best of circumstances, researchers will be able to combine apparent-time data with real-time evidence, with the relative strengths of one approach offsetting the weaknesses of another" (2002: 330). The NECTE corpus, consisting as it does of data collected both from different age-groups and at different times in the 20th century, gives us the opportunity to do just this.

3. A brief history of relativization patterns in English

Romaine (1982) gives an account of the evolution of relativization strategies in English which is summarized in Table 1, below. Of the three strategies used in English, that involving the '*wh*-relatives' is most recent, and these were introduced incrementally according to a grammaticality hierarchy, whereby those with antecedents in the more 'oblique' cases, such as genitive *whose* and object *whom* appeared some 200 years before subject *who*. Moreover, the *wh*-relatives were introduced 'from above', appearing first in more formal styles. According to Romaine, *that* is still frequent in spoken English and "infiltration of *wh*- into the relative system [...] has not really affected the spoken language" (1982: 212). The contact or 'zero'-relative was formerly used with all types of antecedent, but, in Standard English, it became increasingly disfavoured with subject antecedents, such that, whilst sentences such as (1) were produced by Shakespeare, (2) is marked as 'ungrammatical' in Quirk *et al.* (1985: 865) (∅ marks the position of the unmarked relative). Indeed, Schuele and Tolbert (2001) suggest that omission of the "obligatory relativizer *that* or *wh*- relative pronoun" in subject relative clauses is more frequent in the speech of children with specific language impairment.

1)   I have a brother ∅ is condemned to die (*Measure for Measure* II. ii. 34)
2)   *The table ∅ stands in the corner has a broken leg

All this would suggest that, in present-day English, on the one hand, *wh*-markers are confined to written usage, and on the other that the use of the zero or contact relative in subject positions is ungrammatical and/ or pathological. However, research on the syntax of non-standard English dialects, suggests that, in many of these varieties the typical ratio of *wh*- to *th*- and zero relatives lags behind that of present-day Standard English. Data from the *Survey of English Dialects* (SED) shows that traditional dialect speakers in Northumberland (as in many other areas) avoid the use of *wh*- in subject position, but, as predicted by Romaine's model, it is used where the antecedent is possessive (genitive). In response to the question '*HOW WOULD YOU COMPLETE A SENTENCE LIKE*': That man's uncle was drowned last week. In other words, you might say, that's the chap..., wh- relatives in the form of /hwe:z/ or /wi:z/ were given in seven out of nine locations in this county.

Strategy	c. 1100	c. 1400	c. 1500	c. 1600
th-	*that*	*that*	*that*	*that*
wh-	*the*	*of which* *to which* *whose* *whom*	*of which* *to which* *which* *whose* *whom*	*of which* *to which* *which* *whose* *whom* *who*
$\varnothing$-	$\varnothing$	$\varnothing$	$\varnothing$	$\varnothing$

Table 1: The expansion of relative markers in the history of English: a reconstruction
(after Romaine 1982, 53ff.)

4. Comparing real- and apparent-time methodologies

In an earlier study (Beal and Corrigan 2000), we set out (i), to examine specific changes in the patterns of syntactic variation and change in Tyneside English between 1969 and 1994 and (ii) to consider the validity of using apparent-time data for the study of syntactic change in progress. Focussing on changes in patterns of relativization, we conducted a pilot study on a small subsample of the NECTE corpus consisting of nine speakers from the TLS and nine from the PVC subcorpus. We looked at the overall proportions of *wh-*, *that* and zero-relatives across generations within each subcorpus (apparent time), and between speakers of the same generation across subcorpora (real time). Figures 1 and 2 show the patterns of relative marking by age-group (apparent time) in the TLS and PVC corpora respectively.

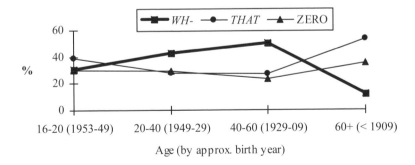

Figure 1: Relative marking by age-group , TLS corpus.

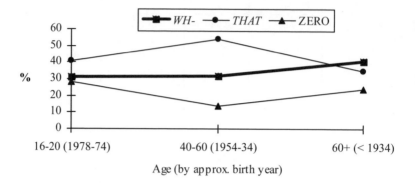

Figure 2: Relative marking by age-group: PVC corpus

What is striking about figure 1 is the sharp rise in the use of *wh-* between the oldest age group (60+) and the 40–60-year olds. These oldest speakers would have been born at the end of the 19th century, and so are contemporary with the SED informants who, as we have seen, tended not to use *wh-* except in the genitive. Use of *wh-* reaches a peak in the 40–60 age group and then levels off, until for the youngest age group it has a distribution equal to that of the zero relative (30%) and close to *that* (40%). Taken alone, this evidence could either point to a change in Tyneside English, introduced in the early 20th century, or to an 'age-grading' effect whereby the middle-aged are more affected by considerations of 'correctness' than either the elderly or the young. If we look at figure 2, we see that the former explanation is more likely. Here, the oldest age-group has the highest proportion of *wh-*relatives, and this again levels off to 30% in the usage of the youngest group. Those who were aged 60+ in 1994 would be part of, or at least overlap with, the same cohort of speakers who were aged 40–60 in 1969, so this suggests that the generation born in the 1920's and 30's, reaching adolescence and early adulthood during World War II, were involved in the increase of *wh-* usage in Tyneside English. In comparing the TLS and PVC age cohorts, we have introduced a 'real-time' element which dispels any concerns about age-grading, but both the nature of the change and its timing could have been inferred from apparent-time studies using either the TLS or PVC material alone. In figure 3, we have conflated the TLS and PVC material into a single dataset, with speakers categorised according to their decade of birth, regardless of when they were recorded (there are no data from 1960's-born informants because the TLS did not record children in 1969, and the PVC did not record any informants in their late 20's or 30's in 1994).

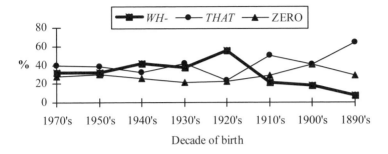

Figure 3: Relative marking by decade of birth, TLS + PVC

Here, it is clear that the 1890's-born informants, like those of the SED, very rarely use *wh-*, and that, whilst *wh-* usage increases gradually in the 1900's and 1910's-born cohorts, the dramatic rise is in the speech of those born in the 1920's. Thereafter, *wh-*usage levels off, until the proportions for the 1950's and 1970's-born cohorts are very similar. What is also striking about the latter groups is that *wh-*, *that* and zero are fairly evenly distributed. The conclusions that we reached in this (2000) study were as follows:

• Both real- and apparent-time methods demonstrate an increase over time in the use of *wh-*relatives in Tyneside English.
• This reaches its peak with those born in the 1920's whose usage is calculated at 55% .
• The increase in *wh-* eventually stabilises: the figure for informants born in the 1970's, has dropped to 32% .
• The infrequency of the *wh-* variant amongst speakers born in the 1890's – who produce the variant only 7% of the time and who greatly prefer *that,* reflects usage in the SED, whose informants would also have been born at the close of the nineteenth century.
• It seems to be inconsequential whether the data is analysed by either real-time or apparent-time methodologies.

Beal and Corrigan (2000) demonstrated that there had been a change in patterns of relativization in Tyneside English and that this change was revealed whether real- or apparent-time methodology was used. However, as a small-scale pilot study, it had a number of limitations. The small numbers of informants used could mean that results could reflect individual idiosyncrasies rather than changes in progress, but the consistency of our findings between the TLS and PVC subcorpora would indicate that this is not the case. More importantly, the study did not differentiate restrictive from non-restrictive relatives, nor did it differentiate between antecedent types. Ball warns that "the effect of personal versus non-personal antecedent on the choice of relative marker is particularly strong" (1996: 228f., 232f.). In order to gain a clearer and more reliable picture of variation and change in the relativization system of Tyneside English, it is necessary to differentiate tokens of relative markers according to whether they are restrictive or non-restrictive, and according to antecedent type. In Beal and Corrigan (2005), we compared the overall use of relativization strategies in the NECTE data with comparable data from the *Survey of Sheffield Usage* (collected 1981) and differentiated restrictive relative clauses by antecedent type. The results for the NECTE sample are presented in Figure 4, which shows the proportion of *wh-*, *that* and zero used in restrictive relative clauses.[1]

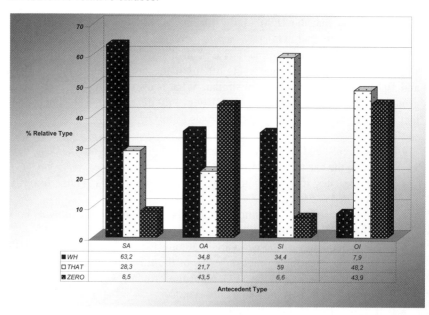

	SA	OA	SI	OI
■ WH	63,2	34,8	34,4	7,9
□ THAT	28,3	21,7	59	48,2
■ ZERO	8,5	43,5	6,6	43,9

SA=subject animate, OA=object animate, SI=subject inanimate, OA=object inanimate
Figure 4. Restrictive relatives by antecedent type in a subsample of the NECTE corpus

---

[1]   Figure 4 excludes all instances of sentential relatives, the very small number of genitive relatives, both of which had *whose*, and the single example of relative *what*.

Perhaps the most striking feature of Figure 4 is the polarity between the preference for *wh-* when the antecedent is both the subject of the sentence and animate as in (3) (63.2%) and for *that* when it is the subject and inanimate as in (4) (59%).

3)   I can remember my poor little mother who was less than five foot (PVC/ J13)
4)   There's some things that were threepence and sixpence (PVC/J13)

This pattern certainly refutes Romaine's claim that "infiltration of *wh-* into the relative system [...] has not really affected the spoken language" (1982: 212), but, even in the context most favourable to *wh-*, the 'infiltration' into Tyneside English still lags behind that of Standard English, since Quirk's (1957) study shows *wh-* to be near-categorical (91%) with animate subject antecedents.

Figure 4 also shows that the link between *that* and inanimacy is also apparent with object antecedents: although *that* is used in all types of restrictive relative clause, it is the most frequent type when the antecedent is both the object and inanimate, as in (5). This is the context in which *wh-* is least frequent: *which* is very rare in this subsample of the NECTE corpus. On the other hand, zero is strongly associated with object antecedents, whether they are animate, as in (6), or inanimate, as in (7).

5)   We used to get a lot of second-hand toys that had been done up (PVC/J13)
6)   When I think of the way that we, and all the people ∅ we knew lived through … the war (PVC/J13)
7)   He can't understand some of the stuff ∅ he watches on the television (TLSG312)

Figure 4 was produced for a study (Beal and Corrigan 2005) which was essentially diatopic rather than diachronic, comparing relativization in the dialects of Newcastle and Sheffield. The data on which it is based are taken from all age groups and both subcorpora (TLS and PVC), so figure 4 really represents a 'snapshot' of Tyneside English in the 20th century. In order to determine whether the tendencies noted above represent changes in progress (as our deliberate use of the phrase 'lags behind' would suggest), we need to analyse the data according to both antecedent type and real/apparent time. Figures 5–8 below show the results of this analysis.

Joan C. Beal and Karen P. Corrigan

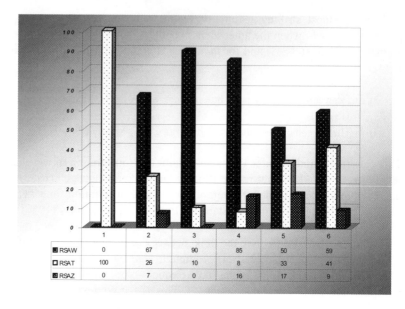

Figure 5: Distribution of relative markers with animate subject antecedents.

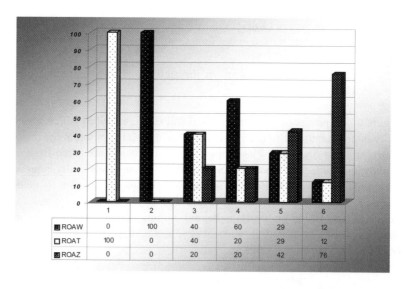

Figure 6: Distribution of relative markers with animate object antecedents

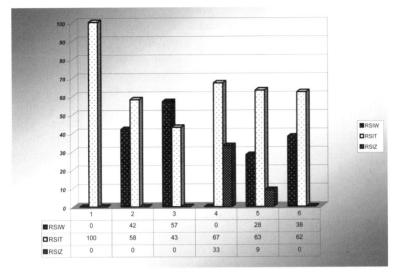

Figure 7: Distribution of relative markers with inanimate subject antecedents

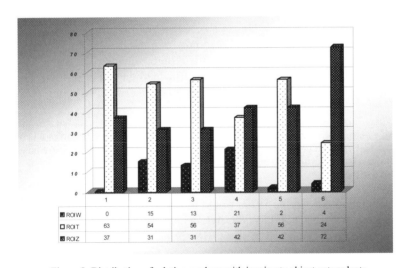

Figure 8: Distribution of relative markers with inanimate object antecedents

In figures 5–8, the results are presented with age / time on the X axis, moving left to right from oldest to youngest age-group in the TLS subsample, then oldest to youngest in the PVC subsample. If we look at the oldest/ earliest group first, the TLS informants who were over sixty at the time of recording, we can see that *wh-* is not used by this group at all when we exclude sentential *which* and non-restrictive relatives. For this group *that* is categorical except with inanimate object antecedents, where *that* is used in 63% and zero in 37% of instances. The figures for the next age group in the TLS subsample show an extraordinary reversal: for this group, *wh-* is categorical when the antecedent is animate and the object, and is used in 67% of cases where it is animate and the subject. This tendency for *wh-* to be associated with animate antecedents persists, but for the next age group, the TLS informants who were under 40, *wh-* is most frequently used when the antecedent is both animate and the subject. This is the pattern which prevails, even when the increase in *wh-* usage levels off, as shown in the results from the PVC subsample. We noted above that figure 4 shows a strong association between *wh-* and animate subject antecedents: what this diachronic study demonstrates is that the sudden increase in *wh-* usage amongst the generation born in the 1920s and 1930s, as shown in figures 1 and 3, is associated with this tendency. Of course, the link between *wh-* and animacy is one that is very strongly promoted in prescriptive grammars. Robert Lowth, perhaps the most famous and influential of all 18th-century grammarians, commented that *that* "is used indifferently both of persons and things: but perhaps would be more properly confined to the latter" (1762: 134). This statement is almost identical to that made by Burchfield in his revision of Fowler's *Modern English Usage*: "normally use *who* as the relative pronoun following a human antecedent and *that* (or *which*) following an inanimate antecedent" (1996: 773).[2] Fowler himself was, if anything, less prescriptive than either Lowth or Burchfield on this matter: his primary focus was on recommending readers to use *that* in 'defining' (i.e. restrictive) and *which* in 'non-defining' (non-restrictive) clauses. Otherwise, he writes:

> Whereas it might seem orderly that, as *who* is appropriate to persons, so *that* should have been appropriated to things…we find in fact that the antecedent of *that* is often personal…. Such peculiarities are explicable, but not now curable; they are inherent in the relative apparatus that we have received & are bound to work with. (Fowler 1926: 634f.)

The generation born in the 1920s would be one of the first to benefit from the provision of the 1918 Education Act, which raised the minimum school-leaving age in England and Wales to 14 (it had been raised to 12 as late as 1909). Given the popularity of works such as Fowler's in the period during which this cohort received their education, it is likely that the introduction of

---

[2] Readers who have only encountered Lowth through the filter of 20th-century commentators might be surprised to note that the tone of his statement is actually rather less prescriptive than that of Burchfield (see Beal (2004: 89–123) for further discussion of this).

wh- into the speech of Tynesiders, and the association of this innovation with animacy, represents a 'change from above'. To be more certain of this, we would need to determine what texts were used in English lessons in Tyneside schools in the 1930s and 1940s. One likely candidate is *Pitman's Common-sense English Course Book* (Potter 1931), a whole series, each book of which "contains sufficient material for a full year's course of systematic reading, language study and composition, together with a large number of graded exercises" (1931, inside front page). Book 1 of the 'Senior Series' contains a number of exercises on relative pronouns, the first of which requires students to "insert the correct relative pronoun *who, whom, whose, which, that, what*" in six sentences, the first of which is 'The man ----- robbed the shop has been caught' (1931: 57). Exercise 3 requires students to 'rewrite correctly' sentences which "contain relative pronouns wrongly used". The 'incorrect' sentences are:

a) Here is the girl who I gave it to.
b) This is the place what I told you about.
c) The man what thinks this is wrong.
d) It was doubtful whom had done it.
e) The people as were here were friends of ours. (Potter 1931: 57)

Lastly, suggestions for composition are provided. Students are invited to write letters of thanks:

1. To an uncle who has sent you ten shillings on your birthday.
2. To your godfather who has sent you £1 for Christmas.
3. To a friend who has lent you a book, which you are returning.
4. To a friend or relative with whom you have recently spent a holiday
5. To a friend who has offered to look after your dog while you are away.
   (Potter 1931: 57)

This provides an intriguing glimpse of the kind of normative instruction being received by schoolchildren in the 1930s. Book 1 of the Senior Series would probably have been used by 11–12 year olds. Whilst no explicit prescription about use of *who* with animate subjects is provided here (indeed, the focus in the 'incorrect sentence' exercise is firmly on proscribing the non-standard relatives *what* and *as*), the preferred model is subtly introduced in the titles for composition exercises: here only *who* and *whom* are used with animate antecedents, and *which* introduces a non-restrictive clause in 3. This would have provided a model for students to follow, in which *wh*- relatives were favoured, especially with animate antecedents.

The 'levelling off' of this rise in *wh*-usage amongst those born in the 1950s and later coincides with the period in which more descriptive ideas about the teaching of English filtered through to schools. Those who received their education in the 1960s and later had acquired a variety into which *wh-* had infiltrated, but would no longer be influenced by the prescriptive model that advocated only *wh-* with animate antecedents.

The other change which is evident in figures 5–8 is the rise in the use of zero relatives, and the increasing association of this with object antecedents. The oldest cohort, those who were over 60 in 1969, use zero only with inanimate object antecedents, but this accounts for 37% of relatives in this category. For the youngest cohort, those who were under 40 in 1994, this has risen to 72%.[3] Where the antecedent is both animate and assumes object function, the introduction of zero appears to come later, and to increase in apparent time through the PVC age cohorts. In this case, the absence of zero in the TLS subcorpus and its greater frequency in the PVC may be partly due to the different methodologies of the two surveys: the TLS data was collected by means of semi-structured, one-on-one interviews, whilst the PVC project used dyadic conversations in which the fieldworker played no part. The latter methodology would be more likely to result in the kind of informal discourse in which zero relatives are more likely to occur. Nevertheless, the distribution of zero relatives across apparent time, as shown in the three right-hand columns of figures 6 and 8, does show a consistent increase in the use of zero with object antecedents. If this does indicate a change in progress, that change could be either from 'above' or 'below': on the one hand, zero is frowned on in prescriptive grammars, so the increase in the use of zero through the later 20th century could represent a change from below, but, on the other hand, this increase is constrained by the 'rule' of Standard English that zero should only appear where the antecedent is the object. The change could therefore be caused by the influence of Standard English on the speech of Tynesiders.

5. Conclusion

This examination of a small subsample of the NECTE corpus has demon-strated that, whether we employ 'real'- or 'apparent'-time methods, or whether we take a synchronic approach as in Beal and Corrigan (2005), certain trends are apparent in patterns of relativization in Tyneside English:

1) *Wh-* is favoured when the antecedent is the subject and animate, and this tendency increases in time;
2) Object antecedents favour the use of zero, and this, too, increases in time;

---

[3]   We need to bear in mind here that, for the PVC informants, the 'under 40' category is in effect 'under 30' since no informants in their 30's were interviewed.

3) Inanimate antecedents favour *that*. This is most apparent in figure 4, but figures 7 and 8 show that there is no diachronic change involved here as the figures fluctuate. *That* seems to be the default relative in Tyneside English: it has always been used, and for the oldest age cohort is categorical for all types of antecedent except those that are inanimate and object. As *wh-* is increasingly used with animate and zero with object antecedents, *that* remains as an option where, for whatever reason, these constraints have less effect.

In all the diachronic studies discussed here, the most dramatic change is the sudden, steep increase in *wh-* use amongst the cohort born in the 1920s. This change is certainly a change 'from above', introducing a relativization strategy, and constraints on that strategy, associated with Standard English. This generation would have been exposed to education for a longer period than those born in the 1890s, but they were also the generation which came into adolescence and early adulthood during World War II, when conscription and evacuation broke up social networks and exposed young people to the speech of other social groups and geographical regions. The oldest cohort of TLS informants demonstrate patterns of relativization identical to those used by the traditional dialect speakers interviewed for the SED. In his *Introduction* to the SED, Harold Orton states that his motivation for undertaking such a large-scale survey of traditional English dialects was to preserve these before the changes in post-war society led to their demise. Perhaps he was right.

Of course, this study is based on a very small subsample of the NECTE corpus, and, as such, can only point to possible trends. Now that the whole corpus is available, we hope to examine the distribution of these patterns of relativization across a much larger sample. Given the complex nature of the constraints which appear to be operating, we intend to subject this data to multivariate analysis, using a package such as *Goldvarb*. It would also be interesting to investigate further the possible impact of education, and of English teaching in particular, on the language of those informants born in the 1920s who seem to be responsible for introducing *wh-* relatives into the spoken English of Tyneside.

References

Bailey, Guy. 2002. Real and apparent time. In Jack K. Chambers, Peter Trudgill and Natalie Schilling-Estes (eds.), *The Handbook of Language Variation and Change*. Oxford: Blackwell, 312–322.
Ball, Catherine N. 1996. A diachronic study of relative markers in spoken and written English. *Linguistic Variation and Change* 8: 227–258.
Beal, Joan C. 2004. *English in Modern Times*. London: Arnold.

Beal, Joan C. and Karen P. Corrigan. 2000. New Ways of Capturing the 'Kodak Moment': Real-time vs. Apparent-time Analyses of Syntactic Variation in Tyneside English, 1969–1994. [paper presented at VIEW conference, University of Essex, September 2000].

Beal, Joan C. and Karen P. Corrigan. 2005. A Tale of Two Dialects: Relativisation in Newcastle and Sheffield. In Markku Filppula, Marjetta Palander, Juhani Klemola and Esa Penttilä (eds.), *Dialects across Borders* Amsterdam: Benjamins, 211–229.

Burchfield, Robert. 1996. *The New Fowler's Modern English Usage* 3rd ed. Oxford: Clarendon Press.

Cukor-Avila, Patricia. 2000. *The Stability of Individual Vernaculars.* University of North Texas MS.

Foulkes, Paul and Gerard Docherty (eds.). 1999. *Urban Voices: Accent Studies in the British Isles.* London: Arnold.

Fowler, Henry W. 1926. *Modern English Usage.* Oxford: Oxford Univ. Press.

Labov, William. 1963. The social motivation of a sound change. *Word* 19: 273–309.

Lowth, Robert. 1762. *A Short Introduction to English Grammar.* London: J. Hughs for A. Miller and R. and J. Dodsley.

Milroy, James, Lesley Milroy and Gerard Docherty. 1997. *Phonological Variation and Change in Contemporary Spoken British English.* [ESRC, unpublished final report, Dept. of Speech, Univ. of Newcastle-Upon-Tyne].

Potter, Frederic F. 1931. *Pitman's Common-sense English Course.* London: Sir Isaac Pitman & Sons Ltd.

Quirk, Randolph. 1957. Relative clauses in educated spoken English. *English Studies* 38: 97–109.

Quirk, Randolph, Sidney Greenbaum, Geoffrey Leech and Jan Svartvik (eds.). 1985. *A Grammar of Contemporary English.* London: Longman.

Romaine, Suzanne. 1982. *Socio-Historical Linguistics: Its Status and Methodology.* Cambridge: Cambridge University Press.

Schuele, C. Melanie and Lesley Tolbert. 2001. Omissions of obligatory relative markers in children with specific language impairment. *Clinical Linguistics and Phonetics* 15: 257–274.

Strang, Barbara M.H. 1968. The Tyneside Linguistic Survey. In Ludwig Erich Schmitt (ed.), *Verhandlungen des Zweiten Internationalen Dialektologenkongresses, Marburg/Lahn, 5.–10. September 1965* (Zeitschrift für Mundartforschung, Beihefte N. F., 4), vol. 2. Wiesbaden: Steiner, 788–794.

DAVID DENISON (MANCHESTER)

Syntactic surprises in some English letters: the underlying progress of the language

1. Introduction

There are three themes interwoven in this paper:

- Change from below
- Recent change in English syntax
- A Corpus of Late Eighteenth-Century Prose

I will start by saying a little about each, then look from various angles at the question of what 'change from below' might mean. The contexts I will discuss are all recent changes in English syntax as played out in examples from my eighteenth-century corpus. Despite my title, not all of the facts are surprises, but even a non-surprise can be instructive.

2. Change from below

'Change from below' notoriously means one of two things: either a change initiated by those socially lower down the scale, or a change driven by systematic factors below the level of conscious awareness. Often, but not always, the two definitions go together. Keeping them apart has always been difficult in sociolinguistic investigation of historical periods. Indeed discussions of historical change sometimes do not – maybe cannot – distinguish change from below and change from above at all: we just observe that 'the language' changed in some respect between period A and period B.

For the social meaning of change from below, Labov (2001) observes that it is not the most peripheral (here the lowest) social classes who lead change. He also states principles which apply especially to modern urban societies, and to phonology. Women often lead change, and also adolescents. Labov's principles may need modification for non-urban or premodern societies. Phonological change may operate differently from change in domains like syntax where functional pressure and meaning have more sway. Therefore it is not straightforward to apply Labov's observations to my material, since (a) society was not as urbanised as now, (b) women are poorly represented and adolescents hardly at all, and (c) I shall be discussing syntax.

3. Recent change in English syntax

I move now to change in syntax. In my work over the last ten years, I have concentrated mostly on late Modern English and Present-day English (henceforth PDE). One of the problems we face in this area is how to identify change at all. We can do so, for example,

- by personal observation and serendipity, comparing different periods.
- by comparing different varieties (British and American English, for example), and assuming that at least one must have diverged from a common source.
- from the comments of contemporary observers.
- and, once a change is known about, by looking for instances either of the old or the new usage.

Identifying patterns of change must precede any statistical work. In my chapter in the *Cambridge History of the English Language* (Denison 1998), I had recourse to all of the above, and for data I used various sources, including comedies and especially informal letters, but typically of educated middle-class speakers. This was taking change from below to mean change below the level of conscious awareness.

4. A Corpus of Late Eighteenth-Century Prose

Now I turn to my third theme, a corpus recently compiled at Manchester (and available to any interested scholar). It consists of letters held in the John Rylands University Library in Manchester, transcribed by Linda van Bergen and Joana Soliva, about 300,000 words in all.[1] The letters were all written to Richard Orford, a steward of Peter Legh the Younger at Lyme Hall in Cheshire. They span the period from 1761 to 1790. Their language varies from utterly standard to barely literate, but none of the letter-writers – apart possibly

---

[1] For a fuller description of the project see van Bergen and Denison (2007). The corpus marks deviant word division with an underscore, but deviant word joining has been suppressed in the examples given here. Where appropriate, italics mark the relevant word(s).

from lawyers – is writing with posterity or permanent record in mind, so the letters often come close to ordinary spoken language. Much of the content concerns collection of rents, sending of goods, coal-mining, farming, the sending of money (whether bills, cash or banknotes – the last-named often sent in two halves by separate posts). There is a fair amount of personal information interspersed. We hear of illness, of travellers taking the waters at Bath or sea-bathing at Liverpool for the supposed health benefits, of men who get drunk and fall in coal-pits, and of at least two unfortunate young men who hang themselves – on which no further information is given. But the personal information is scrappy and at times frustrating. Consider this potentially salacious opening:

(1)   Dear Sir. John Atherton is gone off with Geo. Cundliffs wife on friday
       Morning he has cntracted a greate many debts in the Neighborhood, more
       then you can Imagin in short every_body has suffer'd that had any thing to do
       with him, as Abraham Naylor has been Bro^t: up in the Coal pits and won that
       may be trusted, I have put him into Johns place at presant. if you Approve of
       him he may stay in it, if not, hope you will apoint another. (Samuel Rigby, 12
       Jan. 1784)

The writer, however, is more concerned to report the loss of an employee and the extent of his debts than to gossip about marital relationships. Example (2) comes at the end of what is otherwise a purely business letter:

(2)   Truly Glad I am to hear M^rs, Orford has met with a Son Dick (Harry Richard-
       son, 20 Jun. 1773)

This *envoi* is odd, even if *Dick* should be intended to refer to the letter's recipient, Richard Orford, because in that year, 1773, the Orfords had a daughter, Ellen (Morgan 2005); perhaps the correct year is 1778.

5. Data

5.1 Progressive passive

I turn now to a number of constructions whose history can be illuminated by the corpus and which may be of relevance to the theme of change from below, starting with the progressive passive, as in *The interview was being recorded*. This particular combination of auxiliaries arrives far later in English than any other pairing. It is first found in the 1770s, is uncommon till the 1790s and

then only in diaries and personal letters, and once it appears in print it gets
fiercely attacked by commentators through most of the nineteenth century.
Before it was accepted, one of the common expedients for expressing the same
thing was the passival – a progressive which is active in form but 'passive in
meaning', as in (3) – (12) below. So the period of the corpus is exactly when
we might expect a new sighting of an early progressive passive.

There is not a single one, and not for lack of opportunity: the passival
occurs at least 10 times:

(3)   in my accounts which *are* now *printing* (Josiah Birch, 5 Aug. 1778)
(4)   that ye meanest & lowest arts *are practising* by ye friends of y^e. present
      ministry (Thomas Davenport, 21 Feb. 1784)
(5)   When you came over the other day to view ^the^ Road now *making* in Taxal.
      (John Dickenson, 26 Jan. 1771)
(6)   in consequence of some new works *carrying* forward by M^r. Iacson for taking
      out the Water from the River Goit (Thomas Nicholson, 4 Mar. 1785)
(7)   but I tould him there *was* no preperation *making* for Marling (James
      Grimshaw, 30 Sep. 1782)
(8)   I am told sev^l. applications *are making* for the office (Michael Hall, 20 Dec.
      1773)
(9)   but sometime afterw^ds. I found proceedings *were carrying* on (Walter Kerfoot,
      13 Aug. 1776)
(10) About 3 Weeks ago I had a puncheon of Rum from my Son at Jamaica
      quantity 100 Gallons, 65 Gallons of which *is* now *Casing* up (C. Ridley,
      ?1772)
(11) I have been at LiverpooLe but there is no ship Sailing out for Maryland, M^r.
      Drinkwater who gives his Compliments to you will let you know when any *is
      fitting* out (Harry Richardson, 3 Feb. 1771)
(12) how in the name of Goodness is it possable that two such Coalworks as we
      have *carrying* on can be so wanting in our Inspection to want Brick at either
      work. (Harry Richardson, 27 Apr. 1771)

Furthermore, there is another example where the progressive passive appears
to be being avoided,[2] and we have passive only:

(13) I went to Mr Whites & order'd the Tea, which woud have sent by last nights
      Coach, only Mr White had no Lead large enough to Contain the Quantity but
      is sent by the Coach this Even^g (W. Burchal, 18 Jul. 1771)

---

[2]   However, *is sent* in (13) could also represent PDE *has been sent* rather than *is being sent*.

And finally, there is one instance of a double -*ing* construction which some scholars associate with the grammar of that stage of the language before the progressive passive was enabled (Denison 1993: 441f., Warner 1995: 537f., 544f.), and which is last found regularly in Jane Austen:

(14) the time of your Comeing to Derby *being* now *Approaching* (Richard Hole, 1 Oct. 1783)

So the grammars of the texts in the corpus do not appear to license the progressive passive, insofar as largely negative evidence can be trusted. Is this a surprise?

Actually, no, according to one sociolinguistic account of the origin of the progressive passive (Pratt and Denison 2000), which suggests that it was first found in an area very close to Bristol. The earliest examples currently known are from Malmesbury (23 miles from Bristol), then in a writer from Trowbridge (less than 20 miles away), and then the construction is taken up by a coterie of radicals living in the Clifton area of Bristol from c. 1793–5, sympathetic to the French Revolution and at one time planning to start a commune in America. The core membership was made up of Robert Southey, Samuel Taylor Coleridge, William Wordsworth, Charles Lloyd, Charles Lamb, Amos and Joseph Cottle, and Robert Lovell. They were introduced by Southey's childhood friends the Fricker sisters, and indeed Lovell married Mary Fricker in 1794, Coleridge married her elder sister Sara in October 1795, and one month later Southey married a third sibling, Edith. Another early user of the construction was the Irish novelist, Maria Edgeworth, who lived in Clifton in 1792–3, and whose full sister Anna married Dr Thomas Beddoes of 3 Rodney Place, Clifton, who was close to the Coleridge-Southey circle. I suggested that two dense and multiplex social networks – the Coleridge-Southey circle in the 1790s, and Lamb and Coleridge plus Keats, Shelley, etc. in the 1810s – were responsible for the spread of the construction. The earlier network seems to have used the construction in part subversively, to cock a snook at the literary and political establishments.

As for change from below, here the concept is rather murky, both from the point of view of social positioning of the speakers involved and of their awareness of what they were doing. The very earliest known users of the progressive passive are James Harris, 1st Earl of Malmesbury, and his mother, Elizabeth – probably higher gentry. The Southey-Coleridge circle can be roughly labelled as middle class. I have some evidence, but not at all certain, that the construction might have become a *marker* for them, a usage deliberately adopted as a badge of membership of a social group (or of opposition to the establishment). The later opposition to the 'barbaric' innovation sometimes regarded it as an affectedly schoolteacherish usage. So what seems to us now an entirely natural part of English grammar, usefully expressive and making the auxiliary set-up particularly symmetrical and systematic, may not have been a change from below.

Now the Orford letters of my corpus represent a completely different world from that of the Southey-Coleridge circle. These are busy, working people. If their politics show, they are loyal tenants of the landed gentry and colliery owners and work for elections on their lord's behalf. They live in Lancashire and north Cheshire. So it is convenient for my hypothesis about the progressive passive that it does not show up here at such an early date. However, the hypothesis is very vulnerable to the discovery of new data from the 'wrong' time or place, and I would love to have access to many collections of private writing from different parts of the country between, say, 1760 and 1820. The general point I draw from this is that we cannot always talk about *the* history of English: the English language at any one epoch is a patchwork of different geographical and social dialects and different registers of use, and sometimes change is surprisingly local. Perhaps always, at first.

5.2 Perfect *have*

I turn now to another change in the auxiliary system. The infinitive of the perfect auxiliary *have* is often associated with non-occurrence or unreality, as in these invented PDE examples:

(15) Be careful with that: you might *have* hurt someone.
(16) They couldn't *have* managed it if they'd tried.

In earlier English it was common to insert an infinitival *have* – superfluous by PDE standards – to signal this meaning:

(17) I forgot when you was at Haydock to *have* had some discourse about it (Shaw Allanson, 10 Nov. 1788)
(18) was Oblig'd to Discount a bill of 54..3 [...] I did not Intend to *have* done it but the Weather has been so exceeding bad of late hurts our Trade —— (W. Burchal, 16 Jan. 1772)

This *have* is generally unstressed and often reduced in speech to *'ve* or *a*. The latter is common in the corpus both in 'superfluous' and standard positions:

(19) I should *a* Come over to norbury this week but you comeing may answer the same purpose (Shaw Allanson, 14 Jan. 1784)

(20) I Should *a* Com my_Self.but Have been Ill for Som time (William Bass, 16 Mar. 1772)

(21) his money Shall be redy against The 25th of March; it wod *a* Shuted me better to *a* paid it in July or Auget; (John Buller, 21 Jan. 1774)

(22) If I had nown Hee Could *A* sould It I Could like to *A* Boug[t]: It (John Mercer, 2 Aug. 1790)

(23) We sh[d]. *a* Set the pit upon hard to_day & get up the Eye CoaL tomorrow had the Weather been good. (Harry Richardson, 1 Sep. 1767)

(24) he sh[d], *a* been at Warrington yesterday at which time I c[d]. *a* seen James Leigh but as he went to Manchester last night i'ts out of my Power to see him today (Harry Richardson, 16 Apr. 1772)

(25) had it been in any other Quarter all the whole Fabric must *a* come down. – The damage done is but little. & of a fire c[d], never *a* been better in any part. of the House: (Harry Richardson, 6 Feb. 1773)

(26) I sent for Ri. Melling to *a* come with the underlooker last monday Morning to *a* consulted him in regard to powder ^Sinking^ &c, he was taken bad just when mounting and promis'd he w[d]. be with us as soon as possable he c[d], stir out. (Harry Richardson, 20 Jan. 1774)

Sometimes *have/'a* is lost entirely.

(27) when I put the Letter into the poste did not know of sending so soon for the Colt or woud ø post_pond it (William Buller, 11 Oct. 1789)

(28) he hath livd with M[r]. Whitle at Hollingworth 13 or 14 years, and mostly taken care of the Cattle and might I beleive ø been there yet, had he not left to follow the Cotton Business (Abel Hyde, 22 Dec. 1778)

These could be simple mistakes, but the numerous parallels in Visser (1963–73: 2038ff.) suggest that it is the genuine end-point of phonetic reduction.

What happens when *have* is reduced, but less so, so that the /v/ is retained? Then we get the notorious confusion between unstressed *have* and unstressed *of*, sometimes leading to the spelling <of> where standard English would demand <have>. Until recently, *OED* was claiming that the usage was jocular, citing examples from 1837 and 1844:

(29) Soposing seven hundred and sixty [servants] to *of* advertised and the same number not to *of* advertised. (1837 W. Tayler, *Diary* 10 May in J. Burnett *Useful Toil* (1974) II. 181 [*OED*])

(30) I never would *of* married in the world, ef I couldn't *of* got jist exactly suited. (1844 *Southern Lit. Messenger* 10 486/2 [*OED*])

I found an earlier one in a letter of the poet John Keats from 1819 (Denison 1998: 142):

> (31) Had I known of your illness I should not *of* written in such fiery phrase in my first Letter. (1819 Keats, *Letters* 149 p. 380 (5 Sep.))

The March 2004 draft revision of *OED* has one from an 1814 poem:

> (32) I never could *of* thought that force Could turn affection in its course. (1814 J. H. Reynolds, *Safie* 57 [*OED*])

Interestingly, the *Dictionary of National Biography* says of the author of (32):

> In October 1816 Reynolds met Keats at Leigh Hunt's house in the Vale of Health in Hampstead. The two young men had much in common: born within a year of each other, they were from similar backgrounds and shared a fervent, idealistic commitment to poetry.

Is this a coincidence? I doubt it. Linguistic usage spreads among people in contact. The use of *of* for *have* has been available, if non-standard, for a long time. In any event, we can now demonstrate that it had been available for some time before Reynolds and Keats were born. The corpus allows us to push the date back another 40 years, as there are two clear instances in the eighteenth-century corpus. Example (33) certainly and (34) probably are by female correspondents:

> (33) the servant to the old Lady I sho~ld not *of* thought of after what had past, but I wonder at no_thing, wood will soon be a married woman, all_tho two cheshire men was named to me and when I say~d I Knew it to be fals I was not at all beleived however I shall tell you more when I see you all_tho I was won of those that did not beleive nor cold beleive what the old Lady say~d (Ann Legh, 27 Apr. 1773)
> (34) I should be very happey to *of* seen m^rs. Orford at Leek (D Langham, 18 Sep. ?1774)

This is where written evidence is immensely frustrating. If the spelling <of> represents unstressed [əv], then we have a purely graphic phenomenon, though one presumably correlated with a certain lack of education. It doesn't represent indubitable proof that the writers were not identifying this form with the perfect auxiliary have, though it is suggestive. Literary writers since the mid-nineteenth century have used that spelling as 'eye dialect'– visual evidence of usually comical illiteracy, but probably representing exactly the same pronunciation that they themselves would have used in conversation. However, we know from the present day that many speakers genuinely identify the word with *of* and not with *have* and – crucially – are happy to give it a stressed pronunciation as [ɐv]. When that happens, we know for sure that we have a significant reorganisation of the auxiliary system. I would argue that the word has become an invariant, enclitic particle – not a verb at all – with a grammatical meaning to do with non-fulfilment or unreality. Corroboration for this includes frontings like

(35) What *would've* you done? (1989–95 corpus, cited by Boyland (1998: 3))
(36) a sentiment he *would have probably* denied (1961 Brown corpus G65 (1880))
(37) '1 *should've never* went on a stupid blind date. They never work out.' (1992 Armistead Maupin, *Maybe the Moon* xv.225)

for which I only know of recent evidence, and the construction

(38) Little Dombey was my friend at old Blimber's, and would have been now, if *he'd have lived.* (1848 Charles Dickens, *Dombey and Son* xxxii.445.12)

which dates back to maybe the fifteenth century, though perhaps only the nineteenth in the form given above.

The spelling *of* within the verbal group is certainly a change from below in the 'unconscious' sense, and probably also to some extent in the 'underclass' sense.

5.3 Preposition stranding

Preposition stranding seems to occur in the corpus with almost 100% regularity. Here are three examples from among many:

(39) but she is proper care taken *of* (Edward Ackers, 21 Mar. 1788)
(40) and her_self and two Daughter are the lives she fixis *on* (Thomas ?Manck or Bancks, 2 Aug. 1779)
(41) The person whom I paid it *to* has been at a deal of trouble to find out the person whom it is drawn *upon* but without any success. (William Birchal, 15 Oct. 1790)

Notice that there is little alternative to preposition stranding in the passive of (39), though the word order is highly idiosyncratic, while in both the non-standard (40) and the rather formally couched (41) the potential alternative of 'pied piping' (*on whom she fixes, to whom I paid it*) is not selected. There are hardly any occurrences at all of pied piping in the corpus. Here is one, though odd:

(42) however I can let him see what I have done with the money I have already received, and *from who*, the remainder is due; (Henry Porter, 17 Nov. 1777)

I defer discussion of preposition stranding until another particle usage has been considered.

5.4 Phrasal verbs

Phrasal verbs in PDE have a very interesting phonological constraint, namely that the verb is nearly always monosyllabic or an initial-stressed disyllable. Consider these sets of PDE phrasal verbs from a similar semantic domain, some of them semi-productive:

(43) get [somebody] down
(44) cheese/piss/put/turn [somebody] off
(45) freak/gross/put [somebody] out, etc.

It is presumably the phonological constraint which prohibits

(46) *annóy [somebody] off, *írritate [somebody] out

Now this constraint did not operate – at least to the same extent – in the *Paston Letters* of the fifteenth century (Denison 1981: 148), nor does it appear to have had much effect in the eighteenth-century corpus, where we find:

(47) adjourn out, declare off, inquire out [somebody], repair [something] up, return [somebody] back

Particle usage in English is notoriously problematic for formal models of syntax, but I believe that these two phenomena involving prepositional and adverbial particles are also a little problematic for the concept of sociolinguistically driven change. Both patterns, preposition stranding and the phrasal verb, are routinely (and correctly) regarded as characteristic of informal usage. It does not follow, however, that their growth is simply a matter of change from below. Consider each in turn. Although preposition stranding is certainly the informal variant compared to pied piping, it is also historically the *older* variant, which is inconvenient for a simplistic model in which change from below replaces an older usage with a newer one. As for the phrasal verb, it is in widespread use in the corpus and apparently *less* constrained than it is in PDE. This paper does not attempt a serious study of frequencies, but even if it could be demonstrated that the long-term history of the Modern English period shows a continual rise in frequency of tokens and possibly types of phrasal verb, what (47) implies is that in at least one respect – its rhythmic shape – the pattern has recently become more tightly focused in the last two centuries. Change, then, is not merely a matter of numbers.

5.5 Pronouns

My last contexts concern pronoun usage, beginning with the complementation of double object verbs – those which take both an indirect (iO) and a direct object (dO). In Old English we find both orders, iO–dO and dO–iO (Koopman 1990). In standard PDE, [nonprepositional] indirect object precedes direct object:

(48) Sue sent *her boyfriend the information.*
(49) Sue sent *him it.*

In some dialects, especially if both iO and dO are pronominal, we find dO–iO:

(50) Sue sent *it him.*

In the late eighteenth-century corpus, there are 10 instances of dO–iO, such as:

(51) Shaw wished I wo'd write to you to know if you had given *it him.* (James Grimshaw, 8 Mar. 1788)

There is only one instance of the standard PDE order with pronouns, iO–dO. In context, however, this fact is not surprising. First, the order dO–iO is still normal in the Lancashire-Cheshire area today, and in standard nineteenth-century English it was far more widespread generally than it is now (Denison 1998: 239). In order to make sense of the 10:1 ratio noted above, it would be necessary to compare that result with similar corpora from other areas, in order to distinguish general chronological change from dialectal peculiarity. I have no information on the social distribution of the two word orders, but it seems safe to assert that any change in usage has been a change from below at least in the 'unconscious' sense.

The second pronoun usage I wish to discuss is case choice in coordinated noun phrases. In coordinated subjects it is well known that objective case is readily used in colloquial speech where strict propriety might have expected a subjective form. The corpus furnishes a number of examples:

(52) when *either him or me* will attend you at Groppenhall (Francis Ashley, 20 Nov. 1783)

(53) Sur Ii hope you will Concider That *me* and my famely has been on It for this Hundred Yeare and upwards (Arthur Barton, 2 Sep. 1773)

(54) for less Money, than both *me*, and my Servant, at Bid him (James Brown, 13 Jul. 1772)

(55) My Wife & *me* are both between 28 & 29 Years of Age. (William Dumbell jr., 21 Jan. 1771)

(56) that *nethar them nor himselef*, is wiling J shoud leve the hous (Richard Edensor, 21 Jun. 1767)

(57) & either *him* or his Son, whoud bring it to Lyme (John Egerton, 23 May 1773)

There is an interesting 'mixed' example in:

(58) as *him and I* Agreed (Joseph Drabble, 21 May 1771)

Here we have objective case in *him* but preservation of subjective case in *and I*. This form above all often appears when traditional grammar would demand an objective case:

(59) If agreeable to you I sho^{d}. be very glad that a whole day might be dedicated at Hancocks of Disley for you *and I* and the Tenant and my mason and a mason or Carpenter of yours to settle this Business amicably in the Lump (B. Bower, 24 Jun. 1788)

(60) which Butcher Ellam will not give up the key neither – to m^{r}. Grimshaw *nor I* – but has a_bused me and Call^{d}. me wors then a Chimney Sweep (James Bayley, 23 Jul. 1777)

(61) J shall submit it to yourself, is it not a pity that the misunderstanding betwixt M^{r}. Jacson & *J* shoud not have a period put to it? (John Dickenson, 12 Sep. 1783)

Defaulting to objective case in coordination, as in (52)–(57), is clearly a change from below in the 'unconscious' sense. Conversely, the extension of subjective case in coordination, as in (59)–(61), especially in the sequence *NP and I*, looks like hypercorrection and so has elements of change from above. The social distribution of both types is complex.

6. Conclusion

My aim in this paper is modest. All I hope to have demonstrated is that, valuable and often neglected though it is as a factor in linguistic history, *change from below* has two potentially distinct interpretations, and furthermore, each of those interpretations can conceal quite complex paths of change.

References

van Bergen, Linda and David Denison. 2007. A corpus of late eighteenth-century prose. In Joan C. Beal, Karen P. Corrigan and Hermann L. Moisl (eds.), *Creating and digitizing language corpora*, vol. 2, *Diachronic databases*. Basingstoke: Palgrave, 228–246.

Boyland, Joyce Tang. 1998. A corpus study of *would* + *have* + past-participle. In Richard M. Hogg and Linda van Bergen (eds.), *Historical linguistics 1995: Selected papers from the 12th International Conference on Historical Linguistics, Manchester, August 1995*, vol. 2. Amsterdam and Philadelphia: Benjamins, 1–17.

Denison, David. 1981. *Aspects of the history of English group-verbs: With particular attention to the syntax of the Ormulum.* University of Oxford DPhil dissertation.

Denison, David. 1993. *English historical syntax: Verbal constructions.* London and New York: Longman.

Denison, David. 1998. Syntax. In Suzanne Romaine (ed.), *The Cambridge history of the English language*, vol. 4, *1776–1997*. Cambridge: Cambridge University Press, 92–329.

Koopman, Willem F. 1990. The order of dative and accusative objects in Old English. In Willem Koopman (ed.), *Word order in Old English: With special reference to the verb phrase.* Amsterdam: n.p, 133–223.

Labov, William. 2001. *Principles of linguistic change*, vol. 2, *Social factors.* Malden MA and Oxford: Blackwell.

Morgan, Daniel. 2005. *Descendants of Thomas Orford.* http://www.mit.edu/~dfm/genealogy/orford.html

Pratt, Lynda and David Denison. 2000. The language of the Southey-Coleridge circle. *Language Sciences* 22: 401–422.

Visser, Frederikus Theodorus. 1963–73. *An historical syntax of the English language*, 4 vols. Leiden: Brill.

Warner, Anthony R. 1995. Predicting the progressive passive: Parametric change within a lexicalist framework. *Language* 71: 533–557.

RICHARD DURY (BERGAMO)

YOU and THOU in Early Modern English: cross-linguistic perspectives

The story of English YOU in the period 1300 to 1700 has two main chapters: the extension of originally-objective YOU to the subjective; and the use of the second-person plural pronoun as a polite singular and its eventual extension in use to the exclusion of the original singular pronoun. Numerous aspects of these episodes exemplify 'language change from below': the spread of subject YOU and the abandonment of THOU undoubtedly took place below the level of awareness, with (among the written evidence) typically speech-related written genres showing most advanced use in both cases, and with women and middle classes playing an important role in the diffusion of change. In the following study an important aspect in the abandonment of THOU is also identified in the contact of standard spoken language and other dialects. In addition, bearing in mind the cross-linguistic interests of the 'language history from below' group, parallel developments in related languages are examined as a clue to explaining change.

1. The origin and spread of subject YOU[1]

1.1 Timing of the origin and spread

The Old English pronouns of address were singular ÞŪ (> THOU) and plural GĒ (> YE) with their declined forms, in particular (for the purposes of this study) singular object ÞĒ (> THEE) and plural GŪ (> YOU). In the early sixteenth century, this object form YOU spreads rapidly in subjective uses to the virtual exclusion of YE. Old English (like the older forms of all the Indo-European languages) lacked a polite pronoun of address, but in a development roughly

---

[1] Other terms that have been used for this process: 'the syncretism of *ye* and *you*', 'the extension of oblique *you* over the subjective', 'the disappearance of *ye*', 'the merger of the second-person pronoun paradigm'.

contemporaneous, but not synchronised, with the spread of subject YOU, the plural pronoun began to be used as a polite singular pronoun, and then in the late sixteenth and early seventeenth centuries it is generalized (in the standard dialect), to the point of losing its polite function to become the normal unmarked singular pronoun of address. But let us start with the first of these developments: the spread of originally-objective YOU to subjective uses.

Though subject YOU is found sporadically in the fourteenth century, and more frequently in the fifteenth,[2] a recent (and rare) corpus study of the change shows that the take-off for subject YOU in appreciable numbers only occurs in the late fifteenth century, with rapid diffusion of the new use in the first half of the sixteenth century, and the change practically completed (for writers represented in the Corpus of Early English Correspondence) by 1560 (Raumolin-Brunberg 2005: 59f.). In Henry VIII's official letters, subject YOU is rare before 1535 while after that date "it is the majority variant" (ibid.: 65). His daughter Elizabeth I (born 1533) uses only YOU for both subject and object. Naturally, for some speakers the change (in both singular and plural use) was completed earlier, judging from the fact that already in 1530 John Palsgrave does not use the form YE anywhere in his *Eclarcissement de la langue françoise*, not even among the personal pronouns listed in Book II (Stein 1997: 462).

Raumolin-Brunberg's study shows that the change is associated with written genres close to speech: in the texts from the 1500–1570 part of the Helsinki Corpus the trial transcript has 225 cases of subject YOU and only one case of subject YE,[3] and in all the texts classed as 'oral genres' YOU occurs in 68% of the total number of uses of subject YOU or YE, compared with 58% in 'literary genres'. In the texts in the Corpus of Early English Correspondence written between 1500 and 1519, YOU is found for 28% of total subject YOU/YE use in the family letters but only for less than 2% of cases in the non-family letters.[4] There are also indications of greater middle-class use of the innovation in the early period before 1500 and a clearly greater frequency in its use by women writers in the later period after 1500 (Raumolin-Brunberg 2005: 61–70).

The earliest datings for the parallel case of subject THEE come slightly *earlier* than for subject YOU, with *Middle English Dictionary* (MED) first

---

[2]   The sequence of dates for the earliest citations of singular subject *you* in the MED is: c1330, c1395, c1400, c1460.

[3]   This is, however, near the end of the period of diffusion (1554).

[4]   The article (Raumolin-Brunberg 2005: 65) actually says "[between 1500 and 1519] YOU occurs in 28% of the family letters, while the corresponding figure for nonfamily letters is less than 2%"; presumably this means in 28% of occurrences in family letters, not in 28% of the documents.

citations for c1300, c1330 and 1340).[5] Although this use does not survive in the standard dialect (perhaps because here THOU was increasingly confined to high register text-types where usage was carefully monitored and influenced by knowledge of the historically 'correct' form), subject THEE is found in Quaker speech and writings from the seventeenth to the twentieth century (Finkenstaedt: 216ff.), and survives as the common form of the pronoun in modern traditional West Midlands and S.W. dialects (Upton et al. 1994: 486; Ihalainen 1991: 106, 115f.).

Like the generalization of YOU, the generalization of THEE spreads from below the level of awareness in both Western dialects and Quaker speech, since it takes place despite the constant example of THOU and THEE distinction in the prestigious Bible translation. This familiar text did not prevent even university-educated Quakers (especially in America) from using subject THEE constantly in speech and private correspondence: in the early twentieth century Mary and Alys Pearsall Smith even used the form in their private letters to their non-Quaker husbands, Bernhard Berenson and Bertrand Russell.

1.2 Explanations for the change

(a) YOU functionally reinterpreted as stressed form

The OED (in the final volume, published 1921) adds an explanatory comment to the section on plural subjective YOU: "In early use sometimes app[arently] for emphasis, as opposed to *ye* unemphatic".[6] This sounds like a case of "functional reinterpretation of forms" with paradigmatic forms assigned to accented/non-accented roles (Howe 1996: 188f.). Unfortunately, the earliest dictionary citations do not support this view. Here are the earliest citations of plural subject YOU (the first two from the OED, the others from MED):

(1)   Vnto mi blis haf ȝue na right (13.. [redated by MED to a1400] Cursor Mundi (Göt Theol 107) 23160)

---

[5]   The MED citations come with the caveat that 'some examples may represent the unstressed form of *thou*'. First OED citations are c1375, c1470, 1596. Lutz's comment that '[the] singular forms *thou* and *thee* show no signs of confusion of their traditional syntactic roles' (1998: 197) refers to Graband's 1965 study of the works of Beaumont and Fletcher only, but the lack of any other comment in the article leaves the reader with the impression that the syntactic role of *thee* was non-problematic.

[6]   The origin of this comment may be Spies (1897: 103), who mentions that in stressed position *you* is usually preferred to *ye*.

(2)   And, as *yo* [sc. Æneas and Hector] counsell in the cas, I comaund be done.
      (*c*1400 [for MED 'c1540 (?a1400)'] *Destr. Troy* 7600)

(3)   In swinc ðu salt tilen ði mete ... Til *gu* beas eft in-to erðe cumen. (a1325
      (c1250) Gen.& Ex.(Corp-C 444) 359,365)

(4)   At Stonhenges, wite *ou* [vr. ȝe] wel, Ther he hit made everuch del. (c1330
      SMChron. (Roy 12.C.12) 333; referent of indefinite number)

(5)   Ye shew your lady lyttille love That *you* so herttly preysse (a1500 (a1400)
      Ipomedon (1) (Chet 8009) 1808).

(6)   Hertely welcum shall *yow* bene (?a1525 (?a1475) Play Sacr. (Dub 652) 76)

Of these six examples of earliest use, only examples (1) and (5) seem
associated with the metrical beat and none of them would seem to require a
stressed form in normal speech (for emphasis or contrast). The picture is the
same for the earliest citations of subject YOU with singular reference (the first
two citations from the OED, others from the MED):

(7)   'Syr Gye,' he seyde,...'To morowe schall *yow* weddyd bee.' (14.. [redated by
      MED to a1500] *Guy W.* (Cambr. MS.) 4192)

(8)   Bot the gret part to ȝow tuk 3e, That slew iiij off the fyve *ȝow* ane. (1489
      Barbour's Bruce VI. 657 (Edin. MS.))

(9)   Is it soþ *you* tel it me? (c1330 SMChron. (Auch) 210)

(10) Lord, so wel vs liketh *yow* And al youre werk, and euere han doon, that we
      Ne kouden nat vs self deuysen how We myghte lyuen in moore felicitee.
      ((c1395) Chaucer CT.Cl.(Manly-Rickert) E.106)

(11) On þe autre þu þam lay, Als þare offrand *yow* lay þam þare. (c1400 St.Anne
      (1) (Min-U Z.822.N.81) 511)

(12) Ha Wif ... how trowe *you*, telle me verylye? (c1460 Dub.Abraham (Dub 432)
      327)

Here, only (10) seems to coincide with a metrical beat and none seem to
correspond to normal stressed use.
    The association of subject YOU and stress has been taken up by other
commentators (e.g. Brunner 1960–1962, vol. II: 102, 112), though never (as

far as I know) strengthened by any hard evidence.[7] The evidence seems to suggest that YOU did not become the stressed subject/object form, but that instead YOU (both strong and weak forms) simply spread from object to subject-and-object function. The comment of the OED probably originating from the observation that the form spelt *ye* must often correspond (in Chaucer, for example) to an unstressed object form /jə/. In other words, Chaucer's object *ye* is clearly not a realization of the morpheme YE but a common weak form of both YE and YOU and so is not involved in any 'functional reinterpretation of forms' at all. Confusion between strong and weak *ye* would be impossible as the strong variant (for YE) and weak (for YE or YOU) would be phonetically different. The possible confusion of weak object *ye* (as a realization of YOU) and strong subject *ye* (a realization of YE) is something that could only happen on paper: speakers would have been able to change weak *ye* either to strong *ye* or *you* in slow speech without any problem.

To the hypothesis of reinterpretation of YOU as the stressed form, there are three objections:

(i)   the earliest uses of subject YOU recorded in the dictionaries are not found most frequently in obviously stressed positions;

(ii) the PDE form YOU derives not from ME /juː/, which would have become *yau* with the Great Vowel Shift, but from a weak form, /ju/, from which a strong form was later created by lengthening of the vowel (Franz 1939: 257; Strang 1970: 140), which suggests that it was the weak form that was most frequently used during the central GVS period (c. 1400–1600), approximately the same period as when YOU is generalized to subjective roles;

(iii) in PDE Northern and South-Western dialects, the object pronoun is employed in *unemphatic* contexts (Wakelin 1977: 114f.; Trudgill 1990: 89–93; Ihalainen 1991: 105f.), with the subject pronoun occurring instead in emphatic contexts (as in 'We don't know, do us?' and 'Give the bag to *they*, not *we*').[8]

---

7   Common-case *jo* in West Friesian and *jou*, *joe* frequently found as a subject in the Zeeuws dialect of Dutch and sporadically in the Zaans dialect (all historically objective forms like their cognate *you*) have also been seen as accented forms (Howe 1996: 188, 169). I would suggest that this is true to the extent that *jou* etc. are the present-day strong forms of the more common *je*, but would like to see convincing proof that original subject forms were ever reinterpreted as unaccented forms and original object forms as accented forms.

8   Wagner (2004: 158) says 'the subject forms are used when the respective form is emphasized while the oblique forms are used in all other contexts'; she also finds the SW object-for-subject area covers Devon and bordering counties, while the subject-for-object area covers Wiltshire and east Somerset (i.e. the two phenomena – in the SW at least – rarely occur together with the same speakers). She also remarks that this phenomenon of pronoun exchange is now 'all but dead in its former homelands' (159).

The second point above casts doubt on the idea of 'confusion' between even the two weak forms of YE and YOU, which may have been distinctively /jə/ and /ju/.

(b) YOU functionally reinterpreted as unstressed form

The pragmatic importance of the unstressed pronoun of address is an interesting question. In Modern Dutch, the weak (unstressed) form *je* of the Dutch T-pronoun *jij* is a common subject/object form that can be used for a wider range of interpersonal situations than the stressed forms of the pronoun. It would seem that the lack of prominence of *je* helps to remove face-threatening risks of inappropriate use.

The same phenomenon of phonetic reduction producing a 'safer' pronoun of address is found in German, where generic-*du* can be reduced in a *Sie*-environment to avoid misinterpretation, so that *weißt du?* can become *weißte?* and *siehst du?* can be reduced to *siehste?* And this increases the acceptability of a familiar pronoun form (Hickey 2003: 416).

In common colloquial English an unstressed form of YOU (and related forms) seems to be used in part to mark informality: *y'know*; *y'can, y'mus, see ya*. Notice also the use of sentence-final *yerself* ('yourself') to substitute *you* and so avoid the obligatory strong form in that position

(13) a. What about 'you?   b. What about yer'self?

Where, despite the greater length of 'yerself', the first element, clearly a 'weak' form of 'you', acts as an index of informality. And even *How's yerself?* (where the 3rd person verb adds further indirectness). The form can also be used to substitute strong *you* in other positions:

(14) a. Did 'you go?   b. Did ye go yer'self?

These remarks would seem to complement the observation that, in contrast, the prominent (repeated or markedly-stressed) use of the pronoun of address – even if appropriate to the interaction – can be face-threatening (as in 'You, what do you want?'). Black English and rappers' *yo* for calling attention and challenging undoubtedly derives from the pronoun *yo* 'you' and is certainly both phonetically prominent and potentially face-challenging.

The idea that PDE YOU derives from a weak form and that PDE dialects use object pronouns for subjects in unstressed position suggests that IME YOU could have been functionally reinterpreted, not as a stressed form, but, on the contrary, as an unstressed form. This lack of stress could have been associated with pragmatic advantages. While Dutch has an unstressed T-pronoun as safer for the wavering speaker, it is possible that in EModE an unstressed V-pronoun could have had a similar function. In other words, a V-pronoun realized in an unstressed form, may have been used, in a historical situation of extending use of YOU, to attenuate the risk of inappropriate or too prominent pronoun choice. It may have been seen as a less problematic pronoun of address: less face-threatening because less prominent.

(c) YOU reinterpreted as (unstressed) postverbal form

The view of YOU as possibly an unstressed form seems to be in harmony with scholars who associate early examples of subject YOU with post-verbal position (Kellner 1892: §§ 212f.; Abbott 1870: §§ 205, 212), (and 6 of the 12 earliest dictionary citations of subject YOU have the pronoun in this position). Here are two typical early postverbal uses (cited in Lutz 1996: 200):

(16)   What thynge aske you of me? (Caxton, *Aymont* 246/20)

(17)   tell me, how thynke you? (ibid. 170/10).

Early examples of subject YOU are also found where it has clearly been syntactically reinterpreted from earlier oblique uses: after imperatives ('hark you'), after impersonal verbs ('if it like you', 'if you like') and also in the ambiguous 'accusative and infinitive' construction ('I pray you come this way').

   All these contexts seem typically unstressed positions and associated with weak forms. Subject *thee* also seems to occur frequently in unstressed postverbal position: Abbott (1870: § 205) says it is frequently used in Shakespeare as a subject in questions and requests because there 'the pronoun is especially unemphatic' and also after imperatives 'which, being themselves emphatic, require an unemphatic pronoun' (§ 212).

(d) Analogous extension of the *thou* vowel

The use of subject YOU has frequently been seen as due to analogous reshaping of the paradigm so that the strong second-person subject and object forms had the same rhyming vowel: subject THOU and object THEE causing a switch to subject YOU and object YE (Jespersen 1894: 261; Franz 1939: 257f.; Baugh and Cable 1959: 293; Mustanoja 1960: 124f.; Graband 1965: 243, 237; Strang 1970: 144; Lutz 1998: 193f.). Lutz sees this facilitated in a situation of 'linguistic instability' and with frequent switches between singular and plural pronoun for the same person (so that singular addressees as subject of the verb became associated with the THOU-vowel). However, singular object addressees do not seem to have been associated with the THEE-vowel at all: object YE never catches on, in particular not in the *singular*: the MED lists a few examples of objective plural YE (YE 3(a)), but none for objective singular YE apart from one questioned example with YE as object of a preposition from a1500 (YE 3(b)).

Basically, while the rhyme of THOU and YOU (and Chaucer rhymes them)[9] was perhaps causing the latter to be seen as a subject form, YE remained as an alternative subject form and speakers were not attracted by rhyming THEE to perceive it as an object form. Indeed, while both object THEE and object YOU were extended to subject roles, both THOU and YE resisted the reciprocal change, THOU in particular never being used as an object. So, analogy may have been at work, but there must have been other factors operating to block the simple 'pronoun exchange' and to favour instead the generalization of the originally-objective forms.

(e) General extension of object pronouns to subject roles

The development of subject YOU must also be viewed in the context of three phenomena that have strangely been rarely if ever brought into the discussion:

(i)   a tendency for object personal pronouns to spread to subject uses that we find in other European languages (Swedish 3 psn. pl. object-for-subject *dem, dom*; Dutch 3 psn. pl. *hun*; Norwegian 3 psn. pl. *hun*; Afrikaans 1st psn. pl. *ons*; North Italian dialects 1 and 2 psn. sing. *me* and *te*);
(ii)   the tendency in English (but also other languages) for object pronoun forms to be preferred in all positions except immediately pre-verbal (Brunner 1962: ii 110–114; Kjellmer 1986: 445; Wales 1996: 19–20; Denison 1996), as in *stronger than him* and *us Anglos*;[10]
(iii) the tendency in various English dialects for personal pronouns to be levelled in favour of the object form even in preverbal position (e.g. in Northern and S.W. dialects and in several overseas varieties[11]) (Wales 1996: 90f; Wakelin 1997: 112f.; Upton et al. 1994: 486–488; Kortmann and Szmrecsanyi 2004: 1142–1202).

---

[9]   However, at some point the pronunciation diverged and, as mentioned above, a weak form /ju/ seems to have been the most frequent form of YOU and the origin of the present-day strong form.
[10] Cf. Zeeland dialect *ons Zeeuwen* 'us Zealanders' (van der Wal 1992: 415).
[11] Newfoundland English, Belize Creole, Jamaican Creole, Fiji English, Hawaii Creole, Ghanaian Pidgin (Kortmann and Szmrecsanyi 2004: 1142–1202).

Subject YOU can therefore be seen as part of a common tendency of the extension of object pronouns, yet to be fully explained, though the clear syntactic marking of subject and object by position since the mid-fifteenth century (Howe 1996: 169; Busse 2002: 252) is undoubtedly part of the story, since it removed the need for case distinctions.

Concerning our specific case of the object-to-subject extension of a second person plural pronoun, there are several interesting cases in other European languages, accompanied in some instances, as in the history of English, by the use of the same pronoun as a V-pronoun:

(i)   West Friesian *(j)y* has been totally replaced by the originally-objective form *jo(u)*, a change dating from the seventeenth century (Howe 1996: 187f.);

(ii)   in the Zeeland and Zaans dialects of Dutch originally-objective and plural (but now singular) *jo(u)* is occasionally used as a subject T-pronoun (Howe 1996: 214), presumably after being first used as a singular V-pronoun, as in the history of standard Dutch;[12]

(iii) in Modern East Frisian, Siebs reports in 1901 that in the Saterland area jie was replaced by the object pronoun *jou* as a sign of 'ganz besonderer Höflichkeit' ['exceptional politeness'] in addressing old people (Howe 1996: 190);

(iv)   in Faroese a second-person plural object pronoun has become the common-case singular V-pronoun *tygum* [tiːjʊn] (Howe 1996: 342, 345);

(v)   in Dutch the originally-objective (now common-case) second-person plural pronoun *u* is identical in form with the present common-case singular V-pronoun *u* and may have contributed to its evolution,[13]

(vi)   in Norwegian Bokmål a second-person plural object form *dere*[14] has been extended to the subject, though in this case it remains plural.

In the above cases from the North Atlantic area, with the exception of Bokmål, the levelling has been associated with the use of the originally-objective form as a more polite pronoun of second-person singular address, a linking of the two phenomena that we also find in English. Sieb's interesting remark on the greater politeness of the object form, though quite unsubstantiated, causes one

---

[12] A study of this present-day phenomenon could throw light on the history of English subject YOU.

[13] The alternative (and generally preferred) explanation is a derivation from an abbreviated form of the honorific title *Uwe Edelheit* 'Your Honour'; the first possibly subjective use of *u* dates from the mid-sixteenth century; for a summary of the debate see Haeringen 1960 (104) and Howe 1996 (227–9).

[14] The general acceptability of this change seems to date from the early twentieth century (Howe 1996: 325).

to wonder if the syntactical obliqueness of the successful forms or an associated lack of stress, could be connected with their attractiveness as V-forms. In this respect, it is interesting that an eighteenth-century commentator says that Quakers use the object pronoun THEE as a subject "from an imaginary superior *softness* of the term THEE" (J. Rutty 1756, cited in Finkenstaedt 1963: 131; my italics). The linking of the two phenomena would be strengthened if it emerged that there was indeed a greater frequency of early subject YOU with polite singular than with plural reference. The study by Raumolin-Brunberg (2005) unfortunately throws no light on the subject as her corpus of personal letters contains too few plural pronouns of address. This, then, would be an interesting area for further corpus research.

2. The abandonment of THOU

2.1 Languages without a special pronoun of respect

I now turn to look at the abandonment of THOU – again from a generally comparativist point-of-view. We should remember that though the English lack of differential pronominal recognition of status is rare, it is by no means unique. Indeed we find only one pronoun of address and non status-coding in a variety of languages from a variety of geographical areas and historical periods:

(i)   Classical Latin and Greek and the older forms of the Germanic languages (and so presumably in Indo-European as a whole);
(ii)   Irish Gaelic (sing. *tú* for everybody);
(iii)   North and East Frisian (sing. *dü, du* for everybody);
(iv)   traditional Flemish, after the abandonment of *du* in the sixteenth century (sing. *gai/ge* for everybody) (Deprez and Geerts 1980: 260);
(v)   Netherlands Dutch for several centuries (spoken *jij* for everybody is found into the nineteenth century, ModDu polite *u* being rarely attested before then) (van der Wal 1992: 266, 270);
(vi)   traditional Afrikaans (sing. *jy* for everybody);
(vii)   various German and Dutch dialects can be seen as 'lacking a V-form' as effectively they are only spoken to people that one is familiar with, so that any use of a V-pronoun will be accompanied by some kind of code-

switching: traditional Low Saxon (sing. *du* for everybody),[15] the dialect of the isolated area of Urk in the Netherlands (on the Ijsselmeer) (sing. *jie/je* for everybody);[16] and Jakob Grimm reports the same situation as generally true for rural dialects of Switzerland and Tirol in the early nineteenth century;[17]

(viii) the same phenomenon can be found in various isolated central and southern Italian dialects that only have one second person pronoun, *tu*, and where less educated speakers when speaking Italian will often slip from polite *Lei* to *tu* (Renzi 1995: 355);

(ix)   in most of inland Andean Colombia and parts of Venezuela, Ecuador, and Chile originally-polite *usted* is the pronoun of choice for all situations: although other pronouns are also available, in some cases their use can be seen as accommodation to speakers from outside the community;[18]

(ix)   some exotic languages have no social encoding in the pronoun system, e.g. one or two from New Guinea (Mühlhäusler and Harré 1990: 134).

There seems to be a North Atlantic linguistic area where at present a polite pronoun is either absent (English, Irish, North Frisian, Low German and Flemish) or more restricted in use (Icelandic, Norwegian, Swedish, Danish, Finnish and even Dutch) than in the more central and southern European language communities. It is possible to see this as a fringe area at a distant point to the centre of original change, assuming a cultural diffusion of polite

---

[15] In Low German communities the use of a polite (originally plural) pronoun can be seen as putting on airs and shifting to a *geel* ('yellow', non-genuine) High-German influenced variety of the dialect (R. F. Hahn, LOWLANDS-L electronic discussion list, 25/6/01).

[16] Mathieu van Woerkom (LOWLANDS-L electronic discussion list, 26/6/01): 'There is no polite second-person, just *jie* or *je*. Urk is also a very isolated, non-metropolitan and close-knit community. The village used to be on an island (but is now part of the Flevoland polder), and is very religious (and therefore very close-knit).' To some extent, dialect speech is 'familiar speech' closely associated with speaking to people who know each other or belong to the same group: here, any use of a distancing pronoun could be seen as creating a speech situation that is other than that associated with dialect.

[17] 'Der gemeine Bauer in vielen deutschen Gegenden, z.B. in Tirol und der Schweiz spricht noch heutestages *du* selbst zu dem Vornehmen und Fürsten, niemals *ihr*; in Schweden und Norwegen mag das noch häufiger der Fall sein' (Grimm 1819–1837, vol. I: 341f.); 'in einigen gegenden, namentlich Tirol, hat das ganze volk an dem *du* festgehalten, und sich zu keinem *sie* bequemt' (Grimm 1819–37, vol. IV: 311).

[18] Alvarez and Barros (2000) report in particular on the city of Mérida in Venezuela where the common use of *usted* to all is seen as a characteristic of the local speech, though it is not exclusive. it is 'el pronombre personal más usado en esa población, en todos los estilos, en hombres y mujeres... la comunidad parece preferir el usted a expensas del tú y la dicotomía +/- reverencia tiene poca vitalidad funcional. El uso del tú puede atribuirse quizás, a la afluencia de gente de otros lugares.'

pronouns from Latin in southern Europe (5th c.), to the vernacular in southern Germany (9th c.), France and Spain (in the earliest literary texts, 11th c. and 12th c.), to Dutch (late 12th c.), English (late 13th c.), Danish (early 14th c.), Czech (late 15th c.), Polish (early 16th c.), Swedish and Icelandic (early 17th c.).[19]

2.2 Timing of the change and its spread

Examples of polite YE/YOU with singular reference seem to predate the examples previously seen of subject YOU: they are found sporadically in the thirteenth (rather than the fourteenth) century.[20] However, the use of the new V-pronoun appears clearly for mutual respectful address only in the courtly literature of the second half of the fourteenth century (Shimonomoto 1986: 6), and until the late fourteenth century the lower classes still use THOU even when addressing the king and nobles, ladies and priests and without this being taken as an insult (Stidson 1917: 20–50, 81). In the fifteenth century it was adopted by wealthy townspeople in a package-deal along with the ideal of 'curtesie' (Burnley 2002: 34). A status distinction was established so that high-status speakers now expected to receive YOU but would use THOU to lower-status interlocutors.

The introduction of a V-pronoun is a good example of conscious language change from above, but its spread and often complete generalization is carried out on the pragmatic interface of interpersonal exchanges in largely subconscious choices. Despite starting earlier, the extension of the plural to the singular has a longer history than the extension of subject YOU: the latter was completed by 1560 according to the recent corpus study, but the former change was still incomplete in 1600: THOU is still a common form in the late sixteenth

---

[19] Latin: Finkenstaedt 1963: 21 (the earliest examples are from Valentinian, a bishop in S.E. Gaul, and Sidonius Appolinaris, bishop of Clermont-Ferand); Guitier (1961: 201) confirms that after sporadic early uses from 3rd c., *vos* is first widely used in the 5th c.; German: Finkenstaedt (1963: 45(; French: *Trésor de la langue française*, Paris, Centre National de Recherche Scientifique/Institut National de la langue française, Nancy/Gallimard, s.v. *Vous*; Spanish: *Cantar de Mio Cid* (12th c.); Dutch: Stoett (1977: 21); Danish, Swedish and Icelandic: Howe (1966: 199, 350); Czech and Polish: Betsch (2000: 48, 53).

[20] MED gives examples of singular subject YE from a1225, c1300 (2 cases), c1325, c1330, a1375, and singular object YOU from c1250, c1300 (6 cases), a1325 (2 cases), c1330, a1375. In contrast, the earliest dictionary citations for subject YOU are a1325, c1330 (2 cases), c1395 etc.

century[21] and the declining use of the pronoun continues for some centuries; indeed, for specialized uses it can even be considered to be still 'part of the language' today.

2.3 Sociolinguistic explanations for the change and its spread

(a) A product of a new non-contact culture

Despite the similar cases cited above, the single pronoun in English has sometimes been taken as so unusual as to suggest that it must be the product of an exceptional social situation. One idea is that modern English culture is a non-contact culture (as reflected in interpersonal space, eye-contact, body-contact) and the lack of a familiar/intimate pronoun reflects this. Wierzbicka (1991: 47) suggests that the lack of a T pronoun in ModE is connected to the importance of 'privacy' and that English YOU is a 'distance-building device' which cannot convey the intimacy signalled by the choice of a T-form. Finkenstadt (1963: 250f.) also sees the disappearance of THOU as connected with the new ideals (perhaps connected with non-contact) of 'the gentleman', 'tolerance' and 'restraint'. However, other European cultures which might be considered 'non-contact' (e.g. Norwegian) have a polite and a familiar pronoun of address. In addition, are we right to assume that English was a non-contact culture in the sixteenth century when the use of THOU was becoming increasingly restricted? In the early years of the century, Erasmus says that the English kiss more often than Continentals: 'Wherever you go, you are welcomed with kisses by everybody; when you depart, you are dismissed with kisses; you come back, and your kisses are returned to you; wherever you turn, everything is full of kisses' (letter to Faustus Andrelinus, cit. in Facer 1963: 3).

(b) Upward social aspiration

The spread of YOU seems to coincide with social changes evidenced in the contemporary downward spread of titles of respect associated with the use of V-pronouns (*sir*, *madam*, *Mr.* and *Mrs.*), a process that seems to indicate a generalization of honorific forms to avoid threats to face (Nevalainen and Raumolin-Brunberg 1995: 588). The process was also actively promoted and

---

[21] Though with residual marked uses and not commonly associated with asymmetrical exchanges (Walker 2002: 339), and though many speakers by then seemed to use only YOU with everybody (cf. also Hope 1993, Hope 1994a, Jucker 2001).

imitated from below as a way of gaining status. As with other examples of sociolinguistic evolution, it is the members of the rising class that adopt new forms most quickly (cf. the miller's wife in the Reeve's Tale who insists on being called *dame*).

Against all this, we have to say that honorific titles were generalized in other European cultures but did not lead to the abandonment of the differentiated pronoun system. The famous 'rising middle class' was also famously present in other urban centres where pronominal recognition of status did not disappear.

(c) London

The special sociolinguistic situation of London seems to have played a part in the abandonment of THOU: the geographical distribution of relic areas of THOU -use (the traditional dialects of the North and South and West) by itself suggests that the innovation spread from the south-east. Some commentators have suggested that Londoners found difficulty in ascertaining the relative status of interlocutors that they met on the city streets and "in all cases of doubt one would rather be polite than run the risk of giving offence" (Strang 1970: 139; cf. also Barber 1976: 210, Wales 1983: 117–119).

However, well-dressed strangers who seemed gentleman-like received honorific titles and the pronoun of respect in other European language communities without the familiar pronoun disappearing. Added to this, the 'safest bet' hypothesis does not explain why speakers abandoned the use of THOU with their friends and family.

(d) Negative connotations of THOU

Another hypothesis is that THOU acquired negative connotations by its association with Quakers, rural-speakers, uneducated speakers, and from its use in angry and offensive speech (Brown and Gilman 1960: 268).[22] However, it is difficult to see, even if angry and offensive uses of THOU created negative associations, why THOU did not continue in these uses (if associated with verbal attacks, it would make a handy insult). Quakers were a small group and their movement started in the 1650s, when the singular pronoun had already been relegated to residual uses by many speakers.

---

[22]   Cf. also 'Perhaps the usage of *thou* in general acquired unfavourable associations from Quaker usage: old-fashioned, politicized, rural, regional', Graddol, Leith and Swann 1996: 156.

2.4 Other explanations for the change

(e) Morpho-phonological factors

It is sometimes suggested that the abandonment of THOU is associated with a tendency towards simplification of morphology (Brown and Gilman 1960: 268; Finkenstaedt 1963: 220; Wales 1993: 132; Mausch 1991–93). With (i) the -*est* forms avoided by speakers with an internal model of a simplified paradigm, and (ii) -*est* forms creating difficult consonant clusters *promised(e)st* etc., the morphology together with the associated pronoun fell out of use. The use of YOU had the advantage of not being associated with this strange and inconvenient inflection.[23] A problem here is that the -*est* inflection was frequently dropped on modal and past-tense verbs in the early modern period: the reasons why this was not extended to other verbs (if the inflection was problematic) have yet to be explained.

(f) dialect contact

A more promising direction of enquiry is to investigate possible connections with the spread of Standard English. The official and court language of London was closely associated with YOU because it was a language for public relationships. The mechanism for the spread of YOU as the sole pronoun of address can be summed up succinctly as a situation in which THOU, the normal rural form, was "hypercorrected to YOU by urban aspirants to rank" (Mühlhäusler and Harré 1990: 152). However, "urban aspirants to rank" may give the wrong impression: hypercorrection may be made by those with no personal aspirations, but who want to accommodate to the speakers of another dialect or who want to help children or grandchildren by speaking to them in a dialect with greater social advantages. Indeed, one important moment for the spread of new forms must be in the transmission of language from one

---

[23]   Aalberse (2004) sees parallels with the loss of *du* in Dutch, both motivated by a similar trend towards simplification of the verb-inflectional paradigm and avoidance of morphology that explicitly identified 'address'; the retention of *thou* in the North of England would be explained by the fact that here 2 p sing verb inflections had already been simplified. Mausch (1991–93) proposes a rule of syncretism according to markedness: a tendency for the more marked pronoun forms to extend to areas of the less marked forms where they are (as in *ye/you*) transparently related.

generation to another. Hence one of the necessary stages in the abandonment of THOU must be when parents start to address their children with YOU.[24]

There has been a situation in some ways similar to sixteenth-century England in twentieth-century Flanders. Speakers of Flemish traditionally had only one singular pronoun of address (*ge/gij*) and no T/V distinctions, but then Northern (Dutch) polite *u* began to be used as well (first reported in Antwerp speech in 1930) and has been increasingly used since the Second World War thanks in part to increasing exposure to standard Dutch polite *u* and familiar *je* through the schools. Since they met with the standard Dutch pronouns only in formal situations a number of Flemish speakers have overgeneralized the use of *u*, some mothers and grandmothers using this pronoun to their children (van der Wal 1992: 407f.; Deprez and Geerts 1980: 370).[25]

Deprez and Geerts in their long (130-page) study of pronoun use (1980) in Duffel near Antwerp found that:

(i) 20% of interviewees chose the Dutch polite pronoun *u* rather than the familiar *je* in two sentences of clearly informal interaction – the new polite form being seen as always better in any situation;
(ii) syntactic function, position and stress all influenced the choice of pronoun, the new polite pronoun being used in greatest conformity to standard usage in questions (probably because people have more practice with polite questions than with statements with *u*), least correctly in SVO sentences.

The Flemish situation reported in the same article of older family members using the polite pronoun to children might give us a clue as to a stage that must also have been important in the history of the abandonment of THOU in sixteenth-century England: when parents start using it to children and then perhaps, more in general, when senior speakers start using it with junior interlocutors (if the parent-child dyad is the 'model' for these). The mechanism could be as follows:

---

[24] This is only one of the necessary stages, unless other dyadic relationships associated with T-pronouns were 'mapped' onto the primal and first-learned parent-child one. If T-use in other dyadic relationships is independent of the parent-child dyad (e.g. mutual use by lower classes), then study of the abandonment of *thou* (from the point-of-view of its abandonment in typical dyadic relationships) would have to look for the moment and the mechanism associated the abandonment of *thou* in each. Hope (1994b: 57) lists typical relational pairs in a table, within the framework of Brown and Gilman, reciprocal vs non-reciprocal.

[25] Interestingly, the uncertainty about which pronoun to use also leads to 'pronoun shifting' even within the speech-turn by Flemish speakers similar to that which we see in fourteenth- to sixteenth-century English texts.

(i) non-court speakers live most of their lives using only singular THOU,

(ii) learning standard English for formal situations they mainly learn the formal YOU, and in any case consider it 'better' because of its standard-language associations,

(iii) as they adopt standard English for more situations, they continue to use YOU, including use to their own children, partly because they have wrongly analysed YOU as the standard-language pronoun of address, partly because they want to teach their children what they see as the 'better' of two alternative forms.

If the inhabitants of rural areas of England can be seen as similar to those present-day continental populations of isolated rural areas with only a T pronoun, then perhaps part of the picture of the abandonment of THOU would be not only users of familiar and polite pronouns abandoning one of them, but also (as in Flanders) users of a single pronoun adopting a new dialect and a new pronoun of address and overgeneralizing its use.

Though there is undoubtedly a 'conspiracy' of factors both linguistic and sociolinguistic in the important pronoun changes in English, the study of other language histories has helped us put the matter in a wider perspective and has shown us a possibility of some link between the two main changes in the history of YOU. In addition, the study of recent pronoun-use in Flanders has given us a suggestion concerning a vital stage of language change from below, the moment when parents teach and address their own children.

References

Aalberse, Suzanne. 2004. Waer bestu bleven? De verdwijning van het pronomen "du" in een taalvergelijkend perspektief. *Nederlandse Taalkunde* 9: 231–252.

Abbott, Edwin. 1879. *A Shakespeare Grammar*. London: Macmillan.

Alvarez Alexandra and Ximena Barros. 2000. Sistemas en conflicto: las formas de tratamiento en la ciudad de Mérida, Venezuela. *Lengua y Habla*. Mérida: Universidad de Los Andes <http://www.linguisticahispanica.org/aam/alvarez_17.htm> (accessed 14.03.2007).

Barber, Charles. 1976. *Early Modern English*. London: Deutsch.

Baugh, Albert C. and Thomas Cable. 1959. *A History of the English Language*. 3rd ed. London: Routledge & Kegan Paul.

Betsch, Michael. 2000. *Diskontinuität und Tradition in System der tschechischen Anredepronomina (1700–1850)*. München: Sagner.

Brown, Roger and Albert Gilman. 1960. The Pronouns of Power and Solidarity. In Thomas A. Sebeok (ed.), *Style in language*. New York: Wiley, 253–276.

Brunner, Karl. 1960/62. *Die englische Sprache. Ihre geschichtliche Entwicklung*, 2 vols. 2nd ed. Tübingen: Niemeyer.

Burnley, David. 2003. The T/V pronouns in later Middle English Literature. In Irma Taavitsainen and Andreas H. Jucker (eds.), *Diachronic Perspectives on Address Term Systems*. Amsterdam, Philadelphia: Benjamins, 27–45.

Busse, Ulrich. 2002. *Linguistic Variation in the Shakespeare Corpus: Morphosyntactic Variability of Second Person Pronouns*. Amsterdam, Philadelphia: Benjamins.

Denison, David. 1996. The Case of the Unmarked Pronoun. In Derek Britton (ed.), *English Historical Linguistics 1994*. Amsterdam, Philadelphia: Benjamins. 287–299.

Deprez, K. and G. Geerts. 1980. Pronominale Problemen: GE, U en JE in Duffel-Lier. *Levense Bijdragen* 69: 257–381.

Facer, Geoffrey. 1963. *Erasmus and his Times*. London: Bell.

Finkenstaedt, Thomas. 1963. *'You' und 'thou'. Studien zur Anrede im Englischen. (Mit einem Exkurs über die Anrede im Deutschen)*. Berlin: Mouton de Gruyter.

Franz, Willhelm. 1939. *Die Sprache Shakespeares in Vers und Prosa unter Berücksichtigung des Amerikanischen entwicklungsgeschichtlich dargestellt*. 4th ed. Tübingen: Niemeyer

Graband, Gerhard. 1965. *Die Entwicklungen der frühneuenglischen Nominalflexion. Dargestellt vornehmlich aufgrund von Grammatikerzeugnissen des 17. Jahrhunderts*. Tübingen: Niemeyer.

Graddol, David, Dick Leith and Joan Swann (eds.). 1996. *English: History, Diversity and Change*, London, New York: Routledge.

Grimm, Jacob. 1819–37. *Deutsche Grammatik*. Göttingen: Dieterich.

Guiter, Henri. 1961. L'extension successive des formes de politesse. *Boletim de Filologia* [Lisboa] 18: 195–202.

Haeringen, Coenraad van. 1960. *Netherlandic Language Research. Men and Works in the Study of Dutch*. 2nd ed. Leiden: Brill.

Hickey, Raymond. 2003. The German address system. Binary and scalar at once. In Irma Taavitsainen and Andreas H. Jucker (eds.), *Diachronic Perspectives on Address Term Systems*. Amsterdam, Philadelphia: Benjamins, 402–425.

Hope, Jonathan. 1993. Second person singular pronouns in records of Early Modern "spoken" English. *Neuphololologische Mitteilungen* 94: 83–100.

Hope, Jonathan. 1994a. The use of *thou* and *you* in Early Modern spoken English: evidence from depositions in the Durham ecclesiastical court records. In Dieter Kastovsky (ed.), *Studies in Early Modern English*. Berlin and New York: Mouton de Gruyter, 141–152.

Hope, Jonathan. 1994b. *The Authorship of Shakespeare's Plays*. Cambridge: CUP.

Howe, Stephen. 1996. *The personal pronouns in the Germanic languages. A study of personal pronoun morphology and change in the Germanic languages from the first records to the present day.* Berlin and New York: de Gruyter.

Ihalainen, Ossi. 1991. On Grammatical Diffusion in Somerset Folk Speech. In Peter Trudgill and Jack K. Chambers (eds.), *Dialects of English: Studies in Grammatical Variation.* London and New York: Longman, 104–119.

Jespersen, Otto. 1894. *Growth and Structure of the English Language.* Leipzig: Hirzel.

Jucker, Andreas H. 2001. *Thou* in the history of English: a case for historical emantics or pragmatics? In Christiane Dalton-Puffer and Nikolas Ritt (eds.), *Words: Stucture, Meaning and Function.* New York and Berlin: Mouton de Gruyter. 153–163.

Kellner, Leon. 1892. *Historical Outlines of English Syntax.* London: Macmillan.

Kjellmer, Göran. 1986. "Us Anglos are a cut above the field": on objective pronouns in nominative contexts. *English Studies* 5: 445–509.

Kortmann, Bernd and Benedikt Szmrecsanyi. 2004. Global synopsis: morphological and syntactic variation in English. In Bernd Kortmann et al. (eds.), *A Handbook of Varieties of English*, vol. 2: *Morphology and Syntax.* Berlin and New York: Mouton de Gruyter, 1142–1202.

Lutz, Angelika. 1998. The interplay of external and internal factors in morphological restructuring: the case of *you.* In Jacek Fisiak and Marcin Krygier (eds.), *Advances in English Historical Linguistics (1996).* Berlin and New York: Mouton de Gruyter. 189–210

Mausch, Hanna. 1991. Democratic *you* and paradigm. *Studia Anglica Posnaniensia* 25: 143–153.

Mühlhäusler, Peter and Rom Harré. 1990. *Pronouns and People: the Linguistic Construction of Personal Identity.* Oxford: Blackwell.

Mustanoja, Tauno F. 1960. *Middle English Syntax*, vol 1: *Parts of Speech.* Helsinki: Société Néophilologique.

Nevalainen, Terttu and Helena Raumolin-Brunberg. 1995. Constraints on Politeness: The Pragmatics of Address Formulae in Early English Correspondence. In Andreas H. Jucker (ed.), *Historical Pragmatics. Pragmatic Developments in the History of English.* Amsterdam and Philadelphia: Benjamins. 521–580.

Nevalainen, Terttu and Helena Raumolin-Brunberg. 1996. Social Stratification in Tudor English? In Derek Britton (ed.), *English Historical Linguistics 1994.* Amsterdam and Philadelphia: Benjamins, 301–326.

Raumolin-Brunberg, Helena. 2005. The diffusion of subject YOU: A case study in historical linguistics. *Language Variation and Change* 17: 55–73.

Renzi, Lorenzo. 1995. La deissi personale e il suo uso sociale. In Lorenzo Renzi, Giampaolo Salvi and Anna Cardanaletti (eds.), *Grande grammatica italiana di consultazione*, vol. 3: *Tipi di frase, deissi, formazione delle parole*. Bologna: il Mulino. 350–375.

Shimonomoto, Keiko. *The Use of ye and thou in the Canterbury Tales and its correlation with terms of address and forms of the imperative*. M.A. dissertation, Sheffield University. [Repr. Keiko Shimonomoto, *The Use of 'ye' and 'thou' in the Canterbury Tales and Collected Articles*. Tokyo: Waseda University Enterprise. 2001]

Spies, Heinrich. 1897. *Studien zur Geschichte des englischen pronomens im XIV. und XVI. Jahrhundert (Flexionslehre und Syntax)*. Halle: Niemeyer.

Stein, Gabriele. 1997. *John Palsgrave as Renaissance Linguist. A Pioneer in Vernacular Description*. Oxford: Clarendon Press.

Stidson, Russell O. 1917. *The use of "ye" in the function of "thou" in ME literature from the MS Auchinleck to MS Vernon*. Stanford: Stanford University Press.

Stoett, F. 1977. *Middelnederlandische Spraakkunst*. 5th ed. 's-Gravenhage: Nijhof.

Strang Barbara M.H. 1970. *A History of English*. London and New York: Methuen.

Trudgill, Peter. 1990. *The Dialects of England*. Oxford: Blackwell.

Upton, Clive, David Parry and John Widdowson. 1994. *Survey of English Dialects: The Dictionary and the Grammar*. London and New York: Routledge.

Wagner, Susanne. 2004. English dialects of the south-west: morphology and syntax. In Bernd Kortmann et al. (eds.), *A Handbook of Varieties of English,* vol. 2: *Morphology and Syntax*. Berlin and New York: Mouton de Gruyter, 154–174.

Wakelin, Martyn. 1977. *English dialects: an introduction*. London: Athlone.

Wal, Marijke van der. 1992. *Geschiedenis van het Nederlands*. Utrecht: Spectrum.

Wales, Kathleen M. 1983. *Thou* and *you* in early modern English: Brown and Gilmore re-appraised. *Studia Linguistica* [Lund] 37: 107–125.

Wales, Kathleen M. 1996. *Personal Pronouns in Present-day English*. Cambridge: Cambridge University Press.

Walker, Terry. 2000. The choice of second person singular pronoun in authentic and constructed dialogue in late sixteenth century English. In Christian Mair and Marianne Hundt (eds.), *Corpus Linguistics and Linguistic Theory. Papers from the 20th ICAME Conference, 1999*. Amsterdam and Atlanta: Rodopi. 375–384.

Wierzbicka, Anna. 1991. *Cross-Cultural Pragmatics. The Semantics of Human Interaction*. Berlin and New York: Mouton de Gruyter.

KRISTIN KILLIE (TROMSØ)

On the history of verbal present participle converbs in English and Norwegian and the concept of 'change from below'

1. Introduction: aims and organization

In this paper I discuss the history of constructions such as those italicized in (1) and (2) below.

(1)   *Writing the paper*, the professor got a new idea.
(2)   Next morning I woke up late, *feeling very ill.*

I will refer to the *-ing* form in constructions such as those above as present participle converbs. A converb is a non-finite verb form whose main function it is to mark adverbial subordination, i.e. it is the head of an adverbial subclause (Haspelmath 1995: 3). This paper focuses on present participles in this function. It discusses one particular aspect of present participle converbs, namely their ability to take verbal complementation such as direct objects, subject and object complements, and adverbials, cf. the examples above. This property will be discussed from a diachronic perspective. In what follows the term 'converb' refers to a present participle converb which takes verbal complementation. Adverbial *-ing* forms that are not verbal in this sense are referred to simply as 'participles'.

Converbs are typically assumed to be a heritage from Latin, but while they have become an established feature of English grammar, they have become completely marginalized in Norwegian. One objective of the present paper is to try to explain this fact. It will be argued that English converbs became naturalized because there were other developments that supported their use and because Latin style was held in high esteem, while the opposite was the case in Norwegian (or Dano-Norwegian, cf. section 4). The second aim of this paper is to discuss the naturalization of English converbs and the demise of Norwegian ones in relation to the concept of 'change from below'. It will be argued that none of these changes are in themselves regular changes from below. However, the history of the English converb became interwoven with a true change from below, viz. the grammaticalization of the progressive, and, seen from that perspective, it is in part a change from below.

The structure of the paper is as follows. In section 2 I provide some historical background to the use of converbs in Germanic. In section 3 I discuss why these converb structures developed differently in Norwegian and English, while in section 4 I look at these changes in relation to the concept of change from below. Finally, section 5 provides a brief summary.

2. The historical development of converbs in Germanic

The category of converbs is highly interesting from a comparative Germanic perspective, given that the Germanic languages show varying use of converbs both synchronically and diachronically. Thus, while current English uses converbs extensively, the other Germanic languages use them much more sparingly (Kortmann 1995: 189, 192). However, all the older Germanic languages seem to have made extensive and varied use of converbs (Callaway 1901: 330). Some examples from Old English and Old Norse are given in (3)–(6).[1]

(3) and æffrem þa spræc mid grecisum gereorde, *god herigende* (Ælfric's *Lives of Saints* 3. 522)
     'and Effrem then spoke with Greek tongue, God praising'

(4) and þæt folc... ham gewende, *ðancigende þam Ælmihtigan ealra his goda* (ÆCHom II. 578.28, cited in Mitchell 1985: 600)
     'and that people... home went, thanking the almighty God for all his good deeds'

(5) tekr hann vel við honum *bjóðandi honum til ágætrar veizlu* (from Hanssen, Mundal and Skadberg 1975: 158)
     'takes him well with him, inviting him to a better meal'

(6) hon misgørði *etandi af tréssins ávexti* (from Hanssen, Mundal and Skadberg 1975: 158)
     'she sinned eating of the tree's fruit'

Present participles seem to be native to the Germanic languages, but it is assumed that they were originally exclusively adjectival, having no verbal

---

[1] As the examples in (3) and (4) show, the English present participle suffix at this stage is *-ende* (with the variants *-ande* and *-inde*). This suffix is of course cognate with the corresponding suffixes in the other Germanic languages. However, during the Middle English period (c. 1100–1500), probably from the 12th century onwards, the English present participle suffix for unknown reasons merged with the *-ing* suffix.

properties (Nygaard 1966: 247; Hanssen, Mundal and Skadberg 1975: 157), as in (7) below. They were also used in adverbial function, but were in those cases typically derived from intransitive verbs, as in (8) and (9) (Lund 1862: § 149; Falk and Torp 1900: §68, 2 b, §139, 1.b; Callaway 1901; Nygaard 1966: 238).

(7)   hversu hræddr ok *skjálfandi* maðrinn mun verða (from Hansen, Mundal and Skadberg 1975: 158)
       'how frightened and shivering man may become'
(8)   hann fagnaði henni *hlæjandi* (from Hansen, Mundal and Skadberg 1975: 158)
       'he greeted her laughing'
(9)   kom hann þá *hlaupandi* (from Hansen, Mundal and Skadberg 1975: 158)
       'came he then running'

It is commonly assumed that the use of present participles with verbal complementation in older Germanic texts is due to influence from Latin models (Einenkel 1887: 273; Falk and Torp 1900: 100; Callaway 1901: 297ff., 307ff.; Blatt 1957; Nygaard 1966: 247; Moessner 1997). In translating Latin texts, scribes often mechanically rendered the original text word by word, thereby transferring Latin patterns into the target text. As far as verbal present participles are concerned, what is assumed to have happened is that the translators used a native form, the present participle, but endowed it with characteristics it did not originally have, namely verbal properties (Callaway 1901: 351; Diderichsen 1968: 8f.). Latin makes quite extensive use of appositive participles (the so-called *participium coniunctum*) with verbal complementation (Callaway 1901: 351), and it was first and foremost these that were translated word by word into Germanic texts, but also some gerunds in the ablative and occasionally certain other constructions (Callaway 1901).[2]

The hypothesis that converb use in Germanic is a Latin heritage is supported by the stylistic distribution of converbs in older Germanic texts. While texts written in the so-called 'learned style' (typically translations) contain a large number of converbs, texts written in the 'popular style' mostly contain participles of the non-verbal type (Blatt 1957; Falk and Torp 1900: 100; Nygaard 1966: 247).

---

[2]   The term 'appositive participle' has been used differently by different scholars. While to some appositive participles correspond to converb uses, to others the term includes both converbs and adjectival uses, i.e. participles occurring in relative clauses (cf. Callaway 1901: 144–149 for a discussion). Callaway belongs to the latter group. What all appositive participles have in common is the fact that the auxiliary *be* and the participle do not form a VP together; rather the clause containing the present participle is in apposition to the clause that contains the auxiliary.

While converbs came to be a rather marginal stylistic device in the other Germanic languages, including Norwegian, they became an established feature of English. In fact, the verbal properties of the English converb have even been extended beyond those of its Latin models in the sense that present-day English converb clauses may include tense, aspect, and voice markers, as in (10) below. Converbs have thus been affected by the general historical process which may be referred to as the 'complexification' of the English verb phrase, and which involves increased use of auxiliaries such as *have* and *be* to express distinctions of voice and aspect (Denison 2000).

> (10)   *Having been cancelled* twice already, your flight to Berlin is not very likely to
>   be cancelled a third time (Kortmann 1991: 7)

It has also been shown that English converbs have spread through styles and registers. Thus, even though they predominantly occur in written texts, they no longer exclusively occur in formal, learned styles, but are in fact most common in narrative texts (Kortmann 1991: 2, 39; 1995: 195). This development goes back to the 16th and 17th century (Kohnen 2003). Thus, the English converb has both undergone its 'own' changes and has been affected by more general changes in English. This clearly demonstrates that it has developed from being a Latin construction to becoming a naturalized, truly English one. By contrast, the use of adverbial present participles in current Norwegian is rather similar to the original Germanic use exemplified in (8) and (9).

Assuming that converbs are an import from Latin, we need to explain why English was influenced by Latin syntax to such an extent, while, for example, Norwegian (or Dano-Norwegian) was not. Below I argue that this is a result of both linguistic and socio-linguistic factors.

3. Explaining the development of converbs
in Norwegian and English

3.1 Sociolinguistic factors: the influence of the Danish purist movement

In studying the development of Norwegian, it is important to remember that Norway does not have a history which is separate from those of its neighbouring countries. Its history is closely intertwined with those of Iceland, Sweden, and Denmark, due to colonization and unions. Of the various unions it is the one with Denmark from 1380–1814 which is assumed to have had the greatest influence on the Norwegian language, since Danish was the official language of Denmark-Norway. Some of the sociolinguistic events and developments which I refer to below, and which I suggest may have influenced the development of converbs in written Norwegian, took place in the Dano-Norwegian period. The events in question affected the use of converbs in written Danish, but indirectly also in Norwegian, given that one of the Norwegian written standards, i.e. Bokmål (also referred to as Dano-Norwegian), is a direct descendant of the Danish language.

From the 17th century onwards, there was some interest in the grammar of the Danish language, and this interest increased significantly in the 1740s, when Danish began to be studied in a scientific way and codified through the publication of grammars and a standardized spelling system (see Killie to appear for more details). In the mid-1700s a number of language purists also entered the Danish linguistic scene (Indrebø 2001: 386–392). The main goal of the purists was pragmatic: they wanted to make the scientific literature accessible to the average Danish speaker (Kristiansen 2003: 82). For this to be possible, the language of science had to be Danish, and that Danish had to be a 'pure' Danish, i.e. it should not be made inaccessible by foreign influence. Therefore, the purists wanted to rid the language of Latin and French loanwords and create new Danish ones. In addition, they wanted to get rid of the 'heavy', hypotactic Latin style and establish a 'natural' Danish style instead. This style was to be based on parataxis, and the goal was a written language that was closer to speech, i.e. the speech of the common man. It is generally assumed that the purists indeed managed to influence Danish style. Although it seems that prescriptivists often fail to make an impact, it appears that in this case they may have been able to do so. A main reason for this is probably the fact that the use of Latinate structures, including converbs and participal relative clauses, was more or less restricted to learned styles and, hence, had never become a part of the grammar of the general speaker. In addition, the purists seem to have been rather unified in their goals.

The influence of the Danish purists also reached Norway. In fact, Indrebø (2001: 386, 387) argues that the purist movement continued to exert considerable influence after the dissolution of the Dano-Norwegian union in 1814, when Danish came to be used as the administrative language of Norway (being now referred to as the 'mother tongue'). Via Danish, prescriptive rules concerning the 'good' use of language disseminated into Norwegian (to the extent that the two languages can be kept apart), and in particular into Bokmål. However, there was also another allegedly important promoter of simple styles within the Norwegian context, namely Ivar Aasen. Aasen is the father of 'Nynorsk' ('Neo-Norwegian'), i.e. the other written Norwegian standard (cf. Jahr in this volume). This standard was created in the mid-19th century on the basis of the Norwegian dialects, and as a reaction to the widespread use of Danish in Norway. Aasen strongly advocated the use of a natural, Norwegian style. He warned against the use of the academic, Latinate style, which was said to make the written language inaccessible to the common man (Indrebø 2001: 460f.).

Summing up, it appears that, thanks to the Danish purists, to the high status of and widespread use of Danish in Norway before and after 1814, and possibly also to Aasen and his followers, the Norwegian language has gone through a long-lasting 'purification process'. During this process, language users have come to favour a simpler, more paratactic style over the complex, heavily hypotactic and Latin-based style that was so common a few centuries ago. Further, the use of subordinate clauses has come to involve the use of finite rather than non-finite participial clauses.

The purist movement in England (which started approximately two centuries before the Danish one) does not seem to have had the same impact as the Danish one had. True, there was a rather heated debate about the excessive use of Latinate – and Greek – words; the so-called 'Inkhorn Controversy'. There was also some discussion of Latinate syntax, or style. Some advocated against the long Latinate sentences and took pains to write shorter ones, the goal being a more 'English', speech-based, paratactic style (cf. Gordon 1966: chapters 7 and 8). However, the English generally seem to have held Latin syntax, rhetoric, and style in high esteem, finding that English had a great deal to learn from this language in terms of elegance and logic. According to Knowles (1997: 71), '[t]he Latin sentence, unlike Latin vocabulary, has never been socially contentious, and (leaving aside some twentieth-century writers such as James Joyce) has never been challenged. At most, there have been minor variations, making the English sentence more or less close to the Latin model'. Indeed, as noted by Blatt (1957: 49) and others, the Renaissance translators of Latin texts openly declared that one of their goals was the 'Amelioration of the English Language'. This state would be attained both by introducing new Latinate words and by using Latinate syntax. Apparently, one of the Latinate features that was adopted for this purpose was precisely the extensive use of verbal present participles, including both converbs and relative clauses (cf. Killie to appear). Workman (1940: 43ff.) finds that there is a shift around 1470–1480: from this time on, texts written in the vernacular make increasing use of hypotaxis, before this time such features were associated with texts translated from Latin and French).

3.2 Linguistic factors

We have now looked at some socio-historical factors that may have been important to the development of converbs in English and Norwegian. However, it has been claimed that for a foreign syntactic structure to be borrowed into a language, there must be other structures in that language which are consistent with it and, hence, may support its establishment (cf. Vachek 1962 and the references therein; Sørensen 1957: 133; Aitchison 1995: 3). Thus, Smith claims that "failure in grammatical change, like 'success', is to do with the way in which an innovation correlates with the larger contextual drift of the language" (1996: 153, cf. also 151). In what follows I argue that there were certain trends in English which supported the development of present participle converbs, while there were no corresponding trends in Danish and Norwegian (or Dano-Norwegian).

3.2.1 English

As mentioned earlier (cf. footnote 1), in Middle English the participle suffix changed from *-ende* to *-ing*. This turned the English *-ing* suffix into a highly poly-functional form, with nominal, adjectival, adverbial, prepositional, and verbal uses. Most important to our purposes here is the fact that *-ing* participles were increasingly used with verb-like functions and properties. Three different categories are of interest here: 1) the progressive, 2) the gerund, and 3) converbs (and other appositive participles, cf. footnote 2). Examples of gerunds are given in (11) below, while (12) provides examples of progressives.

(11a) She regretted *having told him the truth* (direct object)
(11b) *Telling him the truth* was the only decent thing to do (subject)
(11c) In *aiming for such a theory*, I shall begin with a number of interrelated assumptions (from Kortmann 1995: 200) (object of a preposition, adverbial at a higher level)
(12a) She *was telling* him the truth.
(12b) I *have been aiming* for such a theory.

The structures under discussion here have very different functions at the sentence level. Thus, while the progressive is verbal, the gerund is nominal and the converb clause adverbial. However, the relevant structures are syntactically rather similar in the sense that they may all take verbal complementation. Interestingly, all these categories experienced a huge growth in frequency at approx. the same time, i.e. from the 15th and 16th century onwards (Dennis 1940; Strang 1982; Houston 1989: 176ff.; Elsness 1993: 13; Fanego 1996: 118ff.).

Given the shared properties of these various *-ing* categories, viz. their similar morphology and syntax, and the fact that their frequencies go up at approximately the same time, it seems likely that they may have influenced each other. It is, however, extremely difficult to trace the precise relations between the various constructions, i.e. the channels of – and direction of – the influence between them. Certain hypotheses have been put forth in the literature on the gerund. For example, it has been suggested that the verbal gerund has developed from present participle converbs (Koma 1987; Houston 1989). It has also been hypothesized that the gerund acquired its verbal properties as a result of the formal merger between the verbal *-ende* and the nominal *-ing* suffix (e.g. Poutsma 1923; cf. Jack 1988: 24ff. for an account). This hypothesis is rejected by Jack (1988: 26f.; cf. also Houston 1989: 179f.). According to him, the verbal properties of the gerund cannot have been 'inherited' directly from the progressive, as in the north of England the verbal gerund developed before the two suffixes merged. Jack nevertheless concedes that it is quite possible – even likely – that the merger of *-ende* and *-ing* and the huge increase in the use of the progressive promoted the use of the gerund (Jack 1988: 27; cf. also Fanego 1996: 135). I agree that this does seem like a likely scenario. In addition to the concurrent increase in the use of all three constructions, another fact that invites such a hypothesis is the fact that there does not seem to have been any clear-cut division line between verbal and nominal uses of *-ing* forms until fairly recently. Texts from the Early Modern English period (c. 1500–1700) abound in constructions that modern linguists refer to as 'hybrid constructions', i.e. structures that have both nominal and verbal properties at the same time. Some examples are given in (13)–(16) below.

(13)   euen while I *was in wryting of thys letter* (1533 St. Thomas More. *Wks.* (1557) 962 H4 [Visser 1963–1973: §1871], cited in Fanego 1996: 103)

(14)   then cam the men rydyng, carehyng of torchys (Helsinki Corpus, period HCE1, 1553–59 Machyn *Diary* 101, cited in Fanego 1996: 104) then came the men riding, *carrying of torches*

(15)   ... and after dinner came two Cauelliers, and a Moore being one of their slaues to the watering place, where our men *were filling of the caske*... (Helsinki Corpus, period HCE2, NN TRAVCOVERTE 12, cited in Elsness 1993: 14)

(16)   *The quickly doing of it*, is the grace (1610 Ben Jonson, Achemist (Everym.) IV, ii, p. 62, cited in van der Wurff 1993: 366)

It is also interesting to note that at some stage all the three constructions under discussion had become verbal to such an extent that they partook in the syntactic development which was referred to in section 2 as the complexification of the English verb phrase (Jespersen 1914–1940, vol. IV: 94; Houston 1989: 189f.; Denison 1998: 143ff. and 2000: 129ff.; Fanego 2004: 8).

3.2.2 Norwegian

Having argued that there were linguistic structures and trends in English that supported the development of converbs, we may ask whether similar structures and developments existed in Norwegian. The answer to this question appears to be *no*. To be sure, both Old and Middle Norwegian to some extent used the present participle in a progressive-like manner, also with transitive verbs (Nygaard 1966: 241f.; Pettersen 1975–1991: 571ff.). Thus, there were certain V*ende* + DO constructions upon which a Norwegian converb could have been modelled. However, such verbal uses of the participle never spread and grammaticalized in the way that the English progressive did. Furthermore, Norwegian never seems to have had a gerund-like construction. Therefore, the use of V*ende* + DO constructions in Norwegian was most probably not extensive enough to support the naturalization of converbs in this language.

4. The development of converbs:
a change from below or from above?

Given that this volume is entitled 'Language history from below', I wish to discuss the relevance of this consept to the change under discussion. In what follows, I focus on the notions of 'change from below' vs. 'change from above', although this dimension represents only one aspect of the concept of 'language history from below' (for a more comprehensive view, cf. Elspaß in this volume).

The distinction between 'change from below' and 'change from above' is based on Labov. Labov (1994: 78; cf. also Labov 1966) starts by noting that "[a]bove and 'below' refer here simultaneously to levels of social awareness and positions in the socioeconomic hierarchy". He then goes on to explain the concepts of 'change from below' and 'change from above' in terms of these two dimensions. Changes from above and below are said by Labov to have the following characteristics:

> *Changes from above* are introduced by the dominant social class, often with full public awareness. Normally, they represent borrowings from other speech communities that have higher prestige in the view of the dominant class. Such borrowings do not immediately affect the vernacular patterns of the dominant class or other social classes, but appear primarily in careful speech, reflecting a superposed dialect learned after the vernacular is acquired. (Labov 1994: 78)

Changes from below are quite different, both with respect to the social status and the consciousness dimension:

Changes from below are systematic changes that appear first in the vernacular and represent the operation of internal, linguistic factors. At the outset, and through most of their development, they are completely below the level of social awareness. No one notices them or talks about them, and even phonetically trained observers may be quite unconscious of them for many years. It is only when changes are nearing completion that members of the community become aware of them. Changes from below may be introduced by any social class, although no cases have been recorded in which the highest-status social group acts as the innovating group. (Labov 1994: ibid.)

Certain aspects of the description of change from above are compatible with the introduction and early development of converbs in English. They were introduced by the 'dominant' (or at least privileged) class. We are talking about a prestigious feature from a prestigious language, and the change did not affect the vernacular at first. However, Labov never intended his terminology to cover cases of change originating in the written language. Both the terms 'change from below' and 'change from above' were meant to describe more 'natural' changes, i.e. the spread of linguistic features through speech.[3] Therefore, neither the naturalization of converbs in English nor the demise of such structures in Norwegian qualifies as changes from below – or from above. On the other hand, if it is correct that the development of converbs became interwoven with the grammaticalization of the progressive, things are different. The grammaticalization of the progressive has been claimed to represent a change from below. Thus, Arnaud (1998: 141) argues that:

[a]part from a few stereotypes it was a change from below. It was usually unconscious even for people who, as writers, were sensitive to language. It was also from below in the sense that it came from the vernacular, informal style and from the ordinary people. It was a grammatical change, affecting one of the major constituents of the auxiliary system.

If it is true that the development of the converb was partly triggered or driven by the grammaticalization of the progressive, it was to some extent a change from below. This means that the history of the converb involves both conscious and subconscious elements, the written and the spoken language, and influences from the higher/literate classes as well as from the lower classes. Such a mixture of apparently opposite elements may in fact not be entirely exceptional. The development of the English progressive is a case in

---

[3] In addition, he was only discussing sound change. However, others have applied his ideas to morphology and syntax as well. For example, Wolfram (1969) studies the use of multiple negation in Detroit speech, as well as the presence/absence/form of auxiliary *be* in sentences such as *he's ready, he be ready, he ready* (Wardhaugh 1992: 141f.). Cf. also the discussion of the English progressive below.

point. Even though the development of the progressive is a change from below (i.e. both in terms of social awareness and socioeconomic status), certain 'subcomponents' seem to carry the hallmarks of a change from above. Thus, the passive progressive was apparently adopted as the conscious linguistic use of a restricted group of people, the so-called Coleridge-Southey circle, which facilitated its adoption into the grammar of 'ordinary' speakers (Denison 1993: 152–154, this volume; Pratt and Denison 2000). A linguistic change, then, need not necessarily be either a change from below or a change from above; it may include elements of both, and the naturalization of converbs in English may be one example of this.

5. Summary

In this paper I have discussed the naturalization of converbs in English and the disappearance of such structures from Norwegian. I have argued that in English converbs became naturalized because there were other developments that supported their development and because Latin style was held in high esteem, while the opposite was the case in Norwegian. I have also argued that the naturalization of the English converb can be seen partly as a change from below. This is the case because the development of the converb became interwoven with the grammaticalization of the progressive, which was in the main a change from below.

References

Aitchison, Jean. 1995. Tadpoles, cuckoos, and multiple births: language contact and models of change. In Jacek Fisiak (ed.), *Linguistic change under contact conditions*. Berlin and New York: Mouton de Gruyter, 1–13.

Arnaud, René. 1998. The development of the progressive in 19th century English: a quantitative survey. In *Language Variation and Change* 10: 123–152.

Blaisdell, Foster W. Jr. 1965. Some observations on style in the riddarasögur. In Carl F. Bayerschmidt and Erik J. Friis (eds.), *Scandinavian studies: essays presented to Dr. Henry Goddard Leach on the occasion of his eighty-fifth birthday*. Seattle: University of Washington Press, 87–94.

Blatt, Franz. 1957. Latin influence on European syntax. The classical pattern of modern Western civilization: language. *Travaux du Cercle linguistique de Copenhague* 11: 33–69.

Callaway, Morgan. 1901. The appositive participle in Anglo-Saxon. *Publications of the Modern Language Association of America* XVI: 141–360.

Denison, David. 1993. *English historical syntax: verbal constructions*. London: Longman.

Denison, David. 1998. Syntax. In Suzanne Romaine (ed.), *The Cambridge history of the English language*. Vol. IV: 1776–1997. Cambridge: Cambridge University Press, 92–329.

Denison, David. 2000. Combining English auxiliaries. In Olga Fischer, Anette Rosenbach and Dieter Stein (eds.), *Pathways of change: grammaticalization in English*. Amsterdam and Philadelphia: Benjamins, 111–147.

Dennis, Leah. 1940. The progressive tense. Frequency of its use in English. *Publications of the Modern Language Association of America* 55: 855–865.

Diderichsen, Paul. 1968. *Dansk prosahistorie I, 1*. København: Gyldendal.

Einenkel, Eugen. 1887. *Streifzüge durch die mittelenglische Syntax unter besonderer Berücksichtigung der Sprache Chaucer's*. Münster/Westfalen: Schöningh.

Elsness, Johan. 1993. On the progression of the progressive in early Modern English. *ICAME Journal* 18: 5–25.

Falk, Hjalmar and Alf Torp. 1900. *Dansk-norskens syntax I historisk fremstilling*. Kristiania: Aschehoug.

Fanego, Teresa. 1996. The gerund in early Modern English: evidence from the Helsinki Corpus. *Folia Linguistica Historica* 17: 97–152.

Fanego, Teresa. 2004. On reanalysis and actualization in syntactic change: the rise and development of English verbal gerunds. *Diachronica* 21/1: 5–55.

Gordon, Ian A. 1966. *The movement of English prose*. London and New York: Longman.

Hanssen, Eskil, Else Mundal and Kåre Skadberg. 1975. *Norrøn grammatikk: lydlære, formlære og syntaks I historisk framstilling*. Oslo: Universitetsforlaget.

Haspelmath, Martin and Ekkehard König (eds.). 1995. *Converbs in cross-linguistic perspective: structure and meaning of adverbial verb forms – adverbial participles, gerunds*. Berlin and New York: Mouton de Gruyter.

Haspelmath, Martin. 1995. The converb as a cross-linguistically valid category. In Martin Haspelmath and Ekkehard König (eds.), *Converbs in cross-linguistic perspective: structure and meaning of adverbial verb forms – adverbial participles, gerunds*. Berlin and New York: Mouton de Gruyter, 1–55.

Houston, Ann. 1989. The English gerund: syntactic change and discourse function. In Ralph W. Fasold (ed.), *Language change and variation*. Amsterdam and Philadelphia: Benjamins, 173–196.

Indrebø, Gunnar. 2001. *Norsk målsoga*. Bergen: Norsk bokreidingslag.

Jack, George. 1988. The origin of the English gerund. *NOWELE* 12: 15–75

Jespersen, Otto. 1914–1940. *A Modern English grammar on historical principles*. London: George Allen, vol. IV.

Killie, Kristin (to appear). Internal and external factors in language change: present participle converbs in English and Norwegian. *Neuphilologische Mitteilungen*.

Knowles, Gerry. 1997. *A cultural history of the English language*. London: Arnold.

Kohnen, Thomas. 2003. The influence of 'Latinate' constructions in Early Modern English: orality and literacy as complementary forces. In: Dieter Kastovsky and Arthur Mettinger (eds.), *Language contact in the history of English*. Frankfurt/Main: Lang.

Koma, Osumu. 1987. On the initial locus of syntactic change: verbal gerund and its historical development. *English Linguistics: Journal of the English Linguistic Society of Japan* 4: 311–324.

Kortmann, Bernd. 1991. *Free adjuncts and absolutes in English: problems of control and interpretation*. London and New York: Routledge.

Kortmann, Bernd. 1995. Adverbial participle clauses in English. In Haspelmath, Martin and Ekkehard König (eds.), *Converbs in cross-linguistic perspective: structure and meaning of adverbial verb forms – adverbial participles, gerunds*. Berlin and New York: Mouton de Gruyter, 189–237.

Kristiansen, Tore. 2003. Danish. In Ana Deumert and Wim Vandenbussche (eds.), *Germanic standardizations: past to present*. Amsterdam and Philadelphia: Benjamins, 69–91.

Labov, William. 1966. *The social stratification of English in New York City*. Washington, DC: Center for Applied Linguistics.

Labov, William. 1994. *Principles of linguistic change. Part 1: Internal factors*. Oxford, UK and Cambridge, USA: Blackwell.

Lund, G. F. V. 1862. *Oldnordisk ordföljningslære*. København: Berlingske bogtrykkeri.

Mitchell, Bruce. 1985. *Old English syntax*. Oxford: Clarendon Press, vol. 1.

Moessner, Lilo. 1997. *-ing* constructions in Middle English. In Jacek Fisiak (ed.), *Studies in Middle English linguistics*. Berlin and New York: Mouton de Gruyter.

Nygaard, M. 1966. *Norrøn syntax*. Oslo: H. Aschehoug & Co. (W. Nygaard).

Oxford English Dictionary (2005). (Digital edition.) Oxford University Press.

Pettersen, Egil. 1975–1991. *Språkbrytning i Vest-Norge 1450–1550: språket i vestnorske skrifter i overgangen fra mellomalder til nyere tid. II: Morfologi*. Bergen: Alma Mater Forlag A/S.

Poutsma, Hendrik. 1923. *The infinitive, the gerund and the participles of the English verb*. Groningen: Noordhoff.

Pratt, Lynda and David Denison. 2000. The language of the Southey-Coleridge circle. *Language Sciences* 22: 401–422.

Strang, Barbara M. H. 1982. Some aspects of the history of the BE + ING construction. In John Anderson (ed.), *Language form and linguistic variation. Papers dedicated to Angus McIntosh*. Amsterdam: Benjamins, 427–474.

Sørensen, Knud. 1957. Latin influence on English syntax. The classical pattern of modern Western civilization: language. *Travaux du Cercle linguistique de Copenhague* 11: 131–155.

Vachek, Josef. 1962. On the interplay of external and internal factors in the development of language. *Lingua* 11: 433–448.

van der Wurff, Wim. 1993. Gerunds and their objects in the Modern English period. In Jaap van Marle (ed.), *Historical linguistics 1991. Papers from the 10th International Conference on Historical Linguistics. Amsterdam, 12-16 August 1991*. Amsterdam and Philadelphia: Benjamins, 363–375.

Visser, Frederikus Theodorus. 1963–1973. *An historical syntax of the English language*. 4 vols. Leiden: Brill.

Wardhaugh, Ronald. 1992. An introduction to sociolinguistics. Oxford, UK and Cambridge, USA: Blackwell.

Wolfram, Walt. 1969. *A sociolinguistic description of Detroit negro speech*. Washington, DC: Center for Applied Linguistics.

Workman, Samuel K. 1940. Fifteenth century translation as an influence on English prose. *Princeton studies in English* 18. Princeton: Princeton University Press.

ALEXANDRA LENZ (MARBURG)

The grammaticalization of *geben* 'to give' in German and Luxembourgish[1]

1. Introduction

This paper examines some grammatical 'anomalies' of German and Luxembourgish language associated with the verb *geben* 'to give'. In these, the two Germanic languages differ from most other languages. The paper focuses on the grammaticalization processes which have resulted in the existential construction *es gibt* 'there is', the *geben*-copula, and the passive and subjunctive auxiliary uses of *geben*. It sets out to review and pull together scattered research results which address individual aspects of the phenomena, and further, to document the large number of unresolved issues surrounding the grammatical affinity of German and Luxembourgish *geben*. Selecting from the latter the historical relationship between the grammaticalized *geben* variants, this paper first reviews hypotheses found in the research literature before testing them against the inter- and intrasystemic variation in German dialects and regiolects.

In varieties of German and Luxembourgish, *geben* is much more than just a full verb with up to three complements. As illustrated in (1), several *geben* variants can be interpreted as the result of grammaticalization processes. According to Hopper and Traugott (1993: 2), *grammaticalization* refers to "that subset of linguistic changes through which a lexical item in certain uses becomes a grammatical item, or through which a grammatical item becomes more grammatical". As Kuteva (2001: 1) reminds us, we have to keep in mind that grammaticalization "often does not so much involve single, isolated word forms but rather entire constructions of more than one word form".

---

[1] This contribution is a shortened and slightly modified version of „Zur Grammatikalisierung von *geben* im Deutschen und Lëtzebuergeschen" (Lenz [in print a]). For both this and the German version, I would like to thank a number of people for their comments and (yet unpublished) manuscripts: Cléo Altenhofen, Jacinta Arnhold, Peter Auer, Claudia Bucheli, Stephan Elspaß, Livio Gaeta, Joachim Herrgen, Cédric Krummes, Nils Langer, Mark Louden, Klaus J. Mattheier, John Newman, Damaris Nübling, Matthias Schlesewsky, Jürgen Erich Schmidt and also Mark Pennay.

Examples		Functions
a. Er *gibt* eine Bestellung *in Auftrag.*	'He commissions an order.'	light verb
b. Das *ergibt* eine hohe Summe.	'That adds up to a high amount.'	perfective (prefix) verb
c. *Es gibt* einen Gott.	'There is a God.'	existential verb
d. Er *gibt alt.*	'He gets old.'	copula ('to get, to become')
e. Er *gibt geschlagen.*	'He is hit.'	passive auxiliary ('to be')
f. Er *gäbe schwimmen.*	'He would swim.'	subjunctive auxiliary ('would')

Table 1: Grammaticalized *geben* variants in German and Luxembourgish varieties

The variants in (1) differ in their regional and social distribution. Whereas examples (1a) to (1c) are elements of standard German, the variants (1d) to (1f) are restricted to regional (nonstandard) varieties of German and Luxembourgish, respectively. The following discussion will be concentrated on the functions of *geben* as an existential verb, a copula, a passive, and a subjunctive auxiliary. This selection of phenomena is motivated by the fact that they are peculiarities of German and Luxembourgish varieties which are not to be found in other Germanic languages.

The research literature about the grammaticalization of *geben* is relatively limited. The contributions are mostly confined to the Moselle-Franconian and Luxembourgian areas, and they focus in particular on grammaticalization in the direction of the copula or the passive auxiliary.[2] The papers underline the typological peculiarity of the *geben* auxiliation and point out gaps in the research which motivate a further and intensive analysis of the multi-functionality of *geben*.[3]

From among these unresolved questions, the historical relationship pertaining between the grammaticalized *geben* variants has been selected for this paper. The results presented are the initial products of a larger research project concentrated on the grammaticalization of GIVING and RECEIVING verbs in German and other Germanic languages (*geben* 'to give', *bekommen/ kriegen* 'to get, to receive', etc.). As the analyses of these phenomena are still

---

[2]   On Luxembourgish *geben*, see Newman (1996: 169ff.), Nübling (2000: 65ff.), Nübling (2006), Gaeta (2005), and Krummes (2004). On Moselle-Franconian *geben* in Germany, see Bellmann (1996), (1998), Girnth (2000: 136ff.), and Lenz (in print a). Bellmann (1998) also sheds light on *geben* auxiliaries in other German varieties.

[3]   See Nübling (2000: 71, 73).

in their initial stages, the findings presented need to be interpreted as preliminary results rather than full-blown hypotheses and will have to be verified by further research.

The paper is structured as follows. At the outset, a survey of the varieties in which the focussed *geben* variants can be found is offered. Evidence for the unusualness of German and Luxembourgish *geben* is then presented in a cursory consideration of other languages. In a next step, the central hypotheses about the grammaticalization processes already developed in the research literature are drawn together and discussed on the basis of regional data. The paper closes with an overview of questions for further research.

2. The oddity of *geben* in German and Luxembourgish

In most German varieties (including the standard language), *geben* can function as an existential verb. As such, it (mostly) occurs in the third-person singular in combination with the syntactic expletive pronoun *es*. The 'es gibt' construction can announce the occurrence of an event or the emergence of an entity (2a). It also can be used as a generic statement of existence (2b) or in the sense of 'to exist in a certain context' (German: *vorhanden sein*) (2c).

Examples		Functions
a. Morgen *gibt es* Regen.	'There will be rain tomorrow.'	Ingressive
b. *Es gibt* einen Gott.	'There is a God.'	Generic
c. In Afrika *gibt es* Löwen.	'There are lions in Africa.'	Contextual

Table 2: The existential construction *es gibt* 'there is/are' in Standard German

Whereas the existential function of *geben* can be found in the standard language as well as in most of the German varieties, the copula and passive functions are confined to regional language varieties (*Regionalsprachen*)[4] and dialects. (The nonstandard functions of *geben* are realised by forms of *werden* in Standard German.) The dialects concerned have in common that they are (at least originally) situated in the West Middle German language area left of the Rhine, more precisely in the Moselle-Franconian and, more rarely, the Rhine-

---

[4] *Regional language* (German *Regionalsprache, Substandard*) here means the entire regionally marked oral spectrum 'below' the standard language. It includes both the dialects (base and regional dialects) and the regiolects (German *Umgangssprachen,* including regional accent) (see Lenz 2003 and 2005). For this definition of *regional language* see also Herrgen/Schmidt (in preparation).

Franconian area and the transitional zone between these two.[5] Outside the
range of the German standard language, the phenomena also occur in the
Luxembourgian varieties, in the Pennsylvania Dutch of North America, in the
Banat region dialects straddling the borders of Romania, Hungary and Serbia,
and in 'Hunsrückish' (named after the area of a West German mountain
range), spoken in the South Brazilian state of Rio Grande do Sul.

In the following, the inter- and intrasystemic variation of the grammaticalized *geben* variants are sketched. Looking at Pennsylvania Dutch (PD) in
North America,[6] we can see that a differentiated analysis of the *es gibt*
constructions is useful. While this construction can be used ingressively in PD
(3a), it is the verb *sein* 'to be' that serves as an existential verb with generic
meaning (3b). The contextually limited existential function (neglected in the
following) is realised by *haben* 'to have' (3c).[7] In PD, *geben* also functions as
an ingressive copula verb but only in combination with a noun phrase (3d). As
in Standard German, *werden* has to be used if the copula verb is combined
with an adjective phrase (3e). As the examples in (3) reveal, the perfect
auxiliary of the *geben* copula is *haben* 'to have', whereas the *werden* copula
takes *sein* 'to be'.

Examples	Standard German	
a. Geschder *hot's* Rege *gewwe*.	*Gestern hat es Regen gegeben.*	'There was rain yesterday.'
b. *'s is* en Gott.	*Es gibt einen Gott.*	'There is a God.'
c. *'s hot* Lions in Africa.	*In Afrika gibt es Löwen.*	'There are lions in Africa.'
d. Er *hot* en guder Breddicher *gewwe*.	*Er ist ein guter Prediger geworden.*	'He has become a good preacher.'
e. Er *is* alt *wadde*.	*Er ist alt geworden.*	'He has become old.'

Table 3: Existential constructions and (ingressive) copulas in Pennsylvania Dutch

---

[5] These regions are clearly illustrated in Wiesinger's (1983) dialect distribution map (also
viewable in DiWA, online at <http://www.diwa.info>).

[6] Most of the dialect features of Pennsylvania Dutch can be classified as Rhine Franconian.
Most of the original Pennsylvania Dutch speakers migrated between 1683 and 1775. For
further information see Louden (1988 [Reprint 2004]). Special thanks to Mark Louden for
further information and comments about Pennsylvania Dutch.

[7] For *es hat* versus *es gibt* in the south of the German language area see the "Variantenwörterbuch" of Ammon et al. (2004), Eichhoff (1978: map 106) and also the "Atlas zur
deutschen Alltagssprache", http://www.philhist.uni-augsburg.de/de/lehrstuehle/germanistik/
sprachwissenschaft/ada/dritte_runde/f04c/ (01.02.2007).

Because it is largely comparable to PD, the Rhine-Franconian *geben* will be omitted here. In the western Moselle-Franconian area in Germany, *geben* clearly has more functions than in Pennsylvania Dutch or the Rhine-Franconian dialects. In this West Central German region, the copula *geben* (4b) can be combined with adjectives as well as noun phrases and additionally functions as a passive auxiliary (4c).[8] In contrast to PD, Moselle-Franconian *es gibt* can be used as ingressive, contextual, or generic existential construction (4a). Analogous to other fully grammaticalized German copulas or passive auxiliaries, the perfect of the *geben* copula and auxiliary in the Moselle-Franconian area is formed with *sein* 'to be'. In contrast, the perfect auxiliary for the full verb *geben* is *haben* 'to have'.

Examples	Standard German	
a. *Et git* en Goot.	*Es gibt einen Gott.*	'There is a God.'
b. Hään *äs* krank *gen.*	*Er ist krank geworden.*	'He has become ill.'
c. Hään *äs* geschloon *gen.*	*Er ist geschlagen worden.*	'He was/has been hit.'

Table 4: *Geben* as existential verb, copula, and passive auxiliary
in the Moselle-Franconian area[9]

If we look at recent dialect data from the Moselle-Franconian area,[10] it becomes obvious that for most of the documented local base dialects, the existence of a *geben* passive auxiliary implies the existence of the *geben* copula. Concentrating on the younger generation of informants in the Linguistic Atlas of the Middle Rhine Area (MRhSA),[11] we see an almost perfect congruence of the two grammatical phenomena. With the exception of two localities, the region in which *geben* can act as a passive auxiliary is part of the region where *geben* is a copula. In 89 localities in which *geben* functions as a copula, it is also used as a passive auxiliary. In 13 localities, *geben* serves as a copula verb

---

[8] On *geben* in the Moselle-Franconian area in Germany see Bellmann (1996 and 1998) and Girnth (2000: 136ff.). For alternative passive auxiliaries in German varieties see Wiesinger (1989), Bellmann (1998) and Bucheli/Glaser (2002).

[9] The transcriptions represent the base dialect of the Wittlich region in the Eifel mountains (see Lenz 2003).

[10] See MRhSA (Linguistic Atlas of the Middle Rhine Area) (maps 509, 544/1–2 and 545/1–2) and Cornelissen 1989.

[11] The MRhSA is a bidimensional atlas. That means that it is not only interested in the horizontal, areal dimension of the dialects, but that the social dimension is also taken into account by polling both the traditional NORMs and a second group of informants, i.e. the younger, mobile generation of informants born in the localities. At the time of the recording, they were about 35 years of age (see Bellmann 1994).

for the younger generation but not as a passive auxiliary. Only in two localities does the MRhSA show *geben* as a passive auxiliary and *werden* as the copula.

We can ascribe a comparable functionality to some dialects in the Banat region straddling the borders of Romania, Hungary, and Serbia.[12] The 'Hunsrückish' of Rio Grande do Sul (Brazil) also belongs to the group of German dialects in which *geben* occurs as both a copula and a passive auxiliary. A detailed analysis of *geben* in the Banat and Hunsrückish regions still needs to be done.[13]

The grammaticalized *geben* variants of the Moselle-Franconian area, the Banat region and Hunsrückish can also be found in Luxembourgish (see (5)). In these dialects we encounter two additional peculiarities related to the grammaticalization of *geben*. Firstly, Luxembourgian *geben* also serves as a periphrastic subjunctive auxiliary (the so called '*würde* subjunctive'),[14] and secondly, the Luxembourgian existential construction is characterized by congruence of number between *geben* and the second NP (5b).[15]

Examples	Standard German	
a Zu Bangor *gëtt et* eng Universitéit.	*In Bangor gibt es eine Universität.*	'There is a university in Bangor.'
b. A Wales *ginn et* vill Universitéiten.	*In Wales gibt es viele Universitäten.*	'There are many universities in Wales.'
c. Gëschter *ass* d'Pamela Mamm *ginn*.	*Gestern ist Pamela Mutter geworden.*	'Pamela became a mum yesterday.'
d. Ech *gi* gesond.	*Ich werde gesund.*	'I am getting healthy.'
e. Ech *gi/gouf fond.*	*Ich werde/wurde gefunden.*	'I am/was found.'
f. Ech *géif bleiwen.*	*Ich würde bleiben.*	'I would stay.'

Table 5: *Geben* as existential verb, copula, passive and subjunctive auxiliary in Luxembourg (see Nübling (2000: 67) and Krummes (2004: 15f.))

---

[12] The origin of the Banat 'Swabians', who emigrated in the 18th century, can largely be traced to the Western German area to the left of the Rhine. Aside from Moselle-Franconian dialect features, Banat German has mainly Rhine-Franconian characteristics.

[13] On these two areas, see also Bellmann (1998: 246 a. 257). The hypotheses about Hunsrückish *geben* have found initial support in speech material collected recently by the University of Freiburg (Germany). Special thanks to Peter Auer and Jacinta Arnhold for their information and helpful insights.

[14] On this phenomenon see in particular Nübling (2006) and Krummes (2004).

[15] It has to be mentioned that the DWb (1878: 1704) also has examples of *es gibt* with a second nominative complement. In "Osterlande, in Thüringen, Hessen z. b. sagt man *es gibt ein tüchtiger regen heute, es gibt frischer hering* u. dergl., d.h. das ursprüngliche object ist vollends zum subj. erhoben auch grammatisch, was dem sinne nach thatsächlich ist […]." 'In Osterlande, in Thuringia, Hesse, e.g., people say *es gibt ein tüchtiger regen heute, es gibt frischer hering* etc., i.e. the initial object has been made subject grammatically, in other words, it has thus become the actual subject.' [my translation – A.L.].

The functions of the grammaticalized *geben* variants outlined are drawn together in the following table 6.

	Standard German	Penns. Dutch	Moselle Franco-nian	Banat dialect	Huns-rückish	Luxem-bourgish
es gibt (ingressive)	+	+	+	+	+	+
es gibt (generic)	+		+	+	+	+
Copula + NP		+	+	+	+	+
Copula + AdjP			+	+	+	+
Passive auxiliary			+	+	+	+
Subjunctive auxiliary						+

Table 6: *Geben* as existential verb, copula, and auxiliary
in German and Luxembourgish varieties

Taking a look at existential constructions in other languages, we can observe that the *es gibt* construction is not a very frequent phenomenon at all (see table 7). In the Germanic languages, the verbs *to be*, *to find* and others take over the existential function of German and Luxembourgish *to give*. In the Romance languages, we foremost come across *to have*, which is also an existential verb in the south of the German language and in Pennsylvania Dutch. Apart from German and Luxembourgish, impersonal *give* constructions with existential meaning are found (at least in the research literature) only in Brazilian Portuguese and in Jacaltec, a Mayan language spoken in Guatemala and South Mexico (s. Newman 1996: 164ff.).

Language	'Es gibt (Menschen)'	Existential verbs
English	*There are (people)*	*to be*
Dutch	*Er zijn / bestaan (mensen)*	*zijn, bestaan*
Norwegian	*Det er / finnes (mennesker)*	*være, finne*
Swedish	*Det finns (människor)*	*finna*
French	*Il y a (des gens)*	*avoir*
Italian	*C'è (gente)*	*essere*
Portuguese	*Há (gente)*	*haver*
Spanish	*Hay (gente)*	*haber*

Table 7: Existential verbs in (some) Germanic und Romance languages

A search for *geben* functioning as a copula or an auxiliary in the Germanic or Romance languages also reveals *geben* to be an exception (see (8)). We can see that English makes use of grammaticalized semantic neighbours of *to give* but not *to give* itself. As for the Romance languages, apart from *to have* and *to be* the COMING and GOING verbs chiefly function as a source for auxiliation. It's only in Brazilian Portuguese that – according to Newman (1996: 170f.) – there is something like a copula use of *dar* ('to give'). As for the passive auxiliary, Haspelmath (1990: 48), Kautz (1991: 72), Wong (2004), and Bisang (1992: 178f.) refer to some interesting parallels in Chinese dialects.

Language	Copulas	(Accusative) Passive auxiliaries
English	*to be, to get, to become, to remain*	*to be*
Dutch	*zijn, worden, blijven*	*zijn, worden*
Norwegian	*vaere, få, bli, forbli*	*verte, bli*
Swedish	*vara, bli, fortsätta*	*bli*
French	*être, devenir, rester*	*être*
Italian	*essere, diventare, rimanere*	*essere, venire, andare*
Portuguese	*ser, estar, ficar*	*ser*
Spanish	*ser, estar, resultar*	*ser, estar*

Table 8: Copula and passive auxiliary in (some) Germanic and Romance languages

As to other grammaticalized variants of *to give*, there are many African and Asian languages using *to give* as benefactive, causative, or dative marker.[16] These examples illustrate that it is not the grammaticalization of *to give* that is special in the languages of the world, but the specific grammaticalization that leads to an existential verb, a copula, or to a passive auxiliary.

3. Grammaticalization channels (hypotheses)

As mentioned above, the historical relationship between the grammaticalized *geben* variants has been chosen as the main topic of this paper. We can only find limited answers to the question of the nature of this relationship, but there

---

[16]   On the multifunctionality of *geben* in the languages of the world see Newman (1993a, 1993b and 1996), Newman (ed.) (1998), Lord et al. (2002) and also Heine/Kuteva (2003).

are a number of hypotheses in research literature. Some of these hypotheses – which can only be sketched here – are the following:[17]

- The development of the existential *es gibt* construction and the grammaticalization of the copula are two parallel processes, which „auf der konzeptuellen Ebene ziemlich nahe beieinander liegen" ['are quite close to one another at a conceptual level'; my transl.–A.L.] Gaeta (2005: 204).[18]

- In the process running from the full verb *geben* to the generic existential construction, the ingressive construction is the older one.

- *Es gibt* constructions with an accusative complement are followed by *es gibt* constructions with a second nominative complement.

- In the grammaticalization channel running from the full verb *geben* to the passive auxiliary, the copula constitutes an intermediate stage.

- *Geben* as a copula is first combined with a NP and then – in a next step – with an AdjP.

- Constructions with a 'pseudo' copula plus accusative NP preceeds the 'real' copula plus nominative NP.

- The development from the *geben* copula to the subjunctive auxiliary can be interpreted as a parallel process to that from the *geben* copula to a passive auxiliary.

Figure 1 summarizes the hypotheses about the different grammaticalization stages:

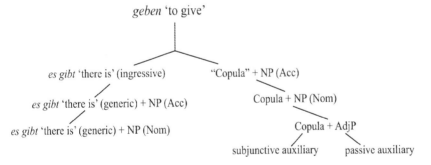

Figure 1: Grammaticalization channels of the full verb *geben* (hypotheses)

---

[17] Because of the limited space here, the hypotheses can only be summarized and sketched. For further details see Bellmann (1998), Girnth (2000: 136–145), Krummes (2004), Newman (1998), Nübling (2000: 65–73), Nübling (2006), Gaeta (2005), and Lenz (in print a).

[18] For a contrasting hypothesis about the chronology see Joseph (2000: 187): "When viewed against the backdrop of there being several verbs in Indo-European meaning both 'give' and 'take', these facts suggest an interpretation wherein the existential sense of *geben* is the archaism, and the meaning 'give' is a Germanic innovation."

4. Evidences from regional varieties of German

Given the limited amount of diachronic evidence available, I searched for synchronic evidence for the different intermediate stages. Once again this is done by examining the regional varieties of German:

On the basis of the intra- and intersystemic variation of *geben* in the German dialect varieties (see table 6), the following can be revealed:

1. Whereas ingressive statements in Pennsylvania Dutch can be verbalized by *es gibt*, the grammaticalization process has not extended to the generic existential construction. We can take this as evidence that the ingressive *es gibt* preceded the generic construction. Danner (1961: 6) refers to some very interesting examples in current 'Dutchified English', which show a substrate influence of Pennsylvania Dutch on the regional English of Pennsylvania Dutch speakers: *It will give a meeting tonight. / What will it give at the meeting tonight?*[19] In contrast, existential *es ist* 'there is' in Pennsylvania Dutch is indeed due to English (superstrate) influence. However, this influence did not displace old *es gibt,* but instead stopped the grammaticalization process before *es gibt* advanced to a generic existential construction.

2. The fact that the first Pennsylvania Dutch people emigrated to North America between 1680 and 1780 supports the hypothesis that the general existential construction had not been established by 1780 and that it is therefore a relatively recent feature of German.

3. Furthermore, Pennsylvania Dutch lends evidence to the thesis that the existential construction and the copula evolved in parallel, at least at a certain point along the grammaticalization channel; *geben* can function as a copula in this variety (if it is combined with a NP), but the development of the ingressive existential construction has not proceeded to the generic one.

4. Turning to Pennsylvania Dutch once more, in this variety, *geben* only functions as a copula in combination with a NP and not with an adjectival phrase. So we could say that Pennsylvania Dutch has been 'frozen' at an intermediate stage along the channel. This variety gives evidence that *geben* as a copula was first combined with a NP.

5. Let's cast a glance at the other dialect varieties (6): *geben* as a passive auxiliary and as a copula plus adjective is only prevalent in those varieties in which *geben* also functions as a copula with a NP. These varieties also reinforce the hypothesis that the copula plus NP construction precedes the copula plus AdjP and the passive auxiliary constructions.

---

[19]   For further examples see Howell (1993: 201). I would like to thank Mark Louden and Stephan Elspaß who called my attention to Danner (1961) and Howell (1993).

6. Support for the suggestion that the copula plus AdjP construction occupies a chronologically intermediate position between the copula plus NP and the passive auxiliary constructions has been found by briefly considering the Moselle Franconian area. From the regional distribution of the *geben*-variants, we can draw evidence for the hypothesis that the copula plus AdjP precedes the passive auxiliary in the grammaticalization channel.
7. The Luxembourgian varieties – intrasystemically as well as in intersystemic comparison to Moselle-Franconian – support the assumption that the periphrastic *gäbe* subjunctive is an ensuing stage to the use of *geben* as a copula.

The focus of the preceding discussion has been on the German dialects on the one hand and the standard language on the other. I would like to close by casting a brief glance at the intermediate varieties in modern German, the regiolects (*Umgangssprachen*). To this end, I have conducted a first pretest on the basis of a questionnaire. With an eye to the region in which their primary socialisation occurred, 316 native speakers of German were asked to evaluate the acceptability of different *geben* constructions in their colloquial language. (The majority of the informants had been raised in the West Central German area.) The survey was feasible because copula constructions of *geben* are also detectable in some current colloquial varieties of German. The central hypothesis was that the native speaker acceptability hierarchies would mirror the diachronic stages of the grammaticalization process of *geben*. There is only space here to summarize the results.

Constructions	Examples	Evaluations (in %)		
		incorrect	collo-quial	proper Standard
Copula + NP (ACC SG)	Vielleicht *gibt* er mal *einen guten Vater.*	48.5	41.3	10.2
Copula + NP (NOM SG)	Tom *gibt* sicher *ein guter Lehrer.*	72.6	23.2	4.2
Copula + NP (PL)	Sie *geben* mal sicher *nette Eltern.*	80.5	17.7	1.9
Copula + AdjP	Wegen dieser Geschichte *gibt* Petra *sauer.*	88.1	11.4	0.6
Impersonal Passive	In diesem Lokal *gibt* nicht *geraucht.*	94.1	2.9	2.9
es gibt + NP (ACC)	*Es gibt* einen Gott. / *Es gibt* Menschen, die	6.2	57.0	36.8
es gibt + NP (NOM SG)	Er hat immer betont, *es gibt* ein Gott.	66.4	22.1	11.5

Table 9: Informant evaluation of acceptablity

The informant evaluation of acceptability increases from the copula plus AdjP to the copula plus NP. Constructions with *geben* as a copula plus nominative NP are evaluated as significantly less acceptable than copula constructions with an accusative NP. From the acceptability hierarchy, we can draw support for the proposal that the 'pseudo' copula plus accusative NP preceeds the copula plus nominative NP. And in comparison with the copula plus AdjP constructions, these copula variants are the historically older ones. With respect to the existential construction *es gibt*, the results of the questionnaire reveal a clear rejection of the constructions with a second nominative element. Consequently, the exhaustive grammaticalization of *es gibt* which has been completed in Luxembourg can barely be detected in the German regiolects, at least at present.

5. Summary and outlook

The paper has focused on special grammaticalized variants of the German and Luxembourgish verb *geben* 'to give'. Apart from the existential construction *es gibt* 'there is', the emphasis has been on the grammaticalization of the full verb *geben* to a copula, a passive auxiliary, and (restrictedly) a subjunctive auxiliary. By taking a glance at other Germanic and Romance languages, it has become obvious that these grammaticalized variants are peculiarities of (some) German varieties and of Luxembourgish, respectively. The historical relationship between the grammaticalized *geben* variants was selected for closer consideration. Given the limited amount of diachronic evidence available, the analysis of different regional varieties of German provided supporting evidence for the broad-brush chronology of the grammaticalization of *geben*. Taking into account German dialects and regiolects, it could be demonstrated that the intra- and intersystemic variation of *geben* supports the hypothesized chronology.

This paper provides initial insights only into the affinity of German and Luxembourgish *geben* for grammaticalization. Many issues remain unresolved, the hypotheses need further specification and supporting evidence. The analysis of a larger corpus would be desirable in establishing the diachrony of events. Such a corpus could also help answer other previously neglected questions. However, many questions remain with regard to the synchronic analysis of the current varieties, e.g.,

- the alternation of *es gibt* 'there is' and *es ist* 'there is / it is' in standard German;
- the regional variation of *haben* 'to have', *sein* 'to be', and *geben* 'to give' as existential verbs in the southwest German language area;

- other grammaticalized variants of *geben* in German (*geben* as a light verb, as a reflexive verb, as a prefix verb);
- the grammaticalization of the semantic neighbours of *geben* (e.g., *bekommen/kriegen/erhalten* 'to get, to receive').[20]

These and other related questions will constitute the objects of further research, in which the analysis of regional data material will play an important role. Apart from this, the explanatory power of other variation dimensions (diastratic, diaphasic, etc.) will also have to be tested.

References

Ammon, Ulrich, Hans Bickel, Jakob Ebner et al. (eds.). 2004. *Variantenwörterbuch des Deutschen. Die Standardsprache in Österreich, der Schweiz und Deutschland sowie in Liechtenstein, Luxemburg, Ostbelgien und Südtirol.* Berlin and New York: de Gruyter.

Bellmann, Günter. 1994. *Einführung in den Mittelrheinischen Sprachatlas (MRhSA).* Tübingen: Niemeyer.

Bellmann, Günter. 1996. Arealität und Sozialität? In Edgar Radtke and Harald Thun (eds.), *Neue Wege der romanischen Geolinguistik. Akten des Symposiums zur Empirischen Dialektologie. Heidelberg/Mainz, 21.–24.10.1991.* Kiel: Westensee-Verlag, 50–77.

Bellmann, Günter. 1998. Zur Passivperiphrase im Deutschen. Grammatikalisierung und Kontinuität. In Ernst Peter and Franz Patocka (eds.), *Deutsche Sprache in Raum und Zeit. Festschrift für Peter Wiesinger zum 60. Geburtstag.* Wien: Edition Präsens, 241–269.

Bisang, Walter. 1992. *Das Verb im Chinesischen, Hmong, Vietnamesischen, Thai und Khmer. Vergleichende Grammatik im Rahmen der Verbserialisierung, der Grammatikalisierung und der Attraktorpositionen.* Tübingen: Narr.

Bucheli, Claudia and Elvira Glaser. 2002. The Syntactic Atlas of Swiss German Dialects: Empirical and Methodological Problems. In Sjef Barbiers (ed.), *Syntactic Microvariation. Electronische publicatie van Meertens Instituut en NIWI.* <http://www.meertens.knaw.nl/books/synmic>, 41–74.

Cornelissen, Georg, Peter Honnen and Fritz Langensiepen (eds.). 1989. *Das rheinische Platt. Eine Bestandsaufnahme. Handbuch der rheinischen Mundarten. Teil 1: Texte.* Köln: Rheinland-Verlag.

---

[20] On the so called "Rezipientenpassiv" (dative passive) in German see Leirbukt (1997) and Lenz (in print b).

Danner, Edwin R. 1961. *Pennsylvania Dutch Colloquialisms.* York, Penn.: William Penn Senior High School.

DiWA = Jürgen E. Schmidt and Joachim Herrgen (eds.). 2001ff. *Digitaler Wenkeratlas (DiWA). Bearbeitet von Alfred Lameli, Alexandra N. Lenz, Jost Nickel und Roland Kehrein, Karl-Heinz Müller, Stefan Rabanus. Erste vollständige Ausgabe von Georg Wenkers „Sprachatlas des Deutschen Reichs". 1888–1923 handgezeichnet von Emil Maurmann, Georg Wenker und Ferdinand Wrede.* Marburg: Forschungsinstitut für deutsche Sprache „Deutscher Sprachatlas". (www.diwa.info).

DWb = Jacob and Wilhelm Grimm. 1878. *Deutsches Wörterbuch. Vierten Bandes erste Abtheilung. Erste Hälfte.* Leipzig: Hirzel.

Eichhoff, Jürgen. 1978. *Wortatlas der deutschen Umgangssprachen.* Bern and München: Francke Verlag, vol. 2.

Gaeta, Livio. 2005. Hilfsverben und Grammatikalisierung: Die fatale Attraktion von *geben.* In Torsten Leuscher et al. (eds.), *Grammatikalisierung im Deutschen.* Berlin: de Gruyter, 193–209.

Girnth, Heiko. 2000. *Untersuchungen zur Theorie der Grammatikalisierung am Beispiel des Westmitteldeutschen.* Tübingen: Niemeyer.

Haspelmath, Martin. 1990. The Grammaticalization of Passive Morphology. In *Studies in Language* 14/1: 25–72.

Heine, Bernd and Tania Kuteva. 2003. *World Lexicon of Grammaticalization.* Cambridge: Cambridge University Press.

Herrgen, Joachim and Jürgen E. Schmidt. (in prep.). *Sprachdynamik. Eine Einführung in die moderne Regionalsprachenforschung.* Berlin: Schmidt.

Hopper, Paul J. and Elizabeth Closs Traugott. 1993. *Grammaticalization.* Cambridge: Cambridge University Press.

Howell, Robert B. 1993. German Immigration and the Development of Regional Variants of American English: Using Contact Theory to Discover Our Roots. In Joseph C. Salmons (ed.), *The German Language in America, 1683–1991.* Madison, Wisconsin: Max Kade Institute, 188–212.

Joseph, Brian D. 2000. *What gives* with *es gibt?* Typological and Comparative Perspectives on Existentials in German, Germanic, and Indo-European. In *American Journal of Germanic Linguistics and Literatures* 12.2: 187–200.

Kautz, Ulrich. 1991. *Aktiv und Passiv im Deutschen und Chinesischen. Eine konfrontativ-übersetzungswissenschaftliche Studie.* Heidelberg: Julius Groos.

Krummes, Cédric. 2004. *The Lëtzebuergesch Verb* ginn *'give'. Grammaticalisation from Lexical Verb to Copula, Existential Construction, Passive Auxiliary, and Conditional Mood Auxiliary.* BA Hons English Language Dissertation. Department of Linguistics and English Language. University of Wales, Bangor. [unpublished manuscript]

Kuteva, Tania. 2001. *Auxiliation. An Enquiry into the Nature of Grammaticalization.* Oxford: University Press.

Leirbukt, Oddleif. 1997. *Untersuchungen zum* bekommen-*Passiv im heutigen Deutsch.* Tübingen: Niemeyer.

Lenz, Alexandra N. 2003. *Struktur und Dynamik von Varietäten. Eine Studie zum Westmitteldeutschen (Wittlich/Eifel).* Stuttgart: Steiner.

Lenz, Alexandra N. 2005. Hyperdialektalismen und Hyperkorrektionen. Indizien für Varietätengrenzen. In Alexandra N. Lenz and Klaus J. Mattheier (eds.), *Varietäten – Theorie und Empirie.* Frankfurt/Main: Lang, 76–95.

Lenz, Alexandra N. (in print a). Grammatikalisierung von *geben* im Deutschen und Lëtzebuergeschen. In *Zeitschrift für Germanistische Linguistik.*

Lenz, Alexandra N. (in print b). Zur variationslinguistischen Analyse regionalsprachlicher Korpora. In Werner Kallmeyer and Gisela Zifonun (eds.), *Sprachkorpora. Datenmengen und Erkenntnisfortschritt.* Berlin and New York: de Gruyter.

Lord, Carol et al. 2002. Grammaticalization of 'give'. African and Asian Perspectives. In Ilse Wischer and Gabriele Diewald (eds.), *New Reflections on Grammaticalization.* Amsterdam, Philadelphia: Benjamins, 217–235.

Louden, Mark. 1988. *Bilingualism and Syntactic Change in Pennsylvania German.* Michigan: UMI.

MRhSA =Günter Bellmann, Joachim Herrgen and Jürgen E.Schmidt. 1994–2002. *Mittelrheinischer Sprachatlas (MRhSA).* 5 vols. Tübingen: Niemeyer.

Newman, John. 1993a. The semantics of giving in Mandarin. In Richard A. Geiger and Brygida Rudzka-Ostyn (eds.), *Conceptualizations and mental processing of language.* Berlin and New York: Mouton de Gruyter, 433–485.

Newman, John. 1993b. A Cognitive Grammar approach to Mandarin *gěi.* In *Journal of Chinese Linguistics* 21: 313–336.

Newman, John. 1996. *Give: A Cognitive Linguistic Study.* Berlin and New York: Mouton de Gruyter.

Newman, John. 1998. The Origin of the German *es gibt* Construction. In: Newman, John (ed.), 307–325.

Newman, John (ed.). 1998. *The Linguistics of Giving.* Amsterdam and Philadelphia: Benjamins.

Nübling, Damaris. 2000. *Prinzipien der Irregularisierung. Eine kontrastive Analyse von zehn Verben in zehn germanischen Sprachen.* Tübingen: Niemeyer.

Nübling, Damaris. 2006. Auf Umwegen zum Passivauxiliar – Die Grammatikalisierungspfade von GEBEN, WERDEN, KOMMEN und BLEIBEN im Luxemburgischen, Deutschen und Schwedischen. In Claudine Moulin and Damaris Nübling (eds.), *Perspektiven einer linguistischen Luxemburgistik. Studien zur Synchronie und Diachronie.* Heidelberg: Winter, 171–202.

Wiesinger, Peter. 1983. Die Einteilung der deutschen Dialekte. In Werner Besch et al. (eds.), *Dialektologie. Ein Handbuch zur deutschen und allgemeinen Dialektforschung.* Berlin and New York: de Gruyter, vol. 2, 807–900.

Wiesinger, Peter. 1989. Zur Passivbildung mit *kommen* im Südbairischen. In Wolfgang Putschke et al. (eds.), *Dialektgeographie und Dialektologie. Günter Bellmann zu seinem 60. Geburtstag von seinen Schülern und Freunden.* Marburg: Elwert, 256–268.

Wong, Kwok-shing. 2004. The acquisition of polysemous forms. The case of *bei2* ("give") in Cantonese. In Olga Fischer et al. (eds.), *Up and down the Cline – The Nature of Grammaticalization.* Amsterdam: Benjamins, 325–343.

KOEN PLEVOETS, DIRK SPEELMAN AND DIRK GEERAERTS
(LEUVEN)

A corpus-based study of modern colloquial 'Flemish'

1. Background

Historically speaking, Flanders (the Dutch-speaking region of Belgium) did not develop a standard language of its own, but adopted the Dutch standard that already existed in The Netherlands. Due to the strong language policy efforts in the post-war period, this language variety – referred to as the Belgian national standard variety of Dutch – ultimately gained widespread recognition as the common standard for Belgian Dutch (see Jaspaert 1986). Its use, however, remained restricted to the formal and/or written registers, whereas in the colloquial registers, the original Flemish dialects were still being used. This division of labour between standard Belgian Dutch on the one hand and the Flemish dialects on the other witnessed a drastic change from about the mid-1980's onwards, as the use of the dialects for colloquial speech came to be replaced by the so-called 'tussentaal' (literally 'in-between language'). This 'tussentaal' is a supraregional language variety that is highly similar to Belgian standard Dutch in many ways, but that still retains a lot of properties of the – Brabantic – dialects.[1] By consequence, the emergence of the 'tussentaal' can be said to quite typically exemplify a 'standardisation from below'.

2. Research question

Given the intrinsic hybridity of the 'tussentaal' – as the name itself already indicates – the primary question is to what extent does it constitute a uniform language variety. Do the typical characteristics of the 'tussentaal' occur with systematically equal probability, or are some characteristics more frequent and hence more common than others? If the latter is the case, along which dimensions can these differences be accounted for? Previous studies already

---

[1]   Also cf. the contribution by Reinhild Vandekerckhove in this volume

indicated significant differences among the various 'tussentaal'-characteristics on the basis of a single and very specific type of speech situation; see, for example, Van Gijsel 2001 for language in radio and TV advertisements, and Geeraerts 2001 for language in soap series. This paper complements these studies in that it will take several speech situations into account. The objective is to accommodate for the observed (register) variation by looking for some underlying dimensions.

3. Methodology

The methodology will be quantitative and corpus-based. The corpus on which the analysis will be performed is pre-release 5 of the Spoken Dutch Corpus ('Corpus Gesproken Nederlands' – CGN). This corpus is particularly suited for the purpose of this analysis, as it is subdivided into 11 sub-corpora, each sub-corpus containing data from a different type of speech situations. They are the following:

> c01: face-to-face conversations
> c02: private interviews
> c05: public interviews and discussions
> c06: discussions, debates and meetings (political)
> c07: classroom lectures
> c09: sports commentaries
> c10: newsreports
> c11: (short) news items
> c12: prepared commentaries
> c13: lectures and speeches
> c14: read aloud text

Important to notice with respect to these subcorpora is the fact that they exhibit an inherent structure: Subcorpora 01 to 07, for instance, are types of speech situations that are more dialogic, while from subcorpus 09 onwards the type of speech situations is more monologic.

4. Linguistic variables

The 'tussentaal' involves all sorts of dialectal elements, various aspects of which have already been studied: phonological variation in Van de Velde (1996), and lexicological variation in both Geeraerts, Grondelaers and Speelman (1999) and Grondelaers, Van Aken, Speelman and Geeraerts (2001). For the purpose of this analysis, however, the scope will be narrowed to the inflectional variation only. The reason for this is the fact that the inflectional characteristics of the 'tussentaal' are commonly considered to be the most predominantly, prototypically 'substandard' ones. These inflectional characteristics, then, can in turn be subdivided into three types: adnominal characteristics, diminutive characteristics, and pronominal characteristics.

The adnominal characteristics of the 'tussentaal' are various determiners and/or attributive elements that are inflected with the dialectal suffix -e(n), in contrast to Belgian standard Dutch where they are not inflected. Table 1 lists a few examples of determiners for both standard Dutch and 'tussentaal', together with a translation:

Standard	Tussentaal	Translation
mijn	*mijn-e(n)*	'my'
elke	*elke-n*	'each'
die	*die-(n)e(n)*	'this'
...	...	...

Table 1: Adnominal variation in Belgian Dutch

The diminutive characteristics of 'tussentaal' also involve a suffixation scheme, but this time in contrast to an existing one in standard Dutch: standard Dutch already has a diminutive system, the so-called J-system; whereas the 'tussentaal' has an alternative one, the K-system. They are listed in Table 2:

Standard	Tussentaal	Translation
bloem-etje	*bloem-eke*	'small flower'
...	...	...

Table 2: Diminutive variation in Belgian Dutch

The most intricate set of 'tussentaal'-characteristics, finally, are the pronominal ones. On the one hand, there are again variants to standard Dutch elements (table 3). They typically occur in post-verbal, enclitic position:

Standard	Tussentaal	Translation
ik	*ekik*	'I'
-ie	*'m*	'he'
...	...	...

Table 3: Pronominal variation in Belgian Dutch

The pronouns of address, on the other hand, even reflect complete alternative (sub-)systems. There exists one system for polite speech, the U-system. For

182   Koen Plevoets, Dirk Speelman and Dirk Geeraerts

familiar speech, however, Belgian Dutch speakers can select out of two/three systems, as shown in table 4:

	subject		object
	− inversion	+ inversion	
polite	*u*	*u*	*u*
familiar	*je/jij*	*je/jij*	*je/jou*
	ge/gij	*ge/gij/-de(gij)*	*u*

Table 4: The pronouns of address

Standard Belgian Dutch prescribes the J-system for familiar speech. The alternative, which is therefore often deemed 'substandard', is the G-system (which moreover incorporates a deficient D-system, which is an historical relic from the Flemish dialects; synchronically, however, the distinction between G- and D-system has been blurred). This situation is the outcome of the Belgian language policy: the standard J-system originally belongs to the Northern Dutch dialects as spoken in The Netherlands (and adopted by Flanders). Therefore, it is an exogenic system for Flanders, which renders it necessarily marked for Belgian speakers. The G-system, by contrast, belongs to the Southern Dutch dialects, and consequentially is the endogenic, unmarked system for pronominal address. This paradox concerning the pronouns of address has been frequently commented upon in the literature (see, for example, Vandekerckhove 2004), and will prove particularly interesting, as it will appear in the analysis later on.

5. Analysis

On the basis of the 'tussentaal'-characteristics outlined in the previous section, 80 linguistic variables are selected for the analysis, which are operationalised as the frequency count of one particular form. These do not only contain the substandard forms but also their corresponding counterparts in Belgian standard Dutch. For the analysis at hand, these 80 linguistic variables will be the statistical objects.

The variables for the analysis will be the 11 CGN-subcorpora. As a consequence, the dataset to be analysed is a 80x11-matrix of linguistic objects by register variables, which geometrically amounts to a data-cloud of 80 objects in an 11-dimensional (register) space.

In order to account for the register structure within this data-cloud, the analysis will try to uncover some underlying factors that optimally fit the observed variation (thus constructing some sort of 'colloquialism measure'). The technique by which this will be done is the Principal Components Analysis.

Three preliminary transformations are performed on the data-matrix. The first one is the standardisation of the 11 register-variables, i.e. setting both their mean to zero and their variance to one. This is necessary because the 11 sub-corpora are not of equal size, which entails that the frequency counts in one sub-corpus differ from those of another sub-corpus, without this difference, however, being attributable to register variation but merely to sample size. Second, the bare frequency counts are log-transformed. The reason here is to correct for the alleged skewness of word frequencies. The last correction consists in weighting the 80 linguistic objects by their 'surprise-value' log(1/p), the logarithm of the inverse of the relative frequency. This correction is reasonable because some words – like articles, for example – are structurally more frequent than others, these differences again being totally unrelated to register variation. The surprise-value, then, gives the infrequent items a high weight, while a low weight to the more frequent items. This standardised, log-transformed, weighted data-matrix will be the input for the analysis.

The first step in the PCA consists in the computation of the scree-plot, which displays how much of the total variance is explained by each underlying factor (or 'Principal Component'). The scree-plot shown below (Figure 1) points out that the first principal component explains the bulk of all the variance, and that there is not much accumulation in explained variance from the second principal component onwards:

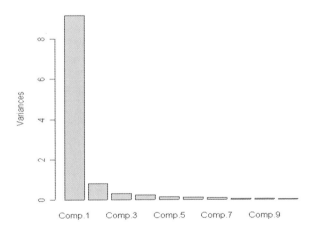

Figure 1: Scree-plot

Consequentially, a structure with the first two principal components can be retained to fit the data.

The next step in the PCA is the computation of the loadings, which are the correlations between the 11 variables on the one hand and the two principal components on the other. Correspondingly, figure 2 shows which of the 11 variables are themselves correlated, and therefore tend to cluster into one register.

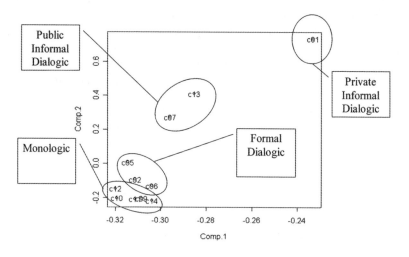

Figure 2: Loadings

Apart from some slight curvature, the loadings display an almost linear trend among the correlations from variables that are negatively correlated with both principal components (bottom-left corner of the plot) to variables that are proportionally more positively correlated with the principal components (top-right corner). As a consequence, the register clusters themselves can be interpreted along these same lines. At the top-right corner of the plot, then, the first subcorpus of the face-to-face conversations (c01) forms a singleton register. More offset, subcorpus 07 of the classroom lectures clusters with subcorpus 13 of the speeches. The difference between this cluster and the face-to-face conversations is that the latter typically consists of two people talking to each other, and hence constitutes a somewhat private type of speech situation. The former cluster, on the other hand, involves speech situations in front of a full and live audience and are therefore more public. A third register is formed by all other subcorpora at the left-hand bottom of the plot. As this cluster contains types of speech situations such as political debates (c06), and/or newsreels (c11), the – admittedly tentative – interpretation is that these subcorpora reflect formal types of speech situations, whereas the previous two clusters are more informal. After a more thorough inspection of this third cluster, however, a more finegrained structure can be discerned. The three subcorpora 02, 05, and 06 are all at a clear distance from subcorpus 09, 10, 11, 12, and 14, which are in turn completely at the corner of the plot. Aside from subcorpus 13 whose hybrid nature remains unclear for the moment and can therefore only be taken as a plain fact, these are the more monologic speech situations, while the subcorpora in the other three clusters are more dialogic. In conclusion, it can be assumed that there are four registers to be distinguished in Belgian Dutch, which can be discriminated along the oppositions of private-public, informal-formal, and dialogic-monologic; the poles of private, informal, and dialogic furthermore being proportionally more positively correlated with both principal components than their respective counterpoles.

The last step in the PCA is the computation of the scores for the 80 linguistic objects on the space spanned by the two principal components. The first principal component (Figure 3) displays the following structure:

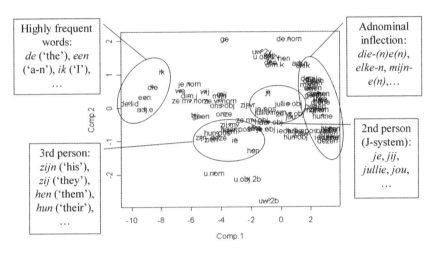

Figure 3: Principal Component 1

On the left-hand side of the plot there is a clearly separate cluster containing articles, the pronoun *I* and so on; in other words, elements that are highly frequent and very common. Somewhat more to the right, there is a cluster with all the third person pronouns. These are still common but slightly less so than the articles. Even more to the right, there is a cluster with 2nd person pronouns, and more particularly those belonging to the J-system. As has already been mentioned, this is an exogenic and marked system of address for Belgian Dutch, and is therefore not so common in usage. Finally, on the right-hand side of the plot, where the scores become positive, there is the highly dense cluster of the adnominal elements from the 'tussentaal'. Again, these elements are marked and restricted in usage, only this time not because they would be exogenic – on the contrary, they are endogenic – but because they are substandard. Taking into consideration, then, the inherent ambiguity in the use of the concept of 'markedness' – the J-pronouns are marked because they are exogenic, while the adnominal elements are marked because they are substandard – the first principal component can be concluded to form a range from elements that are neutral and common to all registers to elements that are restricted to the more colloquial registers (where the 'tussentaal' is used).

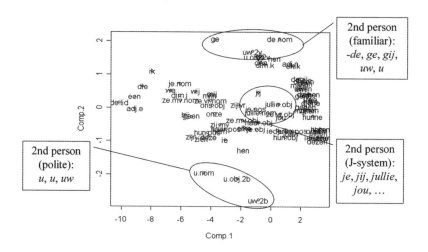

Figure 4: Principal Component 2

Although the second principal component accounts for much less variance (according to the scree-plot), it exhibits some interesting structural differences concerning the pronouns of address that are not visible on the first principal component alone. At the negatively scored bottom of figure 4, for instance, the 2nd person U-pronouns for polite speech are clustered separately from all other variables. Next, the cluster of the J-system has already been pointed out in the middle of the plot. Located at the positively scored top of the plot, finally, are the pronouns of the G-system, which has been stated as the unmarked system of familiar address for Belgian Dutch. The second principal component, then, ranges from unmarked forms for familiar speech (of the 'tussentaal') over marked ones to forms for polite speech. As a consequence, it will become clear now why a geometrical space of two dimensions is retained, and not just of one. As has been pointed out, the bulk of the register variation can be accomodated for by a range from neutral/common to marked/restricted. On top of that stylistic axis, however, a range of conversational variation between familiar and polite speech can be identified that is not reducible to the stylistic first axis. The interpretation of the two register dimensions – and the location of the 'tussentaal'-characteristics on it (at the top-right corner) – concludes the analysis of the scores.

6. Conclusion

By means of Principal Components Analysis, two register dimensions can be distinguished that together define four registers for Belgian Dutch. The four registers are to be discriminated along the oppositions private-public, informal-formal, and dialogic-monologic speech, with the poles of private, informal, and dialogic being proportionally more positively correlated with the two principal components than their respective opposite poles (public, formal, and monologic). The scores of the linguistic objects on the two principal components reveal the 'tussentaal'-characteristics to be located at the top-right corner of the space, and hence by association to be typically used in speech situations that are private, informal, and/or dialogic. The horizontal first principal component that accounts for the bulk of the register variation can be interpreted as a stylistic range from words common to all speech situations (left) to words that are restricted to the colloquial ones only (right). On top of that, the vertical second principal component accomodates for the conversational range from polite speech (bottom) to familiar speech (top). As neither type of variation is reducible to the other, it must be concluded that the 'tussentaal'-characteristics do not occur with systematically equal probability over various registers. There are indications, in sum, that the 'tussentaal' is not a uniform language variety.

References

Geeraerts, Dirk. 2001. Everyday language in the media: The case of Belgian Dutch soap series. In Matthias Kammerer, Klaus-Peter Konerding, Andrea Lehr, Angelika Storrer, Caja Thimm and Werner Wolski (eds.), *Sprache im Alltag. Beiträge zu neuen Perspektiven in der Linguistik. Herbert Ernst Wiegand zum 65. Geburtstag gewidmet.* Berlin and New York: de Gruyter, 281–291.

Geeraerts, Dirk, Stefan Grondelaers and Dirk Speelman. 1999. *Convergentie en divergentie in de Nederlandse woordenschat.* Amsterdam: Meertens Instituut.

Grondelaers, Stefan, Hilde Van Aken, Dirk Speelman and Dirk Geeraerts. 2001. Inhoudswoorden en preposities als standaardiseringsindicatoren. De diachrone en synchrone status van het Belgische Nederlands. *Nederlandse Taalkunde* 6: 179–202.

Jaspaert, Koen. 1986. *Statuut en structuur van standaardtalig Vlaanderen.* Ph.D. dissertation. Leuven: UP.

Vandekerckhove, Reinhild. 2004. Waar zijn je, jij en jou(w) gebleven? Pronominale aanspreekvormen in het gesproken Nederlands van Vlamingen. In Johan de Caluwe, Georges de Schutter, Magda Devos and Jacques van Keymeulen (eds.), *Taeldeman, man van taal, schatbewaarder van de taal.* Gent: Vakgroep Nederlandse Taalkunde-Academia Press, 981–993.

Van de Velde, Hans. 1996. *Variatie en verandering in het gesproken Standaard-Nederlands (1935–1993).* Ph.D. dissertation. Nijmegen: UP.

Van Gijsel, Sofie. 2001. *Taalgebruik in reclame: Een variationele en functionele analyse.* Leuven: unpubl. M.A. thesis.

REINHILD VANDEKERCKHOVE (ANTWERPEN)

'Tussentaal' as a source of change from below in Belgian Dutch. A case study of substandardization processes in the chat language of Flemish teenagers

1. Introduction

In the past decades, quite a lot of research has been inspired by the question whether Belgian Dutch is converging towards Netherlandic Dutch, which constitutes the official standard language norm, or whether diverging tendencies are prevalent. From halfway of the 20th century onwards, Dutch linguists were convinced that Flanders would need only a few more decades to catch up its historical retardation in the standardisation process, and that it would do so by adopting the northern, Netherlandic Dutch, standard language. Judging from present-day written language and public formal speech, we can conclude that the prediction was fulfilled (Goossens 2000: 4). But present-day colloquial speech reveals opposite tendencies which increasingly seem to lead to the development of a Flemish alternative for the Netherlandic Dutch norm, which has been promoted in Flanders for many decades now. Flemings increasingly use a supraregional language variety with strong Brabantic influence. In academic publications on the subject, this variant now is generally called *tussentaal*, i.e. 'interlanguage' or 'intermediate language variety' because, from a structural perspective, it is situated in between the standard language and the Brabantic dialects of northern Belgium.[1] So the central Brabantic area appears to be 'trend-setting'. The Brabantic area comprises the province of Flemish-Brabant (capital: Leuven) and the province of Antwerp (capital: Antwerp).

---

[1]   Also cf. the contribution by Plevoets, Speelman and Geeraerts in this volume.

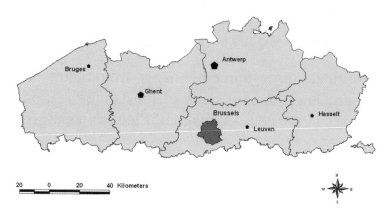

Map 1: Dutch-speaking northern Belgium (=Flanders) with its five provinces.

In order to uncover and analyse these 'changes from below', we need alternative corpora documenting present-day colloquial speech. This paper reports on the analysis of chat language produced by Flemish teenagers. This kind of netspeak combines a high level of informality with the need of supraregional language use, since the participants come from different regions in Flanders. These young chatters share a particular repertoire that has a lot of typical netspeak characteristics. Most of these netspeak characteristics can be explained in terms of the tension between using a written medium and producing colloquial speech: they use a lot of elliptic sentences and all kinds of acronyms, they insert smileys or emoticons, they break with spelling norms in many respects and hardly use punctuation. But these appear to be universal chat language characteristics (cf. Crystal 2001), which will not be focused on in this paper. Instead, we want to analyse to what extent this Flemish chat language is symptomatic of the present state of (or the present day changes in) colloquial speech in Flanders, notwithstanding its typical netspeak characteristics and also its typical teenage talk characteristics, which might and probably will be subject to age grading.

The linguistic features that will be dealt with are two morpho-syntactic variables, the variants of which are markers of Belgian Dutch versus Netherlandic Dutch. Research on the relation between Belgian Dutch and Netherlandic Dutch has mainly dealt with lexical or phonological variables. By focusing on morpho-syntactic variables and by using a relatively unexplored type of corpus, for Flanders at least, we might be able to add a new dimension to the discussion.

2. The corpora

The chat-corpus analysed for the purpose of this paper consists of some 33,500 words.[2] The corpus was copied from the website 'place to be' (www.place.to.be). All of the utterances were produced within a chatroom that is aimed at teenagers aged 11 to 16. The data were collected on ten different days in October 2003 and between February and July 2005. Several utterances clearly show that participants come from all over northern Belgium. The exact number of participants cannot be retrieved: all of the participants use a nickname, but we cannot be sure that every participant uses only one single nickname, although this is probably the most common practice. The corpus contains 416 different nicknames. The actual number of chatters whose utterances have been registered could be lower than 416, but it might approximate that number.

For both variables we did parallel research on the Spoken Dutch Corpus (SDC), which is a large digital database of contemporary Standard Dutch as spoken by adults in the Netherlands and Flanders at the beginning of the 21st century.[3] The findings of the chat language research will be compared with the findings of the research on the SDC. The corpus contains several text types. For the present study only the so-called spontaneous face-to-face conversations from the Flemish part of the corpus were used, more particularly the available orthographic transcriptions of those conversations which were conducted by two or three informants. The corpus' choice of informants aims at a well-balanced geographical representation of the different dialect groups. For northern Belgium, the four main dialect regions are represented (cf. map 1), i.e. West-Flanders (capital: Bruges), East-Flanders (capital: Ghent), Limburg (capital: Hasselt), and, finally, the Brabantic area, which comprises the provinces of Flemish-Brabant (capital: Leuven) and Antwerp (capital: Antwerp). We analysed data of 71 informants, 35 men and 36 women, nearly all of

---

[2] One third of the corpus was collected by Annelies Van Rooy who has written an MA thesis (unpublished) on the chat language of Flemish teenagers (Van Rooy 2004): *Chattaal van Vlaamse jongeren. Een kwantitatieve studie naar de impact van jongerentaal, netspeak en tussentaal op de chattaal van Vlaamse jongeren.* University of Antwerp, Department of Linguistics), cf. Vandekerckhove and Van Rooy (2005). The rest of the corpus was collected by Reinhild Vandekerckhove.

[3] Information on the Spoken Dutch Corpus can be found on: http://lands.let.kun.nl/ cgn/home.htm. The data presented here were extracted from the sixth release of the Spoken Dutch Corpus.

them highly-educated.[4] Two age groups were distinguished: the informants of the youngest group were born between 1967 and 1982. The informants of the older generation were born between 1938 and 1956. In this paper we focus on the group of younger adults. 48 hours of speech were extracted.

Nearly all of the informants were conversing with a friend or an acquaintance for three hours, though not continuously, at home, without a researcher being present. Consequently, the situation can be characterized as informal, in spite of the presence of a small digital recorder. The informants were free to choose the topic of their conversation. Highly relevant for the interpretation of the results, however, is the fact that all of the informants were asked to speak Standard Dutch.

3. The diminutive suffix

The first morphological variable that this paper will focus on is the realisation of the diminutive suffix. For Flemish speakers of Dutch, two diminutive suffixes are available: /jə/ and /kə/. Both of them have a number of allomorphs, depending on the phonetic context in which they are used:

/jə/: [jə], [ətjə], [pjə], [tjə]: e.g.: resp. *knoopje* ('small button'), *mannetje* ('small man'), *boompje* ('small tree'), *boontje* ('small bean')

/kə/: [kə], [əkə], [skə]: e.g.: resp. *knoopke* ('small button'), *manneke* ('small man'), *bankske* ('small bench')

The *-ke*-suffix is a typical exponent of colloquial Belgian Dutch, the *-je*-suffix is the Standard and Netherlandic Dutch realization:

Standard Dutch	Colloquial Belgian Dutch
-je	*-ke*: in most phonetic contexts
	-je: in a limited number of phonetic contexts

Table 1: Diminutive Suffixes in two Dutch varieties

---

[4] 67 of the 71 informants have a high level of education, 4 informants have a middle-high level of education. The latter group contains two informants from the young Brabant generation and two informants from the older Brabant generation. None of the informants has a low level of education.

The -*ke*-suffix is strongly represented both in the dialects of Dutch speaking Belgium and in supraregional colloquial Dutch in Belgium. However, its counterpart -*je* does not mark Netherlandic Dutch exclusively. In most dialects of Dutch-speaking Belgium both -*je* and -*ke* are present. The distribution of these morphemes and their allomorphs is determined by the phonetic context. In the northern and western part of West-Flanders, the -*je*-suffix is used in all phonetic contexts. The other extreme can be found in the southern part of the Brabantic area, where the -*ke*-suffix is used in all phonetic contexts[5]. As such, the suffix -*ke* is a typical Brabantic realization, although in large parts of the Brabantic area the -*je*-suffix is present as well, though only in a very limited number of phonetic contexts; words ending in /n/ preceded by a long vowel, a diphthong or a schwa nearly everywhere require the diminutive suffix -*je*: e.g.: *tuin-tje* ('small garden'), *teen-tje* ('small toe'). The same is true for words ending in /t/ preceded by a long vowel or a consonant, e.g. *straat-je* ('small street'), *krant-je* ('small newspaper'). In all other contexts, the Brabantic dialects require -*ke*. This also holds true for the supraregional colloquial language which is used in the Brabantic area and beyond the borders of that area. In fact, this wide distribution of the suffix -*ke* and limited distribution of the suffix -*je* marks the so-called 'intermediate variety', which is increasingly used as a kind of general Belgian Dutch (Flemish) colloquial variety (e.g. in TV programmes focusing on entertainment[6]). Moreover, it implies a clear morphological distinction between the Belgian Dutch colloquial variety and Standard Dutch. The latter is marked by an exclusive use of the -*je*-suffix in all phonetic contexts.

Consequently, one can ask oneself which diminutive suffixes are used by Flemings nowadays and, more particularly, by Flemings who intend to speak a supraregional variety. When analysing the realisation of the diminutive suffix by the Flemish teenagers, we eliminated those words in which suffixing -*ke* is blocked because of the phonetic context. We found only two exceptions with the suffix -*ke* in one of the so-called blocking contexts. Generally speaking, -*je* appeared to be categorical in the speech of these teenagers in the same contexts as the ones which can be derived from public use of the Belgian colloquial variety; in those contexts -*ke* hardly seemed to be an option. In all other

---

[5]   The area includes large parts of Flemish-Brabant and the southern edge of the province of Antwerp. The city of Leuven constitutes the centre of this exclusive -*ke*-area. The city of Brussels and most of its suburbs have the 'mixed system' demanding either -*ke* or -*je* depending on the phonetic context (cf. Pée 1936/1938, De Vriendt 2000).

[6]   Some 40 MA-students from the department of linguistics of the University of Antwerp analysed the realisation of a number of linguistic variables in popular Flemish TV programmes broadcast in the first half of 2005. The data for the diminutive suffix generally confirm this complementary distribution of the *je*- and the *ke*-suffix. Cf. also Geeraerts et al. (2000).

contexts, *-ke* and *-je* are real variants and in those cases the question whether *-ke* or *-je* is used is a most pertinent one.

As will be demonstrated, the quantitative analysis of the relative frequency of both suffixes in the speech of the Flemish teenagers needs to be supplemented by a qualitative analysis of the functional distribution of both diminutives.

Figure 1 presents some quantitative data:

(a)   teenage chat: chat language of Flemish teenagers
      n = 368 (*-ke*: 70.65%, *-je*: 29.34%)
(b)   young adults: spontaneous speech of young adults (<Spoken Dutch Corpus)
      n = 859 (*-ke*: 44.47%, *-je*: 55.52%)
(c)   young Brabantic adults: spontaneous speech of young Brabantic adults
      (<Spoken Dutch Corpus)
      n = 332 (*-ke*: 60.84%, *-je*: 39.15%)

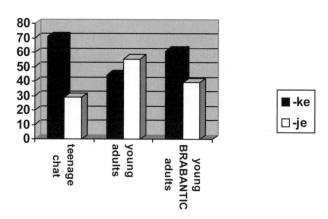

Figure 1: Diminutive suffix in colloquial speech in Flanders

As can be deduced from figure 1, the *-ke*-suffixes by far outnumber the *-je*-suffixes in the chat language of the Flemish teenagers: they are used more than twice as much (1a).

By way of comparison, some figures on the relative frequency of both suffixes in the spontaneous speech of the young adults from the SDC are added (1b). However, we should be very careful when comparing these data with those of the chatters, not only because we are comparing spontaneous speech with chat language, but also because the informants for the SDC were asked to speak standard Dutch, whereas the chatters were of course free to use whichever variety they liked. Of course the informants of the SDC were free to interpret the notion of Standard Dutch any way they liked, and there was no one present to correct them or to comment on their performance, but they knew they were supposed to speak Standard Dutch.

Even in the Flemish part of the SDC the *-ke*-suffixes are well represented, but the *-je*-suffixes clearly outnumber them. However, it must be added that there are considerable regional differences. In the speech of the Brabantic informants the *-ke*-suffixes appear to be dominant, whereas in the speech of the young West-Flemish informants, for example, the *-je*-suffix has a relative frequency score of 83%.

The suffix *-ke* is more prominent in the colloquial speech of the young Brabantic adults than the suffix *-je* (1b). Moreover, these young adults show a higher preference for the *-ke*-suffix than the Brabantic adults from the older generation. In the speech of the latter group, the *-je*-suffix appears to be dominant, with a frequency score of 62% (cf. Vandekerckhove 2005). In other words, the indigenous suffix *-ke* is used more frequently by the younger generation than by the older generation in the trendsetting Brabantic area.

All these quantitative data are highly significant in their own right. They illustrate the strong position of the *-ke* suffix in present day supraregional colloquial speech in Flanders. In the chat language of the Flemish teenagers, the *-ke-* suffix is by far the dominant form (even if the categorical *-je*-suffixes are included in the analysis).

However, a closer analysis of the distribution of *-ke* and *-je* suffixes in the speech of the young chatters reveals a number of interesting patterns, which give additional information on the exact position of both suffixes in present day colloquial speech. When analysing the 108 tokens with *je*-suffixing in contexts in which *-je* is optional and not categorical (taking in account the phonetic context), we come across many 'stereotypical' or 'reproductive' diminutives. In the category of 'stereotypical' or 'reproductive' diminutives, we include those diminutives that (a) are fixed forms in the standard language, (b) have a high frequency in the standard language, that (c) are typically linked to standard language contexts, and (d) are quotations. There is some overlap between these four subcategories. Subcategory (a) includes words that always require the diminutive suffix in the standard language and that are marked by a narrowing down of meaning. This implies that the meaning of the diminutive is not just small x, where x stands for the meaning of the base. An example is *vluggertje* ('quickie'). *Vluggertje* is derived from *vlug* ('quick'), but the noun **vlugger* does not exist in Dutch. In subcategory (b) we find a word like *meisje* ('girl'), which has a high frequency in the corpus. **Meis* does not exist in Dutch, but – unlike *vluggertje* – *meisje* has an equivalent with *-ke* in colloquial Belgian Dutch: *meiske* (also: *maske*). *Meisje* represents 36.11% of the diminutive tokens with *-je*-suffix, whereas *meiske* and *maske* represent only 18.07% of the diminutive tokens with *-ke*-suffix. Subcategory (c) includes a number of words that are typically used in standard language contexts and its diminutives can often be found in children's stories or child (and parental) talk, for instance; e.g: *bengeltje* ('little rascal'), which does not alternate with *bengelke* in Belgian Dutch because *bengel* is typical of written language and hardly used in colloquial speech. *Beertje* ('small bear') and *prinsesje* ('little princess') belong to *child-contexts* as well. Diminutives with *je*-suffixing that appear within quotations of songs or, in one case, in the name of a rock group are included in subcategory (d), e.g. the atypical rock group named *Heideroosjes* (literally: 'heath flowers').

Obviously, it is not always easy to delineate the category of stereotypical or reproductive diminutives in an objective way. But even when this category is interpreted narrowly, at least half of the non-categorical *-je*-diminutives (63/108 = 58.33%) might be characterised as stereotypical or reproductive diminutives. This finding calls for a nuanced interpretation of the productivity of the standard Dutch *-je* suffix in the speech of these Flemish teenagers.

The suffixing of the diminutive morpheme to English words provides further relevant information regarding the relative productivity of the *-je-* and the *-ke*-suffix. The essential characteristic of productive morphological processes is their applicability to new words. The chat language of the Flemish teenagers is interspersed with English words. To 52 of these English loans a Dutch diminutive morpheme is added. The relative representation of the *-ke-* and the *-je-* suffixes is striking: *-je* is suffixed to only 3 of the 52 loans, *-ke* to all the rest. Some examples from the first category are: *loverke, babeke, ghostyke, happyke, duckske, heykes, girlke, angelke,* and *womenke*. *Puppiefaceje, queentje,* and *hawkje* are the three exceptions with *je*-suffixing.

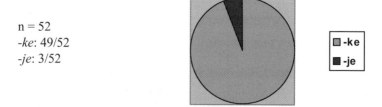

n = 52
-ke: 49/52
-je: 3/52

□ **-ke**
■ **-je**

Figure 2: Diminutive suffix added to English loans in the chat language of Flemish teenagers.

Womenke is a striking example: the spelling of the English base suggests that this is a plural noun, but the context and the absence of plural *-s* added to the suffix make clear that it is intended to be singular. Most interesting, however, is that in this phonetic context (schwa + *n*) Flemish colloquial speech normally demands the suffix *-je* (cf.: **lakenke* as opposed to *lakentje* ('small sheet')). In other words, in this case the use of the diminutive suffix *-ke* is extended to a phonetic context in which it even cannot be used in colloquial Flemish Dutch.

Both the observations on the English loan words and the finding that a majority of the diminutives with the -*je*-suffixing can be characterised as stereotypical or reproductive diminutives imply that the diminutive suffix -*ke* is far more productive in the speech of the young Flemish teenagers than the suffix -*je*. And yet, only the diminutive suffix -*je* is considered to be standard language in Flanders; suffixing by -*je* is what these teenagers learn in school, what they read in the newspapers and what they hear in the media (especially in formal speech). But all this hardly affects the colloquial speech of young Flemings. On the contrary, in supraregional colloquial speech, the suffix -*ke* seems to be more productive than ever.

4. The single pronouns of address

The second variable that is illustrative of present day language use in Flanders is the realisation of the personal pronoun of the 2nd person singular. Our analysis illustrates how a qualitative analysis of, in this case, the pragmatic function of the particular variants within the chat language of the Flemish teenagers reinforces the quantitative analysis of the relative frequency of the variants.

For the pronominal paradigm of the 2nd person singular, there was and is an essential difference between indigenous colloquial Belgian Dutch and Netherlandic-based Standard Dutch. Apart from some formal differences, there is also a structural difference. Unlike the Standard Dutch paradigm, the Belgian Dutch paradigm contains no contrast between polite and informal forms. It is neutral with respect to semantic power and solidarity. Neither the presence or absence of hierarchical relations nor the presence or absence of solidarity has repercussions for the choice of the pronoun because there is no distinction between V-pronouns and T-pronouns (cf. Brown and Gilman 1964).

Table 2 offers a survey of the pronouns in both varieties. In the cells containing two pronouns, the first one is the weak (unaccented) variant (e.g. *je*), while the second one is the strong (accented) variant (e.g. *jij*).

	Subject	Object	Possessive
Standard Dutch informal	*je / jij*	*je / jou*	*je / jouw*
Standard Dutch formal/polite	*u*	*u*	*uw*
(Colloquial) Belgian Dutch informal + formal	*ge / gij*	*u*	*uw*

Table 2: Pronouns of address in two Dutch varieties

Example: (1) *You sleep a lot* (subject)
                (a) Informal Standard Dutch: *je slaapt veel*
                (b) Formal Standard Dutch: *u slaapt veel.*
                (c) Informal + formal (colloquial) Belgian Dutch: *ge slaapt veel*

The object and possessive paradigms are beyond the scope of this paper.[7] Only the subject variants will be focussed on. In informal colloquial speech, two variants are available for the Flemish speaker of Dutch: informality and familiarity can either be expressed by the standard Dutch pronouns *je* and *jij* or by the indigenous (and essentially Brabantic) pronouns *ge* and *gij*. The pronominal paradigm for the 2nd person singular used in, for instance, written language, in education, in the media (except for some tv programs focusing on entertainment) is the northern standard Dutch paradigm. 25 years ago two Dutch linguists, Deprez and Geerts, stated: "the problem is that JE presupposes familiarity and solidarity, whereas for most Flemings only GE has those connotations" (Deprez and Geerts 1977: 371). However, in those days most Dutch linguists supposed that it would not take long before the northern pronoun *je* and its variants would be integrated into the colloquial speech of Flemings. They assumed Flemings would gradually get familiar with the pronoun and this growing familiarity would be reflected in an increasing use of *je*. There were reasons to assume this was the most probable scenario. The 1960s and 1970s were marked by intensive campaigns both in education and in the media to make Flemings familiar with the northern Dutch standard language. The pronoun *je* was systematically propagated in secondary schools from 1960 onwards.

The central question within the scope of this paper is to what extent the Netherlandic Dutch pronouns *je* and *jij* have been integrated in colloquial Belgian Dutch, more than four decades after they entered the public scene in Flanders. The chat data will immediately be compared with the data from the SDC (figure 3).

(a)   teenage chat: chat language of Flemish teenagers
       n = 418 (*ge/gij* (+ clitical *-de/-te*): 82.29% / *je/jij*: 17.70%)
(b)   young adults: spontaneous speech of young adults (<Spoken Dutch Corpus)
       n = 4601 (*ge/gij*: 60.83% / *je/jij*: 39.16%)

---

[7]   They are discussed in Vandekerckhove (2005), which does not deal with chat language but presents an analysis of data from the Spoken Dutch Corpus.

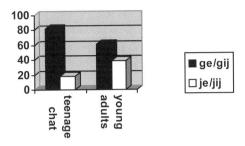

Figure 3: The subject pronoun 2nd person singular in colloquial speech in Flanders

Both the chat corpus and the SDC illustrate the dominance of indigenous *ge* and *gij* in Belgian colloquial Dutch, but once again the chatting teenagers show a higher preference for the indigenous forms than the young adults participating in the SDC-project. Another point of similarity between the data for the pronouns of address and the diminutive forms lies in the fact that the speakers from the Brabantic area in the SDC manifest a stronger preference for the indigenous forms than those from other areas. Moreover, the Belgian Dutch pronoun *ge* is even better represented in the speech of the younger Brabantic informants of the SDC than it is in the speech of older informants from the same region (with frequency scores of 85% and 64% respectively).

As far as the distribution of the pronoun is concerned, it is equally striking that the pronoun 'je' in subject function is far more frequent in enclitic position than in proclitic position. This implies that example (a) is less likely to occur in the corpus than examples (b) or (c):

(a) *Je komt* ('you come')
(b) *Kom je* ('Do you come')
(c) *Ik hoop dat je komt* ('I hope that you come')

The relative presence of *je* in enclitic position amounts to 21.40%, in proclitic position to 11.80%. The chat corpus contains 74 *je*-tokens, 55 of them (= 74.32%) are used in enclitic position.

Two factors may account for this. First, in terms of the dialect geography of northern Belgium, the *je*-pronoun is better represented in enclitic position than in proclitic position in the west of Flanders (cf. Devos 1986). Even more relevant may be the fact that the *je*-pronoun is less conspicuous in enclitic position. This aspect cannot be elaborated within the limits of the present article but deserves close attention in future research.

Highly symptomatic of the position of the pronominal variants is their pragmatic function within the chat language of the Flemish teenagers. This will be illustrated by focussing on the 19 tokens of *je/jij* which are used in proclitic position. The term 'proclitic' should not be interpreted in the narrow sense of pronouns functioning as real clitics. The category of proclitic pronouns includes all pronouns that do not follow a verb (cf. example (b) above) or a subordinate conjunction (cf. example (c)), but which occur in sentences of type (a).

The 19 *je*-tokens in proclitic position form a small minority in comparison with the 142 *ge*-tokens in proclitic position. The analysis of the utterances in which proclitic *je* is used reveals one common feature: in 14 of the 19 cases, the use of *je* or *jij* seems to function as a marker or an index. The use of *je* conveys an intention from the side of the speaker and is informative and meaningful to the receiver. If speakers switch from the pronoun *ge*, which they generally use in proclitic position, to the pronoun *je*, this can be characterized as a 'metaphorical switch' because the speakers "build on their own and their audience's abstract understanding of situational norms to communicate metaphoric information about how they intend their words to be understood" (Gumperz 1982: 61). The metaphorical switch allows the speakers to "tap into the contextualised meaning of a code in order to convey an oblique message" (Wei 2003: 141). Some examples may illustrate this:

(1)   *jij doe dat ni meer e* ('you must not do that again')
(2)   *je moet openstaan e voor dinge* ('you have to open your mind to things')
(3)   *je zijt de oud* (*de* = spelling mistake: *te*) ('you are too old (to participate in this chatroom)')
(4)   *je komt er niet meer in hoor* ('you must not enter (this chatroom) again')
(5)   *je moet hier weg* ('you have to go away')
(6)   *jij probeert mijn overstemming te bemiddelen en je kan er niks van* ('you try to act as an arbitrator but you do not make much of it')

In all these utterances from the chat corpus, the speaker admonishes or reprimands the addressee. He sends a kind of warning to the addressee. The use of the pronouns *je* and *jij* is indexical of the authoritative role the speaker has taken. In (3) and (4), e.g., the speakers are addressing another chatter whom they think to be older than 16 and, in other words, too old for their chatroom, which is meant for teenagers aged 11 to 16. They want the man to leave their chatroom. (2) is an ironic remark to some extent, but it has the same authoritative tone. (6) is somewhat nonsensical because of the word *overstemming*, which could be a perfect Dutch word, but to which a relevant meaning cannot be assigned within this context. It resembles the words *stemming* ('mood'), which would be more appropriate within this context because the speaker is in a very bad temper. He is quarreling with one of his fellow chatters, and he is irritated by the pedantic attitude of the one whom he is addressing. (4), (5), and (6) also are interesting because they are spelt according to the Dutch spelling norms. This is quite exceptional within this chat corpus. It is really hard to find utterances which conform to the spellings norms from beginning to end; as such these utterances are also marked with regard to standard orthography.

These observations are highly similar to observations made by Jürgen Jaspers (2004) on linguistic sabotage by Maroccan school boys in a secondary school in Antwerp. Jaspers' research shows that these boys have several linguistic repertoires at their disposal, one of which is Standard Dutch, and that they handle these repertoires very skilfully and manipulate them intentionally. In switching to Standard Dutch, these boys often evoke a school setting and imitate a teacher-pupil relationship. And this is exactly what seems to happen within the chatroom too. Finally, it is also worth mentioning that the Standard Dutch pronouns *je* and *jij* are also used in fixed formulas; e.g. *je moet eerst twaalf werken doen* (*you have to do twelve labors first*, cf. the myth of Hercules). These kind of *reproductive sentences* resemble the reproductive diminutives which were dealt with in section 3.

In view of the very limited number of tokens of proclitic *je*, we should be very careful when interpreting these data. Yet, we can discern some clear patterns. It cannot be denied that the Standard Dutch pronouns *je* and *jij* belong to the linguistic repertoires of the young chatters, but their use is highly restricted and marked in proclitic position. In Standard Dutch *je* and *jij* are pronouns indicating informality, familiarity, and solidarity. In the colloquial speech of the Flemish teenagers, the use of these pronouns signals exactly the opposite: it is indicative of distancing and absence of solidarity. The use of *ge* and *gij*, on the contrary, implies group membership.

A priority for future research is the extension of this type of qualitative analysis to the SDC, in order to substantiate the present findings.

5. Conclusion

The northern standard Dutch variants which these young Flemings learn at school and see and hear in all kinds of media on a daily basis may belong to their linguistic repertoire, but they are not integrated into their colloquial in-group language. These variants even seem to be excluded from their in-group 'speech' intentionally. The use of the word 'speech' is somewhat ambiguous here, as we are dealing with a written medium. It is worth considering that Flemings are used to write Standard Dutch but not to write 'interlanguage'. It is clear that electronic chatting is a genre in itself, "a form of communication which relies on characteristics belonging to both sides of the speech/writing divide" (Crystal 2001: 28). However, the obvious ease with which these teenagers use a non-standard language variety in a *public written* medium with a *wide communicative reach* may well be symptomatic of an autonomous Flemish standardisation process taking place right now. This implies that Dutch is increasingly becoming a 'pluricentric' language with two centres of standardization (cf. Clyne 1992), one of them being the Brabantic area in northern Belgium. Additional data should be analysed, but the quantitative data from the Spoken Dutch Corpus show our findings cannot simply be reduced to peculiarities of the electronic medium or to characteristics of teenage talk.

References

Brown, Roger and Albert Gilman. 1964. Pronouns of Power and Solidarity. In Thomas A. Sebeok (ed.), *Style in Language*. Cambridge and Massachusetts: M.I.T. Press, 253–276.

Clyne, Michael. 1992. Pluricentric Languages – Introduction. In Michael Clyne (ed.), *Pluricentric Languages. Differing Norms in Different Nations*. Berlin and New York: Mouton de Gruyter, 1–9.

Crystal, David. 2001. *Language and the Internet*. Cambridge: Cambridge University Press.

Deprez, Kas and Guido Geerts. 1977. *Lexikale en pronominale standaardizatie. Een onderzoek van de ontwikkeling van het Algemeen Nederlands in West-Vlaanderen*. Antwerpen: University of Antwerp.

Devos, Magda. 1986. Het persoonlijk voornaamwoord 2^e pers. enk. in het Westvlaams: geografie en historiek. In: Devos, Magda and Johan Taeldeman (eds.), *Vruchten van z'n akker (Festschrift V.F. Vanacker)*. Gent: University of Ghent, 167–189.

De Vriendt, Sera. 2000. Diminutieven in het Brussels. In: *Taal en Tongval* 52: 293–307.

Geeraerts, Dirk and An Penne and Veerle Vanswegenoven. 2000. *Thuis*-taal en *Familie*-taal: taalgebruik in Vlaamse soaps. In: Steven Gillis et al. (eds.), *Met taal om de tuin geleid. Opstellen voor Georges De Schutter*. Antwerpen: University of Antwerp, 161–170.

Goossens, Jan. 1975. De ontwikkeling van het gesproken Nederlands in Vlaanderen. *Nu nog* 23: 51–62.

Goossens, Jan. 2000. De toekomst van het Nederlands in Vlaanderen. *Ons Erfdeel* 43: 2–13.

Gumperz, John J. 1982. *Discourse strategies*. Cambridge: Cambridge University Press.

Jaspers, Jürgen. 2005. *Tegenwerken, belachelijk doen. Talige sabotage van Marokkaanse jongens op een Antwerpse middelbare school. Een sociolinguïstische etnografie*. Brussels: VUBpress.

Pée, Willem. 1936/1938. *Dialectgeographie der Nederlandsche diminutiva*. Part I (1936) and Part II (1938). Tongeren: Michiels

Vandekerckhove, Reinhild and Annelies Van Rooy. 2005. De chattaal van Vlaamse jongeren. *Over Taal* 44: 30–33.

Vandekerckhove, Reinhild. 2005. Belgian Dutch versus Netherlandic Dutch: new patterns of divergence? On pronouns of address and diminutives. *Multilingua* [Journal of Cross-Cultural and Interlanguage Communication] 24: 379–397.

Wei, Jennifer M.Y. 2003. Codeswitching in Campaigning Discourse: The Case of Taiwanese President Chen Shui-bian. *Language and Linguistics* 4: 139–165.

III. Language norms and standardization
in a view form below

CHRISTA DE KLEINE (BALTIMORE)

Surinamese Dutch: The development of a unique Germanic Language variety

1. Introduction

Despite a 300-year history of the use of Dutch in Suriname, the legitimacy of Surinamese Dutch as a separate language variety was denied until well into the twentieth century (Gobardhan-Rambocus 1993). Only recently this has begun to change, with publications acknowledging its unique lexicon (van Donselaar 1989) and its distinct grammar (de Kleine 2007).

This paper examines the history of the use of Dutch in Suriname, in an effort to explain the uniqueness of the grammar of modern Surinamese Dutch (henceforth SD). It is followed by an account of future tense marking in SD, and argues that SD is a variety of Dutch unlike any other variety of European Dutch (henceforth ED), primarily as a result of the strong influence of the local English-lexifier creole language, Sranan – an influence which dates back hundreds of years.

2. The history of Surinamese Dutch

The history of the Dutch language in Suriname can be traced back as far as 1667, when the region first became a Dutch colony. Since then Dutch has functioned as the official language in Suriname. However, the language has not always been used as extensively in society as its official language status might suggest.

From its very beginning, the Dutch colony was a multilingual society, in which Dutch was never the main language used. An English-lexifier creole language, Sranan, had already begun to develop during the early British colonial period, and continued to be used among and with the slaves after the Dutch took over Suriname from the British. Furthermore, despite Dutch possession of the colony, the colonizers were by no means exclusively Dutch. There was a sizeable Jewish community among the planters, who were of Portuguese and German origin, in addition to a group of French colonists.

There was even a small group of British who remained in Suriname (although most left when the Dutch seized the colony). Indeed, evidence indicates that the Dutch were outnumbered by non-Dutch colonist during the seventeenth century (van Lier 1977: 24, Essed-Fruin 1990: 55). Thus, it is hardly surprising that these non-Dutch Europeans initially maintained the languages with which they had arrived in Suriname, and did not adopt Dutch. The use of languages other than Dutch was indeed so common, even in official correspondence, that the colony's government deemed it necessary to publish an ordinance in 1688 stating that documents in languages other than Dutch would no longer be accepted, as the frequent submission of such documents was causing the government great difficulties (Essed-Fruin 1990: 54f.).

The linguistic situation did not alter significantly during the eighteenth century. The European population continued to include a significant non-Dutch element, and as a result Dutch remained restricted to a small group of speakers. Furthermore, the European colonists, including the Dutch, were often transient, as most went to Suriname with the intention of accumulating wealth in a short time, after which they typically returned to their home countries (van Lier 1977: 29). Moreover, many colonists were single males (ibid. 31), that is, there were very few Dutch families with children, thus removing a strong motive among the Dutch-born colonists for the use of the Dutch language (Rens 1953: 90). In fact, it has been argued that the Dutch-born colonists may have used Sranan for the most part rather than Dutch (ibid.), including among themselves (Eersel 1987: 127, van Trier-Guicherit 1991: 35). Evidence lending support to the predominant use of Sranan among the colonists comes from two early teaching manuals for Dutch speakers to learn Sranan (van Dijk [1765], Weygandt 1798). These manuals include many dialogues for possible model conversations, including between colonists, suggesting that Sranan was indeed used among whites. Such a scenario would make perfect sense in light of the fact that the many of the colonists were from non-Dutch language backgrounds, and thus were in need of a lingua franca, and furthermore already had a certain command of Sranan, which they needed for use with the slave population (Rens 1953: 89).

The above could easily lead one to believe that an actively Dutch-speaking community was virtually non-existent throughout the eighteenth century in Suriname, with Dutch merely functioning as the official language of government, and, for the Dutch-born population, education and religion, and that it was Sranan that served as the main medium of social interaction among most of the white population. However, this would be an inaccurate portrayal of the use of Dutch in those days. In the course of the eighteenth century an important new social class emerged consisting of free blacks and people of mixed, that is, African and European (also known as 'Creole') racial background, whose numbers increased rapidly towards the end of the eighteenth century (van Lier 1977: 71). It has been argued that as a means of distinguishing themselves from the slave population, this non-white population deliberately chose to speak Dutch (Essed-Fruin and Gobardhan-Rambocus 1992: 10). Although no explicit information is available to support such a claim, there is indeed indirect evidence available for this hypothesis. McLeod (1994), for instance, in a very interesting in-depth study of the life of Elisabeth Samson, a free black woman, shows that a number of free blacks held prominent positions in Surinamese society, and accumulated great wealth, as Samson herself did. Archival materials establish that Samson must have had at least a reasonable command of Dutch, as she conducted her own correspond-dence with her business representatives in Holland, and even went there to clear her name in a defamation suit in a Dutch court of law. Although Elisabeth Samson's position as a wealthy free black woman was no doubt exceptional, historical documentation shows that in the eighteenth century there were in Suriname numerous people of mixed racial (Creole) background with education, high social position, and wealth (McLeod 1994: 96). It is al-most inconceivable that these people, given their education and social position in a society that used Dutch as official language, would not have had a good command of Dutch. Quite plausibly then, this group was functionally bilingual in Sranan and Dutch, and may very well have used the latter regularly in social life, if only as a way to distinguish themselves from other less fortunate non-whites. In such an admittedly somewhat speculative scenario, it is likely that a distinct and frequently-used variety of SD would have developed in the course of the eighteenth century among this Surinamese-born bilingual group. The van Dijk teaching manual mentioned before lends further support to the possibility of a distinct variety of Dutch having emerged as early as the eighteenth century, as van Dijk's Dutch translations of Sranan phrases and sentences contain many features also present in modern SD (de Kleine 1994).

The nineteenth century eventually saw a drastic change regarding the use of Dutch in Suriname. Initially, however, the linguistic situation that had characterized the eighteenth century persisted into the nineteenth. The European population continued to consist of colonists of various countries, with varying language backgrounds. Furthermore, by the beginning of the nineteenth century, free non-whites had begun to outnumber the white population of Paramaribo. This is significant information because although we cannot be fully certain that a sizeable Dutch-speaking community of locally-born, racially-mixed speakers had developed in the early eighteenth century, evidence abounds that by the beginning of the nineteenth century such a speech community had indeed been formed. We know, for instance, that from the beginning of the nineteenth century, children from well-to-do families of mixed racial background were often sent to Holland for further education, attesting to the fact that this group must have had a good command of Dutch. It is also in the beginning of the nineteenth century that a class of non-white intellectuals emerged in Suriname, who typically received at least part of their education in Holland. Some of these held prominent positions in Surinamese society, and even published in Dutch. There was, for instance, Hendrik Focke, who was the co-founder of the journal *West-Indië*. He is probably best-known for his *Neger-Engelsch woordenboek* (1855) ('Negro-English dictionary'), its excellent quality clearly illustrating his bilingual background (Voorhoeve and Lichtveld 1975: 7). In other words, an elite social class had started to form among the non-whites, who without any doubt were native speakers not only of Sranan, but also of Dutch.

Despite the relatively small size of this elite Sranan-Dutch bilingual group, it is quite probable that this newly emerged social class exerted a substantial influence on the development of Dutch in Suriname. Most importantly, members of this elite group held high social status – albeit not equivalent to the European-born upper class – often having accumulated wealth and occupying prominent positions in the colony, enabling them to exert linguistic influence as well. Crucially, quite unlike the transient white community, they resided permanently in Suriname, and hence were able to develop a stable Dutch-speaking community. This social group probably provided the backbone of the Dutch-speaking community of Suriname in the first part of the nineteenth century, and their Sranan language background is likely to have affected their use of Dutch.

Thus far education had had a limited impact on the use of Dutch in Suriname, but this began to change in the beginning of the nineteenth century when the government began regulating elementary and secondary education. The language of instruction was Dutch, which no doubt strengthened the position of Dutch in Suriname. It has to be born in mind, though, that the slave population, which constituted a majority, was not allowed to receive education until 1844, and when they were given permission, the language of instruction was Sranan. In other words, it was still only a small segment of the population that was educated in Dutch.

This situation changed dramatically in 1876, when following the abolition of slavery in 1863, the Dutch government introduced compulsory education for every child aged 7 to 12. Furthermore, as part of an assimilation effort in which Suriname was supposed to be transformed into another Dutch province, the Dutch government decided to make Dutch the only language of instruction. This meant that after two hundred years of reserving the Dutch language for a small elite, the colonial government now went to the other extreme by forcing a Dutch-only policy onto the Surinamese, actively suppressing the use of Sranan in education (Rens 1953: 134).

The effect on Dutch language use in Suriname of this change in policy must have been profound. Whereas up until then Dutch had been used by a limited number of speakers, it was now introduced into society on a large scale, particularly in the city – the countryside remained relatively unaffected. Moreover, until 1876, children receiving education in Dutch, who constituted a small minority, had typically acquired Dutch as a first language, possibly along with Sranan. By contrast, from 1876 onwards the great majority of pupils entering the school system had a language background that did not include Dutch, resulting in the massive second language learning of Dutch. This, then, is likely to have affected the structural properties of SD, introducing an increasing number of Sranan features, as well as features typically associated with second language learning.

By the twentieth century, a clear distinction had emerged between those that acquired Dutch as a first language and those that acquired it as a second language. The elite group that had formed in the nineteenth century among the Creoles in Paramaribo, while bilingual in Dutch and Sranan, continued to speak Dutch at home, and thus the children of this upper class acquired Dutch as a first language. In addition, Creoles of a middle class background, most of whom also lived in the city, emphasized Dutch language use in the home from the late nineteenth century on, as this group, too, viewed Dutch as the vehicle for social advancement now that it had become the language of instruction in schools (Eersel 1987: 131). In fact, children from middle and upper class families were often forbidden to speak Sranan, and were severely punished if caught doing so (Voorhoeve and Lichtveld 1975: 9).

By contrast, the ex-slaves, who after abolition relocated in the city, forming the lower classes among the Creoles, remained predominantly Sranan-speaking (Veer 1962: 22, Reinecke 1937: 445, Hellinga 1955: 16). They (and their des-cendants) were the ones who mostly acquired Dutch as a second language in the classroom, and so their command of Dutch was not equivalent to those speakers who acquired it as a first language. This fact created a linguistic gap between the higher and the lower social classes – a process that was exacer-bated by the school system (Hellinga 1955: 20, van Wel and Vervoorn [1974]: 12).

In addition to class differences related to the command of Dutch manifested among the Creoles, an even sharper distinction developed with respect to the city versus the countryside during this century, and along with this, a distinction between various other ethnic groups. As the ex-slave population moved to the city in increasing numbers after abolition, new immigrants of Asian decent, primarily from then-British India, and Java, replaced them in the countryside. As a result, until the middle of the twentieth century, a disproportionate number of Creoles lived in the city, while the majority of Asians, in particular the East Indians and Javanese, were found in the country-side (Hellinga 1955: 10). The latter groups lived in relative geographical as well as cultural isolation, maintaining the use of their ancestral languages, even as the language of instruction in education (Essed-Fruin and Gobardhan-Rambocus 1992: 113). In general, Asian immigrants in the countryside experienced little exposure to Dutch in the first few decades of the twentieth century. It is therefore unlikely that the ethnic groups of Asian decent affected the formation of SD in any significant way at that time.

Even though the East Indian population began to immigrate to the city after the Second World War (Brons 1952: 25), thereby gaining more exposure to Dutch, many of the overall patterns regarding the use and command of Dutch that were established in the first half of the twentieth century persisted into the second half: the discrepancy between city and countryside continued to exist (van Wel and Vervoorn [1974]: 11, Essed-Fruin 1990: 56), as did the gap between the lower classes, using predominantly Sranan and their other respective (Asian) group languages, and the higher classes, among whom Dutch is more common, the majority of whom is Sranan-Dutch bilingual. In general, for many Dutch has continued to function as a second language, prompting the Ministry of Education in 1974 to officially declare Dutch a second language in the Surinamese school system (Gobardhan-Rambocus 1989: 68).

Massive second language learning among users of Dutch, in addition to Suriname's geographical distance from the Netherlands, and its political independence since 1975, together could then easily have led to a radically different variety of Dutch. That this has not occurred, however, to the extent it might have can be explained by the continued strong influence of ED in Suriname throughout the twentieth century. Until Suriname became an autonomous state within the Dutch Kingdom in 1954, high governmental positions were typically occupied by Dutch-born residents, as were other prominent positions. More significantly, a great number of teachers in post-elementary education, particularly those who taught on the secondary level and at teachers colleges, were typically recruited in the Netherlands. This practice continued up to independence in 1975. Thus, students receiving education beyond the elementary level, which included most middle and upper class children, were primarily exposed to ED in the classroom until as recently as the 1970s.

When Suriname gained independence in 1975, Dutch presence virtually came to an end. One would expect this momentous political change to have had a significant linguistic effect, and to a certain extent it indeed has, as positions formerly occupied by ED speakers, including those of high governmental officials and teachers, were now filled with Surinamese-born speakers. Additionally, during the period of military dictatorship in the 1980s in particular, an increasing number of speakers of lower class background were all of a sudden found in leadership positions in society, and thus SD forms generally perceived to be more non-standard were increasingly heard in public communication and specifically in the media, a situation that has continued to date. Furthermore, many of the speakers who used to form the (predominantly

Creole) elite group in Suriname, who spoke a variant of SD that was probably closest to ED, have left the country since independence. All these factors, then, resulted in decreased influence of the ED variety on SD.

Paradoxically, however, to a certain extent independence has also resulted in increased exposure to ED. Since the mid-1970s, a large number of Surinamese have emigrated to the Netherlands. As a consequence, today approximately a third of the Suriname-born population resides in the Netherlands, thus creating strong ties between the two countries, as almost everyone in Suriname now has relatives overseas. Moreover, many second generation Surinamese immigrants in the Netherlands now speak a variety of ED, to which their Surinamese-born relatives are exposed when communicating with their family members. In addition, in the media ED can be heard on a daily basis, as some radio stations in Paramaribo broadcast news excerpts copied directly from Dutch media sources. Finally, as Suriname's university as of yet does not offer a full range of academic programs, Surinamese students continue to travel to the Netherlands for further education, albeit in reduced numbers due to the economic situation the country finds itself in today. Thus, despite ever weakening political relations between Suriname and the Netherlands, the influence of ED persists up to the present day.

To conclude, the use of Dutch in Suriname spans over 300 years, with one ethnic group in particular, the Creoles, having the longest history of use, including as a native language along with Sranan. It is therefore hardly surprising, then, that modern SD, certainly as employed by this segment of the Surinamese population, is heavily influenced by Sranan. One area of the grammar of SD which has been particularly affected by Sranan is its tense-mood-aspect system (de Kleine 2007), of which an illustration is provided in the following section.

3. Morphosyntactic differences between ED and SD: The case of future tense marking

The remainder of this paper explores the unique properties of future tense marking in SD,[1] and as such, highlights the complexity of some of the

---

[1] The following account is based on an extensive study of Surinamese Dutch as spoken among the Creole population of Paramaribo (de Kleine 2007). Claims in this paper therefore refer to the SD variety of this particular ethnic group only, and are restricted to the use of Dutch in Paramaribo. The original study analyzed the speech of twenty-two informants, from various class backgrounds.

differences between ED^2 and SD. It is argued here that the camouflaged identity of some of the differences between SD and ED, of which future tense marking constitutes a prime example, provides an explanation why the uniqueness of SD among dialects of Dutch has been underestimated until now.

The basic inventory of forms that can carry future tense in SD and ED is identical: the verbs *gaan* ('to go') and *zullen* ('shall') can be used to mark future tense, along with the form also employed for the simple present, though the latter is rare in future contexts in SD. As the neutral form to express future in ED, the simple present is used most frequently in that language variety (Haeseryn et al. 1997).[3] However, the simple present is not always available in ED, as it is also used for other tense and aspectual categories. The context generally determines the appropriate interpretation of a simple present verb, with the present tense being the default interpretation. Particularly in cases where the verb complex carries additional aspectual categories – most notably progressivity and habituality – a future interpretation is typically cancelled out in favor of a present interpretation. Examples can be found in *Zij leest veel* 'She reads a lot', where the verb carries habitual aspect, or *Zij studeert dus laat haar met rust* 'She is studying so leave her alone', where the verb carries progressive aspect; in both cases, the aspectual values automatically rule out a future tense interpretation. In instances, then, where the simple present form would otherwise assume a present tense reading, either *zullen* or *gaan* must be employed in ED to express future tense, i.e. to disambiguate. Although either form can be used in this disambiguating role, *gaan* additionally carries the notion of intention on the part of the (animate) subject in ED, and is therefore not available in contexts that are incompatible with this notion. This can be seen in the example *Hij gaat dat vergeten* 'He is going to forget that', which is highly awkward in ED, as forgetting something in the future is usually not something one does intentionally. Hence, when an interpretation is incompatible with the notion if intention, *zullen* must be used.

SD differs from ED in that SD employs *gaan* rather than the simple present form as the neutral future tense marker; as such, it is used in many more contexts than in ED, including in those in which it would be unacceptable in

---

[2]   ED refers to the standard European Dutch variety as documented in Haeseryn et al. (1997), by far the most comprehensive grammar of Dutch (though the account presented here does not always follow Haeseryn et al.'s analyses).

[3]   Haeseryn et al. (1997) observe that while (in future contexts) the simple present is the dominant form in spoken ED, *zullen* is more prevalent in written ED. The focus in this paper is on spoken Dutch.

ED.[4] For instance, as a neutral future tense marker, *gaan* does not carry the notion of intention with animate subjects in SD (although it may be compatible with it), as illustrated in the following example:

1.   Ik *ga* die dingen verwaarlozen, het *gaat* me zeker niet lukken
       'I will neglect those things, I am definitely not going to manage'

The context in which this sentence appeared made it very clear that the act of neglecting on the part of the speaker was a prediction rather than an intentional act; similarly, his predicted resulting failure was certainly not his intention either, rendering both clauses highly awkward in ED; yet, as these are future contexts, SD requires the use of *gaan* in both clauses.

In addition, as the default future tense marker in SD, *gaan* does not fulfill a disambiguating role, i.e., it is not used to prevent a sentence from acquiring a non-future tense reading. Hence, *gaan* is also found in sentences which would not have been at risk of assuming a non-future interpretation had no overt marker been used. This can be seen in the following sentence where the inherent semantic properties of the verb *komen* (lit. 'to come') automatically result in a future interpretation; nevertheless, *gaan* is used:

2.   Er *gaat* een nieuwe [TV station] komen
       'There will be (lit. come) a new [TV station]'

By contrast, ED would have employed a simple present verb form here; indeed, the sentence above is highly awkward if not fully ungrammatical in ED.

Furthermore, in ED there is a purely grammatical restriction with respect to the use of future *gaan*: it can never be used in combination with the verbs *worden* 'to become', *hebben* 'to have', *zijn* 'to be', *gaan* (as a main verb), and any modal verb. The same restrictions hold for the semi-auxiliaries *(be)horen* 'should, ought to', *dienen* 'should, ought to', and *durven* 'dare to' (Haeseryn et al. 1997). By contrast, none of these restrictions on the use of *gaan* apply in SD, where *gaan* is found in combination with any of the aforementioned verbs, as in:

3.   Jenny *gaat* je toch niet *kunnen* wijzen
       'Jenny will not be able to show you'

4.   Wanneer *gaat* het land goed *worden*?
       'When will the country get better?'

---

[4] Haeseryn at al. (1997) indicate that non-standard Belgian Dutch, particularly as spoken in West Flanders, displays different future tense marking patterns, allowing *gaan* in more contexts than standard ED. These patterns appear to resemble SD more closely (Vandenbussche, personal communication).

5.   Want morgen *ga* ik weg *gaan*
      'For tomorrow I will go away'

Despite the prevalent use of the neutral form *gaan* to express future tense, *zullen* is also encountered in SD. This form, however, has acquired another grammatical function for many speakers of SD, and can be encountered when the speaker is uncertain whether a state or event will be realized in the future, as in:

6.   Ik weet niet zozeer wat die dame ermee *zal* doen
      'I do not really know what the lady will do with it'

This is in contrast to the form *gaan*, which is typically used when something is indeed expected to happen in the future (and would therefore have been awkward in the sentence above, with *ik weet niet zozeer ...* indicating uncertainty). The contrast between *gaan* and *zullen* is particularly clear in utterances containing both verbs, as in the following example:

7.   ...ze *gaat* boos op je worden, misschien maanden lang. Maar ze *zal* eens inzien dat je gelijk had, toch?
      '...she will get mad at you, maybe for months. But one day she will see that you were right, right?'

The overall context in which this example appeared revealed that the informant had good reason to assume the certainty of the first statement, whereas the second was a lot less certain, thus explaining the use of both verbs in the same sentence (de Kleine 2007: 63).

Table 1 summarizes the main differences between ED and SD:

Form	Function in ED	Function in SD
Simple present	marking future tense *(neutral/default)*	(rarely used for future tense marking)
gaan	marking future tense + conveying intention	marking future tense *(neutral/default)*
	disambiguating	(+certainty)
zullen	marking future tense	marking future tense
	disambiguating	+uncertainty

Table 1: Future Tense Marking in ED and SD

The grammatical functions of *gaan* and *zullen* in SD can be traced to Sranan. The latter uses similar forms, *go* ('go') and *sa* ('shall'), with *go* carrying future tense combined with the notion of certainty, and *sa* expressing future tense with less certainty (cf. Holm 2000: 175), thus mirroring the grammatical functions of *gaan* and *zullen* in SD. In other words, transfer of grammatical function from Sranan has occurred, resulting in a category – certainty – that is not grammaticalized in ED. Furthermore, this transfer of function is not accompanied by a transfer of form(s) – SD employs forms also found in ED to express this 'new' grammatical function only found in SD – resulting in the use of the same grammatical forms but with different meanings.

From a cross-dialectal perspective, this means that the identities of the grammatical forms of *gaan* and, to an even greater extent, *zullen*, are camouflaged (cf. Spears 1982, Stewart 1987, 1990). When such camouflaged forms are used, for the speaker of dialect A there is on the surface no indication that the utterance of the speaker of dialect B carries a different meaning than the interpretation that the speaker of dialect A assigns to it based on his own linguistic background, resulting in what Stewart (1990) has labeled 'pseudocomprehension': the interlocutors do not merely misunderstand each other, but rather, altogether fail to realize that they have misunderstood each other. This phenomenon is nicely illustrated with an anecdote from my early days of doing research in Suriname. As a speaker of ED, I once made a promise to a speaker of SD to bring him money the following weekend, using the sentence *Ik zal u het geld zeker brengen* (in ED, 'I will definitely bring you the money'). The use of the adverb *zeker* 'definitely' left absolutely no room for doubt in my ED interpretation: I was making a firm promise. Not yet being fully aware of all of the differences between ED and SD, to my great surprise my Surinamese conversation partner responded in astonishment, with the utterance *Nee, nee, je moet het geld brengen!* 'No, no, you have to bring the money!', a response that made no sense at all in a ED interpretation. Obviously, my use of a form of *zullen* had led him to interpret my statement as implying that it was not at all certain that I would bring the money, triggering his 'odd' response. This example, while anecdotal, demonstrates how the subtle differences between future verb forms in SD and ED can lead to radically different interpretations, which can go unnoticed easily in inter-dialectal communication. Indeed, the unique functional distribution of *gaan* and *zullen* in SD had gone undetected altogether until recently (de Kleine 2007), with references to future tense marking in SD being limited to constructions using *gaan* that are fully unacceptable in ED, in particular those with *gaan* in combination with main verbs that do not allow this in ED (cf. Healy 1993 286f., Essed-Fruin 1990: 57, Essed-Fruin and Gobardhan 1992: 18). Clearly, as discussed here too, these constitute the more salient differences between SD and ED with regard to verb forms carrying future tense, in particular from the ED speaker's perspective. However, as the account presented in this article demonstrates, the use of *gaan* in such constructions merely constitutes 'the tip of the iceberg', with the overall ED and SD future tense marking systems being fundamentally different, with differing default markers and different additional notions conveyed by the various non-default forms.

4. Conclusion

This paper has explored the history of Dutch in Suriname, and some of the unique properties of SD as they relate to future tense marking. Historical evidence suggests that the use of SD has deep roots in Suriname, particularly among a local-born speech community of (mostly middle-class) Dutch-Sranan bilinguals which has existed since the eighteenth century. As this speech community must have laid a significant part of the foundation of modern SD, it is not surprising to find a strong influence of Sranan in modern SD, as illustrated by its future tense marking system discussed here. It seems likely that the camouflaged nature of (some of) the differences between SD and ED, as for instance found in future tense marking, has contributed significantly to the lack of recognition that this unique variety of Dutch has experienced during the past several centuries. Fortunately, this situation has now – finally – begun to change.

References

Brons, J. C. 1952. *Het Rijksdeel Suriname*. Haarlem: De Erven F. Bohn N. V.

De Kleine, Christa M. 1994. An analysis of van Dijk's Dutch in 'Nieuwe en nooit bevoorens geziene onderwijzinge in het Bastert Engels of Neeger Engels'. Unpubl. manuscript, CUNY Graduate Center.

De Kleine, Christa M. 2007. *A Morphosyntactic Analysis of Surinamese*. München: Lincom Europa.

Eersel, Christian H. 1987. Taalpolitiek en sociale mobiliteit in Suriname, 1863–1985. *OSO* 2: 127–136.

Essed-Fruin, Eva D. 1990. Het Nederlands in Suriname. *Ons Erfdeel*: 53–61.

Essed-Fruin, Eva D. and Lila Gobardhan-Rambocus. 1992. Het Nederlands in Suriname. *Neerlandica Extra Muros*: 10–21.

Focke, Hendrik C. 1855. *Neger-Engelsch woordenboek*. Leiden: Van den Heuvell.

Gobardhan-Rambocus, Lila. 1989. Taalbeleid en taalemancipatie in Suriname sinds het Statuut (1954). *OSO* 1: 65–76.

Gobardhan-Rambocus, Lila. 1993.   Het Surinaams Nederlands. In Lila Gobardhan-Rambocus and Maurits S. Hassankhan (eds.), *Immigratie en ontwikkeling. Emancipatie van contractanten.* Paramaribo: Anton de Kom Universiteit, 140–158.

Haeseryn, W., K. Romijn, G. Geerts, J. de Rooij and M. C. van den Toorn (eds.). 1997. *Algemene Nederlandse Spraakkunst.* 2nd rev. ed. Groningen/ Deurne, Martinus Nijhoff uitgevers/Wolters Plantyn. [Retrieved June 10, 2005, from http://oase.uci.kun.nl/~ans/.]

Healy, Maureen. 1993. The parallel continuum model for Suriname: a preliminary study. In Francis Byrne and John Holm (eds.), *Atlantic meets Pacific. A global view of pidginization and creolization.* Amsterdam: John Benjamins, 279–289.

Hellinga, Wytze G. 1955. *Language problems in Suriname. Dutch as the language of the schools.* Amsterdam: North-Holland.

Holm, John A. 2000. *An Introduction to Pidgins and Creoles.* Cambridge: Cambridge University Press.

McLeod, Cynthia. 1994. *Elisabeth Samson. Een vrije zwarte vrouw in het achttiende-eeuwse Suriname.* Paramaribo: Vaco.

Reinecke, John E. 1937. The Negro English dialects of Surinam and British Guiana. *Marginal languages: a sociological survey of the creole languages and trade jargons.* Ph. D. dissertation, Yale University. Ann Arbor: University Microfilms International, 426–479.

Rens, Lucien Leo Eduard. 1953. *The historical and social background of Surinam Negro-English.* Amsterdam: North-Holland.

Spears, Arthur K. 1982. The Black English semi-auxiliary *come. Language* 58: 850–872.

Stewart, William A. 1987. Coping or groping? Psycholinguistic problems in the acquisition of receptive and productive competence across dialects. In Peter Homel, Michael Palij and Doris Aaronson (eds.), *Childhood bilingualism: aspects of linguistic, cognitive and social development.* Hillsdale, N. J.: Lawrence Erlbaum, 281–298.

Stewart, William A. 1990. From xenolect to mimolect to pseudo-comprehension: structural mimicry and its functional consequences in decreolization. In Edward Herman Bendix (ed.), *The uses of linguistics.* New York: the New York Academy of Sciences, 33–47.

Van Dijk, Pieter. [ca. 1765]. *Nieuwe en nooit bevoorens geziene onderwyzinge in het Bastert Engels of Neeger Engels.* Amsterdam: Jacobus van Egmont.

Van Donselaar, J. 1989. *Woordenboek van het Surinaams Nederlands.* 2nd ed. Muiderberg: Coutinho.

Van Lier, Rudolf. 1977. *Samenleving in een grensgebied. Een sociaal-historische studie van Suriname.* 3rd ed. Amsterdam: Emmering.

Van Trier-Guicherit, I. 1991. De eerste taalgids Sranan-Nederlands. *OSO* 1: 31–47.
Van Wel, Freek J. and A. J. Vervoorn. [ca. 1974]. *Het Nederlands in Suriname.* Den Haag: Kabinet voor Surinaamse en Nederlands-Antilliaanse Zaken.
Veer, W. N. 1962. Taal en volk. *Schakels* 46: 19–23.
Voorhoeve, Jan and Ursy M. Lichtveld (eds.). 1975. *Creole drum: an anthology of Creole literature in Surinam.* New Haven: Yale University Press.
Weygandt, G. C. 1798. *Gemeenzame leerwyze om het Basterd of Neger-Engelsch op een gemakkelyke wyze te leeren verstaan en spreken.* Paramaribo: W. W. Beeldsnyder.

ANA DEUMERT (CAPE TOWN/MONASH)

"Zoo schrijve ek lievers my sort Afrikaans" – Speaker agency, identity, and resistance in the history of Afrikaans

Der kleine Mann scheißt sich was auf die große Zeit. Er will ein bissel ins Wirtshaus gehn und Gulasch auf die Nacht.

'The little man doesn't give a shit about a great era. All he wants to do is to drop into a bar now and then and eat goulash for supper.'

(Bertolt Brecht, *Schweyk in the Second World War*, Scene I)

1. Introduction – "Bringing speakers back in?"

In 2003 I published a paper which, taking the cue from Homans' seminal article *Bringing Men Back In* (1964), examined the epistemology of speaker-oriented explanations of language change. Like Homans in his critique of sociology, I reviewed functionalist and structuralist explanations of language change and argued that historical linguistics as a discipline should be firmly grounded in a theoretical perspective which takes due recognition of the calculative and purposive behaviour of individuals (while, at the same time, developing a keen understanding for the limitations of action theory as an explanatory model).

Whereas historical linguists have long favoured system-internal approaches to language change – as reflected, e.g., in Lass' (1997) provocative argument for a speaker-free linguistics –, historical sociolinguists have since the early 1980s developed a research program which foregrounds social context and social interaction, sociolinguistic variability, metalinguistic discourses (often termed 'language ideologies'), and speaker agency as central, rather than marginal, factors in language change (see Deumert 2003 for a review of the literature). The notion of speaker agency has also received considerable attention in language contact studies and creolistics, in particular in the work of Thomason (e.g. 2001). And indeed, evidence is accumulating that speakers can and do make rather sweeping changes to their languages and linguistic practices. This includes not only relatively well-recognized examples of pragmatic and lexical change and the creative invention, which, at times, accompanies language standardization, but also structural change in non-standard languages:

(a) Laycock (1982) gives the example of Uisai – a Papuan language – where speakers deliberately switched masculine and feminine gender agreement markers in order to make the local dialect more different from the dialects of neighbouring villages.

(b) Thomason (2001) reports that speakers of Ma'a (or Mbugu) in Tanzania deliberately maintained the non-Bantu (Cushitic) /ł/ phoneme (a voiceless velar fricative) to emphasize their cultural distinctiveness, and to mark the group's non-Bantu origin.

(c) Kulick (1992) describes an equally intriguing example from his field work in Papua New Guinea: at a local village meeting a conscious decision was taken by the villagers to change the form of one central word; instead of the usual word for 'no', *bia*, a new word, *buɲe*, was to be introduced as a marker of local identity. Again, the purpose of this change was to emphasize the village's difference from the surrounding villages, whose residents used a similar form of speech. Kulick, somewhat provocatively, interprets the high degree of linguistic diversity in the Pacific region as a direct consequence of such acts of identity, which mark distinction and difference across closely related speech communities.

What is needed at this stage is to move beyond such somewhat anecdotal evidence, which shows individual instances of language change as being initiated and negotiated by speakers, and to conduct careful socio-historical studies which describe in detail how speaker agency can affect substantial language change at a given point in time and across a range of variables and, thus, shape the historical trajectory of a language. This includes, as Mattheier (1987: 1434) has put it, uncovering linguistic *Umwege und Holzpfade* ('detours and wrong tracks'), i.e. changes or variation patterns which did not take root, but nevertheless form part of a language's full historical development. The aim of this article is to develop further the notion of speaker agency in language history, looking not only at speakers as agents of change, but also as resisting change. The data comes from my previous work on Afrikaans (Deumert 2004 and 2005), more specifically the *Corpus of Cape Dutch Correspondence* (1880–1922) and the so-called *Nanny-Letters* (1923–1924).

2. Afrikaans historical linguistics
and the language-political debate of the 1870s

Apart from a focus on speaker agency, there are other reasons why the study of Afrikaans can be of interest to a general audience in historical sociolinguistics:

(a) Afrikaans is the only language with pidgin/creole ancestry which has succeeded in replacing its lexifier, that is Dutch, in all domains and shows full standardization.

(b) Moreover, the standardization of Afrikaans was an exceptionally rapid process: from 1875 onwards we see first efforts at language codification, and in 1925 – i.e. only 50 years later – Afrikaans was granted full official status, alongside English and Dutch. By the 1920s a fully codified Afrikaans standard norm was firmly in place and was promoted through various institutions: the education system, the political administration, the church, and the press.

(c) And finally, we are in an exceptionally fortunate situation in that low-level historical data are available for the time period in question, including large collections of private letters from various social groups, comprehensive official correspondence, newspapers, language-political manifestos, and so forth. These allow us to reconstruct sociolinguistic patterns of variation as well as public attitudes and debates about language in considerable detail.

Before turning to the sociolinguistic analysis, a few words on the language-political context in the 19th and early 20th century are expedient (a more detailed discussion and references are available in Deumert 2004).

The advent of British rule in the early 19th century did not only change the political conditions at the Cape, but also had far-reaching sociolinguistic consequences. From early on, the British Colonial Office advocated a policy aimed at assimilating the Dutch-speaking inhabitants into the English culture and language, and in 1822 a government proclamation granted official status to English only. Dutch was thus reduced to the private sphere and the church. From the 1860s onwards, social life in the colony was significantly anglicized, and there is extensive historical evidence for inter-generational language shift in traditionally Dutch/Afrikaans speaking families. Initially, only few dissenting voices were heard, and many accepted that English would indeed be the future language of the colony. However, in the 1870s, following the advent of Responsible Government in 1872, there emerged a vigorous public debate between advocates of English, Dutch – in its various guises ranging from metropolitan standard Dutch to simplified Cape Dutch –, and also Afrikaans, an emerging local language norm.

The language-political debate at the Cape was always passionate, often amusing, and never boring. The pages of local newspapers were filled with editorials and letters, language congresses took place to debate the linguistic future of the country, grammars and linguistic descriptions were published, and petitions were organized. Scholars, teachers, clerics, and writers – the entire colonial intelligentsia – were deeply involved in these discussions, and even outsiders – such as the Dutch linguist Jan te Winkel – contributed to the debate. The line between scholarship and propaganda was thin and frequently and habitually crossed. In these popular discussions we are witnessing a prime example of what Blommaert has called a language-political debate in his 1999 volume: it was a debate about national and cultural identity, authenticity, and distinctiveness which shaped linguistic practices at the Cape and contributed to the speed and direction of language change.

Before turning to the analysis of everyday language use in private documents, it is necessary to mention another aspect of the public face of the 19th century language debate – namely, the humorous and playful represent-tations of local, non-standard speech which started appearing in the colonial press from the 1820s onwards. These so-called *praatjes* ('dialogues') and *boerenbrieven* ('farmers' letters') were a popular genre in the emerging colonial mass media and constituted a distinct literary tradition which formed the linguistic blue-print for the expression of Afrikaner nationalism.

3. 'A set of defining characteristics' – Linguistic stereotyping and the formation of an Afrikaans proto-standard

In the 1820s the dialect writing tradition at the Cape started with the publication of a series of humorous letters in *De Verzamelaar* ('The Collector'), written by the paper's editor Josephus Suasso De Lima, who had arrived at the Cape in 1818. These letters used the local vernacular to comment satirically on events of political and social importance. The genre was taken up and elaborated by other writers and newspapers in the following decades and gained popularity among readers. From the 1860s onwards, dialect texts became a regular feature in the colonial press and the stream of contributions, although fluctuating, steadily increased (see Figure 1).

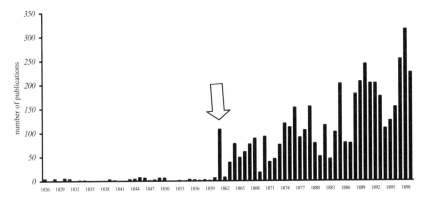

Figure 1: Publication of vernacular texts in newspapers and magazines in the Cape Colony
1826–1899 (number of texts per year; based on Nienaber 1966)

The turning point of 1860 – which is indicated in Figure 1 – was triggered by Meurant's *Klaas Waarzegger* ('Nicolas Truthsayer') dialogues, which appeared in that year. The *Klaas Waarzegger* dialogues were exceedingly popular in the colonial society; they were widely read – even memorized by the readers – and were quickly incorporated into the popular culture of the time (cf. Deumert 2005).

While there is no doubt that these texts were very popular in the colonial society, there is some disagreement on the type of language or linguistic variety they reflect. What – if anything – can they tell us about the historical development of Afrikaans? Are they, as argued by some Afrikaans historical linguists (e.g. Raidt 1968: 117), a largely unmediated reflection of the contemporary spoken language?

Outside of South Africa historical linguists have treated such literary variety imitations cautiously. While 'eye dialects' can be useful for identifying the presence or absence of linguistic features, they often impose – through processes of generalization and stereotyping – linguistic uniformity on highly variable spoken vernaculars. Mesthrie (2002), for example, found in his quantitative analysis of a South African popular radio series from the 1940s (*Applesammy and Naidoo*) that, although the texts showed salient features of South African Indian English, frequencies were considerably higher than had been observed for basilectal speakers in the 1980s and 1990s, and forms had been generalized to new linguistic environments. In other words, it is likely that the relatively uniform dialect texts we see in the colonial press reflect a stylized image of the colonial vernacular, an amalgamation of different non-standard features, which did not necessarily co-exist – in general or in a given frequency – in the speech of any individual, but which endowed the texts with the stereotypical characteristics of local, non-standard speech. Moreover, the dialect literature provided prospective writers with a blueprint of how to write 'the vernacular', and their efforts in turn constituted the model for new generations of writers. Through this process a focused public expectation of how to write what was now termed 'Afrikaans' was created: a 'proto-standard' was born (see Deumert 2004, chapter two, for details).

The earlier mentioned *Klaas Waarzegger* dialogues by Meurant were not only a quantitative turning point in the history of the nineteenth-century dialect literature at the Cape – leading to a general rise in the publication of such texts – but also initiated a qualitative shift in the symbolic meaning of dialect writing. The authors of the pre-1860 tradition were European-born and thus outsiders to the colonial society. They used the vernacular primarily to inscribe 'other-ness' into the text, i.e. to represent (and ridicule) the residents of the colony, their often naive and uneducated beliefs and preoccupations. Meurant, on the other hand, was locally born and grew up in a rural Afrikaner family. In his writings we do not find the projection of 'the other' but, instead, – for the first time – a sense of 'our-own-ness', giving a unique and authentic voice to local experiences and cultural identity.

The dialect literature established linguistic forms and topics of talk and created communities of practice among writers and readers in the colony. Gradually – through increasing use and conventionalization – the dialect texts shed their elements of artificiality and stylization, and the linguistic forms popularized in these texts became markers of colonial identity. With each (playful or serious) imitation and repetition, these forms became more natural and more 'authentic'. And, gradually, they came to be used in new communicative domains, in domains outside of the public sphere, in private letters and diaries. The historical process – which I have dubbed "from the broadsheets to the drawing room" (Deumert 2005) – is captured by Jane Hill's (1986) concept of a 'leaky' boundary between public and private spheres in modern or modernizing societies and growing sociolinguistic work on the appropriation and naturalization of media discourses and styles in every-day conversational encounters (e.g. Schiffman 1998, Coupland 2001, 2003).

The appropriation of the linguistic style or variety characteristic of the dialect literature is clearly visible in the *Corpus of Cape Dutch Correspondence* (*CCDC*), a comprehensive socio-historical corpus, which includes private documents from over 130 individuals. Most of the texts were written between 1890 and 1910 (see Deumert 2004, chapter three, for details). The linguistic analysis of the corpus data (Deumert 2004) shows young, educated writers as 'early adopters' of the new literary norm they employ – initially rather play-fully and sometimes daringly – in their private correspondence with siblings and peers. With regard to frequencies of morphosyntactic regularization,[1] figure 2 illustrates

(a) the linguistic similarities and continuities between the popular local dialect literature (represented by Meurant's early dialogues), the early Afrikaans standard as promoted by the first Afrikaans language society (*Die Genootskap van Regte Afrikaners* 'The Society of True Afrikaners'), and the in-group language use of young, educated Afrikaner nationalists, and

(b) the existence of alternative variation patterns (acrolectal and meso-lectal Cape Dutch), which are equally prominent in the historical record (see Deumert 2004 for a detailed quantitative and qualitative analysis of these varieties).

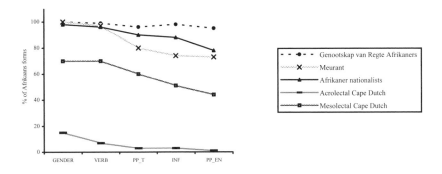

Figure 2: Linguistic practices at the Cape 1860 to 1922: private letters by young Afrikaner nationalists (*CCDC*, 1880–1922), acrolectal Cape Dutch (*CCDC*, 1880–1922), mesolectal Cape Dutch (*CCDC*, 1880–1922), Meurant's *Zamenspraak* (No.1; 1860), and 'Afrikaans' as used in publications of the *Genootskap van Regte Afrikaners*.

With regard to their social location, acrolectal writers and the young Afrikaner nationalists belonged to what has been called 'the new professional classes', an emerging privileged group consisting of white-collar professionals such as doctors, lawyers, teachers, and ministers. These were members of an educational élite, who possessed few liquid assets or property but scored high

---

[1] The following variables were included: loss of neuter gender (understood as loss of agreement between article/ demonstrative and neuter noun; variable: GENDER), loss of person and number distinction in the present tense, main verbs only (variable: VERB), loss of inflection in the infinitive (variable INF), and loss of inflectional endings in the past participle, loss of -*t* and -*en* considered separately (variables PP_T and PP_EN).

on what Bourdieu (1984) has called cultural capital (for a general discussion of the rise of the professional classes in the late 19th century cf. Perkin 1989; also Hofmeyer 1987: 93). The mesolectal writers belonged to what is conventionally known as the 'petty bourgeoisie', including independent farmers, shop owners, and small-scale producers as well as economically successful artisans (see Deumert 2004, chapter three, for a detailed discussion of these social groupings).

4. The spread of the new norm: 'Slow, slow, quick, quicker, bang'?

The Afrikaans writer and language activist C.J. Langenhoven described the spread of Afrikaans in a speech in 1914 as exponential: "a steeply mounting curve, not only rising sharply but doing so at a rapidly increasing ratio" which would soon reach a point "up there in the blue sky":

> As ons nou hier in die saal af'n ry pale sou plant, tien pale, om die laaste tien jaar voor te stel, en aan elke paal'n merk sou maak op'n hoogte van die vloer af ooreenkomende met die betreklike skryfgebruik van Afrikaans in die respektiewe jaartal, en'n streep deur die merke trek van die eerste af hier naby die vloer tot by die laaste daar anderkant teen die solder, dan sou die streep'n snelstygende boog beskryf, nie net vinnig opgaande nie, maar opgaande na'n vinnig vermeerderende rede. Laat ons nou in ons verbeelding die boog verleng vir die tien komende jare van nou af. Sien u menere waar die punt sal wees, daar buite in die bloue lug hoog oor Bloemfontein, in die jaar 1924.

> 'If we plant a row of poles in this hall now, ten poles, to represent the last ten years, and on each pole we make a mark at a height from the floor corresponding to the relative written use of Afrikaans in the respective year, and we draw a line, from the first here near the floor to the last over there against the loft, then the line would describe a steeply mounting curve, not only rising sharply but doing so at a rapidly increasing ratio. Let us now, in our imagination, extend the curve for the ten coming years from now. See you, sirs, where the point shall be, outside in the blue sky high over Bloemfontein, in the year 1924.' (Versamelde Werke, vol. 10)

Langenhoven's words portray a process of linguistic change which Denison (2003) summarized succinctly as 'slow, slow, quick, quicker, bang!' – a model of change which provided the inspiration for the central shape of the Afrikaans language monument in Paarl (Figure 3). In the picture the colonnade to the left symbolizes the European origin of Afrikaans, the podium and a low wall in the middle of the monument the African and Malay contribution. Together they form the base of the hyperbola (visible to the right in the picture), which represents, following Langenhoven's imagery, the exponential rise of Afrikaans in the early 20th century.

Figure 3: The Afrikaans Language Monument, Paarl (http://www.museums.org.za/TaalMon/).

But is the idea of an exponential, hyperbolic rise an appropriate model for the history of Afrikaans? Or – as noted by Denison (2003) – for any language history? If one looks at the real-time diffusion of Afrikaans variants across the *CCDC*, one does indeed see a steep and sudden increase after 1910 (Figure 4). The process of language or variety spread started in the 1880s and by 1920 – following its recognition as medium of instruction in primary schools (1914), the publication of the first official spelling rules (1915–1917), its introduction in the civil service and some universities (1918), and finally, its acceptance by the church (1919) – the new standard of Afrikaans was well established as a code choice in the written domain, both in private and official communication. However, this increase was not so much exponential as following the well-established model of an S-curve, since "[a]fter the phase when the new form gains ascendancy rather rapidly, the process of change slows down again as the last remnants of the older state linger on" (Denison 2003: 56). In the case of Afrikaans, Dutch relics, "the older stage", are still evident after 1910 (i.e. over 30% of the variants included in the analysis for Figure 4 still belong to the system of Dutch, 1911–1922) and can be found in private correspondence until the 1930s.

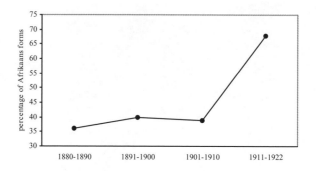

Figure 4: Percentage of Afrikaans forms in the *CCDC* across time (Deumert 2004).

The diffusion of the new colonial norm was certainly not a 'big bang', but a process of many steps, where different variants followed different trajectories and histories. Once we focus our attention on individual variables and social groups, we see that in many cases a period of 'quick, quick' was followed by a rather 'sluggish' diffusion pattern, once a certain frequency plateau was reached.

In order to describe these patterns in some more detail, a second sociolinguistic corpus, the so-called *Nanny-Letters*, is of interest. This is a pragmatically cohesive corpus of 27 application letters (1922–24) for the position of a nanny in the house of Colin Steyn, son of the former President Steyn of the Orange Free State and a passionate supporter of Afrikaner nationalism (see Deumert 2005 for details of the corpus). The young women who applied for the position belonged to the petty bourgeoisie, and their social location is comparable to those writers described as mesolectal in the *CCDC* (see above). However, the sociolinguistic conditions under which they wrote were different, since the new norm of Afrikaans was now firmly established in the written domain (newspapers, books) and recognized in official, high-prestige contexts (including the education system and the government sector, see above).

A comparison of four morphosyntactic variables (loss of neuter gender, loss of infinitive marking, loss of affixation in the weak and strong participle) across the two corpora is instructive (Figure 5). Noticeable in the *Nanny-Letters* is the high maintenance of neuter gender and the almost completed regularization of the infinitive. The overall variation pattern in these 20th century letters is unlike the historical pattern evident in the *CCDC*, which shows a stable hierarchy of morphosyntactic reduction: GENDER > PP_T ≥ INF > PP_EN. It appears that some changes-in-progress slowed down (gender) in the 20th century, while others accelerated (regularization of the infinitive; here we see a classic sociolinguistic cross-over pattern). The continuing variation until well into the 20th century runs counter the conventional dating of Afrikaans, which assumes full diffusion of all defining linguistic features (linguistically, socially, stylistically, and geographically) for no later than 1850 (e.g. Raidt 1983).

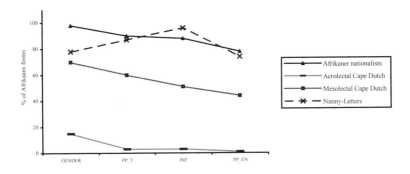

Figure 5: Morphosyntactic regularization in the *CCDC* (1880-1922) and the *Nanny-Letters* (1923/1924). The variable VERB (see Figure 2) was excluded from the analysis, since token numbers were too low in the *Nanny-Letters*.

In the *Nanny-Letters* high frequencies of usage (80+%) are found for the *n*-less Afrikaans first and third person singular possessive pronouns *my* ('my') and *sy* ('his', 'her') and the first person singular pronoun *ek* (instead of Dutch *ik*). Extensive variation with no visible tendency towards generalization exists for the Afrikaans double negation or *nie*-2. This is a linguistic feature which, although well established in the above mentioned dialect literature (represented by Meurant's dialogues from 1860) and codified in the first Afrikaans grammar of 1876, remains highly variable in both the private letters of the *CCDC* and in the *Nanny-Letters* (Figure 6). *Nie*-2 does not occur in the acrolectal letters of the *CCDC*.

In an earlier publication (Deumert 2005) I advanced three explanations to account for the fact that many features characteristic of the Afrikaans standard norm were only partially diffused at a time when the norm was already codified and categorical usage common in formal domains.

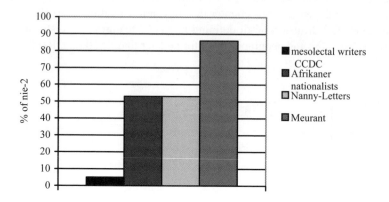

Figure 6: *Nie*-2 (%) in the CCDC,
the Nanny-Letters and Meurant's Zamenspraak (1860).

The limits of ideology – Although language-ideological debates, which (typically) accompany standardization processes, have the potential to influence linguistic practices, their ability to do so competes with the speakers' engrained sociolinguistic habits (including long-standing variation patterns), which persist through time.

Tolerance towards variation – Writers did not consider it important to be consistent at a time which is best seen as a transition period; variation was not yet stigmatized in certain written genres.

Precarious identity management – Judging from attitudes expressed in the historical record, the use of forms which were seen as 'Afrikaans' was initially associated with the speech of people of colour and the lower classes (see Deumert 2004, chapter two, for a discussion of popular attitudes towards early 'Afrikaans'; see also Roberge 2000 with regard to the stigmatization of *nie*-2). That writing 'Afrikaans' could at times be risqué is indicated in this extract from a letter by Hester van der Bijl to the father of her fiancée. She carefully flags her use of Afrikaans by acknowledging that it might be considered 'disrespectful':

Ek kan niet H.Hollandsch schrijf, ek meen nie goed nie .... zoo schrijve ek lievers mij sort Afrikaans, maar dit lijk toch zoo ‚disrespectful' om aan u zoo te schrijf.

'I cannot write High Dutch, I mean not well ... therefore I prefer to write *my* type of Afrikaans, but it seems just so ‚disrespectful' to write to you in this way'. (Hester van der Bijl to C.P. Hoogenhout 13/2/1906, *CCDC*)

The potential of leaving a negative impression by using high frequencies of Afrikaans forms is certainly important in the context of the *Nanny-Letters*. How did the young women who applied for the position of a nanny present themselves linguistically?

5. *U dienswillige dienares* ('Your willing servant')

At the time when these letters were written, unemployment was pervasive in the colony, and the so-called *arme blanke* ('poor whites') were the object of much political and charitable attention. This socio-historical context is reflected in the *Nanny-Letters*, where references to poverty and the need for employment are a common theme.

> U verstaan seker dat ek maar 'n arm meisie is daarom is ek verplig om uit te kyk vir 'n diens al wil ek graag studeer. ... Wat van ons arm mense gaan word weet ek nie maar ek word benoud as ek oor my toekoms dink.

> 'You will certainly understand that I am but a poor girl and am thus obliged to look for work although I would like to study. ... What will happen to us poor people I don't know, but I feel anguish when I think about my future.' (Mara Henning, 9/9/1924)

Positive self-representation is central in such a situation, and using elements of the traditional Dutch standard might have allowed writers to indicate their educatedness and sophistication to a prospective employer. At the same time, by using forms belonging to the emerging standard of Afrikaans writers they were able to affirm, within the context of South African politics, their national and cultural identity, which would have been received positively in the Afrikaner nationalist household of the Steyn family (who, like other Afrikaner nationalists, made use of Afrikaans in their own private correspondence). In the remainder of this section, I will briefly discuss three letters from the corpus to show how writers combined the two norms when writing and moved, seemingly seamlessly, from one to the other.

The letter by one Anna Moelich (dated 30/3/1922, Letter 1) shows a preponderance of Dutch relics; *ik* instead of *ek* for the first person singular, maintenance of word-final /t/ and word-internal /g/ (*eerst*, *vragen* instead of Afrikaans *eers*, *vra'e*), maintenance of neuter gender (*het stasie, het postkantoor, het reiskaartje*), and the irregular inflection of 'to be' (*ik ben*), use of Dutch inflectional morphology in the present tense (*sy levert*), the infinitive (*hebben, ontmoeten*), and the past participle (*gegeven*). Yet, the letter also contains forms which are unambiguously marked as +Afrikaans; infinitives and past participles are not marked throughout the text (*te hou, angeneem, aangestur*), some spellings are clearly influenced by the Afrikaans orthographic norm (*getuigskrifte* rather than *getuigschrifte*, *sal* instead of *zal*), and in the relative clause the writer uses the Afrikaans invariant relativizer *wat* instead of the more common Cape Dutch form *die* (see Deumert 2004, chapter 6, for a discussion of relative pronouns in Cape Dutch).

Letter 1

Angora,
P.K. Bonnie Vale
Dist. Swellendam

Mev. Collin Steyn
"Onse Rust"
Kaalspruit
O.V.S.

Waarde Mev.
     In antwoord op u advertensie in de Burger van 28ste dezer, wil ik my aanbevelen voor die betrekking maar ik sou garne eerst de antwoorden van de volgende vragen hebben.

(a) Hoe lang u plan is om die aplikante te hou wat aangeneem word.
(b) Of u ver van het spoorweg stasie is, naam van stasie en hoe ver het Postkantoor is-van u huis is?
(c) Wanneer applikante in dienst moet treden?
(d) Of er vry logies gegeven wordt
(e) Of er 'n deel van het reiskaartje betaal word
(f) Wat u voorneme is applikante te betalen indien sy goed werk levert.
    Ik ben een liefhebster van naaldwerk en ook van kinderen.
    Ik ben van gesonde ligaamsbou en uit 'n opregte Afrikaanse familie.
    Getuigskrifte sal spoedig aangestuur word op onvangst van u brief indien het voor my mogelik is het te aanvaren. Of u applikante self op het stasie sal ontmoeten?

De Uwe
Mej. Anna Moelich

'Dear Madam,
in answer to your advertisement in the Burger from the 28th of this month, I would like to suggest myself for the position but I would first like to get answers to the following questions.

(a) For how long you are planning to keep the applicant who will be taken.
(b) Whether you are far from the railway station, name of the station and how far the post office is from your house?
(c) When the applicant should start the position?
(d) Whether there will be free board
(e) Whether part of the travel ticket will be paid
(f) What you are planning to pay the application if she delivers good work.
    I like needle work and also children.
    I am healthy and come from a respectable Afrikaans family.

References will be send speedily following the receipt of your letter whether it will be possible for me to begin. Will you meet the applicant at the station yourself?

Yours, Miss Anna Moelich'

Letter 2 shows several forms that are clearly marked as Afrikaans (*ek* as the first person singular pronoun, loss of inflectional marking in the infinitive, *hulle* as third person plural pronoun), yet still uses a number of Dutch spelling conventions (<z> instead of <s>, <ch> instead of <g>) and Dutch lexical variants (e.g. *hun* instead of *hulle* as third person plural possessive pronoun). Spelling variation is a prominent feature of the letter: e.g. /t/ apocope as well as /t/ maintenance in *slech* ('bad') and *recht* ('right'), <sch> and <sk>, *schryf* ('write') and *getuigskrifte* ('references').

Letter 2

    Klipfontein
    P.K. Kaallaagte
    9 ap 1923

    mevr Colin Steyn
           Waarde mevr ek het uwe advetensie in die volkblad gezien dat u een zorg van tweejarige seuntjes nodig heeft ek zal ze verpleeg tegen £ 5 per maand en ek zal u een waarborgen gee dat ek zal hullie goed behandel ek het ondervinding doch nooit getuigskrifte geeist en dan verlang ek vrye logies en inwoning dan zal ek hun naalde werk ook doen maar niet hun waschgoed
    Schryf my of u tevrede is ermede ja of neen
    zo blyf ek de uwe
    S. Meyer
    p.s. en als u eenig sins achter kom ek my slech gedra in u huis heeft u de recht my te vergaan

    'Dear madam,
    I saw your advert in the Volksblad[,] that you need care for two-year old boys[.] I will look after them for £ 5 per month and I will give you an assurance that I will treat them well[.] I have experience but did not ask for references[.] And then I request free board and accommodation[,] and then I will do their needlework but not their washing.
    Write to me whether you are content with this[,] yes or no
    I remain your
    S. Meyer
    P.S. and if you ever notice that I behave myself badly in your house[,] then you have the right to dismiss me.'

A Dutch-Afrikaans mixed style is also characteristic of Letter 3. Linguistically surprising – from the perspective of the Afrikaans standard – is, for example, the maintenance of the preterite (*sag*), the use of *myn* (instead of *my*) as the first person singular possessive pronoun, and the rather archaic use of the non-emphatic pronoun *ge* as a marker of politeness (embedded in a sentence which conforms entirely to the norms of Dutch, both morphologically and orthographically).

Letter 3

Venterburg
2nd April 1923

Mevr. Colin Steyn
"Onze Rust"
Kaalspruit

Seer Geagte Mev.
    Ek sag u applicatie in die Burger, omtrent een blanke ongetroude meisie om voor u seuntje te sorg, ek is gereed sulks te doen daar ek een liefhebber van kinders is, en is ook goed bekwaam met naaldwerk.
Myn ouderdom is 23.
Heeft ook goede vorige ondervinding
Schryf my u aanbiedende salaris
Ingesloten vind ge een getuigschrif
Hoop het sal voldoende wees.
Met die beste verwagting
Blyf Ik,

Joey v. d. Merwe

'My dear madam,
I saw your application in the burger regarding a white unmarried girl to look after your son, I am ready to do this because I like children and I am also skilled with needle work. My age is 23. Have also good previous experience. Write me the salary you're offering[.] Enclosed you'll find a reference [.] Hope this will be sufficient. With best regards
I remain, Joey v. d. Merwe'

The three letters are typical examples from the corpus, and their combination of Dutch and Afrikaans forms is reminiscent of intra- as well as inter-sentential code-switching. Persistent variation between Dutch and Afrikaans is not limited to this corpus, and letters written in a similar style can be found in the historical record until the 1930s. In the postscript to a family letter written in 1932, Hester van Huyssteen acknowledges the existence of a standard norm but shows little inclination to change her highly variable writing habits to conform to either standard Afrikaans or standard Dutch. She left it up to her step-daughter Katie to impose normativity in the process of reading and concludes her letter: "Lees toch maar al myn fouten reg hoor!" ('But just read all of my mistakes right, OK!', South African Library, Manuscript Collection, 853-5-1).

6. Resistance in the history of Afrikaans

In concluding this paper, I would like to make a few comments regarding the notion of 'resistance' in language history. Resistance, that is "the act, on the part of persons, of resisting, opposing, or withstanding" (OED Online 2005), is a useful concept for historical sociolinguistics, as it allows us to capture an important aspect of speaker agency and intentionality in language change. Broadly speaking, resistance can either lead to conscious innovation, that is the creation and propagation of new, alternative forms, as speakers strategically assert an oppositional identity, or to a slowing down of linguistic change, as speakers resist innovations and fail to adopt them, despite their growing preponderance in the speech community (i.e. the 'slow, slow' part of the S-curve).

The very formation and diffusion of Afrikaans can be interpreted as an act of overt resistance, challenging what Mesthrie (1996: x) has called the 'double colonial hegemony' of English and Dutch. The language-political debate at the Cape reflects a symbolic conflict between the traditional colonial elite of church leaders, high-ranking officials and the grand bourgeoisie, and the emerging, socially mobile counter-elite of 'the new professional class', who questioned the hegemony of linguistic tradition and put forward a radical proposal for a new colonial standard norm, which they self-consciously and deliberately enacted in communicative encounters (cf. also Holliday 1993). Although identity politics were important, the success of the movement depended to a considerable degree on the language activists' ability to establish a clear conceptual opposition between authentic and pure (*zuiwer*) Afrikaans and the traditional norms of metropolitan Dutch. The historical sources provide numerous examples of early language purism and the various types of discourse and reasoning by which sociolinguistic distinction and differentiation was established within the colonial speech community (see Deumert 2004 and 2005 for examples and discussion).

However, next to the well-documented and meta-linguistically articulated resistance against Dutch and English and the proposal and propagation of a well-defined and clearly distinct alternative Netherlandic standard, we find another type of resistance, less articulate, less spectacular, less self-conscious, less organized: the everyday resistance of writers from subordinate social positions who showed little willingness to conform to either of the two standard norms (i.e. metropolitan Dutch and Afrikaans), and who continued to use a form of speech which was situated half-way between the two competing norms (and their associated ideologies of educatedness and tradition vs. national identity and change).

In his anthropological study *Weapons of the Weak* (1985), Scott reflects in some detail on such forms of covert, everyday resistance that has been epitomized in the foot-dragging behaviour and feigned ignorance of the good soldier Schweyk. The aim of such resistance, as noted by Scott, is not to change or transform the system, "but rather to survive it" (p. 301); or in the words of Hobsbawm (1973: 7), "working the system to [...] minimum disadvantage". The mixed Dutch-Afrikaans letters discussed in the previous section could, of course, be interpreted simply as a reflection of the writer's inability to conform to either standard. And, indeed, this has been the default interpretation in Afrikaans historical linguistics. Yet, this conventional interpretation is based on the assumption that it is the writer's intention to conform to the codified standard norm (or any other prestige norm) and fails to consider the myriad of alternative intentions and motivations all too familiar to sociolinguists. The term 'covert prestige' (Labov 1972) has been coined to explain the seemingly paradoxical maintenance of non-standard, low-prestige dialects *vis à vis* the high-prestige standard, and, similarly, code-switching has been shown not to be a mark of the speakers' inability to express themselves in either language, but as a strategic use of linguistic resources to project, at times almost subversively, a hybrid and bi-cultural identity.

While employing a range of features of the new norm and thus "hiding behind the mask of public compliance" (Scott 1985: 34) in the context of growing Afrikaner nationalism, many of the writers remain stubbornly attached to Dutch forms and use them throughout their letters (albeit at varying frequencies). Could this be a case of what Scott has called "calculated conformity, cautious resistance"? (Scott 1985, chapter seven). That is, a form of resistance which implicitly also reflects "a struggle over the appropriation of symbols, a struggle of how the past and present shall be understood and labelled" (ibid.: xvii) by calling into question the linguistic purism which had become the hallmark of the standardization of Afrikaans? As so often in historical linguistics, to answer this question we rely on conjecture and interpretation, aiming to provide a coherent narrative which makes sense of the facts. We should not be too quick to equate non-compliance to standard norms with linguistic inability as a result of lack of education, but acknowledge that we might be dealing, at least in part, with Schweikian acts of ideological resistance – the linguistic equivalent of his foot dragging, partial compliance, and feigned ignorance in the face of authority. And indeed, Afrikaans language activists, such as the grammarian Malherbe, were concerned about such mixed language use and saw the continuing presence of Dutch forms as a danger to the success of the Afrikaans language movement.

> Ook van die kant van Nederlands dreig ons 'n gevaar. Ons weet hoe moelik dit vir 'n openbare spreker was wat gewoon geraak het aan sijn soort Nederlands om 'n Afrikaanse anspraak te lewer. Hy verval onbewus in Nederlandse vorm. Dit geld ook van schrijwe ... Eers in die laaste jare na veel studie en bewuste strewe, kan 'n mens 'n groot verbetering opmerk. Dit gaan hand aan hand met 'n toenemende

hoogskatting van ons taal wat op sijn beurt met jaloerse nouwgesetheid 'n so suiwer moontlike gebruik eis. Die "Brandwag"-artiekels vergelijk vandag pragtig met dié van vroeër jaargange. Tog word nog so gedurig foute gemaak.

'There is also danger from the Dutch side. We know how difficult it was for a public speaker who had got used to his kind of Dutch to deliver an Afrikaans speech. He falls unknowingly into the Dutch form. This is also true for writing … Only in recent years after much study and conscious endeavour, can one notice a great improvement. This goes hand in hand with an increasing esteem for our language which in turn demands with jealous conscientiousness a use as pure as possible. The "Brandwag" articles compare today splendidly with those from earlier years. However, mistakes are still being made.' (Malherbe 1917: 44)

Resistance to the new 'pure' norm also came from young English-Dutch/Afrikaans bilingual writers – most typically female –, and English-Afrikaans code-mixing practices are a common feature in the earlier *Corpus of Cape Dutch Correspondence*. The following extract comes from a letter by Johanna Brummer. Her linguistic practices show a fair degree of 'foot-dragging'. Despite repeated requests by her fiancee F. S. Malan to please write to him in 'proper', i.e. 'pure', Afrikaans, she continues to send monolingual English letters, and her Afrikaans letters are characterized by extensive code-switching and mixing (switches into English in italics).

Van aand gaan ons *practice* by die pastorie – wil jy ni saam gaan ni? Connie Newnham zal dar wees, en dan zal ons net 'n *jolly* aand deurbring. Ik zal so *like* dat jy ver haar ontmoet. Zy is altyd zo *bright*, al is dit maar treurig in hulle huis dan lag zy altyd. Ons het di *pledge* ge*sign* om ver Dr. Newnham aan te moedig om ver hom terug te hou van di drank. Ons draag now almal wit *ribbons* want ons behort aan di *association*. Een van di dage gaan ons Dr. Newnham vra om di *pledge* te *sign* en dan kry hy oek 'n *'white ribbon'*.

'Tonight we are going to practice at the parsonage – don't you want to come with us? Connie Newnham will be there, and then we will spend such a jolly evening. I would like it so much that you meet her. She is always so cheerful, even if it is sad in the house she always laughs. We have signed the pledge to encourage Dr. Newnham to hold back from the drink. We are all wearing white ribbons because we belong to the association. One of these days we will ask Dr. Newnham to sign the pledge and the he will also get a "white ribbon".'(Johanna Brummer, 10/5/1895)

These popular code-alternation practices stand in sharp contrast to the anti-English attitudes and polemics which characterized the Afrikaner nationalist agenda. From the 1930s anti-English attitudes proliferated in South Africa, and Afrikaners were called upon by cultural and linguistic organizations to keep their language pure of English influence. Many writers now saw themselves under pressure to purge English items from their language.

But language mixing continued and acquired new meanings in the political context of the 20th century. Following apartheid policies of segregation and exclusion after 1948, English-Afrikaans language mixing emerged as an overt provocative and symbolic response to the apartheid government's obsession with racial purity and distinction. This is clearly visible in the struggle poetry of Adam Small, Peter Snyders and Wopko Jensma, in Koos Kombuis' self-stylization as *die wonder van onsuiver Afrikaans* ('the miracle of impure Afrikaans'), and the counter-cultural discourses evident in popular music such as Kwaito. There is now clearly a collective and symbolic dimension to these code alternation practices which are self-consciously and deliberately enacted in the public domain. In other words, forms of covert, everyday and unreflected resistance always have the potential to transform into overt, symbolic resistance – shaping and structuring language histories at different times and reflecting the agentivity of speakers in the histories of their languages.

References

Blommaert, Jan. 1999. The debate is open. In Jan Blommaert (ed.), *Language Ideological Debates*. Berlin: Mouton de Gruyter, 1–38.

Brecht, Bertolt. 1993. Schweyk in the Second World War. In Hugh Rorrison (ed.) *Plays Vol. 4.* (World Dramatists). London: Methuen.

Bourdieu, Pierre. 1984. *Distinction. A Social Critique of the Judgement of Taste.* London: Routledge.

Coupland, Nikolas. 2001. Dialect stylization in radio talk. *Language in Society* 30: 345–375.

Coupland, Nikolas. 2003. Sociolinguistic authenticities. *Journal of Sociolinguistics* 7: 417–431.

Denison, David. 2003. Log(ist)ic and simplistic S-curves. In Raymond Hickey (ed.), *Motives for Language Change*. Cambridge: Cambridge University Press, 54–70.

Deumert, Ana. 2003. Bringing speakers back in? Epistemological reflection on speaker-oriented explanations of language change. *Language Sciences* 25: 15–76.

Deumert, Ana. 2004. *Language Standardization and Language Change. The Dynamics of Cape Dutch.* Amsterdam: Benjamins.

Deumert, Ana 2005. *Praatjies* and *Boerenbrieven*. Popular literature in the history of Afrikaans. *Journal of Pidgin and Creole Linguistics* 20: 15–51.

Hill, Jane. 1995. Junk Spanish, covert racism and the (leaky) boundary between public and private spheres. *Pragmatics* 5: 197–212.

Hobsbawm, Eric. 1973. Peasants and Politics. *Journal of Peasant Studies* 1: 3–22.

Hofmeyer, Isabel. 1987. Building a Nation from Words: Afrikaans language, literature and ethnic identity, 1902–1924. In Shula Marks (ed.) *The Politics of Race, Class and Nationalism in Twentieth-Century South Africa.* London: Longman, 95–123.

Holliday, Lloyd. 1993. The first language congress for Afrikaans. In Joshua Aron Fishman (ed.), *The Earliest Stage of Language Planning: The 'first' congress phenomenon.* Berlin: de Gruyter, 11–30.

Homans, George C. 1964. Bringing men back in. *American Sociological Review* 29: 809–818.

Lass, Roger. 1997. *Historical linguistics and language change.* Cambridge: Cambridge University Press.

Kulick, Don. 1992. *Language shift and cultural reproduction. Socialization, self, and syncretism in a Papua New Guinean village.* Cambridge: Cambridge University Press.

Labov, William. 1972. *Sociolinguistic Patterns.* Philadelphia: University of Philadelphia Press.

Laycock, Donald C. 1982. Melanesian linguistic diversity: a Melanesian choice? In Ronald James May and Hank Nelson (eds.), *Melanesia: Beyond Diversity.* Canberra: ANU Press, 33–38.

Malherbe, Daniel F. 1917. *Afrikaanse Taalboek. Praktiese wegwijser bij die vernaamste moeilikhede in verband met die Afrikaanse grammatica.* Bloemfontein: Nasionale Pers.

Mattheier, Klaus J. 1987. Das Verhältnis von sozialem und sprachlichen Wandel. In Ulrich Ammon et al. (eds.), *Soziolinguistik/Sociolinguistics. Ein internationales Handbuch*, vol. II. Berlin: Mouton de Gruyter, 1430–1452.

Mesthrie, Rajend. 1996. Foreword. In Mohamed. Adhikari (ed.), *Straatpraatjes. Language, politics and popular culture in Cape Town, 1909–1922*, viii–xii. Pretoria: Van Schaik.

Mesthrie, Rajend. 2002. Mock languages and symbolic power: the South African radio series *Applesammy* and *Naidoo. World Englishes* 21: 99–112.

Nienaber, Gabriel Stefanus. 1966. *Register van Afrikaans voor 1900. Deel 1 – Kaapland.* Pretoria: Suid-Afrikaanse Akademie vir Wetenskap en Kuns.

Nienaber, Gabriel Stefanus. 1967. *Register van Afrikaans voor 1900. Deel 2 – Transvaal, Oranje-Vrystaat en Natal.* Pretoria: Die Suid-Afrikaanse Akademie vir Wetenskap en Kuns.

Perkin, Harold. 1989. *The Rise of Professional Society. England since 1880.* London: Routledge.

Raidt, Edith. 1968. *Geskiedenis van die byvoeglike verbuiging in Nederlands en Afrikaans.* Cape Town: Nasau Beperk.

Roberge, Paul T. 2000. Etymological Opacity, Hybridization and the Afrikaans Brace Negation. *American Journal of Germanic Linguistics and Literatures* 12: 101–176.

Schiffman, Harold F. 1998. Standardization or restandardization: The case for 'Standard' Spoken Tamil. *Language in Society* 27: 259–285.

Scott, James. 1985. *Weapons of the Weak. Everyday Forms of Peasant Resistance*. New Haven and London: Yale University Press.

Thomason, Sarah G. 2001. *Language Contact. An Introduction.* Edinburgh: Edinburgh University Press.

MARTIN DURRELL (MANCHESTER)

"Deutsch ist eine *würde*-lose Sprache".
On the history of a failed prescription[1]

The aim of this paper is to try to trace the history of the old schoolmasters' prescription given in the title: "Deutsch ist eine *würde*-lose Sprache." The essence of the prescription is that synthetic forms traditionally referred to as the 'past subjunctive', i.e. *ich käme* are to be preferred in most contexts to the periphrastic form with *würde* and the infinitive, commonly referred to as the 'conditional', i.e. *ich würde kommen*.[2] These forms are seen as semantically equivalent in all contexts, and the periphrastic form is seen as particularly incorrect in the antecedent clause (traditionally referred to as the 'protasis'), if it is permissible to use it in the consequent clause (traditionally referred to as the 'apodosis'). Thus:

(1)   Wenn das Wetter schön bliebe, gingen wir spazieren.
(2)   Wenn das Wetter schön bliebe, würden wir spazieren gehen.

are both acceptable in good *Hochdeutsch* – although some authorities express a clear preference for (2) – the following, with conditional forms in the apodosis, are incorrect, 'bad' German:

(3)   Wenn das Wetter schön bleiben würde, gingen wir spazieren.
(4)   Wenn das Wetter schön bleiben würde, würden wir spazieren gehen.

---

[1]   I must acknowledge a debt of gratitude to Anita Auer, Wini Davies, Stephan Elspaß, and Claudia Law for their help and advice in preparing this paper. The responsibility for any errors, omissions and misjudgements is of course entirely my own.

[2]   I shall use these traditional terms in this paper rather than the term *Konjunktiv II*, which is frequently employed in modern grammars of German. As Zifonun et al. (1997: 1731–1743) point out, this term is by no means unproblematic, and the place of the periphrasis with *würde* in the verbal paradigm of German is not altogether clear, cf. also Eisenberg (1999: 121f.). The traditional terms have the advantage that they allow unambiguous reference to the synthetic and periphrastic forms, and they are widely used in the older works which will be discussed in this paper.

The use of two periphrastic forms in the same sentence, as in example (4), is generally regarded as particularly objectionable.

In order to understand the origin of this prescription we need to consider some relevant aspects of the uses of the conditional with *würde* in modern German and its history. Many accounts of the subjunctive in modern German, e.g. Bausch (1979: 316), Drosdowski/Henne (1980: 625), Helbig/Buscha (1986: 191f.), Jäger (1971: 251ff.), Weinrich (2003: 246), as well as Behaghel (1924: 244f.), treat the conditional as simply an analytic counterpart to the synthetic past subjunctive and assume that the one may replace the other in any context without any distinction in meaning. This is certainly the case in prototypical 'subjunctive' contexts involving a hypothesis, as in the conditional sentences given in examples (1)–(4). However, the conditional with *würde* can also be used to express a 'future-in-the-past', i.e. to refer to an event subsequent to a reference time in the past, e.g.:

(5)   Ich wusste nun genau, was sie machen würde.
(6)   Das Theater, das sich später als ausverkauft erweisen würde, war erst halb gefüllt.
(7)   Mir war völlig klar, dass sie dort sein würde.

In these contexts, it is *not* possible to replace the conditional by the past subjunctive, and the following sentences are ungrammatical[3]:

(8)   *Ich wusste nun genau, was sie machte.
(9)   *Das Theater, das sich später als ausverkauft erwiese, war erst halb gefüllt.
(10) *Mir war völlig klar, dass sie dort wäre.

The use of the conditional in such 'future-in-the-past' contexts was long overlooked in descriptive accounts of German. To my knowledge, the first to point out this usage in modern German was Herdin (1903, 1905), who thought it was a 'new' use in the narrative device now known as 'erlebte Rede', but it is only very recently that it has been identified as a quite distinct use of the conditional which could be considered as belonging rather to the indicative than the subjunctive system, cf. Fabricius-Hansen (1998, 2000), Schanen/ Confais (1986: 154), Vuillaume (2004), Wolf (1995) and, especially, Thieroff

---

[3]   That replacing the conditional by the past subjunctive in such contexts results in ungrammaticality was confirmed in a survey of twelve educated native speakers undertaken in spring 2005. The results of this survey of the use of the past subjunctive and conditional in modern standard German will form the topic of a subsequent paper, but I should like already here to express my thanks to those friends and colleagues who were kind enough to participate.

(1992), who gives a detailed account of it with reference to the pioneering work by Herdin. However, even these writers do not always make it fully explicit that it is ungrammatical to replace the conditional in these contexts by the past subjunctive.

In this light it is also interesting to consider the history of the periphrastic conditional. Its formation is evident, as a combination of the past subjunctive of *werden* with the infinitive, and it is thus in origin a subjunctive counterpart to the ingressive use of the past tense of *werden* with a present participle or infinitive found in earlier German, e.g. from Behaghel (1924: 366):

(11) da ward im sein pferd hinken. (Ulenspiegel 110)

This usage dies out in the sixteenth century, cf. Reichmann et al. (1993: 394), but the subjunctive counterpart, which is first attested in the fourteenth century, cf. Ebert et al. (1993: 392), becomes widespread from the late fifteenth century on, and it is very widely used as an alternative to the past subjunctive from the later sixteenth century, especially, if not exclusively, in the protasis of conditional sentences, as in the following example from Ebert et al. (1993: 421):

(12) wenn schon kein Cardinal were, die kirch wurd dennoch nit vorsincken.
      (Luther, *Adel* 20)

Interestingly, it is also used from the earliest times with the meaning of a future-in-the-past, e.g., from Ebert et al. (1993: 392):

(13) weil sie wol gewust, das mit den Turcken vnd Frantzosen dis iar so stehen
      wurde. (Luther: DWB 14:1, 255)

This has rarely been remarked on by more recent writers on the modern usage of the form – as we have seen, Herdin (1903, 1905) considered the usage to be 'new' – but this could give a plausible explanation for its form as a hypothetical past of the future with *werden*, and its function, since, as Thieroff (1992: 141) points out, many languages, including French, use the same verbal form to express future-in-the-past and hypothetical conditionals.

It is striking that the functions of the German past subjunctive and conditional forms have only been identified and generally accepted quite recently, despite the fact that the functional distinction has been present since the construction arose. It is thus perhaps not surprising that the history of accounts of these forms in grammars and handbooks over the last few centuries has been one of confusion and uncertainty. In practice, as Auer (2005) shows, no grammar before 1800 really provided anything like an accurate account of the forms and usage of the German subjunctive. Typically, the grammarians of the sixteenth century started from the assumption of the universality of the categories of Greek and Latin grammar, and found difficulty in fitting the forms of German into this. They were uncertain what the moods were and how to define them, and because the uses of the German subjunctive did not parallel those of the subjunctive in the classical languages, they often failed to identify the forms of the German subjunctive accurately. For Schottelius (1663: 570ff.), who attempts to establish the categories of German in its own terms, the form with *würde* is simply the 'künftige Zeit' (i.e. 'Future tense') of the 'Weise zufügen' ('joining mood'), or 'modus coniunctivus'. He fails to identify its functional equivalence to the synthetic past subjunctive, although this is amply attested from German in the seventeenth century. It is thus not the case that the later prescriptions in relation to the use of the subjunctive in German derive from the imposition in the seventeenth and eighteenth centuries of rules and categories deriving from the classical languages, as Glück/Sauer (1997: 67) suggest. Only in the later eighteenth century, notably in Adelung (1782: §682), is there a clear realisation that the subjunctive in German has functions distinct from those of the indicative which cannot necessarily be accounted for in terms of the grammars of the classical languages. However, in common with all other grammars before 1800 which mention the form at all, he treats the conditional simply as part of the subjunctive paradigm, and he does not explicitly stigmatise its use in any context. Indeed, Adelung employs the *würde*-form in his own examples indiscriminately with synthetic past subjunctive forms. It is, however, instructive that Adelung (1782: §685) says that *wissen* ought to be followed by an indicative, as it indicates certainty, but in the past tense a subjunctive may be preferred because of the potentially uncertain outcome. However, the example he gives to illustrate this is of a future-in-the-past, i.e.:

(14)   ich wußte es lange, daß er kommen würde.

Quite typically for writers before 1800, the conditional is identified, but its function and use is misinterpreted or wrongly analysed.

The use of the conditional was thus not subject to any kind of prescription until the nineteenth century, when it came to be heavily stigmatised in certain contexts. When, precisely, this happened is not clear. Jacob Grimm (1837: 184f.), despite his predeliction for synthetic forms generally, has no trace of it, and he sees the conditional simply as an equivalent for the past subjunctive, pointing out that in the modern language the conditional can be used instead of the synthetic past subjunctive, except in an optative sense, and he gives no indication that it might be preferred in the protasis of conditional sentences. Nevertheless, the first clear statements I have been able to find of what came to be the traditional prescription are almost contemporaneous with Grimm (1837), i.e. Götzinger (1836) and Heyse (1838). Götzinger (1836: 523) is explicitly concerned, as he says, 'den jetzigen Zustand der Sprache ins Auge zu fassen und darnach ihre Benennungen und Eintheilungen geben', i.e. to consider the present state of the language and base terms and definitions on that. Thus, in what we might see as anticipating the common modern distinction of *Konjunktiv I* and *Konjunktiv II*, he states that *er habe* and *er hätte* do not express distinctions of time, but the former is used primarily to indicate indirect speech, the latter to express a hypothesis. But in dealing with the periphrasis with *würde*, which he refers to as 'der eigentliche Conditionalis', Götzinger (1836: 525ff.) claims that its proper use is to express a fact which could or might occur given certain conditions. According to Götzinger (1836: 526), it should thus only be used in the protasis:

> Der Conditionalis gilt übrigens nur für die Thatsache, welche für bestimmte Fälle gefolgert wird; nie aber kann er in dem Satze eintreten, der den angenommenen Fall selbst enthält, aus welchem gefolgert wird. Hier können alle andern Redeweisen stehen, nur nicht der Conditionalis. Ich kann sagen:
> Wüchsen die Kinder in der Art fort, wie sie sich andeuten, wir hätten lauter Genies. G. [= Goethe – MD]
> Oder mit dem Conditionalis, obgleich hier weniger gut:
> Wüchsen die Kinder ect. – wir würden lauter Genies haben.
> In keinem Falle aber:
> Würden die Kinder in der Art fortwachsen, so hätten wir lauter Genies.

He acknowledges that the past subjunctive (his 'Optativ') is also used in the protasis (and as we see, he prefers this), but predicts that the two forms will eventually become functionally distinct:

> [...] es ist vorauszusehen, daß beide Formen mit der Zeit sich immer mehr scheiden und trennen werden, so daß das bloß vom Verstand Gefolgerte in kommenden Zeiten immer durch den Conditionalis wird gegeben werden.

The use of the conditional in the apodosis (as an 'Optativ' in his terms), he sees as a peculiarity of 'südliche Mundarten' ('southern dialects'), to be avoided in good German.

The account in Heyse (1838: 770) is very similar, although he uses the term 'Präteritum Conj.' rather than 'Optativ' for the past subjunctive, and he employs 'Conditionalis' to designate function rather than form. Heyse (1838) is a comprehensive revision by Karl Wilhelm Ludwig Heyse of the grammar written by his father Johann Christian August Heyse. This originally appeared in 1819 and went through a number of editions up to J.C.A. Heyse's death in 1829, cf. Chorley (1984). I have not yet been able to consult full copies of all these earlier editions; if they make equally clear statements about the correct use of the conditional and the past subjunctive, the inception of the prescription will have to be placed some twenty years earlier. However, its origin will still be unclear.

> Für den Conditionalis dienen ausschließlich die Präterital=Formen, und zwar die einfachen Formen (a) sowohl in dem hypothetischen oder bedingenden, als in dem conditionalen oder bedingten Satze (z.B. wenn er mäßig wäre, so wäre er gesund); die umschreibenden mit ich würde (b) hingegen nur in dem bedingten Satze; z.b. wenn er mäßig wäre, so würde er gesund sein. [...].

Thus, the *würde* periphrasis is only to be used in the apodosis of conditional sentences, where it *may* replace the synthetic past subjunctive, but never in the protasis or in other contexts, where it is (Heyse 1838: 771) 'ein Verstoß gegen den guten hochdeutschen Sprachgebrauch'. Like Götzinger (1836), he claims (without any evidence that I am aware of) that this incorrect usage is particularly prevalent in South Germany. Neither Heyse nor Götzinger cite any source for their rulings, or any earlier authority, and neither make reference to usage in the classical languages as justification for their prescriptions. Heyse (1838: 771) gives a lengthy explanation why past tense forms are suited to the expression of hypotheses (and gives parallels from Latin, Greek, French and the Slavonic languages), but he does not explain why the conditional should be a permitted alternative in the apodosis of conditional sentences. Götzinger (1836: 525) attempts a rationalist explanation for the prescription, claiming that the protasis is in effect a wish, which means that only the 'Optativ' is appropriate there, since the 'Conditionalis', as it expresses a condition, cannot logically be used in the protasis, but only in the apodosis, where it indicates a consequence. This would seem contradictory, or at best a circular deduction from the appelations which Götzinger has chosen to use, since it is precisely the protasis which expresses a condition. We are left with the conclusion that this is a desperate attempt to make some sense of a grammatical usage which he has misinterpreted in order to justify his prescription.

The traditional prescription thus appears to have been first formulated in the early nineteenth century, and we must deduce that it was probably promulgated on the basis of Heyse (1838) (or earlier editions), which was a widely used school textbook and Götzinger (1836), which was also well known and used, since Cüppers (1903) still refers to it with approval. It is not clear, though, whether it originated with them, and the source of the prescription and the initial rationale for it remain a mystery. As we saw earlier, there was a marked tendency in earlier centuries for the past subjunctive to be preferred in the protasis and the conditional to be used, if at all, in the apodosis, although this was not explicitly observed by the grammarians of the seventeenth and eighteenth centuries. We can only assume that Götzinger

(1836) and Heyse (1838) – and possibly predecessors whom I have as yet been unable to trace – observed this tendency in what they regarded as 'good writers' (predominantly Goethe and Schiller, whom Götzinger in particular cites extensively), and elevated it into a rule, justifying it with *ad hoc* arguments. By the end of the nineteenth century, though, the prescription in respect of the use of the past subjunctive and the conditional had been adopted wholeheartedly by traditional guardians of correct usage,[4] and it had evidently become a shibboleth of 'good' German. The pages of the *Zeitschrift für den deutschen Unterricht* and the *Zeitschrift des Allgemeinen Deutschen Sprachvereins* between 1890 and 1920, for example, seethe with fulminations, particularly from secondary school teachers of German, against the reprehensible tendency to ignore it, especially amongst degenerate youth and the popular press, and it features prominently in books on 'good' and 'correct' usage.[5] We find all the typical discourses and attitudes of the upholders of authority in language being employed against its improper use and encounter the characteristic notion of linguistic conservatism that 'old', especially synthetic forms are inherently superior – and knowing them is a mark of good education, cf. Wustmann (1891: 184) – whereas analytic forms are long-winded and unnecessary, that the inherited, correct forms are beautiful and the innovations are ugly, that linguistic change is natural – but to be resisted in this instance because an inherited valuable distinction would be lost – that the rule for the use of these grammatical forms is dictated by logic or common sense, that inherited cultural and linguistic traditions must be defended and preserved from decay – and that it is the role of the school and the schoolteacher to impart these norms and preserve traditional 'correct' German.

Typical expressions of such attitudes from this period are found in Maydorn (1892: 44):

> Niemand wird es leugnen, daß es ein Zeichen des Verfalles ist, wenn alte klangvolle Formen zu vorzeitigem Absterben verdammt werden. [...] Und hier kann die Schule mehr thun, als vielleicht in anderen Dingen, wenn sie recht oft Gelegenheit giebt zum Gebrauche solcher Formen, so daß diese den Kindern geläufig werden, wie die anderen alle, die wir täglich in den Mund nehmen. Ist man aber erst einmal

---

4 The process thus follows the typical process of intervention in language development by such 'guardians', cf. Milroy/Milroy (1999) or 'controllers', as they are termed by Joseph (1987: 115–126), who gives a clear account of the criteria typically employed to justify such intervention and which we see employed in this case too.

5 See in particular the articles from these journals listed in the bibliography. Some are very short, and there was typically a wave of correspondence on this topic over a number of consecutive issues. Other journals and newspapers of the period would doubtless provide many similar examples. Wustmann (1891) is representative of the books of style of this period, cf. Law (2007).

gewöhnt, die alten schönen und kurzen Formen zu gebrauchen, dann bedarf es
besonderer Belehrung nicht mehr, um die Unschönheit und Unzweckmäßigkeit der
Umschreibungen einzusehen.

and, nearly thirty years later, in Mennicken (1919: 199):

Wenn wir auch den Wert einer Sprache nicht, wie oberflächliche Beobachter das
gern tun, nach ihrem Klang- und Formenreichtum abschätzen, so haben wir doch
allen Grund, der Verwilderung und Verarmung unserer Sprache, wie sie der
maßlose Gebrauch des „würde" herbeiführt, entgegenzuarbeiten und den kräftigen
kürzeren Möglichkeitsformen ihr Recht zu wahren.

Cüppers (1903), Mennicken (1919) and Wustmann (1891: 184f.) give typical
accounts of the prescription, claiming, following Götzinger (1836), that the
'conditional' form is only justified logically to express a consequence. That
these prescriptions might be relatively new and represent the elevation of a
tendency to a fixed grammatical rule is of course ignored; they are treated as if
they had been an integral and essential part of the language since time
immemorial. Such an ahistorical view of language is wholly typical of notions
of linguistic correctness. However, we also encounter two particularly German
themes in these discourses about 'good' and 'bad' language. First, that the use
of the periphrasis comes from foreign, especially French models – and is thus,
in the context of contemporary nationalism, by definition reprehensible, as in
Weitzenböck (1893: 134f.):

Ich glaube, daß die weite Verbreitung der häßlichen Umschreibung, Konditionalis
genannt, zu einem guten Teil den französischen Lehrbüchern aufs Kerbholz zu
schieben ist.

Or Scherffig (1905: 131):

Gewiß ist sie [die Umschreibung mit *würde* – MD] unter dem Einfluß der
französischen Sprache zu dem heutigen Umfang ihres Gebrauchs gekommen.

This reflects the contemporary notion, which was particularly widespread
among the members of the *Allgemeiner Deutscher Sprachverein*, that the very
essence of the German language was in danger of being undermined by French
and that the influence of French and Latin over the centuries had been
continuously deleterious, cf. Rudolph (1888). Secondly, we frequently
encounter the claim which we already saw made by Götzinger (1836) and
Heyse (1838), i.e. that the use of the periphrasis outside the permissible
contexts is a peculiarly south German feature. However, by the late nineteenth
century, it is often elaborated by the notion that it has penetrated into 'good'
northern German since unification, cf. Cüppers (1903: 297):

[Dieser Fehler] erhob sich aus seinem angestammten heimischen Bezirk zu einem Feldzug über den Main, eroberte und unterjochte den Norden und säete sich, während die Leute schliefen, als ein böses Unkraut unter unsern Weizen.

Similar claims are to be found in Wustmann (1891: 184f.) and in an editorial footnote in volume 5 (1891) of the *Zeitschrift für den deutschen Unterricht*[6]. This kind of linguistic *Kulturkampf*, the (often tacit) assumption that correct usage is based on northern (Prussian) norms, that deviations from these norms betray the fact that southerners might still not yet be fully integrated into the German nation, and that correctness is associated with Protestant usage, since High German was created by Luther, is another common topos at this time, again particularly in the writings of the *Allgemeiner Deutscher Sprachverein* and scholars associated with it, cf. Kluge (1884) and Matthias (1897). It is instructive to consider the reaction to challenges to this prescription, such as that by Burghauser (1891: 49), who voices what we would now see as a modern opinion, claiming precedence for norms based on usage (and with some expertise, since he cites Paul's *Prinzipien* in support of his views):

Diesem schönen Eifer eines grammatischen Idealismus möchte ich mir eine nüchterne Einwendung entgegenzusetzen erlauben. Die Sprachrichtigkeit ist nichts Unveränderliches, sondern sie ist vielmehr in demselben Maße veränderlich, in welchem sich der Sprachusus, das Sprachgefühl ändert.

However, his contention on this basis that the use of the conditional in writing should be modelled on majority usage, and that it was pointless to attempt to uphold a rule which nobody understood and everyone ignored in practice was subjected to a merciless barrage of criticism in subsequent issues of the journal, notably by von Dadelsen (1891), Maydorn (1892), Reichel (1892), as well as by the editor of the journal in the footnote just referred to. Burghauser was accused of a reprehensible and unpardonable failure to uphold the norms of 'good' German (the fact that he was writing from Prague, and thus from Austria, only made his views even more objectionable). In the typical argumentation of linguistic guardians it is maintained that any deviation from traditional prescriptions would send the language into terminal decline.

The prescription continued to be maintained in the inter-war years, which, as Law (2007) has shown, are characterised by the persistence of the conservative attitudes to the standard language typical of the *Bildungs-bürgertum*. These attitudes also continue for a while after the Second World

---

[6] Pages 268f. The editor at this time was Professor Otto Lyon, so the footnote is presumably his personal intervention.

War with the continuing insistence on the now traditional prescriptions for the use of the *würde*-construction in handbooks of 'good' German. Thierfelder (1950: 89–91) is a good example of this, espousing the typical 'complaint tradition', cf. Milroy/Milroy (1999: 24–46), and seeing the language in a worrying state of decay. Linguistic correctness is a virtue, and bad language is immoral, leads to vice and decadence and to the break-up of the nation. The account of the *würde*-construction in Thierfelder (1950: 91) follows the familiar pattern of prescription:

> Die Konstruktion [*d.h.*: in Bedingungssätzen – MD] kennt keine Ausnahme, aber leider begehen viele den Fehler, auch das Verbum des Nebensatzes mit „würde" zu umschreiben. Die rhythmisch schöne Fügung wird dadurch völlig zerstört. Wir merken uns: Das Hilfszeitwort „werden" kommt in „wenn"-Sätzen nicht vor.

Thierfelder (1950: 90) has no truck with the idea that some strong verb past subjunctives such as *schmölze*, *söge*, *stöbe* or *fröre* may sound unusual or unfamiliar: their use is absolutely obligatory in 'good' German.

However, this insistence on the old prescription was about to break down. It is indicative that barely ten years later, Grebe (1959: 124f.), in the first post-war edition of the authoritative DUDEN grammar, rejects it entirely, proclaiming the primacy of usage and the need for a grammar to describe the language rather than promote outdated prescriptions which are at variance with it:

> Der Liebhaber klanglich schöner und historisch ehrwürdiger Sprachformen wird die überall im Vorrücken begriffene, für ihn farblose und aufschwemmende Umschreibung mit „würde" + Infinitiv ablehnen, er kann aber nicht leugnen, daß sich die einfachen Konjunktivformen auf dem Rückzug befinden. Eine Grammatik der deutschen Gegenwartssprache muß dieser Entwicklung gerecht werden.

Grebe (1959: 536) states in the strongest possible terms that insisting on the use in particular of the synthetic forms of the past subjunctive is untenable and expresses clear contempt and no little sarcasm for backwoodsmen who might still be tempted to try to uphold the traditional prescription:

> Die Umschreibung muß heute überall als k o r r e k t betrachtet werden, wo d i e e i n f a c h e   K o n j u n k t i v f o r m   v e r a l t e t   i s t ,   g e s c h r a u b t   k l i n g t o d e r   m i t   d e r   I n d i k a t i v f o r m   ü b e r e i n s t i m m t . Sie ist nur dort über-flüssig, wo die einfache Konjunktivform noch der natürlichen Sprechweise entspricht.

Berger (1982: 65ff.), in another work from the same publishing house, whose rulings in matters of what is to be considered standard German are generally regarded as authoritative, refers to the *würde*-form, "das die Sprachpfleger doch immer wieder tadeln", and says that it is always to be preferred to the synthetic form in ambiguous cases (i.e. for all weak verbs, and also past subjunctives in -ä- like *er gäbe* which, as Burghauser (1891) had pointed out seventy years earlier, are indistiguishable for most speakers from *er gebe*) and certainly for "eine Anzahl Formen, die uns heute ungewohnt klingen, die als gekünstelt und veraltet empfunden werden". However, his list of the latter does appear rather conservative, since he lists *er gewönne, er hülfe, er würfe, er stürbe* and one or two others as forms, "vor denen wir uns nicht zu scheuen brauchen". In practice few native speakers now actively use such forms, even in writing, as the survey by Jäger (1971: 251–261) on the basis of the Mannheim corpus shows, cf. also Bausch (1979) and Freund/Sundqvist (1988: 491). Over the last forty years the traditional prescription has in effect been rejected by authoritative grammars, and in practice it is almost universally ignored in formal registers. However, this appears not to have percolated down to a few traditional guardians of correctness, since there is evidence that some secondary school schoolteachers are still attempting to uphold the traditional rules on the avoidance of the conditional, cf. Davies (2004: 331). Nevertheless, the cause is now clearly lost in practice, and it is indicative that Bastian Sick, in one of his recent bestsellers on 'good' or 'correct' German, regards the stigmatisation of the *würde*-form as old-fashioned pedantry (Sick 2005: 79–81).

It would perhaps be too simple to consider the story of the German conditional as a case where usage has won out over an antiquated and poorly motivated prescription. After all, there are many counter-instances, in German and in other languages, where pointless prescriptions have been successfully maintained in the prestige language variety against majority usage. It is thus worth considering again the details of this case, and the broad outlines seem clear. It is noteworthy, first of all, that the prescription emerged quite late – in the early nineteenth century – and its origin is not entirely clear. It appears to have been based on the observation of a tendency to use the conditional in the apodosis of conditional sentences and a mistaken assumption that this must reflect the 'correct' use of the distinct *würde*-form. By the end of the nineteenth century, with the institutionalisation of the standard language in the schools of the German Empire, it was firmly established as one of the central shibboleths of 'good' German. Why the stigmatisation of the conditional should have become so firm is unclear, since it obviously never reflected exclusive spoken usage, but metalinguistic comments in the writing about it suggest four possible principal sources of motivation: first, the presumption that synthetic forms are inherently better than analytic forms; secondly the idea that to have two conditionals with *würde* in the same sentence is ugly and unwieldy; thirdly that the category of the subjunctive adds to the prestige of a language, and it should be preserved at all costs; and, finally, that the *würde* periphrasis should have a distinct function to the analytic past subjunctive, i.e. it is a 'conditional' rather than a 'past subjunctive'. In this way, as far as we can tell, the prescription seems to have become established on the basis of *a priori* assumptions about the nature of language in general and German in particular.

It is thus possible that the failure over many years to understand fully the function of the competing conditional and past subjunctive forms underlies the prescription itself and also explains why it was ultimately unsuccessful. After all, a relatively clear understanding of the various forms and functions of the subjunctive has only emerged quite recently. Despite the assumptions and assertions made by prescriptive grammarians, the functions of the *würde*-construction have been pretty well constant since it emerged in Early New High German, although its actual use has increased immensely as it has slowly replaced the synthetic past subjunctive in contexts where it is an alternative to that. However, the eighteenth century grammarians were clearly at a loss to understand forms which failed to fit into the familiar categories of classical grammar, and the *würde*-form, with its apparently curious formation employing the past subjunctive of the future auxiliary, was difficult to reconcile with traditional views of the structure of a verb paradigm. It is thus possible that the existence of distinct forms provoked prescriptive grammarians to try to invent a functional distinction, possibly looking at parallels in French and Latin, between a 'past subjunctive', to be used in the protasis, and a 'conditional', to be used in the apodosis. Given these shaky foundations, the prescription was perhaps always going to be problematic. First, the distinction in function was never clear: the analytic past subjunctive could also always be used in the apodosis, in variation with the *würde*-form, and many guardians of 'good' language who considered synthetic forms as inherently superior preferred this usage anyway. Secondly, as we saw at the outset, the conditional appears long to have been obligatory to express the future-in-the-past, and in these contexts it is ungrammatical to substitute the past subjunctive for the *würde*-form. In this context it is interesting to note that Matthias (1903), in a detailed critique of Herdin (1903), denies absolutely that such future-in-the past contexts exist in German or that the *würde*-form can legitimately be used in them, and the editor of the journal adds that this usage can only be seen as a matter of (poor) style, not of grammar[7]. Here, Matthias and the editor appear to be rejecting out of hand any possibility that the periphrasis might have a distinct function where the past subjunctive is, in effect, ungrammatical. We can only understand this as a rather desperate attempt to uphold the traditional prescription in respect of the use of the conditional in the light of unwelcome evidence that there might be contexts where it has a distinctive meaning. Finally, as has always been pointed out by

---

[7]   Page 192. This seems to be a gratuitous personal comment by the editor (again presumably
       Professor Otto Lyon) on this point, added apparently without reference to the author.

sceptics like Burghauser (1891) and Grebe (1959: 536), there is the problem of trying to uphold a grammatical category which is imperfectly marked morphologically; for the great mass of regular ('weak') verbs, and indeed for many strong verbs, there is no formal distinction between the past indicative and the past subjunctive, and recourse must be had to the periphrasis if subjunctive meaning is to be expressed unambiguously.

In this way, the basis of the traditional prescription has always been largely artificial. It arose through a misinterpretation of the functions of the forms in question, and a desire to maintain a category (the synthetic subjunctive) which is seen as enhancing the status of German. Being inherently artificial it could only be maintained by very strong normative pressures, and it is clear from the material we have considered that this was always an uphill struggle. Even in the early part of the twentieth century a punctilious non-German descriptive grammarian like Curme (1922: 233) was quite clear that 'good authors' have consistently used the *würde*-form in all contexts without thinking any more about it 'since Luther's day', and even Behaghel (1924: 244) hints that he considers the prescription to be artificial. In effect, it was not just ignored by those local newspapers and popular authors who feature prominently as examples of bad usage in the correspondence columns of the *Zeitschrift für den deutschen Unterricht* and the *Zeitschrift des Allgemeinen Deutschen Sprachvereins*, but also by writers who were consistently put forward as models. In practice, the prescription seems to have existed primarily in school grammar books and the imagination of those guardians – predominantly schoolteachers – who regard it as their duty to uphold and transmit the strictest norms of standard German. Ultimately, it did not prove possible to uphold a prescriptive rule which was confusing and inconsistent, and at variance not only with common spoken usage, but also – and probably far more importantly – with the written usage of the educated literary elite.

References

Adelung, Johann Christoph. 1782. *Umständliches Lehrgebäude der deutschen Sprache, zur Erläuterung der deutschen Sprachlehre für Schulen.* 2 vols. Leipzig: Breitkopf.

Auer, Anita. 2005. *Language Standardisation and Language Prescription in the Eighteenth Century. The Subjunctive in English and (Austrian) German.* Unpublished PhD thesis, Manchester.

Bausch, Karlheinz. 1979. *Modalität und Konjunktivgebrauch in der gesprochenen deutschen Standardssprache. Sprachsystem, Sprachvariation und Sprachwandel im heutigen Deutsch*, vol. 1. München: Hueber.

Behaghel, Otto. 1924. *Deutsche Syntax. Eine geschichtliche Darstellung,* vol. 1: *Die Wortklassen und Wortformen. B: Adverbium. C: Verbum.* Heidelberg: Winter.

Berger, Dieter. 1982. *Fehlerfreies Deutsch.* 2nd. ed. Mannheim et. al.: Bibliographisches Institut.

Burghauser, G. 1891. Das Überwuchern der umschreibenden Konjunktivformen mit w ü r d e. *Zeitschrift für den deutschen Unterricht* 5: 49–51.

Chorley, Julie Ann. 1984. *J.C.A. Heyse (1764-1829) and K.W.L. Heyse (1797-1855) and German School Grammar in the First Half of the Nineteenth Century.* Unpublished M.Litt thesis, Oxford.

Cüppers, W. 1903. Mißbrauch der Umschreibung mit „würde". *Zeitschrift des Allgemeinen Deutschen Sprachvereins* 18: 294–298.

Curme, George O. 1922. *A Grammar of the German Language.* Rev. ed. New York: Macmillan.

Dadelsen, Hans von. 1891. Die umschreibenden Konjunktivformen mit w ü r d e. *Zeitschrift für den deutschen Unterricht* 5: 267–268.

Davies, Winifred. 2004. Deutschlehrer und Deutschlehrerinnen (in Deutschland) als Geber und Vermittler von sprachlichen Normen. In Werner Roggausch (ed.), *Germanistentreffen Deutschland – Großbritannien, Irland. 30.9.–3.10.2004.* Bonn: DAAD, 323–338.

Drosdowski, Günther and Helmut Henne. 1980. Tendenzen der deutschen Gegenwartssprache. In Hans P. Althaus, Helmut Henne and Herbert E. Wiegand (eds.), *Lexikon der germanistischen Linguistik.* 2nd ed. Tübingen: Niemeyer, 619–632.

Eisenberg, Peter. 1999. *Grundriß der deutschen Grammatik.* Vol. 2: *Der Satz.* Stuttgart and Weimar: J.B. Metzler.

Fabricius-Hansen, Cathrine. 1998. Über den Platz des *würde*-Gefüges im Tempus-Modus-System des gegenwärtigen Deutsch. In Harald Pors, Lisbeth Falster Jakobsen and Flemming Talbo Stubkjær (eds.), *Sprachgermanistik in Skandinavien III.* Århus: Handelshøjskolen i Århus, 135–158.

Fabricius-Hansen, Cathrine. 2000. Die Geheimnisse der deutschen *würde*-Konstruktion. In Rolf Thieroff, Matthias Tamrat, Nanna Fuhrhop and Oliver Teuber (eds.), *Deutsche Grammatik in Theorie und Praxis.* Tübingen: Niemeyer, 83–96.

Freund, Folke and Birger Sundqvist. 1988. *Tysk grammatik.* Stockholm: Natur och Kultur.

Glück, Helmut and Wolfangang Werner Sauer. 1997. *Gegenwartsdeutsch.* 2nd ed. Stuttgart: Metzler.

Götzinger, Max Wilhelm. 1836. *Die deutsche Sprache und ihre Literatur,* vol. 1: *Die deutsche Sprache. Theil I.* Stuttgart: Hoffmann.

Grebe, Paul (ed.) 1959. *DUDEN. Grammatik der deutschen Gegenwartssprache.* Mannheim: Bibliographisches Institut.

Grimm, Jacob. 1837. *Deutsche Grammatik*, vol. 4: *Syntax.* Göttingen: Dieterische Buchhandlung.

Helbig, Gerhard, and Joachim Buscha. 1986. *Deutsche Grammatik. Ein Handbuch für den Ausländerunterricht,* 9th. ed. Leipzig: Enzyklopädie.

Herdin, Elis. 1903. Würde + Infinitiv als *Indikativ Futuri praeteriti* gebraucht. *Zeitschrift für den deutschen Unterricht* 17: 191–208.

Herdin, Elis. 1905. Über würde mit dem Infinitiv. *Zeitschrift für den deutschen Unterricht* 19: 81–103.

Heyse, Johann Christian August. 1838. *Theoretisch-praktische Grammatik der deutschen Sprache oder Lehrbuch der deutschen Sprache nebst einer Geschichte derselben.* 5th ed., ed. by Karl Wilhelm Ludwig Heyse. Hannover: Hahnsche Hofbuchhandlung.

Jäger, Siegfried. 1971. *Der Konjunktiv in der deutschen Sprache der Gegenwart. Untersuchungen an ausgewählten Texten.* München: Hueber.

Joseph, John Earl. 1987. *Eloquence and Power. The Rise of Language Standards and Standard Languages.* London: Frances Pinter.

Kluge, Friedrich. 1904. *Von Luther bis Lessing. Sprachgeschichtliche Aufsätze.* 4th. ed. Straßburg: Trübner.

Law, Claudia. 2007. *Sprachratgeber und Stillehren in Deutschland (1923–1967). Ein Vergleich der Sprach- und Stilauffassung in vier politischen Systemen.* Berlin and New York: de Gruyter.

Matthias, Theodor. 1897. Geschichte und Sprache. *Wissenschaftliche Beihefte zur Zeitschrift des Allgemeinen Deutschen Sprachvereins.* Reihe 3: 83–103.

Matthias, Theodor. 1903. Eine junge Anwendung der Umschreibung mit w ü r d e . *Zeitschrift für den deutschen Unterricht* 17: 419–424.

Maydorn, Bernhard. 1892. Über die Konjunktiv-Umschreibung mit „würde". *Zeitschrift für den deutschen Unterricht* 6: 44–48.

Meier, H. 1985. Die Verwendung von „würde" in der deutschen Sprache der Gegenwart. *Sprachpflege* 1985/5: 65–71.

Mennicken, Franz. 1919. Jüngere Verwendung von „würde+Nennform" im Schriftdeutsch. *Zeitschrift des Allgemeinen Deutschen Sprachvereins* 34: 197–199.

Milroy, James, and Lesley Milroy. 1999. *Authority in Language. Investigating Language Prescription and Standardisation.* 3rd. ed. London: Routledge & Kegan Paul.

Reichel, Rudolf. 1892. Der Mißbrauch des Konditionals. *Zeitschrift für den deutschen Unterricht* 6: 57–59.

Reichmann, Oskar and Klaus-Peter Wegera (eds.) 1993. *Frühneuhochdeutsche Grammatik.* Tübingen: Niemeyer.

Reiners, Ludwig. 1943. *Stilkunst. Ein Lehrbuch deutscher Prosa*. München: Beck.

Rudolph, Felix. 1888. Die nationale Bedeutung unserer Sprache. *Zeitschrift des Allgemeinen Deutschen Sprachvereins* 3: 156–158.

Schanen, François, and Jean-Paul Confais. 1986. *Grammaire de l'allemand. Formes et fonctions*. Paris: Nathan.

Scherffig, Richard. 1905. Zur Umschreibung mit „würde". *Zeitschrift für den deutschen Unterricht* 19: 130–133.

Schottelius, Justus Georg. 1663. *Ausführliche Arbeit von der Teutschen HaubtSprache [...]* Braunschweig: Zilliger.

Sick, Bastian. 2005. *Der Dativ ist dem Genitiv sein Tod. Folge 2: Neues aus dem Irrgarten der deutschen Sprache*. Köln: Kiepenheuer & Witsch.

Thierfelder, Franz. 1950. *Wege zu besseren Stil*. Mainz: Grünewald Verlag.

Thieroff, Rolf. 1992. *Das finite Verb im Deutschen. Tempus – Modus – Distanz*. Tübingen: Narr.

Vuillaume, Marcel. 2004. Zum Ausdruck von „Zukunft in der Vergangenheit" im Französischen und Deutschen. In Oddleif Leirbukt (ed), *Tempus/ Temporalität und Modus/Modalität im Sprachenvergleich*. Tübingen: Stauffenburg, 169–189.

Weinrich, Harald. 2003. *Textgrammatik der deutschen Sprache*. 2nd ed. Hildesheim: Olms.

Weitzenböck, Georg. 1893. Zur Umschreibung des Konjunktivs mit „würde". *Zeitschrift für den deutschen Unterricht* 7: 134–135.

Wolf, Norbert Richard. 1995. *würde*. Zur Verwendung einer Hilfsverbform. In Heidrun Popp (ed.), *Deutsch als Fremdsprache. An den Quellen eines Faches. Festschrift für Gerhard Helbig zum 65. Geburtstag*. München: iudicium, 193–202.

Wustmann, Gustav. 1891. *Allerhand Sprachdummheiten. Kleine deutsche Grammatik des Zweifelhaften, des Falschen und des Häßlichen. Ein Hilfsbuch für alle, die sich öffentlich der deutschen Sprache bedienen*. Leipzig: Grunow.

Zifonun, Gisela, Ludger Hoffmann and Bruno Strecker. 1997. *Grammatik der deutschen Sprache*, 3 vols. Berlin and New York: de Gruyter.

ROSWITHA FISCHER (REGENSBURG)

To boldly split the infinitive – or not?
Prescriptive traditions and current English usage

1. Introduction

Many native speakers of English occasionally complain about their language being used by other people. Many people *also* worry whether what *they* say is 'correct English' or not. Where this is the case, they can obtain advice from the numerous usage guides on the market[1] – not to mention the numerous general dictionaries with their usage panels and usage notes. One must consider, however, that native speakers master the rules of their mother tongue perfectly – so the question arises where attitudes about correctness and usage come from. We have to go back in history in order to understand these concerns about good and bad language. They are found to stem mainly from scholars of the 17th, 18th, and 19th centuries, who began to codify English and lay down normative rules of the language. The aim of these so-called prescriptivists was to standardize, refine, and maintain the English language, which they did on the grounds of reason, aesthetics, prestige, or merely individual taste.

In this paper, we will consider an area of disputed grammatical usage that has been discussed with particularly strong fervour, the *split infinitive*, i.e. a verbal phrase with one or more words between the infinitival marker *to* and the following non-finite verb. One focus of the study will be on the history of this solecism and former attitudes towards it, and another will be placed on present times. We shall examine how this construction is presented in current usage books and how it is *actually* used today. For this purpose, we will explore some original versions of prescriptive grammars, current usage guides, dictionaries, and text corpora of present-day English. The paper is thus a contribution to the socio-cultural history of the English language, to questions

---

[1] Popular journalists and editors of newspapers and magazines have published guidebooks, and companies like Merriam-Webster, Oxford University Press, or Longman have all published dictionaries of modern usage, with new editions frequently appearing. A list of the latest editions of the most current usage books is given in the reference section.

dealing with the influence of prescriptivism yesterday and today, and to corpus linguistics.

At the outset, the linguistics of the origin and the spreading of the split infinitive will be investigated. After that, the split infinitive will be examined in the light of English prescriptivism, followed by a corpus-linguistic study of its actual usage in current English. It will be seen that prescriptivism is still influential today, especially with respect to written British English. But despite a sometimes more hesitant attitude towards the use of the split infinitive, it can be observed that nowadays the construction has found its place in certain linguistic contexts. It is possible to identify a language change from below[2] which is most prominent in casual speech but is also apparent in written formal English.

2. Historical Aspects

2.1 Old English

In Old English there were two main morphological types of infinitive constructions, both of which originally derived from a nominal form. Firstly, there was an infinitive with the suffix *-an* or *-ian*, which we would call a *bare infinitive* today, and secondly, there was an infinitive with the preposition *to*, which originally meant 'toward', plus the inflected suffix *-anne* or *-enne*. The former type occurs frequently from earliest times onwards, while the occurrence of the latter type was mainly limited to constructions expressing purpose or volition, and this may have been the entry-point for the *to*-infinitive (Traugott 1992: 242). At this period of time, no evidence exists for a verb phrase where another word has been put between *to* and the verb, i.e. for the so-called split infinitive.

2.2 Middle English

In Middle English, however, the situation changed completely. Now the *to*-infinitive was more common, and the bare infinitive became more and more restricted. Several reasons can be named for this development. First of all, the inflections were gradually reduced and lost, and the preposition *to* became a sign for the infinitive form, which was still distinguishable in this way from

---

[2]   I.e. below the level of consciousness and moving away from the socially accepted norm.

other verb forms. Furthermore, Middle English also saw the introduction of the *for...to*-infinitive. Since the particle *to* had become a marker of the infinitive in general, another particle was needed to express purpose and volition. But *for to* suffered the same fate as *to*, since it eventually also came to mark the infinitive in general, becoming obsolete in Early Modern English (Fischer 1992: 317–24). This development from a more specific use to a more generalized one, which is usually accompanied by semantic bleaching and phonological reduction, is an example of *grammaticalization*, which was in this case triggered by the transformation of English from a synthetic into an analytic language. *Grammaticalization* is said to be a universal tendency in the evolution of languages and is believed to be unidirectional and non-reversible. However, Olga Fischer pointed out that, at least in the case of the *to*-infinitive, this is only part of the story. She claims that the concept of grammaticalization is nowadays used too rashly and too carelessly for explanations of language change. In contrast, she assumes that, towards the end of the Middle English period, *to* went back to its original meaning of goal or direction and thus became degrammaticalized, owing to syntactic processes and universal iconic constraints (Fischer 2000: 158). Evidence for this process can also be found in the allegedly new appearance of the split infinitive (ibid., see below). However, since *to* had never totally lost its lexical meaning, it does not seem appropriate to speak of degrammaticalization. It is preferable to assume a case of *partial grammaticalization*, i.e. an ongoing process of grammaticalization that comes to a halt at a certain point in time.

2.3 Modern English

The split infinitive has occurred sporadically from the 14th century onwards, which can be related to the growing numbers of *to*-infinitives in general. The negator *not* could occur between *to* and the non-finite verb form as a pronoun, later also as an adverb and even in combinations of two or more words; see the following examples from Visser (Visser 1966: §978–82):

(1) It is good for to not ete fleisch and for to not drynke wyn. (c1382 Wyclif Mt. Rom, 14, 21)
(2) Thei not rede and studie in the Bible oonly forto it leerne. (c1449 Pecock, Repressor 59)
(3) I know not how I should be able to absolutely forbid him my sight. (1778 Fanny Burney, Evelina LI, 235)
(4) To quietly next day at crow of cock cut my throat (1868-9 Rob. Browning, The Ring & the Book (Cambr. ed., p. 588)

According to Visser, the prejudice of grammarians has kept the frequency of the split infinitive low until very recently. However, since the construction was frequently mentioned by grammarians and other guardians of the English language from the 19th century onwards, it seems likely that it had already gained in popularity by that time, or even earlier. Several linguistic developments facilitated its gradual spread – the increased frequency of the *to-*infinitive itself (see above), the corresponding parallel finite structures (the type 'I greatly wonder'), the restricted position of the adverb from Early Modern English onwards (sic),[3] and the principle of end-focus together with prosody, i.e. the regular pattern of unstressed adverb and stressed non-finite verb ('to greatly wonder' vs. 'to wonder greatly').[4] With respect to socio-historical reasons, we can also name several changes. The population growth in the 19th century was met with the establishment of compulsory schools and libraries and, as a consequence, literacy spread. A new readership mainly turned to newspapers, which became a cheap and genuine mass medium and rapidly increased in number. It seems that, on the basis of literacy and the print media, latent structures like the split infinitive, which might already have been quite common in spoken language for a while, came out into the open. The construction then came to the attention of schoolmasters and other guardians of English usage, who, in the prescriptive spirit of their times, argued against its usage.

3. The prescriptive tradition

In order to understand the prescriptive tradition in England, we need to go back further in time, i.e. to the Late Middle Ages and to the beginning of the modern era. In the Middle Ages, the primary subject of language study had been Latin, the language of learning, literature, church services, and administration.[5] In the Renaissance, European scholars paid increased attention to the Classical languages, but also started to show interest in the modern languages. This interest was accompanied by a growth of nationalist feeling. The invention and expansion of printing stimulated the gradual spread of literacy and a demand for education by means of texts, dictionaries, and grammars. Since Latin in its classical, written form was still considered to be superior to the modern vernaculars, Latin grammar was used as a model for the description of English.

---

[3]   Compare Rissanen (1999: 268f.).
[4]   Compare Spies (1941: 14ff., 17f., 39).
[5]   The liberal arts, which were part of the core curriculum of medieval universities, included the study of grammar, which served as a basis for learning how to read and write Latin.

This admiration for the highly elaborate Latin of the classical tradition had various effects on attitudes towards language: people felt that there should be fixed, correct forms; they thought that written language was superior to spoken language and they viewed the current form of English as having slipped from classical purity. Furthermore, the expansion of the British Empire in the following centuries resulted in an awareness of national identity, which was met by a growing concern for one's own language as an expression of one's own nationality. Against this background, there arose the need to codify English in its purest form. In the late 17th and 18th centuries, language reformers – among them well-known literary figures – proposed an English Academy, which, however, never became established, probably due to the death of Queen Anne, who had not only been a supporter of their ideas but also a suitable patron for their project. Another reason might have been the growing anxiety that such an academy might interfere with people's individual freedom (Baugh and Cable 1993: 263). This gap was readily filled by individual scholars and their publications. We will pursue below the impact of prescriptivism by the examples of three particularly influential men: Robert Lowth, Henry Alford, and Henry W. Fowler.

3.1 Lowth's *English grammar*

The increased concern and market for grammatical correctness resulted in the publication of numerous popular grammar books from the second half of the 18th century onwards. While earlier grammars were generally written for either foreign learners or for native speakers as a basis for learning and studying Latin, most grammatical treatises at this time were intended to help the students learn 'proper' English. Since it was generally believed that linguistic control was achieved through the study of grammar, teachers were in need of English grammar books, which they often wrote themselves as textbooks for their classes, by heavily leaning on already published and widely acknowledged grammars. These manuals resembled general language guides in that they not only dealt with word classes, morphology, and syntax, but also with orthography, figures of speech, and usage.

One of the best known and probably the most influential grammar at that time was Robert Lowth's *Short Introduction to English Grammar.*[6] Between 1762 and 1800, it went through 22 editions, and its influence was also spread by Lowth's followers. Robert Lowth was a clergyman, and as Bishop of

---

[6] According to Tieken-Boon van Ostade (2000), the idea for such a project did not originally come from Lowth, but from the bookseller Robert Dodsley.

Oxford – later of London – and as a professor of Hebrew poetry he was widely acknowledged as an authority on languages.

Lowth's attitude and approach are characteristic of English prescriptivism in the 18th century. He used Latin models and disregarded structural differences between Latin and English. He acknowledged the authority of older usage and assumed that grammar primarily applied to written language. His basic strategy was to lay down rules and illustrate them by 'right' and 'wrong' examples. These language rules were mainly based on personal preference and on his own intuitions. Lowth's grammar remained in standard use throughout English-speaking educational institutions until the early 20th century.

Robert Lowth's grammar states that the preposition *to* is to be placed before the verb (Lowth 1762: 108). Students had to learn by heart and recite aloud verbal patterns such as "to learn, to be learning, to have learned, to have been learning", sometimes also "about to learn" for the future tense. This newly acquired knowledge was then practiced by means of little sayings, such as 'Let us learn to practice virtue', or 'My friend is worthy to be trusted', which conveyed moral values as well. Lowth's view was clearly based on a Latin model, i.e. on a false analogy with Latin, and it probably became the origin for the later proscription of the split infinitive. In Latin, infinitives consist of a single word, whereas in English they can be made up of more than one. Since the Latin infinitive could not be 'split', grammarians reasoned that in English it should not be split either. Lowth, together with other scholars of the 18th century, does not comment on the possibility of putting a word between *to* and the verb at all,[7] which implies that, for a learned man like him, who was firmly rooted in the tradition of the classical languages, it was simply unimaginable. But the missing commentaries also indicate that the split infinitive must have been used only rarely – at least by the educated –, otherwise Lowth and his equals would certainly have made it a subject of discussion.

3.2 Alford's *Queen's English*

Up to the 18th century, matters of usage had been included in grammar books, but from the 19th century onwards, they became published as a topic of their own, which may be related to the growing association of linguistic purity with the moral values of the Victorian age and the resulting practice of "error-hunting" (Nevalainen 2003: 144). The 'correct' use of certain structures

---

[7] At least with respect to the grammars available and examined.

became an index of education and high social status, and their misuse was felt to be a sign of lack of knowledge and education. This social stigma can also be considered the ultimate reason why emotions still rise high when it comes to usage today. Against this background, we can understand why usage today – especially in Britain – is still disputed so often and so vigorously.

In addition to this, newspapers and magazines began to be widely distributed, so that journalists and readers began discussing various matters of usage. As a result of this activity, usage notes were given out for journalists or freelance writers, which eventually became published as books, along with comments and suggestions by the readers (*Merriam-Webster's dictionary of English usage* 1994: 9a). One of the first of these was *A Plea for Queen's English* by Henry Alford (1810–1871) in 1864. Alford was an English churchman, scholar, poet and artist, who was employed as Dean of Canterbury. His *Queen's English* was printed many times and became well-known throughout the country. It can be considered as one of the first (if not *the* first) of a line of numerous usage guides, bringing to life a tradition that has lasted until today.

Alford also seems to be one of the first to mention the split infinitive.[8] In §350 of *Queen's English* he refers to a correspondent's usage of this construction. Firstly, he argues that nobody knows it, and, secondly, that it is superfluous, since there are already two possible ways to express what one wants to convey:

> A correspondent states as his own usage, and defends, the insertion of an adverb between the sign of the infinitive mood and the verb. He gives as an instance, "*to scientifically illustrate.*" But surely this is a practice entirely unknown to English speakers and writers. It seems to me, that we ever regard the *to* of the infinitive as inseparable from its verb. And when we have already a choice between two forms of expression, "*scientifically to illustrate,*" and "*to illustrate scientifically,*" there seems no good reason for flying in the face of common usage. (Alford [5]1880: 227)

Apart from the accidental pun in this quote, it is interesting to note that Alford not only argues by means of logic (a familiar scholarly method related to the classical traditions), but also by means of common usage; and therefore he must have been well aware of the dictates of language in practice. However, he ignores the fact that the correspondent himself is also a representative of the speech community and regards the innovation as wrong. In addition, he

---

[8] According to Heinrich Spies, the first person to comment on the split infinitive was the London bookseller, editor and publisher Richard Taylor (in 1829). Spies then quotes Goold Brown, an American grammarian (1851), and Henry Alford (Spies 1941: 2f.). However, as the author also admits, the sources are not complete because not all the relevant manuals and books could be obtained and inspected.

considers the three expressions to mean the same, and it is up to Henry W. Fowler to point out the differences between them at a later date.

3.3 Fowler's *Modern English usage*

In the early 20th century, it was not a churchman but a teacher who set the future standard. In 1926 Henry Fowler, a teacher of Classics and English and a freelance writer, published his *Dictionary of Modern English Usage*, which became widely known and respected and, in the form of revised editions, is still considered *the* standard usage guide in Britain today. In contrast to Alford, Fowler considered the use of the split infinitive a matter of good or bad writing style.[9] He wrote the following:

> The English-speaking world may be divided into those who neither know nor care what a split infinitive is, those who don't know, but care very much, those who know and approve, those who know and condemn, and those who know and distinguish. (Fowler 1926: 558)

Fowler clearly disapproved of the former grammarians, while at the same time remaining under their influence himself. He believed that the split infinitive should be recommended in certain contexts, which is also the prevailing opinion of the many usage guides today. The modern guides write accordingly that one should not separate *to* from the non-finite verb, unless this leads to clumsiness or ambiguity. For instance, according to the *Oxford guide to English usage*, the sentence "It fails completely to carry conviction" is ambiguous. Either it means "It totally fails", in which case *completely* should precede *fails*, or it means "It fails to carry complete conviction", in which case the infinitive should be split (cf. *Oxford Guide to English Usage*: 217).[10] But, apart from constructions like this, the usage guides recommend avoiding the split infinitive altogether because its use might meet with disapproval.

---

[9]   In their style guide, called at that time *The King's English*, the Fowler brothers already considered the use of the split infinitive a matter of style, though they advised not to take the matter too seriously: "The 'split' infinitive has taken such hold upon the consciences of journalists that, instead of warning the novice against splitting his infinitives, we must warn him against the curious superstition that the splitting or not splitting makes the difference between a good and a bad writer. The split infinitive is an ugly thing, as will be seen from our examples below; but it is one among several hundred ugly things, and the novice should not allow it to occupy his mind exclusively." (Fowler and Fowler [3]1930 [1906]: 329).

[10] If the meaning is 'it fails to completely carry conviction', there is also the possibility to put the adverb after the word *conviction*, which is not mentioned in the *Oxford Guide to English Usage*.

Summing up, we can assume that the split infinitive has generally been rejected by the guardians of the English language. When it occurred only sporadically in Medieval times, no scholar apparently felt the need to comment on it, simply because it was below the threshold of perception and, within the bounds of the Latin model, clearly unthinkable. From the 19th century onwards, it became more popular, was eventually noticed, and viewed with disfavour. But although the disapproval persists, the argumentation has changed from disregard through seemingly logical reasoning to stylistic matters of conciseness and clarity. In order to find out whether the recommendations for the avoidance of the split infinitive were successful, and if so to what extent, an investigation of actual usage of current English is necessary. To this I will turn now.

4. The split infinitive in actual usage

For an examination of the actual usage of the split infinitive, I used several text corpora of different standard varieties in the spoken and written media, and from different periods of time. The FLOB and FROWN[11] corpora were the starting point of the analysis. Both consist of a million words of British and American English respectively and represent the state of the written language of the early 90s. Compared to other corpora available today, these corpora are rather small; however, they are absolutely sufficient for a study of common syntactic phenomena. In addition, we compared the results in these corpora with their predecessors LOB and BROWN, which include corresponding texts from the 1960s. Furthermore, we considered two corpora of spoken English: the LLC, which contains half a million words of British English collected mainly in the 1960s and 70s, and the WSC, which consists of a million words of New Zealand English and contains texts from the late 1980s and early 90s. Eventually, we arrived at the following results:[12]

---

[11] FLOB is the abbreviation for *Freiburg* LOB, and FROWN for *Freiburg* BROWN. The two corpora were compiled under the same premises as their predecessors LOB (short for London-Oslo / Bergen) and BROWN (named after Brown University, Rhode Island). LLC stands for *London-Lund Corpus*, and WSC for *Wellington Spoken Corpus* (named after the places of assembly).

[12] The text corpora were searched by means of the program WordSmith, typing in *to* + spacebar + **ly*. After that, the samples with *to* and a noun or verb ending in *-ly*, such as *Lilly*, *to family* (*values*), *to rely*, *to comply*, and so on were removed. In addition, cases with *to* + *not* and *to* + *all* were included.

Written British English		Written American English		Spoken English	
LOB (1961)	FLOB (1991)	Brown (1961)	Frown (1991)	LLC (mainly 1960s–1970s)	WSC (1988–94)
9	28	33	76	70	187

Table 1: The split infinitive in LOB, FLOB, Brown, Frown, LLC, and WSC (per 1 m words):

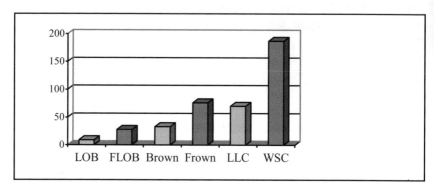

Figure 1: The split infinitive in LOB, FLOB, Brown, Frown, LLC, and WSC (per 1 m words):[13]

The table shows, first of all, that use of the split infinitive is increasing. In the American corpora, the numbers doubled from 1961 to 1991, and in the spoken corpora they even tripled. Comparing the two British corpora, we can also observe a rise in frequency, although it is not possible to make a stronger statement because of the low numbers. With respect to medium and to the national standard varieties, the table reveals that the split infinitive is used much more often in spoken than in written discourse and also occurs more frequently in American English than in British English.

Apart from solely looking at numbers, the type of word involved and its relation to the verb have to be examined. Most of the words used are emphasizers, intensifiers, and focussing subjuncts[14] such as *fully*, *really*, *even*, and *merely*. The restriction of the adverb position in front of the verb goes back to an Early Modern English development, which in turn is related to the fixation of word order caused by the loss of the morphological marking of the object. Throughout the history of English, the placement of adverbs was highly variable and depended on their meaning and their relationship to other sentence elements. The adverb was typically placed in mid- or end-position, either before or after the predicate verb. In Early Modern English, however,

---

[13]   Light grey marks the older corpora, dark grey the later ones.
[14]   Following the terminology of Quirk et al. (1985).

the positioning of the adverb became more restricted, such that the adverb was mostly placed before the verb and not between the verb and its object (Rissanen 1999: 268f.). It seems likely that the increased positioning of the adverb before the verb also influenced the spread of the split infinitive, with the adverb placed before the verb and after the infinitive marker *to*.

Finally, the sentence structures involved have to be considered. The split infinitive is mainly used when the nonfinite verb is followed by a direct object (see the following examples):

(5)   Now, in the person of Mr. Clinton, American voters face the possibility that a generation that once took to the streets *to publicly denounce American policy* will lead it. (FROWN, A A07:19)

(6)   any agreement between local education authorities and teaching unions could be undermined by Whitehall refusing *to fully fund it* [the current system]. (FLOB, B B02:13)

In contrast to this, the adverb is usually postponed when the verb is intransitive or followed by a time or place adjunct which has end-focus:

(7)   And Mr Major will have *to tread carefully*. (FLOB, A 01:44)

(8)   what they are going *to do differently in the coming year* (FROWN, A 22:46)

With respect to verbs with particles, usage is divided. Compare for instance (9) with (10):

(9)   although he was right *to fully cooperate with* the police. (FLOB, A 37:52)

(10) The failure of internal capital *to respond fully to* the PAP's 'second industrial revolution'. (FLOB, J 42: Heading)

If the adverb specifies the finite verb, it is generally placed in front of it:

(11) May be Perot has been telling the truth all along, that he *doesn't really want* to be president. (FROWN, A11:18)

In a few cases, it is also put between the finite verb and the following *to*-infinitive:

(12) In the second procedure, subjects were asked *merely to give* nominal statements of well-formedness. (FROWN, J 34:4)

This construction matches the sentence "It fails completely to carry conviction" from the *Oxford guide to English usage* (see above) and should be avoided because of its ambiguity.

Some uses are rather odd and can be attributed to a conscious avoidance of the split infinitive; these cases occur mostly in the British LOB corpus. See, for instance:

(13) Some observers believe he may *choose publicly to distance himself* from the American plan (FLOB, A 03:33)

(14) *Condemned always to wear* the letter A as a badge of shame, this gifted seamstress has turned it into a resplendent work of art. (FROWN, A44:9)

In these two examples, theoretically there is ambiguity of meaning because one does not know whether the adverb refers to the finite or the non-finite verb. If one associates the adverb with the preceding verb, the resulting meaning does not make much sense – *choose publicly* – *condemned always* – ? What is actually meant is *publicly distance* and *always wear*, i.e. the respective adverb refers to the nonfinite verb. Therefore, the split infinitive would have been appropriate.

The spoken corpora mainly have *actually*, *really*, or *sort of* between *to* and the non-finite verb:

(17) I mean I'd quite like a sort [mod] – modern sort of . single [ein] single lens reflex stuff – . *to actually take photographs* with . (LLC, 310C)

(18) um she needs something *to really get* her going (WSC#DPC326:1445:JI)

(19) just have *to sort of wrap* it around (WSC#DPC077: 0260: MK)

In these cases, the use of the split infinitive is mainly restricted to certain lexical items and thus seems to be lexically conditioned to a certain extent.

5. Conclusion

In this paper, we have addressed the question of the interrelationships between prescriptive tradition and English usage from the 18th century until today, taking as an example the split infinitive. On the one hand, we traced the emergence of this construction and related it to linguistic and social developments; on the other hand, we looked at the attitudes towards usage and the resulting proscriptions. Though the use of the split infinitive coincidentially increased while prescriptivism was blooming, this concurrence of events laid the foundation for the following rejection of the construction. Since then, the line of argumentation against its use has become more moderate and dis-criminative – and the split infinitive more popular. We can therefore dis-tinguish between a language change from above, which was consciously promoted and linked with prestige, and a language change from below, which was below consciousness and took place despite the prohibition by the authorities. Both language changes took place at the same time, with the language change from above being mainly restricted to formal written language, and the language change from below spreading especially in casual conversation. The rising numbers of the split infinitive even in the written text corpora may also indicate that the developments in the spoken language influence the written mode, which corresponds to a tendency subsumed under the term *colloquialization* (Fischer 2005). Nevertheless, the type of discourse involved has a strong impact on the use of the split infinitive and should not be underestimated. Whether the split infinitive will further gain ground, and, if so, under which circumstances this might happen must be left to future consideration.

References

1. Usage guides

Austin, Tim. 1999. *The Times guide to English style and usage.* London: Times Books.

Fowler, Henry W. and Francis Fowler. 1906. *The King's English.* 3rd ed. 1973. Oxford: OUP.

Fowler, Henry W. 1926. *A Dictionary of modern English usage;* Oxford: Clarendon Press. [2nd rev. ed., *The new Fowler's modern English usage,* by Sir Ernest Gowers (1965), 3rd rev. ed. by Robert Burchfield (1996).]

Garner, Bryan A. (ed.). 1998. *A dictionary of modern American usage.* New York: OUP.

Greenbaum, Sidney and Janet Whitcut. 1996. *Longman guide to English usage.* London: Penguin.

Hands, Penny (ed.). 1999. *Chambers essential English grammar and usage.* Edinburgh: Chambers Harrap.

Howard, Geoffrey (ed.). 1993. *The good English guide: English usage in the 1990s.* London: Macmillan.

Johnson, Edward D. H. 1991. *The handbook of good English.* New York: Facts on File.

Merriam-Webster's dictionary of English usage. 1994. Springfield, Mass.: Merriam-Webster.

Partridge, Eric (ed.). 1999. *Usage and abusage: A guide to good English.* 2nd ed. London: Penguin.

Sinclair, John (ed.). 1999. *Collins Cobuild English usage.* London: Harper Collins.

Stevens, John. 1998. *Handbuch des englischen Sprachgebrauchs: ein Ratgeber für Zweifelsfälle.* Stuttgart: Klett.

Weiner Eva S.C. and Andrew Delahunty. 1983 (1993). *The Oxford guide to English usage. The essential guide to correct English.* Oxford: OUP.

2. 18th-century prescriptive grammars

Ash, John. 1763. *Grammatical institutes, or, an easy introduction to Doctor Lowth's English grammar: designed for the use of school.* London: Dilly. [Repr. English Linguistics [= EL]. A collection of facsimile reprints, selected and edited by R.C. Alston. No. 9, 1500–1800. Leeds: Scolar Press, 1967].

Dilworth, Thomas. 1740 (1751). *A new guide to the English tongue.* London: Kent. [Repr. EL, No. 4. Leeds: Scolar Press. 1967].

Fell, John. 1784. *An essay towards an English grammar.* London: Dilly. [Repr. EL, No. 16. Menston: Scolar Press. 1967].

Fisher, Ann. 1750. *A new grammar.* Newcastle upon Tyne. [Repr. EL, No. 130. Menston: Scolar Press. 1968].

Lowth, Robert. 1762. *A short introduction to English grammar.* London: J. Hughes. [Repr. EL, No. 18. Menston: Scolar Press. 1967].

Murray, Lindley. 1795. *English grammar, adapted to the different classes of learners.* Menston: Scolar Press. [Repr. EL, No. 106. Menston: Scolar Press. 1968].

Priestley, John. 1761. *The rudiments of English grammar, adapted to the use of schools, with observations on style.* London: Griffiths. [New York: Garland, 1971].

Ward, William. 1765. *Essay on grammar.* London: Horsfield. [Repr. EL, No. 15. Menston: Scolar Press. 1968].

Webster, Noah. 1784. *A Grammatical institute of the English language comprising an easy, concise, and systematic method of education, designed for the use of English schools in America.* Hartford: Hudson & Goodwin. [Repr. EL, No. 89. Menston: Scolar Press. 1968].

3. Other sources

Baugh, Albert C. and Thomas Cable. 1993. *A history of the English language.* 4th ed. London: Routledge.

Fischer, Olga. 1992. Syntax. In Norman Blake (ed.), *The Cambridge history of the English language, vol. II. 1066–1476.* Cambridge: CUP, 207–408.

Fischer, Olga. 2000. Grammaticalization: Unidirectional, non-reversible? The case of 'to' before the infinitive in English. In Olga Fischer, Anette Rosenbach and Dieter Stein (eds.), *Pathways of change. Grammaticalization in English*. Amsterdam: Benjamins, 149–169.

Fischer, Roswitha. 2005. Discourse levelling in English newspaper language. In Piotr Cap (ed.), *Pragmatics today*. Frankfurt: Lang, 157–172.

Nevalainen, Terttu. 2003. English. In Ana Deumert and Wim Vandenbussche (eds.), *Germanic standardizations. Past to present*. Amsterdam: Benjamins, 127–156.

Quirk, Randolph, et al. (ed.) 1985. *A comprehensive grammar of the English language*. London: Longman.

Rissanen, Matti. 1999. Syntax. In Roger Lass (ed.), *The Cambridge history of the English language, vol. III. 1476–1776*. Cambridge: CUP, 187–331.

Smith, W.M. 1959. The split infinitive. *Anglia* 77: 257–78.

Spies, Heinrich. 1941. Der 'split infinitive' (eine Übersicht). *Anglia* 65: 1–50.

Tieken-Boon van Ostade, Ingrid. 2000. Robert Dodsley and the genesis of Lowth's 'Short introduction to English grammar'. *Historiographica Linguistica* 27: 21–36.

Traugott, Elizabeth Closs. 1992. Syntax. In Richard M. Hogg (ed.), *The Cambridge history of the English language,* vol 1: *The beginnings to 1066*. Cambridge: CUP, 168–289.

Visser, Frederikus Theodorus. 1966. *An historical syntax of the English language*, vol. 2: *Syntactical units with one verb, Part 2*. Leiden: Brill, §977–982.

AMANDA POUNDER (CALGARY)

Norm consciousness and corpus constitution in the study of Earlier Modern Germanic Languages[1]

1. Introduction

The premise that at least some language developments may involve variants associated with informal registers/colloquial speech appears to be an undangerous one, and we can identify variants with system characteristics that predispose them to be candidates for this sort of change under standardization. For example, where in a prestandard or early standard the choice between variants depends on considerations of rhythm, thus by their nature associated with speech, it is to be expected that under the ideology of standardization, the criteria determining choice may be displaced by criteria of uniformity and economy, i.e. a desire of reduction to one invariant form. In order to determine whether such a development has in fact taken place, it would be convenient to be able to examine texts corresponding to informal registers on the further premise that these faithfully reflect oral language and thus provide a basis for establishing distributions and relative frequencies of variants there. Relevant text types under this premise would include personal letters, diaries, dialogue in plays/novels, non-literary prose among others. Unfortunately, after proceeding under this methodological premise, it seems sometimes to occur that texts of these types do not provide a reliable or consistent source of data for informal/colloquial language for the relevant phenomena as expected. From these results arise a number of questions, such as whether we could be mistaken about the supposed change itself (e.g. the location of the variants in the spoken mode or colloquial register.) If not, do we need to revise our expectations of these texts as an automatically reliable data source? If this is so, with what can we replace the data source in order to obtain facts necessary for tracing the development? The present paper considers two phenomena in the early standardization period, namely the choice between deadjectival zero adverb and adverb suffixed in *-ly* in English and the choice between zero form

---

[1] This paper arises from a larger research study on the development of adverb-marking and adjective inflection in West Germanic.

of the inflected attributive adjective and a suffixed form in German. It offers
the tentative conclusion that written texts of early Modern periods may be
selective as to what colloquial traits may (not) appear in them, and personal
letters and diaries in particular may not be as close to spoken language as we
expect them to be today based on our own usage.

2. Adverb-formation in English

While there have always been morphological and lexical criteria governing the
choice between deadjectival zero adverb (*Max runs <u>daily</u>*, *Max runs <u>pretty fast</u>*;
see e.g. Pounder 2004 and references therein for history and distributions),
syntactic and rhythmic factors have also been mentioned by language
historians as possible motivations for the choice in early Modern English. It is
these latter factors that will be the focus of this section.

The first syntactic context we are concerned with is coordinate
constructions. It has been suggested that in these structures, there is a tendency
in earlier Modern English to select the zero adverb for the first conjunct (cf.
Knorrek 1938: 103), as shown in (1).

(1)   *bright and beautifully*

In (1) we have two adverbs conjoined by *and*, with the second only having
undergone suffixation. Insofar as it is purely syntactically motivated, the
structure may be interpreted in two ways: under the first interpretation, the
conversion process has been selected for the first adverb in anticipation of a
suffixed form, whereas under the second interpretation, a suffixation of the
adverb in the first conjunct has been suppressed, to be reconstructed by means
of the suffixed adverb in the second conjunct.

The second context is an adjective or adverb phrase in which an adverb
modifies the head, as in (2). In (2a) the deadjectival degree adverb modifies the
qualitative deadjectival adverb, and appears in its zero form; (2b) shows that
this same pattern can occur even when the modified adverb is not a *ly*-
suffixation.

(2)   a. *exceeding beautifully*
        b. *exceeding well*

It has also been suggested that the choice of deadjectival adverb-formation
type can be motivated by the desire to achieve an optimal rhythmic pattern (cf.
Selkirk 1984), namely an alternation of strong and weakly stressed syllables
(cf. e.g. Schlüter 2002). This would entail that the adverb phrase in (3a), which

provides such a pattern, would be preferred to (3b), which results in a 'stress clash', or succession of stressed syllables.

(3) a. *really well*
     b. *real well*

We get a different preference in (4), however, due to the rhythmic patterns resulting:

(4) a. *real obscene*
     b. *really obscene*

Here, the zero type of the adverb (4a) is preferable, as the suffixed type (4b) results in a sequence of two unstressed syllables. There may be interaction between the syntactic and the rhythmic motivations for adverb formation type in Adverb Phrases in which one derived adverb modifies another: on the rhythmic principle, *real obscenely* and *really beautifully* will both be preferred structures, but only the first will match the syntactic preference. Applying the rhythmic principle should select *bright and beautiful* over *brightly and beautifully*, too, at least if we assume no focus stress on *bright* (5).

(5) a. *bright and beautiful*
     b. *brightly and beautifully*

Furthermore, the syntactic preferences described for coordinate constructions could be interpreted as euphonically motivated, that is, by the desire to avoid a repetition of a suffix in neighbouring items (for discussion of morphological haplology with respect to adverb-formation in English, see Pounder 2004 and references therein).

Assuming these syntactic and rhythmic preferences to have held at some point in the history of Modern English, we want to establish what their strength was at what point in the history of adverb formation in what domains of the language. As these preferences are based at least partially on considerations of euphony, it is a reasonable hypothesis that they will be strongest in the oral mode.[2] We should expect therefore to see structures such as (3a), (4a), (5a) better represented in texts closest to speech. Insofar as grammarians consider spoken language at all, we should expect that if they refer to these preferences, they will attribute them to spoken language.

---

[2] Naturally, we would expect that poetry should also reflect these preferences; however, we will not be considering poetic texts here.

Moreover, we should expect that grammarians who accept the criterion of euphony as an evaluator of linguistic structures will speak favourably of those exemplified by (2a), (4a), and (5a), while those who do not will criticize them, speaking rather in favour of one adverb formation type per base lexeme (criterion of uniformity), namely the *ly*-suffixation (criterion of clarity) where not prevented by other lexical or systemic considerations.

First of all, it must be said that there are very few direct references to these particular structures in contemporary grammars. With regard to zero deadjectival adverbs in general, the usual methods of indicating a preference of *ly*-suffixation are by not mentioning the conversion option at all, or occasionally by such oblique suppressions as illustrated in (6), from Greenwood (1711: 161):

> (6)   Q: Are not Adjectives sometimes used as Adverbs?
>   A: Yes: They often are so used, and there is hardly any Adjective from
>   whence an Adverb in *ly*, may not be formed.

(7) gives Bayly's response (1772: 61) to Lowth's injunction (1762: 56) to use the *ly*-formation-type only:

> (7)   Certainly the ear, which will overrule judgment and theory, taught the use of
>   some adjectives as adverbs without an adverbial termination, and custom hath
>   introduced others....This manner of using adjectives is very animated and
>   frequent [...]

Although Bayly is one of those grammarians who accepts both euphony and custom as evaluation criteria of linguistic structures, he does not make explicit reference to coordination structures or to rhythmic patterns. In (8) we find an objection (Sedger 1798: 71) to a sequence of adverbs suffixed in -*ly*, or to a sequence of zero adverbs (interestingly, *remarkably hasty* does not seem as objectionable to him as does *extraordinarily fine*).

> (8)   But when I say, *He speaks remarkably hastily*, I mean, he speaks in a
>   *remarkably hasty manner*. Now I could wish that two adverbs might not come
>   together, any more than two adjectives, when this can be avoided. Then I
>   could say, *He speaks remarkably hasty*, or *remarkable hastily* [...]

His proposed solutions allow not only for structures such as (2a), where the suffixed adverb is the final one, but also the reverse, where it precedes a zero adverb. Crucially, then, two formally like adverbs should not occur in sequence.

Lennie (1815[3]: 76) declares categorically that "*ly* is cut off from *exceedingly* when the next word ends in *ly*", which reinforces the notion that the zero adverb participates in an avoidance strategy (although we need not assume that a deletion process is involved as Lennie suggests). As an example of a bad structure, he offers *They used me exceedingly discreetly*. For Lennie, unlike Sedger, it would seem that there is only one option: the zero adverb must be the first of the two in sequence.

Where the zero adverb is not recommended as in the illustrations above, then it is globally condemned in all constructions (with lexical and other systemic exceptions). Note especially that the coordinate constructions in (1) are not discussed in any contemporary grammar of English that I have found.[3]

From these slender gleanings, let us proceed to distributions in texts. Unlike Beckmann (1880), Knorrek (1938), and Schlüter (2003), the present attempt to determine the distribution of zero adverbs in the defined contexts is based mainly on non-literary prose texts, especially diaries and private letters, as well as dialogue in fictional texts. In (9)–(16) below are presented examples from two 17th and 18th century diaries. It should be noted that in these and all other texts examined, the *ly*-suffixation type of deadjectival adverb heavily predominates in all functions.[4]

(9) shows two adverbs in a coordination construction, corresponding to (1) above.

(9)   a. At noon, Sr W. Pen and ... dined with me *very merry and handsomely*.
       (Pepys diary: Vol III:8, 12/1/1662)

       b. and so I [...] consulted about drawing up a fair state of all my Lord's accounts; which being settled, he went away and I fell to writing of it very neatly, and it was very *handsome and concisely* done.
       (Pepys diary: Vol III:138, 16/7/1662)

Both (a) and (b) demonstrate that the construction containing a contrast in adverb-formation types does occur. It is significant that no examples were found in which the first conjunct contains the *ly*-adverb and the second the zero adverb. Again, by far the most common construction was that in which both conjuncts contained suffixed deadjectival adverbs, as in (10).

(10)   [...] I find him a fine gentleman and one that loves to live *nobly and neatly*...
       (Pepys diary: Vol III: 300, 31/12/1662)

---

[3]   Sundby et al. (1994) focus exclusively on phenomena evaluated negatively, so that positive recommendations or neutral descriptions go unindexed.

[4]   No statistical counts were made to make this description more precise. Space restrictions force us to omit discussion of fictional dialogue.

(11) shows two adverbs in sequence, whereby the first modifies the second.

(11) [...] the Captain would by all means have me up to his cabin; and there treated
      me *huge nobly*, giving me a barrel of pickled oysters [...]
      (Pepys diary: Vol I: 113, 21/4/1660)

Sequences of two derived adverbs are very rare in the text studied. There are
no examples in which the first adverb is suffixed with -*ly* and the second is a
conversion, and sequences of two *ly*-adverbs did not occur. There were
likewise no examples of two zero adverbs in sequence found. Note that in (11)
a stress clash results from the choice of adverb formation type; it would seem
that at least here, the rhythmic principle is superseded by the avoidance of
repetition of suffixes.

The rhythmic principle could be invoked for (12), in which deadjectival
zero adverbs have been selected to modify adjectives. In each case the choice
of the zero adverb optimizes the rhythmic pattern: *mighty pretty* results in a
regular trochee, while in *infinite fond*, two unstressed syllables in sequence,
while not ideal, is preferable to three.

(12) [...] a little daughter that is *mighty pretty* of which he is *infinite fond*
      (Pepys diary: Vol. IX: 128, 6/4/1668)

On the basis of these examples, we can say that while the *ly*-adverbs
predominate at any rate, the zero deadjectival adverb may on occasion be
produced in accordance with the patterns presented in (1a), (2a), and (4a).
Before leaving the Pepys diary, it is worth mentioning that the diary is
generally written in shorthand, which would indicate the writer's confidence
that none but he should easily read it, and also – contrastingly – that the writer
chose to make a first draft, likely rough notes, and then rewrite the entries
every week or so, elaborating and likely 'repairing' the text (Pepys diary
Vol. I: xcviiiff.). In other words, what has come down to us is a carefully
prepared document, if a private one.

The 'country parson' J. Woodforde keeps his diary approximately one
century later. Again, the content is personal and intimate; one can assume that
the diary was not intended to be read by others[5]. Coordination constructions
occur in which just one deadjectival adverb is suffixed, but this need not be the
last one, as we might expect from the Pepys data: in (13), it is the first that is
suffixed in -*ly*.

(13) Everything was done *decently, handsome and well* (Woodforde: 22/5/1771)

---

[5] For example, Woodforde makes plentiful remarks critical of others, reports (in his student
     days) on drunken incidents, etc.

However, structures of this type are very rare; this was the only example found in the first 240 pages of text. Woodforde also frequently uses two zero adverbs in coordination constructions, as in (14), as well as a zero adverb in conjunction with *well* (15).

(14) [...] his Lordship behaved *exceedingly handsome and free* (Woodforde: Apr/12/1775)

(15) Poor Gooch [...] talked *pretty cheerful and well* (Woodforde: 1/3/1778).

In constructions with two deadjectival adverbs in sequence, Woodforde consistently chooses a different strategy to Pepys's: it is the modifying or first adverb that is suffixed, while the second is converted, as demonstrated by (16).

(16) a. his brother has behaved *surprisingly kind* to all his relations (Woodforde: 29/9/1768)
      b. she went off *extremely easy* (Woodforde: 17/2/1768)
      c. he came and drew my tooth, but *shockingly bad* indeed, he broke away a great piece of my gum (Woodforde: 4/6/1776)

Only in (b) does the rhythmic pattern match the optimal according to the rhythmic alternation principle; it would seem that considerations of euphony ensure that there is no sequence of *ly*-adverbs, but do not make any sacrifices to obtain ideal rhythms.

It would be interesting to know whether the differences between Pepys and Woodforde with respect to sequences of adverbs are due to a change having taken place in the intervening century, or rather result merely from personal preferences. However, it turns out that while these two diarists reliably produce zero adverbs in a variety of contexts, the same cannot be said of most others for whom we have examined diary- or letter material (see references). In these, an intensifying adverb modifying another adverb or an adjective may be a zero formation, but there are very few or no occurrences in other functions or in coordinate constructions. These results contrast with the grammarians' descriptions indicated above, where the intensifying zero adverb is accounted very common and at least some reference to its role in adverb sequences is made. How, then, to account for the data? A possible hypothesis is that zero adverbs in general and zero adverbs in the constructions that ought to promote their selection are not, contrary to expectation, characteristic of colloquial language, especially in the oral mode. Under this hypothesis, Pepys and Woodforde would exceptionally be importing conventions from another register into their diary-writing, while the other diarists and correspondents would be accurately recording speech-like colloquial usage. The zero adverb as a typical feature of colloquial, casual register in the oral mode in 20th century English would then be an innovation. A contrary hypothesis is that while the zero adverb may have been alive and well in colloquial, casual speech in earlier Modern English just as in the present day, it did not generally find its way into the written mode, even in text types assigned to casual registers. Under this hypothesis, speakers, even those unused to expressing themselves in writing, would be conscious of a difference in terms of selection of systemically available devices between spoken and written modes, that might or might not be distinct from notions of grammatical 'correctness', and might or might not have been subject to normative pressures. It is possible that as intonation would have disambiguated between adverb and adjective in sequences, speakers would have been aware of the increased potential ambiguity in writing. While the path for zero adverbs of the qualitative, intensifying, and sentence sort would have been a fairly continuous one, the choice of the zero adverb in coordination constructions and in rhythmically appropriate contexts would have undergone significant change, such that the patterns found to hold for e.g. Pepys and Woodforde would have become extinct.

3. Adjective inflection in Early Modern German / early Modern German

In early Modern German there can be observed competing patterns in adjectival concord involving zero formation. In those we will consider here, the zero form is a paradigmatic alternative to suffixed forms in the 'strong' neuter set (17) for the category values 'nominative' and 'accusative' and in the 'strong' masculine set (18) for the category value 'nominative'.

(17) strong neut. nom/acc.
  – vs. *-es*: (*ein*) *schön Haus*   vs. (*ein*) *schönes Haus*

(18) strong masc. nom.
  – vs. *-er*: (*ein*) *schön Mann*   vs. (*ein*) *schöner Mann*

Both zero and suffixed alternants in this context had been available since Old High German; the suffixed forms, however, become increasingly frequent over the standardization period in printed texts. In Modern Standard German, only the suffixed forms are considered correct, the zero form persisting in a few idiomatic expressions and currently enjoying a certain reemergence in highly colloquial spoken German and its written reflection (e.g. *Lecker Bier!* (H. Spiekermann, p.c.)).

In early Modern German, the 'zero variant' is relatively common in the Neuter and much rarer in the Masculine. Favourable environments for its selection parallel some of those for the English zero deadjectival adverb. It typically occurs in the first conjunct of coordinate structures, while the second conjunct will contain the suffixed equivalent, as shown in (19) for the Neuter and (20) for the Masculine.

(19) *ein alt und ansehnliches Gebäude*

(20) *ein alt und ansehnlicher Mann*

Similarly, sequences of attributive adjectives will sometimes consist of a combination of zero and suffixed forms, whereby it is generally the last that is suffixed. As in the case of the English deadjectival adverbs, there are various ways of analyzing these patterns: it may be that the syntactic environment allows computing of congruence values, such that the suffix is interpreted as functioning for each adjective (in which case we must interpret the zero form as uninflected), or rather, the zero form is selected and interpreted as expressing the relevant category values.

Phonological environments promoting rhythmic alternation may select a zero adverb accordingly: where a zero form allows an alternation of strong and weak syllables, it may well appear, as in (21).

(21) a. *ein alt Gebäude*   vs. *ein altes Gebäude*
      b. *ein alt Betrug*   vs. *ein alter Betrug*

To the extent that rhythmic considerations are most crucial in the oral mode, variation between zero and suffixed form could be expected to be typical of speech. It would be expected that those grammarians who admit spoken usage and custom/frequency as criteria for accepting linguistic structures would approve of this variation, while others would advocate the use of the suffixed variant in all cases.

Pölmann (1671) recommends the zero form for neuter nominative and accusative values generally and for masculine nominative in order to avoid a dactyl (e.g. *ein unbesonnen Man* 'a foolish man' is better than *ein unbesonnener Man*, where the last two syllables in *unbesonnener* are unstressed); he indicates a lower preference for zero-forms with masculine nouns where the dactylic danger is not present (Jellinek 1913–14, vol. II: 384). Much later Becker (1829: 188) remarks that adjectival suffixes are often omitted due merely to rhythmic considerations; Grimm (1893[2]: 590) makes similar remarks, although he limits his observations to literary language. Other grammarians admitting or approving zero forms as in use, without mention of rhythm, include Stieler 1691, Prasch 1687 (both Takada 1998:182f.), Freyer

1722, Wahn 1723, Steinbach 1724, Hentschel 1729, Martini 1738, Antesperg 1747 (all Voeste 1999).

Adelung (1782: 636) recommends full suffixation of attributive adjectives in order to distinguish them clearly from adverbs and criticizes the use of zero forms as frequently found "im gemeinen Leben", i.e. in colloquial language. Other critical voices include Tscherning 1659, Zesen 1668, who attributes the zero form to 'the common man' (both Takada 1998: 181f.) Hempel 1754, (in Voeste 1999), Bauer 1828 (395f.).

Adelung (1782: 637) discusses the choice of form in coordinate structures, saying that adjectives may be 'abbreviated' in the 'vertraulichen Sprechart', i.e. in speech amongst intimates, in non-final conjuncts, with (22) as an example.

(22)   *ein roth und weisses Gesicht*

Wahn (1723: 107, as presented by Voeste 1999: 153) gives examples in which the adjectives in both conjuncts have the zero form.

As far as the grammarians go, then, we have some indication that the selection of the zero form is not an uncommon occurrence in colloquial or casual speech in the syntactic and phonological contexts focused on here. Note that the phenomenon is regionally indifferent, although there may be regional differences in the distributions of subtypes (Solms and Wegera 1994). Behaghel (1926: 199) refers to zero forms of adjectives in the modern dialects. Let us now examine the textual evidence: do we find zero forms in these contexts in diaries and correspondence, as claimed by e.g. Schirmunski (1962: 467) for the 18th century (Voeste 1994: 64)?

The diary of Albrecht Haller contains numerous examples of selection of the zero adjective in the contexts mentioned, and in other contexts as well. This diary is an account of Haller's travels as a medical student, through Germany, the Netherlands, and England. A manuscript version still exists; it is clear that Haller constructed the diary from notes taken during these travels and that he edited it to some extent (Haller, XIIf.).[6]

Beginning with coordinate structures, (23) shows a zero adjective in the first conjunct modifying a neuter noun, while (24) shows the same for modification of a masculine noun. These and many similar examples confirm that the pattern described by early Modern grammarians exists.[7]

---

[6]   Haller was Swiss; the text does not noticeably contain many Swiss features - for example, the diminutive suffix he uses is *-gen*. A consistent feature is *-e* in the 1.Sg.Pret.Ind; this is recommended by 17th-century east central German grammarians such as Stieler and was common in the south (Takada 1998: 207f.).

[7]   Frequency counts of adjectival structures were made for the complete text.

(23) *ein finster und anmuthiges Thal* (Haller 1723–7: 106)

(24) *ungemein schlimm und tiefer Weg* (Haller 1723–7: 86)

The same pattern may be found in sequences of attributive adjectives without a conjunction, as in (25).

(25) *Hannover, ein zimlich groß, etwas befestigter Ort* (Haller 1723–7: 56)

However, we also find other patterns. In (26) it is the first conjunct that contains the suffixed adjective, while the second contains the zero adjective; at best, one could say that the latter choice provides a rhythmic advantage.

(26) *Die Börse ist ein altes und unansehnlich Werk* (Haller 1723–7: 39)

In (27) we find the zero form in both conjuncts; again, choosing the zero form in the second conjunct does conform better to the rhythmic alternation principle.

(27) *Die Johanns Kirche ist ein lang und ungeziert Gebäude*
      (Haller 1723–7: 2)

As for phonological motivation, we find many examples in which the chosen form of the attributive adjective results in an optimal rhythmic pattern (28).

(28) a. *ein groß Geheul von Weibern* (Haller 1723–7: 90)
      b. *über gefroren Meer ... reisete* (Haller 1723–7: 44)
      c. *ein altes Schloß* (Haller 1723–7: 41)

In (28a) and (28b) the zero form prevents two unstressed syllables from appearing in sequence; in (28c) a zero form would have resulted in a stress clash. However, it must be said that Haller often selects the zero form, even if two stressed syllables then appear in sequence (29).

(29) a. *Schaffstatt, klein Dorf in einem Walde* [...] (Haller 1723–7: 76)
      b. *ein verflucht Land* (Haller 1723–7: 55)
      c. *Stark Paß* (Haller 1723–7: 77)

With Haller's diary, then, we seem to be embarked on a clear path: there is variation between the zero and suffixed form of the attributive adjective in the expected contexts, and there seem to be a number of available patterns, some clearly dominating. There can be found earlier and later personal texts presenting similar data (e.g. S. Birken, J. W. von Goethe (diaries); E. Goethe, J. W. von Goethe (personal correspondence)). However, it must be said that many other diaries and letters from the 17th, 18th, and 19th centuries do not manifest any examples of zero forms of attributive adjectives whatsoever (see reference section). Some non-literary prose texts also provide examples, such as von Hellwig (1718); none were found amongst those sources published after 1800, however.[8]

Just as in the English case, then, we find that a phenomenon is described as typical of spoken language and has systemic characteristics that would make this likely; however, it is not consistently found in written texts that ought to be close to colloquial speech.

4. Discussion and Conclusions

We have presented two systemically similar phenomena in German and English for which there is at least some indication that they belonged primarily or also to colloquial speech, but which are at the same time inconsistently attested in texts that one would expect to reflect this mode and register. We should note at this point that our problem does not appear to be unique: for example, Nevalainen and Raumolin-Brunberg (1994) wish to maintain the hypothesis that the possessive form *its* is of colloquial origin, yet they cannot find any examples of the item in texts of the appropriate types and time. In this section we will pursue two main lines of thought: we need to come to a better understanding of the relationship between writing and speech in the early Modern period, and the lack of data means that, while some accounts might be more likely than others, the historical details of the phenomena under investigation may remain in obscurity.

It is evident from private texts of the 17th and 18th centuries that even those whose education was limited and/or who were unused to writing had a clear notion that writing was distinct from speech, and that some level of formality was appropriate to writing, even with an audience of intimates. See here e.g. the remarks of Austin (1994: 285) on the letters of the Clift family:

> When I first began to analyze the Clift letters I believed that they would reveal a language similar to speech or as near speech as we could now reasonably hope to find. Over the years I have become convinced that this is not the case. It is clear that as soon as these people took up a pen they framed their minds to a formal mode of thinking [...]

Remember that our initial hypotheses regarding these zero variants did not include any kind of social marking, at least not before the 19th century. We expected therefore to find examples of zero variants in private writing of those

---

[8]   Bauer (1828) provides (and criticizes) examples from 19th century religious texts.

with education and high or secured social standing, and so we did, to a greater extent than in writing of those positioned lower. One could suppose that those with confidence both in their education and their social standing might be less concerned with their written language appearance, and might be more likely to allow leaking of spoken language forms into written texts.

It is not the case that these private texts, although they are in general more formal and stylistically careful than their modern correspondents, are entirely lacking in colloquial features, however, or that they are linguistically identical to the modern standard in all respects. Why, then, would, of all features, variation involving zero forms be so noticeably absent, while variation in verb forms, say, is common? Here we can only speculate, but it seems likely, as Hope 2000 suggests, that the evaluation criteria for standard languages are easily and naturally learnt. It would be relatively easy, then, for speakers to use invariant, maximally unambiguous, 'full' forms for adverbs in English and adjectives in German writing, which in most cases involve morphological processes but no lexical access, but harder for them to apply the principle of "No variation!" in the domain of the English perfect participle, say, when one has to access a lexically recorded form.

Hope (2000: 51) claims that prescriptivism follows, rather than precedes, standardization. His suggestion (2000: 52) that "[...] we think of standardiz-ation as a set of 'natural' linguistic processes (selections, self-censorships) which are started when language users encounter formal written texts, and become unconsciously sensitive to linguistic variation" certainly seems appropriate to what we observe in these private texts for the relevant linguistic phenomena (see here also Stein 1994, Lass 1994). If our zero adverbs and zero-inflected adjectives were part of spoken language in the colloquial register, then perhaps this sort of censorship is being applied to them when selecting forms for writing even private texts.

If private texts may not always be relied upon to reflect colloquial speech, how can speech of a historical period be recovered? Literary dialogue is certainly less reliable. As McIntosh (1994) shows for the early 17th and late 18th century English and Keating (1971) for 19th, dialogue does not reflect speech, nor does it accurately reflect social and geographic origins. As for other sources, Stein (1994: 14) and Lass (1994: 108) suggest that the wider range of variants listed in contemporary grammars may more closely reflect reality than corpus data from a range of text types or one text type in particular, in that (some) grammarians take all registers and modes into account, including spoken language. It is true in the present case that we have descriptions and examples from contemporary grammarians that suggest that the phenomena are more widespread than our text evidence suggests; of course, one would not want to rely on contemporary grammarians alone.

288   Amanda Pounder

It seems we must recognize a distinction between oral and written language separate from register and recognize that this distinction was in place well before the eighteenth century, even if, as McIntosh (1998) shows for English, it was enhanced and reinforced then. It is possible that some speech patterns do not find their way onto the page such as to allow their prevalence and distribution to be accurately determined. Therefore, as we use private writing to reveal oral language to us, we cannot assume that complete discovery will result.

References

Selected Primary Sources

P. don Constanz Arzonni. 1733. *Hilff= und Trostreiche Marianische Wochen / Ein Glückseeliges End zu erlangen; Welcher beygefügt Ein geistlicher Weegweiser zu den siben Heil. Fest=Tägen der unbefleckten Jungfrauen und Mutter Gottes Mariae, In welchem begriffen schöne außerlesene Gebett, so das gantze Jahr hindurch von einem Fest biß zu dem anderen / sehr Trosstreich zu gebrauchen.* Einsiedeln: Eberlin.
Aulnoy, Marie. 1708 (transl.). *The ingenious and diverting letters of the Lady's travels into Spain.* London: Crouch.
[Beethoven] Brandenburg, Sieghard (ed.). 1996. *Ludwig van Beethoven: Briefwechsel,* vols. I and II. München: Henle.
[Birken, S.] Kröll, Joachim (ed.). 1971. *Die Tagebücher des Sigmund von Birken.* Würzburg: Kommissionsverlag Schöningh
Böckler, Georg. 1683. *Nützliche Haus- und Feld-Schule.* Nürnberg: Fürst.
[Boswell] Pottle, Fred. 1950. *Boswell's London Journal 1762–1763.* New York: McGraw-Hill.
Brady, Frank and Fred Pottle (eds.). 1957. *Boswell in Search of a Wife 1766– 1769. The Yale Editions of the Private Papers of James Boswell.* Vol. 6. Melbourne, London and Toronto: Heinemann.
Brun, Friederike. 1800. *Tagebuch einer Reise durch die östliche, südliche und italienische Schweiz ausgearbeitet in den Jahren 1798 und 1799.* Copenhagen: Brummer
Dickens, Charles. 1966 [1837–39]. *Oliver Twist.* Harmondsworth: Penguin.
[Dutch Tutor] Anon. 1659. *The Dutch Tutor.* [Repr. Menston: Scolar Press 1970]
Eleonora, Maria Rosalia. 1710. *Duchess of Troppau and Jägerndorf. Frey-willig-Auffgesprungener Granat-Appfel dess christlichen Samaritans.* Wien: Voigt.

Eliot, George. 1996 [1859]. *Adam Bede*. Oxford: Oxford University Press.

[Evelyn, J.] Bowle, John (ed.). 1983. *The Diary of John Evelyn*. Oxford: OUP.

Fielding, Henry. 1961 [1742/41]. *Joseph Andrews and Shamela*. Boston: Houghton Mifflin.

[Forster, G.] Zincke, Paul and Albert Leitzmann (eds.). 1914. *Georg Forsters Tagebücher*. Berlin: Belers.

Gaskell, Elizabeth. 1994 [1855]. *North and South*. London: Penguin Books.

[Goethe] Köster, Albert (ed.) 1968. *Die Briefe der Frau Rath Goethe*. Leipzig: Insel-Verlag.

Goethe, Johann Wolfgang von. *Digitale Bibliothek,* vol. 10: *Goethe: Briefe, Tagebücher, Gespräche*. http://www.digitale-bibliothek.de/band10.htm

Greene, Graham. 1938. *Brighton Rock*. London: Heinemann.

Gunby, David, David Carnegie and McDonald Jackson (eds.). 2003. *The Works of John Webster*. Vol. II. Cambridge: CUP.

[Haller, A.] Hintsche, E. (ed.). 1948. *Albrecht Hallers Tagebücher seiner Reisen nach Deutschland, Holland und England (1723–1727)*. St. Gallen: Hausmann

Hassell, F. Wilhelm. [soldier] 1790. *Briefe aus England.*

Haydn, Franz Josef. 1795. *Tagebuch aus der Zeit seines zweiten Aufenthaltes in London.* [facsimile 1909]. Leipzig: Breitkopf und Härtel.

von Hellwig, Christoph. 1718. *Neue und curieuse Schatzkammer oeconomischer Wissenschaften*. Frankfurt: Niedten.

Hines, Philip. *The Newdigate Newsletters*. ICAME.

Knapp, Lewis (ed.). 1970. *The Letters of Tobias Smollett*. Oxford: Clarendon.

Kytö, Merja et al. *Helsinki Corpus of English Texts, Diachronic Part. Early Modern English*. ICAME.

Captain Martin's Journalls Feb 1689–Sept 1690. Ms, British Library.

Magazin für das Neueste aus der Physik und Naturgeschichte. 1781–95.

Maidl, Peter. 2000. *"Hier ißt man anstadt Kardofln und Schwartzbrodt Pasteten". Die deutsche Überseewanderung des 19. Jahrhunderts in Zeitzeugnissen*. Augsburg: Wißner.

Nevalainen, Terttu et al. *Corpus of Early English Correspondence Sampler*. ICAME.

[Osborne] Smith, G.C. Moore (ed.). 1928. *The Letters of Dorothy Osborne to William Temple*. Oxford: Clarendon Press.

[Pepys letters] Heath, Helen (ed.). 1955. *The Letters of Samuel Pepys and his Family Circle*. Oxford: Clarendon Press.

[Pepys diary] Latham Robert and William Matthews (eds.) 1976. *Diary of Samuel Pepys*. Vols. I–V and IX. Berkeley: University of California Press.

Ringrose, Basil [pirate]. *A Journal into the South Sea*. Ms., British Library.

Schmied, Josef et al. *Lampeter Corpus of Early Modern English Tracts*. ICAME.

[Sheridan] Rhys, Ernest (ed.). 1906. *The Plays of R.B. Sheridan*. London: Dent.

Smollett, Tobias. 1979. *Travels Through France and Italy*. [Repr. Frank Felsenstein (ed.) Oxford: OUP].

Smollett, Tobias. 1990. *The Expedition of Humphry Clinker*. [Repr. O. Brack (ed.) Atlanta: University of Georgia Press].

Strother, Jeremy [tailor]. *Diary 1784–1985*. Ms., British Library.

Swift, Jonathan. 1710–1712. *Journal to Stella*, vol. I. [Repr. Herbert Williams (ed.). Oxford: Clarendon, 1948].

Swift, Jonathan. 1733–42. *Instructions to Servants and Miscellaneous Pieces*. [Repr. Herbert Davis (ed.) Oxford: Basil Blackwell, 1964].

[Twain, Mark.] [1884]. *The Adventures of Huckleberry Finn*. [Repr. Walter Blair (ed.) Berkeley: University of California Press, 1988].

Twiss, Richard. 1775. *Travels Through Portugal and Spain*. London: Robinson, Becket and Robson.

Webster, John. 1612. *The White Devil*. [Repr. Menston: Scolar Press 1970].

Westcott, John [Army bandmaster]. *Journal*. Ms., British Library.

Wilder, Thornton. 1957. *Three Plays: Our Town, The Skin of Our Teeth, The Matchmaker*. New York: Harper and Brothers.

[Woodforde] [1758–1781] *Diary of a Country Pastor*. John Beresforde (ed.) Oxford: Oxford University Press.

Wycherley, William. 1675. *The Country Wife*. [Repr. Menston: Scolar Press 1969].

Selected Contemporary Grammars

Adelung, Johann Christoph. 1782. *Umständliches Lehrgebäude der Deutschen Sprache: Zur Erläuterung der Deutschen Sprachlehre für Schulen*, 2. vols. Berlin: Voß. [Repr. Hildesheim: Olms 1971].

Adelung, Johann Christoph. 1792. *Deutsche Sprachlehre*. Wien: von Trattner.

Bayly, Anselm. 1772. *A Plain and Complete Grammar of the English Language*. London: J. Ridley.

Bellin, Johann. 1661. *Syntaxis Præpositionum Teutonicarum*. Lübeck: Michael Volck.

Greenwood, James. 1711. An Essay Towards a Practical English Grammar. [Repr. Menston: Scolar Press1968].

Lennie, William. 1815. *The Principles of English Grammar, Comprising the Substance of all the most approved English Grammars extant*. 3rd ed. Edinburgh: Oliver and Boyd.

Lowth, Robert. 1762. *A Short Introduction to English Grammar With Critical Notes*. [Repr. Menston: Scolar Press 1967].

Pölmann, Isaac. 1671. *Neuer hoochdeutscher DONAT.* Berlin: self-published.

Priestley, Joseph. 1761. *The Rudiments of English Grammar.* [Repr. Menston: Scolar Press 1969].

Sedger, John. 1798. *The Structure of the English Language.* [Repr. Menston: Scolar Press 1970]

Secondary Sources

Austin, Frances. 1994. The Effect of Exposure to Standard English: The Language of William Clift. In Dieter Stein and Ingrid Tieken-Boon van Ostade (eds.), *Towards a Standard English 1600–1800.* Berlin: de Gruyter, 285–313.

Bauer, Heinrich. 1828. *Vollständige Grammatik der neuhochdeutschen Sprache.* Berlin: Reimer. [Repr. 1967 Berlin: de Gruyter].

Beckmann, E. 1880. Über die doppelförmigen englischen Adjektivadverbien. *Archiv für das Studium der neueren Sprachen und Literaturen* 64: 25–27.

Behaghel, Otto. 1923. *Deutsche Syntax. Eine geschichtliche Darstellung.* Vol. I. Heidelberg: Winter.

Berger, Dieter. 1978. *Die Konversationskunst in England 1660–1740. Ein Sprechphänomen und seine literarische Gestaltung.* München: Fink.

Cusack, Bridget (ed.) 1998. *Everyday English 1500–1700.* Edinburgh: Edinburgh UP.

Chafe, Wallace. 1984. Speaking, writing, and prescriptivism. In Deborah Schiffrin (ed.), *Meaning, Form and Use in Context: Linguistic Applications.* Washington: Georgetown UP.

Dörfer, Anja. 1999. *Autobiographische Schriften deutscher Handwerker im 19. Jahrhundert.* Berlin: Verlag im Internet.

Frank, Thomas. 1994. Language Standardization in 18th century Scotland. In Dieter Stein and Ingrid Tieken-Boon van Ostade (eds.), *Towards a Standard English 1600–1800.* Berlin: Mouton de Gruyter, 51–62.

Grimm, Jakob. 1893. *Deutsche Grammatik*, vol. I. 2nd ed. Gütersloh: Bertelsmann.

Jellinek, Max. 1913. *Geschichte der Neuhochdeutschen Grammatik von den Anfängen bis auf Adelung*, 2 vols. Wien: Winter.

Keating, P.J. 1971. *The Working Classes in Victorian Fiction.* London: Routledge and Kegan Paul.

Kjellmer, Göran. 1974. Why Great:Greatly but not Big:Bigly? On the Formation of English Adverbs in -ly. *Studia Linguistica* 38: 1–19.

Hickey, Raymond. 2000. Salience, Stigma, and Standard. In Laura Wright (ed.), *The Development of Standard English 1300–1800.* Cambridge: CUP, 57–72.

292   Amanda Pounder

Knorrek, Marianne. 1938. *Der Einfluß des Rationalismus auf die englische Sprache. Beiträge zur Entwicklungsgeschichte der englischen Syntax im 17. und 18. Jahrhundert.* Breslau: Priebatschs Buchhandlung.

Lass, Roger. 1994. Proliferation and Option-Cutting: The Strong Verb in the Fifteenth to Eighteenth Centuries. In Dieter Stein and Ingrid Tieken-Boon van Ostade (eds.), *Towards a Standard English 1600–1800.* Mouton: Berlin. 81–113.

McIntosh, Carey. 1998. *The Evolution of English Prose, 1700–1800. Style, Politeness, and Print Culture.* Cambridge: CUP.

Milroy, James. 2000. Historical Description and the Ideology of Standard English. In Laura Wright (ed.), *The Development of Standard English 1300–1800.* Cambridge: CUP, 11–28.

Nevalainen, Terttu and Helena Raumolin-Brunberg. 1994. Its Strength and the Beauty of it: The Standardization of the Third Person Neuter Possessive in Early Modern English. In Dieter Stein and Ingrid Tieken-Boon van Ostade (eds.), *Towards a Standard English 1600–1800.* Berlin: Mouton de Gruyter, 171–216.

Ono, Mitsuyo. 1986. *Morphologische Untersuchungen zur deutschen Sprache in einem Stadtbuch der Prager Neustadt vom 16.–18. Jh.* Marburg: Elwert.

Percy, Carol. 1996. 18th century Normative Grammar in Practice: The Case of Captain Cook. In Derek Britton (ed.), *English Historical Linguistics 1994.* Amsterdam: Benjamins, 339–362.

Pounder, Amanda. 2004. Haplology in English Adverb Formation. In Christian Kay et al. (eds.), *New Perspectives on English Historical Linguistics Volume 1: Syntax and Morphology.* Amsterdam: Benjamins, 193–211.

Pounder, Amanda. 2005. *Syntactic Haplology, Morphological Ellipsis, and Phonological Aesthetics.* [talk presented at Workshop on Interfaces With Morphology, Schloss Freudental, Feb 9–13].

Raidt, Edith. 1968. *Geskiedenis van die byvoeglike verbuiging in Nederlands en Afrikaans.* Kaapstad et al.: NASOU.

Rohdenburg, Günter. 1997. Grammatical Variation and the Avoidance of Stress Clashes in Northern Low German In Jenny Cheshire and Dieter Stein (eds.), *Taming the Vernacular: From Dialect to Written Standard Language.* London: Longman, 93–109.

Schlüter, Julia. 2002. Morphology Recycled: The Principle of Rhythmic Alternation at Work in Early and Late Modern English Grammatical Variation. In Teresa Fanego et al. (eds.), *English Historical Syntax and Morphology.* Amsterdam: Benjamins, 255–281.

Selkirk, Elizabeth. 1984. *Phonology and Syntax: The Relation Between Sound and Structure.* Cambridge: MIT Press.

Stein, Dieter. 1994. Sorting out the Variants: Standardization and Social Factors in the English Language 1600–1800. In Dieter Stein and Ingrid

Tieken-Boon van Ostade (eds.), *Towards a Standard English 1600–1800*. Berlin: Mouton de Gruyter, 1–17.

Sundby, Bertil, Anne Bjørge, and Kari Haugland. 1991. *A Dictionary of English Normative Grammar 1700–1800*. Amsterdam: Benjamins.

van Ostade, Ingrid Tieken Boon. 1994. Eighteenth-century letters and journals as evidence: Studying Society Through the Individual. In Roger Sell and Peter Verdonk (eds.), *Literature and the New Interdisciplinarity. Poetics, Linguistics, History*. Amsterdam et al.: Rodopi, 179–191.

van Ostade, Ingrid Tieken Boon. 1996. Social Network Theory and 18th Century English: The Case of Boswell. In Derek Britton (ed.), *English Historical Linguistics 1994*. Amsterdam: Benjamins, 327–337.

Povejšil, Jaromír. 1980 *Das Prager Deutsch des 17. und 18. Jahrhunderts.* Hamburg: Buske

Rühl, Karl. 1909. *Unflektierte (nominale) und starke Form im Singular des attributiven Adjektivs in den hochdeutschen Mundarten.* Diss. Giessen. Darmstadt. Menzlaw.

Schoch, Johann. 1657. *Comoedia vom Studenten=Leben.* [Repr. Hugh Powell (ed.) Bern and Frankfurt: Lang, 1976].

Semenjuk, Natalija. 1972. Zustand und Evolution der grammatischen Normen des Deutschen in der ersten Hälfte des 18. Jahrhunderts. In Günter Feudel (ed.), *Studien zur Geschichte der deutschen Sprache.* Berlin: Akademie-Verlag, 79–166.

Solms, Hans-Joachim and Klaus-Peter Wegera. 1991. *Grammatik des Frühneuhochdeutschen*, vol. VI: *Flexion der Adjektive.* Heidelberg: Winter.

Steglich, Wilhelm. 1902. Über die Ersparung von Flexions- und Bildungssilben bei Copulativen Verbindungen. *Zeitschrift für deutsche Wortforschung* 3: 1–52.

Stricker, Stephanie. 1996. Zu Ellipsen von Wortbestandteilen bei J. W. von Goethe. *Sprachwissenschaft* 21: 37–108.

Takada, Hiroyuki. 1998. *Grammatik und Sprachwirklichkeit von 1640–1700. Zur Rolle Deutscher Grammatiker im schriftsprachlichen Ausgleichsprozess.* Tübingen: Niemeyer.

Törnvall, G. E. 1917. *Die beiden ältesten Drucke von Grimmelshausens "Simplicissimus" sprachlich verglichen.* Uppsala: Appelberg.

Voeste, Anja. 1999. *Varianz und Vertikalisierung. Zur Normierung der Adjektivdeklination in der ersten Hälfte des 18. Jahrhunderts.* Amsterdam and Atlanta, GA: Rodopi.

Vorlaat, Emma. 1979. Criteria of Grammaticalization in 16th and 17th Century English Grammar. *Leuvense Bijdragen* 68: 129–140.

Watts, Richard. 2000. Mythical Strands in the Ideology of Prescriptivism. In Laura Wright (ed.), *The Development of Standard English 1300–1800*. Cambridge: CUP, 29–48.

ANJA VOESTE (AUGSBURG)

Variability and professionalism as prerequisites of standardization

1. The problem of heterogeneity

Texts from the Early New High German period (1350–1650) have one specific feature in common: their orthographic schemes differ extremely. At the close of the previous Middle High German period, poets tried to avoid regional differences and showed efforts towards a more uniform spelling, as it is, e.g., ascertained by Gärtner (2003) for the manuscripts of the commentaries of the Song of Solomon. This changed in the late 13th century. Within the same text we find graphic variants of the same word, even though the writers of the day had a good command of another language that shows no variation: Latin. Nevertheless – texts like the following ooze heterogeneity, cf. *pfalltz ~ pfaltz, bey ~ bej, Reyn ~ Rein, ī ~ in, Bairn ~ bayrn, ſeiner ~ ſeyner, lynij ~ lyni* 'Linie' (cf. Chronik und Stamm […] 1501: aijv.):

> ſchlåchten pfalltzgrafen <u>bey</u> Reyn vnd herczo
> gen *ī* **Bairn** ic · Phillipps pfaltzgrafe <u>bej</u> Rein
> vnd herczog *in* **bayrn** Curfürſt mit *ſeiner* l̶y̶n̶i̶j̶
> Albiecht herczog in bayrn zů Münchē mit *ſey*
> *ner* l̶y̶n̶i̶ · Johanns pfaltzgrafe <u>bey</u> Rein zů ſy=

Today non-uniform, inconsistent writing is interpreted as meaningless and arbitrary. The homogeneity of written German is a national symbol, which – as a cultural asset – is safeguarded by purists and language custodians. Also we are aware – not least because of our school attendance – of its importance as a touchstone of social acceptance:

> Wer nicht richtig schreiben kann, kann gar nichts. Ihm fehlt es an Bildung und Dis-
> ziplin, wahrscheinlich auch an Intelligenz.

> 'Those who are not able to write correctly are incapable in every way. They lack
> education and discipline, probably even intelligence.' (Eisenberg 2001: 60; my
> translation – A.V.)[1]

Standardized orthography as normalized and verifiable writing goes along with
a rigid norm-consciousness that accepts one and only one spelling as the
correct one; variatio *non* delectat. In the 20th century this motto was still
applied to school pupils in often quite punitive ways. A child that misspelt a
word would be required to write it out correctly fifty times or even worse: it
was 'explained' by means of the cane.

Between these two extremes – heterogeneity to a large extent in the 16th
century and a rigid norm-consciousness today – a fundamental change must
have taken place. Variability not only disappeared almost completely, but was
a key issue in the transformation of language attitudes, partly brought on by
the rising professionalism of printers, typesetters, and proofreaders.

The main interest of historical linguistics still lies in the teleological view,
in the evolution of the written standard. Therefore, German linguists mostly
refer to variation as a condition of the 'Dark Ages', from which emerged the
'modern' concept of a unified standard, while ignoring the fact that variability
did not emerge until the late 13th century. It is not surprising that the Early
New High German period was denied the status of an own epoch in the 19th
century. J. Grimm characterized the features of early modern German as un-
couth and lacking 'flourishing poetry' (cf. Grimm 1822: X–XI). It smelled of
'debit and credit, collection and interest rate' (Schirokauer [2]1957: 871; my
translation – A.V.). Besch (1993: 136) states with obvious relief that in the
18th century written German has finally become a dignified tool for academic
purposes, poetry, and – above all – for the classical period of German
literature.

Whereas theories of language change make a distinction between those
innovations that exist only temporarily and those which are incorporated in the
standard, the interest of historical linguists is quite a different one: emphasis is
on that part of the spectrum which lies on the main pathway towards the New
High German standard. The principles of innovation as such have never been
of interest for traditional language historians. They even raise the question of
whether the theory of language change should not leave the theory of variation
aside and focus on the selection of innovations as, for example, Mattheier
(1998: 827) proposes.

---

[1]   It goes without saying that Eisenberg does not agree with this opinion.

Haas (^{2}1998: 843) points out a decisive obstacle that seriously interfered with the embedding of variability into theories of language change. The methods of structuralism, which were mainly used, are based on the assumption that we deal with contrasting distinctive features. Structuralism lacks categories for describing and analysing variability. The segmental description of different variants as secondary forms of a main variant is based on the model of structural phonology. The explanation of those variants and their importance in diachronic change is beyond the interest of structural linguistics.

In what follows I argue that it is precisely a theory of innovation that can best help us to understand phenomena of language change as a whole. Innovations are already a crucial part and not only the precursors of language change. In order to back up such a theory of innovational change, I will propose a system of categorization that could – as I hope – provide us with a new means of describing this kind of language change. I shall also address several alternative explanations of variability.

2. Categories of innovational change

Innovational change can relate to the structural means and/or the ends. Consider the following cultural-historical innovations: the emergence of script, the employment of quills as writing utensils, and the invention of the typewriter. The emergence of script shows *new* means (written characters) for *new* ends (fixing of knowledge). The employment of quills as writing utensils implies *old* means (feathers) for *new* ends (writing on paper-like material). The invention of the typewriter serves *old* ends (production of written characters) by *new* means (print-like characters). I distinguish between three categories: *anastasis*, *exaptation*, and *neoplasia*.

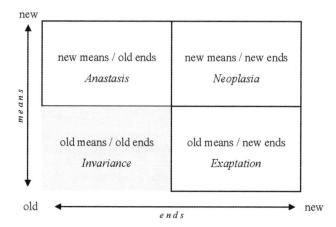

2.1 Anastasis

The term *anastasis* is derived from the so-called anastatic printing process. Up to the 19th century facsimiles were produced by treating the original with acid or oil and pressing it on limestone or zinc plates for reprinting. This way, the original was transformed into a new structure without its contents being changed. With the term anastasis I refer to a kind of language change that gives rise to new means without changing the previous ends.

The alinea (¶), often used in printed texts of the 16th century, is an example of anastasis. It indicates and distinguishes the beginning of a new semantic unit in the text. Its function is not new, as this was formerly – since the Old High German period – achieved by capital letters. The choice of the alinea is due to the increasing use of capital letters within sentences since the 14th century. The following example may illustrate this increased use:[2]

> Anno 1571 den 20. Aprilis aúß beúhelch eines Erbarn Raths haben. herr Michael Peyer Thomas werner vnnd Chriftoff Lift Stadtfchreiber, vff die Einem Erbarn Rathe Zúe gekhombene Articúl, den Gefangenen Chriftoff Amman, gúetlich befprachen laffen Jn kegenwúrt Mathiafen Schmidts Gerichtfchreibers am hoff bej Regenfpúrg vnd wolffen Leppoldingers, des Entleibten brúders vnd hat Chriftoff Amman gúetlich dis aúßgefagt [...].[3]

---

[2]   For a detailed examination of the increasing use of capital letters cf. Bergmann and Nerius (1998).

[3]   From the *Egerer Urgichtenbuch*, cited in Reichmann and Wegera (1988: 61).

The alinea takes over the task to distinguish a new semantic unit:

> ¶ Planearius ſpricht daz zwobeln weychen den buch [*Bauch*; 'belly'] vnd brengen dorſt ¶ Der ſafft gemiſchet mit honig vn̄ die dūckeln augen vſſen an do mit geſchmieret machet ſye clare vnd hūbſch. ¶ Jtem zwobeln gemiſchet mit ſaltz vnd vff die wartzen geleyt [*gelegt*; 'put on'] heylet die von grunde vß […].[4]

We also find anastasis when Early New High German spelling variants show the spreading of an ⟨h⟩, like in *jahr, ehre, ohr*. It indicates the smooth syllable cut or rather the decoding of a long vowel, which – up to this time – could be marked by a circumflex. This example also reveals new means for old ends:

MHG *jâr, êre, ôr(e)*	ENHG *jahr, ehre, ohr*
'year', 'honour', 'ear'	
The circumflex (^) marks the pronunciation of the vowel	⟨h⟩ marks the pronunciation of the vowel

2.2 Exaptation

The term *exaptation* is used by Lass (1990) in his article 'How to do things with junk'. It is – like the more familiar *adaptation* – adapted from evolutionary biology. It describes the re-purposing of old means for new ends, the use of feathers for flying, for example, even though they originally served as thermal insulation.

We find exaptation when the Early New High German writers double letters like in *mutter, himmel, ſollen*, even though the consonants are not pronounced this way. The pattern for those geminates goes back to Middle High German, where they actually were pronounced. The writers maintain the pattern, but they change the ends: geminates indicate an abrupt syllable cut or rather a preceding short vowel, as well as a following neutral vocal, *Schwa*. This is an example for old means, or – as Lass puts it – old junk getting new ends. After the loss of pronounced geminates in late Middle High German (for the reasons cf. Voeste and Wischer 2004), the structure of double consonant letters became obsolete. The written geminates fulfilled a new function and were even generalized. For this reason we cannot derive the MHG form from later written geminates:

---

4   From the *Gart der Gesundheit* 1485, cited in Reichmann and Wegera (1988: 177).

Mitte < mitte	*Butter < buter*	*Natter < nâter*	*Mutter < muoter*
'centre'	'butter'	'adder'	'mother'
geminate	short vowel	long vowel	diphthong
in MHG	in MHG	in MHG	in MHG

Another example for using old junk is the continued spelling of ⟨ie⟩, a former diphthong like in *liebe, vliegen, triefen*. After the ENHG monophthongization the spelling became obsolete, but was now used to indicate the long vowel *i*. It also occurs in words without former ⟨ie⟩.

Liebe < liebe	*Sieg, Wiese < sic/sige, wise*
diphthong in MHG	short vowel in MHG

2.3 Neoplasia

Neoplasia is the rising of new means with new ends. In the narrower sense it was the evolution of something completely new. You do not often find this in language history. In the wider sense of borrowing of structures from other systems, however, it is quite common. When, for example, the Greeks borrowed the Phoenician script, they did not need the character *aleph,* which stood for the glottal stop. Instead, according to its name, they interpreted it as a vowel; it became the letter *alpha*, which, evidently, is no longer a glottal stop.

Finding examples of neoplasia in Early New High German spelling is difficult. While there are a lot of cases in the emergence of punctuation in the 16th century – the question mark, the exclamation mark, quotation marks – these are rarely found with spelling variants. However, a very interesting example is discussed by Macha (1998). He describes the borrowing of Southern variants like *khomen* or *zue* by writers from the Rhineland and Westphalia. Those variants did not simply replace the Northern ones. Instead, they were used in special contexts, when the writers wanted to show their affinity to the counter-reformation.

3. The functions of variants

Anastasis, exaptation, and *neoplasia* may help to classify variants, but they do not explain them. The functional explanations usually applied here refer to linguistic subsystems: diaphasic, diastratic, diasituative, diachronic, and diatopic.

Diaphasic variants refer to different phases in a writer's life. During their lifetime writers or typesetters do not always stick to the same spellings. Spelling differences between different generations of writers and typesetters are also diaphasic: the spellings of a writer with decades of experience in a chancellery may differ from those of a younger novice.

Diastratic variants focus on social differences. The social background of a person and – as a result – the level of schooling can cause spelling variants, cf. the following excerpt from a petition letter which was written in 1893:

> Der selbe mich Beleidigte und sagte das ich mein Ausgeding bekome wo das nicht der Fall ist ich bin nur gest [*jetzt*; 'now'] aus Gnade bei meine Tochter weil ich nirgends habe zu bleiben so lange mein Schwiegersohn mich behält und wen er mich raus jagt mus ich zu fremden sein und von was soll ich leben den Essen Ferlangen kan ich nicht es ist sein guther Wille wen sie mich etwas Reichen.[5]

Diasituative variability may reflect different intentions related to different genres. Documenting, legitimizing, informing, or entertaining the reader result in different linguistic forms. The intention of the author and the form of the text are not arbitrarily related, but are rather conventionalized (cf. Reichmann and Wegera 1988: XII). A legal text differs e.g. from a medical receipt. The legal text shows differences in its linguistic shape, which follows the conventionalized and stereotyped legal wording:

> Jch regina fuggerin hanſſen paumgartnerß des elltern eelicher gemachel beken mit diſſer meiner hand geſchrift waß in diſſem liwel [*libel(lus)*] geſchryben ſtat […].[6]

> Einen fålenden [*faulenden*; 'rotting'] zan/ an dem ort/ da er ſchwartz iſt/ ſoll man ſchaben/ vñ ſchmiren mit geſtoßner roſen blůmen vermiſchet mit vier teylen eychôpfel […].[7]

Variants are called *diachronic* when old, established forms and modern ones appear at the same time. Here, traditional variants get mixed up with modern

---

[5]   Cited in Tenfelde and Trischler (1986: 299f.). Cf. Fairman and van der Wal (this volume) for examples from English and Dutch.

[6]   From the marriage contract of Hans Paumgartner and his wife Regina, née Fugger (after 1519), cited in Reichmann and Wegera (1988: 25).

[7]   From the German translation of the *de medicina libri octo* 1531, cited in Reichmann and Wegera (1988: 193).

ones in order to increase or to guarantee comprehensibility. This is the case when writers put e.g. MHG *mânôt* and the younger form *monat* side by side and write *manot adder monat*. Twin forms as *mit Fug und Recht* may also contain those diachronic variants.

Comprehensibility is another object of *diatopic* variants, e.g. when nowadays I refer to a *lift or elevator* or an *estate car* or *station wagon*. Diatopic variability refers to different regional conventions or pronunciations which are reflected in the written forms. Fabian Frangk points out diatopic differences in his *Cantzley vnd Titel büchlin* 1531:

> Es fpricht der Oberlender [*Oberdeutsche*; 'Upper German speaker']/ Bezal mir mein wein vnd gehe mir aus meinem haufe.
> Der Dôring [*Thüringer*; 'Thuringian']/ Zal mir myn wyn/ vnd geh mir vfs mym hufe.
> Der Niderlender [*Niederdeutsche*; 'Low German speaker']/ Tal my myn wyn/ vnd ga my vt mym hufs.[8]

Specific regional characteristics can be chosen as a courtesy to the addressee. In this case, regional features do not show the characteristics of the sender's language, but those of the (supposed) language of the addressee (cf. Möller 1998).

4. Spelling variation as an aesthetic principle

In spite of this apparent wealth of possibilities for explanation, a lot of ENHG texts still cause confusion. Two findings interfere with common functional explanations. First, a lot of spelling variants appear on the same page, cf. *Jahr ~ Jhar ~ Jar* (Spangenberg 1572: 6r) or *pfalltzgraf ~ pfaltzgraf ~ pfaltzgraff* (Chronik und Stamm […] 1501: b6r):

> oder wie Panthaleon fchreibet / ift er allererft geboren worden im 1787. **Jahr** nach Anfang der Welt (Auentino tefte) im 130. **Jhar** nach verlauffung der Sûndflut / als fein Anherr Noah (den die Heidnifchen Scribenten fonft Janum heiffen) noch gelebet/vnd 730. **Jar** alt gewefen/vnd jn felbft zum Herrn vber die Lande zwifchen

> mit feym gemahel **pfalltzgraf** bey Rein ward ·
> Vom felben ottē viel dʒ land auf feī fun herczog
> ludwigen ward **pfaltzgraf** bey Rein herczog in
> bairn vñ Curfürft · Von dem felben ludwig viel
> es nach feī tod auf fein eynigen fun **pfaltzgraff**

---

[8]   Frangk 1531, cited in Müller (1882/1969: 106).

Secondly, frequent words like articles (*die* ~ *dje* ~ *dye*) or prepositions (*ī* ~ *in* ~ *inn* ~ *jn* ~ *jnn* ~ *yn* ~ *ynn*) are typically affected, although it would have been easy to use a uniform spelling. Looking at a text by one and the same writer or typesetter,[9] diaphasic variability can be excluded. Uncertainty due to social factors (diastratic variability) seems unlikely: why should a writer not have been able to write frequent words like *die, in, bei* in an identical shape – especially when he was able to write Latin? Diasituative variability does not play a role, as the differences occur in the same text. And even diachronic and diatopic variability may not explain the existence of several spelling variants next to each other.

Therefore, I propose an additional explanation. Spelling variability may often be considered as a search for new visual word schemata, arising from variation being seen as a stylistic imperative. I take spelling variation as an aesthetic principle, comparable to today's variations as a lexical imperative:

> *Boyle published his first novel, the well-known author argues, he describes, the writer claims.*

Looking at the beginning of the early modern age, there seems to be strong evidence for the fact that it was not appropriate to repeat words in the same monotonous spelling. This would explain why heterogeneous spellings occur on the same page, and why common words are written in different shapes. *Variatio delectat* meant more than just giving pleasure to the eye. It meant demonstrating one's writing skills through the calculated use of alternation. Anastasis, exaptation, and neoplasia are the tools to guarantee variation. We should not forget that this has provided us with a set of strategies that are still used in orthography today, e.g. spellings like *Ball, Stadt, Jahr, Wiese, Schuh*.

I have depicted one of the two extremes I introduced at the beginning: heterogeneity. But the question of the transformation of language attitudes and the role typesetters played in this process remains. Assuming variability had been a stylistic imperative, the decline of variability in the 16th and 17th centuries seems even more inexplicable than before: why should such an aesthetic principle fall out of favour?

5. The role of the typesetters

My theory is that the developing professionalism of typesetters was partly responsible for the erosion of variability. Not only did the technical and

---

[9]   For the problem of different typesetters setting one text cf. Fujii (1996).

economic demands influence the work cycle and the various relevant crafts of the printing process. They also had an influence on spelling. The letter case used by typesetters marked the limits of the typographic possibilities: double types ($r \sim \mathfrak{z}$, $u \sim \mathring{u}$), abbreviations, and most of the ligatures were removed from the letter case in order to speed up the printing process. Variants including these letters could no longer be set.

types	examples
d^{s}	abbreviation for: *der*
$\mathfrak{z}$	as in: *o\mathfrak{z}t, her\mathfrak{z}*
$\mathring{u}$	as in: *g\mathring{u}t, z\mathring{u}*
$-\bar{a}, -\bar{e}, -\bar{\imath}, -\bar{o} -\bar{u}$	as in: *d\bar{e} (dem), v\bar{o} (von)*
v\bar{n}	abbreviation for: *vnd*

A statistical study based on a corpus of some 200,000 words collected from chronicles of 30 German printers of the 16th century (cf. Voeste in prep.) demonstrates the decline of those spellings. Counting the variants of *und* in my corpus, one can trace the decline of the spelling with the titled letter (*v\bar{n}*):

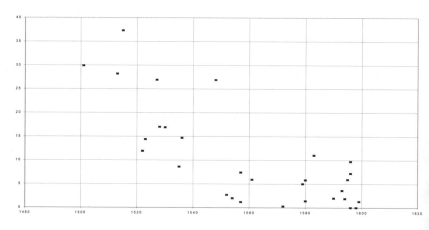

Figure 1: Correlation year of print/percentage *v\bar{n}* ($\tau = -0,51$)[10]

---

[10]   Instead of the correlation *r* I am using Kendall's τ. This nonparametric correlation makes it possible to calculate the significance of the results. In this case $p = 0.0002$.

In the course of the 16th century, the modernized methods of typesetters led to discrediting the earlier 'unprofessional' methods. At the close of the 17th century, Moxon (1683/84: 237) described those means as a sign of bungling:

> If the *Compositor* is not firmly resolv'd to keep himself strictly to the Rules of good Workmanship, he is now tempted to make *Botches*; viz. *Pidgeon-holes* [i.e. 'holes' in the line], *Thin-Spaces*, no *Space* before a *Capital*, *Short* &s, *Abbreviations* or *Titled Letters*, *Abbreviate Words*, &c.

In addition, aesthetic principles were a key factor in the emergence of regulated spelling variants. Under the surface of stochastic variation, the typesetters developed graphotactic word patterns. Using the segments of the letter case to set words, they considered and changed the width of the consonantal word margins. A word like *land* could be extended in the right margin (*Vergewichtung*, 'compensatory extension'):

Irrespective of the stylistic imperative, regulated variants emerged, corresponding to aesthetic patterns. The counting of 2.189 words with *l, r, m, n* + *dt* like *waldt, herdt, hemdt, bandt* in the corpus has shown that words without a left margin like *endt* are written with ⟨dt⟩ four times as often as those with one segment in the left margin like *handt* – not counting the records with *l-* or the great many of *und*-variants.

We therefore have to take into consideration that aesthetic principles are not only responsible for the imperative to make variations. They also played an important role in the emergence of regulated, aesthetically shaped spelling variants. Some of those aesthetic patterns became an integral part of today's orthography: we still do not extend the right margin of a word if the left one already shows a cluster of three or four consonants, cf. *Schwahn* (Schwan),*Strohm* (Strom), *Schahl* (Schal).

6. Conclusions

Typography seems to have been a key factor in establishing logographic patterns. While the writer of a manuscript was never able to copy a word in an identical shape, the production of uniform, printed texts allowed words to be identically replicated. The reiterative process of printing had an effect on visual perception. Words became more than semantic entities: now a prototypical logographic pattern had been superimposed onto them. The principle of the uniform writing of morphemes had been established.

The imperative to make variations was replaced by a new motto of self-confident craftmanship: variatio *non* delectat. The rapid success of this motto might be attributed to different factors. We can be certain that one of them is the aspiring bourgeoisie, which – being without financial resources – was forced to use language as a status symbol.

References

Bergmann, Rolf and Dieter Nerius. 1988. *Die Entwicklung der Groß-schreibung im Deutschen von 1500 bis 1700*. 2 vols. Heidelberg: Winter.

Besch, Werner. 1993. Regionalität – Überregionalität. Sprachlicher Wandel zu Beginn der Neuzeit. *Rheinische Vierteljahrsblätter* 57: 114–136.

Chronik und Stamm der Pfalzgrafen bei Rhein und Herzoge in Bayern. 1501. Die älteste gedruckte bayerische Chronik, zugleich der älteste Druck der Stadt Landshut in Bayern [rather Munich: Hans Schobser, cf. VD 16: I 110; A.V.]. [Repr. Georg Leidingen (ed.) Straßburg: Heitz. 1901]

Eisenberg, Peter. 2001. Sprache, Schrift, Orthographie. *Jahrbuch der Henning-Kaufmann-Stiftung 1995–1999*. Schliengen: Schmitt, 58–72.

Fujii, Akihiko. 1996. Zur Methode der Exzerption älterer Drucke. Ein Beitrag zum Problem des Setzerwechsels in Frühdrucken. *Zeitschrift für deutsche Philologie* 115: 393–432.

Gärtner, Kurt. 2003. Variation im Mittelhochdeutschen am Beispiel der Handschriften des Hoheliedkommentars Williram von Ebersberg († 1085). In Michèle Goyens and Werner Verbeke (eds.), *The Dawn of the Written Vernacular in Western Europe*. Leuven: University Press, 415–426.

Grimm, Jacob. 1822. *Deutsche Grammatik*, vol. 1. Göttingen: Dieterich.

Haas, Walter. 1998. Ansätze zu einer Theorie des Sprachwandels auf lautlicher Ebene. In Werner Besch, Anne Betten, Oskar Reichmann and Stefan Sonderegger (eds.), *Sprachgeschichte. Ein Handbuch zur Geschichte der deutschen Sprache und ihrer Erforschung*, vol. 1. 2nd ed. Berlin and New York: de Gruyter, 836–850.

Lass, Roger. 1990. How to do things with junk: exaptation in language evolution. *Journal of Linguistics* 26: 79–102.

Macha, Jürgen. 1998. Schreibvariation und ihr regional-kultureller Hinter-grund: Rheinland und Westfalen im 17. Jahrhundert. *Zeitschrift für deutsche Philologie* 117 [Spec. issue 'Regionale Sprachgeschichte']: 50–66.

Mattheier, Klaus J. 1998. Allgemeine Aspekte einer Theorie des Sprach-wandels. In Werner Besch, Anne Betten, Oskar Reichmann and Stefan Sonderegger (eds.), *Sprachgeschichte. Ein Handbuch zur Geschichte der deutschen Sprache und ihrer Erforschung*, vol. 1. 2nd ed. Berlin and New York: de Gruyter, 824–836.

Möller, Robert. 1998. *Regionale Schreibsprachen im überregionalen Schriftverkehr. Empfängerorientierung in den Briefen des Kölner Rates im 15. Jahrhundert.* Köln et al.: Böhlau.

Moxon, Joseph. 1683/84. *Mechanick Exercises on the Whole Art of Printing.* London. [Repr. Herbert Davis and Harry Carter (eds.) New York: Dover Publications. 1978]

Müller, Johannes. 1882/1969. *Quellenschriften und Geschichte des deutschsprachlichen Unterrichts bis zur Mitte des 16. Jahrhunderts.* Gotha. [Repr. Monika Rössing-Hager (ed.) Hildesheim et al.: Olms. 1969, 92–110]

Reichmann, Oskar and Klaus-Peter Wegera (eds.) 1988. *Frühneuhochdeutsches Lesebuch.* Tübingen: Niemeyer.

Schirokauer, Arno. 1957. Frühneuhochdeutsch. In Wolfgang Stammler (ed.), *Deutsche Philologie im Aufriß*, vol. 1. 2nd ed. Berlin: Schmidt, 855–930.

Spangenberg, Cyriacus. 1572. *Manßfeldifche chronica. Der Erfte Theil.* Eisleben: Petri. [Repr. Leonhard Boyle and Elmar Mittler (eds.) 1991. *Bibliotheca Palatina. Druckschriften.* München et al.: Saur, II 76.]

Tenfelde, Klaus and Helmuth Trischler (eds.) 1986. *Bis vor die Stufen des Throns. Bittschriften und Beschwerden von Bergleuten im Zeitalter der Industrialisierung.* München: Beck.

VD 16 = *Verzeichnis der im deutschen Sprachbereich erschienenen Drucke des 16. Jahrhunderts.* 1983–2000. Ed. by the Bayerische Staatsbibliothek in München together with the Herzog August Bibliothek in Wolfenbüttel, 25 vols. Stuttgart: Hiersemann.

Voeste, Anja [in prep.]. *Orthographie und Innovation. Die Segmentierung des Wortes im 16. Jahrhundert.* Ms. to be submitted as Higher Doctorate (Habilitation).

Voeste, Anja and Ilse Wischer. 2004. Der Zusammenhang von quantitativem und qualitativem Lautwandel in der deutschen und englischen Sprachgeschichte des 12.–16. Jahrhunderts. In Matthias Fritz and Ilse Wischer (eds.), *Historisch-Vergleichende Sprachwissenschaft und Germanische Sprachen. Akten der 4. Neulandtagung der Historisch-Vergleichenden Sprachwissenschaft in Potsdam 2001.* Innsbruck: Institut für Sprachen und Literaturen der Universität Innsbruck, 191–204.

EVELYN ZIEGLER (MARBURG)

Putting standard German to the test: some notes on the linguistic competence of grammar-school students and teachers in the nineteenth century

1. Conceptual preliminaries

It is a widely held view in German historical linguistics that the development of a written German standard language was completed by the end of the eighteenth century, at least as far as codification of written German was concerned, and that the educational spread and social diffusion of these norms took place in the nineteenth and twentieth century. Since little attention has so far been paid to the teaching and learning of Standard German, I focus here on the ritual of essay writing[1] as a clue to students' and teachers' linguistic competence. More specifically, I will concentrate on matriculation essays and investigate the actual use of and variation in certain stylistic and linguistic features.

Essay writing can roughly be defined as an artificial writing practice with an audience consisting of both student and teacher. Students know that their writing is, on the whole, a ritual performance, produced only to be marked and commented upon by the teacher. But as this ritual triggers a maximum display of written language norms, an investigation of this text genre can provide us with more information on the actual command of these norms. On this basis, we can determine more precisely the effects of standardization, that is the differences between norm prescriptivism and norm realization.

The obvious point of departure for any inquiry into the effects of implementing a standard variety is an appropiate concept of standardization. As contemporary research on the theory of standardization shows, it is of central importance to consider not only aspects of homogeneity, but also aspects of heterogeneity and also to clarify their possible interactions in the process of standard formation. Standardization, as it is generally understood,

---

[1]   See Deumert (2003) on ritual aspects of language instruction.

has as its aim the reduction of variation. It thus inhibits linguistic variation and change, but it does not prevent it totally. According to Ferguson (1996), the relationship between invariability and variability is best captured in what he calls a 'standardization cycle'. By this metaphor he means that a period of more homogeneity alternates with a period of more heterogeneity, which again results in a period of more homogeneity and, thus, in a new standard language. But the idea that standardization is a circular movement is not really convincing, as new variants are continuously produced to meet new social, functional, and situational communicative constraints. As a natural tendency of any (standard) language, the emergence of new variants results in a permanent tension between the forces of language maintenance and language change, as Edwards (1985: 90) points out. Thus, in the words of Sapir, standardization "leaks" (Sapir 1921: 39) or, in the words of Auer and more appropriate to the general perspective of this volume, standardization "profits from innovations from below" (Auer 2005: 18).

In the light of this reasoning, I decided to investigate not only phenomena of standardization and their realization in actual language use, but also phenomena of destandardization as a matrix from which new norms develop. From a broad perspective, destandardization[2] can be defined as a dialect-standard contact phenomenon, i.e. as an interaction between spoken and written language. This contact results in new, subsistent norms (Gloy 1997), which finally make their way up into the formal, written standard and replace existing standard variants (see Mattheier 1997, Spiekermann 2005). In a historical interpretation of literacy practices, an analysis of these forms may be particularly promising, as these processes mirror the slow acceptance of new changes into the written language.

2. Pedagogical background:
teaching composition in the nineteenth century

In Germany composition instruction started around 1780, but it was not until 1812 that Prussia introduced the *Abitur* (the grammar-school leaving exam, which was required for enrolling at a German university). Thus, essay writing and composition as a grammar school subject developed around the same time. In general, essay writing was conceived as a reflection of a student's *Gesamtbildung*, i.e. humanistic education. Following Deinhardt, a famous contemporary pedagogue, this meant

---

[2]   For a more detailed discussion of destandardization see Daneš (2003)

[a]lles, was der Schüler in einer gewissen Classe geworden ist, in Wissenschaft, Sittlichkeit und Religion, sein Verhältnis zu Gott, zu den Menschen und zur Natur, kurz Alles, was in ihm eine geistige Existenz gewonnen hat, das soll sich in seiner Gesammtheit, in seiner lebendigen Einheit und individuellen Zusammenfassung durch die deutschen Aufsätze offenbaren. Sie sind die Blüthen der Schülerbildung. In ihnen treten die verschiedenen Seiten der Gymnasialbildung in einer individuellen Spitze zusammen. (Deinhardt 1837: 138)

'Everything a student has achieved, in science, ethics and religion, his relationship to god, to humanity, and to nature – in short, everything that provides him with a cognitive existence – should manifest itself in its entirety, in its living unity and individual combination in [his or her] German essays. They are the tender fruit of student education. In them the different facets of a higher education come together in a unique acuteness.'

In order to develop an elaborate style, students were required to

[v]ernünftig und klar sich schriftlich ausdrücken zu können, ist Zeichen höherer allgemeiner Bildung. [...] Wir beabsichtigen nicht, die Fähigkeit auszubilden, worin die alten Redner so groß sind, in unchristlicher Rabulistik die schlechteste Sache durchzufechten, sondern schlichte, sachgemäße Abhandlungen zu schreiben. Wir verzichten auch darauf, Ciceros schönen und gesättigten, wahrhaft künstlerisch entwickelten Stil nachzubilden. (Laas 1868: 142ff.)

'writing in a prudent and clear style is an indicator of higher education. We do not intend to develop those abilities in which the orators of old were so great, railing through even the worst of premises with unchristian sophistry, but rather [teach them] to write plain and appropriate essays. We also abstain from recreating Cicero's beautiful, dense, and truly adroitly developed style.'

These ideals were a late effect of the 'Enlightenment', of which Gottsched was a primary proponent. His rationalistic "Versuch einer critischen Dichtkunst vor die Deutschen" (A critical approach to poetry, 1751) rejected poetic fancy and conceits, stressing purity and ease of understanding. Although these ideals became increasingly popular among pedagogues around the middle of the nineteenth century, they met with much resistance. Most grammar-school teachers and students favoured an ideal of style associated with Ciceronian ornamentation and syntax. Hildebrand, a harsh critic of over-elaborate language use, diagnosed this practice as "intended latinate style", indexed by lengthy sentences based on complex, "blown up" noun phrases and parenthetical participial clauses (Hildebrand 1867: 57f.). Nevertheless, such language use lasted well into the twentieth century. Metalinguistic commentators responded by creating stigmatizing labels such as "Zopfsprache" (literally: 'pony-tail language', i.e. a rather old-fashioned, outdated style).

The standard model for teaching essay writing was a rhetorical scheme based on three stages of text production:

1. The *inventio*, which refers to the teacher's finding of a topic and formulation of theme. The student then meditates on the theme to find the appropriate content.
2. The *dispositio*, which refers to the text structure and the logical arrangement and sequencing of ideas, appropriate to the topic.
3. The *elocutio*, which refers to the choice of vocabulary, rhetorical figures, and verbal ornamentation according to the rules of purity, propriety, and perspicuity.

In sum, the aim of this ritualized writing practice was to produce a well-formed text. In other words, grammar school students' linguistic and stylistic elaboration was guided not so much by the idea of a correct reproduction of codified norms of a written language (this went without saying), but was rather based on the overarching idea of educatedness, a primarily aesthetic concept. This fixation on educatedness also dominated the choice of topics. Moral, philosophical, historical, and literary topics were clearly preferred to topics of every-day life, especially in the latter decades of the nineteenth century.

According to the range of thematic choices, the following types of style were taught at school: commercial style (*Geschäftsstil*), dogmatic style (*Lehrstil, wissenschaftlicher Stil*), letter-writing style, and historical style. The type of style adopted most often was the dogmatic style, characterized as a style "worinn einzelne oder mehrere allgemeine Wahrheiten vorgetragen, erkläret, bewiesen und angewandt werden" ('in which particular or several common truths were brought forth, explained, proven and employed', Adelung 1785, II: 110). The appropriate style level students were required to use was the so called middle style, representing the mean between the ornate, elevated style and the very plain style. To qualify as middle style, rhetorical features and ornamentation were to be employed carefully.

The macro-genre essay writing was taught according to three sub-genres. In the first half of the nineteenth century, the following so-called 'objective' sub-genres were taught: narration (*Erzählung*), description (*Beschreibung*), and argumentation (*Abhandlung*). This classification was based on the general idea that texts are primarily a product of what in modern sociolinguistic theory is called 'audience design'. This means that stylistic devices and linguistic features were chosen on the basis of their rhetorical effectiveness and appropriateness. Because of the de-rhetoricization of composition writing and the new conception of style as an expression of individuality, a new system was introduced after 1850.[3] This new system comprised the following sub-

---

[3]   See Hildebrand (1867).

genres: report (*Bericht*), characterization (*Schilderung*), and contemplation (*Betrachtung*). It was identified with an author-centred approach. Style was no longer a matter of stylistic norms determined by the demands of different text-genres but of individual choices and preferences. This conception was based on the idea that style could not be taught but could only be learned by extensive reading of approved classics of German literature. This approach moved away from pragmatic dimensions, e.g. rhetorical power, to subjective dimensions found to mirror the inner characteristics of the text producer.[4]

3. Corpus

My analysis draws on a corpus of 60 essays, which span the period from 1821 to 1920. The corpus was divided into two subsets, covering the years from 1821 to 1870 and 1871 to 1920, to investigate any changes resulting from the *Reichsgründung*. Many language historians, for example v. Polenz (1999) and Mattheier (2000), advocate this caesura and point out the very important changes taking place in the education system especially. These changes include the general introduction of German lessons on all levels of schooling, the development of a curriculum, and the establishment of a widely accepted literary canon.

The essays were written by students from Lower Saxony, mainly Hannover, Göttingen, and environs. All texts were produced for the final secondary, i.e. matriculation, examinations. Unfortunately, due to the poor data situation, I do not have sets of essays written by whole classes, but single essays only. All texts were written by male students, as girls were not allowed to attend grammar schools regularly in those days. I do not have any detailed information on the social background of the students. It is however most likely – as sociohistorical studies show (see Nipperdey 1993, Wehler 1995) – that for the first decades it can be assumed that 70% of them had an upper-middle-class background, compared to only 59% in the last decades. This decrease is due to increasing numbers of students from the lower middle class, who aspired to the higher standards of educatedness.

It is evident that this rather small corpus only allows explorative findings.

---

[4] For more information about the history of teaching composition in the nineteenth century see Ludwig (1988).

4. Analysis

Before going into the details of my analysis, it is necessary to sketch out first the formal conditions under which the matriculation essays were written.

1. Students had – at least in the second half of the nineteenth century – about four hours' time to write the essay.
2. In general, there was no thematic choice.
3. Compositions were corrected by one teacher only.
4. Norms of correction did not exist in the first half of the century, even grading was not compulsory.

Moreover, matriculation essays were perceived not only as a means of final assessment, but also as a pedagogical ritual with which to improve a student's skills. This tendency is indicated by two facts: (a) sometimes an elaborated endnote summarizes the teachers' marking practice, which is more than a focus on errors and grade justification; (b) students quite often consider and utilize feedback by writing a correction or revision of their original composition. This is a significant deviation from marking practice today, where students' corrections do not occur.

4.1 Global characteristics

As a first step of my analysis, I investigated the formal characteristics of the texts, that is text length and use of paragraphs. It turns out that the average text length for the compositions written between 1821 and 1870 is 984 words, with a minimum of 404 and a maximum of 1939 words. Between 1871 and 1920 the average text length rises to 1225 words, with the variation-coefficient slightly smaller in this period. The higher figures for the second period run somewhat counter to the results of Sieber (1998: 83), whose analysis of Swiss matriculation essays records an average text length of 789 words for essays written in the years 1881 to 1921.[5]

The use of paragraphs as a text structuring device begins in the eighteenth century. The texts show that the students make wide usage of this device, as the average number of nine paragraphs for the texts between 1821 and 1870

---

[5] The figure of 789 words is the mean value of the following figures listed by Sieber: 895 words average text length for essays written in 1881, 852 words average text length for essays written in 1891, 813 words text length for essays written in 1901, 818 words text length for essays written in 1911, and 567 words text length for essays written in 1921.

and of twelve paragraphs for the texts between 1871 and 1920 indicates. This is a proportional increase. Again, this tendency marks a contrast to Sieber's analysis (1998: 80), who reports an average use of 10 paragraphs[6] for an average text length of 789 words.

As a second step, I looked at the thematic choices. Table 1 presents the percentages for the categories 'national history' (e.g. "Bismarck, der nationale Heros"), 'philosophy/ethics' (e.g. Socrates: "Die Wurzel der Bildung ist bitter, die Frucht aber ist süß!"), 'literature' (e.g. "Schicksal und Schuld in Schillers Wallenstein"), and 'daily life' (e.g. "Bitte eines Jünglings um ein Stipendium an einer Universität").

	1821–1870	1871–1920
National History	14%	57%
Philosophy/Ethics	48%	23%
Literature	--	11%
Daily Life	38%	8%

Table 1: Thematic choices in student essays

As the table shows, the thematic choices clearly differ in both periods. In the first decades, topics from daily life to philosophical issues dominate. The choice of daily life topics is probably due to a pedagogical tendency of the late Enlightenment, which prefers themes with a practical relevance; in the later decades of the nineteenth century, themes concerned with national history are – unsurprisingly – chosen very often. Literary themes in general and those related to classical German literature in particular (preferably Goethe, Schiller, and the Romantics) became popular only after the *Reichsgründung*, due to the establishment of a national literary canon. In sum, the choices mirror the degree to which essay writing was conceived of as an indicator of a so-called *Gesamtbildung*.

I further examined the use of the adjective *deutsch* (including derivations) and the noun *Deutschland* as a linguistic indicator of the link between topic choice and growing nationalistic feeling. These frequencies are given in table 2:

	1821–1870	1871–1920
deutsch	33	215
Deutschland	22	70

Table 2: Linguistic indicators of the nationalization of topic choice in student essays

---

[6]   The figures fluctuate between 7 and 13 paragraphs (see Sieber 1998: 80f.).

The third approach I took was to look for any remarkable stylistic trends. The texts under investigation display a certain partiality for rhetorical devices which goes beyond the demands of a middle style.[7] This partiality is based on a fairly diffuse idea of what an educated style should look like. Therefore, it may not be surprising that the tendencies are quite complex. See table 3:

	rhetorical question	exclamation	superlative	quotation
1821–1870	59% (45)	25% (19)	24% (33)	0.3 (per text)
1871–1920	41% (31)	75% (58)	76% (102)	2.1 (per text)

Table 3: Rhetorical devices in student essays

The pattern that emerges is quite an interesting one: while the use of exclamations, superlatives and quotations gradually increases during the course of the century, the use of rhetorical questions decreases. The latter development runs indeed counter to the overall tendency: according to Adelung (1785/1974), the use of exclamations makes a text more vivid. In addition, a closer look at individual instances reveals that exclamations and quotations are very often coded in confessions of national feeling, such as "Ja, deutsche Einheit und Einigkeit!" ('Ah, German unity and concord!'), or "Süß ist es, für das Vaterland zu sterben" (Horace's 'dulce et decorum est pro patria mori'). The same holds for the increasing use of superlatives as expressions of national enthusiasm ("der gerechteste aller Kriege", 'the most justified of all wars', 1870[8]). As to the counter tendency with respect to the use of rhetorical questions (e.g.: "Und wer waren die Sieger? Wir waren es, die Deutschen, die lange verachtete und bespöttelte Nation." – 'Who won? We did, the Germans, the formerly despised and sneered-at nation', 1872), a post-hoc explanation might be found in three overlapping developments. First, students probably became acquainted with this device in their Greek lessons. Rhetorical questions make up an important part of the Greek philosophical tradition and a central part of 'maieutics', a method of teaching introduced by Socrates. Given the fact that classical Greek was taught with fewer lessons per week in the second half of the nineteenth century than in the first half of the nineteenth century, the decrease is not surprising. Secondly, as I have pointed out before, composition instruction shifted from audience-centred patterns of style to

---

[7]   This subjectice impression is also supported by teacher's comments, which point to 'unnecessary ornamentation' as in the following comment from 1821: "Der Verfasser hat hier zu sehr nach dem Schmuke des Ausdruckes gesucht, und den klaren Gedanken jenem untergeordnet."

[8]   This expression refers to the Franco-Prussian War of 1870/1871.

author-centred patterns of style in the second half of the nineteenth century, thus mirroring the general rejection of rhetorics, especially as a means of deception; thirdly, philosophical themes (see table 1) were less popular after 1871. As a result, fewer opportunities were provided to employ rhetorical questions in argumentative text genres.

4.2 Grammatical variables

With regard to the level of codification of and variation in standard features,[9] the following grammatical variables were chosen for the analysis:

(1) Dative-*e* marking:

According to Adelung (1782) and Heyse (1838), dative-*e* marking in the singular of strong masculine and neuter nouns is obligatory (*dem Manne* 'to the man'). Adelung (1782: 399) points out that *-e-* is a characteristic case ending which should not be omitted in the genitive and dative of genuinely German words.[10] Heyse, going into further detail, formulates certain constraints governing the use and omission of dative-*e*. While words containing *-es-* in the genitive case form their dative by adding an *-e-*, the suppression of *-e-* is allowed in prepositional phrases where no article precedes and as a way of avoiding a hiatus.

> Alle Wörter, welche im Genitiv es anhängen, haben im Dativ die Endung *e*. Das Dativ-*e* bleibt überall erhalten außer im Hiatus und in artikellosen Präpositional-verbindungen. (Heyse 1838: 488f.)

Nevertheless, dative-*e* dropping has been going on for centuries. It is a result of a natural phonological process in spoken language and affects unstressed syllables. As the dropping of *-e-* is a supraregional phenomenon, it results on a national level in de-standardization. Wustmann, along with many other contemporary language critics, complained about the loss of inflection and argued that this development was detrimental to stylistic euphony and sentence prosody (Wustmann 1896: 5).

---

[9] For a discussion of grammatical variation in the nineteenth century see Schieb (1981).
[10] "Das *e* ist ... ein characteristischer Biegungslaut, daher derselbe, in eigentlich Deutschen Wörtern, im Genitiv und Dativ der Einheit nie verbissen werden sollte."

(2) Comparative particle *als*

According to Heyse (1838) and Becker (1841), the use of comparative markers is functionally distributed. Thus, *wie* is used after the positive of adjectives indicating similarity: "ich bin ebenso groß, wie du" (Heyse 1838: 577), *als* is used after the comparative of adjectives indicating difference: "schneller als ein Pfeil" (Becker 1841: 308). Exceptions to this rule were only allowed in poetic prose when serving stylistic functions and in oratorical style when serving pragmatic purposes, e.g. foregrounding. The use of *als wie* instead of *wie* after a positive and instead of *als* after a comparative was quite common in colloquial language, although only allowed in literary style (see Becker 1845). Although the *als/wie* rule was – and is – generally recommended by grammarians, it has never been thoroughly established in actual usage.[11] In the nineteenth century, many language critics complained about the incorrect usage of the particle *wie* after the comparative of adjectives and marked this language use as "uneducated". Yet, the formulation and implementation of the *als/wie* rule can be interpreted as a case of suppressing optional variation. Although both structures are linguistically equivalent, the use of *wie* following the comparative of adjectives is rejected on grounds that they are linguistically arbitrary but socially non-arbitrary (even though the *wie* construction is the more economical construction, as the comparative is already marked by the *-er*-morpheme).[12]

(3) Double negation[13]

Double negation is a phenomenon concerning the syntax-semantics-interface, i.e. logical form and syntactic structure. The Latin rule that two negatives make an affirmative had gained more and more ground among eighteenth and nineteenth century grammarians. They rejected negated sentences with more than one negative element as ungrammatical and referred to the principle of logic (Engelien 1878: 429ff).[14] But the double negative is often to be found in the literary language of the classical period: "Man sieht, daß er an *nichts keinen* Anteil nimmt." (Goethe). Here double negation adds emphasis to the negative idea that is contained in the statement. The double negative is also quite common in German dialects, e.g. in Bavarian dialects: "er war *nirgends*

---

[11] The use of *wie* after the comparative is still frequent in colloquial German.
[12] See Milroy (2000: 13) on similar cases of fixing prescriptive rules in English.
[13] For an overview of mono- and polynegation and their areal distribution in the history of German see Langer (2001).
[14] Double negation was also rejected on the grounds of redundancy (see Schötensack 1856: 557f.).

nicht zu finden", where there are sometimes even three negatives: "Hat *keiner kein* Geld *nicht*?" (Zehetner 1977) Despite all endeavours to establish the rule of mononegation, the double negative persisted in spoken and written language in the nineteenth century. Particularly writers from the south of Germany used double negatives not only in private, but also in formal contexts, as the following example, taken from an instruction manual, illustrates: "Wenn das Bier einmal sauer wird, so ist es *kein* gesundes Getränck *nicht* mehr für den Menschen." (Scharl 1814)

(4) *e*-extension

The loss of e-extension in verbs marks another process of change, i.e. de-standardization, since most nineteenth century grammarians considered e-extension for the 2nd person singular and plural as in *du hilfest* vs. *du hilfst* and *ihr sehet* vs. *ihr seht* and for the plural imperative as in *sehet!* vs. *seht!* to be out of use. While Adelung (1782: 764) still allowed the use of e-extension in those cases where it served euphony and ease of articulation, Becker (1845: 111) already considered forms with e-extension as old, although basic variants (dating back to Middle High German) and forms with e-dropping as new variants. By the end of the century, e-extension was overtly rated archaic in prose but permissible in poetic and pathetic style (see Blatz 1896). Seen from this angle, e-extension is a good example for the recycling of variants left over from morphological simplification. In terms of established sociolinguistic concepts, the stylistic redefinition of e-extension can be interpreted as a case of 'reallocation' (Trudgill 1986).

(5) Afinite construction

By the end of the fifteenth century, in the Early New High German period (c. 1350–1650), it became possible to drop finite auxiliaries from embedded clauses, e.g.: "Die große Not, welche sie in dem Kriege ausgestanden (haben), [...]" This construction has been referred to as the 'afinite construction' by grammarians of Early Modern German (see Admoni 1990) and 'auxiliary ellipsis' by grammarians of contemporary German. It was argued that the information coded in the finite auxiliary was redundant and could therefore be dropped. With the stylistic changes after 1700, the afinite construction gradually lost credit, contributing to a more natural, less hypotactic style. A basic line of argumentation was that the auxiliary ellipsis represented a violation of the principle of perspicuity. In consequence, its usage was only allowed in highly restricted contexts, i.e. elevated and poetic style (see Adelung 1782: 394ff.). A second line of argumentation was based on the principle of completeness and put forward, for example, by Herling (1832:

133), who argued that a subject in a sentence usually requires a verb as its complement.

(6) Verb first construction

In the nineteenth century, inversions such as verb first constructions were considered good style and an important resource for highlighting semantic as well as pragmatic functions. As Adelung put it: inversion adds zest to a sentence, and taking advantage of this syntactical flexibility expresses literacy (Adelung 1785: 292–304). It was argued that a text in which every clause begins with the subject sounds mechanical. At the same time, while it was not wrong, it was considered inappropriate to use verb first constructions all the time. Thus, an exaggerated usage was sanctioned as 'affected' and 'tasteless' ("maniriert und geschmacklos", Heyse 1830: 276). Four different mechanisms of deriving verb-initial order can be distinguished:

- main clause:
   a) perfect participles and infinitives may come into this position as in: "Geschrieben ist es noch nicht." and "Fragen wollte er dich."
   b) after omission of *es* as in: "Sah ein Knab' ein Röslein stehn." (Goethe). This construction is only allowed in spoken language and poetic style.
- before *doch* as in "Kenn ich sie doch kaum!" to make some statement more impressive in form of an exclamation.
- conditional clauses without subjunction: "Läßt man ein Kind allein auf die Straße, dann…"

(7) *der/welcher*

At the beginning of the nineteenth century, many grammarians regarded the relative pronoun *der* as a characteristic feature of spoken language, the relative pronoun *welcher* as a characteristic feature of written language. The usage of both forms was less a question of grammar than of style, although Heyse, in a nitpicking manner, insisted on a semantic difference. According to him, *der* referred to a person, whereas *welcher* referred to an object (Heyse 1838: 542). By the end of the century, most grammarians preferred *der* to *welcher* in written language and branded *welcher* as lengthy and 'clumsy' (Vernaleken 1863: 454), restricting the latter to a well considered argumentative style (see Sanders 1880: 236a). Language critics, however, were less unanimous in their evaluation of both forms. Schopenhauer, for example, advocated vehemently the usage of *welcher* in written language and mocked the usage of *der*: "Die, die die, die die Buchstaben zählen, für klägliche Tröpfe halten, möchten vielleicht nicht so ganz Unrecht haben" (Schopenhauer 1923: §13). In sharp contrast to Schopenhauer, Meyer, who published a very popular style manual at the beginning of the twentieth century, disliked *welcher* and coined the derivation *welchern* to describe Gustav Freytag's overdosed usage of *welcher* (Meyer 1906: 15).[15]

The overall view of the analysis of the seven variables is provided by table 4:

	1821–1870		1871–1920	
Dative-*e*	92%	(136/12)	81%	(239/56)
als after comparative	90%	(35/1/4)	93%	(27/2/1)
Double negation		--		--
e-extension	100%	(19/0)	100%	(6/0)
Afinite construction	53%	(28/25)	29%	(25/60)
der (vs. *welcher*)	57%	(110/83)	56%	(197/153)
Verb first construction		8		25

Table 4: Results of seven grammatical variables in students' essays

(1) Dative-*e* marking

The results show that the dative singular ending -*e*- is widely used throughout the nineteenth century and almost categorically employed in prepositional phrases as "zum Wohle der Menschheit". Nevertheless, as the frequencies slightly drop from 92% to 81% around the turn of the century, they nicely reflect the ongoing process of destandardization. i.e. intrusion of nonstandard forms into the written language. Counter to the prescriptive norm, the loss of dative-*e* in spoken and written language illustrates the limits of prescriptive work. As to the constraints governing the loss of dative-*e*, there seems to be no obvious contextual pattern. I would rather suggest that this is a case of optional variation, as -*e*- dropping occurs on the intrapersonal level (that is within the same text) and the lexical level, that is with the same noun as in "dem norddeutschen Bund(e)".

(2) Comparative particle *als*

The figures indicate that most students knew when to apply the particle *als*. Only in 10% respectively 7% of all instances do they not comply with the rule. This result corresponds exactly with Elspaß' analysis of educated and experienced letter writers in the nineteenth century (Elspaß 2005: 35). Yet, *als*, which should only follow a comparative adjective, is also used after the

---

[15]   For a critical discussion of the range of arguments used by prescriptive grammarians in the nineteenth century see Lühr (1992).

positive as in the combination "ebenso gefährlich als heilsbringend" in a very few instances (essay 1853). In connection with *ebenso* fluctuation of both particles was allowed, although *wie* was more common than *als*. Apart from this special construction, the usage of *als* was tolerated (see Becker 1845) under the condition that degree and intensity were to be expressed. This may explain its usage in a composition from 1856: "kein Laster wurzelt so tief im menschlichen Herzen als Undank".

(3) Double negation

No cases of double negation occurred in the corpus. Compared to Elspaß (2005: 30), who reports a frequency of 5% for writers from the Low German dialect area, the students' categorical usage of mononegation is probably due to the highly formalized text genre and a successful grammar instruction, but first and foremost to the fact that double negation is a very rare feature in the Eastfalian city dialects of Hannover and Göttingen.

(4) *e*-extension

The analysis illustrates that instances of *e*-extension are restricted to two contexts: 2nd person plural and plural imperative. As regards the 2nd person singular, no single instance was found. This distributional pattern is determined by the text genre and its identification with an impersonal style. However, a significant finding is that all students systematically prefer *e*-extension to *e*-dropping in the given contexts and throughout the nineteenth century. This result is surprising, since nineteenth century grammarians not only allowed *e*-dropping in the inflectional system, but also dismissed *e*-extension as archaic. In addition, this tendency also runs counter to the students' language use as regards the dative-*e*, where they slowly but gradually adopt the nonstandard variant, i.e. the *e*-less variant.

(5) Afinite construction

As far as the afinite construction is concerned, the analysis reveals that this feature is still quite variable, with relative frequencies of 53% for the earlier decades and 29% for the later decades. Although the overall tendency indicates a sharp decline in the use of this construction, the result is still confusing, as language historians have pointed out that afinite constructions had almost completely disappeared in the eighteenth century.

However, as we know from sociolinguistic studies, linguistic change does not take place simultaneously in all styles and text genres, but sooner in some styles and text genres than in others. With regard to my corpus, it appears that essay writing is obviously one of those text genres lagging behind the general development, provided historical linguistics gives us a true account of the 'afinite construction story'.

(6) *der/welcher*

The relative frequencies indicate that the students use *der* and *welcher* alternatively. No pattern whatsoever emerged in the analysis. Moreover, it appears that the students are more conservative than nineteenth century grammarians, who preferred the shorter pronoun, especially at the end of the nineteenth century.

(7) Verb-first construction

The inverted word order for verbs is a feature rarely used by the students, as the low number of instances indicates. This result is probably due to the fact that the ability to manage this syntactic pattern requires a good command of grammar, since topicalization affects the whole sentence structure. Against this background, it may not be surprising that most cases of verb-initial order are either conditional clauses omitting *wenn* or clauses starting with *und*. While verb-first constructions in conditional clauses not introduced by a conjunction correspond to the rule, verb-first constructions in clauses starting with *und* are generally regarded as a rule violation or at best as 'commercial style' (see Schötensack 1856: 778). However, making use of verb first after *und*, as in the sentence "Das [sic!] beide Vermutungen nicht blindlings ohne festen Grund aufgestellt sind, darf wohl keinen Zweifel unterliegen, und mag es mir dafür gestattet sein, zu beweisen, welche von beiden Meinungen als die richtigere anzusehen ist" (1872), must have been fairly popular in those days, as Keller (1879: 157f.) reports in his "Antibarbarus". Provided that Keller's observation is true, the students' linguistic behaviour corresponds to the general trend, which obviously deviates from the prescriptive norm. Yet, in relation to stylistic features that are easier to incorporate, it is remarkable that the use of verb-first constructions after 1871 increases just as much as the use of exclamations and quotations.

All in all, the students' linguistic behaviour reveals a dialectic tendency: (a) a progressive undercurrent that is orientated towards new developments taking place in spoken language (this holds for the dropping of dative-*e*) and (b) a conservative undercurrent that resists changes as demonstrated by the invariability of the *e*-extension in the 2nd person plural, the plural imperative, and the stagnation of the *der/welcher* substitution.

5. Teachers' assessment strategies and linguistic competence

Teacher marking practices can be classified into two types: local responses and global responses. The local response represents a strategy that uses marginal comments. In most cases these comments refer to global issues such as text organization and content. Less often local concerns such as logic and clarity are addressed. Further investigation shows that there is a disparity between the stylistic tasks which students are assigned in essay writing as well as the language skills which are expected of them and their low priority in teachers' responses. This tendency is probably due to the fact that grammatical correctness as well as verbal and stylistic ornamentation were conceived of as linguistic subskills, whereas logic for the invention and arrangement of arguments was regarded as a primary competence. In those few cases where grammatical errors are referred to, they are simply located and stated. Only in one composition, written in 1909, are errors classified using an error code. In a few cases, corrections involve a reformulation or substitution.

Most teachers prefer global responses. In this strategy, comments are collected in an endnote as a response to student writing. In the first half of the nineteenth century, such comments are the only form of response strategy, while in the second half of the nineteenth century marginal notes in combination with endnotes dominate. However, most comments emphasize content, structure, and coherence, while only sparsely addressing grammar and lexis. The comments are usually rounded off with an explicit grade. However, two teachers display a very relaxed attitude and refuse to give grades or to comment on the compositions.

The following example, a global teacher comment concerning issues such as text structure, content, and linguistic elaboration, is taken from a composition written in 1870. It gives an insight into the criteria applied and the use of impressionistic evaluations of style like *durchsichtig* ('transparent'), *gefällig* ('pleasant'), and *gewandt* ('elegant').

Example 1

Die Gedanken, welche entwickelt wurden, sind richtig, wenn auch nicht in strengster Disposition durchgeführt. Abgesehen von einer falschen Auffassung der deutschen Verhältnisse, wie sie nach dem siebenjährigen Kriege lagen, liegt der in das Gebiet des Thema gehörende Stoff einfach klar vor Augen. Die Diction ist durchsichtig, gefällig, zuweilen gewandt.   Note: "gut"   (Aufsatz 1870)

'The thoughts developed are correct, albeit not worked through in the most rigorous arrangement. With the exception of a misunderstanding of the conditions in Germany following the Seven Years War, the material relevant to the topic is presented clearly and openly. The style is transparent, pleasant, at times elegant. Grade: "good"' (Essay 1870)

The second teacher comment shows that local errors concerning grammar, spelling, and punctuation are also mentioned in endnotes. In particular, the practice illustrates that the errors to which attention is drawn are discussed on a 'wildcard basis', as it is left open whether these errors are recurrent or simply chosen and discussed as representative or illustrative examples.

Example 2

Der Eingang dieser Rede sollte einfacher seyn, und größere Klarheit haben. Der Verfasser hat hier zu sehr nach dem Schmuke des Ausdruckes gesucht, und den klaren Gedanken jenem untergeordnet. Über das Thema selbst in seinen drei Theilen hat er übrigens grammatisch und logisch mit belohnendem Eifer im Ganzen abgehandelt, obgleich auch hier einzelne Ausdrücke nicht ganz richtig gewählt oder nicht schön dargestellt sind; z. B. erglimmen, mit Dornen besäht; euch als Jüngling, so herrliche blühen; vortheilhaft gewählt scheinende Umweg; fleckenloser Ruhm; u.a. sind grammatische Fehler. (Aufsatz 1821)

'The introduction of this speech should be simpler and clearer. The author has searched too hard for elaborate expression and subordinated clear thinking. As a whole, he has grammatically and logically developed the three parts of the topic itself with rewarding diligence, although here too individual expressions are not well chosen or are badly placed, e.g., *erglimmen, ... fleckenloser Ruhm;* etc. are grammatical mistakes.' (Essay 1821)

My material indicates that it is worthwhile to not only look at the errors detected by teachers, but also at those phenomena that went unnoticed. On the whole, teachers do not mark cases of the comparative particle *als* after positive adjectives, cases of verb-first constructions after *und*, or cases of dative-*e*-dropping. As far as the particle *als* is concerned, a possible explanation might be that some grammarians allow the use of *als* after positive adjectives in the interest of emphasis (see Becker 1845). However, a closer investigation of the contexts does not provide any evidence for a rhetorical purpose. As to the verb-first constructions after *und*, I do not really have an explanation. Maybe this is a case where prescriptivism and usage differ and a 'subsistent', implicit norm is favoured or at best tolerated by the teachers. Finally, in the case of dative-*e*-dropping, it seems that teachers are undecided how to react to ongoing, natural changes as a result of articulatory ease and indicators of destandardization. Although dative-*e*-dropping is one of the most prominent features discussed by contemporary grammarians and language critics, teachers do not comment on those cases. This is even more surprising as their own language behaviour displays a categorical usage of dative-*e*. Thus, it remains unclear whether the teachers are tolerant or ignorant of variation.

6. Conclusion

The main findings of my inquiry into the standard competence of students and teachers can be summarized as follows:

1. Contrary to the criticism of many contemporary language critics, the linguistic performance of the students exhibits a high degree of norm compliance.

2. Students' norm orientation displays a dialectic tendency that includes progressive and conservative target norms. In particular, clinging to conservative norms seems to be more likely in those cases where the variants carry stylistic meaning (e.g. *e*-extension in the 2nd person plural and plural imperative). This interpretation is supported by the students' general tendency to fill their texts with pathetic rhetorical devices.

3. During the first half of the nineteenth century, teachers seem to be more interested in correcting phenomena concerning global aspects such as text archtitecture and style (e.g. use of quotations and superlatives). Grammatical errors are not marked consistently, but rather picked out and discussed 'representatively' in an endnote.

4. Finally, variation is a collective but obviously unconscious practice and restricted to certain features. In general, it goes unnoticed, which in the case of dative -*e*- dropping is surprising, all the more so, as many grammarians stubbornly insist on the dative -*e*- as the one and only norm.

References

Adelung, Johann Christoph. 1782. *Umständliches Lehrgebäude der deutschen Sprache, zur Erläuterung der deutschen Sprachlehre für Schulen.* 2 vols. Berlin: Voß [Repr. Hildesheim and New York: Olms 1971].

Adelung, Johann Christoph. 1785. *Über den deutschen Styl. 3 Teile in einem Band.* Berlin: Voß [Repr. Hildesheim, New York: Olms 1974].

Admoni, Wladimir. 1990. *Historische Syntax des Deutschen.* Tübingen: Niemeyer.

Auer, Peter. 2005. "Europe's Sociolinguistic Unity, or: A Typology of European Dialect/Standard Constellations." In Nicole Delbecque, Johan van der Auwera and Dirk Geeraerts (eds.), *Perspectives on Variation. Sociolinguistic, Historical, Comparative.* Berlin and New York: de Gruyter, 7–43.

Becker, Karl Ferdinand. 1841. *Organism der Sprache.* 2nd ed. Frankfurt/Main: Kettembeil. [Repr. Hildesheim, New York: Olms 1970].

Becker, Karl Ferdinand. 1845. *Schulgrammatik der deutschen Sprache.* 5th ed. Frankfurt/Main: Kettembeil.

Becker, Karl Ferdinand. 1848. *Der deutsche Stil.* Frankfurt/Main: Kettembeil [Repr. Hildesheim, New York: Olms 1977].

Blatz, Friedrich. 1896. *Neuhochdeutsche Grammatik mit Berücksichtigung der Entwickelung der deutschen Sprache.* 2 vols. 3th ed. Karlsruhe: Lang.

Daneš, František. 2003. The present-day situation of Czech. *International Journal of the Sociology of Language* 162: 9–18.

Deinhardt, Johann Heinrich. 1837. *Der Gymnasialunterricht nach den wissenschaftlichen Anforderungen der jetzigen Zeit.* Hamburg: Perthes.

Deumert, Ana. 2003. Standard Languages as Civic Rituals – Theory and Examples. *Sociolinguistica* 17: 31–51.

Edwards, John. 1985. *Language, Society and Identity.* Blackwell: Oxford.

Elspaß, Stephan. 2005. Language Norm and Language Reality. Effectiveness and limits of prescriptivism in New High German. In Nils Langer and Winifred V. Davies (eds.), *Linguistic Purism in the Germanic Language.* Berlin and New York: de Gruyter, 20–46.

Engelien, August. 1878. *Grammatik der neuhochdeutschen Sprache.* 2th ed. Berlin: Schultze.

Ferguson, Charles A. 1996. Standardization as a Form of Language Spread. In Thom Huebner (ed.), *Sociolinguistic Perspectives. Papers on Language in Society, 1959–1994.* New York: Oxford University Press, 189–200.

Gloy, Klaus. 1997. Sprachnormen als 'Institutionen im Reich der Gedanken' und die Rolle des Individuums in Sprachnormierungsprozessen. In Klaus J. Mattheier (ed.), *Norm und Variation.* Frankfurt/Main: Lang, 27–36.

Gottsched, Johann Christoph. 1751. *Versuch einer critischen Dichtkunst.* 4th ed. Leipzig: Breitkopf [Repr. Darmstadt: Wiss. Buchgesellschaft 1982].

Herling, Simon Heinrich Adolf. 1832. *Grundregeln des deutschen Styls, oder der Periodenbau der deutschen Sprache. Ein Lehrbuch für den stilistischen Unterricht.* Frankfurt/Main: Kettembeil.

Heyse, Johann Christoph August. 1838. J. C. A. *Heyse's ausführliches Lehrbuch der deutschen Sprache. Neu bearbeitet von K.W.L. Heyse.* Hannover: Hahn'sche Hofbuchhandlung.

Heyse, Johann Christoph August. 1830. *Theoretisch-praktische deutsche Schulgrammatik oder kurzgefaßtes Lehrbuch der deutschen Sprache, mit Beispielen und Aufgaben zur Anwendung der Regeln.* 9th ed. Hannover: Hahn.

Hildebrand, Rudolf. 1867. *Vom deutschen Sprachunterricht in der Schule und von deutscher Erziehung und Bildung überhaupt.* Leipzig: Klinkhardt.

Keller, Karl Gottlieb. 1878. *Deutscher Antibarbarus. Beiträge zur Förderung des richtigen Gebrauches der Muttersprache.* Stuttgart: Liesching & Comp.

Laas, Ernst. 1868. *Der deutsche Aufsatz in der ersten Gymnasialclasse (Prima). Ein Handbuch für Lehrer und Schüler, enthaltend Theorie und Materialien.* Berlin: Weidmannsche Buchhandlung.

Langer, Nils. 2001. *Linguistic Purism in Action. How auxiliary tun was stigmatized in Early New High German.* Berlin and New York: de Gruyter.

Ludwig, Otto. 1988. *Der Schulaufsatz: Seine Geschichte in Deutschland.* Berlin and New York: de Gruyter.

Lühr, Rosemarie. 1992. Gleichartigkeit, Vollständigkeit, Vermeidung von Redundanz. Prinzipien von Sprachbewertungen im 19. Jahrhundert. *Muttersprache* 102: 341–359.

Nipperdey, Thomas. 1993. *Deutsche Geschichte 1800–1866. Bürgerwelt und starker Staat.* München: C.H. Beck.

Mattheier, Klaus J. 1997. Destandardisierung, Umstandardisierung, Standardisierung in europäischen Sprachen. In Klaus J. Mattheier and Edgar Radtke (eds.), *Standardisierung und Destandardisierung europäischer Nationalsprachen.* Frankfurt/Main: Lang, 1–10.

Mattheier, Klaus J. 2000. Die Herausbildung neuzeitlicher Schriftsprachen. In Werner Besch, Anne Betten, Oskar Reichmann and Stefan Sonderegger (eds.), *Sprachgeschichte. Ein Handbuch zur Geschichte der deutschen Sprache und ihrer Erforschung.* 2nd ed. Berlin and New York: de Gruyter, vol. 2, 1085–1107.

Meyer, Richard Moritz. 1906. *Deutsche Stilistik.* München: Beck.

Milroy, James. 2000. The ideology of the standard language. In Laura Wright (ed.), *The Development of Standard English, 1300–1800 – Theories, Descriptions, Conflicts.* Cambridge: Cambridge University Press, 11–28.

Polenz, Peter von. 1999. *Deutsche Sprachgeschichte vom Mittelalter bis zur Gegenwart. Vol. III: 19. und 20. Jahrhundert.* Berlin and New York: de Gruyter.

Sanders, Daniel. 1880. *Deutsche Sprachbriefe.* 2nd ed. Berlin: Langenscheidt.

Sapir, Edward. 1921. *Language: an introduction to the study of speech.* New York: Harcourt, Brace & World.

Scharl, Benno. 1814. *Beschreibung der Braunbier-Brauerey im Königreich Baiern.* München: Lindauer [Repr. Hildesheim, New York: Olms 1976].

Schieb, Gabriele. 1981. Zu Stand und Wirkungsbereich der kodifizierten grammatischen Norm Ende des 19. Jahrhunderts. *Beiträge zur Erforschung der deutschen Sprache* 1: 134–176.

Sieber, Peter. 1998. *Parlando in Texten: zur Veränderung kommunikativer Grundmuster in der Schriftlichkeit.* Tübingen: Niemeyer.

Schopenhauer, Arthur. 1923. Über die Verhunzung der deutschen Sprache. In Paul Deussen (ed.), Arthus *Schopenhauers Sämtliche Werke,* vol. 6. München: Piper.

Schötensack, Heinrich August. 1856. *Grammatik der neuhochdeutschen Sprache. Mit besonderer Berücksichtigung ihrer historischen Entwickelung.* Erlangen: Encke.

Spiekermann, Helmut. 2005. Regionale Standardisierung, nationale Destandardisierung. In Ludwig M. Eichinger and Werner Kallmeyer (eds.), *Standardvariation – Wie viel Variation verträgt die deutsche Sprache?* Berlin, New York: de Gruyter, 100–126.

Trudgill, Peter. 1986. *Dialects in contact.* Oxford: Blackwell.

Vernaleken, Theodor. 1863. *Deutsche Syntax. Zweiter Theil.* Wien: Braumüller.

Wehler, Hans Ulrich. 1995. *Deutsche Gesellschaftsgeschichte Vol. 3, Von der 'Deutschen Doppelrevolution' bis zum Beginn des Ersten Weltkrieges 1849–1914.* München: C.H. Beck.

Wustmann, Gustav. 1896. *Allerhand Sprachdummheiten. Kleine deutsche Grammatik des Zweifelhaften, Falschen und des Hässlichen. Ein Hilfsbuch für alle, die sich öffentlich der deutschen Sprache bedienen.* 2nd ed. Leipzig: Grunow.

Zehetner, Ludwig G. 1977. *Bairisch. Dialekt / Hochsprache Kontrastiv. Sprachhefte für den Deutschunterricht.* Düsseldorf: Schwann.

IV. Language choice and language planning

Steffen Arzberger (Erlangen)

The choice between German and French for the German nobility of the late 18th century

1. Introduction

Monsieur
Mon tres cher Cousin
Son Altesse Madame La Margrave; vous fait faire ces grand compliments; et vous
prie davoir La bontez de demanter, Monseigneur Le Margrave, si il vouloit qu'elle
viene avant son depart pour Driesdorff prentre conger de lui; Mais vous dever avoir
La complaisance Cher cousin; de lui parler en particulier – et non en presence de M;
pour le reste vous le pourieè tire en presence de qui vous voutiez; elle assure aussi
de ces compliments a Madame votre chere Epouse; et de moi sil vous plait de mes
amitièe; edant avec beaucoup destime; et avec la plus hautte conssideration;
Monsieur
Mon tres Cher Cousin
Votre tres obeisante servante
de Forstner la veuve
neé de Pölnitz

'Sir, my very dear cousin, Her Highness the Margravine presents her compliments
to you and begs you to have the kindness to ask the Margrave [title of a high
German noble – S.A.] if he wishes for her to come and bid him farewell before his
departure for Triesdorf. Although, my dear cousin, you must do her the favour of
speaking to her privately – and not in M.'s presence. As to everything else, you may
talk to him in presence of whomever. She also sends her compliments to your dear
wife, and I beg you to assure her of my friendship. Yours faithfully, Sir, my dear
cousin, your most obedient servant (Mrs) von Forstner widow, née von Pölnitz'

The above was taken from a letter by Baroness Forstner, who wrote to her
cousin Baron von Gemmingen on 19th October 1789 (State Archive, Nuremberg, Repository 314: Estate of State Minister Karl Friedrich Reinhard Baron
von Gemmingen (1739–1822); No. 11: Letters by Baroness Forstner 1789).
The letter is a typical example of correspondence between German nobles of
the late 18th century and shows that, from the 17th century onwards, the
French language had been established as the language of correspondence for
the German high nobility. The lower nobility subsequently tried to imitate the

princes in their behaviour and language choice, and the bourgeoisie tended to copy the landed gentry and the patricians.

In the course of the 18th century, however, the bourgeoisie or upper middle class began to emancipate itself. In the process of the 'European Enlightenment' it formed a new educated elite, and by the beginning of the 20th century, it had already replaced the nobility as the former elite of state. Being thus put on the spot, the nobility reacted to this in many ways. Some noblemen came to terms with the middle class conventions that were asserting themselves and took tuition not only in fencing, dancing, riding, and French, but increasingly in academic subjects, too. Others ignored the social changes, stuck to their old traditions and norms and remained farmers, military officers, and senior clergymen.

My concern in this paper is how this process manifested itself in their choice of language and how the nobility's choice of language differed from the middle classes'. Who wrote to whom about what in which language? Since there are contradictions in its representation even today, we do not yet know enough about the actual extent and functional contribution of French and German to communication in 18th and early 19th century Germany. Thus, a study as to what extent the two languages were used in written correspondence has been overdue.

In this paper I outline the Erlangen project *Adelssprache* and show how it can eventually answer the question which of the two languages was used in which proportion in what kind of written correspondence in the 18th and 19th centuries. Huge parts of the corpus which the project makes use of – mostly letters that were kept in several German archives – have already been assessed.

2. State of research

Klaus J. Mattheier (1995: 475; 1997: 34) mentions that French was especially widespread in the type of text used in correspondence and that we find "[s]chon im 17. und dann vermehrt im 18. Jahrhundert [...] Briefwechsel unter Deutschen in französischer Sprache" ('correspondence between Germans written in French even in the 17th century and with increasing frequency in the 18th century'). He claims that French tended to be used especially in 'official' letters between persons of different social rank.

In Frederick II of Prussia's chancellery, however, it had been the case that many subjects, including high-ranking officers, had to be addressed in German because they were not able to read French (Petersilka 2005: 171–175). First impressions from the letter collections in the State Archive in Nuremberg seem to confirm neither the one custom nor the other. Thus, the circumstances surrounding the actual choice of language must be examined more closely.

Our knowledge on the proportion of French that was used in written texts is based almost entirely on published correspondence by well-known and literary persons. According to these data, French was most frequently used at the princes' courts, and since the high nobility was related across territorial borders even, Francophone contacts were not uncommon in the family.

The best known case in this respect is that of Frederick II of Prussia and the Prussian court (see Petersilka 2005). Although it is in no way representative, Frederick's linguistic behaviour has formed the prevailing image of language use in the 18th century because he almost exclusively spoke and wrote in French. However, things were different at other courts. In 1774 Clairon, the mistress of Margrave Alexander of Ansbach-Bayreuth, reports in French:

> [O]n trouve à peine à la cour une douzaine de personnes qui puissent avoir une conversation en françois, et tout le reste n'en entend pas un mot
>
> 'there are hardly a dozen people at court who can converse in French, the rest don't understand a word.' (Brunot 1967: 611)

Petersilka (2005: 39–45) also describes the situation at the Habsburg court in Vienna. She emphasizes that the common opinion that all noblemen spoke French is actually false. She says that, on the contrary, choice of language was individual and differed greatly in many respects. She holds that "there was a tendency for protestant courts to be more French than the catholic ones were", which remains to be investigated more thoroughly.

For our purposes, we can state that the majority of the lower nobility definitely acquired a style of writing that was in accordance with the high nobility's. Peter von Polenz (1994: 71f.), for example, describes the use of French and German in the writings and letters of the Prussian reformer Karl Baron vom und zum Stein, who lived from 1757 to 1831. According to von Polenz, two thirds of Stein's letters were written in German and one third was written in French, with the proportion of those written in French decreasing during the latter stages of his life.

When adopting previous academic contributions on the subject, it must be taken into account that nearly all of these have an impressionistic character, and that their general conclusions cannot be verified empirically. Consequently, the aim of the *Adelssprache* project is to provide an empirical foundation for further studies on the subject.

3. The *Adelssprache* project

The project *Adelssprache* is being designed as a corpus-based study on German-French bilingualism, ranging from 1750 to 1825. By choosing the region of southeast Germany, also known as *Franken* (Franconia), as an example, the proportion of French and German in the correspondence of German noblemen can be ascertained.

3.1 Types of text

The project is based on a corpus of so far unpublished letters. In a situation of bilingualism, letters are entirely suitable for an examination of language choice, since they are authentic sources whose authors, addressees, and dates are known. Correspondence by letter was a particularly wide-spread form of communication in the 18th and 19th century. It is therefore possible to compile a representative corpus of sub-divisions covering the private, official, and commercial domains.

3.2 Time span

The period from 1750 to 1825 proves to be interesting for several reasons. 1750, the starting point for the study, coincides with both the peak of the absolutist regime and the peak of the European 'Enlightenment'. French can thus be seen both as the language of absolutism, with Versailles standing as a model for the rest of Europe, and as the language of the Enlightenment, with French and British philosophers being the most important representatives of the movement. The date for the starting point of the study therefore is the French language's moment of strongest presence in Germany (cf. Brunot 1967: 558–616 and von Polenz 1994: 66–71). After this, Francophilia declined in favour of a slowly increasing linguistic nationalism in Germany.

3.3 Selection of region and sociological spheres

A regional delimitation was necessary. There are several reasons for choosing Franconia as an example, one of which is that nowhere else in Germany was there such a great social diversity of noblemen. The high nobility was mostly represented by the Franconian Hohenzollern princes, who ruled the principalities of Brandenburg-Anspach and Brandenburg-Bayreuth until 1792 and were linked to other courts such as the royal Prussian court in Berlin.

There were both Roman-Catholic and Protestant families in Franconia, and until the time of secularisation, territorial rule was in many cases in the hands of spiritual principalities such as the diocese of Würzburg. Apart from the old self-governing princes and counts of the Empire, there were knights and patricians in free cities of the Holy Roman Empire such as Nuremberg, landed gentry and young nobles who were former bourgeois civil servants. Therefore, in choosing this particular German region, both a confessional and social differentiation became possible.

In order to get a sociological cross-section, two or three representatives of each type of nobleman were selected. The two major confessions, Roman-Catholic and Lutheran, are equally represented in the project. As far as this was possible, both sexes of each rank were included.

The writers selected for this study did not only write to Franconian noblemen. They held contacts with noblemen in other German and European countries and had correspondence with the middle classes also, e.g. priests and local administration officials. In one and the same fascicle, we often find letters written by different persons who had written to each other. Considering these findings, the language of Franconian noblemen can easily be compared to that of non-Franconian noblemen and to middle-class writers.

The writers as such are represented by short biographies that include their educational profile, i.e. whether they learnt French in a special college for noblemen or by mediation of a francophone nurse or a francophone tutor. Addressees are also documented biographically. One further consideration is that ruling princes had their own chancelleries and had someone to write their letters for them instead of writing them personally. This fact may have an impact on the quality of the language, and it should also be ascertained whether this could affect the choice of language.

3.4 Procedure: data base and statistical analysis

All letters forming the corpus are put into a data base which allows quick access to and combination of the various social and communicative data such as the sender's and addressee's name and sex, the type of the letter, and its subject. The different areas are then statistically compared to each other, and it is analysed which percentage of French and German was used by male or female writers and by Protestants and Catholics respectively. The most important question concerns the possible functional distribution of the two languages. Since, from the 17th century onwards, the address on the reverse side of or on the envelope was mostly written in French, the salutation and the closing phrase were also frequently written in French, even where letters were otherwise completely or partly written in German.

3.5 Further analysis

The main body of the letters needs to be analysed with respect to the qualification and qualitative distribution of German and French. Here it is important to note which percentage of the whole they comprise, and which passages were written in which language. Likewise, the content and purpose of the communication requires special attention.

The question of how the employed languages were seen by their users is very important, too. What was associated with French, what kind of ideas were connected with German? Was French seen as the language of absolutism and feudalism or as *the* modern language of the Enlightenment? It is also necessary to investigate whether German was considered as progressive or as a conservative, national language. In order to do that, metalinguistic comments in the letters are being investigated and will then be gathered and analysed.

One aspect of the study is dedicated to those aspects of the chosen languages that are due to interference and variety. As far as French is concerned, it is above all interference by the speakers' native language that promises the most interesting results. Some of the letters show strong German usage and dialectal (i.e. Franconian) interference in particular. Apart from other orthographical and grammatical mistakes, quantity and quality of interference may be taken as indicators of the writers' grade of language competence.

The German texts, too, must be analysed for linguistic variance. Above all, the question to be looked into is whether the variety used correlates with the communicative situation and the writer's social position.

4. Examining the corpus

4.1 Examples of interference

In order to illustrate German-dialectal interference in French texts, let us take a closer look at Baroness Forstner's letter to Baron von Gemmingen, which was mentioned at the beginning of this paper:

> Monsieur
> Mon tres cher Cousin
> Son Altesse Madame La Margrave; vous fait faire ces grand compliments; et vous prie davoir La bontez de demanter, Monseigneur Le Margrave, si il vouloit qu'elle viene avant son depart pour Driesdorff prentre conger de lui; Mais vous dever avoir La complaisance Cher cousin; de lui parler en particulier – et non en presence de M; pour le reste vous le pourieè tire en presence de qui vous voutiez; elle assure aussi

de ces compliments a Madame votre chere Epouse; et de moi sil vous plait de mes
amitièe; edant avec beaucoup destime; et avec la plus hautte conssideration;
Monsieur
Mon tres Cher Cousin
Votre tres obeisante servante
de Forstner la veuve
neé de Pölnitz

Repeatedly French voiced plosives (here: dentals) are rendered by graphemes
for unvoiced plosives: *demanter* instead of <demander>, *prentre* instead of
<prendre>. Conversely, voiceless plosives (here: a dental) are written with
graphemes for voiced plosives: *edant* instead of <étant>. This confusion is
probably due to the writer's dialectal substratum with the characteristic
German consonant weakening, i.e. the absence of the voiced-unvoiced
opposition and the generalisation of all plosives to (unvoiced lenis) weak
unvoiced plosives. One of the consequences of this generalisation is that
dialect speakers tend to be unsure how to write plosives. Another regional
feature is the voiced *s*, which is unknown to the dialects of Southern Germany.
This explains the writing *obeisante* instead of <obéissante>, a written form
that would suggest a voiced [z] according to the French grapheme-phoneme-
correspondence rule that says that an intervocalic <s> is to be pronounced
voiced. The writer apparently makes no difference between the French
phonemes /s/ and /z/.

As an example of a German letter, I quote from a letter by Baron Johann
Sigmund Stromer von Reichenbach (1756–1815). The letter was addressed to
his secretary Mr. Zwingel in Nuremberg and was written in Munich on January
17th, 1784:

> […] gestern erhielte mit vielen Vergnügen Ihren werthen Brief und heute will ich
> ihn beantworten, glauben Sie mir es giebt Augenblicke, wo ich eben so gerne allein
> bin, und die ich nicht für alle Gesellschaften verdauschte, Sie sind es also nicht
> allein, der die Einsamkeit liebt […].

> '[...] yesterday I received your dear letter with great pleasure and today I will
> answer it, believe me there are moments in which I like to be alone just as much as
> you do, and which I would not want to trade in for any kind of society, that is to say
> that you are not alone in loving solitude [...].'

Franconian substratum can be noticed in this German text, too: *verdauschte*
instead of <vertauschte>. Besides phonographic aspects, there may be further
interference and mistakes that are due to dialectal influence on other linguistic
levels. This might also explain the non-standard dative ending in *<vielen>
instead of *<vielem>.

4.2 Karl Friedrich Reinhard von Gemmingen's correspondence

The second example I would like to refer to concerns the correspondence of Karl Friedrich Reinhard von Gemmingen, who was born in 1739 and died in 1822; the letters were accessed in the State Archive in Nuremberg. Gemmingen was State Minister of Margave Alexander of Brandenburg-Anspach.

Out of some 160 letters that could be attributed to his correspondence, about 40 letters were written in German, about 118 in French. 82 of these French letters were written by members of the high nobility, such as King Max Joseph of Bavaria, Margrave Alexander of Brandenburg-Ansbach-Bayreuth, Margravine Friederike Caroline and Lady Elizabeth Craven, the margrave's mistress and the latter's second wife, who was not a German native speaker. 12 of the French letters were written by barons who later became princes (Prince Archbishop Carl Theodor von Dalberg and Karl August von Hardenberg), 24 by members of the lower nobility (4 by Baroness Forstner née Baroness von Pölnitz, 16 by Baron Albert von Seckendorff, 4 by Baron Karl von Gemmingen) and 2 by a middle class citizen (Privy Councillor Schmid). 8 of the letters written in German were composed by princes, namely King Max Joseph, King Frederick William III. of Prussia, Prince and former Count Clemens Wenzel Lothar von Metternich, Prince – former Baron – Carl Philipp von Wrede, 1 by Count Rehberg, 16 by Barons (Gemmingen and Seckendorff), 8 by members of the middle class (Privy Councillor Schmid, the civil servants Dertinger and Schoepf, the merchants Amos and Loesch). 7 letters were written by unknown persons.

My analysis shows that the proportion of French correspondence by princes amounts to 69% and a further 10% consist of social climbers, so that the total amount is approximately 79%. The lower nobility is represented by approximately 20%, the middle class members only amount to 1%. The proportion of German correspondence amounts to 20% written by the high nobility, 43% written by the low nobility, and 20% by members of the middle class; 17% of the letters examined were written by unknown persons. This means that about 80% of the letters written by princes were composed in French and about 20% in German. About 32% of the letters by lower noblemen were written in French, about 68% in German, and for the middle classes we can state that 5% of their letters were written in French and 95% in German.

All letters of the estate written by women were in French, as were all the private letters. As far as official letters are concerned, German is predominant, though not in diplomatic correspondence (e.g. between Hardenberg and Gemmingen). Here both languages are represented.

5. Conclusion

The choice between the German and French language in the communication of the 18th and early 19th century in Germany has hitherto not been empirically and systematically analysed with regard to its functionality. The *Adelsssprache* project aims at finding out which language German noblemen chose in their private, official and business letters, vis-à-vis to whom and why they wrote at all. On the basis of a representative corpus of letters written by Franconian noblemen between 1750 and 1825, the study will provide information on the role of French as a social marker, about the actual acquisition and use of French, and the circumstances in which the German elite would switch from French to German.

Judging form the examples above, we can already discern a preliminary trend in the language use of the writers in question. Apart from the percentages stated, we can further state that all letters written by women and all private letters were composed in French. As opposed to diplomatic letters, official letters tend to occur in German. In diplomacy both languages are equally represented.

References

Brunot, Ferdinand. 1967. *Histoire de la langue française des origines à nos jours.* Paris: Colin.

Mattheier, Klaus J. 1995. Das Französische in Deutschland. Sprach-soziologische Überlegungen zur deutschen Sprachgeschichte im 17./18. Jahrhundert. In Eugène Faucher, René Métrich and Marcel Vuillaume (eds.), *Signans und Signatum. Auf dem Weg zu einer semantischen Grammatik. Festschrift für Paul Valentin zu 60. Geburtstag.* Tübingen: Stauffenburg, 467–479.

Mattheier, Klaus J. 1997. Französisch verdrängt Deutsch? Soziolinguistische Überlegungen zum 18. Jahrhundert. In Bernd Spillner (ed.), *Französische Sprache in Deutschland im Zeitalter der Französischen Revolution.* Frankfurt am Main et al.: Lang, 27–38.

Petersilka, Corina. 2005. *Die Zweisprachigkeit Friedrichs des Großen. Ein linguistisches Porträt.* Tübingen: Niemeyer.

Polenz, Peter von. 1994. *Deutsche Sprachgeschichte vom späten Mittelalter bis zur Gegenwart. Vol. 2. 17. und 18. Jahrhundert.* Berlin u.a.: de Gruyter.

JEROEN DARQUENNES (BRUSSEL)

Flirting at the fringe – The status of the German varieties as perceived by language activists in Belgium's Areler Land

1. Introduction

Though often neglected in contemporary socio- and contact linguistic literature, the Areler Land, i.e. the historically German-speaking area located around the Belgian city of Arel/Arlon, remains one of the most intriguing language contact zones along the Germanic-Romance language border. Since it was attached to Belgium in the early 19th century, the Areler Land has been the playground of ongoing German-French language shift. This article deals with the language shift processes in the Areler Land from a historical perspective and subsequently pays attention to contemporary attempts to maintain the local German varieties. Of special interest here will be the changes in the linguistic classification of the local German varieties by language activists in the Areler Land. We will first provide the necessary background information to situate the Areler Land in the Belgian context.

2. The Areler Land: peripheral part of Belgium

Situated in the southernmost corner of the Belgian province of Luxembourg, the Areler Land roughly coincides with the administrative district of Arel, which consists of 5 greater municipalities since the Belgian municipal reform in the 1970s: Martelingen/Martelange, Attert, Arel/Arlon, Metzig/Messancy and Ibingen/Aubange.[1]

---

[1]   A few villages belonging to the municipality of Arel are to be deducted from the Areler Land, notably the southern francophone villages Deutsch-Meer/Meix-le-Tige, Rösig/Rachecourt und Holdingen/Halanzy (with the exception of the hamlets Bettenhofen/Battincourt and Esch-auf-der-Hurt/Aix-sur-Cloie). A few villages that do not belong to the administrative district of Arel are added to the Areler Land. In the north: Tintingen/Tintange, Warnach, Bödingen/Bodange and Wiesembach/Wisembach as part of the administrative district of Bastnach/Bastogne. In the

Map 1: The Areler land (from Nelde 1979a: 67)

As a former part of the greater Grand Duchy of Luxembourg, the Areler Land joined the territorially unstable Belgian state in 1830. When, as a result of hot international debates, the precise territorial demarcation of the newly founded state was finally settled in 1839, this had major consequences for the Grand Duchy of Luxembourg. The entire French part of the Grand Duchy remained with Belgium and became the Belgian province of Luxembourg. The German part – with the notable exception of the Areler Land and a small area surrounding the village of Bocholz/Bého to the south of St. Vith – was to become the present Grand Duchy of Luxembourg. That the Grand Duchy was

---

north-west: Herzig/Hachy (part of the village of Habich/Habay that belongs to the administrative district of Virton).

not divided according to the Germanic-Romance language border was due to diverse and diplomatically cloaked personal interests on the Belgian side and geopolitical interests on the French side. The linguistic consequences of this bargain soon made themselves known. When French as the favorite language of the Walloon post-office employees and a considerable part of the bourgeoisie had slowly been established as the preferred language of higher administration in the period before Belgian independence, its range of influence grew considerably throughout the following decades. The present situation of German-French asymmetrical multilingualism, in which German clearly overruled French in the form of the local Moselle-Franconian varieties in daily communication on a broad societal level, quite swiftly evolved into societal German-French language shift. In the course of the 19th century, the linguistic landscape was about to change dramatically.

3. Language Shift in the Areler Land: a historical perspective

A glance at historical factors influencing German-French language shift in the linguistically marginalized German-speaking parts of the largely francophone Belgian province of Luxembourg shows that three subsequent periods in history can be distinguished during which the language shift process was sped up: the decades following Belgian independence, World War I, and World War II. Each of these three periods will now be discussed, focusing on both factors that accelerated language shift and attempts to slow it down.[2]

3.1 Belgian independence

Once the borders of the Belgian state had been determined, Arel was turned into the administrative capital of the Belgian province of Luxemburg. The city swiftly lost its rural character and developed into a well-equipped province capital. Due to the influx of mainly francophone civil servants that were sent by the central Belgian government to work in the provincial administration, the court, the railway station, the customs service and in the newly erected schools the Areler population rose from 3,283 in 1831 to more than 12,000 in 1910. Apart from Arel, the communities of Athus and Ibingen near the French border also witnessed population growth. Here it was the ongoing process of industrialization that attracted a Walloon, Flemish, French, and Italian work

---

[2]   Details can be found in Bertrang (1921, 1936), Zender (1939, 1941), Nelde (1979a and b), Pabst (1979), Kern (1999), Triffaux (2002) and Lejeune (2003).

force. Quite naturally, the inhabitants of the rural villages in the north of the Areler Land found their way to the factories in the south as well. Combined with the fact that some educated people left the villages to capitalize their knowledge of German as lower civil servants in the central administration in Brussels, this led to a partial rural depopulation.

The diverging demographical development of the municipalities constituting the Areler Land was soon complemented by a diverging linguistic development. In Arel, Athem, Ibingen, and their immediate surroundings the increase of the non-native population caused an increase in the use of French in everyday life. This influence was not only reinforced by the clear-cut use of French as the administrative language of a centralized state that was ruled by a trans-ethnic francophone elite. Also the augmented use of French in education contributed to the process of frenchification. During the course of the 19th century's second half French replaced (standard) German as the language of instruction in primary schools in Arel and in the industrialized communities. (Apart from primary education, (standard) German had not been used as a language of instruction in the Areler Land). Due to the changing linguistic circumstances the autochthonous nobility and bourgeoisie (most of them traditionally residing in the city of Arel) had almost completely switched to French by 1880. Motivated by this behavior, parts of the native petty bourgeoisie felt obliged to start passing on the language of their employers to the next generation in order to assure its upward social mobility. And when in the course of the 19th century more and more mixed marriages occurred in all layers of society, this also strengthened the societal position of French in the family. Traditionally French rather than German (in its local varieties) was passed on as a mother tongue to the next generation. As a daily means of communication of the autochthonous working population, the local German varieties did not, however, disappear in Arel and the industrialized communities. They were rather submerged into a German-French diglossic pattern in which French was used in public domains and penetrated rather gradually into semi-official and private domains. However, French linguistic pressure was continuously on the increase.

The situation in the rural villages of the Areler Land was totally different. Apart from its use in administration, the range of influence of the French language affected everyday communication in the strongly catholic communities to a lower extent. The church and also the schools (primary schools in which (standard) German was used as the language of instruction) contributed to German language maintenance. The rural villages also accounted for most of the readers of the *Deutsche Arloner Zeitung*, which – with its special attention for agricultural topics – was a welcome alternative in a region that was dominated by francophone media. All in all, the rural communities were not subject to German-French language shift to a large degree. Consequently, when Gottfried Kurth (professor of history at the university of Liège) and Nicolaus Warker (a local poet and teacher) founded the *Deutscher Verein zur Hebung und Pflege der Muttersprache* in 1893, this was not so much the result of the situation in the rural communities, but rather the result of the changing linguistic landscape in Arel and the industrialized communities.

Alarmed by the ongoing Frenchification in Arel and its surroundings, the *Deutscher Verein* – on a local as well as on a national level – strongly pleaded for the use of German in education and administration as well as for the translation of official documents into German. It proved, however, difficult to recruit members. At the peak of its fame the *Deutscher Verein* counted slightly more than 100 members, most of them priests and teachers belonging to the catholic elite. Even though the German-speaking population of the Areler Land showed interest in evening parties, musical evenings, and poetry readings, they could not be persuaded to overtly side with the demands of the association. As a consequence, the elitist *Deutscher Verein* failed to become a contributing factor to language maintenance and language awareness on a broad societal level and ceased to exist with the outbreak of the Great War.

3.2 World War I

When German troops crossed the Belgian border in 1914, the Areler population did not support this undertaking. Attempts to establish German as the official language and to reintroduce German as the language of instruction in Arel and the industrialized communities remained theoretical, since, especially in the frenchified parts of the Areler Land, the initiators met with a wall of resistance. To show their dislike for the Prussian military initiative, the greater lot of the German-speaking inhabitants of the Areler Land overtly turned to French and started using it as a symbol of patriotic unity (Verdoodt 1968: 9). The autochthonous Areler population was ashamed of using its local German varieties, since they were associated with the language of the Prussian occupier. It comes as no surprise, therefore, that the use of German in the post-war years was increasingly limited to the private sphere. Neither is it surprising that no loud opposition was heard when the language-in-education policy of the central Belgian government aimed at a geopolitically motivated reduction of the use of German in education. Alfred Bertrang (1936: 139), secondary school teacher in Arel and advocate of the German language, reports how schools in Arel advised against the choice of German as a foreign language. And when German courses were offered in the curriculum at all, classes were either not organized or often taught by a francophone teacher with hardly any knowledge of German. In the rural communities, similar attempts were made to replace German with French as a language of instruction in primary schools. However, educational authorities were prompted to reconsider this decision, since pupils showed severe difficulties to catch on. All the same, it became more difficult in the rural communities to refrain from the use of French in certain aspects of daily life. On the one hand, this was caused by the stigmatization of German following World War I. On the other hand, it was caused by the social changes that also started to affect life in the more remote parts of the Areler Land:

> Die Ausdehnungen der Beziehungen aller Art, der Aufenthalt in der Kaserne, die Dienstjahre in einer großen Stadt, die Ausübung eines Handwerks in der Fremde, die Nähe romanischer Ortschaften, die Niederlassung Französischsprechender in deutschen Gemeinden, die Verbreitung der Zeitungen, die Fortschritte im Unterrichtswesen, das Besuchen eines Gymnasiums, wenn der Bauernsohn eine gründlichere Erziehung erhalten will, ehe er sich dem Ackerbau widmet: dies alles hat eine tiefe Umwälzung in unserem winzigen deutschen Winkel hervorgerufen. Die Zahl derer, die französisch verstehen, sprechen und sogar schreiben, ist in stetem Wachsen begriffen. (Bertrang 1936: 144)

> ('the increase of all kinds of relationships, life in the barracks, years of service in a big city, the occupation as a labourer abroad, the closeness of Romanic hamlets, the settlement of francophones in German communities, the distribution of newspapers, the progress in education, a farmer's son visiting a gymnasium in pursuit of better education before dedicating his life entirely to farming: all of this has revolutionized our small German territory. The number of those who understand, speak and even write French is constantly growing.')

Here Bertrang describes how the enlargement of individual social networks, the spread of newspapers, the emigration of French-speaking persons as well as the spread of education each contribute to the Frenchification of the Areler Land.

There was no organized opposition against the ongoing frenchification. Heinrich Bischoff, linguistics professor in Lüttich (Liège), was one of the few people who defended the linguistic rights of the entire German population in Belgium; he had formerly been involved in the afore-mentioned *Deutscher Verein*. In 1931 Bischoff founded the *Bund der Deutsch-Belgier*. In a time in which the linguistic rights in Belgium were re-negotiated and the foundations of the linguistic legislation of the 1960s were laid, Bischoff demanded the recognition of all Belgian areas with a German minority as German.[3] In these areas Bischoff, among other things, wanted to (re-)introduce German, which in his opinion should have been recognized as the third national language, as the language of instruction in schools and as the language used in administration. Yet, the demands of the Bund were felt to be so radical that Bischoff experienced strong resistance in the Areler Land. People in the Areler Land would not hear of a reconsideration of the position of German in education, not even when the Belgian minister of education, the Flemish socialist Camille Huysmans, gave a speech in Arel for the benefit of the German language. The fear of facing more anti-German feelings and the knowledge that a considerable part of their fellow citizens was indifferent to the situation prevented the few who would have liked to renegotiate the situation of German in education from taking further actions.

3.3 World War II

The *Deutscher Sprachverein*, founded by the German ethnologue and linguist Matthias Zender in 1941, proved somewhat more successful than the interwar initiatives that were aiming at reviving the interest for the German language (varieties) in the Areler Land. Zender, at that time in the German military, had been asked by his superiors to develop strategies aiming at the promotion and the cultivation of the mother tongue in "des Deutschtums fernstem Westen" ('the most western corner of German civilization'), as it was sometimes referred to. The *Deutscher Sprachverein* (DSV), among other things, organized language courses, founded a *Volksjugend* and a choir, and started spreading the *Areler Volkszeitung* (following the example of the *Arloner Zeitung* in the 19th century). Zender's organization rapidly counted some 1,000 members, many of which belonged to the lower working class. An anonymous military document that was found shortly after the war revealed that the motivations of the members were not purely philological. About 60% of the members had hoped for material advantages, 20% acquired membership out of diplomatic considerations, and 20% were considered to be 'idealists of a special sort'. However, the divergent motivations for membership were not taken into account after the war. Members of the DSV were prosecuted during

---

[3]   Apart from the Areler Land autochthonous German populations lived (and still live) in the areas around Eupen, St. Vith, Malmedy, Montzen (to the south of Eupen) and Bocholz/Bého (to the south of St. Vith). The areas around Arel, Montzen and Bocholz became part of Belgium in 1830 and are – in historical and linguistic literature – often referred to as Old Belgium. The areas around Eupen, St. Vith and Malmedy are referred to as New Belgium. They were added to Belgium after World War I.

the repression. Lists of members' names circulated in the Areler Land, and rumor has it that copies of these lists still exist today and are used to categorize persons as either belonging to the 'good' or to the 'bad' side. In any case, the period following World War II did not prove to be an ideal climate for making yourself known as German. Only few people had the courage to declare themselves as German-speakers. Looking at the results of the 1947-language census (cf. below), it almost seems as if the German language in the Areler Land had been completely wiped out.

To evaluate the results of the 1947-language census, it proves necessary to compare them to the results of previous censuses. For the purpose of this article the results of 1947 will be compared to the results of 1846 and 1930. The results for the census of 1846 are the answers to the question on the habitual language. The results of the censuses of 1930 and 1947 are the answers to the question on the language most frequently used. The results are shown for those villages that give their names to the five greater municipalities in the Areler Land.[4]

	1846		1930		1947	
	G	*F	G	F	G	F
Arel	78.02	16.48	13.45	82.53	0.72	95.07
Attert	99.00	0.99	82.73	14.05	28.28	67.56
Martelingen	96.23	3.76	87.16	10.02	1.56	84.35
Metzig	97.12	2.87	82.22	12.41	8.89	86.30
Ibingen	95.08	4.91	11.75	82.03	0.34	96.02

(G = German, F = French, * including Walloon)

Table 1: Selected results
of the Belgian language census for the district of Arel (from Nelde 1979a)

Table 1 shows that the percentage of German in Arel between 1846 and 1930 had dropped from 78% to 13%. Only 17 years later it had been reduced to 0.72%. Since Frenchification was strongest in Arel, these results could be regarded as more or less reliable at first glance. The same could be argued in the case of Ibingen, an industrialized village that was subject to strong Frenchification, too. Nevertheless, in the light of the observations made by linguists during the first half of the twentieth century, the census results need to be questioned more thoroughly. In his article "Die sterbende Mundart" ('the dying dialect') (1936) Alfred Bertrang points out that, according to his own observations, at least 50% of the population in Arel was able to make perfect

[4] A more extensive list with census results can be found in Nelde (1979a: 70).

use of the local German variety in daily life. Zender came to the same conclusion in 1939. Even if the estimates by both Bertrang and Zender might be somewhat exaggerated, it can be assumed that the census results of 1930 and 1947 in the case of Arel (and Ibingen for that matter) are a little low and, therefore, do not reflect the actual situation at the time. The same goes for the results for Attert, Martelingen, and Metzig, where little progress for French can be noticed when comparing the results of 1846 and 1930. Based on the results of 1947, however, it seems that within a period of 17 years (between 1930 and 1947) German in Martelingen had practically disappeared, whereas the loss of German was considerable in Attert and Metzig. Here too it seems that the results of the 1930 census need to be slightly corrected in favor of German, since the relatively high results for French are likely to be due to the anti-Prussian feelings after World War I, as depicted by Bertrang and Zender. As to the results of 1947, it is clear that the discrepancy between the previous results is so strong that language census results in the Belgian language contact zones need to be interpreted with great caution. Rather than depicting the actual linguistic situation, the statistics need to be interpreted as a declaration of loyalty to the Belgian state by a disrupted population. In the aftermath of World War II people were both afraid and ashamed of identifying themselves as Germans. In this respect, Peter Nelde and Marie-Paule Quix have used the term 'collective neurosis' to label the state the entire Old Belgian population (cf. footnote 3 on the terminology) found itself in after 1945. People did not want to be overtly associated with 'Germanness' anymore. Therefore, they 'interiorized' their Germanness, largely refrained from the public use of the local German varieties and turned to French instead. This was not done because they suddenly wanted to identify themselves as Walloons, but as a means of self-preservation (Quix 1981: 231 and Nelde 1982: 87). This increased turn to French sharply contrasted with the situation that could be observed in the Grand Duchy of Luxembourg. In order to make clear that they did not want to have anything to do with Germany and the German language, the Luxembourgers vehemently started stressing the distinctiveness of their local Moselle-Franconian German varieties (commonly designated as Luxembourgish) from standard German. Luxembourgish gradually became a symbol of national identity, and continuous *Ausbau*-processes would eventually lead to the *Loi sur le régime des langues* of 1984, which gave Luxembourgisch the status of a national language in the Grand Duchy (cf. Kloss 1986, Coulmas 1996, Fröhlich 1996, Newton 1996, Fröhlich/Hoffmann 1997).

4. Post-war efforts on language maintenance
in the Areler Land

Even before and during World War II a strong emancipation of Luxembourgish could be witnessed in the Grand-Duchy, though it took until the second half of the 1950s before people started to overtly promote their local linguistic varieties in the Areler Land again. The following sections describe the efforts of organizations that defended the cause of the local German varieties after World War II. Special attention will be paid to the linguistic classification of the local German varieties by language activists.

4.1 Back to the roots with P.A.F.

In 1955 Julien Bestgen and some of his fellow students founded a cultural organization named P.A.F. The original meaning 'Parti Arlonais Folklorique' was quickly changed to 'Pour Arlon et son Folklore', since 'parti arlonais' had evoked pan-German associations in some circles in the Areler Land. The renaming of P.A.F. thus makes clear that the organizations wanted to serve "la cause du pays d'Arlon et de son parler" ('the case of the Areler Land and its language') in harmony with the francophone fellow citizens. The rather folkloristic activities of P.A.F were organized for a broad audience and involved cabaret nights, suppers, and lectures by meritorious inhabitants of the Areler Land. All of this, as Julien Bestgen (1979: 114) reports in retrospect, took place "à une époque où les notions de retour aux sources, de droit de minorités, de mode rétro, de littérature provinciale, de sous-régions n'était pas encore les tartes à la crème d'aujourd'hui" ('at a time when concepts such as back to the roots, language minority rights, retro mode, provincial literature and devolution weren't as common as they are now').

Although P.A.F. already ceased to exist in the 1960s and had, similar to all the political forces in the Areler Land, refrained from partaking in the debates on the linguistic legislation and the question of language facilities for minorities[5] in Flanders and Wallonia, it had managed to re-awaken the interest in the local German varieties and had furthermore made clear that these

---

[5] The outcome of the Belgian linguistic legislation for the German areas in Belgium was as follows: The areas around Eupen and St. Vith were considered to be the officially German-speaking part of Belgium (but with the obligation to grant so-called 'linguistic facilities' to the French people residing on the territory). All the other areas were considered to be officially French-speaking. Yet, German-speaking persons can appeal to 'linguistic facilities' in the area around Malmedy and in some parts of the area around Montzen. In the area surrounding Malmedy the facilities are used, in the area around Montzen they were never put into effect.

varieties had not reached the stage of language death. In fact, in his early sociolinguistic study *Zweisprachige Nachbarn* (1968) the Belgian linguist Albert Verdoodt estimated the total number of people able to speak the local German varieties in the Areler Land at 50–80% of the population. This means that roughly 22,000–36,000 persons were able to make use of German varieties, which is clearly more than the 7,000 German-speaking persons that lived in the entire Province of Luxembourg, according to the language census of 1947. With more refined methods Peter Nelde would later estimate the number of people using the local German varieties in the Areler Land of the mid-1970s at approximately 66% of the population, which amounts to a number of approx. 30,000 persons. Language domains, which were positively contributing to the maintenance of the local German varieties were the family, the local inns, and the workfloor.

Apart from the scientific interest evoked by Verdoodt and Nelde's *Research Center on Multilingualism*, popular and the political interest for the native linguistic varieties used in the Areler Land also grew in the 1970s. The Provincial Council of the province of Luxembourg even made an appeal to the Cultural Council of the French Community[6] concerning the maintenance of the local German varieties (called 'Luxembourgish dialect' in the document of the Provincial Council) and the consideration of Germanic languages in education "et particulièrement de l'allemand à partir du dialecte luxembourgeois" ('and particularly of German starting from the Luxembourgish dialect'). Although this appeal was never acted upon, it is a clear product of a *Zeitgeist* that was characterized by an ethnic revival (cf. Héraud 1987). Precisely this accentuation of the importance of local elements during the ethnic revival proved to be a welcome gift for those who wanted to skirt the genetic link between the autochthonous linguistic varieties of the Areler Land and the German language.

In the past, associations striving for the cause of the autochthonous linguistic varieties in the Areler Land had generally subsumed these varieties under the roof of 'German'. This had been the case for the *Deutscher Verein zur Hebung und Pflege der Muttersprache*, for the *Bund der Deutsch-Belgier* and certainly for the *Deutscher Sprachverein*. The common use of *Areler Däitsch* and *Plattdeutsch* next to *patois luxembourgeois* to designate the autochthonous linguistic varieties shows that the population of the Areler Land was aware of the genetic affinity between their local varieties and German. The atrocities of the Great War, however, initiated a tendency among the Areler population to avoid stressing this affinity. Towards the first part of the

---

[6]   This was the predecessor of the current government of the Communauté française Wallonie-Bruxelles (cf. www.cfwb.be for details).

20th century large parts of the autochthonous population of the Areler Land
started to accentuate the differences between standard German (*Hochdeutsch*)
and their local varieties, among other things by resorting to *patois
luxembourgeois* rather than *Areler Däitsch* or *Plattdeutsch* to designate their
varieties. Still, it was mainly their loyalty towards the – in their perception
mainly francophone – Belgian state that prevented them from exploiting those
perceived differences between local varieties and standard German in a
process of identity formation very much like their neighbors in the Grand
Duchy had managed to do. It took until the late 1950s and the foundation of
P.A.F. until timid attempts to do so could be observed.

Reading interviews with and articles by the P.A.F.'s founder, Julien
Bestgen, it becomes clear that, in line with the 'back to the roots' philosophy
and the folkloristic leanings of the organization, P.A.F. tended to refer to the
local German varieties in the Areler Land as *Arloner Dialekt*, *parler arlonais*,
or *le dialecte arlonais* (cf. *Contrepoint* 1977). Following this point of view,
Bestgen (1978: 71) explains how the Arel dialect is a Germanic one. But he
also adds that its distance to the German language is undeniable and much
bigger than many of the inhabitants of the Areler Land would realize. Simply
labelling these local varieties as German would therefore be somewhat
inappropriate. Throughout the 1970s it was quite common for language
activists in the Areler Land to start promoting the local linguistic varieties this
way, putting the stress on the local character of the linguistic varieties. But, at
the same time, they were sharply watching the changing status of the mutually
intelligible varieties at the other side of the border.

4.2 Looking across the border with *Arelerland a Sprooch*

The official recognition of Luxembourgish as the national language of the
Grand Duchy of Luxembourg in 1984 was a gift from God for the organization
Arelerland a Sprooch (ALAS). Founded in 1976 in the high days of the ethnic
revival, this organization had long sought for an appropriate way to free the
local Moselle-Franconian varieties (commonly referred to in French as
'luxembourgeois') of the German roof. At first they tended to stress the
'localness' of Luxembourgish, thereby following the example of P.A.F. But
the status-upgrade of Luxembourgish in the Grand Duchy urged Gaston
Matthey, the late president of *Arelerland a Sprooch*, to claim in a Flemish
paper that Luxembourgish is neither German ("Luxemburgs is helemaal geen
Duits", *Belang van Limburg*, 02.08.1988) nor simply a variety of German but a
language in its own right. Time was ripe for ALAS to start promoting
Luxembourgish as the autochthonous (regional) language of the Areler Land
by staging cultural events, initiating the publication of a magazine *Geschwënn*

(published every three months), the publication of a popular *Vollekskalenner*, the organization of church celebrations, and the organization of Luxembourgish classes.

Initially the actions of ALAS evoked the interest of a broad audience. It seemed as if the organization was succeeding in helping to reverse language shift by raising the interest of the population of the Areler Land in their linguistic varieties. At the beginning of the 1990s, however, the board of ALAS had to conclude that the intergenerational continuity of Luxembourgish in the Areler Land had considerably decreased since the 1970s and was, according to the president's catastrophic prediction at that time, facing rock bottom (cf. Triffaux 2002: 99). A lack of cooperation on the part of official bodies (e.g. communal councils and cultural centers) as to the promotion of Luxembourgish on the one hand, and the apparent indifference of the largest part of the population on the other, were seen as the major causes for this decrease. ALAS had to make the observation that people were obviously highly interested in the economic value of Luxembourgish (the numerous Luxembourgish courses organized by ALAS and several language schools attracted people in the pursuit of a well-paid job in the Grand-Duchy) but much less concerned about the value of Luxembourgish as a part of the save-worthy cultural heritage of the Areler Land.

When, towards the end of the 1980s, the vigor of the ethnic revival had diminished all over Europe and much of the organizations and movements striving for the linguistic rights of language minorities were most often wrongfully accused of having right-wing sympathies, this affected ALAS too. It is the merit of ALAS that, despite an often negative press and a lack of interest on the part of the Areler population, they did not give up the struggle for autochthonous linguistic varieties. Next to maintaining the original activities outlined above, at the beginning of the 1990s ALAS increasingly put efforts in language political activities aimed at raising the legal status of Luxembourgish in the Areler Land. When the French Community of Belgium adopted a "Décret relatif aux langues régionales endogènes de la Communauté française" in 1990, Luxembourgish was, due to lobbying on the side of ALAS, one of the regional languages towards which – according to art. 2 the French Community – has "le devoir de les préserver, d'en favoriser l'étude scientifique et l'usage, soit comme outil de communication, soit comme moyen d'expression"[7] ('the obligation to preserve them, to encourage scientific research and to encourage its usage either as a means of

---

[7]   Somewhat strange in this respect is that the autochthonous linguistic varieties used in Bocholz/Bého are mutually intelligible with the ones used in the Areler Land. Contrary to the varieties in the Areler Land they are, however, labeled German.

communication or to express oneself'). And the recognition of Luxembourgish as an autochthonous regional language on the level of the French Community automatically entails its recognition as a regional language in the context of the *European Charter for Regional or Minority Languages* (1992), which aims at protecting regional or minority language communities. The problem today is that Belgium has not yet signed the Charter due to quarrels over the linguistic situation in the Brussels conurbation. Concrete measures in this respect thus remain to be taken. The same is true with respect to the above-mentioned decree of the French Community, which seems to be a mere 'paper tiger'. The hopes of ALAS that the Luxembourgish community of the Areler Land be recognized as a national minority within the *Framework Convention of the Protection of National Minorities* (1995), and that this recognition be used to extort protective measures for Luxembourgish from the Belgian government have, thus far, been in vain. The Belgian state has already signed the framework but has put its ratification on hold until a proper definition of the minority concept is reached, in line with the current linguistic situation in Belgium and, accordingly, with the typical Belgian linguistic consensus strategies. Consequently, the chances that Luxembourgish on a federal Belgian level will be recognized as an autochthonous language are rather small. Former deputy prime-minister Vande Lanotte, e.g., has openly questioned the linguistic emancipation in the Areler Land as articulated by ALAS in wondering how the public would react if people in West-Flanders suddenly started to strive for a status upgrading of their dialect (*l'Avenir du Luxembourg*, 22.03.02).

Now that we have cited the viewpoints of ALAS concerning the status of Luxembourgish in Belgium, it seems legitimate to discuss the altered appraisal of the local autochthonous linguistic varieties in the Areler Land by ALAS and the recognition of Luxembourgish as a regional autochthonous language, on the level of the French Community in Belgium from a contact linguistic point of view.

4.3 Some comments on the status of Luxembourgish in the Areler Land

In the preceding paragraphs we have described how, after a period in which the local character of the autochthonous linguistic varieties was stressed, ALAS has started to promote Luxembourgish (the preferred umbrella term for the autochthonous linguistic varieties) as a (regional) language in the Belgian context and has rejected its classification as a variety (let alone a 'dialect') of German. ALAS legitimizes this point of view by pointing out that Luxembourgish has been recognized as a "langue régionale endogène" in a decree by the French Community (1990) and above all by referring to the

Grand Duchy, where the mutually intelligible linguistic varieties acquired the status of a national language in 1984. In their handbook *Die Volksgruppen in Europa* (2000) Christoph Pan and Beate Sibylle Pfeil use the latter argument in their appraisal of Luxembourgish in the Belgian context[8]. The question is, however, whether a reference to the situation in the Grand Duchy and the recognition in a decree that shows no practical effects suffice to grant Luxembourgish the status of an autochthonous language in a Belgian context from a contact linguistic point of view. For a detailed discussion of this problem, it will be useful to look at the following opinion of the late Heinz Kloss on the classification of a 'form of language' (*Sprachform*) as a dialect or a language as a starting point:

> Eine Sprachform, die die Linguisten eindeutig als Dialekt auffassen, wird nicht dadurch zur Sprache, daß ihre Sprecher stattdessen der Meinung sind, es handele sich um eine Sprache, sondern erst (und bloß dadurch), daß sie daraus tätig die praktische Folgerung ziehen, aus ihrem Dialekt eine Ausbausprache zu machen, sei es mit oder ohne vorherige Einschaltung der Zwischenstufe des 'Ausbaudialektes'. (Kloss 1978: 27)

> ('A form of language that linguists unequivocally assess to be a dialect does not become a language simply because its speakers believe that is a language. It only then becomes a language when its speakers draw the practical conclusion to actively turn their dialect into an *Ausbau*-language, with or without first aiming towards an '*Ausbau*-dialect' as an intermediate.')

Linguists today more or less agree that Luxembourgish in the Grand Duchy is a typical example of an *Ausbau*-language. Over the years the Luxembourgish population has succeeded in elaborating both the functional range and the legal status of those linguistic varieties that are strongly related to German genetically. Notwithstanding certain problems related to the standardization of Luxembourgish, the oral use of it covers all domains of daily life and has given Luxembourgish a clear-cut position next to French and German within the Grand Duchy. Either of the former languages are simply indispensable for the good functioning of the Luxemburgish state. Apart from the fact that the legal status of Luxembourgish in federal Belgium does not match up to that in the Grand Duchy (in Belgium Luxembourgish is not recognized as a national language), it is primarily the difference in its functional range that poses difficulties in considering Luxembourgish to be an *Ausbau*-language on the Belgian side of the border. Subsequent contact linguistic surveys (Nelde 1979, Hermans 1989, Darquennes 2005) have shown that Luxembourgish plays no

---

[8]   Pan and Pfeil (2000: 45) do, however, keep the possibility open of subsuming Luxembourgish in Belgium under the roof of German.

significant role on a societal level in the Areler Land and has been pushed back
to an often limited use in the private sphere and in the work domain (especially
for those who work in the Grand Duchy). ALAS may thus well have
succeeded in having Luxembourgish recognized as a (regional) language on a
legal level, but this did not coincide with the elaboration on a societal level,
where Luxembourgish – at least from a contact linguistic point of view – still
is to be considered as a set of German[9] varieties rather than an *Ausbau*-
language. This, however, does not prevent Luxembourgish (in the form of the
Grand Duchy's *koiné*) from simultaneously acquiring the status of a *foreign*
language within the Areler Land. And rumor has it that knowledge of
Luxembourgish is the key to find a well-paid job in the Grand-Duchy.
Especially speakers who are in their twenties and thirties and on the pursuit of
a job enroll for the numerous Luxembourgish language courses offered in the
Areler region. Their participation in Luxembourgish courses does not,
however, tempt them to start using Luxembourgish in daily life in the Areler
Land, even if they have ancestors who master the local linguistic varieties very
well. Needless to say that this particular linguistic behavior might very well
strengthen the role of Luxembourgish as a foreign language in the Areler Land.
But it simultaneously threatens the survival of the autochthonous linguistic
varieties and prevents these varieties from developing into an (*Ausbau-*)
language.

What has to be done in order to revitalize the use of Luxembourgish on a
local level or try and elaborate Luxembourgish in such a way that linguistic
reality matches its legal status of a (regional) language is hard to say. The
development of a total package of tailor-made and attuned cognitive, social
and affective measures similar to Wales and Catalonia might prove to be the
best possible option. For an area in which a voluntary organization with scarce
financial means is the major actor striving for the revitalization of
Luxembourgish, this might be aimed a bit too high. The initiation of
spontaneous grassroots activities and a pragmatic search for possibilities to
promote Luxembourgish on various levels should, however, be feasible. In this
respect Jörg Horn (2004: 83), a political scientist, has aired the opinion that it
would be wise to rethink the current language political strategies and to
possibly sacrifice the 'Luxembourgish path' in exchange for a 'German path'.
What this means is that stressing the affinities rather than the differences
between Luxembourgish and German (after all one of the three languages
featuring in Belgium's linguistic legislation) could lead to a better chance of
establishing certain linguistic rights in the Areler Land. The following

---

[9]   Cf. Beckers and Cajot (1979: 187–210) for an innerlinguistic description of the Moselle-
Franconian varieties in the Areler Land.

example, however, illustrated that hoping for the better might very well be in vain.

With the decree of 1998 the French Community made it possible to organize immersion education at the level of kindergarten and primary school either in Dutch, English or German. Yet, instead of using the opportunity to obtain a place for Luxembourgish in education by stressing its close affinity to German – something that would have been feasible within the range of the existing legislation – ALAS continued to stress the individual character of Luxembourgish and showed little sympathy for the introduction of German immersion education (in a local primary school in Attert, for example).[10] It looks as if ALAS is determined to go its own linguistic way. Emotional factors related to the Areler Land's history and an apparent urge to flirt with the neighboring Grand Duchy, with which the Areler Land was united 175 years ago, seem to prevent the association from considering more pragmatic 'German' alternatives. Whether this will be the best way to preserve the linguistic inheritance is far from certain.

5. Outlook

Language activists in the Areler Land (and in other language minority settings as well) have the tendency to approach linguistic reality according to their own criteria. In their efforts for more linguistic autonomy many language minorities (e.g. the Silesians in Poland, the Ulster Scots, the Latgalians in Latvia, the Limburgers in the Netherlands, etc.) construct their linguistic identity in such a way that ideological and/or sociological criteria come to overrule linguistic criteria. Therefore, there is a strong need for (contact) linguists to compensate for the sometimes 'libertine' way in which certain language activists classify linguistic varieties (cf. Kronsteiner 2000 and Goebl 2002). Needless to say that an accurate study of the linguistic history of language minorities, from below as well as from above, can help to clear linguistic mist.

---

[10] No direct reference to Luxembourgish was made when German immersion was introduced, since this is forbidden by the legislator.

References

Bertrang, Alfred. 1921. *Grammatik der Areler Mundart.* Bruxelles: Hayez.

Bertrang, Alfred. 1936. Die sterbende Mundart. *Vierteljahresblätter für luxemburgische Sprachwissenschaft* 7: 135–152.

Beckers, Hartmut and José Cajot. 1979. Zur Diatopie der deutschen Dialekte in Belgien. In Peter H. Nelde (ed.), *Deutsch als Muttersprache in Belgien.* Steiner, Wiesbaden, 151–218.

Bestgen, Julien. 1978. About a Germanic Dialect in Southern Belgium. *International Journal of the Sociology of Language* 15: 71–76.

Bestgen, Julien. 1979. Dialecte et langues au Pays d'Arlon. In Fernand Hoffmann (ed.), *Dialektologie heute.* Luxembourg: Institut Grand-Ducal, 107–118.

Bischoff, Heinrich. 1931. *Die deutsche Sprache in Belgien: ihre Geschichte und ihre Rechte.* Eupen: Esch.

Contrepoint. Bulletin d'information de la maison de la culture du sudluxembourg. Mais-Juin 1977.

Coulmas, Florian. 1996. *Gewählte Worte. Über Sprache als Wille und Bekenntnis.* Frankfurt and New York: Campus.

Darquennes, Jeroen. 2005. *Sprachrevitalisierung aus kontaktlinguistischer Sicht. Theorie und Praxis am Beispiel Altbelgien-Süd.* St. Augustin: Asgard.

Fröhlich, Harald. 1996. Luxemburg. In Robert Hinderling and Ludwig M. Eichinger (eds.), *Handbuch der mitteleuropäischen Sprachminderheiten.* Tübingen: Narr, 459–478.

Fröhlich, Harald and Fernand Hoffmann. 1997. Luxemburg. In Hans Goebl et al. (eds.), *Kontaktlinguistik.* Berlin and New York: de Gruyter, 1158–1172.

Goebl, Hans. 2002. Sprachpolitik: auch für und mit Geister- bzw. Traumsprachen. In Peter H. Nelde (ed.), *Sprachpolitik und kleine Sprachen.* Tübingen: Niemeyer, 49–63.

Héraud, Guy. 1987. Renaissances éthniques. In Ulrich Ammon, Klaus J. Mattheier and Peter H. Nelde (eds.), *Brennpunkte der Soziolinguistik.* Tübingen: Niemeyer, 30–45.

Hermans, Stefaan. 1989. *Sprachwechsel im Areler Land. Eine soziolinguistische Untersuchung.* Unpublished thesis. University of Antwerpen.

Kern, Rudolf. 1999. *Beiträge zur Stellung der deutschen Sprache in Belgien.* Bruxelles: Nauwelaerts.

Kloss, Heinz. 1986. Der Stand der in Luxemburg gesprochenen Sprachen beim Jahresende 1984. *Germanistische Mitteilungen* 24: 83–94.

Kloss, Heinz. 1978. *Die Entwicklung neuer germanischer Kultursprachen seit 1800.* Düsseldorf: Schwann.

Kronsteiner, Otto. 2000. Sind Burgenländischkroatisch, Kaschubisch, Sorbisch und Rusinisch eigene Sprachen? In Baldur Panzer (ed.), *Die sprachliche Situation in der Slavia zehn Jahre nach der Wende.* Frankfurt/Main: Lang, 305–311.

Lejeune, Carlo. 2003. 'Des Deutschtums fernster Westen'. Eupen-Malmedy, die deutschen Dialekt redenden Gemeinden um Arlon und Montzen und die 'Westforschung'. In Burkhard Dietz, Helmut Gabel and Ulrich Tiedau (eds.), *Griff nach dem Westen. Die 'Westforschung' der völkisch-nationalen Wissenschaften zum nordwesteuropäischen Raum (1919–1960). Teil I.* Münster and New York: Waxmann, 493–538

Nelde, Peter Hans. 1979a. *Volkssprache und Kultursprache. Die gegenwärtige Lage des sprachlichen Übergangsgebietes im deutsch-belgisch-luxemburgischen Grenzraum.* Wiesbaden: Steiner.

Nelde, Peter Hans (ed.) 1979b. *Deutsch als Muttersprache in Belgien.* Wiesbaden: Steiner.

Nelde, Peter Hans. 1982. Sprachökologische Überlegungen am Beispiel Altbelgiens. *Germanistische Mitteilungen* 15: 81–92.

Newton, Gerald (ed.). 1996. *Luxembourg and Lëtzebuergesch. Language and Communication at the Crossroads of Europe.* Oxford: Clarendon.

Quix, Marie-Paule. 1981. Altbelgien-Nord. In Per Sture Ureland (ed.), *Kulturelle und sprachliche Minderheiten in Europa.* Tübingen: Niemeyer, 225–235.

Pabst, Klaus. 1979. Politische Geschichte des deutschen Sprachgebiets in Ostbelgien bis 1944. In Peter H. Nelde (ed.), *Deutsch als Muttersprache in Belgien.* Wiesbaden: Steiner, 9–38.

Pan, Christoph and Beate Sibylle Pfeil. 2000. *Die Volksgruppen in Europa. Ein Handbuch.* Wien: Braumüller.

Triffaux, Jean-Marie. 2002. *Combats pour la langue dans le pays d'Arlon. Une minorité oubliée?* Arlon: Editions 'La Vie Arlonaise'.

Verdoodt, Albert. 1968. *Zweisprachige Nachbarn: Die deutschen Hochsprach- und Mundartgruppen in Ost-Belgien, dem Elsass, Ost-Lothringen und Luxemburg.* Wien and Stuttgart: Braumüller.

Verdoodt, Albert (ed.). 1978. *Belgium (International Journal of the Sociology of Language 15).* The Hague: Mouton.

Zender, Matthias. 1939. Die deutsche Sprache in der Gegend von Arel. In *Deutsches Archiv für Landes- und Volksforschung,* vol. 3, 1–40.

Zender, Matthias. 1942. *Der Sprachenkampf im volksdeutschen Gebiet um Arel.* Bonn: Scheur.

KRISTINE HORNER (LEEDS)

Language and Luxembourgish national identity: ideologies of hybridity and purity in the past and present

1. Introduction: language history from the center or from the periphery?

Approaching language history 'from below' is a timely endeavor in light of recent challenges to authoritative voices in the narration of historical events. Although critical approaches to historiography are perhaps most widely associated with the work of Hayden White (1981), similar questions have been raised in relation to language history (see Crowley 1996 and Milroy 2002). In spite of the fact that named languages exist in the form of numerous linguistic varieties, the lion's share of historical linguistic work – especially in relation to the modern period – has focused on telling the stories of standard varieties rather than grappling with much of the complexity surrounding actual language use.[1] It may be argued that this emphasis reifies the folk view that the differentiated status of standard and non-standard varieties is based on purely *internal linguistic criteria*. This state of affairs is further perpetuated by the fact that the former are usually equated with named state languages and associated with the quest for nation-state congruence, whereas the latter tend to be classified at best as dialects and at worst as deviations or corruptions due to their perceived incompatibility with the ideal of the homogeneous nation-state (cf. Lippi-Green 1997).[2] Irvine and Gal (2000: 35) remind us that the demarcation and naming of languages is bound up with greater socio-political processes:

---

[1] For a discussion of this issue in relation to the history of 'English', see Trudgill and Watts (2002). Research in dialectology – a field particularly well cultivated in *Germanistik* – has dealt with the description of non-standard varieties, although much of this work does not challenge the hierarchical relationship between standard and non-standard varieties.

[2] The folk linguistics paradigm developed by Niedzielski and Preston (2000) provides a valuable framework for understanding how laypeople participate in the process of evaluating language varieties.

A language is simply a dialect that has an army and a navy – so goes a well-known saying in linguistics. Although only semiserious, this dictum recognizes an important truth: The significance of linguistic differentiation is embedded in the politics of a region and its observers. Just as having an army presupposes some outside force, some real or putative opposition to be faced, so does identifying a language presuppose a boundary or opposition to other languages with which it contrasts in some larger sociolinguistic field.

In order to explore the ways in which linguistic boundaries are drawn, particularly within a given dialect continuum, it is useful to view language history from interdisciplinary perspectives. As the naming and legitimation of languages is linked to the drawing of national boundaries and related nationalist ideologies propagated by state apparatuses, language histories tend to be closely intertwined with national histories (cf. Blommaert 1999, Crowley 1996). Nationalist ideologies and language ideologies reinforce one another, as the legitimate national and/or official languages of the state are those that are named, written, and (usually) the continuous 'product' of standardization processes. It must be stressed that there exist various layers to linguistic Othering on the statewide level, including that of speakers of varieties that are markedly different from the so-called standard variety as well as speakers of minority languages. Furthermore, access to elite bilingualism often constitutes a gate-keeping mechanism. As Grillo (1980) observes, the center-periphery matrix is always multidimensional, and therefore, there is never a clear-cut center-periphery distinction that researchers can simply assume. Thus, states do not coincide with linguistically homogeneous units, in spite of the fact that they are often depicted as such.

   Given the direction of my discussion so far, it will be evident that I value certain questions that have been brought forward by postmodernist and poststructuralist theorists. For example, social constructivist approaches to the processes of group identification and social categorization – especially those emphasizing the centrality of discourse – have led to productive scholarship on the relationship between language and national identity as well as the circulation of nationalist ideologies. At the same time, valid points of critique have been raised in relation to constructivist approaches that overstate the malleability of identity and overlook the persistence of ethnicity (see Grillo 1998, Jenkins 1997, and May 2001). Commentators highlighting the continued salience of ethnicity rightfully point out that the modernist project of nation-state congruence has not yet been abandoned in spite of widespread challenges to it. Morley (1996: 327–331) suggests that postmodernist theory has fallen short of recognizing that modernity has affected people in the 'West', i.e. in Europe and the United States, differently than in other parts of the world. In this light, it is not only the presupposed linear flow of time from the modern to the postmodern era that is to be approached critically, but also the homogenization of the processes of modernity and postmodernity on a global scale. I would like to elaborate on this line of thought by arguing that the emphasis on *present-day challenges* to national identity, the nation-state, and nationalist ideologies depends very much on point of view, even when discussing cases in the European context.

An analysis of debates about Luxembourgish national identity provides fertile ground for critically exploring this strand of postmodernist thought, i.e. that national identities, nation-state congruence, and the circulation of related nationalist ideologies were once secure in the past but are being challenged at this particular point in time. More specifically, I would like to focus on two time periods that have been flagged as significant moments of fluctuation and turbulence both in Europe as a whole and Luxembourg in particular: the turn of the twentieth century and the turn of the century in which we find ourselves today (cf. Grillo 1998). Jenkins (1997: 38) argues against certain dimensions of postmodernist theory, suggesting that the myriad changes taking place now – in the period of late or high modernity – are quantitatively rather than qualitatively different from those in the past, in the heyday of modernity. In all fairness, however, it must be stressed that theorists of various persuasions assert that national identity, just as is the case with any form of identity, seems to be most salient in times of uncertainty and major change.

Language constitutes a key symbol of Luxembourgish national identity and is central to the circulation of related nationalist ideologies, which is not surprising, given the fact that similar observations have been made in relation to other European states (cf. Crowley 1996, Blommaert and Verschueren 1998). However, questions regarding legitimate language are somewhat problematic within Luxembourg and perhaps even more so when viewed from beyond state borders. Which named language is to fulfill this role and serve as a marker of identity and/or as a distinctive feature of national group membership? Through the lens of *Germanistik*, Luxembourgish language varieties are often homogenized and categorized as 'a dialect of German', due in part to their proximity to the Germanic language varieties spoken in the bordering areas of Germany and, to a lesser extent, Belgium and France. I would argue that this categorization hinges greatly on the fact that the Germanic language varieties spoken in Luxembourg are not propagated by state apparatuses in the same way that written varieties of German and French are, perhaps most notably within the framework of the educational system.[3] On the other hand, the statewide, institutionalized use of written German and French is often portrayed as something unique, both by scholars situated in states with monolingual language policies and by intellectuals in Luxembourg seeking to draw an 'acceptable' linguistic boundary between Luxembourg and neighboring states. In this sense, there exist two parallel forms of linguistic identification, emphasizing Luxembourgish and/or the paradigm of trilingualism. Although these strategies need not conflict with one another, putting the weight too heavily on one side of this continuum or the other sometimes creates divisions within Luxembourg. The origins of these forms of linguistic identification can be found in late nineteenth and early twentieth century texts (cf. Spizzo 1995), and similar patterns continue to surface in present-day discourses (cf. Horner 2004).

2. Language and the genesis of Luxembourgish national identity

The turn of the twentieth century was a time of continuity and change in Luxembourg. Following the disintegration of the German Confederation (*Bund*), Luxembourg was declared a neutral state in 1867. At that time the Prussian garrison that had been installed in 1815 was withdrawn and the fortress walls around Luxembourg city were gradually dismantled.[4] However, Luxembourg remained a member of the German Customs Union (*Zollverein*) until the close of World War I and thus maintained close economic ties with the German state until that time. In spite of political autonomy and internationally recognized neutrality, the Luxembourgish economy was dependent on foreign capital as well as labor from abroad. The processes of industrialization were in full swing particularly in the southern part of the country and immigration increased steadily. Another key event of this period was the introduction of obligatory (primary) schooling in 1881, which led to a gradual increase in the overall literacy rate. As is still the case today, literacy

---

[3]   In other words, Luxembourgish is not standardized if we take a sightly revised interpretation of Haugen's (1966) four phase process as the reference point; namely selection, codification, elaboration, and acceptance. Gilles and Moulin (2003: 321) rightfully underline the fact that elaboration and acceptance are not fully underway. At the same time, it must be stressed that debates are taking place as to what should be done with Luxembourgish (see Horner 2005). In relation to this point, Deumert and Vandenbussche (2003) provide an insightful discussion of the pros and cons of Haugen's model.

[4]   Luxembourg was elevated to the status of a Grand Duchy in 1815 but it was not until 1839 – in the aftermath of the Belgian revolution – that Luxembourg became a truly independent state and an autonomous government was installed shortly thereafter.

was taught via standard German, with standard French being added to the curriculum in full by the third year of primary school.[5]

It was also during the early twentieth century that the three major present-day political parties were established, i.e. the Socialists (the current *Lëtzebuerger Sozialistesch Aarbechter Partei*), the Liberal League (today's *Demokratesch Partei*), and the Party of the Right (now the *Chrëschtlesch Sozial Volkspartei*). It was members of the Party of the Right – founded by the so-called Clericalists – that successfully managed to position themselves as representative of the majority of the Luxembourgish people and therewith harness the flow of power on the national level upon the introduction of universal suffrage in 1919. Spizzo (1995) argues that this process was facilitated by their capitalization on key cultural symbols, in particular that of the monarchy, which served as one of the primary means of justifying Luxembourg's independence. He considers the early twentieth century as the 'genesis' of Luxembourgish national identity because:

> les institutions de l'Etat moderne luxembourgeois (et sa structure politique) commencèrent à assumer des contours beaucoup plus précis, un Etat moderne qui en peu de temps allait créer le cadre politique nécessaire à l'apparition du "nationalisme" catholique. (Spizzo 1995: 248)

> 'the institutions of the modern Luxembourgish state (and its political structure) began to assume a much more precise shape, a modern state which in a short period of time began to create the political framework necessary for the appearance of Catholic "nationalism".'[6]

Drawing on the work of Anderson ([1983] 1991), Spizzo (1995: 58f.) discusses the oscillation between the opening and closure of the nation, or the outward and inward directions involved in the construction of Luxembourgish national identity. I would like to build on Spizzo's work by exploring how discourses about language map out onto this movement between the opening and the closure of the nation.[7] Spizzo (1995) underlines the importance of the writings of Nicolas Ries as well as the publications of the *Letzeburger National-Unio'n* in relation to this process. Maintaining that Luxembourgish is a language in its own right, authors of these publications played a key role in establishing the trilingual paradigm that continues to be associated with

---

[5] For further details regarding Luxembourgish history during this period, see Calmes and Bossaert (1996), Spizzo (1995), and Trausch (2002).

[6] All translations are my own, K. H. I am grateful to Jean Jacques Weber for helping me sort out difficulties concerning the French language texts.

[7] For a discussion of similar patterns of linguistic identification in Hungary, see Gal (1991, 2001).

Luxembourgish national identity today, although it will be illustrated that the writings of Nicolas Ries and those of the *Letzeburger National-Unio'n* differ from one another significantly in a number of respects.

Nicolas Ries, a high school (*lycée*) teacher and founder of the journal *Les cahiers luxembourgeois* (cf. Wilhelm 1993),[8] published an influential book in 1911 entitled *Essai d'une psychologie du peuple luxembourgeois*. According to Spizzo (1995: 284f.), Ries' use of the term *Mitteleuropäer* 'middle Europeans', as illustrated in Text 1a, serves as basis of an 'outward' looking manifestation of nationalism. This discursive strategy may be read as an attempt to construct a framework for a nationalist ideology that overtly differs from 'inward' expressions of nationalism rooted in romanticism:

(1a) Nos souvenirs nationaux sont si peu abondants, nos connaissances des autres peuples et des langues étrangères tellement étendues, notre cosmopolitisme tellement général, nos besoins d'un idéal supérieur tellement contrôlés, enfin, l'exaltation du sentiment national si peu cultivée par nos établissements d'enseignement, qu'on ne saurait vraiment parler de patriotisme chez nous au même titre que chez nos voisins. Il s'ensuit que *nous sommes de bons "Mitteleuropäer"*, au sens de Nietzsche, chez lesquels les sentiments internationaux et humanitaires dominent. (Ries [1911] 1920: 267, my emphasis)

'Our national memories are so scarce, our knowledge of other peoples and foreign languages is so extended, our cosmopolitism is so general, our needs of a superior ideal are so controlled, and finally, the exaltation of the national sentiment is so little cultivated by our educational establishments that in our case one cannot really speak of patriotism in the same way as one does of our neighbors. And it follows that *we are good "middle Europeans"* in the Nietzschean sense, in whom international and humanitarian sentiments dominate.'

Building on Batty Weber's (1909) use of the term *Mischkultur*, Ries narrates a hybrid version of Luxembourgish national identity; however, this is a one plus one schema based on the presupposition that there exist clearly defined French and German national characteristics. In this excerpt Ries highlights the role of Luxembourgers as mediators or forming a 'bridge' between civilizations:

(1b) En tout cas, nos voisins allemands et français, sans s'en douter d'ailleurs, ne font que confirmer cette espèce de particularisme (*Mischkultur!*), sanctionné par l'histoire et la politique, en nous reconnaissant, les uns, des qualités purement françaises, les autres des qualités allemandes distinctives … Nous ne formons pas seulement *un pont entre l'esprit allemand et l'esprit français*, mais une synthèse vivante de deux civilisations, et, en apprenant les deux langues, nous acquérons la possibilité de jouir des bienfaits des deux cultures. (Ries [1911] 1920: 124–125, my emphasis).

---

[8] The first edition of the journal was printed in 1923, and it continues to be circulated under the present-day title of *Nos cahiers: lëtzebuerger zäitschrëft fir kultur*.

'In any case, our German and French neighbors, without being aware of it by the way, cannot but confirm this species of particularism (*mixed [hybrid] culture!*), sanctioned by history and politics, by recognizing in us either purely French qualities or distinctive German qualities ... Not only do we form *a bridge between the German spirit and the French spirit*, but a living synthesis of two civilizations and, by acquiring the two languages, we obtain the possibility of enjoying the benefits of the two cultures.'

In this manner, Luxembourgers are portrayed as embodying the best of both worlds. As regards language use and linguistic repertoires, Ries places a strong emphasis on the acquisition of German and French, although he also makes the argument that Luxembourgish should be considered a 'genuine language'. In this manner, he sketches the basis for the trilingual paradigm that continues to be associated with Luxembourg to this day:

(1c) Ici en effet, les langues allemande et française sont superposées et emmêlées depuis des siècles, et la connaissance en a toujours été une nécessité nationale. Aussi, de tous temps les Luxembourgeois quelque peu instruits et tous ceux qui de par leur fonctions sont forcés de se servir indistinctement et alternativement de l'allemand et du français, ont-ils tenu à honneur non seulement de comprendre, mais encore de parler et d'écrire ces deux langues d'une manière parfaite. Mais, ce qui achève d'embrouiller la question, c'est que le Luxembourg est proprement *trilingue*, car la langue maternelle de ses habitants n'est ni l'allemand ni le français, mais l'idiome luxembourgeois, qu'il faut considérer comme une véritable langue. (Ries [1911] 1920: 113, original italics)

'Here in effect, the German and French languages have been superimposed and tangled up with one another for centuries, and this knowledge has always been a national necessity. Furthermore, the somewhat educated Luxembourgers and those who by their functions are forced to use both the German and the French language, have always felt in honor bound not only to understand but also to speak and write these two languages in a perfect manner. But to add to the confusion, Luxembourg is *trilingual* properly speaking, for the mother tongue of its inhabitants is neither German nor French but the Luxembourgish idiom, which should be considered as a genuine language.'

In contrast to Ries, discourses in the journal published by the *Letzeburger National-Unio'n* (LN) tend to concentrate on matters within the borders of Luxembourg rather than attempt to build bridges between neighboring states. Among the founding members of the LN was Lucien Koenig, nicknamed *Siggy vu Lëtzebuerg*, a high school (*lycée*) teacher and literary writer (cf. Hoffmann 1993). The first LN journal appeared in 1911 under the name of

Jongletzeburg.[9] The discourses in this journal often focus on rallying for unity within Luxembourg, and there exist attempts to define the *Stackletzebuerger*:

> (2a) Am Lâf vun de Johrhonnerten hun sech an hirer Mött vu Generatiŏn zu Generatiŏn Sötten, Gebreicher, Jenseitsiwerzêgonken a vrun Allem èng Sprôch erausgebild, dě nur hinnen ege sinn ... Get dûorfir [Naturalisation, KH] *dât frîemt Element* ze stark, da gêt et net am *einhêmeschen* op, mä ömmgekěert: An d'Natiŏn gêt flêten. Wě ass et nun an onsem Hêmeschsland? Hu mir e stârke Kär, dên t'frîemt Element net brauch ze fàrten, ass ons Population stark genug, verměert se sech an ènger Proportion, dě dě Frîem als "quantité négligeable" önnert de *Stackletzeburger* dêt verschwannen? (Jongletzeburg 1911/1912, No. 1: 3, my emphasis)

> 'Over the course of the centuries, customs, traditions, religious convictions, and above all a language have developed from generation to generation, which are theirs alone ... If for that reason [naturalization, KH] *the foreign element* becomes too strong, then it does not dissolve in *the native* [element], but the opposite: And the nation will disintegrate. What is the situation in our homeland? Do we have a strong enough core, so that there is no need to fear the foreign element, is our population strong enough, is the native element increasing in such a proportion that the foreign will disappear as an "insignificant quantity" among the *Stackletzeburger* ['rooted Luxembourgers']?'

A binary opposition between Luxembourgers and non-Luxembourgers is constructed along ethnic lines, and – based on this categorization – there is a call for the only boundary to be between Luxembourgers and non-Luxembourgers:

> (2b) Och fir ons, Jongletzeburger, muß dê Sproch Gesetz gin, och mir musse mâchen wě d'Fransõsen, d'Deitsch, d'Amerikaner, iwerhâpt wě jidwer Vollek dât erstârke wöllt – mir mussen êneg gin a bleiwen. Op onst Land an ons Zeit iwerdrôen, hêscht et matt ânere Wirder: *Jongletzeburg soll kên Ennerschêd mân töschent Liberal, Klerikal a Sozialist.* Fir Jongletzeburg soll dât alles ênt an dât selwécht sin, fir Jongletzeburg soll et nömme Letzeburger oder Netletzeburger gin. (Jongletzeburg 1911/1912, No. 3: 1, original emphasis)

> 'Also for us, Young Luxembourgers, the language must enter into law, also we have to do like the French, the Germans, the Americans, just like every other people that wants to be strong – we have to become and remain unified. Applied to our country and our time, this means in other words: *Young Luxembourg should make no distinction between liberals, clericalists and socialists.* For Young Luxembourg all those should be one and the same, for Young Luxembourg there should only exist Luxembourgers and non-Luxembourgers.'

---

[9] From 1915–1923 the LN journal appeared under the name *d'Natio'n (Organ vun der Letzeburger Nationalunio'n)*. For a detailed discussion of the LN, including their resurgence in the late 1930s, see Blau (2005: 201–276).

Like Ries, contributors to this journal turn to language to construct Luxembourgish national identity, although the emphasis is not on trilingualism but on the centrality of Luxembourgish, which is referred to simply as 'our language', as for example in the following excerpt:

> (2c) Onse letzeburger Karakter wölle mer erhalen an alles wat mat him zesummenhenkt: *Ons Sprôch*, ons Egenarten, ons Sitten a Gebreicher ...Onst Volek soll nun seng Schreftsteller an Dichter kennen, well si sin et dě un der Erhalung vun onser Sprôch arbechten an dodurch onse Karakter, ons Onofhèngegkèt secherstellen. (Jongletzeburg 1911/1912, No. 1: 1, my emphasis)

> 'We want to retain our Luxembourgish character and everything that is connected to it: *Our language*, our characteristics, our customs and practices ... Our people should really know its writers and poets, because they are the ones who work at keeping our language and therewith secure our character, our independence.'

It was members of the LN as well as individuals that were sympathetic to some of their goals who successfully lobbied for the addition of Luxembourgish as a school subject in 1912, although it must be stressed that this addendum to the curriculum entailed reading literary texts and singing songs in Luxembourgish rather than teaching how to write Luxembourgish (cf. Newton 1996: 183–4). Furthermore, members of LN did not advocate the replacement of German and French in the schools by Luxembourgish.

The work of Ries and that of the LN both highlight the role of language in the construction of Luxembourgish national identity, although they diverge as to whether the emphasis is placed on trilingualism or Luxembourgish.[10] The way in which the LN identifies strictly with Luxembourgish corresponds with the inward turn, and they attempt to construct a binary opposition between Luxembourgers and non-Luxembourgers in ethnic terms in the context of increasing levels of immigration. Ries, on the other hand, argues for Luxembourgers to mediate between the German and French states and, on a more general level, to look beyond national boundaries. In this light, it is not surprising that Ries writes extensively about the way in which Luxembourgers speak and write French and German, whereas the LN is primarily concerned with the propagation of Luxembourgish. However, it is also worth noting that Ries calls for more support for Luxembourgish. The situation has not changed

---

[10] The writings of Ries and members of the LN both reflect the dominance of race theory during the period when they were published. Although it is rare to come across explicit references to the work of LN in present-day discourses, Ries' book continues to be fairly widely cited. In 1995, an edition of *Nos cahiers* was dedicated to Ries' memory. See Fehlen (1996) for critical response to some of the contributions in this issue, i.e. those that draw on primordialist paradigms.

a great deal in the last 100 years: at present, identification with both tri-lingualism and Luxembourgish may be two sides to the same coin, as long as the emphasis on the one side does not outweigh the other, which is not always an easy balance to maintain.

3. Language and the continuity of Luxembourgish national identity

The present-day situation in Luxembourg is marked by a series of interrelated social, political, and economic changes. In the post World War II period, the formation of the European Union (EU) allowed key Luxembourgish policy makers to move from a peripheral to a more central role on the European scene.[11] During the 1960s and 70s, a gradual transition towards a more service-oriented job sector began. As was the case at the turn of the previous century, the Luxembourgish economy continues to be dependent on foreign capital as well as labor from abroad. Due to developments on the EU level, particularly the introduction of free movement, there is more competition on the employment market than ever before. The population of Luxembourg currently consists of 40% resident foreigners. In addition, 39% of the workforce consists of *frontaliers* 'border-crossing commuters' (Statec 2006), the majority of whom are predominantly French speakers. The link between the Luxembourgish language and national identity has become highly salient in the Grand Duchy, a development that has been gaining momentum steadily since the late 1970s.[12] The status and value of various languages has fluctuated due in part to the growing number of French speakers in Luxembourg, but also due to greater issues linked to EU expansion and the processes of accelerated globalization, which in turn are serving as an impetus for the increased use of English. These developments have undoubtedly contributed to the momentum to promote the national language. The ratification of the 1984 law provides the first legal recognition of Luxembourgish as the national language, although the same law also recognizes French and German in various statewide, institutional functions.

---

[11]   Luxembourg is one of the six founding EU member-states and Luxembourg city – together with Brussels and Strasbourg – serves as one of the three EU capitals.

[12]   In the 1980s a number of attempts were made to form new political parties, and it was the Greens as well as the right-wing *Aktiounskomitee fir Demokratie a Rentegerechtegkeet* (ADR) that were successful in this process and have managed to secure and maintain a number of seats in the Luxembourgish parliament. In its election campaigns, the ADR has made specific reference to cultural criteria, including the Luxembourgish language. For a discussion of attempts to form extreme right parties during the 1980s and 1990s, see Blau (2005: 518–625).

At present, the parallel identification strategies with trilingualism and with Luxembourgish often continue to coexist alongside one another, as for example in texts 3 and 4:

(3) *the 'Luxembourgeois' are trilingual: they speak Lëtzebuergesch (the national language), French and German.* Most of them also have a good mastery of English ... Luxembourg folk, who are they? They are a cheerful, happy people, *a blend of Latin and Germanic cultures,* fiercely proud of their popular and religious traditions, resolutely European and multicultural ... (Luxembourg National Tourist Office 2003, my emphasis).

(4) Déi meescht Lëtzebuerger kënnen haut, nieft hirem Lëtzebuergesch, och nach Däitsch a Franséisch, muncher och Englesch. An dat soll och esou sin! Mir sin op eis Noperen ugewisen, fir mat Friemen an d'Gespréich ze kommen, musse mir hir Sprooche kennen. (Rasquin et al. [1990] 1994: 22)

'In addition to their Luxembourgish, most Luxembourgers today know German and French, and many also English. And that is the way it should be! We are dependent on our neighbors; in order to have conversations with foreigners, we must be able to speak their languages.'

Text 3, quoted from a tourist brochure, is aimed at an international audience and the emphasis is on the trilingual paradigm, although there is the disclaimer – set off in brackets – that Luxembourgish is the national language. In a similar fashion to Ries ([1911] 1921), Luxembourgers are constructed as a hybrid people, and identification with trilingualism is foregrounded. Taken from a high school textbook targeting a national audience, Text 4 contrasts with Text 3 by directly linking Luxembourgers to the Luxembourgish language, although the learning of German and French is also depicted as an essential tool for communicating with 'foreigners'. An image of a tree filled in with Luxembourgish words appears on the cover of this textbook, thus reproducing the biological metaphor of the *Stacklëtzebuerger* 'rooted Luxembourgers' that appears in the publications of LN (1911/1912). Although Texts 3 and 4 emphasize different dimensions of the link between language and Luxembourgish national identity, there is no indication that they are out of balance.

Official discourses, such as Text 5 by EU commissioner Viviane Reding – written during the European Year of Languages – sometimes go as far as to portray the two identification strategies as complementary and even depict Luxembourg as the model for other EU member-states:

(5) En appliquant avec un succès universellement reconnu le trilinguisme dans ses écoles, le Luxembourg a déjà atteint l'objectif que se fixe l'Union européenne pour les prochaines années: que chaque jeune Européen soit capable, à sa sortie du système scolaire, de s'exprimer dans deux langues en plus de sa langue maternelle. Les Luxembourgeois montrent aussi l'exemple au reste de l'Europe par leur attachement à la langue luxembourgeoise. (Viviane Reding in *Luxemburger Wort,* 27 September 2001: 3)

'By using a trilingual school-system with universally recognized success, Luxembourg has already achieved the aim that the European Union has set itself for the following years: that every young European coming out of the school-system should be able to communicate in two languages in addition to his or her mother tongue. The Luxembourgers also set an example for the rest of Europe through their attachment to the Luxembourgish language.'

However, there also exists a substantial amount of popular discourse, as for example in Text 6 from a letter to the editor, which portrays the current linguistic situation in Luxembourg as problematic and calls urgently for more support for Luxembourgish:

(6) Et as allgemeng unerkannt, datt d'Sprooch den Zement vun der Identitéit duerstellt. Wa mir dat Lëtzebuergescht nët bei eisen auslännesche Matbierger consolidéieren, da riskéiere mir geschwënn, an Europa just nach als klengen Territoire consideréiert ze gin, zwar mat engem schéine Sproochecocktail, mee kaum nach als Land mat Recht op eegen Existenz ... Wann haut an engem Buttek d'Vendeuse seet: "Vous ne pouvez pas parler français comme tout le monde?", da rege mir eis mat Recht op. Wann awer engesdaags d'Lëtzebuergescht nëmmen nach vun enger Minoritéit geschwat gët, da ka kee méi der selwechter Vendeuse eppes verdenken ... Hei zu Lëtzebuerg ware mir eis bis elo ëmmer eens mat den dräi Sprooche Lëtzebuergesch, Däitsch a Franséisch ëmzegoen. Ouni Ëmdenken as de Risk grouss, datt dat Lëtzebuergescht nët nëmmen an den Eck gedréckt gët, mee datt eis Enkelkanner mat enger Sprooch ze du kréien, déi als Emgangssprooch um Ausstierwen as. (A.C. in *Luxemburger Wort*, 4 September 1999: 19)

'It is generally recognized that language is the cement of identity. If we fail to teach our *auslännesche Matbierger* ['foreign co-citizens'] Luxembourgish and thus consolidate the language, we run the risk of soon being considered in Europe as just a small territory, albeit with a beautiful language cocktail, but hardly any longer as a country with a right to its own existence ... When today in a store the saleslady says, "Can you not speak French like everybody else?" [switches to French to quote the hypothetical saleslady, KH] then we are right to get annoyed. If however one day Luxembourgish is only spoken by a minority, then nobody will have a right any longer to be upset with the same saleslady ... Here in Luxembourg we have always agreed so far to use the three languages, Luxembourgish, German and French. Without changing our way of thinking, there is a big risk not only that Luxembourgish will be pushed into a corner, but also that our grandchildren will inherit a language that is dying out as a means of communication.'

Such discourses appear frequently in the letters to the editor column of the major national newspaper, the *Luxemburger Wort*, indicating that there is not complete consensus regarding present-day patterns of language use and therewith revealing a gap between official and popular discourses.[13]

---

[13] For a detailed discussion of the present-day situation, see Horner (2004). The *Luxemburger Wort* was renamed *d'Wort* when the layout was changed from broadsheet to tabloid format in 2005.

4. Conclusion: multidimensional approaches to language history

Past and present discourses about language in Luxembourg are not completely dissimilar from one another, although they diverge in the way they are related to contextually specific processes of greater social, political, and economic change. Thus, present-day discourses continue to refract ideologies of hybridity and purity that correspond to the opening and closure of the nation, with the former being linked to the paradigm of trilingualism and the latter to Luxembourgish. At present the positive self is constructed on the international level by identifying with the paradigm of trilingualism; however, internal group boundaries are sometimes forged via identification with the national language, Luxembourgish. Following Irvine and Gal (2000), it makes good sense to focus our attention on exploring the construction of boundaries rather than attempting to define a community with self-contained and rigid characteristics. It also follows that we need to approach language history from interdisciplinary perspectives, which may be accomplished by putting theoretical concepts such as identity and ideology at the heart of scientific inquiry.

A look at the role of language in the construction of Luxembourgish national identity illustrates that similar questions have been posed in the past and present, but that they are being asked in a different manner at this point in time in comparison to the period at the turn of the twentieth century. Is there really more of a 'national identity crisis' now than in the past? In spite of EU enlargement and globalization, or perhaps for these very reasons, the ideal of the nation-state together with the nationalist ideologies underpinning it are not disappearing from view. At present it is the *status quo* and existing world order that are being challenged. According to Grillo (1998: 218), it is useful to try to get a grasp of what constitutes the postmodern condition, although this does not require researchers to fully embrace the postmodernist intellectual project. I would argue that postmodernist theory would benefit from greater engagement with history and, more specifically, with the role of ethnicity in the formation of group membership. At the same time, postmodernist theory is valuable due to the questions that are being raised in relation to the position of the researcher. It is useful to reflect upon the factors that shape our work, including various dimensions of center-periphery matrix as well as the fact that we tend to view past events through the lens of the present. Looking at language histories from various points of view reminds us of our own bearings, be it on one or more central axes rather than peripheral ones, or situated in the present-day rather than in the past.

Sources of Data

Ries, Nicolas. [1911] 1920. *Essai d'une psychologie du peuple luxembour-geois*. Diekirch: Imprimerie J. Schroell.

Jongletzeburg (Organ vun der Letzeburger National-Unio'n). 1911/1912.

Luxembourg National Tourist Office. 2003. *Luxembourg: Sights and attractions*.

Rasquin, Fernand, Jean Rinnen, Jos Schmit and Paul Schumacher. [1990] 1994. *Lëtzebuergesch Texter*. Lëtzebuerg: Ministère de l'Education Nationale.

Reding, Viviane. Toute langue est une grande langue. *Luxemburger Wort*, 27 September 2001: 3

A. C. Wéi geet et viru *mat* der Lëtzebuerger Sprooch? *Luxemburger Wort*, 4 September 1999: 19

References

Anderson, Benedict. [1983] 1991. *Imagined Communities: Reflections on the Origin and Spread of Nationalism*. Rev. ed. London: Verso.

Blau, Lucien. 2005. *Histoire de l'extrème droite au Grand-Duché de Luxembourg au XXe siècle*. Esch-sur-Alzette: Le Phare.

Blommaert, Jan. 1999. The Debate is Closed. In Jan Blommaert (ed.), *Language Ideological Debates*. Berlin and New York: Mouton de Gruyter, 425–438.

Blommaert, Jan and Jef Verschueren. 1998. The Role of Language in European Nationalist Ideologies. In Bambi B. Schieffelin, Kathryn Woolard and Paul Kroskrity (eds.), *Language Ideologies: Practice and Theory*. Oxford: Oxford University Press, 189–210.

Calmes, Christian and Danielle Bossaert. 1996. *Geschichte des Großherzogtums Luxemburg: Von 1815 bis heute*. Luxemburg: Editions Saint-Paul.

Crowley, Tony. 1996. *Language in History: Theories and Texts*. London: Routledge.

Deumert, Ana and Wim Vandenbussche. 2003. Standard Languages: Taxonomies and Histories. In Ana Deumert and Wim Vandenbussche (eds.), *Germanic Standardizations: Past and Present*. Amsterdam and Philadelphia: Benjamins, 1–14.

Fehlen, Fernand. 1996. La race luxembourgeoise: Le libéral Nicolas Ries et ses épigones conservateurs. *Forum für Politik, Gesellschaft und Kultur* 168: 35–38.

Gal, Susan. 1991. Bartók's Funeral: Representations of Europe in Hungarian Political Rhetoric. *American Ethnologist* 18: 440–458.

Gal, Susan. 2001. Linguistic Theories and National Images in Nineteenth-Century Hungary. In Susan Gal and Kathryn Woolard (eds.), *Languages and Publics: The Making of Authority*. Manchester: St. Jerome Publishing, 30–45.

Gilles, Peter and Claudine Moulin. 2003. Luxembourgish. In Ana Deumert and Wim Vandenbussche (eds.), *Germanic Standardizations: Past and Present*. Amsterdam and Philadelphia: Benjamins, 303–329.

Grillo, Ralph. 1980. Introduction. In Ralph Grillo (ed.), *'Nation' and 'State' in Europe: Anthropological Perspectives*. London: Academic Press, 1–30.

Grillo, Ralph. 1998. *Pluralism and the Politics of Difference: State, Culture, and Ethnicity in Comparative Perspective*. Oxford: Clarendon Press.

Haugen, Einar. 1966. Dialect, Language, Nation. *American Anthropologist* 68: 922–935.

Hoffmann, Fernand. 1993. Lucien Koenig (1888–1961): Siggy vu Letzebuerg. In Paul Dostert (ed.), *Le livre d'or du lycée de garçons de Luxembourg: de l'école industrielle et commerciale au lycée de garçons de Luxembourg 1892–1992*. Luxembourg, 269–270.

Horner, Kristine. 2004. *Negotiating the Language-Identity Link: Media Discourse and Nation-Building in Luxembourg*. PhD dissertation, State University of New York at Buffalo.

Horner, Kristine. 2005. Reimagining the Nation: Discourses of Language Purism in Luxembourg. In Nils Langer and Winifred V. Davies. *Linguistic Purism in the Germanic Languages*. Berlin and New York: de Gruyter, 166–185.

Irvine, Judith T. and Susan Gal. 2000. Language Ideology and Linguistic Differentiation. In Paul V. Kroskrity (ed.), *Regimes of Language: Ideologies, Polities, and Identities*. Oxford: James Currey, 35–83.

Jenkins, Richard. 1997. *Rethinking Ethnicity: Arguments and Explorations*. London: Sage.

Lippi-Green, Rosina. 1997. *English with an Accent: Language, Ideology, and Discrimination in the United States*. London: Routledge.

May, Stephen. 2001. *Language and Minority Rights: Ethnicity, Nationalism and the Politics of Language*. London: Longman.

Milroy, Jim. 2002. The Legitimate Language: Giving a History to English. In Richard Watts and Peter Trudgill (eds.), *Alternative Histories of English*. London: Routledge, 7–25.

Morley, David. 1996. EurAm, Modernity, Reason and Alterity: Or, Postmodernism, The Highest Stage of Cultural Imperialism? In David Morley and Kuan-Hsing Chen (eds.), *Stuart Hall: Critical Dialogues in Cultural Studies*. London: Routledge, 326–360.

Newton, Gerald. 1996. Lëtzebuergesch and the Establishment of National Identity. In Gerald Newton (ed.), *Luxembourg and Lëtzebuergesch:*

Language and Communication at the Crossroads of Europe. Oxford: Clarendon Press, 181–215.

Niedzielski, Nancy A. and Dennis R. Preston. 2000. *Folk Linguistics*. Berlin and New York: Mouton de Gruyter.

Spizzo, Daniel. 1995. *La nation luxembourgeoise: genèse et structure d'une identité*. Paris: L'Harmattan.

Statec. 2006. *Le Luxembourg en chiffres*. Luxembourg: Graphic Press.

Trausch, Gilbert. 2002. Comment faire d'un état de convention une nation? In Gilbert Trausch (ed.), *Histoire du Luxembourg: Le destin européen d'un "petit pays"*. Toulouse: Éditions Privat, 201–274.

Trudgill, Peter and Richard Watts. 2002. Introduction: In the Year 2525. In Richard Watts and Peter Trudgill (eds.), *Alternative Histories of English*. London: Routledge, 1–3.

Weber, Batty. Ueber Mischkultur in Luxemburg. *Beilage der Münchner Neuesten Nachrichten*, 20 January 1909: 121–124.

White, Hayden. 1981. The Value of Narrativity in the Representation of Reality. In William J. Thomas Mitchell (ed.), *On Narrative*. Chicago: University of Chicago Press, 1–23.

Wilhelm, Frank. 1993. Nicolas Ries (1876-1941). In Paul Dostert (ed.), *Le livre d'or du lycée de garçons de Luxembourg: de l'école industrielle et commerciale au lycée de garçons de Luxembourg 1892–1992*. Luxembourg, 250–268.

Ernst Håkon Jahr (Kristiansand)

The planning of modern Norwegian as a sociolinguistic experiment – 'from below'

1814 – independence from Denmark – what about language?

Two solutions emerged to meet the language situation in Norway following the historical events of the year 1814:[1] either a gradual change of written Danish – the Danish standard being the heritage of the union period – or the creation of a new written standard based on contemporary rural dialects. The former solution we usually associate with the grammarian and headmaster Knud Knudsen (1812–95), the latter with the linguist and poet Ivar Aasen (1813–96). Both these solutions were pursued during the 19th century. The competition between them created the Norwegian language struggle, which in the 1960s gave the necessary empirical data to Einar Haugen's well-known model of language planning (cf. Haugen 1966). For us, in the present article, the planning and development of modern Norwegian gives a unique possibility to study the implementation and results of a sociolinguistic experiment through deliberate linguistic changes 'from below'.

Departure from a 'normal' sociolinguistic situation

We will soon return to Ivar Aasen and Knud Knudsen, but first we need to underscore that the sociolinguistic situation in Norway around 1814 was not at all unusual. Norwegians at that time had one written standard (i.e. Danish), which was relatively well-defined and stable. The class of government

---

[1] With the independence from Denmark after more than 400 years. However, until 1905 Norway remained within a personal union with Sweden.

officials,[2] which constituted the country's ruling class after 1814, used a spoken idiom which was relatively homogenous and universally accepted as 'cultured' and which to a great extent was based on the vocabulary and forms of the written (Danish) standard. The class of peasants, amounting to more than 95% of the population, used the local dialects, but these had a low status. Thus, we have reason to claim that the sociolinguistic situation in Norway was 'normal' – and that it never has been more 'normal' than it was in 1814 and shortly thereafter.

It is therefore important to realize that a Norwegian 'language issue' did not necessarily have to develop upon the 1814 dissolution of the union with Denmark. The problem at that time did not primarily reside in the fact that the written language (i.e. Danish) was particularly difficult for Norwegians to learn. On the contrary, Danish and Norwegian are too much alike for this to be the case. Upon the dissolution of the union, however, the written standard became a foreign language, a language 'belonging' to another country and – what was even more important – to another nation: Denmark.

The current situation

Thus, in 1814 Norway had a sociolinguistic community which was quite 'normal' in a European context. In Norway today, however, we have a situation which can be considered unique. What is particularly exceptional about this is that the country has two written standards, both of them Norwegian (*Bokmål* and *Nynorsk*, literally 'Book language' and 'New Norwegian') but no universally accepted spoken standard. Instead, most inhabitants use their local dialects in most contexts. There exist only small linguistic differences between the two written standards, but most Norwegians know that the differences between Bokmål and Nynorsk are sociolinguistically important. The use of Nynorsk or Bokmål frequently signals different values, opinions, and attitudes to many people. Why this is so will become apparent from the following.

Examining our two written standards more thoroughly and comparing them to written Swedish and Danish, we will soon discover that there is an important

---

[2] In 1814 upper-middle classes (less than 5% of the total population) consisted mainly of the educated elite which constituted the group of civil servants. It was not an urban group in principle, but they were scattered around the country. Many of them were priests. The upper-middle classes also consisted of a tiny group of extremely rich merchants who were scattered around the country. The lower classes (then, more than 95%) were mainly peasants, fishermen and workers (but very few workers in 1814). What happened over time in the 19th and 20th centuries was that the number of upper-middle class members increased through the rise of industry and trade. During the same time, working-class members increased too, being recruited from the class of peasants.

difference. In Swedish and Danish there are extremely few double or parallel forms. A word is written in one way and only in this way, and if conjugated, the word is conjugated in one and only one way (with a few exceptions both in Swedish and Danish). Such is not the case in Norway. In each of the written standards there are many double forms. Often one can conjugate a word in many ways. How is that? We may accept that there are two written Norwegian standards, but why are they not more or less fixed, as are standard Swedish and Danish? The reason for this is to be found in the development of the language after 1814.

In Sweden and Denmark dialects have a far lower social status than in contemporary Norway, where e.g. students speak their local dialects in school. Even the School Act states that they have a right to do so. Although not yet investigated enough, it seems that electronic text messages among young people are written in dialect more often than not. The country's School Act states that the teacher should pay due attention to the vernacular used by pupils, and that he or she should not attempt to make them abandon their home dialect. The frequent use of dialects in modern Norway – from kindergarten to university and from local municipalities to Parliament and government – shows a unique position of local dialects in society at large and a sociolinguistic situation probably unparalleled in Europe, to which only the German speaking parts of Switzerland come close (cf. Jahr 1997).

Let us now return to the beginning – the time right after 1814 – and study why and how the current and exceptional Norwegian language situation developed from a fairly 'normal' stage in the early 19th century.

National romanticism

National romanticism emphasized the connection between a nation and its language. A language of its own was the prime characteristic of an independent nation. But in post-1814 Norway the written language was foreign. The Norwegians, therefore, did not meet one very fundamental national romantic requirement as regards the creation of a nation of their own. Without the ideological climate associated with romanticism, it becomes difficult to explain why the 'language issue' during the 19th century developed the way it did, why there, on the whole, was a 'language issue' at all.

How old is Norway?

Most Norwegians today consider the kingdom of Norway to be fairly old. We should at least be able to count the country's age from the glorious or, as some would say, infamous time of the Vikings. To most Norwegians this view has been so ingrained by teaching in school that they rarely would venture to question the fact. Only occasionally someone happens to point out that Norway is in fact a rather young European nation, less than 200 years old. Two different views exist, then, regarding Norway's age. And precisely by formulating questions about the age of the country, we may gain an understanding of why there was a 'language issue' in Norway after 1814, and maybe we will also understand why it took on the form it actually did.

The question about Norway's age may perhaps appear somewhat strange. But it is important for understanding the language debate and the language development during the 19th century. The 'age question' can be said to have been answered in at least two ways, and, depending on the answer, one can also give the answer to an even more important question: who constituted the Norwegian nation in post-1814 Norway? Who – if not everybody – had the right to be called a true or real 'Norwegian'? We will soon discover that these questions have decisive sociolinguistic implications for Norway's language development.

The names of the two most important Norwegian language planners of the 19th century have already been mentioned: Ivar Aasen and Knud Knudsen. Their answers to the two questions just mentioned were totally opposite: Aasen's work indicated that Norway was very old, while Knudsen's program pointed instead to a start in 1814. They therefore represented opposing solutions to how an independent written Norwegian standard was to be developed, and they suggested written standards with markedly different sociolinguistic bases.

Ivar Aasen and the rural dialects: Norway is old

The philosophical basis for Ivar Aasen's work was the national romantic view that an autonomous language was important for an independent nation. For him it was important to establish a connection between the new Norway that emerged after 1814 and the Medieval Old Norse Norway. From this point of view, the four-century long union with Denmark was reduced to an insignificant parenthesis in Norwegian history. It is true that this understanding of Norwegian history has since been accepted by most people, albeit not generally by today's historians.

If one was to establish a relationship between the modern nineteenth-century Norway and the ancient Norse empire straight through the union with Denmark, it should be possible to find connections and concrete contexts showing that the two periods really are connected. It was at this point that Ivar Aasen offered his linguistic evidence. In his first published works (Aasen 1848, 1850) he claimed that the modern dialects spoken by the peasants in rural areas had developed from Old Norse, and that it was possible to describe them on the whole without taking into account Danish. The Danish period thus disappeared, or, rather, it could be disregarded. We can say that Aasen provided the linguistic evidence showing that the period of Danish dominion in reality was merely an episode in the long history of Norway.

While, towards the end of the union, the dialects in Norway were considered dialects of Danish, it now became necessary, Aasen argued, to initiate a national awareness that the dialects within Norway had developed from Old Norse independently of Danish, and that they constituted a separate Germanic and Nordic language. The premise for such a view at that time was a written standard which displayed the national features found in the dialects. Ivar Aasen – a peasant's son from western Norway and a self-taught man – had as his objective to create such a written language, and it became his mission in life to realize it (cf. Aasen 1836).

Between 1842 and 1846, he travelled around the country and collected materials from the rural dialects to make an account of the 'Popular Tongue'. For the most part he covered the southern parts of Norway during these journeys, avoiding the towns, as he thought that there the language would be too influenced by Danish. After 1847 he settled for good in Kristiania [Oslo].

Aasen possessed an unusual ability to systematize a vast linguistic corpus. Still, he did not present a proposal for a new national written standard at once. He first presented the materials collected during his travels in a *grammar* (1848) and a *dictionary* (1850). In those he demonstrated how the modern popular dialects were related to Old Norse.

The next step in his work was to establish a unifying standard, a written expression of all the various dialects. This work took him many years. Only with the publication of *Norwegian Grammar* (1864) and *Norwegian Dictionary* (1873) was the 'Aasen standard' fully elaborated. Aasen himself called his standard 'Landsmål'. Different opinions have been voiced as to whether Aasen's term referred to the 'language of the country' or the 'language of the countryside'. Both interpretations are possible from the term alone. However, this distinction would have been of no consequence to Aasen. As he saw it, the language found in the various towns was far too influenced by Danish to deserve attention when considering a national standard. In relation to the nation as a whole, the language spoken in the countryside therefore also became the language of the country. To Aasen this constituted no contradiction in terms. Only at a much later stage, when it was 'discovered' that the popular dialects of the towns, the working class sociolects, were 'good' Norwegian varieties as well, the ambiguity inherent in the term 'Landsmål' became unfortunate, and attempts to alter the term were initiated. Finally, in 1929 Parliament (the Storting) decided that *Nynorsk* was to be the term instead of 'Landsmål', while at the same time *Bokmål* was to be the term for the other competing standard. (I will in this account use 'Landsmål/Nynorsk' and 'Riksmål/Bokmål' for the two

standards for the period until 1929 and 'Nynorsk' and 'Bokmål' for the two
official written standards from then on.)

The Aasen standard

Four important principles can be distinguished in the Aasen standard of
Landsmål/Nynorsk:

1. There was to be only one valid form of each word. The words were to
   be conjugated in one way only. There were to be no optional parallel
   forms.
2. The forms of the standard were to be based on contemporary spoken
   dialects.
3. The standard ought to be uniform and consistent, that is that words
   which were connected with reference to meaning and etymology should
   reveal this connection by the way they were written.
4. Old Norse was considered the historical point of departure for
   contemporary dialects, this being the final instance of appeal when it
   became necessary to choose between different dialectal forms.

It can be said that Aasen's program was democratic, since he did not build his
standard on one single dialect, but – in principle – on all the dialects. It is an
open question whether the idea to build a national Norwegian standard on one
dialect alone – which was suggested by others – would have stirred the interest
and zeal of people all around the country as much as Ivar Aasen's program has
succeeded in doing ever since the 1850s. The idea that the national language of
Norway was to be a common denominator, a kind of the least common
multiple for all popular dialects, the dialect 'from below' has made people join
the movement to develop Landsmål/Nynorsk and introduce it into ever new
areas.

    In retrospect, the assessment of the Aasen standard as such has differed quite
considerably. Many have been struck by the accomplished and systematic
structure of the standard. Everything is thoroughly and well conceived, and
everything finds its proper place. It is easy to demonstrate that the principle
applied by Aasen, that is to build on the basis of the modern dialects, permeates
the entire fabric. Still, many have claimed that his standard nevertheless was too
old-fashioned and difficult to use. Some have believed that Aasen allowed
himself gradually to be more influenced by Old Norse. This is hardly correct, as
Aasen pursued his own principles. It is, however, clear that there existed an
inner contradiction between, on the one hand, Aasen's wish to create a written
standard for the common people – for the populace that had the least time

available for schooling and practical writing instruction – and, on the other hand, the results of the methods and principles he chose to be lead by when elaborating the standard.[3] This is the contradiction that causes the markedly different opinions regarding how successful the Aasen standard was as a written language for most people, opinions which later were to appear both within the Landsmål/Nynorsk language movement and outside of it.

The theory of the 'two cultures'

Ivar Aasen's work soon led to a national political project, that is the official establishment of an exclusively Norwegian written standard. Through his project Aasen demonstrated a historical view of what should be reckoned as 'Norwegian'. His work suggested a definition of who in the country represented Norsedom (the peasants did), and how the spoken idiom that had been developed during the Danish rule (the spoken variety of the upper classes) was to be evaluated nationally (it had no national value). Aasen's answer to the question who the Norwegians were was clear from the start: only the peasants.

On the basis of his assessment, it was not a long way to the theory of the so-called 'two cultures'. This theory claimed that Norway in reality contained two entirely different cultures. While one was foreign and imported (i.e. Danish), the other was native and national. The upper classes, essentially the upper class of government officials, represented the foreign culture, the colonial culture, whereas the peasants, the populace, represented the indigenous and national (cf. Garborg 1877). Between these two cultures there existed serious competition, which was expressed in the farmer's political opposition to the ruling upper class. Gradually the Aasen's standard, Landsmål/Nynorsk, came to be the javelin edge poised against an extremely important cultural privilege of the ruling class: the language hegemony.

The officials' culture, which had originated in the period of Danish rule, had written Danish as its natural form of expression. The officials commanded this language, and they possessed a spoken variety that to a great extent drew on the said written language as its model (cf. below). Launching attacks against the language hegemony of the officials became an important political measure for the opposition, and here the Aasen standard emerged as a concrete issue with which the opposition could argue and which it could promote. The Parliament decision of 1885 – after the fall of the government of the officials and the introduction of parliamentary rule in 1884 – to grant Landsmål/Nynorsk and the

---

[3]   In particular his puristic attitude of banning all clearly Danish or Low German loanwords from his written standard, necessary as it was from his nationalist point of view.

'Common Language of Books' (= Riksmål/Bokmål) equal status is only explainable in this more general political context. Since the 1885 decision in Parliament, however, Norway has had two written standards with equal official status.

Nationalist and sociopolitical arguments

Ivar Aasen was himself very conscious of the sociopolitical and sociolinguistic content of his own language program. In his argumentation, national romanticism joined with sociopolitical thinking, and he emphasized both elements in his work. From the very beginning, the organized Landsmål movement also comprised both national and social elements. It turned out that these elements in the movement easily entered into a conflicting relationship, depending on the emphasis their supporters put on one or the other aspect. Soon they formed two groups of language activists who opposed one another, representing different policies and strategies in the political language work. While one group emphasized the national aspect in their arguments, the other stressed the social element.

Until 1905 this difference of opinion could nevertheless be evened out because the national and social struggle in society coincided in the general political struggle. Both nationally and socially the peasants' movement faced the same adversary, the officials. The latter were generally in favor of the union with Sweden and opposed a development towards democracy in society.

The advocates of Landsmål/Nynorsk in the Storting (Parliament) used arguments which principally must be labelled democratic, pedagogical, and national. It was argued that it was a democratic policy and pedagogically advantageous to favor a written standard based on the spoken language of the majority of the population. Besides, it was nationally important and necessary, since an independent people or nation needs a written language of its own, and the majority of the population, the peasants, represented what was genuinely Norwegian.

The opponents of Landsmål/Nynorsk in the Storting could hardly disagree with this pedagogical line of reasoning. But they argued that the dialects differed so much linguistically that they could not at all be said to be better represented in the Landsmål of Aasen – the Aasen standard – than in the Dano-Norwegian standard (= Riksmål/Bokmål).

Political advances of Landsmål/Nynorsk

Those who directly opposed the introduction of Landsmål/Nynorsk were consistently a minority in the Storting in the late nineteenth century, and the advance of Landsmål/Nynorsk came as the result of important political decisions of 1878, 1885, and 1892. In 1878 the Odelsting – one of the two chambers of the Storting – decided that the dialects of the pupils should form the basis of oral instruction in primary school and that the teacher should as far as possible utilize the dialect of the region in his teaching (cf. Jahr 1984). This decision on oral language provided the basis for the decision of 1885, already mentioned, when the two written standards were officially declared equal. And this decision was then used to argue in favor of an amendment of the School Act in 1892. It empowered the local schoolboards all over the country to decide in which of the two standards the pupils were to have their written instruction. At the same time it became obligatory for everybody in school to learn to read both standards. Texts in both standards were therefore introduced to school books, especially to the readers.

The Knud Knudsen program: Norway was born in 1814

An entirely different view about what constituted 'Norwegian' is obtained if we consider Norway as a nation established in 1814. The leading politicians were government officials, and the country's independence and constitution of 1814 were founded on the contribution of this social class, which also was to govern the young new state. Their spoken idiom thus had to be accepted as 'Norwegian' and also had to be considered a strong candidate as the norm basis for the development of a Norwegian national language. The particular spoken idiom that had developed during the 18th century by officials and the upper-middle classes was an interesting result of language contact. Colloquial Norwegian and written Danish were mixed, yielding a new linguistic variety which was grammatically simplified with regard to both written Danish and Norwegian dialects (cf. Jahr 1994: 36f.). Following Trudgill (1986), such a new dialect would be termed a *creoloid* or *koiné* variety.

If it had not been for the national romantic ideology of the time, this spoken variety would certainly have been unchallenged as the sole basis for a Norwegian national standard. Alternatively, it would also have been conceivable that the Danish standard might continue to be used in modern Norway like, say, English has been in the U.S, since this spoken variety was so close to written Danish. However, the romantic idea of that particular period triggered the issue of 'true' Norsedom, and here the officials and upper-middle classes – still with their primary cultural ties to Copenhagen and Denmark – could hardly compete with the class of peasants. Knud Knudsen realized that Ivar Aasen's solution represented a linguistic as well as a sociolinguistic revolution. Thus, Knudsen advocated a step-wise development of a national standard with the spoken variety of the officials and upper-middle classes as the norm basis for a step-by-step transformation of written Danish into Norwegian. The Norwegianization of written Danish was to happen gradually, and the resulting standard would then reflect upper-middle class speech (cf. Knudsen 1887).

Aasen and Knudsen – opposite sociolinguistic bases

Knud Knudsen and Ivar Aasen thus emerge as diametrically opposite poles with respect to their assessment of who was to decide what should count as 'Norwegian' and the national standard. Both took contemporary everyday spoken language as their point of departure. Knudsen wanted to build on the language of the officials and upper-middle classes, the classes that had fostered and brought about independence in 1814, and which were the politically commanding and culturally dominant classes in the new nation (and this solution has led to today's Bokmål). Aasen, however, used the popular local dialects of the peasants to establish a link to the Norse past (and his solution has resulted in today's Nynorsk). The sociolinguistic difference between these two standards is still very important today, while linguistically the differences are small and rather trivial.

The view of the upper-middle classes – the reform of 1907

The written standard inherited from the time of the union (i.e. the Danish written standard, but in Norway either called 'the mother tongue' or just 'Dano-Norwegian' up towards the end of the 19th century) represented 'culture' and 'education'. The upper-middle classes in Norway saw no reason whatsoever to change the Danish standard. It was functional and worked fine for them. True enough, they too were influenced by national romantic views and were Norwegian patriots. But they nevertheless saw no motivation for changing the linguistic situation in any way. Even if the populace – according to Ivar Aasen – was 'Norwegian', the sentiment among the upper-middle classes was, nevertheless, that the common people were 'uncultured' and 'uneducated'. As a result of the growth of the political opposition party Venstre (the 'Left' party) and the political turmoil of 1884, the language program of Knud Knudsen became more acceptable only when the Landsmål/Nynorsk policy became directly threatening when, as mentioned, parliamentary rule was introduced. Something had to be done to meet an imminent threat of a sociolinguistic revolution from the Landsmål/Nynorsk movement.

The political success of Landsmål/Nynorsk thus was an important precondition for the preparation of a language report which resulted in the 1907 reform of Riksmål/Bokmål. The reform established the principles of Knud Knudsen, that is that, in Norway, the Danish standard was to be changed into a

Riksmål/Bokmål standard and standardized according to the spoken (creoloid/koiné) variety of the upper-middle classes.

At the turn of the century

At the turn of the century, the principal ideologist of the Landsmål/Nynorsk movement, the author Arne Garborg (1851–1924), summarised his views on the language conflict in the following way:

> And here we face the secret of the language conflict. This bitter, long, passionate struggle, which every now and then flares up, is not a discussion of grammar; it is a struggle for power. It is the old conflict between 'the peasantry' and 'the class of officials' which in new guises continues. [...] – It is a power struggle. By upholding the dominance of its language, the nationalism that lost politically [in 1884] wishes to continue its rule (Garborg 1900: 154).

"The nationalism that lost politically", Garborg wrote. The view on nationalism that built on the idea that Norway was a new nation born in 1814 and not stretching back to the Middle Ages lost its appeal in 1884, when the government of the officials was defeated and parliamentary rule was introduced. But the social and national struggle continued far into the 20th century, and, as a struggle over national issues, it only ended with the advent of the Second World War. More and more, however, in the 20th century the struggle altered, away from national issues and it became dominated by sociopolitical and, therefore, also more salient sociolinguistic questions and differences.

Until 1910 most of the conflict was focussed on the competition between Landsmål/Nynorsk and Riksmål/Bokmål. It was a clear either-or question, and the Landsmål movement was continously on the offensive. The Storting in 1907 decided to introduce an obligatory second language essay for the General Certificate of Education (which gave access to university). This victory of the Landsmål movement, which meant that the candidates for the General Certificate of Education had to write an essay in Landsmål/Nynorsk, was the last in a series of decisions that gave the Landsmål/Nynorsk standard a secure footing in the schools.

The candidates for the General Certificate of Education were predominantly recruited from social groups which had no or very little sympathy for Landsmål/Nynorsk and the language issue as such. Most of them came from the upper-middle classes of the cities and towns, where Landsmål/Nynorsk had virtually no support. Many members of these groups, therefore, considered the proposal and decision about an obligatory subsidiary language essay as a provocation and as an alarming warning that attempts were to be made to introduce

Landsmål/Nynorsk into every new area of society by way of political decisions. Up until about 1910 the struggle was extremely bitter and the parties looked for no compromise whatsoever. The Landsmål/Nynorsk movement established a nation-wide organization, *Noregs Mållag*, in 1906. Riksmål/ Bokmål supporters responded in 1909 with *Riksmålsforbundet*.

New ideas 1910–20

During the decade from 1910 to 1920, however, the language conflict and the language debate changed its character. The dialects of the central part of the South-East and their role in the development of the language came to play an increasingly important role in the debate, with the demand that the eastern dialects should be given greater prominence in the development of the written standards. These dialects were scarcely represented in Aasen's Landsmål/ Nynorsk and did not come to the fore in Riksmål/Bokmål. It was common to refer to the fact that while Landsmål/Nynorsk had the form *soli* (the sun, *-i* being the definite article in the singular of strong feminine nouns) and Riksmål/Bokmål used *solen* (*-en* being the definite article), the South-East and most of the remaining part of the country used *sola* (with *-a* as the definite article). And the latter (*sola*) was a form that was not permitted under any circumstances in the two contemporary standards.

Another important factor that contributed to changing the political language situation between 1910 and 1920 was the evaluation of and view on the town dialects. Until about 1910 the Landsmål/Nynorsk movement had paid little attention to urban dialects. The common view, first expressed by Aasen, was that they were too influenced by Danish and by educated upper-class speech to be considered as 'Norwegian' dialects. And if they nonetheless were to be assessed as 'Norwegian', they would still be so debilitated that they would have little or nothing to contribute to the standardization of the written language. This view coincided with the tenets of Riksmål/Bokmål people as regards these urban dialects. Riksmål/Bokmål advocates commonly thought that these dialects were nothing but vulgar and sloppy varieties of Riksmål/Bokmål.

In 1911 the School Board of the town of Kristiansund decided that the pupils and the teachers in the primary schools of the town were to use Riksmål/Bokmål in oral instruction. This decision accorded with the dominant view among Riksmål/Bokmål supporters that the spoken language in the town was Riksmål/Bokmål on principle, although it was not always 'good and pure'. On the other hand, however, this decision caused an outcry, as the Landsmål/Nynorsk movement now claimed that low-status urban speech (the working class sociolects) were dialects in their own right on a par with the rural dialects and, therefore, that they were 'good' Norwegian dialects.[4] This dispute was brought to a political conclusion when the principles established in the Odelsting Decision of 1878 about the oral instruction in primary school were finally mentioned in the School Acts. In 1915 it appeared in the Act for Country Schools, and in 1917 the Act for Town Schools followed (cf. Jahr 1984).

A pan-Norwegian solution?

The conflict concerning the language to be used in oral instruction in schools introduced another important element into the language debate: the development of a language policy with a view to language unification, a pan-Norwegian solution.

In view of the bitter and unreconcilable tone of the language conflict by this time, it hardly comes as a surprise that other solutions were proposed in addition to those favored by the two chief antagonists: full victory to one of the two standards and, consequently, the defeat of its adversary. Would it not be possible to find a way out which did not imply the defeat of one of the two parties involved?

The idea itself strongly appealed to many. Some considered the antagonistic situation a threat to national unity. Was the nation to be divided into two entirely opposite camps in terms of language and culture (cf. the theory of the 'two cultures')?

It was one thing, however, to imagine a pan-Norwegian solution, but quite a different one to find a concrete language planning policy to arrive at such a result. In this respect, the eastern and the town dialects both seemed to lend themselves to serving as practical linguistic bridges between the opposite camps. Some claimed that the South-East region, with its linguistically more modern dialects than the western part of the country (the western part therefore having been especially important to Ivar Aasen's work), had a historical role to play in furnishing the written standards with sufficient linguistic material in

---

[4] It is worth mentioning that this change of view on the part of the Landsmål/Nynorsk movement was brought about mainly by the results of linguistic research. As early as 1907, the leading Norwegian dialectologist of the time, Amund B. Larsen (1849–1928), published a thorough monograph (Larsen 1907) on the working class dialect of Kristiania (Oslo). This study showed convincingly that this urban dialect was closely related to the rural dialects surrounding the capital, and not to upper-middle class Oslo speech. The early date of Amund B. Larsen's study of the Oslo dialect no doubt makes it unique, also as regards its status within international dialectology research. Later Larsen published additional studies of the dialects of Bergen (Larsen/Stoltz 1911–12) and Stavanger (Berntsen/Larsen 1925).

order to bridge the division between 'the western Landsmål/Nynorsk' and 'the urban Riksmål/Bokmål'.

The years between 1915 and 1917 saw a breakthrough in the Storting for the idea of a pan-Norwegian development. In these years, the MP Johan Gjøstein (1866–1935) of the Labor party agitated vigorously to give the working-class urban dialects in schools a protected status by law because – he insisted – these dialects, the workers' sociolects and not the posh upper-middle class speech, possessed the linguistic capacity to bridge the gap between Landsmål/Nynorsk and Riksmål/Bokmål. As mentioned above, protection by law was given to these low-status sociolects by Parliament in 1917. What is important here, however, is that previously unnoticed spoken varieties 'from below' – were now considered a possible basis for a linguistic reconciliation and the final merging of Landsmål/Nynorsk and Riksmål/Bokmål (cf. Jahr 1978, 1984).

A serious weakness of this analysis, not realized at all at the time, was the total absence of an understanding and appreciation of the important and underlying sociolinguistic differences between the two written standards, as well as between upper-middle class speech and the rural and urban popular dialects. The social distance was indeed far greater than the purely linguistic one.

The reform of 1917 – end of the first language planning period

The language reform of 1917 was in a way the first 'pan-Norwegian reform'. The Riksmål/Bokmål standard of 1917 was divided into two parts. One of them included no popular dialect forms, reflecting, however, upper-middle class speech almost completely and, thus, fulfilling Knud Knudsen's idea and program. The second part was considered extremely radical with frequent use of eastern popular dialectal forms and forms which coincided with those of Landsmål/Nynorsk.[5]

The language reform of 1917 represents the conclusion of the first language planning period, the period that focussed on creating a national written standard. With the reform of 1917, it was obvious that there now existed *two* standards which one could call Norwegian. And both of them were based on spoken varieties found within the boundaries of Norway.

In order to understand the fight that followed in the years after the 1917 reform, it is important to be aware of the fact that the two varieties of Riksmål/Bokmål were characteristic of opposite sides of the most salient

---

[5] Landsmål/Nynorsk, too, was divided into a more traditional – Aasen standard-like – and a more eastern based variety, but, in the case of Landsmål/Nynorsk, this was to be of little consequence compared to the turmoil created by the two Riksmål/Bokmål varieties.

sociolinguistic division of the Norwegian language community, i.e. that between educated upper-middle class speech on the one hand and all the local rural and urban dialects on the other. Linguistically and socially – the latter being the most important – the difference was less between Landsmål/Nynorsk and least traditional 1917 Riksmål/Bokmål than between the two Riksmål/Bokmål varieties.

We may therefore say that the social dimension of the conflict between Riksmål/Bokmål and Landsmål/Nynorsk until 1917 was present even *inside* the official Riksmål/Bokmål and was given expression in the two different varieties of that standard. The words employed by opponents regarding the 1917 reform leave little doubt that the reaction was solely based on a social and political assessment of what had been done to Riksmål/Bokmål by this reform. Nobody protested against 'the Norwegianization' of the Riksmål/Bokmål standard – which was given as a reason by the language planners who had prepared the reform – but against the 'vulgarization', the 'rape of our language', and the 'Bolshevikification' of the standard. These terms give a clear social message: with the low-status words and linguistic forms now introduced as optional (to the individual writer) in Riksmål/Bokmål, the political class struggle, represented by the Labor party and a growing working class, was being introduced as a wedge into the main written standard of the country. The least traditional so-called 'optional variety of Riksmål' represented different social classes more than the more traditional variety did. 'Culture' and 'education' were more under threat than ever, it was argued. Parallel to the Bolshevik political revolution in Russia in 1917, a sociolinguistic revolution 'from below' had taken place in Norway that same year.

That claim, however, was premature, since the sociolinguistic revolution did not occur until 1938, as we will see below.

New fronts

From 1917 onwards the language conflict split into two fronts. Thus, it became considerably more complicated than it had been previously. It is not surprising that the situation appeared totally confusing and intolerable to many people at the time. On the one hand, there was the continued competition between Riksmål/Bokmål and Landsmål/Nynorsk. On the other hand, there now appeared the inner contention in the Riksmål/Bokmål standard between a more traditional variety, which reflected educated upper-middle class everyday speech, and a sociolinguistically radical variety, which to a great extent was built on the popular forms of speech of the urban working class as well as on countryside dialects of south-eastern Norway.

The Riksmål/Bokmål movement, which grew considerably in number and strength after the reform of 1917, concentrated its opposition on the use – in their own standard – of the sociolinguistically radical (low-status) forms in the schools. According to the view of the Riksmål/Bokmål supporters, 'optional Riksmål' now posed a greater sociolinguistic threat than Landsmål/Nynorsk did. 'Optional Riksmål' could be compared to a guerilla army within the country itself, while Landsmål/Nynorsk was somewhat more like an invading army. Many municipalities all over the country opted for the use of the radical Riksmål/Bokmål variety, thinking this variety was more in keeping with the future of the Riksmål/Bokmål standard.

The first half of the 1920s thus was a period of severe language debate. The aftermath of the 1917 reform lasted until 1925–26, with the disagreement about the use of the Riksmål/Bokmål varieties in the schools. In many communities, people experienced language conflict for the first time, and in many places the struggle was hard and bitter. In some communities in the South-East, children were taken from one school district to a neighboring other in order to avoid 'optional Riksmål/Bokmål' as the language of instruction. Around 1926, however, this particular struggle died out, as economic problems gradually gained more importance and became the people's primary concern (cf. Jahr 1978).

The emergence of a socialist sociolinguistic theory of language planning

After the turmoil of the years following the 1917 reform, it was obvious that the nationalist ideology of the previous language planning period (up until 1917) was quite insufficient as a basis for a policy of developing one amalgamated written pan-Norwegian standard, which was now the expressed goal of a clear majority in Parliament.

What was needed was an analysis of the situation, resulting in a theory of language planning aimed at crossing the major sociolinguistic borderline between popular and upper-middle-class speech, i.e. defining the general popular dialects as the linguistic foundation on which Riksmål/Bokmål as well as Landsmål/Nynorsk should be based, while at the same time singling out which popular dialects to use as a means of bridging the gap between the two standards. The analysis and theory required in the 1920s and early 1930s supplied by the growing Labor party.

Ever since the formation of the Norwegian political parties in the 1870s and 1880s, Venstre had been the Landsmål/Nynorsk party, while Høyre (conservative) supported the Riksmål/Bokmål cause. However, the Labor party, which grew stronger and more powerful in each successive election, tried at length to avoid taking a stand in the language question. Officially, the party was neutral and allowed its representatives to vote according to their own liking. In reality, this meant that the Labor party representatives most frequently sided with Riksmål/Bokmål.

In the 1920s there was a development within the Labor party which was to have important consequences for further language planning in the 1930s. In 1920, Halvdan Koht (1873–1965), a professor of history and later Foreign Minister in the Labor government of 1935, was assigned by the party to review the language question, which was to serve as the basis for internal party discussions.

The report was issued in 1921 (Koht 1921), and Koht's main conclusion was that the Labor party should enter a passage to further 'the people's language' in both standards Nynorsk and Bokmål alike in the party program. Koht developed an analysis in which the language situation and the question of language and social class were seen as an integral part of Norwegian history. He and, later, the Labor party focused on promoting what they called 'People's Language' (*folkemål*). This vague concept was claimed to refer to a linguistic reality, an existing, systematic and unifying core in the popular urban and rural dialects. On this core, it was claimed, a pan-Norwegian standard could be founded. This pan-Norwegian standard was termed *Samnorsk*. Samnorsk, then, was understood to be representing the common linguistic system believed to unite all varieties of spoken popular Norwegian, urban as well as rural (but not upper-middle class speech).

In Professor Koht's analysis this sociolinguistic understanding of the situation is fundamental. Koht argued that the only solution to the linguistic question was a socio-political one in which the lower classes of workers and peasants should influence both written standards by introducing increasing amounts of present-day popular speech (reflecting popular phonology, morphology, and lexis) to both of them. The standards would thus, it was claimed, by degrees move towards a fusion and, in the same process, demote and devalue the spoken variety of the upper-middle classes. This demotion of upper-middle class speech was absolutely necessary in order for an amalgamated written standard to emerge and gain the required social status in society, being, as it would be, full of wordforms and morphology usually considered vulgar and low-status by the upper-middle classes.

Halvdan Koht considered contemporary Nynorsk as being too archaic, too removed from present-day popular speech, and Bokmål as too dependent on upper-middle-class speech. By making Nynorsk linguistically more modern by relying more on south-eastern dialects and working class sociolects of the towns, and at the same time – by the same linguistic means – making Bokmål more democratic, less upper-middle class, one could develop a pan-Norwegian, *Samnorsk*, standard.

Koht's conclusion was that the Labor party should include a passage of support for a language planning policy that would further the 'People's Language' in both Nynorsk and Bokmål in the party's program. As he put it: "The struggle to advance the People's Language is the cultural side of the rise of the workers." (On Koht, see Jahr 1992a).

The result of this process was that the Labor party in the early 1930s agreed with the principal view expressed by Koht: a pan-Norwegian standard achieved by an opening up of both the written standards to the same popular forms and features from the rural and urban dialects. (On the Labor party and the language question, see Jahr 1992b).

The language reform of 1938 was consistent with the ideology and sociolinguistic analysis of Halvdan Koht and of the now ruling Labor party, which had been in power since 1935, and with the declared aim of Parliament to pursue the development of pan-Norwegian.

The most prestigious spoken variety in the country was demoted socially by this reform, thereby given a considerably less important role in relation to written Bokmål. Those speakers who were used to consider their own spoken variety to be 'correct', 'nice', and 'proper' no longer could rely solely on their own speech if they were to write Bokmål correctly. Supporters of the (traditional) 1917 Riksmål/Bokmål standard considered the 1938 reform to be an outrage against what they reckoned to be *their* written language. From this point on they termed the written standard they wanted to return to 'Riksmål' (thereby referring to the traditional Riksmål/Bokmål variety of 1917) as opposed to the official 1938 Bokmål standard.[6]

In short, the 1938 reform was viewed and perceived by the 'Riksmål' supporters, and quite rightly so, as a sociolinguistic revolution 'from below'.

Consequences of World War II for the Nynorsk movement

With the Nazi occupation (1940–45) and the events of those years, we can say that the new Norway, the Norway of 1814, completed the building of the nation. The Norwegian nation proved its existence during five hard and difficult years. During the war the question about national attitude had very little to do with a person's linguistic preferences. Bokmål and Nynorsk users proved to be equally good Norwegians. The Nynorsk movement was rendered fairly destitute after the war, despite the huge advance of Nynorsk in the schools between 1938 (22%) and 1943 (34%). The argument that, because of its origin, Nynorsk was more 'Norwegian' than Bokmål – and that therefore those who used and

---

[6]   I will use 'Riksmål' in this way from now on.

supported Nynorsk were more national than those who did not – could no longer serve as a viable argument after the war. The Nynorsk movement thereby lost its most effective recruitment argument up until then (cf. Jahr 1989).

A consequence of this appeared after a few post-war years with a major setback for Nynorsk in the schools and problems for the Nynorsk movement to find convincing arguments to use in the language debate. Instead, there arose an internal and long-lasting conflict within the Nynorsk movement. In reality, it was divided into conflicting branches for many years. With rapid decline of Nynorsk in the schools, and the difficulty to argue effectively in favor of Nynorsk in society at large, a growing number of Nynorsk supporters found it important to try to secure as much as possible of the Nynorsk standard in a future pan-Norwegian standard. The war had created the attitudes necessary for stimulating cooperation and joint efforts in general, and a poll held in 1946 showed that a massive majority of the population supported the development towards pan-Norwegian (Samnorsk). However, strong opposition to such a development soon evolved, too.

The postwar struggle to reverse
the Bokmål sociolinguistic revolution of 1938

During the war, the organization of the traditional Riksmål supporters, Riksmålsforbundet, disgraced itself by making an appeal to Quisling's Nazi government to abolish the 1938 language reform (Fløgstad 2004). This, however, did not happen. Instead, the government introduced its own 'spelling' reform in 1941. It came to exert little influence on how people actually spelled during the war, even though the nazified larger newpapers and dailies adopted it. In the schools it was largely seen sabotaged.

After the war, the poet Arnulf Øverland (1889–1968) reestablished the Riksmål movement. For this it proved important that Øverland was acknowlegded as an ideological war hero of the national resistance. Now he organized the battle, not against Nynorsk, which – and this was new – he accepted as a fully developed standard of culture, but rather against the idea of a pan-Norwegian standard, against *Samnorsk*. The very word itself, *Samnorsk*, soon came to signify the non-conservative Bokmål standard of 1938, the variety of Bokmål which included all the popular ('People's Language') low-status dialect forms (the more official term was 'Radical Bokmål'). The term *Samnorsk* thereby assumed a new meaning, signifying an already existing and official variety of one of the two standards – and not a future pan-Norwegian solution, as had been the pre-war meaning of *Samnorsk*. It was against the use in school of this type of Radical Bokmål that the attacks were directed from the late 1940s onwards. The fight to restore the lost norm position of upper-middle class speech – a sociolinguistic counter-revolution – had begun.

The Riksmål supporters could neither conceive nor accept that the written standard they considered to be *their* language no longer allowed forms they were taught to consider correct, educated, and proper. They saw it as totally unacceptable that the now official written Bokmål standard required their children in school to write words and linguistic forms they had always considered 'sloppy', 'ugly', or even 'vulgar'. That their view meant a social downgrading of speakers who used these declared 'vulgar' forms in their everyday speech was something they could not or would not see nor accept. The Riksmål movement resented the political aim of Halvdan Koht and the Labor party – to promote in writing exactly those forms used in everyday speech by a vast majority of the Norwegian people. To the Riksmål activists the struggle was a fight for freedom against the state's policy of dictating their language and for what they termed a 'free development of language' (*fri sprogutvikling*). For them free development meant a development where the State and the political authorities were not involved in language planning at all. That such a situation would exclusively favor and benefit high-status linguistic forms, i.e. forms used in their upper-middle class speech, was something they were not at all willing to admit. The sociolinguistic content of the fight was obvious, but not at all accepted by those who objected to the Bokmål standard of 1938.

The Riksmål opposition against the low-status ('radical') forms in school books was formidable and appeared in many disguises. 'The Parents' campaign against Samnorsk' (from 1951) was organized from the western part of Oslo but received support for its campaigns from large areas of the country. Action took on many forms: letters to editors, posters or newspaper ads, petitions and demonstrations. In 1953 they initiated a 'correction' of school textbooks. This was done in pen by the parents and mostly concerned pupils in the western parts of Oslo.

The language conflict of the 1950s was both hard and intense and not all the means employed in the struggle were equally fair. For instance, the associations were less than pleasant when, only a decade after the Nazi atrocities, Riksmål supporters made bonfires of school textbooks because they were written in the radical variety of the Bokmål standard.

Even though the Riksmål advocates at the time did not always understand that their cause was steadily winning ground, the fact was that the high level of activity and the vast resources employed by business and private persons paid off in the long run. The repeated and lasting attacks on and incursions against the authorities in the language question caused the ruling party of government, the Labor party, gradually to see its identification with the Samnorsk policy as a negative factor.

That this was the result was partly due to the fact that the Riksmål movement was allowed to dominate the scene in the 1950s and early 1960s. The Nynorsk movement was busily occupied with its own affairs during these years, and the supporters of Samnorsk did not assemble its forces in one effective organisation. The 1950s was a time when political and social considerations in the language question were less in the forefront of the debate. Thus, the only argument left to support the official Samnorsk policy was the practical and economic one: it was too costly and problematic in such a small country to maintain two national language standards of writing. However, this practical argument, even though put forward with enthusiasm by many, was far from sufficient to withstand the much more varied arguments offered by the Riksmål movement: they defended the written tradition dating from the great Norwegian authors of the 19th century (including the playwright Henrik Ibsen and the Nobel laureate Bjørnstjerne Bjørnson), and they launched severe attacks on the popular forms of language in Bokmål as being 'vulgar'. They pointed out that the radical forms often were left standing alone as alien elements in the text, imported or 'borrowed' into the language and could offer striking examples, as they saw it, of bad stylistic judgments found in the school textbooks and readers. And they emerged as defenders of the individual's right to choose his or her freedom of language, a right they argued the State was depriving them of.

Termination of the pan-Norwegian policy

A textbook standard launched in 1959 outwardly signalled that the policy of unification would continue. In reality, however, the battle about the firmly controlled development towards a pan-Norwegian standard based on the 'people's language' was now lost. Things were happening behind the scenes. What counted most was the fact that the Labor party wanted to get out of a binding stand in the pan-Norwegian question. The political right and private enterprise supported the Riksmål movement economically. The language question was in effect the only topic where the political opposition could effectively attack the Labor government, which had a clear majority in Parliament through the 1950s. And without active support from the Labor party, the daring 1938 sociolinguistic experiment of changing the norm basis for written Bokmål from upper-middle class speech to the 'People's Language' was doomed to come to a halt. In the long run the sociolinguistic revolution proved difficult to defend.

The development of the reaction that started in the 1950s, and which led to the formation of an official 'committee for language peace' in the 1960s and to the establishment of a Norwegian Language Council in the 1970s, got its final result in the Bokmål reforms of 1981 and 2005. The authorities have now officially terminated the language planning policy aiming at a pan-Norwegian solution. In a report to Parliament in 2001, the government declared that the pan-Norwegian (the Samnorsk) policy had been a failure and that it should no longer be pursued politically. With this resolution the much weakened Riksmål movement (weakened partly as a result of the reform of 1981) gained a victory the supporters of Riksmål in the 1950s could only have dreamed of. Nonetheless, it was the work carried out in the 1950s and early 1960s that finally rendered the outcome they wanted. The sociolinguistic experiment with elements 'from below' being elevated into Bokmål did not in the long run achieve the necessary political and public support, and it has therefore been aborted.

The second language planning period of modern Norway ends with the report to Parliament about the termination of the pan-Norwegian policy and the 2005 reform of Bokmål. This second period (1917–2001/2005) saw the attempt to resolve the problem with two national written standards – created in the first period (1814–1917). The means employed – elevating linguistic materials 'from below' in Bokmål failed in the end. The fight had been concentrated mainly on the written Bokmål standard; here the sociolinguistic counter-revolution succeeded.

A new platform for Nynorsk

Towards the end of the 1960s, and also during the 1970s, the Nynorsk movement finally found a platform of arguments on which to stand. A new generation of eager Nynorsk activists now assumed power in the movement. Alongside the philosophy connected to the events of 1968 in particular, the results provided by the developing new branches of linguistics – sociolinguistics, sociology of language, psycholinguistics – furnished the Nynorsk movement with new arguments. In the mid 1970s, then, the decline of written Nynorsk in the schools stopped, and later the percentage of usage more or less stabilized at around 16%.

With the termination of the pan-Norwegian policy and the sociolinguistic experiment of 1938, the Nynorsk supporters can claim today that Nynorsk more or less is the only option for those interested in supporting the 'people's language' 'from below'. This in a way represents a return to the situation of the 19th century and to the competition between Landsmål/Nynorsk and Riksmål/Bokmål, but with the one and very important difference that the then politically effective nationalist argument has no effect whatsoever today. Nynorsk's function as part of a cultural counter-movement 'from below' – or representing the periphery, the local communities, versus the center and Oslo especially – is an important aspect of the linguistic situation today.

A lasting result of the sociolinguistic experiment of 1938

Thus, in the end did no lasting result whatsoever come from the unique sociolinguistic experiment of 1938?

One very important sociolinguistic result can be observed and appreciated in the Norwegian society today, which, no doubt, Halvdan Koht himself would have welcomed; it concerns the obvious demotion of upper-middle class Oslo speech as a model for other speakers that has taken place since 1938. In the mid-war period, upper-middle class Oslo speech was the only standardizing target. Today, however, virtually nobody would look to that particular spoken variety as a model to copy. From being more or less accepted by many, perhaps a majority of Norwegians, as standard spoken Norwegian, it is now perceived much more as just one of the many spoken varieties of Norwegian – albeit one of the more prestigious ones. It is not perceived any longer, as was previously the case, as a neutral, unmarked spoken standard variety. This function has been taken over by a variety reflecting official written standard Bokmål instead, especially as regards morphology and root forms of some frequently used words. Since 1938 official written standard Bokmål in its most frequently used form has gradually increased its importance as a target and a norm for those who, for some reason, want to standardize their speech. Standardization of speech is, however, not at all common in Norway and, as mentioned earlier, not demanded from pupils in school. While upper-middle-class Oslo speech between 1917 and 1938 served as the main target variety for standardized speech – especially because it corresponded so closely to the written Riksmål/Bokmål standard during that period –, this is no longer the case. Therefore, while in many respects the *written* Bokmål standard can be claimed to have been restored to a pre-1938 position by the language reforms of 1981 and 2005, the status of upper-middle-class Oslo *speech* as 'Standard Spoken Norwegian' seems to have been definitively lost. This, certainly, is a long-term sociolinguistic effect of the daring 1938 experiment of politically wanted and planned linguistic changes 'from below'.

References

Aasen, Ivar. 1909. Om vort skriftsprog. [On our written language]. *Syn og Segn* 17, 1–5.

Aasen, Ivar. 1848. *Det norske Folkesprogs Grammatik* [Grammar of the popular language in Norway]. Kristiania [Oslo]: Feilberg & Landmark.

Aasen, Ivar. 1850. *Ordbog over det norske Folkesprog* [Dictionary of the popular language in Norway]. Kristiania [Oslo]: Feilberg & Landmark.

Aasen, Ivar. 1864. *Norsk Grammatik* [Norwegian Grammar]. Christiania [Oslo]: Malling.

Aasen, Ivar. 1873. *Norsk Ordbog* [Norwegian Dictionary]. Christiania [Oslo]: Malling.

Berntsen, Mandius and Amund B. Larsen. 1925. *Stavanger Bymål* [The urban dialect of Stavanger]. Kristiania [Oslo]: Bymålslaget – Aschehoug. 2nd edition Oslo: Det Norske Samlaget, 1978.

Fløgstad, Kjartan. 2004. *Brennbart* [Inflammable]. Oslo: Gyldendal.

Garborg, Arne. 1877. *Den ny-norske Sprog- og Nationalitetsbevægelse* [The New Norwegian Language and National Movement]. Kristiania [Oslo]: Cammermeyer.

Garborg, Arne. 1900. Vor nationale situation [Our national situation]. *Samtiden* 11: 148–162.

Haugen, Einar. 1966. *Language Conflict and Language Planning: The Case of Modern Norwegian*. Cambridge: Harvard University Press.

Jahr, Ernst Håkon. 1978. *Østlandsmåla fram! Ei bok om rørsla Østlandsk reisning* [Forward with the dialects of Eastern Norway! A book on the movement *Østlandsk reisning*]. Tromsø, Oslo and Bergen: Universitetsforlaget.

Jahr, Ernst Håkon. 1984. *Talemålet i skolen. En studie av drøftinger og bestemmelser om muntlig språkbruk i folkeskolen (fra 1974 til 1925)* [Spoken language in (Norwegian) schools (from 1874 till 1925)]. Oslo: Novus.

Jahr, Ernst Håkon. 1989. *Utsyn over norsk språkhistorie etter 1814* [Overview of Norwegian language history from 1814]. 2nd rev. edition Oslo: Novus, 1994.

Jahr, Ernst Håkon. 1992a. Halvdan Koht og språkstriden [Halvdan Koht and the language struggle.] In Ernst Håkon Jahr (eds.), *Innhogg i nyare norsk språkhistorie* [Insights into recent Norwegian language history]. Oslo: Novus, 69–81.

Jahr, Ernst Håkon. 1992b. DNA og samnorskpolitikken [The Labor Party and the Pan Norwegian language policy]. In Ernst Håkon Jahr (eds.), *Innhogg i nyare norsk språkhistorie* [Insights into recent Norwegian language history]. Oslo: Novus, 114–24.

Jahr, Ernst Håkon. 1994. See Jahr 1989.

Jahr, Ernst Håkon. 1997. On the use of dialects in Norway. In Heinrich Ramisch and Kenneth Wynne (eds.), *Language in Time and Space. A Festschrift for Wolfgang Viereck on His Sixtieth Birthday, 4 September 1997*. Stuttgart: Steiner, 363–369. [Repr. Klára Sándor (ed.) 2001. *Issues on language cultivation*. Szeged: Juhász Gyula University Press, 75–84.]

Knudsen, Knud. 1887. *Kortfattet redegjørelse for det dansknorske målstræv* [Short account of the strive for a Danish-Norwegian language]. Kristiania [Oslo].

Koht, Halvdan. 1921. *Arbeidarreising og målspørsmål* [Working class uprising and language issues]. Kristiania [Oslo]: Det Norske Arbeiderpartis Forlag.

Larsen, Amund B. 1907. *Kristiania bymål. Vulgærsproget med henblik på den utvungne dagligtale* [The urban dialect of Oslo]. Kristiania [Oslo]: Cammermeyer.

Larsen, Amund B. and Gerhard Stoltz. 1911–12. *Bergen bymål* [The urban dialect of Bergen]. Kristiania [Oslo]: Bymålslaget – Aschehoug.

Trudgill, Peter. 1986. *Dialects in contact*. Oxford: Blackwell.

PÉTER MAITZ (DEBRECEN)

The death of Standard German in 19th-century Budapest. A case study on the role of linguistic ideologies in language shift[1]

1. Linguistic ideologies

By the term 'linguistic ideology' I mean the comprehensive system of collective notions and values of a given period, culture, or speech community within this culture that fundamentally determines the view on questions connected to language (such as the evaluation of languages and language varieties, language use and its preferred or stigmatized forms, multilingualism etc.). Linguistic ideology in this sense provides a certain collective framework of thinking on language. Since it is itself dependent on the given temporal and cultural context, the inherent process of thinking and the very knowledge borne out of it – be this either scientific or naïve – are society- and culture-specific; and they change historically (cf. Barnes, Bloor and Henry 1996). Susan Gal defines the concept of 'linguistic ideology' in a similar vein:

> Linguistic ideologies are the culturally specific notions which participants and observers bring to language, the ideas they have about what language is good for, what linguistic differences mean about the speakers who use them, why there are linguistic differences at all. Both ordinary people and social scientists – linguists, sociologists, anthropologists – hold language ideologies. (Gal 2002a: 197)

However, linguistic ideologies determine not only the subjective views of the speakers on language and language use. It is even more important for our present purposes that these subjective views and opinions on language serve also as a basis for the decisions pertaining to the speakers' language use. From all this the significance of linguistic ideologies for sociolinguistic research inevitably follows: linguistic ideologies play a key role in speakers' decisions about language use and, hence, in speakers' language behaviour. In the present

---

1 The present study was written with the support of the Bolyai Scholarship kindly granted by the Hungarian Academy of Sciences.

article, by discussing one example of a language contact situation, I attempt to demonstrate that linguistic ideologies bear particular significance for the speakers' evaluation of linguistic structures or languages, language varieties and, at the same time, also for their language choice, for instances of language shift and even for language maintenance.

One such dominant linguistic ideology in nineteenth-century Europe was *linguistic nationalism*. This ideology evoked the concept of the 'national language', a common and unified language, which was considered not only as one of the most important symbols, but also as a cohesive force of the nation by the bourgeois society of the period (cf. Edwards 1985: 23ff.). This connection of nation and language made language and language use one of the central questions of politics and public life in the contemporary Hungarian and several other European national societies and also a topic in politics and jurisdiction. Thus, linguistic nationalism became an important issue to all classes of the population.

Sociolinguistic literature and literature related to the history of language has dealt extensively with the question and the significance of nationalism and with its linguistic projections over the last decades (cf. e.g. Edwards 1985, Fishman 1989, Barbour and Carmichael, 2000, Gal 2002a etc.). The perhaps most systematic analysis of German and other nations' linguistic nationalism was published by Andreas Gardt (1999, 2000). The operation and con-sequences of this specific linguistic ideology in a concrete historical language contact and conflict situation and in the language use of concrete speech communities, however, have not been investigated in much detail up to the present. In this respect, my paper is an attempt at investigating the change in the social status of standard German[2] and the causes of its death in nineteenth-century Budapest.

In the first section of my paper, I sketch out the problem, the object of the investigation, and its methods and aims. In the second section, I outline the representative data which show the change in the status of standard German in nineteenth-century Hungary. I am going to analyse the role of linguistic nationalism and how it became important for the subsequent changes pertaining to its status. In section 3 I briefly sketch the historical antecedents and the status and ideological environment of German in the preceding decades. In section 4 I attempt to reconstruct the causal relations between the changes and linguistic nationalism as presented in chapter two.

---

[2]   By the term 'standard German' I mean a prestigious high variety of German orientated towards written language and used foremost by bourgeois speakers.

2. The problem

There had been a several decade long tradition in nineteenth-century[3] Hungary of using German as a mother tongue, including its different standard and non-standard varieties. Moreover, in the standard domains of communication (both oral and literal) German had been the dominant variety for centuries – initially alongside Latin, then instead of it. This astonishingly asymmetrical bilingual situation – astonishing at least to the present – is well-exemplified in the determining role of standard German in one of the typically standard-oriented domains of urban language use: the theatre. At the beginning of the nineteenth century, there were already several German-speaking theatres in Budapest.[4] And in 1812 the continent's most monumental German theatre opened also here in the Hungarian capital: the theatre of Pest housing an audience of 3500 (!) men (cf. Belitska-Scholtz and Somorjai 1995: 14ff., Klemm 1998: 256).

However, in the second half of the nineteenth century, this bilingual situation changed rapidly; moreover, it took a reverse order. Accordingly, the *status* of standard German, i.e. (a) *its social prestige* and (b) *its usage* underwent radical changes. Its social prestige not only decreased, but it turned straight into a stigma. The community speaking this variety thus reached the last stage of language shift.[5] So, for the second half of the nineteenth century, German-Hungarian bilingualism, seemingly stable for decades, became definitely unsteady and, in the course of some generations, ended up in language shift. The theatre of Pest, which burnt down for the second time in 1889, was not even restored. Furthermore, as a result of the more and more

---

3   Based on the practice attributed to periods already widespread in historical social sciences, I use the term 'nineteenth century' as a historical period of language in the sense of 'the long nineteenth century of Europe', that is the period between the French Revolution and the First World War.

4   Budapest, in an administrative sense, i.e. de jure, came into existence in 1873, based on an act passed in 1872 via the union of the previously independent settlements: Buda, Pest and Óbuda. In my paper I use the name Budapest for the sake of simplicity also in cases where I talk about the preceding period, i.e. about the not yet unified Pest-Buda.

5   We cannot talk about similar radical changes pertaining to status in the case of the German dialects in Hungary neither with respect to language use nor to social prestige. During the seventeenth and eighteenth centuries, in the rural, peasant speech communities established as a result of organized settlement operations, the dialects preserved – in most of the cases – their vernacular function in the analyzed period. Similarly, their social prestige did not change either: they were non-prestigious varieties in the previous centuries and they remained the same in the analyzed period. To the circumstances related to the establishments of these peasant speech communities see Manherz (ed. 1998), to the status of German dialects in Hungary in the eighteenth-nineteenth centuries see Hutterer (1961) and Maitz (2005).

violent protests against the German-speaking theatre, there was not a single permanent German-speaking theatre in the Hungarian capital left by the end of the nineteenth century. The Hungarian theatre, on the other hand, was in its glory (Klemm 260ff., Pukánszky 2000/1940: 87ff.).

In this paper I wish to show that the quick and radical change outlined above was ultimately based on a new linguistic ideology that was domineering Hungarian society in the nineteenth century, i.e. in linguistic nationalism. I implicitly want to argue – in line with Fishman (1971) and Gal (2002b) – that we cannot understand the changes connected to the social prestige and usage of languages and varieties nor the phenomenon of language shift and its causal relation *without* investigating and understanding both the outer and quasi objective sociological background and the subjective, mental factors and cognitive processes determining the language use of a speech community's members.

3. The data

3.1. Quantitative changes in language use

In nineteenth-century Hungary, standard German was spoken as a mother tongue first and foremost by the *bourgeoisie*[6] of German or Austrian origin and not least by those of Jewish origin. This German-speaking bourgeoisie concentrated primarily in towns, and it was a decisive part of the population of the capital Budapest, being still multilingual at that time. When studying the quantitative changes of German used as a mother tongue in nineteenth-century Budapest in the light of the contemporary census-data, these data – according to the above delineated points – will chiefly illustrate the customs of language choice and usage of the bourgeoisie speaking standard German.

A look at the contemporary linguistic statistical data shows that within the total population of Budapest, only in the last third of the nineteenth century, between 1880 and 1920 – so in not more than 40 years' time –, the number of people speaking German as a mother tongue was reduced to half its speakers (from 122,454 to 60,425) – as opposed to the rise in the previous decades (Figure 1).

---

6 I use the term 'bourgeoisie' as a synonym for the German 'Bürgertum'. Here I would not attempt to define precisely the social formation denoted by this term as there is not yet a consensus on it in historical science. Let me just refer to the work by Angelika Linke (1996), which investigates this problem during a comprehensive reconstruction of the language culture of the nineteenth-century German bourgeoisie.

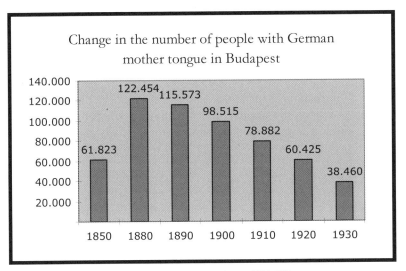

Figure 1 (based on Fónagy 1998: 78)

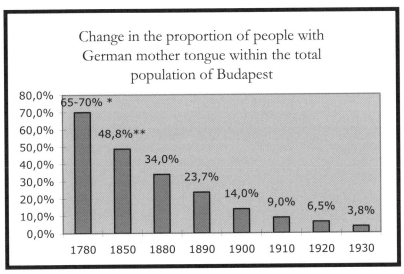

* Based on estimates in the area of today's Budapest (cf. Berza 1993: 182)
** Equals the proportion of speakers with German nationality

Figure 2 (based on Fónagy 1998: 78)

The proportion of Germans within the total population of the capital shows an even quicker and more radical decline (Figure 2). While in 1880 the 122.454 speakers encompassed 34% of the total population of the capital, in 1920 the 60.425 speakers with German as their mother tongue represented only 6.5% of the population. This regression cannot be explained by migration or the rise in mortality. In order to understand the causes of the processes underlying these tendencies, we have to consider that the absolute number as well as the proportion of the Hungarian population rose in a similarly significant fashion in the same period: between 1870 and 1910 it rose from 46% to 85.9% alone (Karády and Kozma 2002: 52).

These numbers indicate that another phenomenon was behind the changes: *language shift*. Based on Weinreich's (1953: 68) classical definition, we can thus state that – in the analyzed period – a significant part of the traditionally German-speaking Budapest bourgeoisie replaced its habitual use of German with Hungarian.

3.2. Changes in the social status of German

As I have mentioned earlier, significant changes in the linguistic consciousness of the contemporary Hungarian society happened parallel to changes in their language use. One could list a multitude of contemporary language reflections to see that standard German did not only lose most of its speakers, but also lost its social prestige during the second half of the nineteenth century. It became a stigmatized language variety within the Hungarian bourgeoisie, both within the Hungarian (being already the majority) and the German speech community. Here two relevant metalinguistic data shall suffice to demonstrate this stigmatisation.[7]

Let us first have a look at the – not at all unique – example of *Jenő Rákosi* (1842–1929), who was one of the most influential personalities of Hungary's intellectual life. Rákosi was born into a family of German origin and with German as his mother tongue in a little village in Western Hungary. His secondary, institutional language socialization was later determined by German-Hungarian bilingualism, and, in the course of a few decades, he shifted from German to Hungarian. This was complete to such an extent that he later – with the permission of the Home Secretary – changed his German

---

7   For further examples and relevant empirical analyses see Maitz (2005) and Maitz/Molnár (2004).

family name (*Kremsner*) to the Hungarian *Rákosi*.[8] We also know that, as a famous Budapest writer and journalist, he considered German to be the biggest danger to Hungarian (cf. Pukánszky 2000: 86ff.). For instance, he was an active member of the contemporary Hungarian language purist movement, the primary targets of which were the numerous German loanwords having entered Hungarian as a result of language contact over several preceding centuries. Rákosi's thoughts given below are significant, since they illustrate a changed social prestige of German. Here, a German-speaking bourgeois no longer acts as a member of the German speech community in the interest and in defence of German, but he clearly articulates the necessity of use and protection of Hungarian:

(1)   [...] a faji jelleget ember és nemzet a nyelvétől kapja [...] a magyar fajt a magyar nyelv termeli nagyban és kicsinyben egyaránt [...] mindent a világon, minden egyéb, ha még oly fontos érdeket is, a nyelv érdekének kell alája rendelnünk.

'[...] man and nation get its racial character from language, [...] the Hungarian race is produced both on a macro and micro level by the Hungarian language, [...] everything in the world and each serious interest whatsoever has to be subordinated to language.' (cited in Pukánszky loc. cit.: 84ff., my translation – P.M.)

The lines below are from a popular contemporary Hungarian etiquette-manuals. Here, we can clearly observe an unambiguously negative attitude towards German that was characteristic of the Hungarian society in the nineteenth century:

(2)   Nézzük ezzel szemben a német nyelvet, mennyire meglátszik rajta, hogy részben a tudósok katedráin, részben a kaszárnyákban fejlődött ki. Unalmas, száraz, nehézkes, szintelen, elvesznek benne a gondolatok s erővel teljes csak akkor tud lenni, mikor – parancsol. S ha van némelyik költőjükben és esztétikusukban némi báj és finomság, az bizonyára francia hatásra termett.

---

8   Rákosi's is by no means an exceptional case. Only within the fifty years between 1867 and 1918 74.500 similar applications – aiming at changing the family name – were approved in Hungary (cf. Karády/ Kozma 2002: 49). The majority of the family names were German, with the majority of the applicants being of German or Jewish origin and having a German or Yiddish variety as their mother-tongue (loc. cit. 52ff). (The Hungarian Jews had German family and first names thanks to Joseph the Second's 1787 decree.) As far as I know, among the European countries only Finland experienced a similar change in family names to such a large extent during the first decades of the twentieth century (cf. Paikkala 1997). Here, on the 12th of May 1906, during the so-called 'Great Name Changing Day' alone, approx. 25000 Finnish citizens changed their Swedish family names to Finnish. (I would like to thank Agnete Nesse (Bodø), who drew my attention to this Hungarian-Finnish parallel.)

'Let us compare our findings with *the German language*. How obvious it is that it was developed in lecterns and barracks. *It is boring, dry, awkward, colourless, thoughts are lost in it. And it only has power when giving orders*. If a few of its poets and aestheticians should possess any charm and gentility at all, it is only due to French influence.' (Gonda 1920: 162ff., my translation – P.M., emphasis added)

But what is the reason for such a quick and radical decay in the status of German in the second half of the nineteenth century? What is the explanation for the language shift of the German-speaking Budapest bourgeoisie within a few decades and the parallel stigmatization of standard German? Since in the framework of the present study there is no opportunity for a wide-ranging and coherent sociolinguistic explanation, I will confine myself to the following subproblem: which role did linguistic nationalism play as a linguistic ideology regarding the radical decline in the social prestige of German and in the language shift of the German-speaking bourgeoisie in nineteenth-century Budapest?

In order to provide an adequate answer, it is necessary to first shed some light on the antecedents related to the social and intellectual history of the period.

4. German and its speakers before the nineteenth century

The German-speaking bourgeoisie of the nineteenth century in Budapest and Hungary's other towns came to Hungary mainly during the course of medieval migration processes, during the so-called 'Ostkolonisation' from the 12th century onwards. Thus, Germans settled in an age when the Hungarian society was a *feudal* one. As it is known, one of the main characteristics of this social form – as opposed to modern civil societies – is that it was basically not founded on ethnical or linguistic grounds, but on dynastic, partly religious and along social and feudal grounds. In other words, the status of an individual in a particular society was not determined by his or her belonging to one ethnic group or speech community, but rather by being a member of the aristocracy, bourgeoisie, or serfdom (Niederhauser 2000: 175). According to this view, at that time the belonging to different speech communities did not automatically imply an affiliation to different interest groups – language had not yet attained the status of a primacy social marker. The state did not intervene in questions on language use, and so we cannot yet talk about institutional language policy in those centuries.

All this shows that belonging to a *German* speech community in *Hungary* in the Middle Ages and in the Early Modern Period was not automatically a source of conflict at all, and why sources from that period did not address ethnic or language conflicts (loc. cit. 175ff.). We can state instead that anybody who wanted to be *a Hungarian patriot* was free to do so and become a part of the feudal Hungarian society, i.e. to become *Hungarian* with respect to his or her social identity after the settlement of the German-speaking urban bourgeoisie (e.g. Budapest bourgeoisie).

Social identity and state patriotism was established in the circle of the German-speaking urban bourgeoisie at the end of the eighteenth century, and as such at the beginning of a century under the banner of *nationalism*. However, after the Enlightenment the situation of the German-speaking bourgeoisie in Hungary outlined above changed radically. In the following I will investigate to what extent this new political and thus linguistic ideology contributed to the stigmatization of German and to the decline of its social prestige and usage.

5. Linguistic nationalism, identity, and language shift in the nineteenth century

From the very beginning, nationalism was connected with the question of language – which was primarily due to the impact of the German romantic philosophy and by thinkers such as Johann Gottfried Herder in particular. The European ideal of 'one nation – one language' was also established in Hungary, and one of the key notions of the contemporary national discourse, the 'national language', was formed. This national language was embodied in the codified standard Hungarian; and in this unified national language and language unity, Hungarian society saw one of the most important factors for an establishment of national unity and national ascension. Consequently, territorial multilingualism, having presented no problems in the previous centuries, gradually became abnormal, was labelled harmful, and provoked several national language conflicts. Due to these conflicts, the multilingual Habsburg Monarchy – Hungary being still part of it – gradually turned into a time bomb (and, as it is known, the bomb indeed exploded).

The non-Hungarian languages and various varieties that were spoken in Hungary at that time were stigmatized by Hungarian society, since they posed a potential threat to national language unity and the purity of a national language, according to the prevailing purist view. This view of linguistic nationalism is the primary reason for the radical decrease in the social prestige of German as it was spoken by the Budapest bourgeoisie of German and Jewish origin in nineteenth-century Hungary. But its stigmatization was also reinforced by two further factors.

One of them is that in his famous work *Ideen zur Philosophie der Geschichte der Menschheit* Herder hinted at the possible death of Hungarian.

This statement was fiercly discussed in nineteenth-century Hungary: it became one of the major reference points of the contemporary language policy and language cultivation, and, naturally, it aggrevated the negative attitudes that were connected with non-Hungarian languages and varieties (as potential trouble sources for the union of nation and the national language). The sentence in its original context runs as follows:

> Das einzige Volk, das aus diesem Stamm sich unter die Eroberer gedrängt hat, sind die Ungarn oder Madjaren. [...] Da sind sie jetzt unter Slawen, Deutschen, Wlachen und andern Völkern der geringere Teil der Landeseinwohner, und *nach Jahrhunderten wird man vielleicht ihre Sprache kaum finden.*

> 'The only people from this tribe [i.e. the 'Finnish tribe' – P. M.] who managed to become conquerors are the Hungarians or Magyars. [...] They are now among Slavs, Germans, Vlachs and other peoples a minority in their own country, and *in a few centuries their language will probably be lost.*' (Herder 1989: 688, emphasis added)

Apart from this, there was significant subversive potential lurking behind the negative Hungarian attitude towards German (cf. Glatz 1974: 255ff.). The former 150-year-long Turkish oppression was replaced by a Habsburg oppression at the end of the seventeenth century, and the country became yet another minor part of a superior Habsburg Empire. The oppression obviously also affected language rights. The Viennese Court – partly as a manifestation of its own linguistic nationalism – observed assimilatory language policies, aiming at the eventual supremacy of German. One major step towards this was taken in 1784, when Joseph II made German the official language of the Empire. And it is no wonder that, after Emperor Franz Joseph II. had put down the Hungarian War of Independence in 1849 at the peak of his reign, German antipathy was rooted in the Habsburg oppression throughout the nineteenth century. Thus, it were first and foremost these two factors, rooted in linguistic nationalism, that provide explanation for the negative attitudes connected with German on the part of the Hungarian speech community outlined in (2).

But how and why did the status of German decrease among its own speakers, in the circles of the German-speaking urban bourgeoisie? To what extent did linguistic nationalism contribute to the changes of (a) their language attitudes and through this to that of (b) their language behaviour, that is to their language shift? In the following I will try to answer these questions.

Social modernization began and accelerated parallel to the expansion of nationalism in Hungary. Due to this modernization process, various social interest groups underwent substantial changes. Feudal and social affiliations, a certain attachment to the state, to a dynasty, or to a religious group gradually lost their identity-building and group-shaping function in the Hungarian society of the nineteenth century, as this was also the case in other European societies (cf. Gardt 1999: 90). These traditional ties were replaced by the nation as an ideological formation, thus the national community developed into the most important social interest group (Barbour 2000: 3).

Consequently, the use of Hungarian emerged as a necessary condition for the individual's national belonging and social integration into nineteenth-century Hungary. For the German-speaking Budapest bourgeoisie this in turn meant that, via their *German* mother tongue variety, they (would have) stigmatized and excluded themselves from a Hungarian national community. We know – and this is crucial – that Hungarian state patriotism had already been established and stabilized before the nineteenth century within the circle of the German-speaking Budapest bourgeoisie. Since, after the appearance and expansion of the political ideology of nationalism, the state as an interest community was replaced by the nation after the turn of the century, the Hungarian state patriotism of the German-speaking bourgeoisie converted into a Hungarian national identity. This is already reflected in Rákosi's sentences quoted in (1) above, where he expresses his opinion 'from within', that is as a member of the Hungarian nation, in defence of Hungarian – as opposed to German – national interests.

We can thus observe that for the speakers the system of linguistic norms in the nineteenth century nationalist society brought about a severe *anomaly*. As the system was adopted by its speakers – arising from their Hungarian national identity –, their traditional language use and their social identities became irreconcilable. Their stigmatized German mother-tongue variety became an obstacle for social integration. Basically, there were two options to get out of this anomaly:

(a) *Transformation of the social identity and preservation of the customary language use.* The German national identity attached to the German mother-tongue variety already established a consistent status conforming the norm in linguistic nationalism, promoting the ideal of 'one nation – one language'. By sticking to German, the consistent relation between national and linguistic belonging would be re-established. However, with German being stigmatized, the conflict of linguistic interests with the domineering Hungarian speech community would not cease to exist, but rather be intensified.

(b) *Change in language attitudes and in language use traditions: language shift while preserving social identity.* The shift to Hungarian would put an end to the former conflict between the use of German and the Hungarian national identity. Furthermore, it would bring an end to the stigmatization of Germans by the Hungarian national society, which was induced by the non-Hungarian mother-tongue variety, which in turn was different from the Hungarian national language.

As the data in figures 1 and 2 suggest, speakers chose the second option: the Hungarian national identity and the language shift. Their national identity thus proved to be more stable and dominant than their language loyalty.

National identity determined their language choice – and not vice versa. From a sociolinguistic point of view, it is crucial that, in the circle of the Budapest and the Hungarian bourgeoisie of German origin in general speaking, German national identity and self-consciousness did not establish itself in the course of the nineteenth century. Consequently, there did not emerge any organized German national movement either, which would have served the German national interests and language loyalty against the Hungarian national and language interests.[9] As illustrated by Rákosi's example in chapter 3.2, the speakers adopted the language use norms of their own national community, namely that of the Hungarian national society. As a consequence of the prevailing linguistic ideology, this system of norms strengthened the positive attitudes connected to Hungarian and the negative ones connected to German. It furthermore accelerated the language shift process: speakers shifted from stigmatized German without social prestige to the use of standard Hungarian, which at that time possessed the biggest social prestige among all language varieties in Hungary. And as a result, we can observe the following relationship of social identity, language attitudes, and language behaviour:

social identity → language attitudes → language behaviour

Naturally, the language shift of the German-speaking Budapest bourgeoisie was motivated by other factors, too. I would briefly like to touch upon only one such factor, namely *language policy*, as it is a means in the hands of a domineering community via which the language shift of a subordinate community can indeed be furthered or even forced. I have studied the practice of language policy in nineteenth-century Hungary in detail elsewhere,[10] so I

---

9   Other works mention several reasons that hindered the establishment of the German national identity – among them several of a linguistic nature. One of them is that during the establishment and spreading of (linguistic) nationalism, Hungary had already been part of the Habsburg Monarchy. Accordingly, German was the dominant language in several – formal and informal – domains of communication in Hungary also and was used by the Hungarian speech community. Due to this, however, the sharp linguistic opposition between the two speech communities was missing (which played a decisive role in the self-definition of several other European nations). German thus could not exercise a group-shaping function, the lack of language opposition neutralized any national segregation attempts. Secondly, the same neutralizing function could have been exercised by the following: for this time – at the turn of the eighteenth to the nineteenth century – among the speakers the process of the natural, voluntary language assimilation, the language shift had already started (cf. Figure 2). This also lead to the equalization of language differences, and, hence, it could have turned into a hindrance to the linguistic segregation's becoming the base for the national self-definition.

10 Cf. Maitz 2005: 93–107, as to the accepted and operative laws between 1867 and 1918 regarding language and language use of the speech community analyzed, see the appendix of this book.

would only want to stress two points. On the one hand, we have to see that not only language use but – in a more direct and more transparent fashion – every language policy is necessarily ideology-dependent. As the nineteenth-century Hungarian language policy originates in the period's domineering linguistic ideology, namely linguistic nationalism, it is without doubt that it encompassed discriminative parts which advanced the language shift of the country's linguistic – e.g. German – minorities. On the other hand, however, the view that the explanation for the language shift of the German-speaking bourgeoisie could be reduced to mere language policy, to the alleged "dramatic Magyarization" (Eichinger 2003: 94ff.), remains untenable. This particular language policy namely guarantees the right to use German in formal language settings (like in school or in court) also. Through its certain orders it did in fact force *bilingualism*. Yet, it never forced language shift; German did not become an endangered language in Hungary (cf. Maitz 2005: 106).

It is not possible – and perhaps it is not necessary either – to expound the language laws and the additional motivational forces influencing the language shift of the German-speaking bourgeoisie in this paper. My purpose merely was to demonstrate the role of linguistic nationalism in the changes related to the language attitudes of the German-speaking Budapest bourgeoisie and, through this, in its language shift. I hope that it was plausibly illustrated that (a) the language shift would not have happened and the linguistic accommodation would not have become necessary if the demonstrated anomaly between the speakers' language use and their social and national identity had not arisen, i.e. if the *Hungarian* national identity and the *German* language use had not become incompatible, and (b) that this anomaly would not have happened if linguistic nationalism had not became a domineering linguistic ideology in nineteenth-century Hungary – similar to several other countries –, and if the ideal of 'one language – one nation' had not come about.

As a result of the analyzed processes, by the beginning of the twentieth century, standard German had died out in Hungary. These days numerous people still speak German as a second language, but, from the beginning of the twentieth century onwards, there have been no native speakers of it. German as a first language today only exists in the form of vernacular, non-standard varieties in Hungary, in mainly rural *'Sprachinseln'*.[11] However, these communities have also reached the last stage of language shift today; their language use is characterized by an asymmetrical and instable bilingualism that is dominated by Hungarian.

---

11 For the present sociolinguistic state of these 'Sprachinseln' see Hutterer (1961), Hessky (1997), the chapter in Manherz ed. (1998), and the studies in Nelde (1990).

6. Conclusion

In order to understand the causal relations of language shift, it is not only necessary to study its sociological factors, but the socio-psychological, mental factors that determine the speakers' language use and their individual system of values within a particular speech community. As Susan Gal puts it:

> these ideas are always positioned in some way, relate to politics, and are influenced by power. There is no "view from nowhere" no opinions about language that are not in some way "neutral or only scientific." (Gal 2002a: 198)

As we were able to observe, the language shift of the German-speaking Budapest bourgeoisie was not directly motivated by sociological circumstances, but by knowledge related to language and by the attitudes and mentalities which linguistic nationalism as a linguistic ideology carried. The language shift of the community under investigation in nineteenth-century Hungary might not have happened if eighteenth-nineteenth century linguistic nationalism had not become a decisive factor of linguistic ideology. Evidence proves that, while the German-speaking bourgeoisie could preserve its language throughout centuries, it went through a language shift in the course of the nineteenth century, after the establishment of linguistic nationalism in the course of a few generations even.

This in turn calls attention to the untenability of one of the widespread and accepted views of sociolinguistics. In several works on multilingualism, we read that, in the case of emigrant minorities, language shift generally happens in the course of three generations (cf. e.g. Borbély 2001: 34, Mattheier 1994: 334, Paulston 1994, Romaine 1989: 35ff. etc.). The case of the German-speaking Budapest bourgeoisie suggests that this does not always have to be the case. The quoted statement can thus only be formulated as a tendency rather than a regularity. This shows that we do not know enough about the phenomenon and its background. The characteristic feature of the emigrant community presented in my investigations was the language maintenance for centuries before the nineteenth century. For the language shift to happen in a few generations' time in the nineteenth century, a new linguistic ideology, namely linguistic nationalism, was needed.

This can be viewed as evidence of the strong ideology-dependence in the process of language shift and the speed of the process. And it is exactly why (historical) sociolinguistics must take into account the significance and the role of linguistic ideologies in the speakers' decisions about language use more precisely when investigating the explanations for language shift and language maintenance and the factors influencing language shift.

References

Barbour, Stephen. 2000. Nationalism, Language, Europe. In: Stephen Barbour and Cathie Carmichael (eds.), *Language and Nationalism in Europe*. Oxford: Oxford University Press, 1–17.

Barnes, Barry, David Bloor and John Henry. 1996. *Scientific Knowledge: A Sociological Analysis*. London: Athlone Press.

Belitska-Scholtz, Hedvig and Olga Somorjai. 1995. *Deutsche Theater in Pest und Ofen 1770–1850*, vol. 1. Budapest: Argumentum.

Berza, László (ed.). 1993. *Budapest Lexikon*, vol. 2. 2nd ed. Budapest: Akadémiai Kiadó.

Borbély, Anna. 2001. *Nyelvcsere. Szociolingvisztikai kutatások a magyarországi románok közösségében*. Budapest: MTA Nyelvtudományi Intézet.

Edwards, John. 1985. *Language, Society and Identity*. Oxford: Blackwell.

Eichinger, Ludwig M. 2003. Island Hopping: vom Nutzen und Vergnügen beim Vergleichen von Sprachinseln. In Jannis K. Androutsopoulos and Evelyn Ziegler (eds.), *'Standardfragen'. Soziolinguistische Perspektiven auf Sprachgeschichte, Sprachkontakt und Sprachvariation*. Frankfurt/Main et al.: Lang, 83–107.

Fishman, Joshua A. 1971. The Sociology of Language: An Interdisciplinary Social Science Approach to Language in Society. In Joshua A. Fishman (ed.), *Advances in the Sociology of Language*, vol. 1. The Hague: Mouton, 217–404.

Fishman, Joshua A. 1989. Language and Nationalism: Two Integrative Essays. In Joshua A. Fishman (ed.), *Language and Ethnicity in Minority Sociolinguistic Perspective*. Clevedon: Multilingual Matters, 97–175, 269–367.

Fónagy, Zoltán. 1998. A budapesti németek lélekszáma. In Vendel Hambuch (ed.), *Németek Budapesten*. Budapest: Fővárosi Német Kisebbségi Önkormányzat, 76–80.

Gal, Susan. 2002a. Language Ideologies and Linguistic Diversity: Where Culture Meets Power. In László Keresztes and Sándor Maticsák (eds.), *A magyar nyelv idegenben*. Debrecen: Egyetem Finnugor Nyelvtudomáyi Tanszéke, 197–204.

Gal, Susan. 2002b. Mi a nyelvcsere és hogyan történik? In Anna A. Jászó, and Zoltán Bódi (eds.), *Szociolingvisztikai szöveggyűjtemény*. Budapest: Tinta, 165–173.

Gardt, Andreas. 1999. Sprachpatriotismus und Sprachnationalismus. Versuch einer historisch-systematischen Bestimmung am Beispiel des Deutschen. In Andreas Gardt, Ulrike Haß-Zumkehr and Thorsten Roelcke (eds.), *Sprachgeschichte als Kulturgeschichte*. Berlin and New York: de Gruyter, 89–113.

Gardt, Andreas (ed.). 2000. *Nation und Sprache. Die Diskussion ihres Verhältnisses in Geschichte und Gegenwart.* Berlin and New York: de Gruyter.

Glatz, Ferenc. 1974. Polgári fejlődés és nacionalizmus Magyarországon a XIX. században. *Történelmi Szemle* 17: 248–260.

Gonda, Béla. 1920. *Jó modor – jó társaság.* 2. kiadás. Budapest. The author's own edition.

Herder, Johann Gottfried. 1989. Ideen zur Philosophie der Geschichte der Menschheit. In Martin Bollacher et al. (eds.), *Johann Gottfried Herder: Werke in zehn Bänden*, vol. 6. Frankfurt/Main: Deutscher Klassiker Verlag.

Hessky, Regina. 1997. Ungarisch – Deutsch. In Hans Goebl, Peter H. Nelde, Zdenêk Starý and Wolfgang Wölck (eds.), *Kontaktlinguistik. Ein internationales Handbuch zeitgenössischer Forschung,* vol. 2. Berlin and New York: de Gruyter, 1723–1731.

Hutterer, Claus Jürgen. 1961. Hochsprache und Mundart bei den Deutschen in Ungarn. In Rudolf Grosse and Claus Jürgen Hutterer (eds.), *Hochsprache und Mundart in Gebieten mit fremdsprachigen Bevölkerungsteilen.* Berlin: Akademie-Verlag, 33–71.

Karády, Viktor and István Kozma. 2002. *Név és nemzet. Családnévváltoztatás, névpolitika és nemzetiségi erőviszonyok Magyarországon a feudalizmustól a kommunizmusig.* Budapest: Osiris.

Klemm, László. 1998. A pest-budai német nyelvű színházkultúra. In Vendel Hambuch (ed.), *Németek Budapesten.* Budapest: Fővárosi Német Kisebbségi Önkormányzat, 254–262.

Linke, Angelika. 1996. *Sprachkultur und Bürgertum. Zur Mentalitätsgeschichte des 19. Jahrhunderts.* Stuttgart and Weimar: Metzler.

Maitz, Péter. 2005. *Sozialpsychologie des Sprachverhaltens. Der deutschungarische Sprachkonflikt in der Habsburgermonarchie.* Tübingen: Niemeyer.

Maitz, Péter and Anna Molnár. 2004. Zur Rolle sprachlicher Ideologien beim Sprachwechsel. Am Beispiel der deutschen Sprachgemeinschaft Ungarns im sprachnationalistischen 19. Jahrhundert. In Dániel Czicza, Ildikó Hegedűs, Péter Kappel and Attila Németh (eds.), *Wertigkeiten, Geschichten und Kontraste. Festschrift für Péter Bassola zum 60. Geburtstag.* Szeged: Grimm, 293–310.

Manherz, Károly (ed.). 1998. *Die Ungarndeutschen.* Budapest: Útmutató.

Mattheier, Klaus J. 1994. Theorie der Sprachinsel. Voraussetzungen und Strukturierungen. In Nina Berend and Klaus J. Mattheier (eds.), *Sprachinselforschung. Eine Gedenkschrift für Hugo Jedig.* Frankfurt/Main et al.: Lang, 333–348.

Nelde, Peter H. (ed.). 1990. *Deutsch als Muttersprache in Ungarn. Forschungsberichte zur Gegenwartslage.* Stuttgart: Steiner.

Niederhauser, Emil. 2000. A magyarországi asszimiláció problémái. Utószó
 Pukánszky Béla könyvének új kiadásához. In Béla Pukánszky (ed.), *Német
 polgárság magyar földön*. Budapest: Lucidus, 174–189.

Paikkala, Sirkka. 1997. Finnische Familiennamen und europäischer Zeitgeist.
 Studia Anthroponymica Scandinavica 15: 113–131.

Paulston, Christina Bratt. 1994. *Linguistic Minorities in Multilingual Settings:
 Implications for Language Policies*. Amsterdam and Philadelphia:
 Benjamins.

Pukánszky, Béla. 2000. *Német polgárság magyar földön*. Budapest: Lucidus.

Romaine, Suzanne. 1989. *Bilingualism*. Oxford: Blackwell.

Weinreich, Uriel. 1953. *Languages in Contact. Findings and Problems*. New
 York: Publications of the Linguistic Circle of New York.

AGNETE NESSE (BODØ)

1750–1850:
The disappearance of German from Bergen, Norway

1. The bilingual city

For more than 400 years, the city of Bergen on the western coast of Norway was a bilingual, Norwegian-German city. Throughout history trade has been a factor that has led to bilingualism and language contact in many places in the world, and Bergen was no exception. In Bergen's case, the trade in question was the early export trade in Norwegian fish. The fish was brought from the fisheries in the northern part of Norway and, on its way to the markets in the southern part of Europe, Bergen served as a place of trade and storage. The city was well suited for the purpose. Geographically it was situated more or less halfway between the fisheries and the markets, its harbour was deep, it afforded good shelter and was surrounded by storage facilities built to handle fish from all sides.

Originally, Norwegians were in charge of this trade, but, during the late Middle Ages, the powerful German Hanseatic League took over. How this could happen has been a source of much discussion among Norwegian historians. One early point of view, represented by Schreiner (1935) in the first half of the 20th century, was that the German shipbuilding skills were superior to those of the Norwegians (this was centuries after the era of the Viking ships), and that this, combined with the increasing dependence on foreign grain, was so important that the Norwegians lost control of the trade. More recent research (Nedkvitne 2004) has emphasized the economic strength and organizational skills (including a high degree of literacy) of the Hanseatic League.

An important feature of the Hanse organization was the distinction between smaller settlements and the major strongholds with extensive privileges, their Kontors. There were four of these, namely in London, Brugge, Novgorod, and Bergen. The Kontor in Bergen, which was established in the middle of the 14th century, led to great demographic changes in the city; at times during the Hanse era as much as a fifth of the population of Bergen consisted of single, German men. Even though the number of Germans, both in absolute and relative terms, fell after the mid 16th century, the Hanse had been present in the city until the mid-18th century, at which time the organization had long ceased to exist in the rest of Europe.

Bilingualism in Bergen during the Hanse era was a receptive or passive bilingualism. For the majority of the city's population, both the Norwegians and the Germans, speaking the other language was not an option. They understood but did not use it. Most of those who could write also used their own language exclusively in their writing. There were individuals, however, who could write in both languages, and they are the ones who translated the documents that needed to be translated; certain categories of legal documents, especially those dealing with property, and some letters written by Norwegians to recipients outside the city.

Why the linguistic situation came to develop in this way in the 14th century, and why it furthermore remained unchanged until the 18th century, is a complex matter, and I will only point out some important factors which are crucial to understanding the process of language change in the 19th century (these matters are discussed in greater depth in Nesse 2002 and 2003).

Due to the policies of the leaders of the Hanse, and partly also due to the policies of the Danish kings, the Hanseatic merchants in Bergen were not integrated into the local community. Due to this lack of integration, the different individuals' identities in the city were very distinct: you were either one of us, or you were one of them. And even though there was some unofficial socialization between members of the two groups, a common or mixed identity was never established as long as the Hanse was present in the city. The groups were not particularly hostile towards one another, but they were kept apart, mostly staying in their own areas of the town, with their own businesses, their own jurisdiction, and their own churches. The Germans had no say in the affairs of the city, and even though the leaders of the Kontor were invited to social functions given by the Bergen elite, they could never become part of that elite.

The most important symbol of these two identities was neither their appearance, rites of confession nor eating habits – it was language. Having a German identity meant speaking German and, conversely, speaking German meant having a German identity. And even though Old Norwegian and Middle Low German were closely related languages, the speakers were never in doubt as to which was which. Due to the centuries-long contact between the two languages, they became even more similar to one another as time elapsed. Loanwords went in both directions; in the sources we find lots of Norwegian loanwords in the German documents (*kleve* 'small room', *dyrr* 'expensive'), and lots of German loanwords in the Norwegian documents (*vorveser* 'leader, chairman'). In the Bergen vernacular, some grammatical alterations also took place as a result of the contact. Most prominent of these were the merger of grammatical genders from three (fem., masc., and neuter) to two (masc. and neuter), and the development of the periphrastic genitive using the pronoun *sin* (Nesse 2002 and 2003).

Both Middle Low German and Old Norwegian ceased to be used in official writing during this period. In brief, we can say that the situation in Bergen from approximately 1600 onwards was characterised by double diglossia. For the Germans, High German was the high variety which was used in writing and in church, whereas Low German was the low variety, the spoken language, also used in 'private' writing until approximately 1650. For the Norwegians, Danish was the high variety and Norwegian the low variety. The transition from one written language to another was not abrupt, it went through heavy mixing. If we look at documents from the 16th century in particular, it is not always obvious whether the language in question should be labelled Norwegian with Danish elements or Danish with Norwegian elements. And the same applies to the varieties of German.

From the 18th century onwards, however, things slowly started to change, first politically and economically, then linguistically. During this period it became more and more common for German merchants who were not members of the Hanse to settle in Bergen. Some were 'new' immigrants from Germany, who took citizenship as merchants or craftsmen, and some were former Hanse merchants who decided to leave the organization but stay in Bergen as Norwegians. These people, though formally Danish, were not required to learn Norwegian in any other way than Germans had learned Norwegian for centuries – receptively. We know of men who had been doing business in Bergen for 20 years as Norwegians without being able to write Danish. There was no need to. One can say that, for the German immigrants of the 18th century, there was a choice of identity. They could remain German, with the linguistic code that followed that identity, or they could become Norwegian. We have examples of both, but the motivations behind the different choices have not yet been thoroughly investigated.

2. The end of the Hanse era

It is generally acknowledged that it was the end of the Hanse Kontor in Bergen in 1756 that led to the disappearance of German from Bergen. It is tempting to imagine shiploads of German men sailing out from the harbour in Bergen, and that, with all the Germans gone, German had disappeared, too. But in fact there was only one German man who left the town as a result of the closure of the Hanse Kontor. Schuckman was the last leader or secretary of the Kontor and, before he left in 1761, he sold the headquarters of the Hanse Kontor. He also wrote a very thorough list of the contents of the Kontor's archives, then packed the same archives, and took them back with him to Lübeck.

Now, even though Schuckman was an important man, the departure of one man does not lead to language change. Furthermore, the recruitment of new Germans did not stop. Until the first half of the 19th century, German boys came to Bergen to become apprentices, and some of the German immigrants went to Germany to find wives, whom they brought back with them to Bergen. If the traders had remained independent, running their firms with their German apprentices, then going home to their German wives and attending services in the German church on Sundays and not demanding more from life, who knows how long a German speech community could have continued to exist in Bergen.

But they did demand more: power and wealth, for example. The independent traders in Bergen, most of them first or second generation Germans, decided to organize themselves in an organisation that could increase their profits. They formed an organization that was very similar to the Hanse Kontor, they even called it the Norwegian Kontor.[1] But whereas the Hanse merchants had to send their firms' profits back to the owners in Germany, the Bergen merchants – whatever ethnic background they might have had – owned their firms and were allowed to keep the profits. In other respects they traded in much the same way as the Hanse merchants had done. And for most people in Bergen, there did not appear to be much difference. To them, the area was the German Wharf, and the organization was the German Kontor. From 1767 we have an example of a spelling mistake made in a letter to the Norwegian Kontor:

Etter de herrer Vorvæsere for det Tydske Contoiret deres forlangende
'On the demand of the leaders of the German Kontor'

In this example we see the German influence also in the words and phrases used. *Vorvæsere* is a German loanword, and the genitive construction using the pronoun *deres* ('their') is a translation loan from German.

People were so used to speaking and writing about the German Kontor that they continued to write it. This writer has seen his mistake and struck out *det tyske*; others did not do so and, as late as 1819, letters were sent to 'The German Kontor in Bergen'.

But even if it did not matter much to other people, the fact that they were not a German organization mattered to the members of the Norwegian Kontor.

---

[1]   Actually, several names were used for this organization during the 150 years of its existence: *Det Norske Comptoir*, *Det Bergenske Handelskontor*, *Det Bergenske Handelssocietet*, or just *Kontoret*.

They wanted to trade like the Germans had done, but they also wanted to be a part of the political and cultural elite of the town. They wanted to matter – not just as merchants. So in order to show the world – or at least the city – that they were something different, that they were the Norwegian Kontor as opposed to the German Kontor, there was only one thing to do: change their language. And since language had always been the most important symbol of German versus Norwegian identity in Bergen, it was the one logical thing to do. There was only one problem with this: many of them were not able to write in anything but German. And these members found it hard when the leaders of the Kontor tried to force them to use Danish. We can see this in a letter written by the leaders of the Norwegian Kontor in 1754. The letter is a reply to a merchant called Carl von der Fehr, a German who had been a citizen of Bergen for approximately 15 years:

> Hr. Carl von der Fehr!
> Deres Skrivelse af 13de hujus paa tydsk skrevet have vi erholdt, menn da Indholden er i Æmbeds Sager, saavidt vi ere Oldermand og Forstander for contoiret, de og vi er Borger og fast Indvaaner, som mange Aar har været her i Byen, saa maathe det behage dem at skrive os til i landets Sprog, da det firnøden dem derpaa skal blive svaret.

> 'Mr. Carl von der Fehr!
> We have received your letter of the 13th of this month, written in German. But since the contents are related to business, and we are leaders of the Kontor, and you and we are citizens and live here, and have been in the city for many years, we would request you to write to us in the language of the country, and you will receive a reply.'

Carl von der Fehr found this reply very provocative. He thought it snobbish that they, all of them German and with German as their mother tongue, should start writing to each other in Danish. Besides, it was expensive for him, as he would have to pay a translator. It ended up being quite a long correspondence, in which the linguistic programme of the Norwegian Kontor is outlined in detail. Carl von der Fehr did spend money on the translation; his original letter shows up in a Danish version in the archives, but in later letters he again uses German. So it seems that, once the point was made, things returned to normal, at least for a while.

It seems that the leaders of the Norwegian Kontor were in fact able to write in Danish, but from the 1760s onwards they solved the 'problem' by hiring a Norwegian clerk, and much of the official writing from the Kontor came from his hand. That way, they could easily ensure that all outgoing and/or business correspondence was in Danish, while continuing to use German between themselves in other matters.

3. The sources for the investigation

The archives of the Norwegian Kontor, from which both examples were taken, have, to my knowledge, not previously been used for language survey purposes; they have mostly been of interest to historians working on economic matters such as fish prices throughout the ages. They are not just business archives, however. Other people lived in the area of Bergen where the Kontor was situated, in the same buildings in which the German Kontor had its premises. The archive therefore includes matters relating to the apprentices, to fire protection, guard duty, the upkeep of houses etc., hundreds of documents written in one of the two languages of the city.

Another important source, which is rather different from the vast archives of the Norwegian Kontor, is a book belonging to a housing community, or a *garten* (< old Norwegian *garðr*), as the Germans called it. In brief, a *garten* consisted of several firms with their quarters close together, sharing responsibilities for common rooms, cooking, fire protection, the behaviour of apprentices etc. There were about 30 of them at the Warf, each with its own name. This one was called Svendsgarten (modern Norwegian: *Svendsgården*), one of the few that had a man's name as the first part of its name. The merchants who stayed in a *garten* called each other neighbours, and hence the book in which the business of the *garten* was put down was called the neighbour record.

The neighbour record for Svendsgarten, which was written from 1598 until 1870, shows the linguistic history of this one *garten*, or rather of the people who lived there through two language shifts. They started writing the record in 1598, in a language we could characterize as typical of the time, predominately Low German, but with some High German influence, such as *nach* for Low German *na* ('after'):

> Dudt Is Der Nabere Unde Gesellen Boeck angefangen nach Christij Unses selich Mackkers Geboerdt Indt Jaer 1598 Den 10 Dach Nofembrys

> 'This is the Neighbours' and head apprentices' book started in the year 1598 after the birth of Christ our late creator on the 10th day of November'

In internal writing, of which this record is an excellent example, Low German was used until well into the 17th century. This was a hundred years longer than Low German was used in the Kontor's external correspondence. How long the spoken language remained Low German, we do not know. Once we come to the 18th century, there are few traces of Low German writing. In 1710 the neighbours in Svensgarten wrote High German:

den 22 October sind sambtligen nachbahrn und gesellen im Schütstauen versamblet worden und klage [...] gekommen, daß die gesellen sich ungebührlich in Schütstauen der gantzen nacht.....

'on the 22nd of October all neighbours and head apprentices gathered in the common rooms and received a complaint [...] that the head apprentices had the whole night in the Common rooms [...] in an inappropriate manner.....'

The word *Schütstauen* stayed Low German for a long time, but the High German form *Shütstube* or *Schötstube* is used later. The word originates from the Old Norwegian *skytningr* or *skytningsstofa*, and in German we also find the short form *Schütting*. The most curious part of the history of this word is actually the modern Norwegian form, *schøtstue*, which is closer to the German than to the Old Norwegian form. The reason for this is that the Germans in Bergen used these traditional common rooms long after they had gone out of fashion among Norwegians, and so it was the German form of the word that survived.

If we compare the neighbour record for Svendsgarten, which must be regarded as internal, with the archives of the Norwegian Kontor, we see that the members of the Svendsgarten held on to the German language longer, but once they started using Danish, only a relatively short period elapsed before they stopped using German all together. Up until 1798 there is no trace of Danish in the book, but then a man called Daniel Wiese wrote a receipt in Danish. By comparison, we can look at a receipt written by Hinrich Rathmann in 1796 (there was no receipt from 1797):

1796 d 20 Decbr: habe ich meinen Gesellen Georg Friedrerick Luseke vorgestellet und an dieses buch bezahlt 4 β Hinrich Rahtmann

'1796 on the 20th of December I have presented my head apprentice Georg Friederick Luseke and to this book paid 4 shillings. Hinrich Rahtmann.'

1798 dn 20 Dec: har ieg efter Con tume for min Gesell Christian Simensen til denne bog betalth 4 β Daniel Wiese

'1798 on the 20th December I have, as is the custom, for my head apprentice Christian Simensen to this book paid 4 shillings. Daniel Wiese.'

The last entry in German in this book appears in 1814, which means that the change from one language to the other took place over a period of 16 years, a period that in Nancy Dorian's terms can be labelled the linguistic 'tip':

A language which has been demographically highly stable for several centuries may experience a sudden "tip", after which the demographic tide flows strongly in favour of some other language. (Dorian 1981, here quoted from Mertz 1989: 103)

During the 16 years which constitute the linguistic tip, we see that one and the same person can write in both languages. This is important. Both from the archives of the Norwegian Kontor and from the neighbour record we can see that, as we approach 1800, a new linguistic situation was emerging in Bergen. After centuries during which both the Germans and the Norwegians were receptively bilingual only, the Germans were now becoming actively bilingual. There is no sign of the Norwegians becoming actively bilingual; they write in Danish only, as they have always done. The new factor is that the Germans started writing in both languages. And if we compare these sources with a third, namely the discussion about language – German or Danish/Norwegian – that should be used in the German church, we can state the following: the change of language in Bergen happened in two phases. First, the Germans went from being receptively bilingual to being actively bilingual. They then became receptively bilingual again, only now (mid-19th century) with Norwegian as their first and active language and German as their second and passive language. By 1900 they were all monolingual Norwegian[2].

It is not always the case that active bilingualism leads to the death of the minority language. On the contrary, minority groups are often bilingual for generations. But in Bergen, where a strict pattern regulated language use and identity, it is not surprising that active bilingualism would stir up conceptions of language versus identity. If they could speak both languages, which group did they belong to?

4. The church

In the discussion concerning whether or not the traditional German church should remain German, those who were opposed to German in the church ridiculed those who wanted to hear German in the church, even though they could not speak but merely understand it. Seen from the perspective of tradition, this makes sense. Traditionally, understanding German but only being able to speak Norwegian was part of being Norwegian in Bergen – and Norwegians did not want German in their churches. So what they were saying, though indirectly, is that if you have the linguistic competence that has always been a part of being Norwegian, how can you then claim to be German? Evidently, these matters are not always well-defined. Things may become unclear as to who belongs to which language community, especially in a

---

[2]   There were, of course, a number of Norwegians who also knew German after this, but now as a foreign language that they learned at school or by going to Germany, not as their mother tongue. German was the most important foreign language in Norway up until the Second World War, when English took over.

situation like this, where sociolinguistic conditions were undergoing rapid change:

> When a language has been in retreat for a long time and its distribution has been shrinking at the same time that its functions have been dwindling, difficulties are very likely to arise in even such basic matters as determining just who should be considered a 'speaker' or a 'member' of the speaker community. The 'native speaker' population itself may not agree on who falls within that category: some people may claim speaker status when others would not accept them as such; some may say they are not speakers when others would include them as speakers. (Watson 1989: 41)

From the viewpoint of those dealing with church matters in Bergen, it was clear that German ethnicity had to do with the nationality of the breadwinner of the family. The widowers that are mentioned below were themselves born in Germany, while the widows had husbands who were German.

In 1831 the members of the German church comprised:

- 17 families where both wife and husband were German, or born in Bergen to German parents.
- 19 families where the husband was German and the wife Norwegian.
- 9 widowers born in Germany, 19 widows whose husbands were German.
- some young men, born in Germany, working at the Kontor.

(taken from Nilsen 1948: 179)

I do not know for certain whether this means that German women married to Norwegian men were not entitled to be members of the church. What we do know is that there were a number of people who did not belong to the German church, who nonetheless wished to have their children baptised or confirmed in the German church. Perhaps some of them were German women married to Norwegian men, who, because of their husband's ethnicity, were not entitled to call themselves German.

Applications from 'non-Germans' to be allowed to hold such ceremonies in the German church were a problem for the pastors in the other churches in town. Part of their income was based on baptism, weddings, funerals etc., and when people who belonged to their church wished to hold these ceremonies in the German church, it meant that they lost part of their income. But as is often the case in such conflicts, even if the background for them relates to economic or other 'practical' matters, the arguments used are linked to ethnicity, nationality, or language. The following quote is taken from a letter from 1831, written by several Bergen pastors to Bishop Neumann, the bishop of Bergen. The bishop was considered to be friendly towards the Germans; he had preached in German on several occasions and had a German wife. The 'applicants' about whom the pastors write were people not entitled to be part of the German church who had applied to have ceremonies performed there:

> [...] og om Supplikanternes Børn, Børnebørn, Børnebørnsbørn o.s.v. – med norsk Modersmaal, Undersaatter af Norges Konge, beskyttede af Norsk Regjering, spisende Norsk Brød, handlende med Norske Producter og Penge, engang ophøre at være et Slags Tydskere eller Amphibier og blive aldeles Norske, saa troe vi, at de deraf have hverken Skam eller Skade eller Undergang at befrygte. (Nilsen 1948: 178f.)

> 'and if the applicants' children, grandchildren, grandchildren's children etc. – with Norwegian as their mother's tongue, subjects of Norway's king, protected by the Norwegian Government, eating Norwegian bread, trading with Norwegian products and money, ever cease being some kind of Germans or amphibians and become totally Norwegian, then we suppose that they will have neither shame nor damage nor damnation to fear.'

This was during the period of Romanticism, when it was quite common, not only in Norway, to use arguments invoking national feelings, the soul or voice of the nation etc. Today, we would certainly not wish to refer to second or third generation 'immigrants' as amphibians.

5. The family

The family was a domain that never became German in Bergen. In the Hanse era, the closest the merchant came to a family, was his apprentices, but this 'family' was not a lasting unit. After making enough money, the merchant would go back to Germany and start a real family there.

From 1700 and onwards, this changed, and there were many German speaking men in Bergen who married and had children. An important question is if these children had German or Norwegian as their first language. The sources available show us that the German merchants' children were brought up with Norwegian as their mother tongue, but that the boys were taught German at school, first in Bergen, later during a year or two in Hamburg or Bremen. In order to start working at the Kontor, one of the most important skills a young boy had to have, was some knowledge of German. For the girls, an active competence in German was not important. It was merely a foreign language they could use in their autograph albums, like others used French or Greek. But they needed to understand some German, since the families went to the German church.

If these children did not learn German in the family despite the fact that German was their father's first language, it must have been because their mothers did not use German. The private correspondence I have found at the

University Library in Bergen, written by women in merchant's families in the late 18th and the 19th century, is with no exceptions written in Danish. Many of these women had German father and German husband who used German at work, and they went to German service at church. So why did they not use German themselves?

Again it seems that we have to go back to the sociolinguistic conditions in the Hanse era to find an explanation. In addition to the close relationship between German identity and German language that existed at the time, there was a close relationship between German language and being a man. There were very few German women in Bergen in the Hanse era, and also later most of the German immigrants were bachelors. So German may well have been considered a male language, not suitable for 'nice' girls.

Also, in the Hanse era, marrying a Norwegian woman was a big step towards becoming Norwegian for the German men. Since such marriages were prohibited, consequences were large for those who did it. They were expelled from the Hanse organization and from the German area, and sometimes violently punished. As late as in 1741 it almost came to a diplomatic crisis when one of the last secretaries of the German Kontor wanted to marry a Norwegian woman. He had to quit his job, and settled in Bergen as a Norwegian merchant. Not long after that does he write his first letter in Danish (Carbiner, in NKB).

We can state that the family sphere was not a German speaking domain in Bergen, and that even those who used German at work, raised their children in Norwegian. The reason for this was that speaking German in the family was not an option for Norwegian women, and the consequence was that German changed from being a minority language to being a foreign language in the city.

6. Conclusion

The disappearance of German from Bergen can be seen as a classic example of how a language loses domain by domain before it is no longer used. The chart below shows the development from 1700 to 1900. Up until 1750 the languages hold the domains they have held since the beginning of the Hanse era in Bergen, at least since the 14th century. We see that the Norwegian authorities always used the national language, which was Norwegian in the beginning of the period, and Danish from approximately 1600 onwards. It must be emphasized that this only holds for the local authorities. Some of the Danish kings would communicate with the Germans in Bergen in German. There are several reasons for this. Several of the Danish kings came from German speaking areas, and thus had Low German as their mother tongue. In addition,

Low German held a generally high prestige in the Copenhagen chancery, at least in the 15th and 16th centuries. Also, as long as the Hanse league was strong and mighty, they did what the powerful most often do – they used their own language no matter who they wrote to, so the Danish kings were used to Low German as the language one addressed the Hanse officials in, whether situated in Germany, Bergen, or even London. But inside Bergen, all correspondence from the authorities was in Norwegian / Danish.

The Hanse Kontor was as consequent in its language use. If they sent a letter to the Bergen council or the Danish king or the Hanse officials in Germany, they always used German. The only language shift we see in this group is a change from Low to High German in external correspondence in 1580, while they use Low German internally until approximately the mid-17th century.

The next group on the chart is the Norwegian Kontor, founded in 1754. Their main way of marking distance to the German Kontor was to use another language: in all external correspondence they used Danish. Since many of the members did not write Danish, they used German in internal correspondence (and book-keeping) for another 50–60 years.

The church was the last stronghold of the German language in the city, and the shift from German to Norwegian seems also to have been less abrupt than was the case for the Norwegian Kontor.

The family language and the female language was Norwegian.

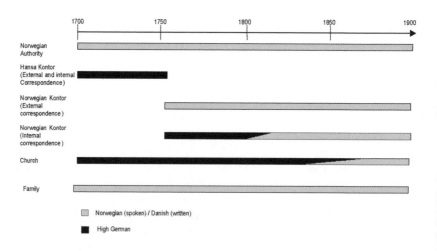

Figure 1: Language change in Bergen, 1700–1900

To sum up, we can say that Language death in Bergen in the early 19th century happened because a group of resourceful men wanted both wealth and power. They wanted the privileges of the old Hanse system, having control of the fish export from Norway to Europe. That they could achieve with German identity and with German language. But they also wanted to be an important part of the city's political and cultural elite. And in order to be that, they had to become Norwegian – both in mind and in language.

References

Mertz, Elisabeth. 1989. Sociolinguistic creativity: Cape Breton Gaelic's linguistic 'tip'. In Nancy C. Dorian (ed.), *Investigating obsolescence. Studies in language contraction and death.* Cambridge: Cambridge University Press, 117–138.

Nedkvitne, Arnved. 2004. *The social consequences of literacy in medieval Scandinavia.* Turnhout: Brepols.

Nesse, Agnete. 2002. *Språkkontakt mellom norsk og tysk i hansatidens Bergen.* Oslo: Novus.

Nesse, Agnete. 2003. Written and spoken languages in Bergen in the Hansa era. In Kurt Braunmüller and Gisella Ferraresi (eds.), *Aspects of Multilingualism in European Language History.* Amsterdam and Philadelphia: John Benjamins, 61–84.

Nilsen, Halkild. 1948. *Kirke- og skoleforhold i Bergen i biskop Jacob Neumanns tid.* Oslo: Gyldendal.

Schreiner, Johan. 1963. Bremerne i Bergen. *Historisk tidsskrift* 4: 291–316.

Watson, Seosamh. 1989. Scottish and Irish Gaelic: The giant's bed-fellows. In Nancy C. Dorian (ed.), *Investigating obsolescence. Studies in language contraction and death.* Cambridge: Cambridge University Press, 61–74.

Sources

NKB = The archive of the Norwegian Kontor in Bergen city archive

The Neighbour's book of Svensgården at Bergen University Library, Manuscript no. 211

Private correspondence from the 18th and 19th century, Bergen University Library

Stefaniya Ptashnyk (Lviv/Wrocław/Tübingen)

Societal multilingualism and language conflicts in Galicia in the 19th century

1. Historical and political premises

The political situation in most of the crownlands of the Habsburg Empire in the 19th century, especially after the civil revolution of 1848, stands out due to the great variety of different nationalities living side by side and being in close contact to each other.

The Galician part of the Habsburg Monarchy, on which my paper will focus, was populated by groups which can be defined by language, religion, and ethnicity on the one hand, and by social diversification on the other (cf. Fellerer 2003: 109). At that time the Galician population comprised the following social groups: Ukrainian and Polish peasants, the Ukrainian clergy, the Polish upper classes, in particular the Polish aristocracy, different ethnic groups of town-dwellers such as Jews, German-speaking protestants and craftsmen, and Polish or polonised citizens.

Poles spoke Polish and wrote Polish or Latin. Galician Ukrainians (Ruthenians) used different western dialects of the Ukrainian vernacular for oral communication (Fellerer 2003: 109). The written Galician Ukrainian was elaborated on the basis of the Galician vernacular, but, until the end of the 19th century, the standardisation of Ukrainian was not completed. German was spoken by Protestants living in Galicia. Beyond that, Yiddish, Armenian, and Hebrew were also used by the citizens of Galicia.

It should be emphasized that German was also the language of the state and of officials who influenced the civil life in Galicia through administrative structures and state institutions, especially in domains such as administration, legislation, and culture. The language of higher education until 1870 was German, and Polish after that. Therefore, the German language had a hegemonial position in Galicia, even if, in general, most citizens of Galicia had Ukrainian and Polish as their native language. Religion was closely connected with language: members of the Roman Catholic Church were regarded as Poles for example, whereas the Greek Catholic (Uniate) Church was a kind of melting pot for all Galician Ukrainians (cf. Fellerer 2003: 109).

Stefaniya Ptashnyk

The Habsburg administration attempted to regulate the asymmetric relationship between ethnic groups by granting them linguistic and cultural equality. The most important step in regulating the relationship between nationalities in Galicia was Article 19 of the Austrian Constitution of 1867. This article guaranteed equality of all nationalities in the monarchy, referred to as "Volksstämme" ('branches of the people') as well as their rights to maintain and use their "landesübliche Sprachen" (i.e. their vernacular languages; literally 'languages usually used in particular region') in school, administration, and public life (Wandruszka and Urbanitsch 1980: 1199). Nevertheless, this article could not prevent certain asymmetries between languages and ethnic groups, as I will demonstrate in my present paper.

Regarding Galicia's multilingual society in the 19th century, we find a situation of diglossia or, better, polyglossia. Rindler Schjerve defines diglossia as the "totality of discursive practices which manifest themselves in terms of a functionally constrained distribution of the languages and in terms of textual realisation" (Rindler Schjerve and Vetter 2003: 57). Polyglossia correlates with subordination and domination of languages in a multilingual society and can be generally conceptualized in terms of the distribution and valorisation of the respective languages. Diglossic orders of discourse always refer to asymmetries in the status ascriptions of ethnic groups to each other and their languages (cf. ibid.: 45).

Social reality, social roles, and social identities manifest themselves in many different texts, which concentrate on the topic 'societal multilingualism' (ibid.: 46). For this reason, all of these texts can be regarded as belonging to the same discourse which can be defined by certain semantic criteria, i.e. by the same topic (cf. Busse and Teubert 1994: 14). Taking this as a starting-point, the phenomenon of diglossia can be described by the method of discourse analysis. Two aspects are relevant for such an investigation; a) historical preferences of certain languages existing in a given social domain and b) textual manifestations of social practices.

For an investigation of societal multilingualism in Galicia by the method of discourse analysis, it is necessary to identify social groups which were involved in Galicia's discourse and which participated in societal practices. These are the basic instruments for the following description of polyglossia.

Ethnic groups involved in social interaction tend to distinguish themselves from one another. In this process, comparisons between different groups are made and group identities are shaped (cf. Rindler Schjerve 1998: 496). Discursive identifications are often accompanied by valorisations which are realised simultaneously in texts and can be described as self-categorisations and categorisation of others.

Polyglossia refers to the functionally constrained distribution of languages in specific domains. Language use in politics, school, legislation, or private life is compartmentalised in various ways. In our analysis of the polyglossic situation under discussion, it is essential to consider specific discursive patterns in different social domains.

In the following I present categorisations of Galician ethnic groups using texts from Polish, German, and Ukrainian newspapers that were published from March until June 1897 in Lemberg (today Lviv), the capital of crownland Galicia. My data corpus consists of written texts from 4 different newspapers: the German *Galizische Presse* (GP), the Ukrainian *Дѣло* (Dilo), and 2 Polish newspapers, the radical *Kurier Lwowski* (KL), and the conservative *Dziennik Polski* (DP). Two important political events are relevant for these texts; these are the Galician election to parliament in April 1897 and the language decree for Bohemia and Moravia, issued by Count Badeni in April 1897. Both the election and the language decree were discussed intensively in the press. The texts chosen reflect the relationship of Galician nationalities and the status of languages in the polyglossic society in the Habsburg Empire.

I will now give a short overview of the categorisation of Galician ethnic groups in the texts.

2. Galician ethnic groups and their discursive categorisations

The Polish citizens of Galicia constituted one of the largest ethnic groups, neutrally called in Polish *poliacy*, *lud polski*, in German *Polen*, in Ukrainian *поляки* (*poliaky*). In the discursive self-categorisation of this group, we can find two characteristic motives. On the one hand, Poles valued themselves as a strong and well developed community with a high cultural level. Poles perceived themselves as "one of the two most important nationalities of the monarchy besides the Czech" (DP 7.04.1897: 1).

On the other hand, Poles saw themselves as one part of a great Polish nation, albeit divided under Austrian, Prussian, and Russian rulers since 1772. This is why Poles tended to categorise themselves as a subordinated and oppressed community:

(1) [...] społeczeństwo nasze, gniecione od stu lat moskiewską nahajką i pruską pikielhaubą (DP 13.05.1897: 1)

'our society, for hundreds of years oppressed by Moscow's whip and Prussian spiked helmet'

This image of the endangered community was also applied to Poles living in Galicia, where their identity was threatened by the experience of living dispersed among Ukrainians:

(2) Jeżeli Polakom, rozrzuconym po Rusi, dziś jeszcze nie brak narodowego poczucia, to wnet to nastąpić może. Mówią oni i śpiewają po rusku i powoli się wynaradowjają. (KL 4.05.1897: 1)

'The Poles, dispersed in the Rus'[1] do not lack national feelings at the moment, but it can come quickly. They speak and sing Ruthenian and denationalise step by step.'

The lexis of foreign categorisation contrasts with self-categorisation. In the Ukrainian press, for example, Poles are valued as *inconsiderate, morally unjust* (the last expression with regard to Polish intellectuals), and *undemocratic*:

(3) [...] у Полякôвъ верховодила и верховодить шляхта та єзуиты, а идеѣ демократизму, свободомысленности и поступовости [...] затерли ся майже цѣлкомъ (Dilo 3. (15.) 04. 1897: 1)

'[...] aristocracy and Jesuits rule among the Poles, and the ideas of democracy, liberal thinking, and progressive thought are almost completely vanished.'

Self-identifications of Ukrainians are particularly interesting in this period. Referred to as *Ruthenen* in German, *rusini, lud ruski* in Polish, and primarily *русини* (*rusyny*), *руський народ* (*rus'kyj narod*) in their own language, the word *Ukrainians* is very rarely used in the texts.

Regarding the self-image of Ukrainians, the foregrounded topics of discourse are their lawlessness, social and economic subordination, and their classification in the *discriminated nationalities* ("народов упослѣдженыхъ") (Dilo 15. (25.) 05.1897: 1). Leitmotifs in the self-categorisation are reflections about Ruthenians' *unhappy destiny, crushed truth and justice* ("подоптану правду и справедливôсть") (Dilo 14. (26.) 03.1897: 2).

In opposition to this image, Ukrainians also categorise themselves by using more positive and optimistic expressions, such as a nation *standing on the principles of democracy, free thinking, and progress* ("стоячи на основахъ демократизму, свободомысленности и поступовости") (Dilo 3. (15.) 04.1897: 1) and as a *quiet nation, but with consciousness of their rights* ("Сей тихій, свѣдомый своихъ правъ народъ") (Dilo 14. (26.) 03.1897: 1).

In the foreign categorisations of Ukrainians, we first find the same motive as in the self-categorisation, but the lexis is more negative, radical, and intense: Ukrainians are presented as people being in *a hopelessly desperate situation*; the discourse is dominated by an image of a *passive* (DP 16.03.1897: 1) and *unhappy people* ("widok nieszczęśliwego, czasami rozpaczliwego położenia,

---

1 "Rus'" means the Eastern part of the Crownland Galicia with dominantly Ukrainian speaking population; in contrast to the people in "Rus'", most people of Western Galicia had Polish as their vernacular language.

w którem się ten naród znajduje") (KL 15.04.1897: 1). Especially the Polish press refers to Ukrainians as *miserable and simple-minded people* ("siermieżne prostaczki") (DP 16.03.1897: 1) *without outstanding representatives*, whose *'intellectuals' can be counted on the fingers of one hand* ("'Inteligencję' ich na palcach można policzyć") (DP 14.05.1897: 1).

The statements of the "Galizische Presse" are similar: *doubtful people* ("in Zweifel geratenes Volk") (GP 20.06.1897: 1), which adheres to *a certain depression of the spirit as an ethnological feature* ("dem schon von Natur aus eine gewisse Depression des Geistes als ethnologisches Merkmal anhaftet") (GP 20.06.1897: 1).

Beyond this, there are further terms with negative connotations, which refer to the Ukrainian nationality as *a peasants' rabble* ("hajdamackich rozruchach rozwydrzonego chłopskiego motłochu") and even *carcass* ("Kadaver") and *servants* ("Knechte") (Dilo 14. (26.) 03.1897:1). In reference to the Ukrainian elite, i.e. the Ukrainian Greek-catholic clergy, the "Galizische Presse" particularly uses such terms as *harpies* ("Harpyen") and *hotheads* ("Hitzköpfe", GP 13.06.1897: 1).

In my small corpus, there is no information about the self-categorisation of Germans (neutrally called *німці [nimci]* in Ukrainian, *niemcy* in Polish, and *Deutsche* in German). I will concentrate on the specific categorisation of Germans by other ethnic groups. First of all, the discursive expressions refer not only to the neighbours living in Galicia, but rather to the Austrian Germans and to the rulers. Implicitly, it is a common practice that Germans are accepted as a great and well-developed nation.

At the same time, they are very often characterised as a nationality with absolute political and social power that decides about the destinies of other (especially Slavic) ethnic groups. For this reason, Germans are discursively characterised as the *enemy* ("противниками") (Dilo 14. (26.) 03.1897: 1), and furthermore as *unreasonable* and *incorrigible*:

(4) Нѣмцѣ невырозумѣли та непоправни: они хотять надъ народами славяньскими задержати давну свою опѣку та гегемонію. (Dilo 2. (14.) 05.1897: 1)

'But Germans are unreasonable and incorrigible: they want to hold their old guardianship and hegemony over the Slavic nations.'

A similar idea is contained in the following quotation from the Polish newspaper "Dziennik Polski":

(5) [...] Niemcy i żydzi [sic!], chcą także narzucić swój język [...] Tych Niemców śmiałoby można postawić na równi z Prusakami lub Moskalami, ale nigdy z nami. [...] ci Niemcy byli zawsze i są ciemnieżycielami. (DP 29.05.1897: 1)

'Germans and Jews also want to force their language on others ... These Germans belong to the same category as Prussians and Russians, but never to us ... These Germans have always been oppressors, and they have remained so until now.'

From the texts, we obtain information about Jewish people in Galicia (neutrally called *Juden* in German, *zydzi* in Polish, and *жиди [zhydy]* in Ukrainian). Expressions in the discourse such as *Ruthenian-Jewish propaganda against Poles* ("rusko-żydowska propaganda przeciw polskości") (DP 17.03.1897: 1) or *Germans and Jews also want to force their language* ("Niemcy i żydzi [sic!], chcą także narzucić swój język") (DP 29.05.1897: 1) illustrate that Jews were seen as enemies of Poles. Ruthenians also consider Jews as their antagonists because they are seen as allies of Poles:

(6) Противниками въ своЪй роботЪ выборчôй мавъ рускій нарôдъ – правительство и Полякôвъ звязаныхъ зъ жидами [...]. Жиды заняли становиско, якъ звичайно, намъ вороже. (Dilo 14. (26.) 03.1897: 1)

'The antagonists of the Ruthenian people during the elections were rulers (the government) and Poles in connection with Jews ... As they usually do, Jews took a hostile position towards us.'

The discourse furthermore contains some positive references from the Polish side towards Jews, for example as *brothers of mosaic confession* ("braćmi mojżeszowego wyznannia") (Dilo 14. (26.) 03.1897: 1). Such examples are rather rare in my corpus.

We can see that the Jewish part of the Galician population, which was not recognised by the government as a nationality, was valued negatively by different ethnic groups but, at the same time, was also exploited for certain political aims.

In general, negative judgements are dominant in the foreign categorisations of national groups. Furthermore, the analysed documents demonstrate major differences between self-categorisation and categorisation by others. They provide evidence that the social and cultural status of the various ethnic groups and the relationship between them was not well-balanced and that this fact resulted in an increase of conflicts between the groups. In our corpus societal multilingualism results in conflict whenever it is paired with asymmetric status and social hierarchy of linguistically distinct groups within a state.

3. The role of the language in the conflict discourse

The next aspect with which I will deal briefly is the valorisation of languages by Galician ethnic groups and the role of language in inter-ethnic struggles. Following the increase of national consciousness during the 19th century, the social groups in the Habsburg Empire developed a kind of corporate identity based on special ethnic features and irrespective of class differences. Dominance by other ethnic groups was less and less accepted.

The relationship between these groups in Galicia was marked by certain difficulties, due to the fact that the commonly used languages of the Galicia region reached different stages of standardisation in the 19th century. The standardisation process of written German had started in the Early Modern period; Polish as a language of literature began to flourish at the beginning of the 19th century. For Ukrainian this process was completed by the end of the 19th century. Yiddish was not at all acknowledged as a "language common to the region". These facts led to a principal asymmetry between the prestige of these individual languages (see Wandruszka and Urbanitsch 1980: 904).

Languages became a symbol of specific national identities, but also of the social and political prestige of their speakers. The analysed texts clearly show that different languages were associated with differences in power and prestige and that speakers of these different languages were evaluated accordingly.

Although there is little evidence of reflections on the role of language in the political conflict in Galicia in my present corpus, a few tendencies can already be observed. With regard to language, three main topics were discussed: (1) language use in specific social domains, (2) the language rights of certain nationalities, and (3) language as a main subject of interethnic struggles.

3.1 Language use in specific social domains

Language use in certain domains of public life, especially in the more prestigious ones, was an important indicator of the relationship between ethnic groups. By restricting the use of a language to specific domains, the political influence and importance of its speakers could be limited or eliminated.

In my texts, most discussions regard the use of Ukrainian. In the politically important domains of public life, this language was only marginally represented, for example, it was not spoken by administration officials:

(7) А що-жъ казати про руску часть Галичины? Не кажучи вже о внутрѣшнôм урядованю, чи богато урядникôвъ знає руску мову, щобы зъ рускими сторонами зносити ся по руски? А и ти, що справдѣ знають, чи хочуть? У насъ урядники зъ засады не хочуть знати рускои мови. (Dilo 22.04. (4.05.) 1897: 1)

'What is there to say about the Ruthenian part of Galicia? To say nothing about the interior administration, how many officials know the Ruthenian language and can speak with Ruthenians the Ruthenian language? And those who know, do they want to? Our officials do not want to know Ruthenian at all.'

Attempts by Ruthenians to extend the use of their language were judged negatively by the German press, referred to as *an outflow [a result] of the national consciousness of some Ruthenian hotheads, overestimating themselves* ("Ausfluss eines sich selbst überschätzenden Nationalbewusstseins einiger ruthenischer Hitzköpfe") (GP 13.06.1897: 2). As we can see, the Habsburg administration tried to keep the hegemonial position of German in the domain of administration by restricting the use of other languages.

3.2 The language rights of Galician nationalities in discourse

Related to the language use in specific domains, the problem of language rights was also discussed. In the German press the subordination of Ruthenian were seen as legitimate because the language is perceived as less valuable. The status of Ruthenian as a national language and a language of literature was, therefore, denied:

> (8) [in Bezug auf das Ruthenische:] [...] dass es nur eine unbegreifliche Unvernunft vermag, eine Sprache als gleichwertig mit den anderen hinstellen zu wollen, welche noch nicht Literatursprache geworden ist, deren Idiome von einander grundverschieden sind und aus diesem Grunde noch nicht als einheitliches Gemeingut des Volkes als Nationalsprache, betrachtet werden kann [...]. (GP 13.06.1897: 2)

> 'Only an incomprehensible fool is capable of perceiving a language as equivalent to the others, which has not yet become literary language, whose idioms are completely different from one another, and therefore cannot be considered as a common heritage of the people, i.e. as a national language.'

Poles had similar aims: they argued in favour of more rights for the use of the Czech language due to the advanced cultural and economic development of the Czech, whereas Germans should be ready to learn the Czech language:

> (9) Czyż wistocie ma być dla Niemców w Czechach nadzwyczajnem nieszczęściem ten fakt, iż ich dzieci nauczą się także po czesku? [...] Nikt, ucząc się języka swego współobywatela, nie czyni ujmy swemu językowi ojczystemu i nie zatraca cech swego narodu. (DP 11.04.1897: 1)

> 'Should the fact that their children will also learn Czech be a big disaster for Germans? [...] Learning the language of one's own fellow citizens, no one will derive disadvantages for the own mother tongue and nobody will lose the features of one's own people.'

As we see, Germans used the status of a language as an argument, trying to maintain their hegemonic position in the Empire and in Galicia. By not offering more rights to Ruthenians, the Habsburg Germans preserved the linguistic status quo, and at the same time they kept their own political hegemony. Poles, on the one hand, tried to retain their language dominance against Ruthenian, but, on the other hand, they were interested in limiting the influence of German by demanding more rights for the Czech language. Ruthenians tried to foster the use of their language in the more prestigious domains of public life, for example in administration, in order to achieve more rights in society.

3.3 Language as the main subject of interethnic conflicts

In the 19th century, and especially after 1848, language played an important role as a proof of identity for the different social groups in the Habsburg Empire, constituted as ethnic and linguistic groups. The role of language as a symbol of the identity of social groups and as a kind of "epicentre" or quintessence of conflicts between the Galician nationalities was also explicitly discussed in newspaper texts. I chose just one quotation from my corpus of examples to show which role the speakers attribute to language in conflict discourse and how they use language in their argumentation.

> (10) Wir stehen im Zeichen der Sprachenfragen. Ueberall stehen dieselben auf der Tagesordnung und bilden das Streitobject, den Erisapfel, der die nationalen Kämpfe erweitert, und ihnen gewissermassen einen neuen Gehalt geben. Es ist der Ausgangspunkt der Defensive oder der Offensive im Kampfe der Nationen und nivellirt alle anderen zur Austragung gelangenden Zwistigkeiten der Völker unter einander. Und mit Recht; denn die Sprache ist ja als der lebendige Ausdruck des Denkens am besten geeignet, die erkämpften Vortheile eines Volkes darzutun und die errungene nationale Selbständigkeit durch die freie Entfaltung der Nationalsprache, welche der getreue Spiegel des Fühlens und des nationalen Empfindens ist, zu beweisen. (GP 13.06.1897: 2)

> 'Today we are concerned with the linguistic question. Everywhere the same questions are on the agenda and form the object of dispute, the apple of Eris, which expands national struggles and gives them a new content. It is the starting point of the defensive and offensive in the struggle of nations and evens out all other disputes carried out between peoples. And rightly so because language as a vivid expression of thought is best used to expose the hard-won advantages and to prove the achieved national independence by means of the free development of the national language that is the faithful mirror of feeling and national consciousness.'

In this quotation language is perceived as the quintessence of the national conflict, and it is argued that language rights and social advantages are interconnected. Such an explicit understanding of language as a symbol of national identity confirms the argument mentioned above. The restrictions of language rights and language use are strategies against the extension of the social rights of their speakers.

4. Summary

In the multilingual Galician society of the 19th century, every single ethnic group that can be identified as a linguistic community sought to foster the use of their own language in the prestigious domains of social life to obtain a better social position and more power, or to maintain its hegemonic role. In these processes, language as an important dimension of group identity was often instrumentalised in the national struggle and being used as an argument for restricting or controlling language use on different levels of discursive interaction.

In such conflicts, which can be defined as language conflicts, language has several functions. First, language is discursively conceptualised as an important component of national culture and as a factor in identity constitution. In this function, language is manifested in texts as the quintessence of national conflict. Secondly, the language use is discussed in discourse, giving evidence for the subordination or domination of a certain national group. Finally, language is used in discourse as a means of argumentation: the valorisation of language correlates with the valorisation of their speakers. A nationality without a standardized and elaborated written language cannot achieve equal rights with other national groups and vice versa.

5. References

Busse, Dietrich and Wolfgang Teubert. 1994. Ist Diskurs ein sprachwissen-schaftliches Objekt? Zur Methodenfrage der historischen Semantik. In Dietrich Busse, Fritz Hermanns and Wolfgang Teubert (eds.), *Begriffsgeschichte und Diskursgeschichte. Methodenfragen und Forschungsergebnisse der historischen Semantik*. Opladen: Westdeutscher Verlag, 10–28.

Deminger, Szilvia, Thorsten Fögen, Joachim Scharloth and Simone Zwickl (eds.) 2000. *Einstellungsforschung in der Soziolinguistik und Nachbardisziplinen. Studies in Language Attitudes*. Frankfurt/Main: Peter Lang Verlag.

Fellerer, Jan. 2003. Discourse and Hegemony: The case of the Ukrainian language in Galicia under Austrian rule (1772–1914). In Rosita Rindler Schjerve (ed.), *Diglossia and Power. Language Policies and Practice in the 19th Century Habsburg Empire*. Berlin et al.: Mouton de Gruyter, 107–166.

Fellerer, Jan. 2005. *Mehrsprachigkeit im galizischen Verwaltungswesen (1772–1914): Eine historisch-soziolinguistische Studie zum Polnischen und Ruthenischen (Ukrainischen)*. Köln, Weimar and Wien: Böhlau Verlag.

Mattheier, Klaus J. 1998. Kommunikationsgeschichte des 19. Jahrhunderts. Überlegungen zum Forschungsstand und zu Perspektiven der Forschungsentwicklung. In Dieter Cherubim, Siegfried Grosse and Klaus J. Mattheier (eds), *Sprache und bürgerliche Nation. Beiträge zur deutschen und europäischen Sprachgeschichte des 19. Jahrhunderts.* Berlin and New York: de Gruyter, 1–46.

Nagl, Johann Willibald and Jakob Zeidler. 1931. Deutsch-österreichische Literaturgeschichte. *Ein Handbuch zur Geschichte der deutschen Dichtung in Österreich-Ungarn,* vol. III–IV. Wien: Fromme.

Neuland, Eva. 1993. Sprachgefühl, Spracheinstellungen, Sprachbewußtsein. Zur Relevanz ‚subjektiver Faktoren‘ für Sprachvariation und Sprachwandel. In Klaus J. Mattheier, Klaus-Peter Wegera et al. (eds.), *Vielfalt des Deutschen. Festschrift für Werner Besch.* Frankfurt/Main: Lang, 723–748.

Paupié, Kurt (ed.) 1966. *Handbuch der österreichischen Pressegeschichte: 1848–1959,* vol. I–II. Wien et al.: Braumüller.

Rindler Schjerve, Rosita. 2000. Diglossie als diskursives Herrschaftskonstrukt. Überlegungen zur Beschreibung diachroner Mehrsprachigkeit. *Sociolinguistica* 14: 42–49.

Rindler Schjerve, Rosita. 1997. Sprachpolitik aus der Sicht einer Sprachwissenschaftlerin. In Umberto Rinaldi et al. (eds.), *Lingua e politica: la politica linguistica della duplice monarchia e la sua attualità; atti del simposio; 31. 5. 1996.* Wien: Istituto Italiano di Cultura, 13–23.

Rindler Schjerve, Rosita. 1998. Italienisch und Deutsch im Habsburgischen Vielvölkerstaat: Zur Beziehung von Diglossie und Sprachpolitik aus historischer Perspektive. In: Cordin, Patrizia, Maria Iliescu, Heidi Siller-Runggaldier (eds.): *Italienisch und Deutsch im Kontakt und im Vergleich. Akten des VII. Treffens der italienischen und österreichischen Linguisten.* Trento: Dipartimento di Scienze Filologiche e Storiche, 487–503.

Rindler Schjerve, Rosita and Eva Vetter. 2003. Historical Sociolinguistics and Multilingualism: Theoretical and methodological issues in the Development of a Multifunctional Framework. In Rosita Rindler Schjerve (ed.), *Diglossia and power. Language policies and practice in the 19th century Habsburg Empire.* Berlin et al.: Mouton de Gruyter, 35–66.

Wandruszka, Adam and Peter Urbanitsch (eds.) 1980. *Die Habsburgermonarchie (1848–1918),* vol. 3.1 and 3.2. Wien: Verlag der Österreichischen Akademie der Wissenschaften.

Левицький К. 1926. *Історія політичної думки галицьких українців 1848–1914. Львів.*

ELINE VANHECKE AND JETJE DE GROOF (BRUSSELS)

New data on language policy and language choice in 19th-century Flemish city administrations

1. Introduction

From a meta-linguistic point of view, the general history with regard to the situation of the Dutch Language in 19th-century Flanders is well-documented. It is clear that Flanders experienced very radical language planning measures, either in favour or at the expense of the position of the Dutch language. Still, concrete data on the impact of the continuous language planning activities of the successive political regimes[1] and their language norms (including different spelling systems) on written Dutch are rather scarce.

With this contribution we want to provide information that can help us to understand this forgotten (or neglected) chapter of the history of Dutch in 19th-century Flanders. It deals with official language use in Flanders at the time and provides a general overview of language choice and language variation within a large number of Flemish city hall administrations during the nineteenth century. The study involves the analysis of an original and extensive corpus of handwritten documents, focussing on the intriguing interplay of language policy and the actual language choice and written language output of city hall scribes. It will be pointed out to what extent the involved city administrations were influenced by and reacted to the various language planning activities, the (imposed) norms, and the often contradictory language policies of the successive regimes.

---

[1] During the nineteenth century, Flanders was governed by three different regimes. Until 1814 Flanders was a part of the French Republic. It was subsequently reunited with the Northern Netherlands until 1830, after which it became part of independent Belgium for the rest of the century.

2. The project

During the 19th century, Flanders witnessed a number of very radical changes both on the general socio-political and on the linguistic level. Although the language measures implemented by the different successive regimes have had an undeniable effect on the development of the Dutch language in Flanders, only little is known, so far, about the actual language use during that specific period.

More specifically, the general linguistic and socio-political situation of 19th-century Flanders is well documented by a large number of secondary sources, but most of these only offer a meta-linguistic account of the relevant institutional, political, and social aspects. Even though the Flemish archives contain piles of primary sources, it appears that, until a decade ago, this original language material has never been used for investigating the actual 19th-century written language use. As such, there were hardly any studies on the historical sociolinguistics of Dutch.

A long-term and large-scale project in historical sociolinguistics was set up at the Centre for Linguistics of the Vrije Universiteit Brussel (VUB) in 1992. Initially this project was concerned with the (socio)linguistic situation in Bruges during the 19th century (Willemyns and Vandenbussche 2000), but the innovative outcomes of the study soon led to a number of sub-research projects focusing on other, but interrelated, aspects of the development and use of Dutch in 19th-century Flanders. The complex situation of the Dutch language is now investigated systematically in all domains of society and with respect to different degrees of formality: *language policy and language planning, language and the media, language and class, language and administration...* (cf. Vandenbussche, De Groof, Vanhecke and Willemyns 2004). This research is conducted on the basis of original source material which has never been used for linguistic research before.

By now the importance of both taking into account a number of relevant sociolinguistic variables and using original sources has become very clear. All results, so far, seem to indicate that a number of 'traditional' beliefs about the 19th-century situation are either based on wrong interpretations of data or not empirically founded (Willemyns 2004).

One part of our socio-historical research project focuses on written language output on official city administrations. The main research question is to what extent city chancelleries reacted to and were influenced by the drastic (and often conflicting) language planning activities of the successive regimes in 19th-century Flanders. The aim is to gain a clear insight into the actual *language choice* and *language use* of town hall scribes and the prevailing connection with the extremely varied historical-political context of that time. To achieve this, we have analysed an extensive corpus of original handwritten documents, i.e. the minutes and reports of the city council meetings of 53 different towns. The present article reports on the most recent findings of this ongoing study.

These results should be interpreted within the relevant social and political context. The following paragraph provides a brief historical overview of the linguistic and political landscape of Flanders in the 19th century. Next, the research data and results are discussed, followed by our concluding remarks.

3. Political-linguistic context

In the 19th century, the Southern Low Countries (i.e. Flanders) experienced three very distinct regimes, each introducing a radical, and also often contradictory, language policy. From 1794 until 1814, Flanders had been annexed by France. For the next 15 years, it was reunited with the Northern Low Countries in the United Kingdom of the Netherlands. In October 1830 Flanders became part of the independent constitutional monarchy of Belgium. Each of these authorities tried to achieve very specific language planning goals, either in favour or at the expense of the position of the Dutch language[2].

Although the foreign authorities who preceded the French annexation[3] favoured French as the language of prestige and administration, they never implemented an actual language policy. Still, this did not prevent the Dutch language from gradually losing its official status and functions, except at the local level (Vandenbussche et al. 2004). By the time the 'Belgian' regions were annexed by France, Dutch remained the language of the people, but French was the *de facto* language of the central administration (Willemyns et al. 2005).

The French were the first to officially implement an extreme language policy of Frenchification, attempting to completely exclude the Dutch language from public and private life. In 1803 it was stipulated by law that, from 1804 onwards, all public and private acts were to be written only in French. As a result, the already dominant position of French became even more important (and officially confirmed), especially in the domains of administration and justice. However, the knowledge and use of French was to a large extent socially determined. In reality, the majority of the Flemish

---

[2]   In her doctoral research on language policy and language planning in 19th-century Flanders, De Groof (2004) explains that the language planning activities did not only originate in the government, but that, especially after Belgian independence, political groupings, unions, and even individuals played a certain role in this process.

[3]   From 1555 until 1714, the Low Countries were ruled by the Spanish. In 1714 the 'Belgian' territories were passed on to the Austrian Habsburgers until they became occupied by the French in 1794.

population had no command of French, and most of them were therefore not able to apply the regulations (De Groof 2004). The same situation occurred in many town hall administrations of smaller communes, where only a few civil servants had any competence in French (Willemyns et al. 2005). Nevertheless, by the time that Flanders was reunited with the Northern Low Countries in 1814, the Dutch language had suffered immense prestige and function loss.

In the United Kingdom of the Netherlands, under the reign of King Willem I, the Flemish regions were once again confronted with a strict policy based on the 'one nation – one language' doctrine. As opposed to the French, who attempted to suppress and even eradicate the Dutch language, Willem I favoured Dutch as the national language. To this end, he counted on the presumed language unity between the Northern and Southern Low Countries in order to unite his kingdom. Indeed, in theory 75% of his citizens were Dutch-speaking (De Jonghe 1967), but the true situation in the southern part of his kingdom was much more complicated. In Flanders, Willem I was confronted with at least three language varieties: 1) French, which was the prestige variety of the social elite, 2) Southern Dutch dialects, and 3) an 'intended' standard Dutch,[4] used by members of middle and lower social classes (cf. Vandenbussche 2003). Furthermore, most Flemish citizens were not convinced of a linguistic link between their own language and the northern standard (Willemyns 2003).

However, this did not restrain Willem I from imposing a strict language policy in order to dutchify (and in this way also de-frenchify) public life in Flanders. In 1819 a law was announced declaring Dutch to be the only national and, hence, also the exclusive administrative language from 1823 onward.[5] In 1822 it was decided that the same law would be applied in the districts of Brussels and Leuven. The period between 1819 and 1823 was intended as a transitional phase, in order to give civil servants sufficient time to change their linguistic habits and learn the Dutch language if necessary. Towards the end of his reign, in 1829 and 1830, Willem I felt obliged to make a number of concessions to the growing opposition to his general policy. He reversed his language policy by introducing complete language freedom and granting facilities for the use of French in Flanders. As such, Dutch lost its position as exclusive official language.

Though the reunion of the Low Countries only lasted for about 15 years, it was extremely important for the future linguistic landscape of Flanders. It

---

[4] The concept of an 'intended standard' was introduced by Mihm (1995) and refers to a language variant of which the formal characteristics do not always correspond to the actual standard language, but which is nevertheless used to function as standard variety.

[5] This law was not intended for the Walloon provinces.

lasted long enough for the Flemings to rediscover "their language for administration, politics, the courts, and education" and inspired a small group of intellectuals (Flemish Movement) to try and (re)establish the Dutch language in administration, education, and cultural life (Vandenbussche et al 2004: 52).

From September to October 1830 the opposition against Willem I escalated in the so-called Belgian Revolution. Belgium became an independent monarchy and, once again, the language-political situation in the Low Countries changed radically.

The Belgian parliament was dominated by the bourgeois elite, who preferred French as the language for administration and public life in general (Vandenbussche et al. 2004). The concept of 'language freedom' continued to exist but would soon be reinterpreted as French unilingualism through a series of language decrees (De Groof 2004). In October and November 1830, the 'Provisional Government' declared French as the only official and administrative language of Belgium and, as a result, the country was ruled almost exclusively in French.

In 1831 the new Belgian constitution was proclaimed. Article 23 of this constitution guaranteed freedom of language choice; language use could only be regulated for administrative and legal matters. Even though the previous language decrees became void as soon as the constitution was announced, they still ought to be considered as the background against which constitutional language freedom was interpreted in practice (De Groof 2004). Besides, the government only appointed French-speaking civil servants, deliberately discriminating the Dutch language (Willemyns et al. 2002). Hence, French *de facto* was the prestige language of administration, justice, education, and army.

As soon as Belgium was declared independent, the Flemish Movement started its long battle against the exclusion of Dutch from official functions. A first request for adopting a number of language laws concerning the use of Dutch in administration, justice, and education was submitted in 1840. However, it took almost 40 years before the first law granting (though only limited) rights for Dutch in administrative matters was passed (1878). Only with the so called 'Equality law' in 1898, Dutch was finally recognized as an official language of Belgium next (and fully equal) to French.

4. Analysis and research results

It is clear that Flanders experienced very drastic political and linguistic changes during the 19th century. Although until recently no in-depth (historical-sociolinguistic) study had been carried out based on original historical sources, and hence no concrete data concerning the actual linguistic situation in Flemish city hall administrations was available, it was (and still is) commonly accepted that Dutch played a minor part in the administration at the time. It is generally agreed that the Flemish administration was completely Frenchified due to the language policy of the French rulers (1794–1814). It is also 'common knowledge' that the language policy of King Willem I failed, and that the Dutch language was not suitable, nor sufficiently developed, for the use in formal and official domains.

The analysis and research results discussed below are a first attempt to determine the actual extent to which Flemish chancelleries reacted to the changing political situation and the often contradictory regulations.

Our study of language choice in 19th-century Flemish chancelleries is based on an extensive corpus of original written language material that has been collected in more than 50 Flemish (town hall) archives. Pilot studies were carried out in Willebroek (Vanhecke 1998) and Grembergen (Van Meersche 2003), and these formed the basis for our core research in Bruges and Antwerp. In each of these cities, handwritten reports of city council meetings or minutes of the meetings of the aldermen were examined with regard to spelling and language choice. In order to determine whether and when the chancelleries used Dutch or French for writing their official administrative texts, the language of all documents was inspected for every year. Next, it was established whether these findings concerning the actual language choice corresponded to the official language rules of that time.

The results emerging from the four detailed case studies led to a number of unexpected conclusions and intriguing assumptions. In general, a major difference can be observed between the language choice in city and smaller town/village chancelleries. It appears that in the smaller towns the language regulations were only partially respected during the French rule. Both in Grembergen and Willebroek many official texts continued to be written in Dutch. On the other hand, during the time of the United Kingdom practically all documents in both town hall administrations were drawn up in Dutch, even before this was mandatory (cf. also Willemyns and De Groof 2004). Soon after Belgian independence in 1830, both administrations switched to the almost exclusive use of French but only continued to do so for less than a decade. Around 1840 French started to lose its dominant position, and by the 1860s French had disappeared almost completely from these small town-halls administrations. In the city hall administrations, quite a different course was pursued. Whereas in Grembergen and Willebroek language freedom was interpreted in favour of the Dutch language, in Antwerp and Bruges this was done in favour of French. Both city chancelleries switched back from Dutch to French as soon as Belgium became independent, and it took decades before French lost its dominant position. In Antwerp, the city government accepted

Dutch as its official language in August 1866, but, apparently, this decision was only gradually applied.[6] In the city administration of Bruges, Dutch was partly reintroduced in 1888; the meetings of the city council were registered in Dutch from 1897 onwards.

Apart from the different linguistic practices in the chancelleries of bigger and smaller towns, there is another interesting observation. It appears that in each of the analysed administrations the switch from French to Dutch and vice versa occurred virtually without any problem (cf. De Groof and Vanhecke 2004). This implies that not only the involved city scribes had the required linguistic competence to function in both French and Dutch, but it also contradicts the generally accepted idea of the so-called uselessness of Dutch for official purposes[7] (cf. Willemyns and Vanhecke 2003).

In order to confirm and refine our initial research results and to get an overview of the situation in the whole of Flanders, similar analyses were carried out in another 49 town hall administrations: Aartrijke, Koekelare*[8], Koksijde*, Loppem, Poperinge, Zedelgem (Province of West-Flanders); Aalst, Lebbeke, Meerbeke, Oudenaarde, Zele (Province of East-Flanders); Boom, Bornem, Geel, Mechelen, Mol, Turnhout, Wilrijk (province of Antwerp); Borgloon, Hasselt, Leopoldsburg, Lummen*, Maaseik, Tongeren (Province of Limburg); Asse*, Brussel, Diegem, Diest, Etterbeek, Evere, Ganshoren, Grimbergen, Haacht, Halle, Hoeilaart, Huldenberg*, Itterbeek*, Jette, Keerbergen, Lennik*, Leuven, Liedekerke, Meise, Overijse, Ruisbroek, Schaarbeek, Sint-Martens-Bodegem, Sint-Pieters-Leeuw, Sint-Pieters-Woluwe, Ternat*, Tervuren*, Tienen, Tildonk, Vorst, Wezembeek-Oppem, Zemst (Province of

---

6   From 27th August 1866 onwards, all reports of the city council meetings were written exclusively in Dutch. However, this does not mean that French had disappeared from these meetings. The 'Municipal Journal', which included all discussions and interruptions of the council members, shows that, despite the fact that the meetings were officially registered in Dutch, many of the members were still using French in meetings. It was not before 1895 that all council members actually attended the meetings using the Dutch language (cf. Beyers-Bell 1978).

7   In 1817 the Bruges-born Minister of Internal Affaires, De Coninck van Outryve, stressed that the tongue spoken in Flanders was useless for official function: "Flemish can, as it is known by them [i.e. the members of various social classes in Flanders], be of use to neither one nor the other, to perform acts of a certain importance [...]. I hold the opinion that one should first and foremost make learn the Dutch language in these provinces, because one does not know that language there, at least not in that way that it could be used by enlightened men in any important discussions." (quoted in Willemyns 2003: 189; translation by Wim Vandenbussche).

8   In the towns marked with an asterisk, the collected data concerns the language choice solely for the acts of the Registry Office (civil state). Bearing in mind that the focus of the present contribution is on the city council meetings, those towns are not considered here.

Flemish-Brabant); Landen, St-Martensvoeren (Province of Luik).[9] Map 1 shows the geographical position of the chancelleries under discussion.

In each of these towns, we likewise compared the official language policy of the successive governments with the actual language choice in the local town hall administrations, i.e. in the minutes of the city council meetings. For every document analysed we verified to what extent the used language conformed with the language regulations of that time.

In order to obtain a visual representation of the relation between the actual language choice in the different chancelleries and the official language policies, all findings are summarized in a series of maps.[10] Each of the following maps shows the language(s) used in the analysed town hall administrations at a crucial moment in the 19th century.

Map 2 reveals the actual language choice in 1819, five years after the end of the annexation by France. The new language regulations of King Willem I (installing Dutch as the only official language in Flanders) had yet to be applied. At the onset of the Dutch government, Dutch had clearly been ruled out almost entirely from the official domain.[11] Although in Brussels[12] documents were registered in both French and Dutch, and in the town hall administrations of Grembergen, Lebbeke, Meerbeke, and Turnhout, Dutch was still used now and then, the general picture here is that French found itself in a very strong and dominant position. The only exception is the town of Mol, where Dutch remained the exclusive language for administration. Only a few years later, in 1823, the situation reversed completely.

Map 3 shows the situation in 1823. It is quite striking to see how strict the decree of 1819, implying that from 1st January 1823 Dutch would be the only official language, was observed. French disappeared almost completely from official documents, even in those areas where formerly only French had been used. Moreover, the research results also prove that many city and town administrations already switched to the use of Dutch before this was

---

[9] The reason for collecting data in these specific cities or towns was mainly practical, taking into account the availability of the desired documents and the cooperation of the archives. Within these constraints, we tried to arrive at the best possible and balanced regional distribution of towns for our research.

[10] The maps were made by Torsten Wiedemann, affiliated to the Department of Modern History at Ghent University and the Belgian Historical IGIS (Interactive Geographical Information System for historical statistics in Belgium 1800–1963/2003).

[11] This holds true for the reports of the city council meetings and the meetings of the aldermen. However, other documents, such as the acts of the registry office, were (still) written in Dutch.

[12] Apparently, in Brussels and its surroundings a bilingual situation continued to exist. Further in-depth study is necessary before any final conclusions can be drawn with regard to this specific area.

compulsory. Only four exceptions were encountered:[13] Brussels, which still shows a bilingual situation; Halle, were Dutch became the dominant language but French was still used sometimes in 1823 only; Zele, where French kept its dominant position, though by the end of the year the chancellery did switch to the exclusive use of Dutch; and, finally, Poperinge, which appears to be a special case. Whereas the minutes of city council meetings were written in French, those of the meetings of the aldermen were noted in Dutch. This peculiar 'bilingual' situation continued throughout the 19th century.

Map 4 shows the situation in September 1830, after King Willem I had introduced language freedom and facilities for the use of French in Flanders. All chancelleries were now free to choose their language of administration themselves. It is remarkable that at this point virtually none of the city administrations seized the opportunity to switch back to French. The most reasonable explanation, so it seems, may be the fact that the Dutch king was still in power, and that Dutch thus remained the 'loyal' chancellery language. The elite of Flanders might have accepted by now that Dutch would remain the official language. Only few city administrations decided to reintroduce French: in Oudenaarde the new French facilities were utilized immediately; in Lebbeke French soon regained its former dominant position, and in Zele French gradually sneaked its way in again.

It appears that, in only two months' time, this picture once again changed radically (map 5). As soon as Belgium became independent, the 'expected' switch to French did occur. Although no specific language regulation had been decreed yet, the Belgian Provisional Government overtly expressed its preference for French as the prestige language of culture and administration. Many city councils that had formerly opted for the Dutch language now immediately started using French in a very determined way. This goes especially for major cities such as Bruges, Antwerp, and Tongeren.

Map 6 shows that many smaller towns would soon massively follow the example of these big cities during the first decade after Belgian independence, especially once the 'freedom of language choice' had been constitutionalized. Although many city councils still used both Dutch and French, the latter quickly became the dominant language. Again, the pace of change is rather amazing. The young Belgian state had no official linguistic regulations whatsoever for local authorities, but since the Provisional Government had given the French example, many city administrations followed the national government's preference.

---

[13] The city administrations of Landen and Sint-Martens-Voeren did not belong to the Flemish provinces and were hence not obliged to use Dutch. Both towns kept on using French during the entire 19th century.

Map 7 clearly demonstrates the ongoing and growing influence of Frenchification: by 1840 the use of French had reached its climax in the chancelleries under discussion. This observation indicates that 1830 may have been the true *annus horribilis* for the Dutch language in Flanders, especially bearing in mind that the government did its utmost to exclude Dutch from any official functions. However, the map also shows that even at this point, contrary to what has been generally assumed so far, Dutch had not been excluded completely from the town halls. In fact, 9 of the analysed chancelleries functioned exclusively in Dutch, in 8 town hall administrations Dutch was still the dominant language, and 6 town councils still used Dutch regularly, though French remained dominant.

Another interesting point is the difference in language choice between administrations in larger and smaller towns. Whereas the first switched back to French almost immediately, this did not happen in the latter, where French never regained its former dominant position. A clear example of this can be found when comparing the city administration of Antwerp with the neighbouring town of Wilrijk. A similar contrast is found in the data collected in the chancelleries of Aartrijke, Loppem, and Zedelgem, when compared to Bruges: the city councils of the first three towns in the surrounding area of Bruges used Dutch almost continuously during the 19th century; Bruges continued to be Frenchified until the 1890s.

Map 8 shows how, forty years later, the linguistic situation had again changed considerably. It appears that after 1840 a growing tendency towards the exclusive use of Dutch had started. Although in 1880 Dutch had not yet been recognized as officially equal to French, it did enjoy a rather strong position within many Flemish town hall administrations. Around the turn of the century, French would disappear completely from most chancelleries. This change in the linguistic landscape of Flanders was mainly due to the initiatives of the Flemish Movement, which was the driving force behind the first language laws in Belgium.

5. Conclusion

Our research of original data from some 50 Flemish chancelleries has led to a number of interesting conclusions which challenge and refute a number of traditionally held ideas concerning the position of Dutch in the 19th century.

Until recently it had been generally assumed that King Willem's Dutch language policy had failed (De Jonghe 1967; Deneckere 1954), especially given the fact that French became the dominant language immediately after the independence of Belgium. However, our research proves that Willem I did succeed in Dutchifying official and public life in Flanders. His language policy was consistently applied. In compliance with the law of 1819, Dutch was effectively implemented in the chancelleries discussed above as the only official language from 1823 onwards and remained the exclusive language of administration until the independence of Belgium in 1830 (cf. also Willemyns and De Groof 2004).

It appears that political loyalty may have been a crucial element in the official reactions of the city administrations towards the different language policies. It is noteworthy that, both under the Dutch rule and after the Belgian independence, the town hall scribes behaved 'politically correct', i.e. their language choice corresponded to what was expected by their new political leaders. Our analysis also illustrates, however, that the actual language choice in the involved city hall administrations did not necessarily correspond to the 'expected' language choice. The massive switch from Dutch to French as exclusive administrative language, for example, did not occur as soon as the opportunity was offered (i.e. 1829), but only after Belgian independence.

Apart from political correctness, linguistic preferences of the scribes may have caused a language switch. Willem's language regulations were sometimes put into practice even before they were compulsory, whereas French language laws were only hesitantly complied with (Willemyns and Vanhecke 2003). During the first decade of Belgium's independence, on the other hand, there was a massive shift from Dutch to French, although this time no official language legislation existed (yet). This prompt shift needs to be interpreted in the light of the general political (and revolutionary) atmosphere. The use of Dutch could easily be seen as a sign of loyalty towards the former king. As soon as the situation had calmed down, the use of Dutch as an administrative language increased again.

Our analysis has, finally, also revealed major differences in language choice between larger and smaller town hall administrations. Apparently, the different political and social context strongly influenced the linguistic situation. Whereas smaller communes like Willebroek and Grembergen interpreted the Belgian language freedom in favour of Dutch, major cities like Antwerp and Bruges preferred to use French (cf. Willemyns, De Groof, Vandenbussche and Vanhecke 2004).

Leaving the particular reasons for the language switches aside, it is striking that most town hall clerks did possess the linguistic competence necessary to switch from one language to the other so quickly. The collected data have shown that a language switch only rarely coincided with a change of scribes. Hence city hall scribes must have had an elaborated linguistic competence in both French and Dutch, and this contradicts the common assumption that Dutch was not appropriate as an administrative and official language in the 19th century. Ongoing research investigating the spelling behaviour in a number of Flemish chancelleries (Antwerp, Bruges, Willebroek, and

Grembergen) already indicated that the scribes were acquainted with the different existing spelling systems and were able to use them virtually flawlessly (Willemyns and Vanhecke 2003). For now, there is no scientifically grounded or empirically based explanation for this remarkable competence, though it is hoped that historical-pedagogical research may be able to provide some answers.

References

Beyers-Bell, Janine. 1978. Jan Van Rijswijck Liberaal Flamingant en burgemeester van Antwerpen. In Lode Wils (ed.), *Kopstukken van de Vlaamse Beweging.* Kortrijk/Heule: UGA, 17–106.

Deneckere, Marcel. 1954. *Histoire de la langue Française dans les Flandres (1770–1823).* Gent: Romanica Gandensia.

De Groof, Jetje. 2004. *Nederlandse taalplanning in Vlaanderen in de lange negentiende eeuw (1795–1914). Een linguïstische analyse met speciale aandacht voor de wisselwerking tussen status- en corpusplanning.* Unpublished Ph thesis. Vrije Universiteit Brussel.

De Groof, Jetje and Eline Vanhecke. 2004. 1830 als taalpolitiek keerpunt, de jure en de facto. In Wim Vandenbussche (ed.), *Terug naar de bron(nen). Taal en taalgebruik in de 19de eeuw in Vlaanderen. Handelingen van het Academiecolloquium van 28 mei 2003.* Gent: Koninklijke Academie voor Nederlandse Taal- en Letterkunde, 55–69.

De Jonghe, Albert. 1967. *De taalpolitiek van Willem I. in de Zuidelijke Nederlanden (1814–1830).* Sint-Andries bij Brugge: Darthet.

Mihm, Arend. 1995. Arbeitersprache und gesprochene Sprache im 19. Jahrhundert. In Dieter Cherubim et al. (eds.), *Sprache und bürgerliche Nation.* Berlin and New York: de Gruyter, 282–316.

Vandenbussche, Wim. 2003. Historische sociolinguïstiek in Vlaanderen. *Thema's en trends in de sociolinguïstiek* 4: 39–49.

Vandenbussche, Wim, Jetje De Groof, Eline Vanhecke and Roland Willemyns. 2004. Historical sociolinguistics in Flanders: Rediscovering the 19th century. In Helen Christen (ed.), *Dialekt, Regiolekt und Standardsprache im sozialen und zeitlichen Raum.* Wien: Praesens, 49–80.

Vanhecke, Eline. 1998. *Enkele aspecten van het ambtelijk taalgebruik in de negentiende eeuw: taal, spelling en woordenschat in de verslagen van het Willebroekse Schepencollege (1818–1900).* Unpublished MA thesis. Vrije Universiteit Brussel.

Vanhecke, Eline. 2005. Taalkeuze in Vlaamse stadskanselarijen in de negentiende eeuw. *Taal en Tongva* 56: 48–64.

Van Meersche, Linda. 2003. *Kanselarijtalen in de negentiende eeuw in Grembergen: een onderzoek naar taalgebruik en spelling.* Unpublished MA thesis. Vrije Universiteit Brussel.

Willemyns, Roland. 2003. *Het verhaal van het Vlaams. De geschiedenis van het Nederlands in de Zuidelijke Nederlanden.* Antwerpen and Utrecht: Standaard Uitgeverij – Spectrum.

Willemyns, Roland. 2004. Terug naar de bron(nen). In Wim Vandenbussche (ed.), *Terug naar de bron(nen). Taal en taalgebruik in de 19de eeuw in Vlaanderen. Handelingen van het Academiecolloquium van 28 mei 2003.* Gent: Koninklijke Academie voor Nederlandse Taal- en Letterkunde, 5–10.

Willemyns, Roland and Jetje De Groof. 2004. Is de taalpolitiek van Willem I werkelijk mislukt? In Saskia Daalder, Theo Janssen and Jan Noordegraaf (eds.), *Taal in verandering. Huldealbum Arjan van Leuvensteijn.* Amsterdam: Stichting Neerlandistiek VU, 185–191.

Willemyns, Roland, Jetje De Groof and Wim Vandenbussche. 2002. Die Standardisierungsgeschichte des Niederländischen im 18. und 19. Jahrhundert. Einige Ergebnisse und Forschungsdesiderate. In Jannis Androutsopoulos and Evelyn Ziegler (eds.), *Standardfragen. Soziolinguistische Perspektiven auf Sprachgeschichte, Sprachkontakt und Sprachvariation.* Frankfurt am Main: Lang, 27–38.

Willemyns, Roland and Wim Vandenbussche. 2000. Historische sociolinguïstiek: het 'Brugge-project'. *Taal en Tongval* 52: 258–276.

Willemyns, Roland and Eline Vanhecke. 2003. Corpus planning in 19th century Flanders and its consequences on public language usage in the administration. *Interdisciplinary Journal for Germanic Linguistics and Semiotic Analysis* 8: 83–96.

Willemyns, Roland, Eline Vanhecke and Wim Vandenbussche. 2005. Politische Loyalität und Sprachwahl. Eine Fallstudie aus dem Flandern des frühen 19. Jahrhunderts. In Elisabeth Berner, Manuela Böhm and Anja Voeste (eds.), *Ein grofs vnnd narhafft haffen. Festschrift für Joachim Gessinger.* Potsdam: Institut für Germanistik, 197–207.

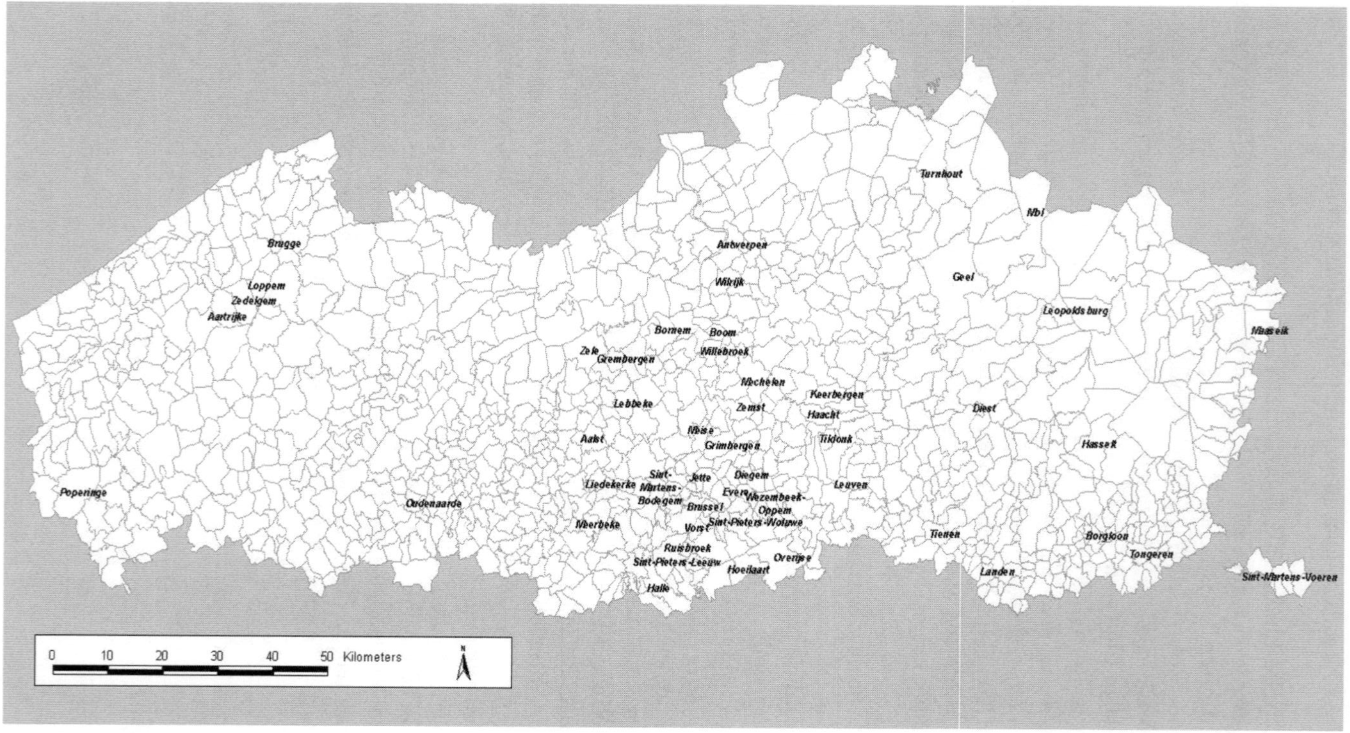

Map 1: Analysed Chancelleries

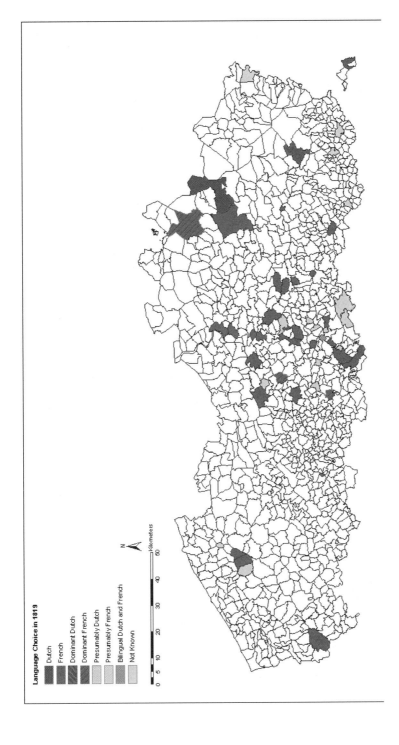

Map 2: Language choice in town chancellors 1819

Language Choice in 1819

- Dutch
- French
- Dominant Dutch
- Dominant French
- Presumably Dutch
- Presumably French
- Bilingual Dutch and French
- Not Known

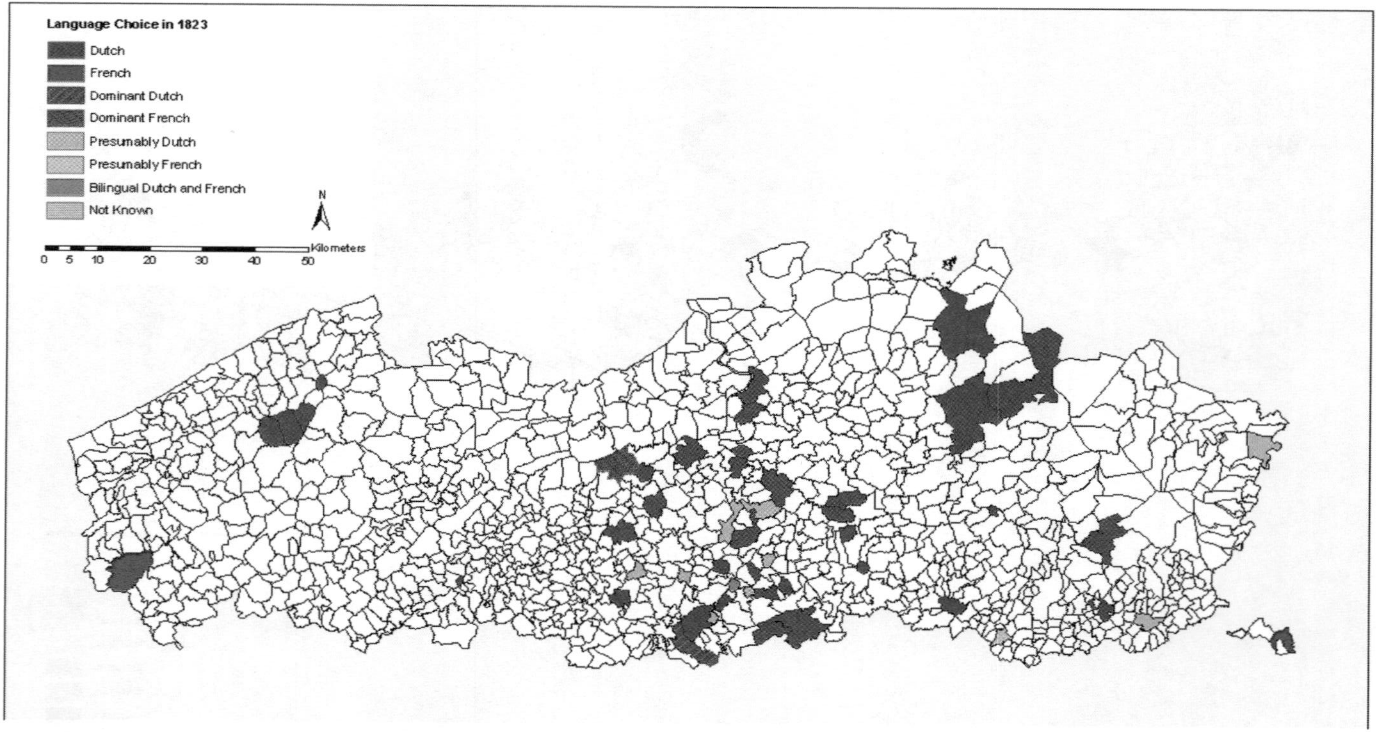

Map 3: Language choice in town chancellors 1823

Language Choice in 1823

- Dutch
- French
- Dominant Dutch
- Dominant French
- Presumably Dutch
- Presumably French
- Bilingual Dutch and French
- Not Known

0 5 10 20 30 40 50
Kilometers

N

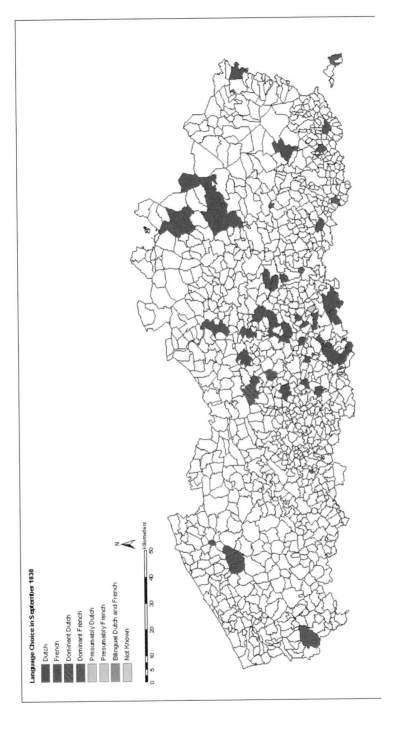

Language Choice in September 1830

- Dutch
- French
- Dominant Dutch
- Dominant French
- Presumably Dutch
- Presumably French
- Bilingual Dutch and French
- Not Known

N

0 5 10 20 30 40 50
Kilometers

Map 4: Language choice in town chancellors September 1830

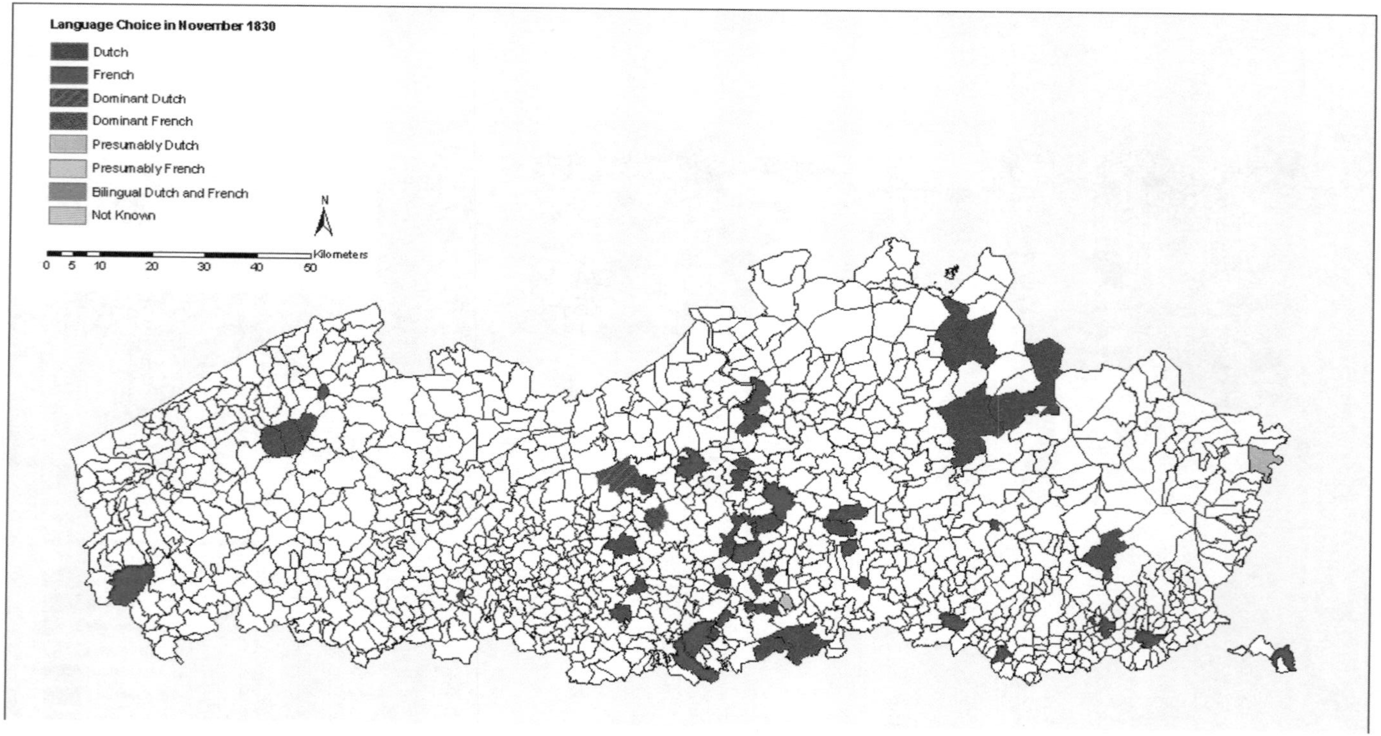

Language Choice in November 1830

- ■ Dutch
- ■ French
- ▨ Dominant Dutch
- ■ Dominant French
- ▨ Presumably Dutch
- ▨ Presumably French
- ▨ Bilingual Dutch and French
- ☐ Not Known

0 5 10   20   30   40   50 kilometers

Map 5: Language choice in town chancellors November 1830

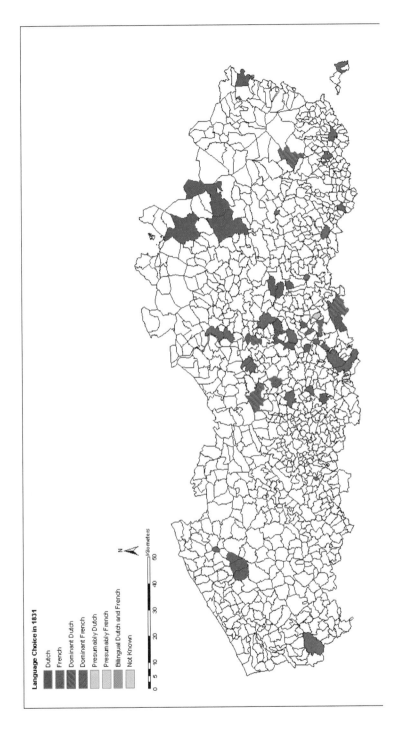

Map 6: Language choice in town chancellors 1831

Language Choice in 1831

Dutch
French
Dominant Dutch
Dominant French
Presumably Dutch
Presumably French
Bilingual Dutch and French
Not Known

N

0 5 10   20   30   40   50
Kilometers

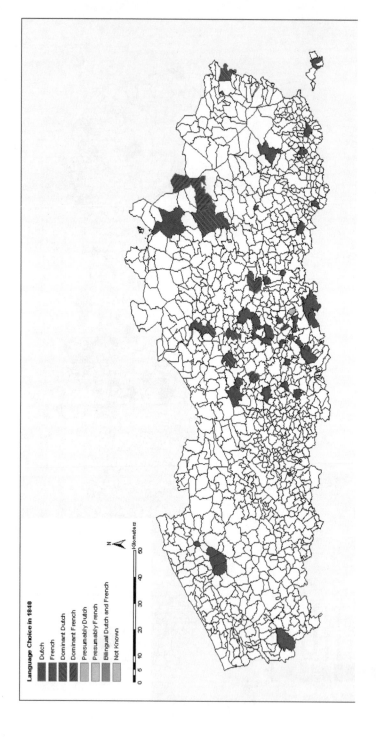

Map 7: Language choice in town chancellors 1840

Language Choice in 1840

- Dutch
- French
- Dominant Dutch
- Dominant French
- Presumably Dutch
- Presumably French
- Bilingual Dutch and French
- Not Known

N

Kilometers
0 5 10   20   30   40   50

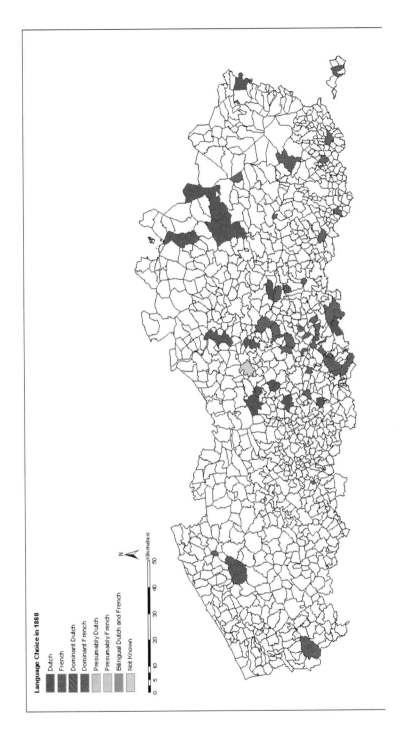

Map 8: Language choice in town chancellors 1880

V. Reflections on alternative language histories

ANGELIKA LINKE (ZÜRICH)

Communicative genres as categories in a socio-cultural history of communication

1. Introduction

On 13 December 1836 Felix Mendelssohn-Bartholdy – despite his young age of 27 already a well known composer – sent a letter from Frankfurt to Berlin. The letter was addressed to his sister Fanny and read:

> Zuweilen möcht' ich ein klein wenig toll werden, wenn ich an die Visiten denke, die morgen losgehen, es sind deren — — — 163, wohlgezählt! — Was sagst Du nun, Kantor? Und bei meinem Bart, ich muss sie alle machen, trotzdem dass ich mich so jämmerlich anstelle, wie mir nur möglich. Aber wahrlich, mir ist das auch einerlei — ich bin zu froh. [...][1]

> 'At times, when I allow myself to think of all the calls due from tomorrow on – 163 in all –, I could go a little mad. What do you say to that, Kantor? Upon my word, I will have to do them all, despite the fact that I always try to be as impossible as possible at doing them. But frankly, I don't really care – I am simply too cheerful […].'

Neither the subject of the letter – the call – nor the actual word Mendelssohn-Bartholdy uses for it, the German word "Visite", sounds very familiar to the contemporary reader. Today, speakers of German are most likely to think of a ward round in a hospital rather than a social event.[2] And even if people are still

---

[1] Letter dating from 13 December 1836, cited in Hensel (1995: 474); the graphic notation follows the print in Hensel.

[2] The German words "Besuch" and "Visite" basically translate as 'visit' and 'call' in English. The older use of the formerly French word resembles the German "Visite" in many ways, especially in terms of its usage in the context of formal social interaction of the 18th and 19th century (compare, e.g., compounds like 'visit-day' or 'visit-paying' in the Oxford English Dictionary 1989 Vol. XIX: 691). It is also quite similar to its contemporary meaning in medical contexts in phrases such as "a professional call made by a doctor on a patient" (Oxford English Dictionary 1989 Vol. XIX: 690). As opposed to the German word, however, the English 'visit' is not restricted to medical contexts but can also be used when referring to

aware of the actual meaning and implication of the word, the communicative genre of the 'call' no longer forms an active part of our "genre spectrum" (Luckmann). Moreover, the genre of the 'cal' bears no real similarity to today's 'visit'. How unfamiliar the term is today also becomes apparent in the surprisingly high number of 'calls' Mendelssohn-Bartholdy has to make. 163 calls in one week seem far too many to us today. And yet, he himself does not seem to be at all surprised by the number of calls, although he could 'go a little mad' if he were to think too much about them. The fact that Mendelssohn-Bartholdy is expected to pay the 163 visits mentioned despite his obvious reluctance in the matter underlines the assumption that the "Visite" must have been a very important genre both to him and his class, the German bourgeoisie. And, in addition to this, he declares he will act as 'impossibly as possible' on the occasion, which would indicate that there are certain rules of conduct he clearly knows of but deliberately fails to observe. What these norms are like is not mentioned in his letter because it is not necessary: His sister knows them as well as he does.

Before turning to Mendelssohn-Bartholdy's dilemma of 163 calls and the question of how such an undertaking might be at all possible,[3] I would first like to introduce the concept of 'communicative genres' as an analytic category, of which the call is a typical example. I will argue that communicative genres can provide helpful entities for a history of communication and that reconstructing historical genres can give valuable insight into sociolinguistic processes. In a second move, I will then discuss a few examples to find out if and how such reconstructions are at all possible; what kinds of sources, even unconventional ones, should be used; what kinds of linguistic and historical-cultural questions could be raised by the concept of communicative genres, and which answers we can hope to get.

2. The term and concept 'communicative genres'

In contemporary German linguistics, 'communicative genre' as both term and concept is closely linked to American *linguistic anthropology* (Hymes 1972, Hanks 1987, 1989, Scollon/Scollon 2003) and Bakhtin's approach to "speech

---

social interaction with friends and relatives: "an act of visiting a person: a friendly or formal call upon, a shorter or longer stay with a person, as a feature of social intercourse" (OED 1989 Vol. XIX: 690). Formal visits are generally referred to as 'calls' rather than 'visits', given that an unexpected official visitor is also a 'caller' rather than a 'visitor' (Longman Language Activator 1998).

[3]   I have already discussed this in greater detail in Linke (1996: 178–191).

genres". The terms "communicative activity" or "activity type" (Levinson 1979, Clarke 1996: 36, Linell 1998: 234ff.),[4] which have contributed widely to theories of pragmatics and the field of discourse analysis, are also closely related. As far as I know, the term 'communicative genres' was first introduced into German research literature by the sociologist Thomas Luckmann,[5] who initially developed it in the context of social science theory (Luckmann 1986, 1988).[6]

In German linguistics Susanne Günthner first made productive use of the term in her research into spoken language.[7] According to her definition, communicative genres are marked by fixed linguistic patterns, whose function is to indicate the socio-cultural significance of an action. Thus, communicative genres are formed in the process of charging communicative practices with socio-symbolic content and it is through these formal patterns that the socio-symbolic significance expresses itself indexically. In other words, "predefined genre solutions are stored in the social memory [...] of a society" and thereby illustrate the fact that they not only bear significance for particular *individuals* in particular situations; but they also comprise communicative tasks[8] "which are linked to those forms of social conduct that are of existential importance for a *society*" (Luckmann 1988: 284; my translation and emphasis – AL). Seen from a historical perspective, this also means that socio-cultural processes can be symbolically connected to both the establishment of communicative genres by means of repetitive communicative actions and – respectively– to the weakening or even complete disappearance of formerly established genres (cf. Luckmann 1988: 248). This relationship will prove theoretically relevant for the concept of a 'history of communication'.

---

[4]   In his Swedish publications this is also called "verksamhetstyp". See Linell (forthcoming) for a more detailed discussion.

[5]   Luckmann worked on this together with Jörg R. Bergmann.

[6]   In Luckmann's work the term "communicative genre" is closely linked to "social institutions", while at the same time being very different. While "social institutions" are "more or less effective and normative *solutions* to social *problems*" (Luckmann 1986: 202; my emphasis – AL), he defines "communicative genres" as "more or less effective and normative *solutions* to particular communicative *problems*" (Luckmann 1986: 202; my emphasis – AL).

[7]   Compare Günthner/Knoblauch (1995), Günthner (1995), Günthner/Knoblauch (1997), Günthner (2000), Günthner/Luckmann (2002).

[8]   I use the term "task" instead of Luckmann's "problem" (a term he uses in inverted commas only). To speak of "problems" presupposes possible resistance or obstacles in social (inter)action. Therefore, I find the term misleading in the given context.

3. Positioning the concept of 'communicative genres'

Still, the theoretical concept of 'communicative genres' remains a tricky one. This has to do with the fact that the "units" we are dealing with here are ethno-categories[9] rather than products of scientific categorisation. Terms like "Visite" ('call'), "Unterrichtsstunde" ('lesson'), "Geburtstagsfest" ('birthday party') all refer to concepts of social events we obviously recognise as being coherent, clearly delimited, and recognisable. Yet, developing analytical criteria based on these pre-scientific categories, seems complicated. It also proves rather difficult to define clear-cut distinctions between communicative genres and other communicative patterns.[10] According to Susanne Günthner (1995, 2000), 'communicative patterns' and 'genre-like patterns' should be distinguished from prototypical genres by certain criteria such as their *level of coinage*, i.e., their degree of fixity and complexity. This, however, leaves us with fuzzy edges in two directions: *downwards*, if we think of small-scale, less complex patterns like 'greetings', 'compliments', or 'congratulations',[11] and *upwards* with regard to 'maxi-genres' as conferences and election campaigns. In either case, a certain degree of linguistic fixity as well as a high degree of complexity are necessary to allow us to categorize a certain communicative activity as a 'communicative genre'.

4. Communicative genres as constant factors in a socio-cultural history of communication

Once established, communicative genres can play a vital role as a kind of cognitive blueprint for dealing with communicative tasks. That way, the individual is not forced to start from scratch and make up his or her own communicative manual.

The downside to this, however, is a normative effect, given that genre knowledge and genre awareness also provide certain social groups with the means for stigmatising 'wrong' or 'inappropriate' social conduct. At the same time, genre knowledge is part of the social competence that might become necessary for expressing a social status or an affiliation to some class. Usually,

---

[9] Compare both Ehlich's and Günthner's remarks on the subject (Ehlich 1986: 53ff., Günthner 1995: 199).

[10] Still, the fact that the lexicon of everyday language contains a huge number of terms for referring to particular communicative or interactive contexts remains one of the main reasons to argue even for a scientific concept of 'communicative genres'.

[11] In accordance with Hymes, Günthner also suggests the term "minimal genres" (Günthner 1995: 199).

this social competence is acquired through socialisation processes within a particular social group (family, peer group) or by means of formal education (school, apprenticeship).

With regard to all of these aspects – genre as a helpful communicative manual, as a normative pattern and as a socially marked form of communicative behaviour – the historical study of communicative genres provides a promising means for the scientific aims of a socio-cultural history of communication.

This is even more the case as the establishment of communicative genres is not to be seen as a mere strategic social act but as an act which perfectly fulfils the requirements of a so-called "invisible hand process" (Keller 1994). This is why characteristics and patterns of communicative genres can be described as indicators of socio-cultural factors, even though the acting individuals are not always aware of their semiotic significance. In other words, practical genre knowledge does not necessarily comprise an awareness of the cultural and semiotic significance of the relevant genre.

From the perspective of cultural analysis, it is therefore imperative to examine closely both the question of what kind of communicative genres prevail in a society and how they refer to particular social tasks, structures and hierarchies. It is also necessary to define and sharply distinguish different genres from each other in order to be able to draw conclusions of their specific appearance and form.

Applying this to our example of the 'call' ("Visite") as a communicative genre, we have not only to prove that this genre was socially important in the bourgeois society of the 18th and 19th century but have to strive for a detailed reconstruction of the communicative patterns involved and discuss which socio-semiotic conclusions we might be able to draw from this. As far as specific communicative genres are concerned, it will therefore be important to not only answer the *how* of a genre, i.e.: how exactly did the communicative genre "Visite" use to be carried out in the first half of the 19th century? Any discussion of a communicative genre will also have to consider the *why* of its formal peculiarity.

5. Characteristics of 'communicative genres'

In most cases, communicative genres can be defined by more than their fix communicative patterns. First, they have a clear limitation in space and time. Secondly, they usually comprise one or more salient elements which characterise the course of their inherent action. More precisely, communicative genres generally possess:

1) A (sometimes formally marked) beginning and end[12] and involve a
    coherent (and to a certain degree variable) course of successive social
    (inter)actions[13]
2) Obligatory verbal and/or nonverbal elements which assist in shaping the
    course of the action and are responsible for the specific 'gestalt' or
    'type' of the genre

In other words, I would like to introduce the category of 'gestalt' to the
concept of 'genre', which can be found in its overall structure.[14] It is the
'gestalt' of a set of communicative actions which allows for recognition and
which makes it possible to talk about communicative genres as conceptual
entities in the stream of everyday activities. We are *at* an interview, *in* class, *at*
an opening of an exhibition, *in* a meeting or *at* confessions. Communicative
genres can therefore denote "sites of meaning" that can assist us in structuring
our life world ("Lebenswelt"), thereby helping us to understand "where we are
and what may be expected of us in a particular situation".[15]

6. The oral nature of communicative genres

Communicative interaction does not necessarily involve verbal language. In
fact, it might be interesting to note historical shifts in the proportion of verbal
elements in communicative genres. The question of whether one actually has
to "speak during conversation", which is raised in an etiquette manual of the
18th century (Schmeizel 1737: 66), clearly illustrates the fact that "con-

---

[12] Clarke calls this an "entry-body-exit structure" (1996: 36). Usually, it is the beginning and the
      end of communicative genres which follow a particular pattern and shape the formal structure
      of the genre.
[13] However, this can also mean that participants of communicative genres are taking part in more
      than one genre at the same time. An examiner, for instance, could receive a telephone call
      during an oral exam. Participants generally know how to distinguish between the genres in
      question.
[14] See Feilke (1996: 37ff.) for a discussion of the concept of gestalt in linguistics. Due to the
      limits of this contribution, it is not possible to elaborate on this concept here.
[15] Goffman emphasized this as early as in 1974. Although his remarks are of a more general
      nature and do not refer to the concept of communicative genres I outline here, he still
      underlines the importance of communicative awareness: "I assume that when individuals
      attend to any current situation, they face the question: 'What is it that's going on here?'
      Whether asked explicitly, as in times of confusion or doubt, or tacitly, during occasions of
      usual certitude, the question is put and the answer to it is presumed by the way the individuals
      then proceed to get on with the affairs at hand." (Goffmann 1974: 8. I owe this reference to
      Goffman to Linell, forthcoming.)

versation" in the sense of social interaction[16] by no means referred to verbal conversations only. Likewise, both the "Promenade" ('promenade') and the "Kartenspiel" ('card game') are prominent examples of communicative genres in the life of 18th century upper classes. However, they were not understood as primarily *verbal* genres. The same goes for lunch and dinner as forms of social intercourse. The growing attention given to the issues of the table *talk* by late 18th and above all the 19th century etiquette manuals provides evidence for the assumption that dining with company only evolved into the dominantly *verbal* genre it is today in the course of the 19th century.

7. How to reconstruct 'communicative genres'

When we recognise the evidence of a particular historical communicative genre like, for instance, the mentioning of the "Visite" in Felix Mendelssohn-Bartholdy's letter, this is but a first step. As a second step we need to reconstruct the genre, i.e., describe its verbal or nonverbal forms, its overall 'gestalt'. This should be done by using sources of different types and closely examining their respective qualities and characteristics.[17] Here, our main focus will lie on linguistic sources. But I would also like to suggest considering rather unconventional types of sources such as paintings as well as material sediments of communicative activities.

7.1 Linguistic sources

When considering linguistic sources, one has to distinguish several types.[18] I distinguish between three different sources, namely *primary sources*, *secondary sources*, and *metalinguistic sources*.

By *primary sources* I mean transcripts or recordings of authentic historical usage, i.e., written texts or – for the recent past – audiovisual media. Relics of communicative genres are documents drawn up for or in a particular genre. Reconsidering the example of the call or visit, the cards used for such an

---

[16] The Zedler Encyclopedia, e.g., defines Lat. "conversatio" as follows: "Conversatio, die Conversation, Gemeinschafft, Gesellschafft, welche also genennt wird, wenn man mit einen (!) persöhnlich umgehet. Conversatio aequalis, ein gleicher, familiairer Umgang mit jemand."

[17] See, e.g., Kilian (2002), Linke (1995) and Gloning (1993) for an in-depth discussion of problems relating to historical reconstruction in diachronic linguistics. Kilian (2002: 140ff.) also points out that a proper criticism of (historical) sources as such has not yet been established in German linguistics.

[18] See Kilian (2002) for classifications regarding the reconstruction of spoken language sources only.

occasion could be such a relic, especially those cards with some individual message written on the front or back connected to the occasion they were used for.[19]

Secondary sources would, on the other hand, comprise written texts or recorded audiovisual media of contemporary usage *purposefully* preserved beyond their historical usage. This includes, for example, transcripts of political debates or private recordings of conversations.[20]

Finally, *metalinguistic sources* refer to linguistic sources which describe, comment or assess contemporary usage, as, e.g., under a *normative* perspective (compare Gloning 1993). Apart from academic or scientific notes on language in grammars or phrase books, this also includes etiquette books or comments on communicative events in private correspondence such as letters, diaries and memoirs.

Distinguishing between these different types of sources can sometimes be difficult, which is why I suggest employing different types of sources as a methodological 'remedy'.

7.2 Pictorial documents

As sources, pictorial documents have so far been mostly neglected in linguistic and historical communicative research.[21] But thanks to the socio-cultural significance of communicative genres, we might get a glimpse of them not only in linguistic sources, but as well in genre paintings, in illustrations in works of literature or popular magazines or in caricatures. These visual re-presentations do not and cannot represent the genre 'in action' but rather convey certain typical details by portraying the people involved, the con-stellation of the participants, their body gestures, etc. The following examples will throw at least some light on the advantages visual documents can offer:

Picture 1 shows a copperplate Daniel Chodowiecki engraved in 1774 for Johann Bernhard Basedow's *Elementarwerk*, which, among other things, intro-duces several social amusements. Picture 2 is taken from an etiquette manual dating from the late 19th century (Adelfels [1888]). Both pictures show the communicative genre of the 'promenade'. Thus, these pictures bear evidence of a historical genre (and its historical continuity over more than a century)

---

[19]   In other words, primary sources could also be seen as 'remains' of contemporary usage which have been preserved for other reasons than for the sake of later generations' linguistic interest.

[20]   Regarding this particular kind of source, Kilian uses the term "secondary performance fragment" (Kilian 2002: 152).

[21]   Reconstructing spoken language from historical graphics and texts was first introduced by Dieter Cherubim (2003).

which today is no longer part of everyday communication, not even in the upper classes represented in the two pictures.

The pictures illustrate both continuity and discontinuity in the moulding of the genre. In both pictures, the promenade appears to be an occasion for the meeting of the sexes. In the 18th century, however, the women appear accompanied by a gentleman; there is no such companion in the picture from the 19th century. In both cases, however, it is the man who greets the woman, which can be seen by his communicative posture. A noticeable bow formed an integral part of greetings in the 18th century. The man had to lower the upper part of his body while taking off his hat to the ladies, ensuring thereby that the inside of his hat was pointing toward the party. The latter is also true for the 19th century, although then the hat did not have to be lowered right to the knees. It was obviously considered enough if it was lowered to head height and the upper part of the male body remained more or less erect. The picture does not show whether a nod of the head or a bow of the upper part of the body would have been part of the ritual. But given that it is not conveyed further in the picture, we can safely assume that lowering the head or the upper part of one's body was no longer a *characteristic* element of the meeting. Body gestures on the other hand appear in both pictures, thereby indicating their vital role in the genre in both centuries.

D. Chodowiecki del.

Picture 1. Taken from Johann Bernhard Basedow [1774] 1909: Elementarwerk, Tab. VII ("Von Vergnügungen").

We cannot be certain about the importance of *verbal* greetings for the genre, even though the participants in picture 2 more likely appear to be talking to each other (as they do have open eye contact) than the ones in picture 1. But if we draw on etiquette manuals as additional sources for the two historical periods respectively, we find that the number of verbal elements in such genres as 'meeting on a promenade' and of greetings in general increases considerably throughout the 18th and 19th century.[22]

Comparing both illustrations of the promenade to the upper part of picture 2 (which illustrates a central element of another communicative genre, the 'ball': 'asking a lady for a dance'), it appears that the male bow as an integral component of (public) greetings in the 18th century has now come to play a major part in the (private) ball room. As opposed to its significance for the public event of the promenade, it now characterises the festivity of the private event. This is also the case for the ladies' fan, which was an important accessory for the promenade in the 18th century but now indicates the genre of the ball. The ladies' parasol on the other hand appears in both illustrations of the promenade.

Picture 2. Taken from Adelfels [1888].

---

[22]   See Linke (1996) for a more detailed analysis.

This example illustrates how visual documents can be valuable means of reconstructing situational settings, the constellation of participants, particular body gestures and props of historical genres, all of which contribute to our understanding of the relationship between non-verbal and verbal elements.

7.3 Material sediments

Finally, material sediments such as occur in the typography of architectural floor plans or in the furnishing of rooms constitute yet another important resource for reconstructing communicative genres.

Here I refer to the ideas of Walther Dieckmann, who coined the term "materialised norms of communication" in his work on political communication (Dieckmann 1983).[23] Both concept and term point to the conclusion that communicative patterns or norms are more than cognitive entities, that they represent more than commands and prohibitions in the *minds* of communication partners. According to Dieckmann, they also materialise in architecture, interior design and seating arrangements. They can also prove very influential when it comes to canalising communicative procedures via topographic arrangements such as the combination of anteroom and office or the ways of postal delivery. As these examples indicate, Dieckmann is referring first and foremost to political or institutional contexts, which is why he interprets material constraints as norms primarily enforced by powerful official bodies. However, if we were to focus on examples that refer to half-official or entirely private contexts such as the 'call', we can classify these materialisations as sedimented products of communicative patterns, originating from collective communicative interaction rather than from prescriptive tradition. In either case, such material sediments of communicative genres contribute to the perpetuation of particular patterns and structures and prove to be a valuable source when it comes to reconstructing genres. Thus, the number of seats and the seating arrangements can provide evidence of the usual number of participants in a certain genre, of their spatial orientation and of the distribution of speaking rights and the speakers' roles at the table. To give an example: During the second half of the 20th century, the communicative genre of the 'meeting' has successfully been introduced as a means of administration and management in modern companies and organisations. This, in turn, has brought forth several material sediments which indicate social and communicative structures dominant in the genre itself, a, for example, the 'conference

---

[23]   Diekmann drew on an idea by Ehlich/Rehbein for the development of the term (Dieckmann 1983: 246).

room' as an obligatory detail in most contemporary office and administrative architecture. There is also the 'conference table', which has become a constitutive piece of furniture in most work-related environments today. Catalogues on office furniture dedicate whole sections to conference room furnishing. And in these, the oval or round shape of the table prescribes a particular spatial and physical orientation of the meeting's participants, indicating the verbal manner of the genre as well as its egalitarian character (see picture 3).

Picture 3. Taken from a catalogue 2005.

The communicative configurations of the "meeting" can be categorised as correlating with a high esteem of flat economic or administrative hierarchies – the oval form of the conference table could therefore be interpreted as expressing the specific socio-cultural significance of the genre.[24]

---

[24] On the other hand, examples taken from politics such as the "runder Tisch" ('round-table talk') also illustrate the fact that these materialisations tend to transcend the simple furthering or preventing of communicative practice.

8. The call – reconstructing a communicative genre

With the call as an example, I would now like to outline how we can reconstruct communicative genres and evaluate their significance within the larger context of a history of communication.

As an ethnographic category, the call is mentioned in several types of historical sources such as diaries, letters, memoirs and in etiquette manuals of the 18th and 19th century especially. These documents are generally documentary or descriptive in nature, as can be seen by Mendelssohn-Bartholdy's letter. When we add up all our sources for consideration, we can reconstruct the structure of the genre[25] as follows.

A call is supposed to be fairly brief: it usually only takes between 10 and 15 minutes. In the case of formal first visits due to the commencement of employment or, as in Mendelssohn-Bartholdy's case, the occasion of an engagement, this can even be reduced to 5 minutes only. Thus, even though 163 calls seem to be an overwhelming task, it is still one that is possible to perform.

Several non-verbal elements can contribute to the gestalt of the genre (the depositing of cards, for instance, which will be discussed in further detail below). And even the verbal parts consist more or less of prefixed patterns. The conversation itself comprises obligatory elements primarily regarding *what* is to be said; suggested topics are, e.g., cultural amusements such as theatre. Typical *formal* patterns mostly apply to greetings and good-byes. This is illustrated by the following passage from an etiquette manual dating from the second half of the 19th century:

> Mit einem höflichen "Ich wollte mir erlauben, meine Aufwartung zu machen", oder: "Ich bin so frei, mich vorzustellen", oder "Ich weiss nicht, ob ich lästig falle" oder "Darf ich mir erlauben, einzutreten?" leitest du deinen Besuch ein, mit einem "Ich darf Ihre Zeit nicht länger in Anspruch nehmen" - "Verzeihen Sie, dass ich Sie so lange aufhielt" - "Ich fürchte, ich habe schon zu lange gestört" - rüstest du dich, den Rückzug anzutreten.[26]

> 'With a polite "I wanted to pay my respects", or "Allow me to introduce myself", or "I hope this is not a bad time", or "May I come in?" you will introduce your visit; with something like "I have already taken up too much of your precious time" - "I am sorry for having taken up so much of your time" – "I feel I have disturbed you long enough" – you prepare yourself to withdraw from the company.'

---

[25] I have already introduced the call as a socio-semiotic communicative form in some detail elsewhere, without drawing on the concept of communicative genres. In the following, I will therefore pick up some of the aspects I discussed in Linke (1996) and adjust them accordingly.

[26] Franken (repr. 1978, chapter VIII [no page numbers]).

Material sediments generated by the call have shaped private housing in a most obvious and lasting way. During the course of the 19th century, the drawing room ("Besuchszimmer", in German also known as "Gesellschaftszimmer", "gute Stube" or "Salon") became a vital room in any bourgeois or later even lower middle-class flat. Certain rules regarding the décor and furnishing of these rooms were introduced. The sofa, for instance, was to provide seating for female visitors only during the call and became just as important to the genre as the private exhibition of engravings and paintings, the possession of a decent bookshelf adorned with "Werken der schönen Litteratur und populärwissenschaftlichen Schriften"[27] ('works of belles lettres and popular scientific writings') and the obligatory "Schale zur Aufnahme der Visitenkarten"[28] ('bowl for depositing visiting cards').

Such insights into material aspects of the genre are provided by the visual evidence we encounter in partly preserved historical furniture settings and décors, or contemporary paintings and photographs.

Further evidence found in etiquette manuals indicates that an essential connection existed between the genre 'call' and the drawing room itself. As chapter headings such as "Zur Visite und im Salon" ('The call and how to behave in the drawing room'), which is taken from Eufemia von Adelfelds' book *Guter Ton und feine Sitte* (1895) suggest, it is the drawing room itself that requires a particular form of social conduct. Furthermore, the sources clearly point out that the call as a communicative genre is socially marked: All etiquette manuals of the 19th century which discuss the call address bourgeois readers, and even private sources reporting on the genre originate from members of the bourgeoisie and middle classes.

This was my brief reconstruction of the genre. If we now turn briefly to its formal aspects and verbal character we can draw the following conclusions:

Even though the call is on the whole a verbal genre – this can be seen in several of the manuals, which offer pages of dialogue patterns including rigid formal requirements – it can in fact be reduced to one central non-verbal element: 'leaving one's card'. In such cases as Mendelssohn-Bartholdy's tour de force on the occasion of his engagement, there are even complex rules for avoiding the actual realization of the call without offending anybody. In these cases, we meet a somewhat bizarre interplay of signals and signs which both parties – the callers and the persons or families to receive them – need to have a command of. In the end, the cards were indeed deposited without any

---

[27]   Adelfels ([1888]: 285).
[28]   Ebhardt (1880: 8).

physical and verbal contact of the parties at all.[29] But even in this down-sized version of the genre the physical appearance of the callers in front of the homes of those to be called upon would be a necessary element. It was not possible to simply send cards via mail as a symbolic substitute for the call.

Hence, the physical meeting of persons can be seen as the genre's primary purpose and appears to be far more important than its verbal elements; even more so, since the short duration of the event did not allow for meaningful conversation anyhow. As the quotation above indicates, fixed verbal patterns were characteristic especially for the beginning and the end of the genre, thus overemphasizing their importance for an event which, otherwise, was comparatively brief.

Moreover, the cultural-analytical question 'why is it done like this and not in a different way?' highlights the fact that the verbal patterns and idioms provided by etiquette manuals refer to the visitor's role only.[30] Based on this, the following hypothesis can be posited.

As could be seen with the example of Mendelssohn-Bartholdy's letter, it is *not* on the host to suggest or initiate a call. It is the caller himself who has to know whom he should pay a formal visit.[31] Thus the social 'mechanism' of the call offers the opportunity to call at the house of someone who is personally unknown to the caller, given that the person calling is a member of the same class. So viewed, the visit implies a socially aggressive act,[32] although the visitors are obliged to perform it in accordance with contemporary social rules and cultural habits. The fact that etiquette books concentrate on behavioural rules and verbal formulas for the *caller* could therefore be interpreted as the consequence and expression of the act's latent aggressive potential. The semiotic 'expense' of words and ritualized formulas on the part of the caller confirms and re-establishes the social role of the person called upon, whose 'territory' he has threatened by initiating the call.

---

[29]   This particular example of *non-communication* also includes procedures such as the depositing of the card via servant, while remaining seated in the carriage within sight of the host's home. In these cases, the residents have to pretend that they are 'not in at the moment', which is usually done by sending a servant of their own who will then accept the card on behalf of his master or mistress and also apologise for their absence (see Linke 1996: 179ff. for further details on this).

[30]   There are only a few exceptions from this rule to be found in the etiquette manuals I analysed. A. Kistner, for instance, provides a different perspective on the caller – host relationship in his *Schicklichkeitsregeln für das bürgerliche Leben* (1886).

[31]   In relation to this, the call bears significant similarities to the telephone call, which has assumed many of the call's functions since the beginning of the 20th century.

[32]   According to Brown and Levinson (1987) and their concept of politeness, this could also qualify as a 'face-threatening act'.

Taking all this into account, the call proves to be a genre which is not only socially relevant but also precarious. This is what the letter Felix Mendelssohn-Bartholdy writes to his sister presents evidence for: his poor performance on these occasions appears to be extremely embarrassing to him, otherwise he would not have brought it up so explicitly.

Finally, by considering the formal structure of the call, it becomes obvious that the main focus rests on its beginning and end, i.e., the framing of the contact established by the parties in question. And even though this contact can be reduced to the formal depositing of cards without any *verbal* encounter, the call still requires the physical presence of the caller. In other words, the sources clearly indicate that the physical presence of the caller is the ends of the genre rather than its means. This also explains the specific architectural materialization of the call – the "Salon" or "Gesellschaftszimmer" –, since calls are typically made at home and take place in a surrounding furnished and decorated for this purpose only.

Both the element of the physical encounter and its link to a specifically designated location for the purpose of the call reflect a constitutive element of bourgeois life in the 18th and 19th century: the increasing separation of the private from the public. Older forms of socialization such as *personal* acquaintances, *immediate* personal contact and the acquaintance of whole *families* rather than individuals live on in the condensed character of the call, but have been minimalized to such an extent that they allow for socializing within a widely ramified social network, thus complying with the needs of the new urban middle classes.[33] Furthermore, although the locus of contact, the drawing room, belongs to the private domain of the bourgeois home, it is designed to form an island of reduced privacy in this otherwise explicitly private surrounding, mainly due to the specific semiotics of its interior. This semi-privacy both corresponds to the semi-public character of the call, at the same time as it serves the purpose of neutralizing its latent aggressive potential – the intrusion into private territory. According to these characteristics, we can

---

[33] Under urban circumstances in particular, the genre of the call contributes to both the establishment and administration of those social networks: "In Kreisen, die viel Verkehr haben, ist es üblich, dass zu Beginn jeder Saison von neuem Besuche gemacht werden. Besonders die jüngeren Herren geben ihre Karten ab in all den Häusern, in denen sie im Winter vorher verkehrt haben, und lassen damit den Wunsch erkennen, wieder zu den gesellschaftlichen Veranstaltungen herangezogen zu werden." ('It is quite common for circles with frequent social interaction that calls have to be made at the beginning of each season. Younger gentlemen especially will deposit their cards in all the houses they visited last winter, thereby indicating that they would also like to be considered for this season's social events.' Ebhardt 1913: 230). The upside to this procedure obviously lies in the simple fact that disagreeable contacts can be broken up quite easily by simply not calling at someone's home anymore.

describe the main socio-cultural significance of the call as bridging the gap between private and public, while at the same time underlining the difference of these spheres.

If we agree to this interpretation the marginalization of the call in the course of the 20th century might indicate a change in the formation of the private and the public sphere even in classes which drew upon this distinction as a means of socially defining themselves. One could of course as well argue that the marginalization of the call results from broadly reorganizing a social environment which now – among other things – is marked by the contrast between mediated communication and direct communicative contact, i.e., by media modality.[34]

In any case, the disappearance of the call as a communicative genre and the fading of the term "Visite" from the vocabulary of the later 20th century indicate a structural change in fundamental social settings which transcends both communicative and linguistic change.

9. Conclusion

Both the analytical concept of the 'communicative genre' and its significance for a history of communication require further research. However, the above should have shown that

1) there is a general connection between the stereotypical patterns of linguistic interaction and its socio-cultural significance. This connection can be described systematically by employing the concept of communicative genres. The concept itself rests upon the assumption that constructing and sustaining social and cultural order rely to a great extent on everyday communicative actions. Therefore, the concept of communicative genres seems particularly interesting for further linguistic analysis towards a history of social and cultural communication.

2) The reconstruction of certain communicative genres or the communicative household from particular historical epochs allows typical formal characteristics and communicative structures to come forth, thus providing insight into constitutive cultural values and social identities or hierarchies of the period in question.

---

[34] Preliminary interpretations of mediated communication as being public and non-mediated communication being private prove erroneous when faced with the contemporary reality of the 'new media' as computer or SMS/MMS. Even traditional print or audio-visual media do not allow for such a clear-cut distinction (cf. Linke 2001).

3) When reconstructing communicative genres, one should always try to consider several different types of sources such as texts and visual documents or material sediments like architecture and furniture.

4) It is not possible to distinguish sharply between the reconstruction of communicative genres on the one hand and their socio-cultural interpretation on the other. This, however, should not be considered as a handicap but rather as a challenge for future analysis.

References

Adelfels, Kurt o.J. [Vorwort 1888]: *Das Lexikon der feinen Sitte. Praktisches Hand- und Nachschlagebuch für alle Fälle des gesellschaftlichen Verkehrs.* Stuttgart: Levy & Müller

Adlersfeld, Eufemia. 1895. *Katechismus des Guten Ton und der feinen Sitte.* 2nd ed. Leipzig.

Bakhtin, Mikhail M. 1979/86. The problem of speech genres. In Caryl Emerson and Michael Holquist (eds.), *Speech genres and other Essays.* Austin: University of Texas Press, 60–102.

Basedow, Johann Bernhard. 1774. *J. B. Basedows Elementarwerk.* [Repr. Theodor Fritsch (ed.), *Kritische Bearbeitung in drei Bänden. Mit den Kupfertafeln Chodowieckis u. a.* 1909. Leipzig: Wiegandt]

Benker, Gertrud. 1984. *Bürgerliches Wohnen. Städtische Wohnkultur in Mitteleuropa von der Gotik bis zum Jugendstil. Aufnahmen Helga Schmidt-Glassner.* München.

Briggs, Charles L. and Richard Bauman. 1992. Genre, Intertextuality, and Social Power. *Journal of Linguistic anthropology* 2/2: 131–172.

Brown, Penelope and Stephen C. Levinson. 1987. *Politeness. Some universals in language usage.* Cambridge: Cambridge University Press.

Cherubim, Dieter. 2003. Sprechende Bilder. Zur Darstellung und Rekonstruktion gesprochener Sprache in historischen Text-Bild-Kombinationen. In Wilhelm Heizmann and Astrid von Nahl (eds.), *Runica – Germanica – Mediaevalia.* Berlin and New York: de Gruyter, 128–145.

Clarke, Herber H. 1996. *Using Language.* Cambridge: Cambridge University Press.

Dieckmann, Walther. 1983. Materialisierte Normen in Prozessen institutioneller Kommunikation. In Walter Dieckmann (ed.), *Politische Sprache. Politische Kommunikation.* Heidelberg: Winter, 246–254.

Ebhardt, Franz. 1880. *Der gute Ton in allen Lebenslagen. Ein Handbuch für den Verkehr in der Familie, in der Gesellschaft und im öffentlichen Leben. Unter Mitwirkung erfahrener Freunde und autorisirter Benutzung der Werke Madame d'Alq's.* 4th rev. ed. Berlin.

Ebhardt, Franz. 1913. *Der gute Ton in allen Lebenslagen. Ein Handbuch für den Verkehr in der Familie, in der Gesellschaft und im öffentlichen Leben.* 17th rev. ed. Leipzig: Klinkhardt.

Ehlich, Konrad. 1986. Die Entwicklung von Kommunikationstypologien und die Formbestimmtheit sprachlichen Handelns. In Werner Kallmeyer (ed.), *Kommunikaionstypologie.* Düsseldorf: Schwann, 47–72.

Feilke, Helmuth. 1996. *Sprache als soziale Gestalt.* Frankfurt/Main: Suhrkamp

Franken, Constanze von. 1907. *Katechismus des guten Tons und der feinen Sitte.* 13th ed. Leipzig.

Franken, Constanze von. 1978 [1st edn unkown, 7th edn 1871]. *Wovon soll ich reden? Die Kunst der Unterhaltung.* [Reprint, 1978 München: Rogner & Bernhard]

Gloning, Thomas. 1993. Sprachreflexive Textstellen als Quellen für die Geschichte von Kommunikationsformen. In Heinrich Löffler et al. (eds.), *Dialoganalyse.* Vol. IV: *Teil 1.* Tübingen: Niemeyer, 207–217.

Goffman, Erving. 1974. *Frame Analysis.* Cambridge, MA: Harvard University Press.

Günthner, Susanne. 1995. Gattungen in der sozialen Praxis. Die Analyse ‚kommunikativer Gattungen' als Textsorten mündlicher Kommunikation. *Deutsche Sprache* 3: 193–218.

Günthner, Susanne and Hubert Knoblauch. 1995. Culturally Patterned Speaking Practices. The Analysis of Communicative Genres. *Pragmatics* 5 (1): 1–32.

Günthner, Susanne and Hubert Knoblauch. 1997. Textlinguistik und Sozialwissenschaft. In Klaus Brinker, Gerd Antos, Wolfgang Heinemann and Sven F. Sager (eds.), *Text- und Gesprächslinguistik.* Berlin and New York: de Gruyter, 811–820.

Günthner, Susanne. 2000. *Vorwurfsaktivitäten in der Alltagsinteraktion. Grammatische, prosodische, rhetorisch-stilistische und interaktive Verfahren bei der Konstitution kommunikativer Muster und Gattungen.* Tübingen: Niemeyer.

Günthner, Susanne and Thomas Luckmann. 2002: Wissensasymmetrien in interkultureller Kommunikation. In Helga Kotthoff (ed.) *Kultur(en) im Gespräch.* Tübingen: Niemeyer, 213–244.

Günthner, Susanne and Hubert Knoblauch. 1994. Forms are the food of faith. Gattungen als Muster kommunikativen Handelns. *Kölner Zeitschrift für Soziologie und Sozialpsychologie* 4: 693–723.

Günthner, Susanne and Hubert Knoblauch. 2000. Textlinguistik und Sozialwissenschaften. In Klaus Brinker, Gerd Antos, Wolfgang Heinemann and Sven F. Sager (eds.), *Text- und Gesprächslinguistik.* Berlin and New York: de Gruyter, 811–819.

Hanks, William F. 1996. Language form and communicative practices. In Stephen C. Levinson and John Gumperz (eds.), *Rethinking Linguistic Relativity*. Cambridge: Cambridge University Press, 232–270.

Hanks, Williams F. 1987. Discourse Genres in a Theory of Practice. *American Ethnologist* 4/14: 668–696.

Hensel, Sebastian. 1995. *Die Familie Mendelssohn. 1729 bis 1847.* Frankfurt/Main: Insel.

Hymes, Dell H. 1972. Models of the Interaction of Language and Social Life. In John Gumperz and Dell H. Hymes (eds.), *Directions in Sociolinguistics: The Ethnography of communication.* New York: Holt, 35–71.

Rudi Keller. 1994. *Sprachwandel*, 2nd ed. Tübingen: Francke.

Kilian Jürg. 2002. Scherbengericht. Zu Quellenkunde und Quellenkritik der Sprachgeschichte. In Dieter Cherubim, Karlheinz Jakob and Angelika Linke (eds.), *Neue deutsche Sprachgeschichte. Mentalitäts-, kultur- und sozialgeschichtliche Zusammenhänge.* Berlin and New York: de Gruyter: 139–166.

Kistner, A. 1886. *Schicklichkeitsregeln für das bürgerliche Leben. Ein A-B-C-Buch.* Guben: König.

Levinson, Stephen. 1979. Activity types and language. *Linguistics* 17: 365–399.

Linke, Angelika. 1995. Zur Rekonstruierbarkeit sprachlicher Vergangenheit: Auf der Suche nach der bürgerlichen Sprachkultur im 19. Jahrhundert. In Andreas Gardt, Klaus J. Mattheier and Oskar Reichmann (eds.), *Sprachgeschichte des Neuhochdeutschen. Gegenstände, Methoden, Theorien.* Tübingen: Niemeyer, 369–397.

Linke, Angelika. 1996. *Sprachkultur und Bürgertum. Zur Mentalitätsgeschichte des 19. Jahrhunderts.* Stuttgart and Weimar: Metzler.

Linke, Angelika. 2000. Informalisierung? Ent-Distanzierung? Familiarisierung? Sprach(gebrauchs)wandel als Indikator soziokultureller Entwicklungen. *Der Deutschunterricht* 3.

Linke, Angelika. 2001. Trauer, Öffentlichkeit und Intimität. In Ulla Fix, Stephan Habscheid and Joseph Klein (eds.), Zur Kulturspezifik von Textsorten. Tübingen: Stauffenburg.

Linell, Per. Forthcoming *Samtalskulturer. Analys av samtal och språkliga möten som kommunikativa verksamheter.* (Unpublished manuscript.)

Linell, Per. 1998. *Approaching Dialogue. Talk, interaction and contexts in dialogical perspectives.* Amsterdam and Philadelphia: Benjamins.

Luckmann, Thomas. 1986. Grundformen der gesellschaftlichen Vermittlung des Wissens: Kommunikative Gattungen. In *Kölner Zeitschrift für Soziologie und Sozialpsychologie*, Sonderheft 27: 191–211.

Luckmann, Thomas. 1988. Kommunikative Gattungen im kommunikativen „Haushalt" einer Gesellschaft. In Gisela Smolka-Koerdt, Peter M.

Sprangenberg and Dagmar Tillmann-Bartylla (eds.), *Der Ursprung von Literatur. Medien, Rollen, Kommunikationssituationen zwischen 1450 und 1650*. München, 279–288.

Raible, Wolfgang. 1980. Was sind Gattungen? Eine Antwort aus semiotischer und textlinguistischer Sicht. *Poetica* 12: 320–349.

Scollon, Ron and Suzie Wong Scollon. 2003. *Discourses in Place: Language in the Material World*. London: Routledge.

RICHARD J. WATTS (BERN)

Deconstructing episodes in the 'history of English'

1. Introduction

In our editorial introduction to *Alternative Histories of English*, Peter Trudgill and I take the view that the discourse of the history of English has become so naturalised and so narrowly conceived over time that it effectively represents the history of 'standard English' rather than that of the multitude of present-day varieties of English across the world. It was our aim in that book to present a necessarily restricted set of approaches to the history of English which, in a modest way, might help to challenge the hegemony of the traditional discourse.

Despite the restriction imposed by space, the availability of contributors and the normal constraints of the publishing business, it was our intention to contribute towards research aimed at revealing the ideological bases of the discourse of the history of English. David Crystal points out in his epilogue to the book that there are innumerable stories that can be told and that many may appear to present contradictory interpretations of 'what happened'. He is of course correct, but implicit in the idea of alternative stories is that any new retelling of a story involves a deconstruction of the one that it replaces. It involves a challenge to part of a hegemonic discourse on language, and in this sense an 'alternative' story is a counter-discourse, perhaps even an anti-discourse.

Deconstructions call for reconstructions, and these, in their turn (and particularly if they ever become the accepted dominant discourse), are also open to deconstruction. Such is the nature of historical sociolinguistics. A successful deconstruction, however, must produce a strong, and, wherever possible, empirically grounded argument to challenge accepted beliefs. In this paper I shall produce evidence to challenge three such beliefs at three different time periods within the history of English:

(1)   the belief in the longevity of the English language;
(2)   the belief that the major distinction between modern English and the English of the Middle Ages was the Great Vowel Shift;

(3)   the belief in the social construction of 'standard English' as the language of
       the 'polite class' of society.

The first of these challenges focuses on the dispute over the dating of the epic
poem *Beowulf*, the second on the validity of the Great Vowel Shift and the
third on the social construction of 'polite' society in the 18th century. But
before I embark on those deconstructions, I wish to provide a framework for
my argumentation which is heavily indebted to Tony Crowley's inspiring book
Standard English and the Politics of Language ([1989] 2003).

2. The 'history of language' vs 'the history of the language'

At a time when the study of language in continental Western Europe in the
early 19th century began to close in upon itself and, like the study of other
areas of knowledge, be subjected to a rigorous and objective scrutiny of how
things came to be as they were, i.e. when the study of language as a human
phenomenon acquired a discursive historicity which constructed it as
'linguistics', it seems strange that 'comparative grammar' (Schlegel 1808), or
'comparative philology' as it was later called, did not take a firm foothold in
Britain. The term 'philology' itself was, of course, in use, but it referred to the
scholarly study of Classical languages and their literatures (Crowley 2003: 18–
19). It was not until the 1830s and 1840s that a very specific form of historical
study of language arose, the study of the history of English itself, and it arose
at a time of great social unrest in Britain caused by the emergence of Chartism
in the 1830s at the end of the first phase of the Industrial Revolution.

Crowley sees the development of a 'history of the English language' as a
reflex to the extreme anxiety created in the upper levels of the social hierarchy
by Chartism. The 'history of the language' discourse congealed around the
need to provide some sort of answer to the wide and explosive social gulf
between the new working classes and other social levels. If anything could
bridge this gulf, it was an extension of the voting franchise, education for all
and the development of a feeling of national patriotism. As Crowley points
out, the two driving forces behind the implementation of these solutions were
religion and language.

Britain's own unique form of historicism in language study, the 'history of
the language' discourse, spawned other related discourses which are still with
us today and have already undergone a great deal of historical deconstruction. I
refer to the 'Standard English' discourse, the discourse of 'education for all',
the discourse of 'the literary canon', the discourse of 'good' vs 'bad' English,
the discourse of 'falling standards' (linguistic, educational and moral), etc. In
the course of time, the 'history of the language' discourse led to the definition

of Standard English as a social 'dialect', to the establishment of English Literature as a subject within the university system and to the cementation of the dichotomous and divisive social class system in Britain.

The major achievement of this early phase of the 'history of the language' discourse was the setting up of a committee to compile a new, historically based dictionary of English, the *New English Dictionary*, which later became the *Oxford English Dictionary*. One of the first major tasks of the committee was to decide on a period in time at which one could reasonably maintain that the words to be included in the *NED* were 'English'. They decided on the end of the 13th century for the simple reason that the number of texts available in what could reasonably be called 'English' date from that period. As the 19th century wore on, however, the idea of 'standard English' required that linguists take a longer view of the history of the language. The notion of a 'national language' provided symbolic support for the historic consciousness of a strong nation-state whose roots could be traced back through time, and if the 'English state' could be traced back to pre-Norman Conquest Anglo-Saxon times, then the 'national language' must have existed at that time too. One of the fundamental beliefs in the 'history of the language' discourse is thus the discourse of the longevity of the English language, and it is that belief that I shall now call into question.

3. The longevity of English

Throughout the first half of the nineteenth century, study of the English language in the tertiary sector of the education system meant the study of what was called 'Anglo-Saxon'. Although it was clear that Anglo-Saxon was a precursor of English, it was also clear that its structure was so different from that of even post-Conquest late medieval English that it could be seen as a different language. In his prologue to *Alternative Histories of English*, Jim Milroy makes this point very forcefully:

> The standard view of the transition from Old to Middle English is that, although it appears in the texts to be abrupt, it was actually gradual, and this of course backs up the idea of the ancient language and unbroken transmission. Old English, however, is structurally very unlike Modern English or most of Middle English in a number of ways. To show that it is the "same" language on purely internal grounds requires some ingenuity. It is much easier to show that it is different. (Milroy 2002: 19)

The discourse of the longevity of English depends on the linguistic ingenuity of scholars of Old English (or, rather, Anglo-Saxon) to trace the unbroken transmission from Old to Middle English, but it also depends on the existence of texts from which one can demonstrate that transmission both during the period of Anglo-Saxon (ca. 5th century AD onward) and during the 'transition period' from Anglo-Saxon to Middle English. The early compilers of the NED (OED) only considered the 'best' texts as sources for the words they wished to include in the dictionary, and, as we might expect, the 'best texts' were literary. Now, while one can sympathise with this tendency in the middle of the 19th century, there are sound reasons to reject the reliance on the 'best texts' at the end of the 20th century and the beginning of the 21st.

Notwithstanding objections to this method, the central text to argue for the longevity of English during the Old English period has always been *Beowulf*, and not Old English recipes, chronicles, wills and other legal documents, etc. The reason is obvious: *Beowulf* is considered to be an epic poem, which places English into the same illustrious bracket as the classical languages Latin and Greek. If the dating of *Beowulf* can push its genesis as far back into the Old English period as possible, the 'classical', literary prestige of English is greatly enhanced.

In the 1980s and early 1990s, a dispute broke out over the dating of *Beowulf*, following on the publication of *Beowulf and the Beowulf Manuscript* by Kevin Kiernan in 1981 (reprinted as a paperback in 1997). Only one manuscript of the poem has survived, and we are extraordinarily lucky to have that, since it was rescued from a fire in 1731 in Ashburnham House in which the Cottonian Library was housed. The manuscript dates from the early 11th century, and Kiernan argues that it is likely to have been the only manuscript of *Beowulf* ever to have been prepared. Kiernan's arguments are based on a painstaking empirical study of the extant manuscript, and on piecing together the conclusions he has come to with respect to the original writing of the manuscript and its possible authorship, on the one hand, and the socio-political events in England at the time of its preparation, on the other.

Kiernan's approach is very convincing, although there is ultimately no way of knowing whether or not the manuscript was the copy of an earlier text. Let us assume for the moment that it *is* the only copy of *Beowulf* ever compiled, and that the two scribes who were involved in compiling it were effectively its 'authors'. I hesitate to use this term too literally, but one might assume that they were committing to writing what appear to be two unrelated, (possibly poetic) oral stories that had been circulating in the Danelaw area of England for some time. *Beowulf* has always puzzled literary analysts by appearing to be more 'cobbled together' than a coherent text. However, the 'art' in the manuscript lies in the cobbling. The two stories have been 'stitched' together in a fascinating way by inventing the homecoming episode to link Beowulf's exploits at Hrothgar's court as a young warrior and his heroic, but unsuccessful fight against the dragon as an old man.

No dating of a vellum manuscript can ever be exact, but if we consider the socio-political events of the time, then the most likely date is some time after 1016. In 1016 the Danish king, Cnut, acquired the English throne and set about incorporating the kingdom of England into his short-lived 'empire', consisting of Denmark, Norway, England, and parts of Southern Sweden. Cnut made every effort to uphold the social structures and traditions of Anglo-Saxon England. The struggle against Danish military incursions had lasted throughout most of Ethelred the Unready's reign, eventually leading to the latter's flight to Normandy in 1013 after Svein Haraldsson's invasion of England. Ethelred returned in 1014, but died in 1016. For a few brief months, Ethelred's son, Edmund Ironside, reigned in England till he was ousted by Svein's son Cnut.

The history of Ethelred's struggle against Danish incursions does not make it at all likely that the manuscript of *Beowulf* was prepared prior to 1016. On the other hand, Cnut's efforts to ingratiate himself with the English certainly do argue for the preparation of an epic poem extolling the virtues of a southern Swedish prince at the Danish court of Cnut's ancestor, written as it was in the traditional poetic idiom of Anglo-Saxon. Kiernan's efforts to provide a strong, empirically grounded alternative explanation for the genesis of *Beowulf* have led to a viable alternative discourse to the discourse of the longevity of English. He provides a set of arguments which appear more convincing than the speculative assumption that the only extant manuscript of *Beowulf* is the end-product of a set of copies of an original text composed at least two-and-a-half centuries prior to the present text. Part of the counter-discourse might be the separation of the history of English from the mythical historical roots of the English 'state'. It might also lead to a re-examination of the status of Anglo-Saxon and the feasibility of a theory that the rupture between it and the forms of Middle English that we see at the end of the 13th century was indeed more sudden and cataclysmic than historical linguistics has hitherto considered to be possible. The connection between Anglo-Saxon and Middle English may not have been quite so unbroken as is assumed.

4. The Great Vowel Shift: Constructing the periodicity of English

In the previous section, I put into question the commonly held assumption that the history of English represents an unbroken line between Old English (Anglo-Saxon) through Middle English and Early Modern English to Modern English. Such a presentation of the periodicity of English is in any case focused on the eventual emergence of a standard form of English and automatically cancels out any alternative efforts to tell the stories of other varieties.

I turn my attention now to the myth of the Great Vowel Shift, which is used implicitly as the major watershed between Middle English and Early Modern English. In Watts (2003b) I argue that the term 'Great Vowel Shift' itself implies that "[t]here is a sense of uniqueness, unitariness, of grandiose proportions and perhaps even of historical significance in the term 'great'" (2003: 13). I focus on the disputes revolving around the GVS, which concern not only its dating, but also the linguistic processes involved in its development and whether or not it can be seen as a unitary development.

The last two types of dispute are not unimportant. If we can reconstruct the ideological discourse of the GVS to show that it was in fact a series of smaller vowel shifts taking place at different points in time in different parts of the country, and that there were certain areas in which some (or even many) of those shifts did not take place at all, then we have a strong argument for looking at language change on a more local level, i.e. for looking at language history from below. The fact is, however, that the tradition of presenting the GVS as one 'great' unitary phenomenon constitutes another ideology naturalised within the discourse of 'the history of the language' (cf. Ellis 1869; Sweet 1874), and one which needs to be deconstructed to allow a bottom-up rather than a top-down approach to the history of English.

The period during which the GVS is assumed to have taken place covers almost 300 years from the early 15th to the late 18th century. The second of these two dates is interesting in that it is only in the last 40 years of the 18th century that we see attempts to construct and prescribe a standard oral language, e.g. Thomas Sheridan's *A Course of Lectures on Elocution* (1762) and John Walker's *Elements of Elocution* (1781) and *A Critical Pronouncing Dictionary* (1791). The latter part of the 19th century and the first 25 years of the twentieth century saw a concerted effort to locate that oral standard socially, and it is precisely the legacy of those efforts which haunts the requirement written into the National Curriculum for English that pupils be given access to standard oral English. As Tony Bex and I point out in *Standard English: The Widening Debate* (1999: 116), "to teach standard spoken English requires that we take on the task of showing what it is". This has not been done, and I suggest that this is because it cannot be done.

What about the first of the two dates marking the presumed beginning of the GVS, the early 15th century? As Giancarlo (2000) argues, it allows us to construct a convenient borderline between the outgoing Middle Ages as represented by the literary genius of Chaucer and the period of early modern English as represented by Shakespeare. It allows us to claim Shakespeare as "one of us", and while not disclaiming his greatness, to place Chaucer into the camp of those who did not speak English as we do. It allows us to define the language of Shakespeare as 'modern English', albeit 'early modern English', and to locate the 'true' beginning of standard English at the end of the 16th century. It is part of the ideology of the 'history of the language' discourse that what I call the 'funnel view' of the history of the language focuses narrowly on the development of standard English to the detriment of the dialects, creoles, and other colonial varieties of English and, as Jim Milroy (2002) astutely points out, to the detriment of seeing the historical development of varieties of English in relation to that of other Germanic languages.

Again, I am not able to go into great detail here, but it is important to note that the traditional accounts of the GVS have not gone unchallenged. The work of deconstructing the ideology was begun in the early 1980s by Stockwell and Minkova, and it has been continued by a number of important articles in the 1990s, notably Johnston (1992), Smith (1993) and Guzman (1994). The most detailed of these is Johnston (1992), who gives well-documented evidence to suggest that, in the Plain of York, low-vowel raising preceded not only the chain shift in the long high vowels, but also Open Syllable Lengthening itself in the 13th century – perhaps even earlier.

We can conclude from the story of the GVS that if we are interested in researching into how the traditional discourse of 'the history of the language' has been constructed, the issue of what the GVS was and how it should be deconstructed loses none of its compulsive power. We might add here that sociolinguistic research into other varieties of English in the US and New Zealand gives undisputed present-day evidence into other vowel shifts currently taking place. It seems that speakers of English, wherever they are, whichever variety they speak, are simply inveterate vowel shifters.

5. Deconstructing the social construction of oral 'standard English'

My final deconstruction focuses on how it has become practically impossible to separate, from within the 'history of the language' discourse, the tracking of language change from the construction of the canon of English literature. However, since I take up the extreme position that there is no such thing as oral standard English, or at least not until we have shown unambiguously what it is (or should be), I shall have to retrace my steps to the early 18th century.

In his second edition of *Standard English and the Politics of Language*, Crowley adds an extra chapter to bring the reader up to date on what we might call the 'state of the standard English question'. The first edition took us up to the end of the 1980s and the bitter dispute between Conservative politicians, the media and self-appointed guardians of the language, on the one hand, and linguists, educationalists and teachers on the other. The 1990s saw the rejection of the Kingman Report, the embarrassment over the Cox Report and the final implementation of the National Curriculum in England and Wales. The definition of standard oral English, however, has still not been adequately tackled, and when we read reputed linguists like Quirk, Greenbaum, Leech and Svartvik in their grammar (1985) referring to 'Standard English' as educated English or even Peter Trudgill (1995) referring to it as "the variety which is normally spoken by educated people", they begin to sound suspiciously like John Honey in *Language is Power* (1997). Crowley is acutely aware of the dangers here, and he reminds us of what Raymond Williams had argued in *Communications*:

> At the roots of much of our cultural thinking is our actual experience of speech. In Britain the question of good speech is deeply confused, and is in itself a major source of many of the divisions in our culture. (Williams 1962: 102)

The argument that I wish to trace out and deconstruct here is the perhaps not so subtle transformation of the 18th century discourse of politeness into a discourse of educatedness.

Within the last 30 years, we linguists have experienced the so-called 'pragmatic turn' in linguistics. So we may be forgiven for missing out on the fact that literary studies have experienced a number of their own 'turns' in the post-modern era. The turn in literary studies that promises to produce the most fruitful forms of collaboration between linguists and literary theorists in helping to deconstruct 'the history of the language' discourse and solve the 'question of good speech' once and for all is what I will call the 'cultural turn'. The cultural turn represents an attempt to embed the study of literature (and of course the same goes for the study of language) into the study of cultural movements in general. It places literature and linguistics within what is frequently called 'cultural studies'.

My present focus will be on one tiny, but very significant snippet in the cultural history of the English language, the 18th century obsession with politeness and the prescriptive grammarian's urge to 'fix', or, as we would say today, 'standardise' the English language. Milroy and Milroy (1985) have called this latter urge 'the ideology of the standard', and I have called the former obsession 'the ideology of politeness' (Watts 2002, 2003b). In forging and interweaving these ideologies in the 18th century, creative writers, literary critics, grammarians and other writers on language were involved in constructing the emergent standard language as a natural feature of polite society. In doing so, they paved the way for the social construction of oral 'standard English'.

As a first illustration of the cross-fertilisation of literature, literary criticism and linguistics, consider Samuel Johnson, the 'father' of the English dictionary. Johnson was not just a dictionary writer; he was also a poet, an essayist, and a literary critic. In 1747, at a time when he was gathering his ideas and materials for the dictionary, Johnson published *The Plan of a Dictionary of the English Language*, in which he states that the major aim of the dictionary is "to preserve the purity and ascertain the meaning of our English idiom" and "to fix the English language". In order to do this, it was his intention to select "the words and phrases used in the general intercourse of life, or found in the works of those we commonly stile *polite* writers". Like many other critics in the first half of the 18th century, Johnson assumed that English had already achieved a level of purity and that it had to be prevented from changing, since "[a]ll change is of itself evil, which ought not to be hazarded but for evident advantage". The 'polite writers' to whom he refers turn out to be 'the best writers', although we learn little in this text about what makes them 'best'. Beyond this, however, the dictionary also aims to achieve the equivalent of Boileau's proposal to the Académie Française that "they should review all their *polite* writers, and correct such impurities as might be found in them, that their authority might not contribute, at any distant time, to the depravation of the language".

In the event, when it was published in 1755, the *Dictionary* took a more liberal view of change in language and no attempt was made to 'correct impurities' in any 'polite' writer's work. Looked at from our present-day perspective, of course, it seems preposterous to imagine that a linguist should castigate an author for mistakes in her/his grammar or lexis, let alone claim the right to correct any such 'mistakes' that might be noticed. But throughout the 18th century, criticism of the 'best' authors – the 'polite' authors – by grammarians and other language 'experts' was relatively common. We can perhaps excuse Johnson, since he *was* himself a poet and essayist, but when we read in Bishop Robert Lowth's *A Short Introduction to English Grammar* (1761) a statement like the following:

> It will evidently appear from these Notes, that our best Authors for want of some rudiments of this kind [i.e. rudiments of English grammar – R.W.] have sometimes fallen into mistakes, and been guilty of palpable errors in point of Grammar. (Lowth 1761: viii–ix)

we can only conclude that grammarians placed themselves *above* the 'best authors'. The notes that Lowth refers to here are copious notes placed at the foot of most of the pages of the grammar illustrating and explaining for the benefit of the non-polite reader 'mistakes' made by authors such as Pope, Addison, Milton and even the *Authorised Version of the Bible*. Nor should we underestimate the influence of grammarians on authors. Leslie Arnovick discusses Swift's 'corrections' in his use of the modal verbs *will* and *shall* in the manuscript versions of his humorous *Directions to Servants*. She attributes this to the influence of the prescriptive grammarians of the early 18th century:

> Swift's practice of revising and correcting questionable usage substantiates the usage quandaries troubling eighteenth-century writers. The dean's uncertainty also underscores the practical need shared by others writing English. Their requirement is satisfied by the grammars. Where common use is proscribed, correct use is prescribed and praised. (Arnovick 1999: 45)

But who were the 'polite' writers referred to by Johnson and Lowth – and also, by the way, by Swift himself? What did the term 'polite', here in reference to writers, mean throughout the 18th century? Why were grammarians so concerned that their 'best' authors should write 'polite language', and what gave them the authority to decide on this? What effect did this insistence on authority have on the emergence of standard English? Why is it important in tracing out these cultural developments in the emergence of the standard to consider works of literature and the work of literary critics?

This is a long list of questions, so let us start from the perspective of a historian, Paul Langford (1989), who has charted the 18th century English obsession for politeness and the ways in which it was interwoven with the obsession for commerce in England from 1727 to 1783. Langford goes so far as to call the attempts of the new, upwardly mobile middle classes of society to achieve polite values a 'revolution', which he describes as follows:

> Nothing unified the middling orders so much as their passion for aping the manners and morals of the gentry more strictly defined, as soon as they possessed the material means to do so. This was a revolution by conjunction rather than confrontation, but it was a revolution none the less, transforming the pattern of social relations, and subtly reshaping the role of that governing class which was the object of imitation. The aspirants sought incorporation in the class above them, not collaboration with those below them [...]. (Langford 1989: 63)

He describes politeness as "an ambiguous term" which was "naturally associated with the possession of those goods which marked off the moderately wealthy from the poor". He defines "the essence of politeness" as "that *je ne sais quoi* which distinguished the innate gentleman's understanding of what made for civilized conduct" (1989: 71). It was, in other words, an extremely elusive term. To get to the bottom of it, one would need to trace its beginnings back into the 16th century in the late Renaissance ducal courts of Italy and from there to plot its development into the 17th century royal court in France. I will refrain from going into detail here, but it is interesting to note that at the court of Louis XIV the terms 'politesse' and 'poli' were virtually synonymous with 'courtoisie' and 'courtois'. In the period after the Glorious Revolution of 1688 in England, 'politeness' had become almost synonymous with 'gentility', but not with 'courtesy'. It had been appropriated by the class of the landed gentry and was no longer uniquely associated with appropriate forms of behaviour at the royal court.

Let us try to piece together the rough meaning of 'politeness' as it was used in literary and philosophical texts around the turn of the 18th century. The lexeme *polite* is derived from the Latin past participle *politus* meaning 'polished, refined, cultured', and it is sometimes used interchangeably with or in close contiguity to *polished*. Here is an example from Daniel Defoe's *An Essay on Projects* (1697):

The work of this society should be to encourage *polite* learning, to *polish* and refine the English tongue, and advance the so much neglected faculty of correct language, to establish purity and propriety of style, and to purge it from all the irregular additions that ignorance and affectation have introduced; and all those innovations in speech, if I may call them such, which some dogmatic writers have the confidence to foster upon their native language, as if their authority were sufficient to make their own fancy legitimate. (my emphasis – R.W.)

Defoe's text contains a number of projects, most of which are economic. The quotation here is taken from the project for a language academy along the lines of the Académie Française, and as we can see, the aim of the academy would be to "encourage polite learning", "to polish and refine the English tongue", "to advance the [...] faculty of correct language" and "to purge it from all the irregular additions that ignorance and affectation have introduced". Note that he places the blame for those faults that need to be corrected squarely on the shoulders of the presumed authority of certain 'dogmatic writers'. Here we have a first clear example of a writer in his role of critic passing moral judgment on fellow writers on the grounds of incorrect language and innovations in speech. So polite, or polished, language can be equated with correct language, purified language, language in which no change is condoned, etc. In a word, what we have here is a statement about the need to standardise English, a statement from an ideological discourse on standardisation which was soon to develop into the dominant discourse on language during the 18th century (cf. Milroy and Milroy 1985; Watts 1999 and 2002) and was destined to become the lynchpin of the 'history of the language' discourse.

Defoe's conditions for admission into this academy give us further clues as to the meaning of 'politeness' and 'polite language' at the beginning of the 18th century:

Into this society should be admitted none but persons eminent for learning, and yet none, or but very few, whose business or trade was learning. For I may be allowed, I suppose, to say we have seen many great scholars mere learned men, and graduates in the last degree of study, whose English has been far from *polite*, full of stiffness and affectation, hard words, and long unusual coupling of syllables and sentences, which sound harsh and untuneable to the ear, and shock the reader both in expression and understanding. (my emphasis – R.W.)

"Persons eminent for learning" have a place in Defoe's proposed academy, but not scholars from the two universities Oxford and Cambridge, since their language is "far from polite", i.e. "full of stiffness and affectation", full of "hard words" and with "long and unusual coupling of syllables and sentences". So polite language must be fluent, easy to understand and without unnecessary syntactic complexity. It must be "easy" and "melodious" on the ear and it must not shock the reader either in what it expresses or in the way it is expressed. Note also that it is not acquired in the major seats of learning.

Defoe then goes on to talk about the "spoilers and destroyers of a man's discourse", and he asks his reader "a little to foul his mouth with the brutish, sordid, senseless expressions which some gentlemen call polite English, and speaking with a grace". Those who claim to speak 'polite English' but who lower themselves to use "brutish, sordid, senseless expressions" have "the character of a gentleman with a good estate, and of a good family, and with tolerable parts", but they do not cut a polished figure "for want of education". There are, in other words, gentlemen and gentlemen, and the difference is polite and impolite English. But where is a member of the landed gentry to acquire the art of speaking and writing polite English if not at the universities?

The answer to this question can be found in the work of Robert Ashley Cooper, the 3rd Earl of Shaftesbury, a contemporary of Defoe's. In a number of important articles on Shaftesbury and his time and in particular in *Shaftesbury and the Culture of Politeness: Moral Discourse and Cultural Politics in Early Eighteenth-century England* (1994), Lawrence Klein shows how Shaftesbury aims to further the study of moral philosophy outside the universities and outside London. Philosophy was to be taken from the universities and introduced into the drawing-rooms of the landed gentry, and the touchstone of that philosophy was the notion of politeness. So for Shaftesbury and his contemporaries politeness was to be freed from courtly society and urbane civilisation and to become a set of moral values associated with the landed gentry. In other words, it became a quality marking out social class distinctions. As the 18th century moved on, the intertwining of the ideology of politeness with the ideology of standardisation became a potential means to brand Langford's members of the middling orders seeking incorporation into the social class above them as not worthy of incorporation. The stage was set for a distinction between standard and non-standard English along the lines of social class and wealth.

Politeness, in Shaftesbury's terms, was to "advance philosophy on the very foundation of what is called agreeable and polite", and in order to do this, 'morals' must be equated with 'manners'. Shaftesbury represents himself as endeavouring to show "that nothing which is found charming or delightful in the polite world [...] can any way be accounted for, supported, or established, without the pre-establishment or supposition of a certain taste". Politeness incorporates 'the study and love of beauty', 'the study and love of symmetry and order', and it is associated with 'decorum and grace'.

Allow me to summarise briefly before I move on:

a. Politeness was equated with *civilised* behaviour, i.e. with the behaviour of the landed gentry and social classes above them, but not the behaviour of the royal court or the capital.

b. Politeness took on *aesthetic* values such as 'decorum and grace', 'the study and love of beauty', 'the study and love of symmetry and order', etc.

c. Politeness took on *moral* values, since it caused a man 'to prosecute the public good or interest in his species with more zeal and affection than ordinary'.

d. Politeness was *rational* behaviour.

Polite *language* was the language of all those who propagated these values and behaved in accordance with them. It was

a. a socially marked language, and
b. the language of the 'best authors'.

It should

a. be fluent and easy to understand,
b. be without unnecessary syntactic complexity,
c. be 'easy' and 'melodious' on the ear,
d. not shock the reader,
e. represent the aesthetic and moral values defined by Shaftesbury.

It could not be acquired at the universities, and it should not change but should retain the assumed purity of English.

In addition, it was literary critics and grammarians who assumed the authority to 'police' polite English, or, we might more innocently say, to codify polite English and standardise it. In case there should be any doubt that this was the case, consider the following statement by Shaftesbury's *alter ego* critic in his *Miscellaneous Observations*:

> For this reason we presume not only to defend the cause of critics, but to declare open war against those indolent supine authors, performers, readers, auditors, actors or spectators who, making their humour alone the rule of what is beautiful and agreeable, and having no account to give of such their humour or odd fancy, reject the criticising or examining art, by which alone they are able to discover the true beauty and worth of every object.

This effectively gives *carte blanche* to critics, and among the critics I would not hesitate to number the prescriptive grammarians of the 18th century.

The ideology of politeness, of course, concerns many more forms of social behaviour than simply language usage, but its greatest effect can be seen in the codification of the English language throughout the 18th century. The beginnings of codification in English can be traced back at least as far as the first half of the 16th century, but a focus on written text rather than oral language production seems to dominate the first half of the 18th century. Driven by the obsession for politeness, it was inevitable that standardisation should rapidly crystallise into an elitist social discourse. Both McIntosh (1998) and Watts (1999, 2002, and 2003a) use the term 'gentrification' to refer to those changes in language which had become social class distinctions by the middle of the century. In the quotation given above, Macintosh suggests that "the presumption of a system of social rank is deeply implicated in the language itself", and he ventures the tentative opinion that it "may sometimes have served to exclude unschooled writers from the circles of influence and power". But at the same time he also allows for the possibility that those same forces may have helped the 'unschooled' to gain access to circles of power through the acquisition of the standard. I would argue that the mechanism of social exclusion is likely to be more accurate.

The pace of codification during the 18th century was so fast that attempts were also made in the second half of the century to codify pronunciation, culminating in John Walker's *A Critical Pronouncing Dictionary* in 1791. 'Polite pronunciation', however, was made popular by Thomas Sheridan in the late 1750s and early 1760s. Sheridan was an Irish actor, who took it upon himself to teach the upwardly mobile 'middling orders' of Langford's social scale the 'correct' (i.e. polite) way to pronounce English by offering a series of public lectures on elocution and other related matters to large audiences up and down the country in the late 1750s. At each of these lectures, he offered the members of the audience the opportunity of putting their names down on a subscribers' list, i.e. of committing themselves to buying the published version of the lectures, which were finally published under the title *A Course of Lectures on Elocution: Together with Two Dissertations on Language and Some other Tracts relative to those Subjects* in 1762. The list of over 200 subscribers was dutifully added to the beginning of *A Course of Lectures on Elocution*, and it gives us fairly solid evidence that Sheridan more than covered the costs of the publication by selling the book in this way. The number of names indicating that the subscribers were members of the landed gentry or the aristocracy was extremely small.

Sheridan lectured to packed halls across the country and an admission fee was charged, so we can imagine the large sums of money he must have earned just by holding the lectures. He need only have mentioned the subscribers' list very casually to have picked up enough subscribers at each lecture to finance the publication. Sheridan, then, was cashing in on the obsession for politeness. Clearly, the ideology of politeness had come to dominate the discourse of standardisation to such an extent that even pronunciation could not escape its beady eye. What we have with Sheridan's work and John Walker's *Dictionary of Pronunciation* are the beginnings of a discourse that was to construct RP towards the end of the 19th century and in the first half of the 20th century as the only socially acceptable form of speech – at least in Britain and the British Empire.

In my work on the prescriptive grammarians of the 17th and 18th centuries, I have referred to them as a 'discourse community', and I define this term as follows:

> [...] a set of individuals who can be interpreted as constituting a community on the basis of the ways in which their oral or written discourse practices reveal common interests, goals and beliefs ... The members of the community may or may not be conscious of sharing these discourse practices. Thus, a discourse community may show strong or weak affiliation to the values of the community, and the community itself may only become 'visible' through the course of time. (Watts 1999: 43)

The term 'discourse community' is equivalent to the term 'community of practice' as it is used in modern sociolinguistic work. There is evidence that each grammarian was aware of the work of at least a number of other grammarians, and sometimes we find wholesale lifting of segments of text out of previous grammars, a practice that would be condemned today as plagiarism. The locus of activities in a community of practice may be widely distant in terms of time and space, and members of the community may not even be aware of their own membership in it. But the term is entirely applicable to grammarians, dictionary writers, lecturers on elocution, writers of periodicals, and literary critics in the 18th century.

The community of practice may even be considerably wider than this. Lynda Mugglestone (1995), for example, deals with books on language etiquette, magazines, cartoons, etc. throughout the 18th and 19th centuries in tracing the development of standard pronunciation and accounting for the construction of language shibboleths like the dropping of word-initial 'h'.

In Watts (2002) I have also shown how, in the modern discourse on standard English, polite language, particularly with reference to the socially acceptable version of the spoken language, was unobtrusively transformed into the language of the educated, and Crowley (1989) gives evidence of how this came about with the extension of universal education in the 19th century. In doing so, it lost none of its socially divisive force. If we consider the teaching of English in schools across Britain and how the transformation from polite to educated language came to the fore during the virulent debate over the National Curriculum in the 1980s, we will see that both literary scholars and linguists were deeply involved.

6. Conclusion

I began this paper by arguing that a challenge to a belief or set of beliefs on language can lead to the deconstruction of a hegemonic discourse and the construction of an alternative, or even a counter-discourse. I would also suggest that sets of beliefs that are reproduced through forms of discourse represent ideologies of language. As historical linguists we are particularly prone to represent the events of the past in as coherent a way as possible, but in doing so we tend to forget that at the time when the changes were taking place those involved can hardly have had a sense of where they would lead.

As sociolinguists we need to consider alternative methods of explaining those changes retrospectively which allow us to achieve the maximum degree of explanatory power available, and this entails consideration of extralinguistic information, much of which will be socio-cultural in the widest sense. The arguments that we advance must have a higher degree of empirical groundedness than those currently in use in the ideological discourse we are deconstructing. Obviously, such counter-discourses are themselves also open to alternative interpretations.

In the case of the discourse of the longevity of English, Kiernan's arguments offer an alternative way of viewing the connection between a 'literary' text and the historical 'pedigree' of English. It opens us to the awareness that that discourse is ideological in linking the presumed antiquity of *Beowulf* with a coherent development of the English language. It raises the issue of whether it makes sense to talk of 'Old English' at all, or whether there might not have been a fundamental disruption in the development from Anglo-Saxon to Middle English.

The periodisation of English is also focused on in the 'standard' explanations of the Great Vowel Shift, but if we have concrete evidence that elements of this discourse may also be contested, then we are forced to question terms such as 'Middle English' and 'Early Modern English'. In particular, we need to consider that the GVS is an ideological means to explain a coherent development from Middle English to modern 'standard' English. If we challenge the validity of that discourse, we automatically open up investigation into other forms of English in which many of the changes of the GVS never took place, and others in which vowel shifting continues today, e.g. New Zealand, the Northern Cities vowel shift in the USA, etc.

The third ideological discourse which I focused on in a little more detail than the other two offers a socio-cultural explanation for the development of the social divisiveness of 'standard' English by linking it up explicitly to 18th century concepts such as 'polite society' and 'polite language'. Looked at in this way, the Milroys' argument that we are confronted with an ideological discourse of the standardisation of English gains considerable support from the far-reaching socio-political, socio-economic, and socio-cultural changes of the 18th century, changes which paved the way for the Chartist movement in the 1830s and the resultant 'history of the language' discourse.

In conclusion, therefore, as sociolinguists we need to remember that, no matter how hard we try to look at language dispassionately and 'objectively' from the outside, we are still within language and language is still within us. In

Verbal Hygiene (1995) Deborah Cameron puts a convincing case for the argument that language has always been evaluated normatively and morally. If we are to make further progress in deconstructing the 'history of the language' discourse and offering alternative discourses, we must take on board the inherent normativity of people's judgments of language, including their own.

References

Arnovick, Leslie K. 1999. *Diachronic Pragmatics: Seven Case Studies in English Illocutionary Development*. Amsterdam: Benjamins.

Bex, Tony and Richard Watts (eds.) 1999. *Standard English: The Widening Debate*. London: Routledge.

Cameron, Deborah. 1995. *Verbal Hygiene*. London: Routledge.

Cooper, Anthony Ashley, the 3rd Earl of Shaftesbury. 1711. *Characteristics of Men, Manners, Opinions, Times: An Enquiry Concerning Virtue and Merit.* London.

Crowley, Tony. 1989 (2003). *Standard English and the Politics of Language.* London: Palgrave Macmillan.

Crystal, David. 2002. Broadcasting the non-standard message. In Richard Watts and Peter Trudgill (eds.), *Alternative Histories of English*. London: Routledge, 233–244.

Defoe, Daniel. 1698. *An Essay on Projects.* London.

Ellis, Alexander J. 1869–89 (1968). *Early English Pronunciation*. New York: Maskell House.

Giancarlo, Matthew. 2000. The rise and fall of the Great Vowel Shift? The changing ideological intersections of philology, historical linguistics, and literary history. *Representations* 76: 27–60.

Guzman, Trinidad. 1994. The Great Vowel Shift revisited. In Francisco Moreno Fernández, Miguel Fuster and Juan Jose Calvo (eds.), *English Historical Linguistics 1992: Papers from the 7th International Conference on English Historical Linguistics*. Amsterdam: Benjamin, 81–89.

Honey, John. 1997. *Language is Power: The Story of Standard English and its Enemies*. London: Faber.

Johnson, Samuel. 1747. *The Plan of a Dictionary of the English Language.* London.

Johnston, Paul A. Jr. 1992. English vowel shifting: One Great Vowel Shift or two small vowel shifts. *Diachronica* 9: 189–226.

Kiernan, Kevin S. 1981 (1997). *Beowulf and the Beowulf Manuscript.* New Brunswick, N.J.: Rutgers University Press.

Klein, Lawrence. 1994. *Shaftesbury and the Culture of Politeness: Moral Discourse and Cultural Politics in Early Eighteenth-Century England.* Cambridge: Cambridge University Press.

Langford, Paul. 1989. *A Polite and Commercial People: England 1727–1783.* Oxford: Clarendon Press.

Lowth, Robert. 1761 (1967). *A Short Introduction to English Grammar.* Menston, UK: Scolar Press.

McIntosh, Carey. 1998. *The Evolution of English Prose, 1700–1800.* Cambridge: Cambridge University Press.

Milroy, James. 2002. The legitimate language: Giving a history to language. In Richard Watts and Peter Trudgill (eds.), *Alternative Histories of English.* London: Routledge, 7–25.

Milroy, James and Milroy, Lesley. 1985 (1999 3rd edn). *Authority in Language: Investigating Standard English.* London: Routledge.

Mugglestone, Lynda. 1995. *'Talking Proper': The Rise of Accent as Social Symbol.* Oxford: Clarendon.

Quirk, Randolph, Sidney Greenbaum, Geoffrey Leech and Jan Svartvik. 1972. *A Grammar of Contemporary English.* London: Longman.

Schlegel, Friedrich. 1808. *Über die Sprache und Weisheit der Indier.* Heidelberg: Mohr & Zimmer.

Sheridan, Thomas. 1762. *A Course of Lectures on Elocution: Together with Two Dissertations on Language and Some other Tracts relative to those Subjects.* London: Millar, Dodsley et al.

Smith, Jeremy. 1993. Dialectal variation and the actuation of the Great Vowel Shift. *Neuphilologische Mitteilungen* 94: 259–277.

Stockwell, Robert P. and Donka Minkova. 1988. The English Great Vowel Shift: Problems of coherence and explanation. In Dieter Kastovsky and Gero Bauer (eds.), *Luick Revisited.* Tübingen: Gunter Narr, 335–393.

Stockwell, Robert P. and Donka Minkova. 1990. The Early English modern vowels: More o' Lass. *Diachronica* 7: 199–214.

Stockwell, Robert P. and Donka Minkova. 1999. Explanations of sound change: Contradictions between dialect data and theories of chain-shifting. *Leeds Studies in English* 30: 83–111.

Sweet, Henry. 1874. *A History of English Sounds.* London.

Trudgill, Peter. 1995. *Sociolinguistics: An Introduction to Language and Society,* 4th edition. London: Penguin.

Walker, John. 1781. *Elements of Elocution,* vols. I and II. [Repr. Menston, UK: Scolar Press. 1969].

Walker, John. 1791. *A Critical Pronouncing Dictionary.* Menston, UK: Scolar Press.

Watts, Richard. 1999. The social construction of standard English: Grammar writers as a 'discourse community'. In Tony Bex and Richard Watts (eds.), *Standard English: The Widening Debate*. London: Routledge, 40–68.

Watts, Richard. 2002. From polite language to educated language: The re-emergence of an ideology. In Richard Watts and Peter Trudgill (eds.), *Alternative Histories of English*. London: Routledge, 155–172.

Watts, Richard. 2003a. *Politeness*. Cambridge: Cambridge University Press.

Watts, Richard. 2003b. Was the Great Vowel Shift really "great"? A re-appraisal of research work on an elusive linguistic phenomenon. In Cornelia Tschichold (ed.), *English Core Linguistics: Essays in Honour of D. J. Allerton*. Bern: Lang, 13–30.

Watts, Richard and Peter Trudgill (eds.) 2002. *Alternative Histories of English*. London: Routledge.

Williams, Raymond. 1962. *Communications*. London: Penguin.

Index